CONTENTS

1	POPULATION	4
2	SETTLEMENT	18
3	URBANISATION	24
4	MIGRATION	42
5	SHOPPING	54
6	TRANSPORT	58
7	FARMING	70
8	ENERGY	90
9	INDUSTRY	108
10	PLANNING	130
11	TOURISM	136
12	TRADE	154
13	WORLD DEVELOPMENT	160
14	LANDFORMS	168
15	WEATHER, CLIMATE AND VEGETATION	190
16	ENVIRONMENTAL HAZARDS	210
17	ENVIRONMENTAL LOSS	224
	INDEX	240

Distribution and density

Distribution describes the way in which people are spread out across the earth's surface. This distribution is very uneven and changes over periods of time. *Density* describes the number of people living in a given area, usually a square kilometre. It is found by dividing the total population of a place by its area. On a global scale, patterns of distribution and density are mainly affected by major environmental factors such as relief, climate, vegetation, natural resources and water supply. On a regional, or a more local scale, patterns are more likely to be influenced by economic, political and social factors.

Figure 1.2 shows, by the use of dots, the distribution of people over the world. Some places are very crowded with a high population density. Other places are not crowded and have a low population density. Figure 1.1 gives some reasons, with specific examples, for this uneven distribution. When using Figure 1.1 it should be noted that:

1 For any given place there are usually several reasons for its sparse or dense population distribution rather than only the one given here, e.g. how many of the factors listed contribute to the fact that the Amazon rainforests in Brazil are sparsely populated?
2 Even within areas there are variations in density, e.g. parts of Japan have exceptionally high densities yet less than one-fifth of the country is inhabited while Manaus, on the Amazon River in Brazil, has over one million inhabitants.
3 There is a temptation to fill in every space in the table to avoid leaving gaps. Sometimes this can lead to questionable examples, e.g. is the Paris Basin a 'grassland area' and is it at all 'densely populated'?

Figure 1.1
Factors affecting distribution and density of population

Sparsely populated areas	Example	Factor
Rugged, high fold mountains, especially those with active volcanoes Ancient, worn down Shield lands	Andes Canadian Shield	**Physical (relief)**
Areas of very little rainfall throughout the year Areas of very low temperatures throughout the year Areas of extremely high humidity Savanna areas with seasonal drought and unreliable rainfall	Sahara Desert Greenland Amazon rainforest Sahel countries	**Climate**
Areas covered in dense forests such as (i) the tropical rainforests and (ii) the coniferous (Boreal) forests	(i) Amazonia (ii) Canadian Shield	**Vegetation (natural)**
Thin soils as found on high mountains Soils which have been leached (nutrients washed out); acidic	(i) Scottish Highlands (ii) Lake District	**Soils**
Lack of supply resulting from drought, seasonal irregularities, lack of reservoirs and clean drinking water	Ethiopia	**Water supply**
Areas affected by mosquitoes, tse-tse fly, locusts	East Africa	**Disease and pests**
Areas lacking in mineral wealth or local energy supplies	Sudan	**Resources**
Areas where vegetation, climate and topography (relief) act as barriers	Himalayas	**Communications**
Those which are poorly developed such as nomadic and shifting cultivation	Lappland	**Economies**
Lack of investment in rural areas in comparison with urban centres	Scottish Highlands	**Political policies**

DAVID WAUGH

The WIDER WORLD

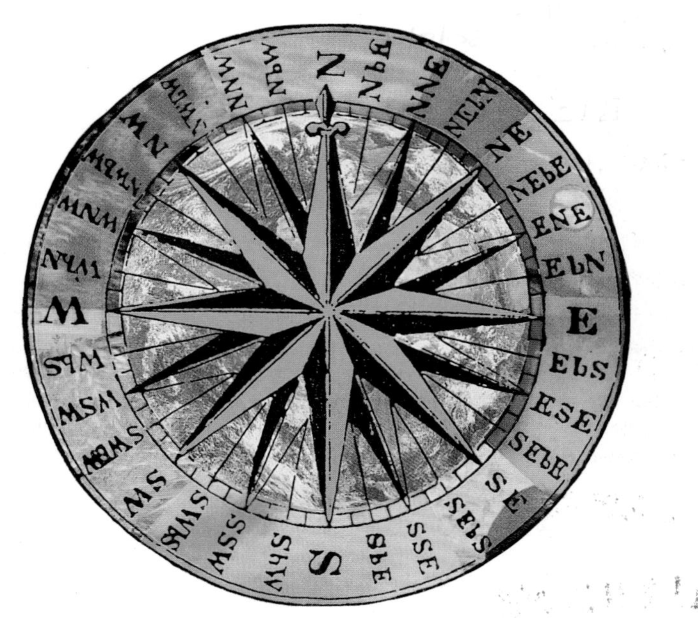

Nelson

Thomas Nelson and Sons Ltd
Nelson House Mayfield Road
Walton-on-Thames Surrey
KT12 5PL UK

Thomas Nelson Australia
102 Dodds Street
South Melbourne
Victoria 3205 Australia

Nelson Canada
1120 Birchmount Road
Scarborough Ontario
M1K 5G4 Canada

First Published by Thomas Nelson and Sons Ltd 1994

I(T)P Thomas Nelson is an International Thomson Publishing Company

I(T)P is used under licence

ISBN 0-17-434309-4
NPN 15

Printed in China

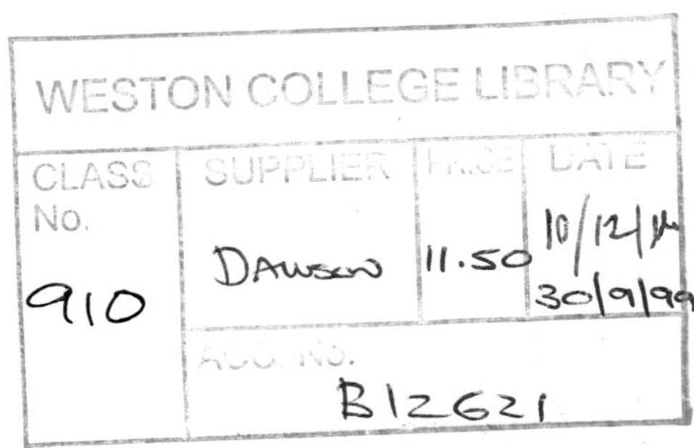

Acknowledgments

Photography:

Aerofilms: 132.
Ancient Art and Architecture Collection: p.146 (left, bottom right).
B P: p.90 (right), 99 (left), 99 (right).
Basilicata: p.78.
Comstock: p.61 (bottom).
Danish Embassy: p.77 (top).
David Waugh: p.20 (top), 28, 31 (top right), 34 (left), 55 (middle bottom), 56 (top), 72 (top), 80 (left), 81 (background, right), 88, 124, 125 (background, top middle and right), 130, 132, 146 (top right), 148 (bottom right), 149 (middle, bottom right), 172, 179 (bottom right), 185 (bottom left), 197 (bottom left), 198 (top right), 225 (middle left, bottom left), 232 (bottom).
Dundee University: p.195 (top left, top right, bottom right).
Environmental Picture Library: p.93, 94 (bottom), 95 (right).
Eye Ubiquitous: p.31 (top), 59 (bottom left), 75 (top), 80 (right), 98, 101, 133 (top), 133 (bottom), 166 (bottom right), 199 (top right), 203 (bottom left), 234.
Frank Lane Picture Library: p.179 (bottom left), 212 (left), 215 (2), 236.
Geoscience: p.149 (middle), 181 (bottom right), 182 (bottom left), 183 (bottom left, bottom right), 185 (top right), 201 (bottom right).
Hutchison: p.33 (bottom), 36 (bottom), 51 (top), 55 (middle top), 61 (top), 82/83 (top), 82 (left), 84 (middle), 91, 94 (top), 95 (left), 119, 141 (top), 182 (bottom right), 183 (top right), 198 (bottom right), 207 (bottom right).
Images: p.138 (top).
Impact: p.28 (top right), 29 (top right), 35 (top right), 36 (top) 49 (top), 51 (bottom), 55 (bottom left), 70 (right), 76, 90 (left), 227, 230 (top), 236 (background).
Imperial War Museum: p.110 (left).
Intermediate Technology: p.123 (2), 129.
James Davis: p.20 (bottom right), 31 (bottom right), 75, (left), 75 (right).
Japan Archive: p.225 (right).
Japan Information & Cultural Centre: p.120
John Cleare/Mountain Camera: p.180 (top right).
John Mills Photography: p.118.
Lupe cunha: p.153 (a & b).
Maggie Murray/Format: p.30 (bottom).
Mazda, Japan: P.121 (2).
NHPA: p.148 (bottom middle, top middle).
Ordnance Survey Map p.21.
Panos: p.149 (top), 161 (middle), 166 (bottom left).
Peak National Parks: p.139 (bottom).
Peak National Trust: p.139 (top right).
Penni Bickle: p.29 (top left), 713 (top, bottom right), 174, 177, 178 (middle), 201 (bottom left), 202 (middle, bottom right).
PHI: p.161 (bottom right).
Photo Air: p.20 (bottom left), 27, 110 (right), 113, 179 (top right).
Picturepoint: p.31 (top left), 49, 60, 103.
Port of Felixstowe: 62(2).
Rex Features: p.43, 63 (bottom).
Robert Harding: p.30 (Background), 37, 55 (top), 72 (bottom), 74 (bottom left), 74/75 (background), 84 (bottom), 226, 233.
S & R Greenhill: p.56 (bottom).
Science Photo Library: p.175, 178 (top left, top right), 181 (bottom right, bottom left), 196 (bottom right), 199 (bottom left), 202 (top right).
Sheffield Local History Library: p.114.
Simon Warner: p.185 (top right, bottom right (2)).
Skishoot/Offshoot: p.144.
Still Pictures: p.35 (left), 217 (bottom), 220, 225 (top), 230 (bottom), 231.
Thomas Paupach/Argus p.217.
Thomson Tour Operations: p.142 (bottom), 143 (top), 144 (top right).
Tony Stone Associates: p.149 (bottom left).
Zefa: p.30 (top), 34 (right), 59 (bottom right), 63 (top), 64 (bottom), 70 (left), 81 (left), 83 (right), 83, 84 (top), 92, 104.

Additional Material:

Donars
The Meteorological Office, Bracknell
New Internationalist (May 1986)
NRA South West Region - Hydrometric Services
Office of Population Census and Surveys/ HMSO
Ordnance Survey
Oxfam
Social Trends
Thomson Tours
Unesco
World Bank

Every effort has been made to trace the owners of copyright, but if any have been inadvertantly overlooked, the publishers will be pleased to make the necessary arrangement at the first opportunity.

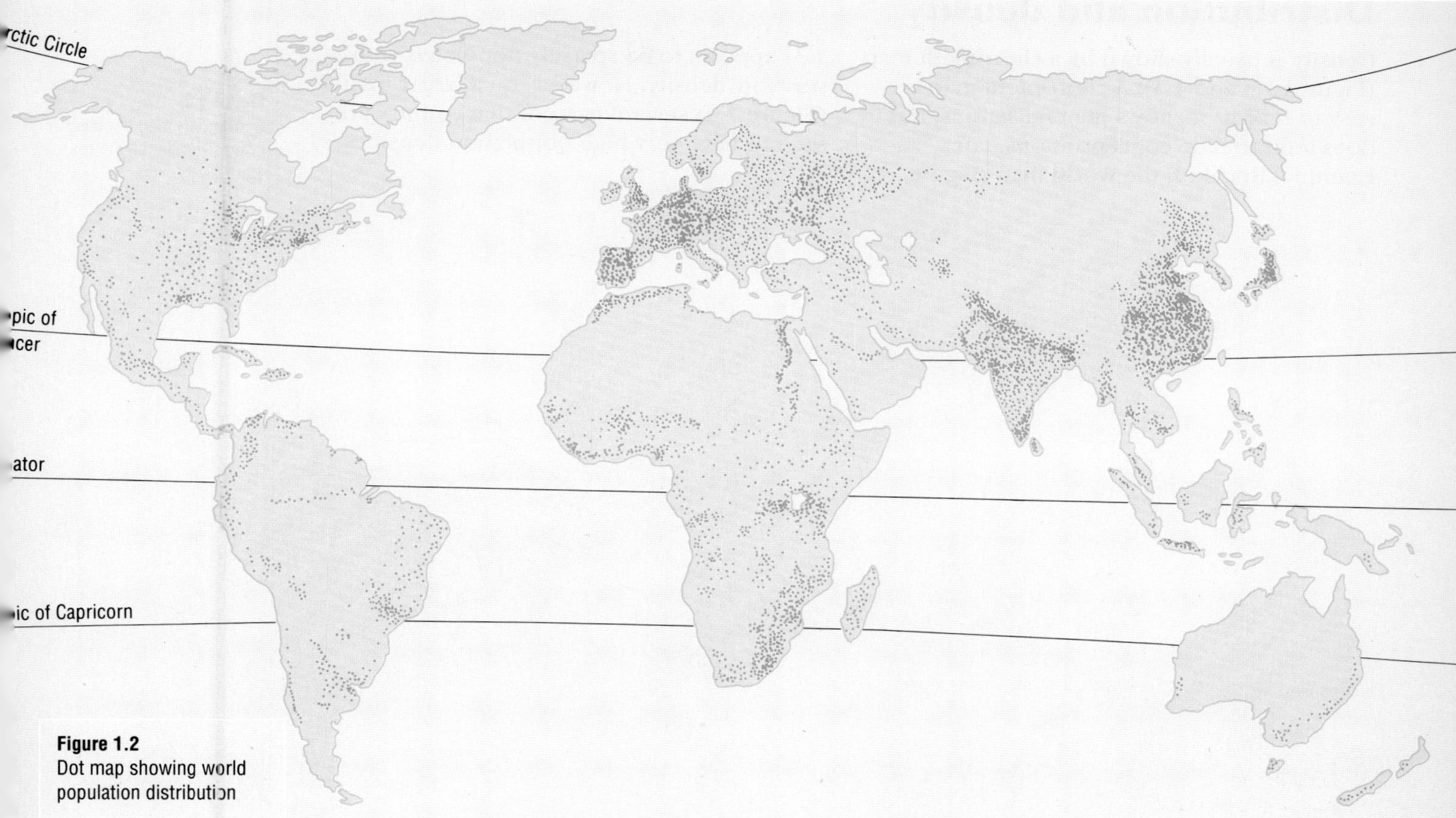

Figure 1.2
Dot map showing world population distribution

Densely populated areas	Example
Flat, extensive plains and low-lying undulating areas	Ganges Valley (India)
Foothills of active volcanoes	Mount Etna
Areas with a reliable, evenly distributed rainfall and with no extremes in temperature	North-west Europe
Areas with (i) high sunshine totals or (ii) heavy snowfalls encouraging tourism	(i) Mediterranean coastal areas (ii) Alps
Monsoon with heavy seasonal rainfall allowing high-yielding crops to be grown	Bangladesh
Open grasslands, especially in temperate latitudes	Paris Basin
Alluvial soils deposited by rivers	Nile Valley
Areas with rainfall spread evenly throughout the year, with reservoirs to store water and the provision of clean drinking water	North-west Europe
Areas without climatic extremes and with money for pest control and health facilities	Eastern USA
Areas with numerous, easily obtained mineral resources with plentiful energy resources	Great Britain
Areas with good road and rail links (originally water)	Germany
Ports and route centres	Japan
Those with a high level of technological development	California
Capital cities with their associated administration and service jobs	London
Where governments have created new towns, are investing in rural areas, or are opening up new land	Around London Dutch Polders

Distribution and density

Density is usually shown by a choropleth map (Figures 1.3 and 1.4). A choropleth map is easy to read as it shows generalisations, but it does tend to hide concentrations. For example, Brazil on the world map (Figure 1.3) appears to be sparsely populated with a very low density. However, on a larger map (Figure 1.4) several parts of that country are seen to have very high population densities.

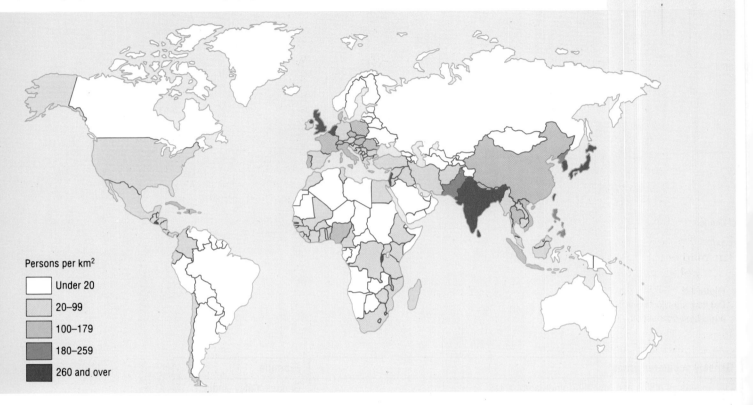

Figure 1.3
Choropleth map showing population density in the world

Persons per km²

Under 20
20–99
100–179
180–259
260 and over

Distribution of population in Brazil

The population density map of Brazil (Figure 1.4) shows a relatively simple pattern. Over 90 per cent of Brazilians live near to the coast in the south-east of the country. Going inland towards the north-west, the density declines very rapidly with some of the more remote areas being virtually uninhabited.

The highest population densities occur either at irregular intervals along the coast or around the cities of São Paulo and Belo Horizonte. Although the coastal climate is hot and wet and flat land is limited due to mountains often reaching the sea, these high density areas have a good water supply. Salvador and then Rio de Janeiro became the first two capital cities. Both had good harbours which encouraged trade, immigration, industry and, more recently, tourism (Photo page 125). The world's second fastest growing city after Mexico City, São Paulo (page 24), and Belo Horizonte

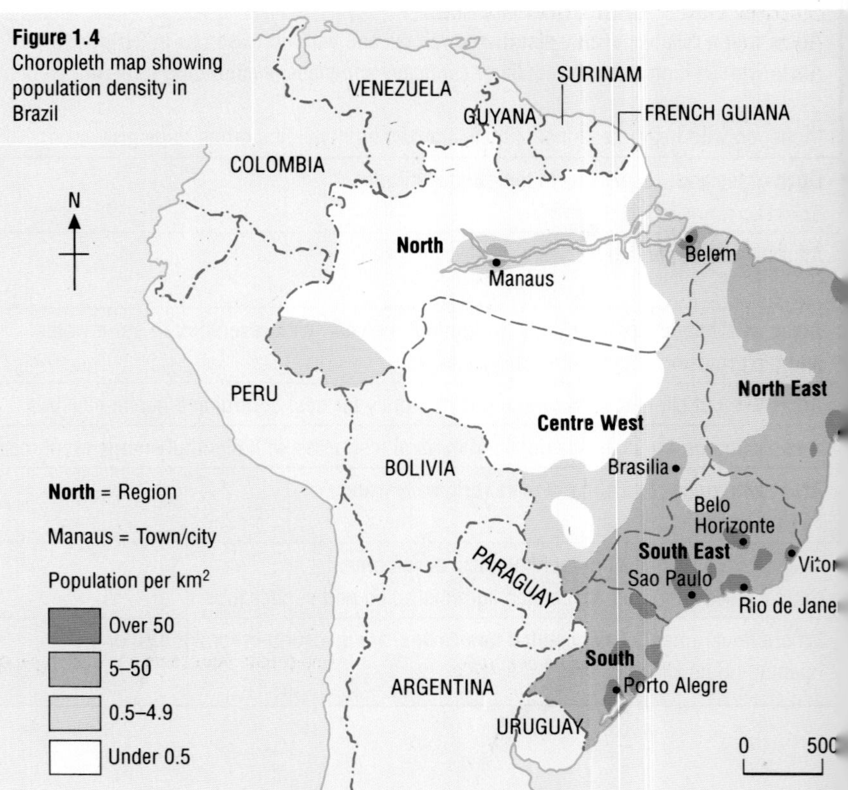

Figure 1.4
Choropleth map showing population density in Brazil

grew up on the higher, cooler, healthier plateau. The rich soils around São Paulo were ideal for the growing of coffee (page 83). Later the presence of nearby minerals, such as iron ore, and energy supplies allowed the city to develop into a major industrial centre. This region has the best transport system in Brazil, the greatest number of services and receives the most government help.

Population density decreases with distance from the coast. This is because places further inland have fewer natural resources and cannot support as many people. Those areas shown as having an average population density have a less favourable climate, a less reliable water supply, and fewer raw materials than places in the south-east of the country. Brasilia is an anomaly. An anomaly is something unusual. Brasilia was chosen in 1960 as the site for the new federal capital. The area then was virtually uninhabited. Today Brasilia has a population of over 1.5 million. It was built to try to spread out Brazil's population more evenly. (Page 130)

The sparsely populated region to the north-west is drained by the Amazon River and its tributaries. The area is very hot, wet and unhealthy. Transport through the tropical rainforest (page 230) is difficult. Soils are poor and there are few known natural resources. There is a lack of the basic services of health, education and electricity. Birth and death rates (page 10) are high and life expectancy is low. There are two anomalies in this region. Manaus was originally the centre of the rubber collecting industry and is now a large river port, whereas several places near to the mouth of the Amazon have benefited from the discovery of iron ore and bauxite and the production of hydroelectricity (page 230).

Topological maps

The map of Europe (Figure 1.5) is a topological map. In a topological map shapes are distorted and distances and directions are inaccurate. However, the map does allow easy comparisons between places to be made. In this example the scale is based upon the total population of each European country rather than upon the size (area) of each country as is more usual.

Some interesting comparisons are seen. For example, Sweden is twice the actual area of England, Scotland and Wales, while Iceland is three times the area of the Netherlands. However on the topological map (Figure 1.5) the relative sizes of the countries are distorted.

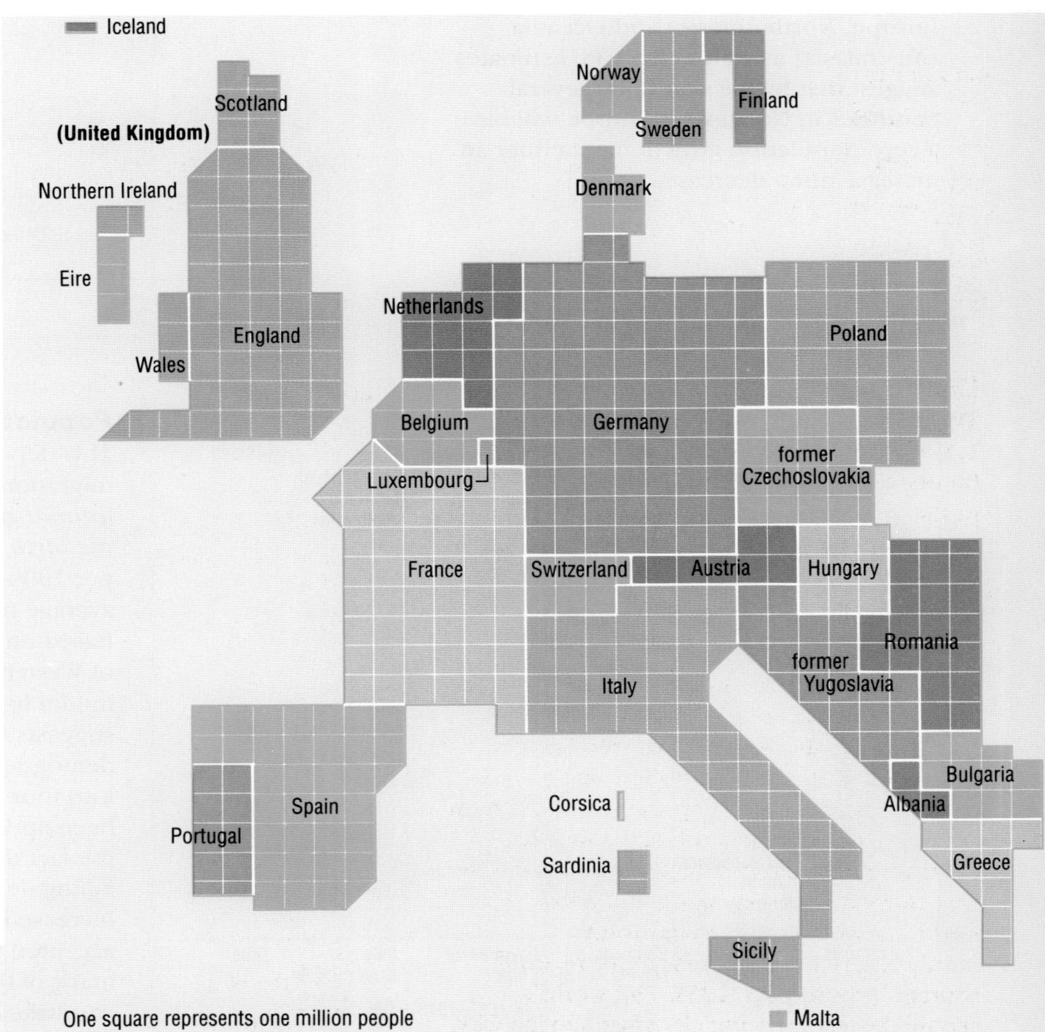

Figure 1.5
Topological map showing the population of Europe

Population growth

The annual growth rate of the world's population rose slowly but steadily until the beginning of the nineteenth century. Since then it has grown at a faster rate. Figure 1.6 is a bar graph showing the growth in population for this century in each continent. As well as emphasising the uneven distribution in population described on Page 4, it shows that:

- The continents with the greatest increase in population are the developing ones of Asia, Africa and Latin America. One UN estimate suggests that by the year 2000, 39 per cent of the world's population will live in the two countries of China and India. Already in 1990 (Figure 1.7) the three developing continents were home to 84 per cent of the world's inhabitants.
- The continents with the slowest increase in population are the developed ones of Europe, North America and Oceania (Australasia) as well as the CIS. Estimates suggest that by the year 2000 several countries in North-west Europe will have a zero population growth, i.e. neither an increase nor a decrease.

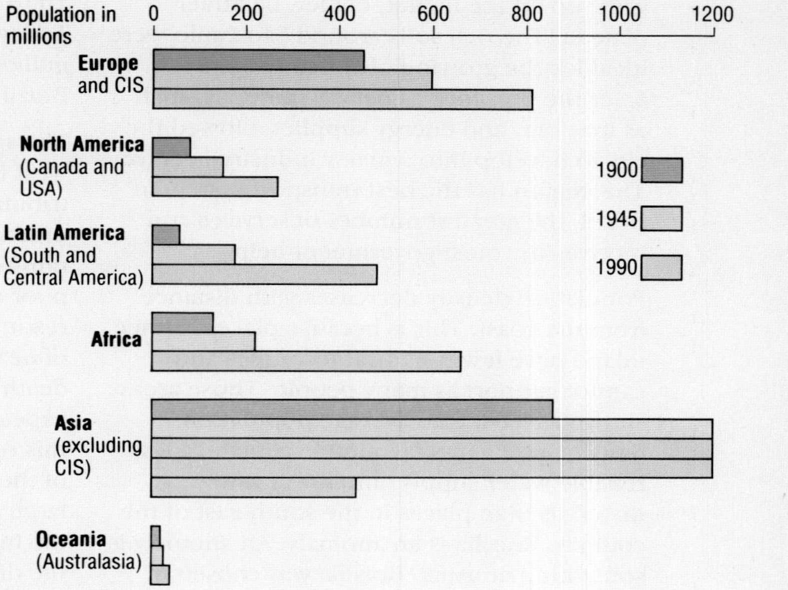

Population in millions
0 200 400 600 800 1000 1200
Europe and CIS
North America (Canada and USA)
Latin America (South and Central America)
Africa
Asia (excluding CIS)
Oceania (Australasia)
1900
1945
1990

Figure 1.6
Bar graph showing world population growth

Figure 1.7
Percentage bar graphs of population per continent in 1950 and 1990

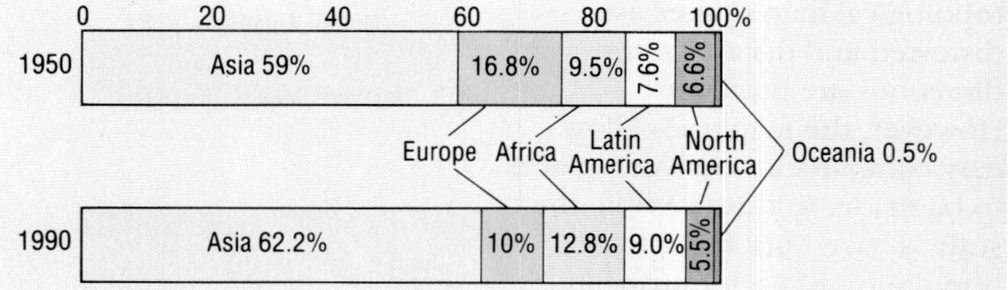

0 20 40 60 80 100%
1950: Asia 59% | 16.8% | 9.5% | 7.6% | 6.6%
Europe Africa Latin America North America Oceania 0.5%
1990: Asia 62.2% | 10% | 12.8% | 9.0% | 5.5%

Figure 1.8
Demographic transition model

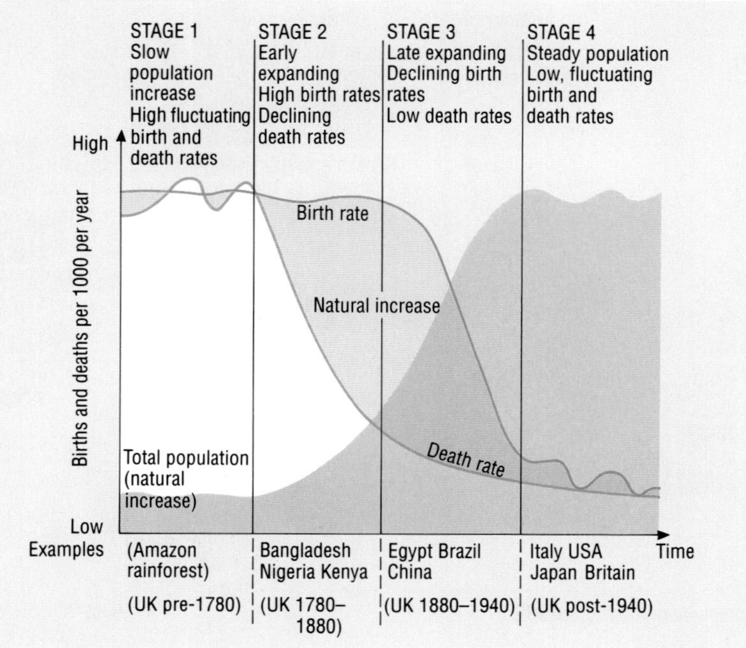

Population change

This depends on birth rate, death rate and migration. The natural increase or the *annual growth rate* is the difference between the *birth rate* (the average number of births per 1000 people) and the *death rate* (the average number of deaths per 1000 people). Based on growth rates in the industrial areas of Western Europe and North America, a model has been produced (Figure 1.8) which suggests that the population (or demographic) growth rate can be divided into four distinct stages. This model has also been applied to developing countries despite the fact that the model assumes that the falling death rate (Stage 2) is a response to increased industrialisation, a process now accepted as being unlikely to take place in many of the less economically developed countries.

Stage 1 Here both birth rates and death rates fluctuate at a high level (about 35 per 1000) giving a small population growth.

Birth rates are high because:
- ◆ No birth control or family planning.
- ◆ So many children die in infancy that parents tend to produce more in the hope that several will live.
- ◆ Many children are needed to work on the land.
- ◆ Children are regarded as a sign of virility.
- ◆ Religious beliefs (e.g. Roman Catholics, Moslems and Hindus) encourage large families.

High death rates, especially among children, are due to:
- ◆ Disease and plague (bubonic, cholera, kwashiorkor).
- ◆ Famine, uncertain food supplies, poor diet.
- ◆ Poor hygiene – no piped, clean water and no sewage disposal.
- ◆ Little medical science – few doctors, hospitals, drugs.

Stage 2 Birth rates remain high, but death rates fall rapidly to about 20 per 1000 people giving a rapid population growth.

The fall in death rate results from:
- ◆ Improved medical care – vaccinations, hospitals, doctors, new drugs and scientific inventions.
- ◆ Improved sanitation and water supply.
- ◆ Improvements in food production (both quality and quantity).
- ◆ Improved transport to move food, doctors, etc.
- ◆ A decrease in child mortality.

Stage 3 Birth rates fall rapidly, to perhaps 20 per 1000 people, while death rates continue to fall slightly (15 per 1000 people) to give a slowly increasing population.

The fall in birth rate may be due to:
- ◆ Family planning – contraceptives, sterilisation, abortion and government incentives.
- ◆ A lower infant mortality rate therefore less need to have so many children.
- ◆ Increased industrialisation and mechanisation meaning fewer labourers are needed.
- ◆ Increased desire for material possessions (cars, holidays, bigger homes) and less for large families.
- ◆ Emancipation of women, enabling them to follow their own careers rather than being solely child bearers.

Stage 4 Both birth rates (16 per 1000) and death rates (12 per 1000) remain low, fluctuating slightly to give a steady population.*

*In several Western European countries birth rates have begun to fall below death rates. This could result in a Stage 5 with a declining population.

Population change in developing and developed countries

Many of the least economically developed countries still fit into Stage 2, with a high birth rate and a falling death rate, whereas most of the more economically developed countries have reached Stage 4 with low birth and death rates (see Figure 1.9).

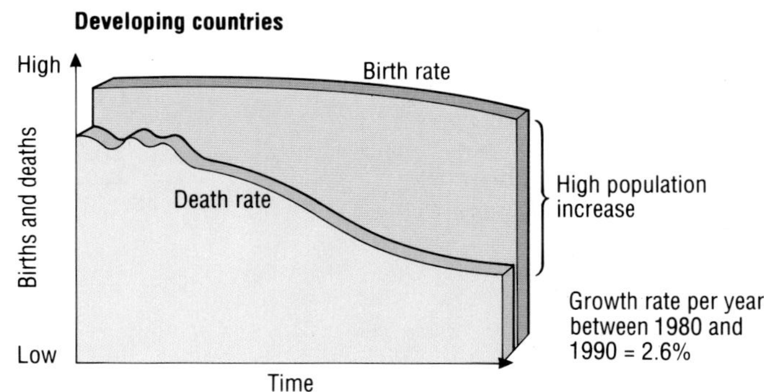

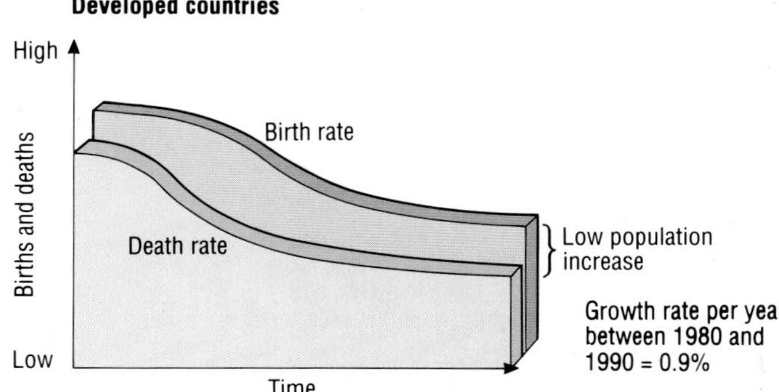

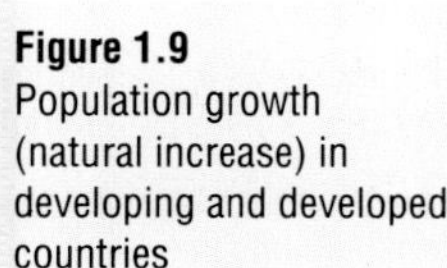

Figure 1.9
Population growth (natural increase) in developing and developed countries

Population structures

The rate of natural increase, birth rate, death rate and life expectancy (*life expectancy* is the number of years that the average person born in a particular country can expect to live) all affect the population structure of a country. The population structure of a country can be shown by a population pyramid or, as it is sometimes known, an age-sex pyramid. The population is divided into five-year age groups (e.g. 5–9 years, 10–14 years), and also into males and females. The population pyramid for the United Kingdom is shown in Figure 1.10. The graph shows:

- A narrow pyramid indicating approximately equal numbers in each age group
- A low birth rate and a low death rate indicating a steady, or even a static, population growth
- More females than males live over 70 years
- There are more boys under 4 years of age than girls
- A relatively large proportion of the population in the pre- and post-reproductive age groups, and a relatively small number in the 15–64 age group which is the one that produces children and most of the national wealth. This can be shown as the *dependency ratio* which can be expressed as:

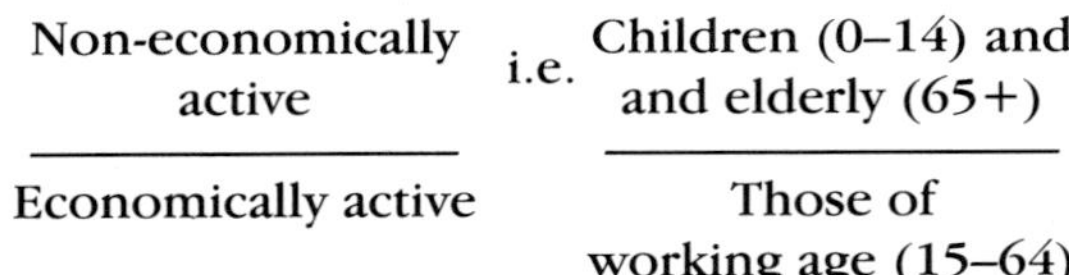

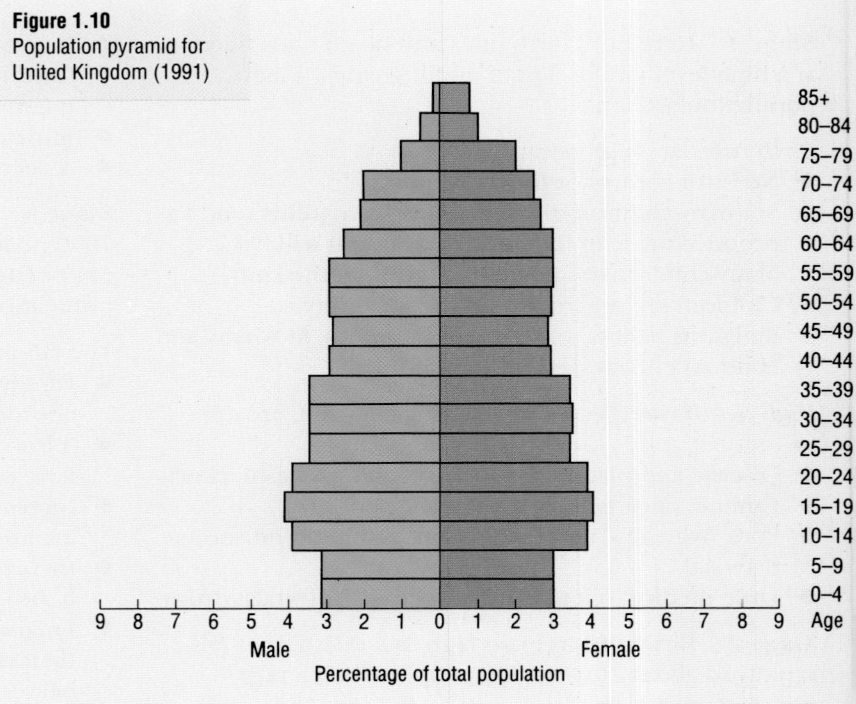

Figure 1.10
Population pyramid for United Kingdom (1991)

e.g. **UK 1971** (figures in millions)

$$\frac{13.387 + 7.307 \times 100}{31.616} = \text{Dependency ratio of } 65.45$$

That means that for every 100 people of working age, there were 65.45 people dependent upon them.

UK 1990 (figures in millions)

$$\frac{10.799 + 8.683 \times 100}{37.281} = \text{Dependency ratio of } 52.26$$

Figure 1.11
Changing population structures

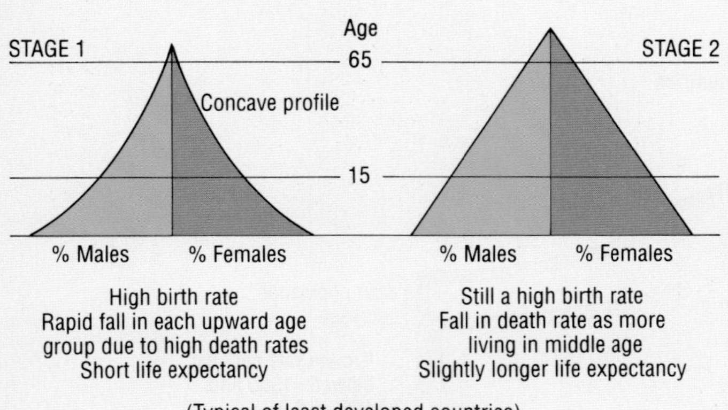

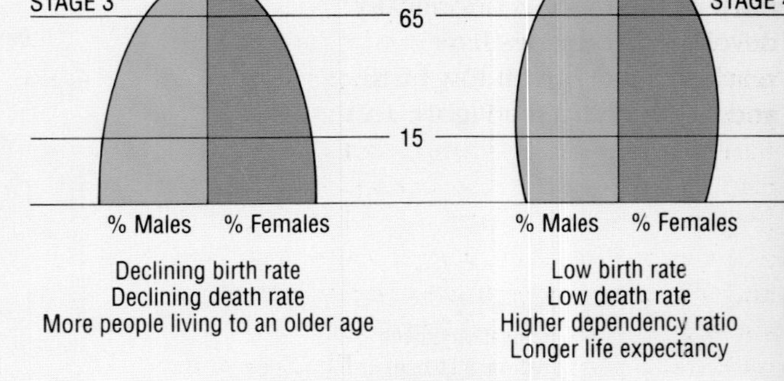

That means that for every 100 people of working age, there were 52.26 people dependent upon them.

Compared with 1971, the dependency ratio had fallen slightly. This was because despite a fall in Britain's birth rate, there had been an increase in the number of economically active people and an increase in life expectancy. (The dependency ratio does not take into account those of working age who are unemployed.) Most developed countries have a dependency ratio of between 50 and 70, whereas in developing countries the ratio is often over 100 due to the large numbers of children.

Population pyramids enable comparisons to be made between countries, and can help a country to plan for future service needs such as old people's homes if it has an ageing population or fewer schools if it has a declining, younger population. Unlike the demographic transition model (Figure 1.8), population pyramids include immigrants, but like that model they can produce four idealised types of graph representing different stages of development (Figure 1.11).

Three countries which will be referred to in several later chapters are Bangladesh, Brazil and Japan. The most recent population pyramids for these countries are given in Figure 1.12. How well, do you think, the three pyramids fit with the models shown in Figure 1.11? Figure 1.12 confirms the point that population structures change over periods of time. Bangladesh is the least wealthy of the three. Its wide base confirms that it has the highest birth rate and that its population declines rapidly due to a high infant mortality rate. Brazil, slightly more wealthy, has its birth and infant mortality rate both declining. This is shown by the narrower base (0–4 years) and relatively more people reaching child-bearing age (e.g. 20–24 years). Both countries have a rapidly narrowing pyramid, indicating a high death rate and a short life expectancy. The pyramid for Japan shows, by contrast, a low birth rate, a low infant mortality rate, a low death rate and a long life expectancy. The graphs also show that in Japan and Brazil, in common with most countries in the world, there are slightly more male than female births; but that females have the longer life expectancy.

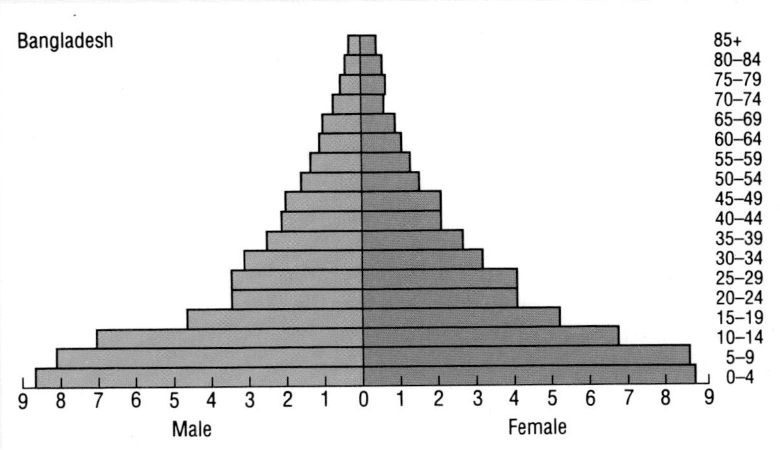

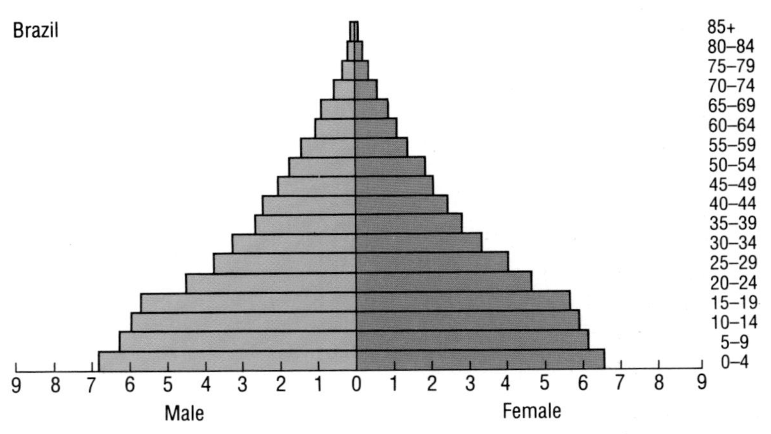

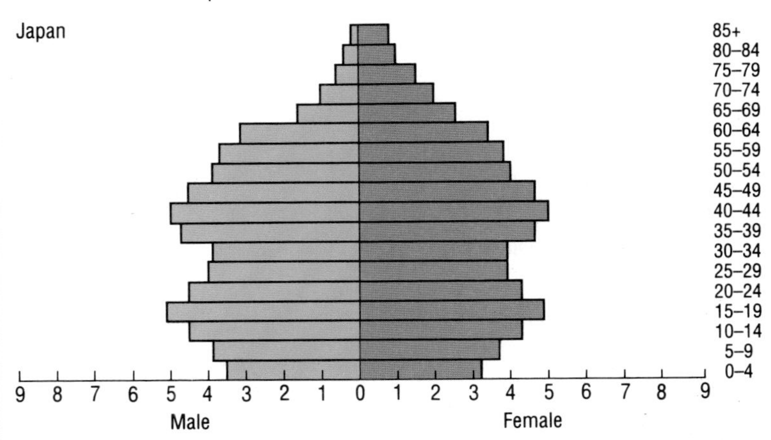

Figure 1.12
Population pyramids for Bangladesh, Brazil and Japan

Future trends

Since the concern expressed during the 1970s at the increased growth rate in world population, evidence has shown that fertility in nearly all countries is now declining. The 1992 United Nations estimate claimed that the annual growth rate of 2 per cent in 1965 had dropped to 1.6 per cent and could fall to 1.5 per cent by the year 2000. This means that the world's population will reach 6300 million by AD 2000 (Figure 1.13) instead of the 7600 million it would have reached had the growth of the period 1950–1980 continued. Even so, the rapid growth in the developing countries in Africa and Asia could mean the world population total of 1988 could double by 2025.

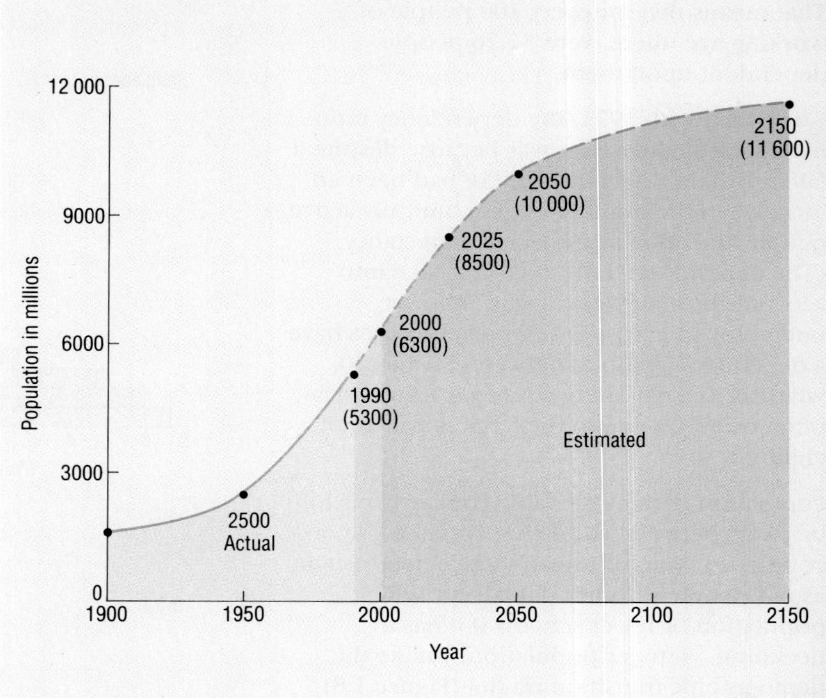

Figure 1.13 World population growth

Changing population structures

The increase in children under 15

To maintain a stable world population, without growth, each mother should have two children. In many developed countries the average family has less than two children which, in time, will cause their populations to decrease. However, attitudes towards children differ in developing countries where the average is still often over five children who live beyond infancy (remember that many mothers may have given birth more than ten times – Figures 1.15 and 1.16). This means (Figure 1.14) that while developed countries have less than 30 per cent of their populations aged under 15, in developing countries the corresponding figure exceeds 40 per cent. This increase in potential mothers will outweigh any decrease in family size – a major cause of the predicted continued growth in world population.

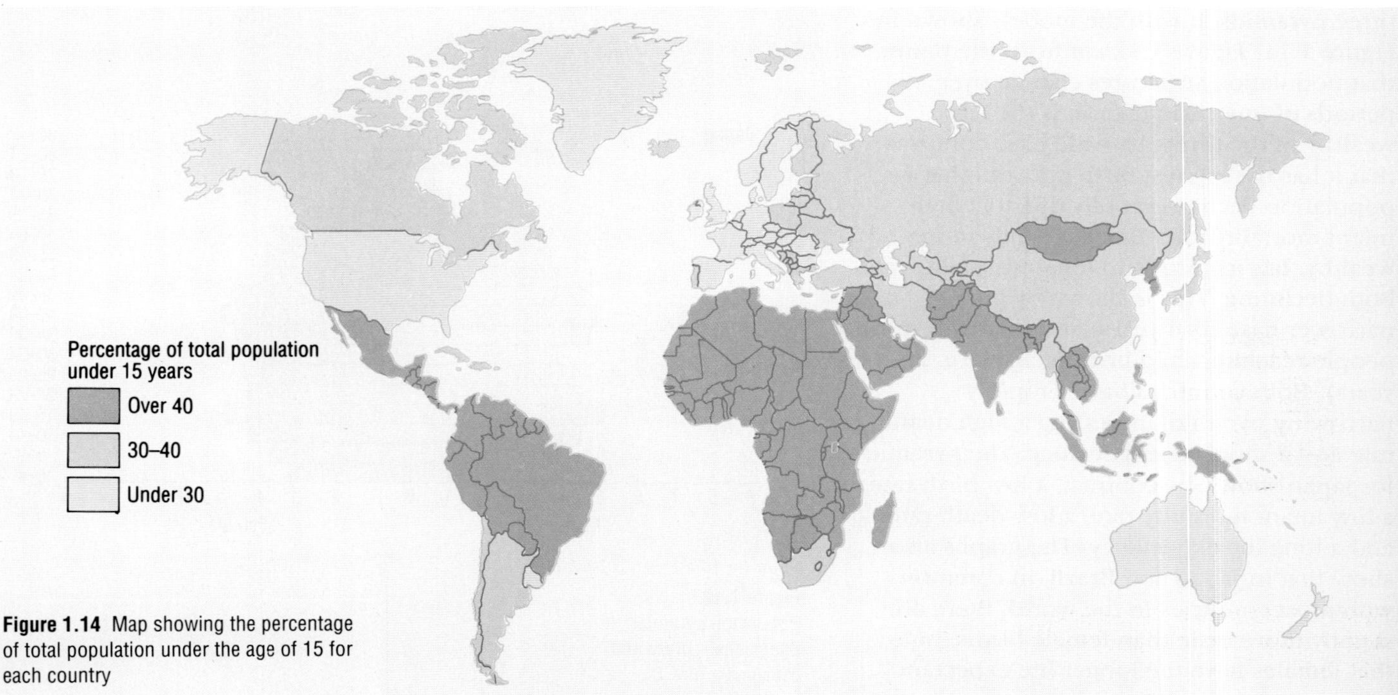

Figure 1.14 Map showing the percentage of total population under the age of 15 for each country

The world's ageing population

Due to improvements in medical facilities, hygiene and vaccines, life expectancy has increased considerably. This will mean more elderly people for whom care will be necessary. Several developed countries (Figure 1.17) already have over 16 per cent of their populations over pensionable age, a figure likely to reach 20 per cent in Japan and the UK within the next decade. This will lead to increases in demands for more pensions, money from the National Health for medical care, residential homes and other social services. As the number of pensioners increases, fewer people in the economically active age groups will be earning the money needed to support them. This problem will be even greater in developing countries. Assuming life expectancy continues to increase, and there continues to be a fall in the death rate, these countries will have insufficient money to support the growth of their elderly populations.

Figure 1.15
Having children in a developing country

"Families with children into the double figures are very common in north-east Brazil. Rural mothers in this state, Rio Grande do Norte, have an average of more than seven living children. A quarter of them have ten or more. And that is not counting the dead ones. You often meet women like Luisa Gomez, a slight, small, thirty-nine-year-old. She married at fourteen. Since then she has been pregnant sixteen times, one every eighteen months. For half her adult life she has been pregnant, and for the other half breast-feeding the most recent addition. Only six of those sixteen are still alive. There were three stillbirths and seven died in their first year. Ten wasted pregnancies. Seven and a half years of drain on an already weak organism for nothing. Worse than nothing, for all the anxiety, all the care, all the concern, and then the grief."

Figure 1.16
Attitudes towards children in the developing and developed world

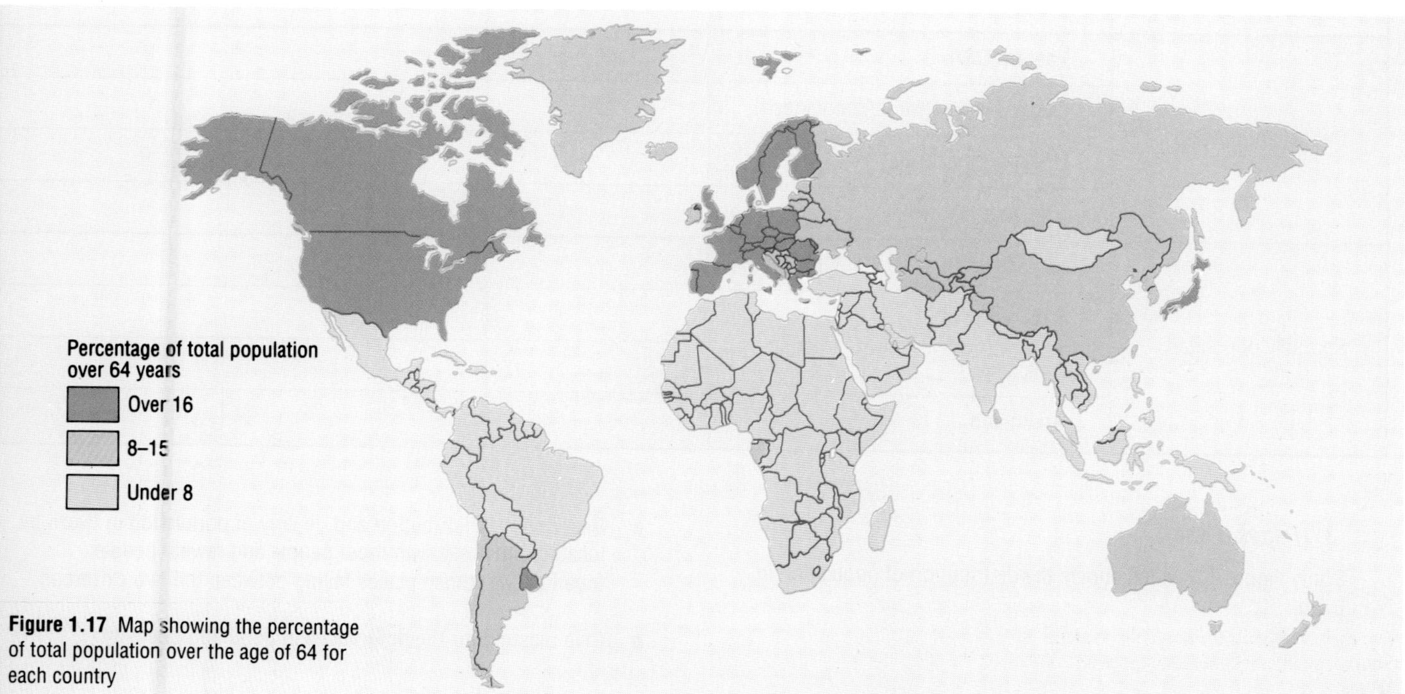

Figure 1.17 Map showing the percentage of total population over the age of 64 for each country

QUESTIONS

1 *(Page 4)*

a What is meant by the terms: i) Population Distribution and ii) Population Density? *(2)*
b How is population density calculated? *(1)*

2 *(Pages 4 and 5)*

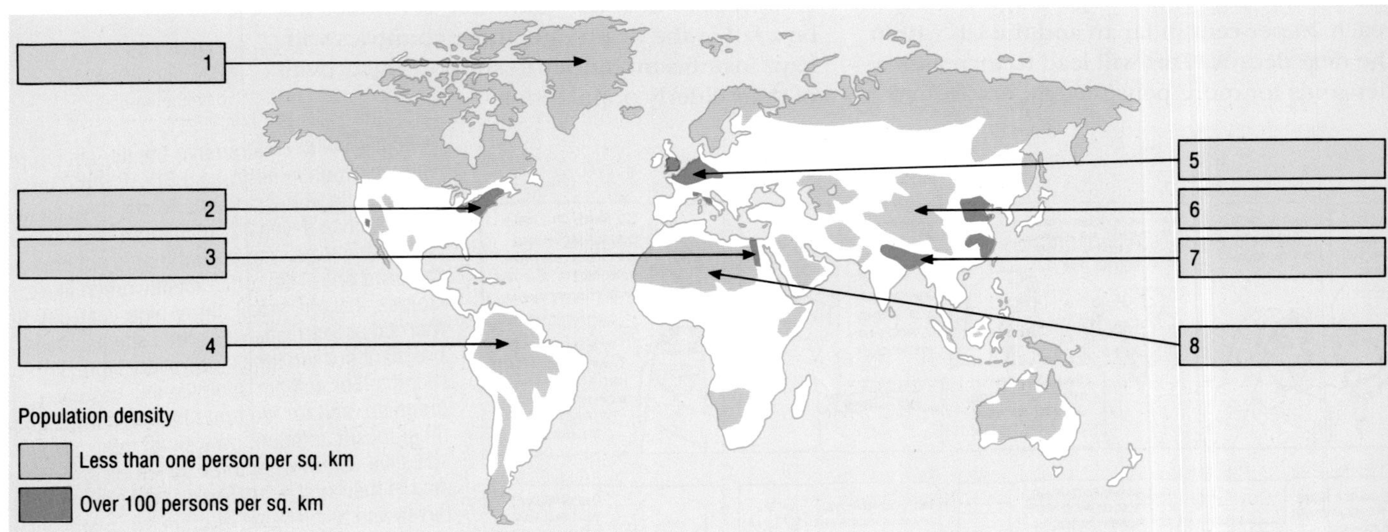

a Make a copy of the table below.
b Match the numbers on the map with the places named in the table. *(8)*
c Give reasons for the population density of each place. The list (right) should help you with your answer. Each label in the list may be used more than once. *(16)*

No extremes of climate • too hot • too wet • too dry
good water supply • low lying • many resources
few resources • flat land • fertile soil • too mountainous
good transport • money for development

Population density	Place	Number on map	Reasons
Densely populated	Eastern USA		
	Ganges valley (India/Bangladesh)		
	North-west Europe		
	Nile Valley (Egypt)		
Sparsely populated	Himalayas		
	Sahara desert		
	Amazonia		
	Greenland		

3 *(Pages 6 and 7)*

Study Figure 1.4 which shows the distribution of population in Brazil.

a Describe the distribution and density of population in Brazil by locating the areas with most people and fewest people, together with those places falling between the two extremes. *(6)*
b Give reasons for the differences in population density. *(9)*

4 *(Figures 1.6 and 1.7 on Page 8)*

a What was Asia's population in 1900? *(1)*
b Which continent had the second largest population in 1945? *(1)*
c Which two continents more than doubled their population between 1945 and 1990? *(2)*
d i) By how many millions did North America's population increase between 1945 and 1990?
ii) Express this increase as a percentage. *(2)*
e In 1990 what percentage of the world's population lived in:
i) The three developing continents?
ii) The three developed continents? *(2)*

5 *(Pages 8 and 9)*

a What is meant by the following terms?
i) Birth rate ii) Death rate iii) Natural increase *(3)*
b Using the demographic transition graph for Brazil opposite:
i) Give the birth rate and the death rate for the present day. *(2)*
ii) Give the figure 'per 1000' by which the population is increasing at the present day. *(1)*
iii) Say which of the following periods was the one during which the population of Brazil grew most rapidly: 1900–1910; 1920–1930; 1940–1950; 1960–1970. *(1)*
c Give three reasons for a high birth rate in Brazil. *(3)*
d Give three reasons why Brazil's death rate has fallen rapidly since 1940. *(3)*
e Using the graph:
i) Complete the total population for Brazil for the years 1920 to the present day. *(1)*
ii) Predict what the birth rate and death rate for Brazil might be in the year 2000. *(1)*
iii) Give reasons for your prediction. *(2)*

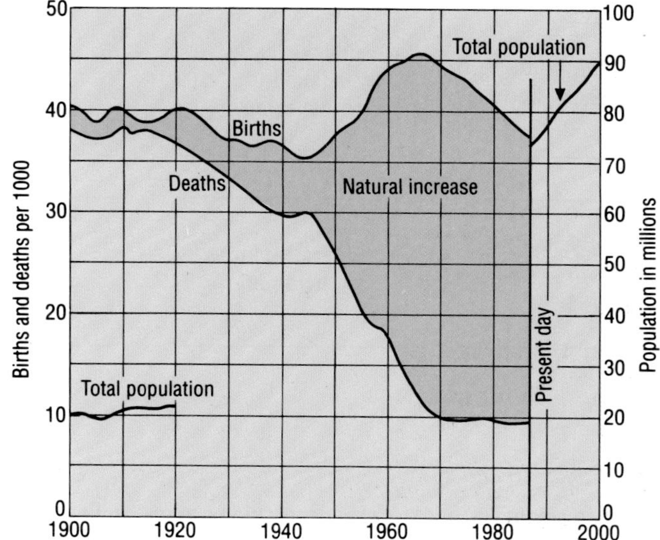

6 *(Pages 8 and 9)*

The figure below is a simplified diagram showing how population changes are likely to take place over a period of time. It is called a demographic transition model.

a i) Make a copy of the figure and the table below it.
ii) Add labels to show birth rate and death rate. *(2)*
iii) Complete the birth rate and death rate part of the table by adding the words: **high**, **low** or **decreasing** in the correct places. *(4)*
b i) On your diagram draw a line to show total population. Start at X. *(2)*
ii) Complete the population change part of the table by adding: **steady decrease**, **slow increase** or **rapid increase** in the correct places. *(2)*
c i) Describe and give reasons for the population change in Stage 3. *(4)*
ii) When was the UK at this stage of population growth? *(1)*

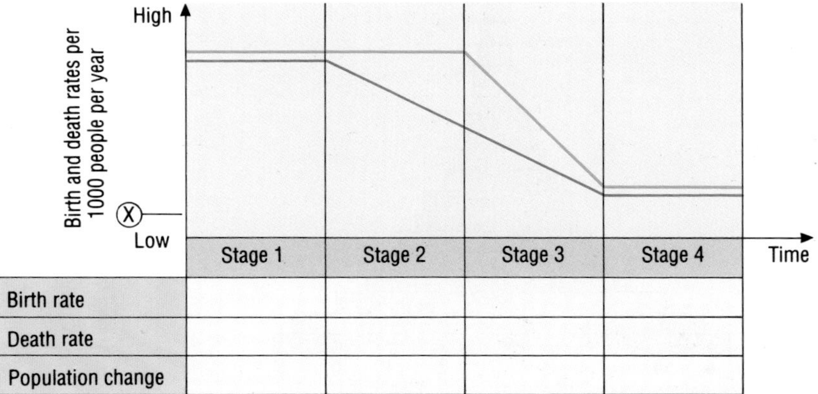

	Stage 1	Stage 2	Stage 3	Stage 4
Birth rate				
Death rate				
Population change				

7 *(Page 10)*

Study the diagram which compares population structures typical of less developed (poor) countries and more developed (rich) countries.

a Make a larger copy of the diagram.

b Describe the main features of population structure by adding the following labels in the correct places: *(10)*

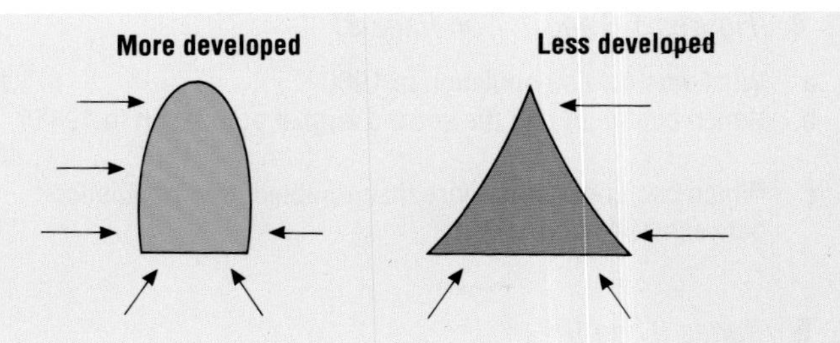

High birth-rate, many children	**Many elderly, long life expected**	**Squat-pyramid shape**	**Many people die when young**	**Many middle aged**
Nearly equal numbers at each age	**Generally narrow pyramid**	**Many more young than old**	**Low birth rate, few children**	**Few elderly, short life expectancy**

8 *(Pages 10 and 11)*

The two graphs, (a) and (b), show population pyramids for two countries in different parts of the world.

a i) Describe any three differences between the two graphs. *(3)*

ii) State which graph is more typical of a developing country and which more typical of a developed country. *(1)*

iii) In graph (a) what percentage of the female population is aged between 40–44 years? *(1)*

iv) What percentage of the total population in graph (b) is: over 60 years of age; under 15 years of age? *(2)*

b Which country, (a) or (b) has:

i) The higher birth rate?

ii) The higher death rate?

iii) The more rapid population growth?

Give reasons for your answers. *(6)*

c i) What is meant by the term *dependency ratio*? *(1)*

ii) Compare the size of the dependent population for country (b)with that of country (a). *(2)*

iii) What are the consequences for countries with a rising dependent population? *(2)*

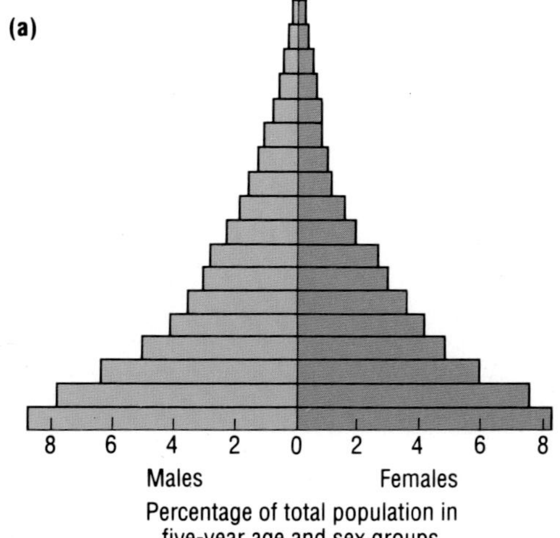

85+
80–84
75–79
70–74
65–69
60–64
55–59
50–54
45–49
40–44
35–39
30–34
25–29
20–24
15–19
10–14
5–9
0–4

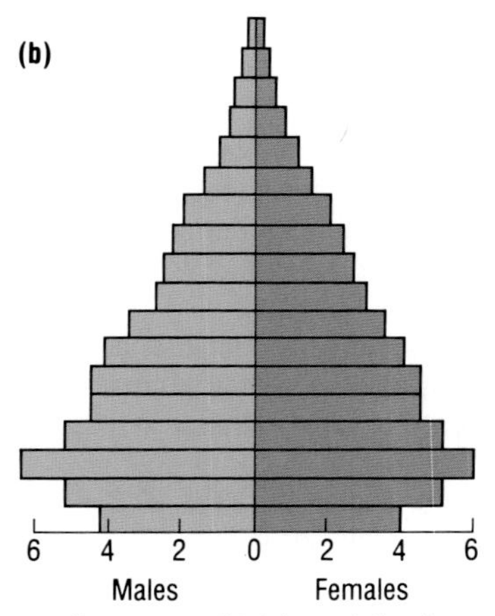

9 *(Pages 8 to 11)*

Country	Total population millions	Population density per sq km	Birth rate per 1000	Death rate per 1000	Infant mortality per 1000	Life expectancy in years
Brazil	135	16	31	8	84	63
Egypt	47	47	38	13	113	57
Ethiopia	36	30	49	22	143	43
India	761	232	33	13	118	53
Italy	57	189	13	10	14	74
Japan	120	323	12	7	50	77
Philippines	55	182	32	7	50	65
UK	56	227	13	12	12	74

a i) Which country has the largest population? *(1)*
ii) Which country has the greatest density of population? *(1)*
iii) The rate of natural increase in population is the birth rate minus the death rate. Which three countries have the biggest rate of natural increase? *(3)*
iv) Life expectancy is the average age to which people may expect to live. In which three countries is life expectancy the lowest? *(3)*

b i) Name four countries from the table above which have all of the following features:
High birth rate
Moderate death rate
High infant mortality
Low life expectancy *(4)*
ii) State two ways in which countries like these may try to increase the life expectancy of their population. *(2)*

10 *(Pages 12 and 13)*

a i) What percentage of the UK's population is aged under 15? *(1)*
ii) Why is the percentage in this age group in the UK falling? *(1)*
iii) Why are there fewer people aged under 15 in the UK than in developing countries? *(4)*

b i) What percentage of the UK's population was aged over 65 in 1980? *(1)*
ii) What percentage of the UK's population is expected to be aged over 65 in 2025? *(1)*

c What effect might these changes in Britain's population have on:
i) education services
ii) health services
iii) the economy *(6)*

11 *(Page 6)*

Study the diagram which shows some ways to reduce the birth rate.

a Choose four of the factors shown on the diagram and explain why they reduce birth rates. *(4)*

b Why have developed countries been more successful than developing countries in lowering their birth rates? *(4)*

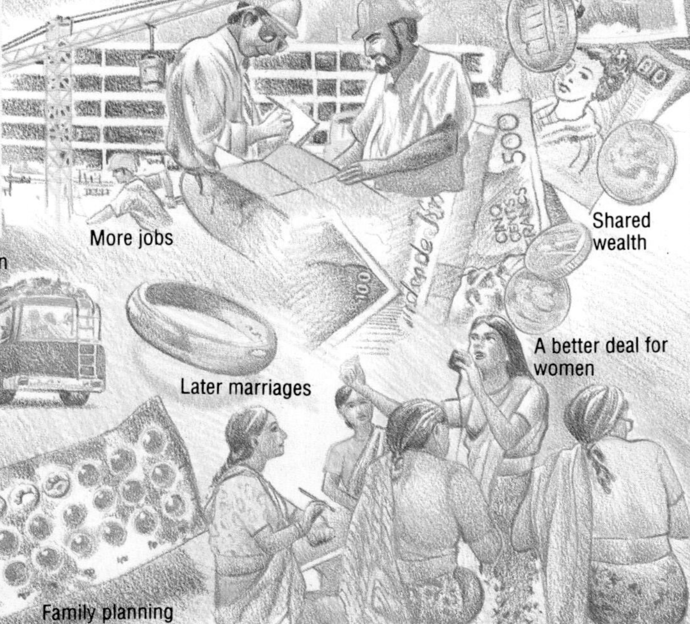

2 SETTLEMENTS

Site and situation

Site describes the point at which the town (village, farm, industry) is located. It is concerned with the local relief, soils, water supply, etc. It is the initial determining factor in the growth of a settlement.

Situation describes where the settlement (or farm/factory) is located in relation to surrounding features such as other settlements, rivers and communications. The settlement's situation becomes a predominant factor in its continued rate of growth. Paris, for example, had the site advantage of being on an island in the River Seine which could be defended and which made bridging easier. However, it continued to grow because it was the centre of a major farming area where several routes (rivers) converged.

Early settlements These developed initially within a rural economy which aimed to be self sufficient. They were influenced mainly by physical factors which included:

Wet-point sites, especially in relatively dry areas, e.g. springs at the foot of chalk escarpments. Water was needed frequently throughout the year, and was heavy to carry. In times of early settlement rivers were sufficiently clean to give a safe, permanent supply.

Dry-point sites which may have been 'islands' in an otherwise marshy area, e.g. Ely.

Building materials which had to be located nearby and which ideally included stone, wood and clay.

Defence against surrounding tribes. Such sites may have been protected on three sides by water (Durham) or on a hill with steep sides and commanding views (e.g. Edinburgh).

Fuel supply which was essential for heating and cooking and which, in earlier days, was usually wood (still applicable today in developing countries).

Food supply from land which was suitable for animal grazing and, nearby, land which could be used for growing crops.

Nodal points where several valleys (natural routes) met to give a route centre; or which commanded routes through the hills (e.g. Guildford).

Bridging points, originally possibly a ford in the river, e.g. Bedford, where natural routes were able to cross rivers.

Shelter and aspect In Britain it was an advantage to be sheltered from winds blowing from the north, and to be facing south which meant more sunlight (e.g. Torquay).

Study Figure 2.1 which shows an area of land available for early settlement.

1 List the advantages and disadvantages of each of the five sites labelled A to E.
2 Is there an ideal site?

Figure 2.1
Which would be the best site for an early settlement?

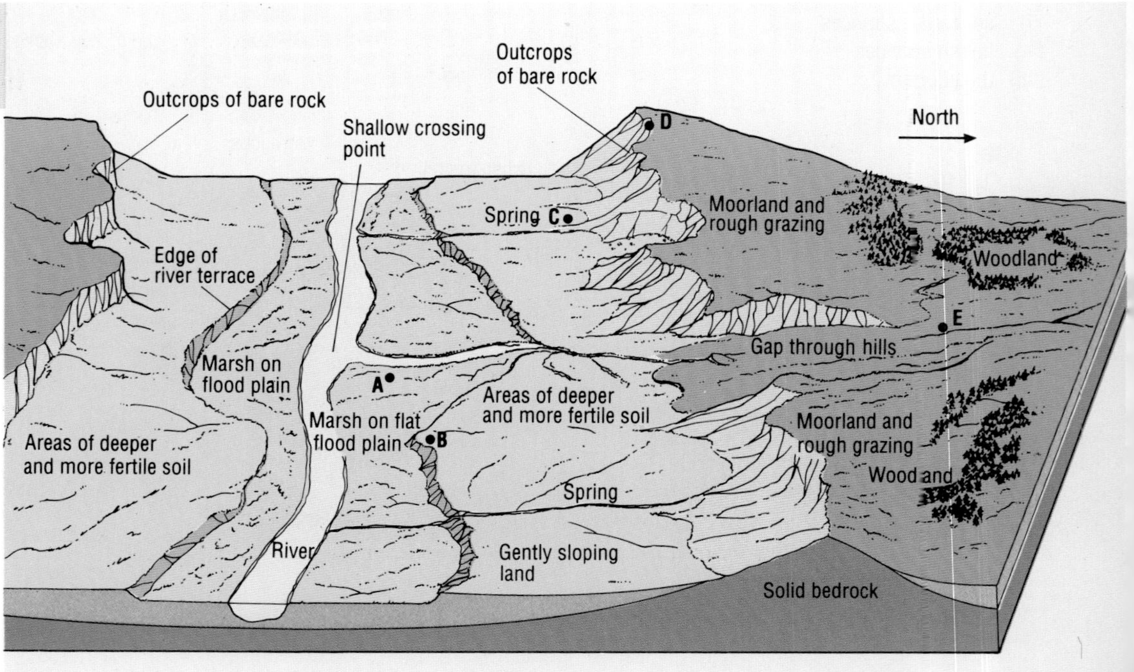

Figure 2.2
Annotated sketch map showing the site of Hedon

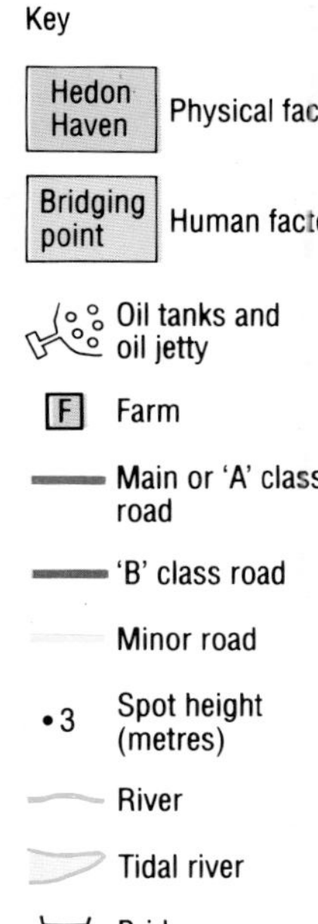

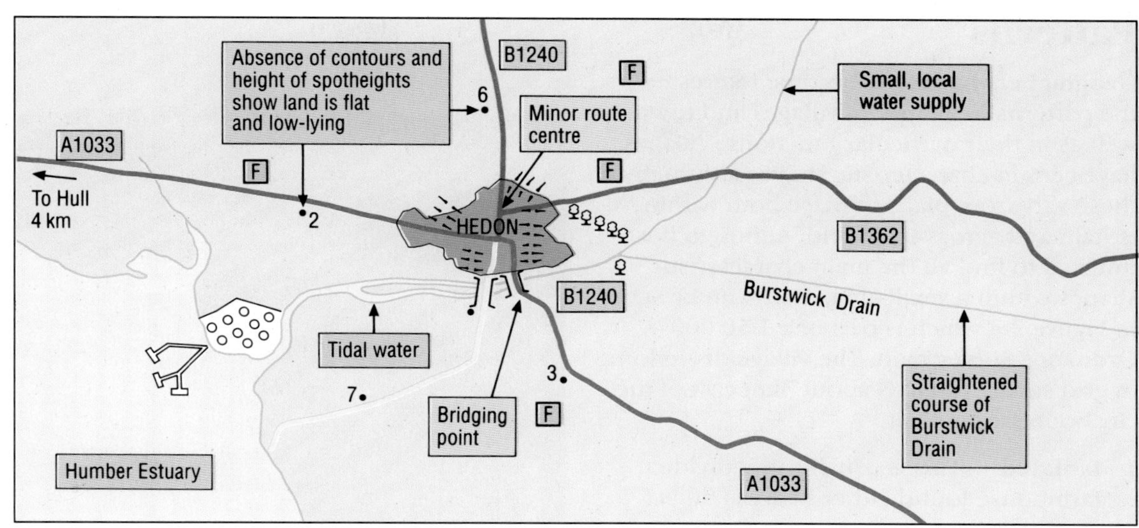

Functions

The *function* of a town relates to its economic and social development. In some cases the original function is no longer applicable, e.g. British towns no longer have a defensive function. Many attempts have been made to classify towns according to their main functions. Classifications are valuable if, for convenience, towns which have similar characteristic functions can be grouped together. Some classifications are too simple and general, e.g. dividing all towns into three groups based on primary, secondary and tertiary (service) industries (see page 108). Other classifications are far too detailed to be applied easily, and so are not convenient to use.

Market towns originally started as collection and distribution centres for the surrounding farming area. Today their functions will probably include the manufacturing and servicing of agricultural machinery and the processing of agricultural produce (e.g. Winnipeg, York).

Mining towns have grown due to the exploitation of a local fuel or mineral (e.g. coal at Treorky in the Rhondda Valley and iron ore at Schefferville in Labrador).

Manufacturing/industrial towns have grown where raw materials are processed into manufactured goods (e.g. Birmingham, Toronto).

Ports include those on coasts, rivers, and lakes (e.g. Southampton, Thunder Bay). These have grown at points where goods are moved from land to water, or vice versa.

Route centres are located at the junction of several natural routes or at nodal points resulting from economic development (e.g. Carlisle, Paris).

Service centres have grown to provide the needs of a local community. Such services may include shopping, recreation, education and health (e.g. Cambridge).

Cultural and religious settlements attract people from many parts of the world, even if only temporarily, to live and study (e.g. Oxford, Rome).

Administrative centres may vary from smaller regional centres (e.g. county towns such as Exeter) to capital cities (e.g. Ottawa).

Residential towns are those in which the majority of the inhabitants are either retired or work elsewhere. In the widest definition this could include commuter, overspill and new towns (e.g. Cumbernauld).

Tourist resorts (with the exception of spa towns, such as Bath) are modern in origin. Most are on coasts or in mountains (e.g. Blackpool, Aviemore).

Today, especially in the developed world, most towns tend to be multi-functional (i.e. they have several functions) though a particular function may be predominant. Also, many towns may have had a change in function from their original one, e.g. a Cornish fishing port may now be a tourist resort (e.g. Penzance), a mining village may have become a new town with some manufacturing industry (e.g. Washington, Tyne and Wear).

Patterns

Geographers have now become interested in the patterns or shapes of villages and towns as well as in their particular functions. Villages have certain characteristic shapes although these vary from place to place both within Britain and across the world. Although it is unusual to find all the main characteristic shapes within a small area, many can be seen in Figure 2.3 which is part of a 1:50 000 Ordnance Survey map. The village of Hedon, in grid square 1928, is about 3km east of the city boundary of Hull.

1 **Isolated** This is usually an individual farmhouse found either in areas of extreme adverse physical conditions as in the Highlands of Scotland, or in areas of pioneer settlement where land was actually divided into planned lots (e.g. the Canadian Prairies). Isolated or, more accurately in this case, individual farms can be seen in Figure 2.6 in grid squares 1630 and 2230.

2 **Dispersed** (Figure 2.3) This consists of groups of two or three buildings, perhaps forming a hamlet, and separated from the next small group of buildings by two or three kilometres (e.g. Lelley in 2032). Such settlements are common in the central Pennines.

3 **Nucleated or compact** (Figure 2.5) These are found every three or four kilometres in rural England, so that there is enough land around the village to make it self sufficient with its own crops and its own animals. The buildings are grouped together for defensive purposes as well as for social and economic ones. The village of Preston, in grid square 1830, illustrates the grouping of buildings at a crossroad. Mediterranean hilltop villages fit this pattern (page 119).

4 **Loose knit** These are similar to the nucleated type in that they are found at crossroads and junctions, but here the buildings are more spread out as in Burstwick (grid square 2227) and Burton Pidsea (grid quare 2431).

5 **Linear or street** (Figure 2.4) Here the buildings are strung out along the minor road between Burstwick (2227) and Camerton (2226) or, in the case of the Netherlands, along a dyke or canal.

Figure 2.3
Dispersed settlement in Northumberland

6 **Planned villages** These include suburbanised villages which are near enough to large cities to house their workforce, as in square 1533 at Bilton. They tend to contain small crescent-shaped estates with individual buildings. These are also seen on the Dutch Polders.

Naturally some villages show characteristics of more than one pattern, e.g. Thorngumbald (2026) has a nucleated centre with some linear development, while Hedon (1828) includes nucleated, linear and planned patterns.

Figure 2.4
Linear settlement at Parson's Drove, Cambs

Figure 2.5
Nucleated settlement in South Sumatra

Figure 2.6
Part of map sheet 107 Kingston upon Hull

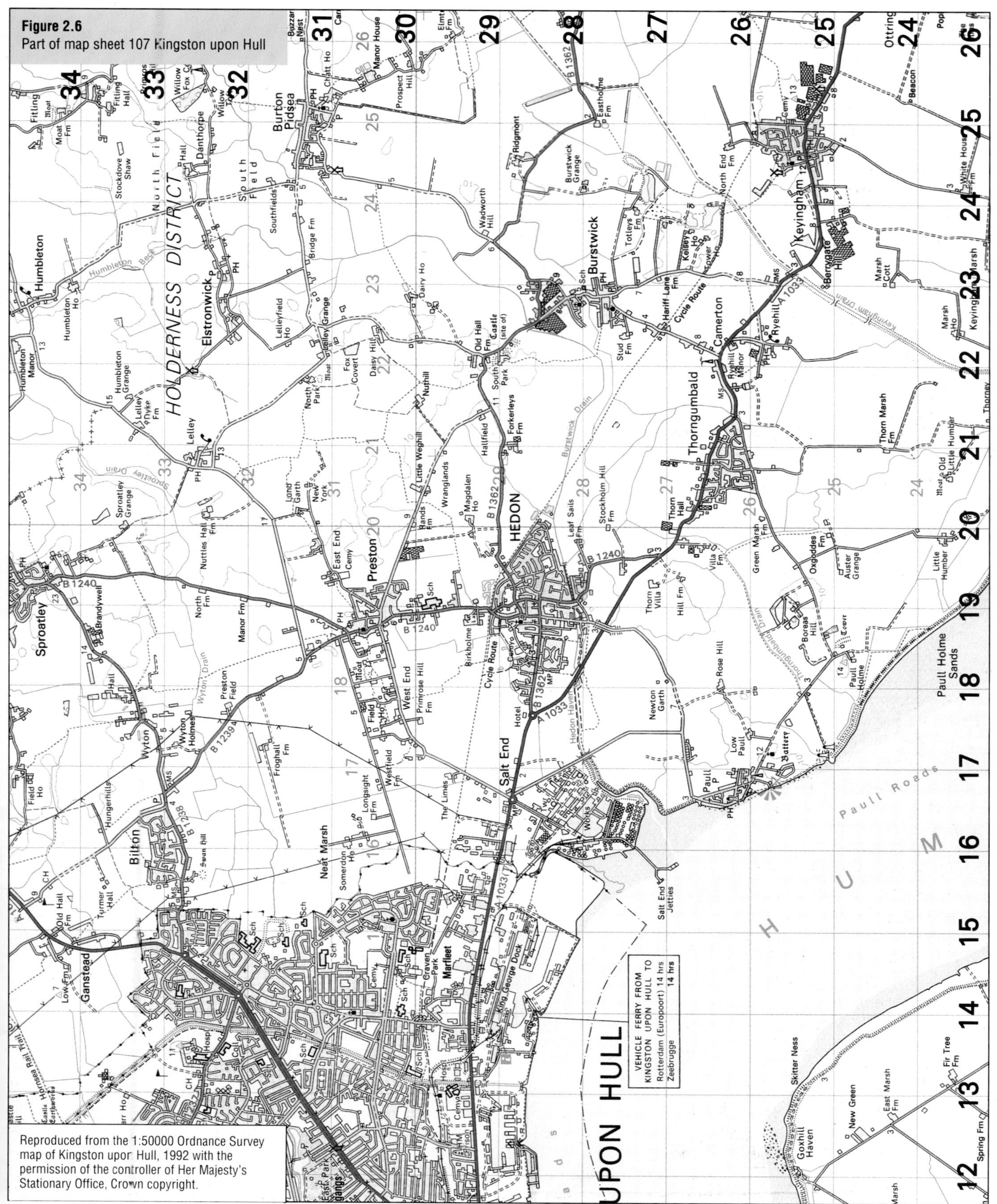

Hierarchy

This term refers to the arrangement of settlements within a country in 'an order of importance' – usually from many small hamlets and villages at the base of the hierarchy, to one major city, usually the capital, at the top. Three different methods to determine this order of importance have been based on:

1 The area and population of the settlement, i.e. its size.
2 The range and number of functions and/or services within each settlement.
3 The relative sphere of influence of each settlement.

Size Early attempts to determine a hierarchy were based on size. However, no-one has been able to produce a commonly accepted division between, for example, a hamlet and a village, and a village and a town. Indeed, many villages in China and India are as big as many British towns. Figure 2.9 lists a fairly conventional hierarchy in terms of type of settlement, and a debatable 'division' based on actual numbers (more applicable to Britain than elsewhere).

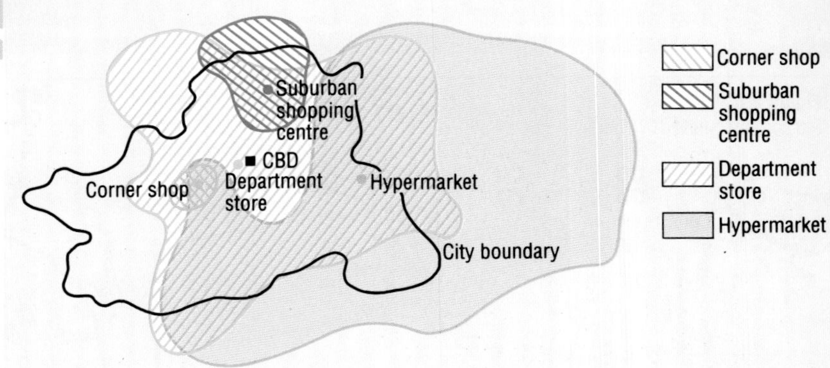

Figure 2.7
Spheres of influence of shops in and around Sheffield

Figure 2.8
Hierarchy of settlements according to services

Hamlet	Perhaps none
Village	Church, post office, public house, shop for daily goods, small junior school
Town	Several shops, churches and senior school, bus station, supermarket, doctor, dentist, banks, small hospital and football team
City	Large railway station, large shopping complex, cathedral, opticians and jewellers, large hospital and football team, museum
Capital	Cathedrals, government buildings, banking HQ, railway termini, museums and art galleries, main theatre and shopping centre

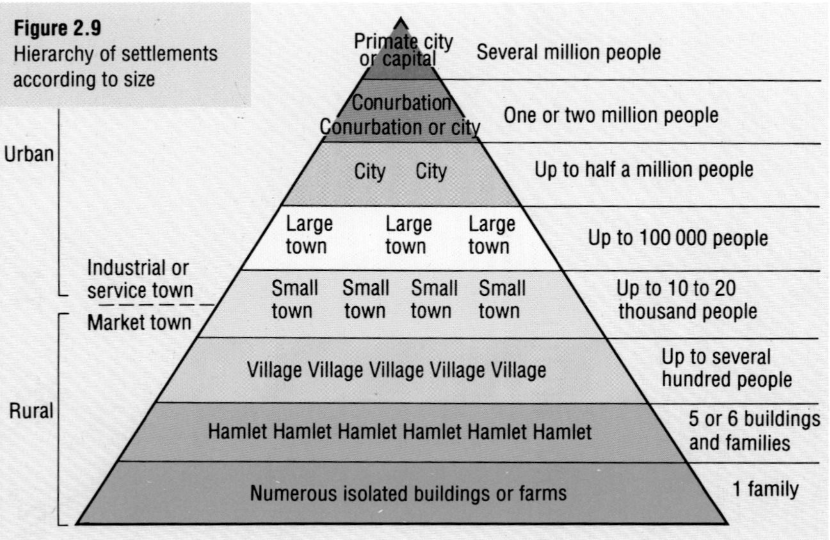

Figure 2.9
Hierarchy of settlements according to size

Range and number of functions or services These, like the size of the settlements, must also be based upon arbitrary criteria. The table in Figure 2.8 is a starting point which you could test for yourself in the field if you live in or near a rural area.

Sphere of influence This may be defined as the area served by a particular settlement. The size of this sphere of influence depends on the size and functions of a town and its surrounding settlements, the transport facilities available and the level of competition from a rival settlement. Two main ideas should be noted:

1 A *threshold population* is the minimum number of people needed to ensure that demand is great enough for a special service to be offered to the people living in that area. For example, estimates suggest 350 people are needed to make a grocer's shop successful, 2500 for a single doctor to be available, and 10,000 for a secondary school. Boots the Chemist prefers a threshold of 10,000 people in its catchment areas, Marks & Spencer 50,000 and Sainsburys 60,000.
2 *Range* is the maximum distance that people are prepared to travel to obtain a service. Figure 2.7 shows that people are not prepared to travel far to a corner shop, but will travel much further for a hypermarket – presumably because of the range and volume of stock and competitive prices.

Changes in time Few settlements remain constant in size. Most villages have increased (to suburbanised villages) or have become towns, while towns have become cities and cities have merged into conurbations. A few settlements have decreased in size, notably villages in isolated areas and, more recently, conurbations.

1 *(Page 18)*

Imagine that a group of settlers has sailed up the river shown on Figure 2.1. As their leader you have to choose the best site for a village. Your scouts have reported good possibilities at A, B, C, D and E.

i) Copy the following table. It shows several important factors that you will have to consider before choosing the best site.
ii) Complete the table for each possible site. *(5)*

Give a score of 1 to 5 for each factor for each site:
1 = Very good; 2 = Good; 3 = Average;
4 = Poor; 5 = Very poor.

Resource	Site A	Site B	Site C	Site D	Site E
Water Crop land Grazing land Fuel Building materials Defence Flat land which does not flood					
Total					

iii) State which you consider to be the best site (the one with the lowest score). *(1)*
iv) With help from the map, describe the location of the chosen site. *(3)*
v) Give your reasons for choosing this site. *(3)*
vi) What will be the main problems of living at this site? *(2)*

2 *(Pages 19 and 20)*

a i) What is meant by the term 'function of a town'? *(2)*
ii) What are the main functions of your nearest town or city? *(2)*

b Explain what is meant by the following terms: *(3)*
i) Dispersed settlement
ii) Nucleated settlement
iii) Linear settlement

3 *(Pages 21 and 22)*

An Ordnance Survey map can give some help in deciding the range and number of services found in different settlements. Look again at Figure 2.6 and find the settlements of Hedon, Preston, Thorngumbald, Burstwick, Lelley, Burton Pidsea, Bilton and Keyingham.

If a settlement is on a main road, give it two points. If it is on a 'B' class road, award one point. Give one point for every public house, church, school, post office and telephone box that each place has. For example, Keyingham is on the main road (two points) and has two churches and a post office (three more points) giving a total of five points. Obviously not all services or functions are shown on the OS map, but you could produce a rank order and see if this appears to agree with the differing sizes of the settlements. *(10)*

4 *(Page 22)*

Refer to the diagram below.

a i) What does the term 'sphere of influence' mean?
ii) Which service has the smallest threshold?
iii) Which service has the largest threshold?
iv) How far is it between the village and the town? *(4)*

b Give a reason why the sphere of influence of the theatre is larger than that of the chemist. *(1)*

c If a main road were built linking the village to the town, how might this affect the spheres of influence of the theatre, chemist and supermarket? *(3)*

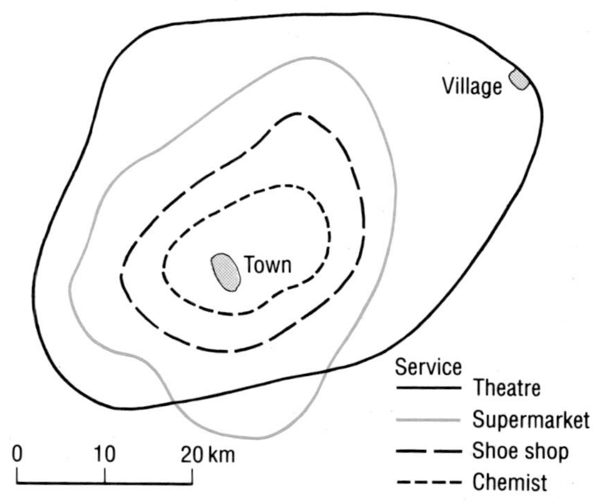

5 *(Page 22)*

The graph below shows a settlement hierarchy.

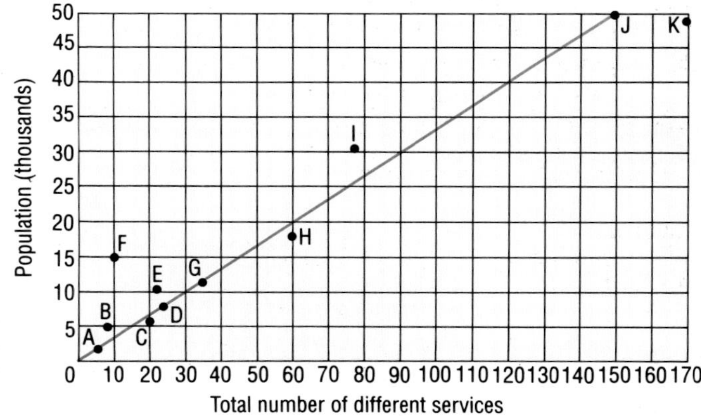

a i) Which settlement has the fewest services? *(1)*
ii) Which settlement has the most services? *(1)*
iii) What is the population of Settlement F? *(1)*
iv) How many services has Settlement F? *(1)*

b i) Describe the relationship between the population size and number of services in a settlement. *(1)*
ii) Suggest a reason for this relationship. *(1)*

c i) Which town has fewer services than you would expect for its size? *(1)*
ii) Suggest a reason for this. *(1)*

Growth of cities

Urbanisation means an increase in the proportion of people living in towns and cities. Even in the early civilisations of Mesopotamia, the Nile Valley, the Indus Valley and the Huang-He (North China), towns were important. However, it was not until the growth of industry in the nineteenth century that large-scale urbanisation occurred. In Great Britain, where the industrial revolution began, only 10 per cent of the population was living in towns in England and Wales in 1801, compared with 93 per cent in 1990. On a global scale, whereas only 15 per cent of the world's population lived in towns and cities in 1900, by 2000 this figure is expected to exceed 50 per cent.

Figure 3.1 shows the percentage of people living in urban areas in 1990. In parts of the more developed world, i.e. North America, North-west Europe and Oceania, over 75 per cent live in cities. However, recently the most rapid growth has been in the developing world where the 5 per cent of 1920 had grown to over 30 per cent by 1990 (Figure 3.1).

Two additional factors are the growth of very large cities which exceed one million inhabitants and the changing distribution of these cities (Figures 3.2 and 3.3).

- In 1850 there were only two 'million' cities – London and Paris. This number increased to 70 by 1950 and to 286 in 1990. There has also been a recent, rapid increase in the number of cities with populations of over five million.

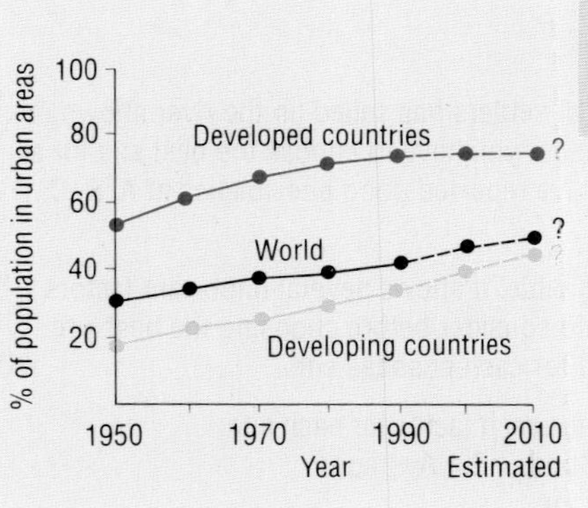

Figure 3.1
Percentage of world population in urban areas

- Prior to 1940 the majority of 'million' cities were found in the developed countries, in the temperate latitudes of the northern hemisphere. Since 1940 there has been a dramatic increase in the number of 'million' cities in the developing countries, the majority of which are found within the tropics.

Figure 3.5 shows the rank order of the world's twelve largest cities over a period of years. In 1970 half of these were still in the industrialised, developed continents of North America and Europe. By 1985 there were no European cities in the top twelve. Estimates suggest that by the year 2000 the two largest cities will be in Latin America and nine of the top ten will be in Latin America and Asia.

Both São Paulo and Mexico City are growing by an estimated half a million people a year. Can you imagine all the inhabitants of Leeds or Sheffield suddenly arriving in São Paulo or Mexico City in one year? Think of the problems that it must pose for both the newcomers and the city authorities.

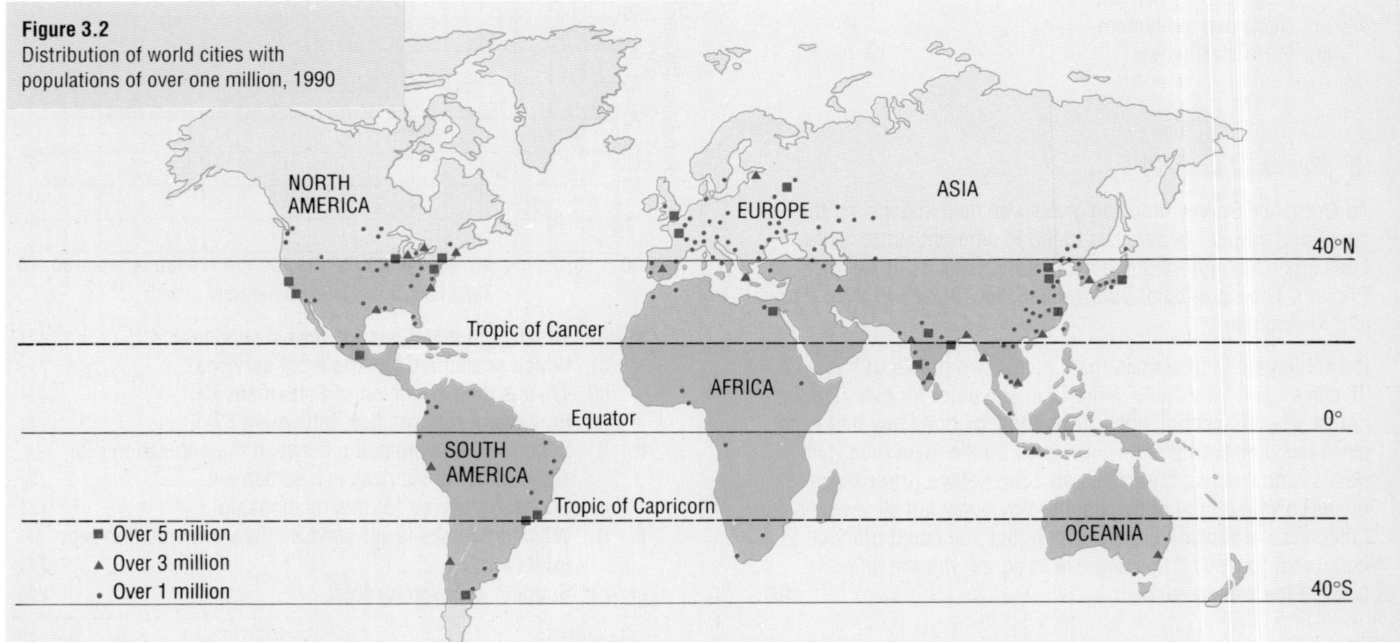

Figure 3.2
Distribution of world cities with populations of over one million, 1990

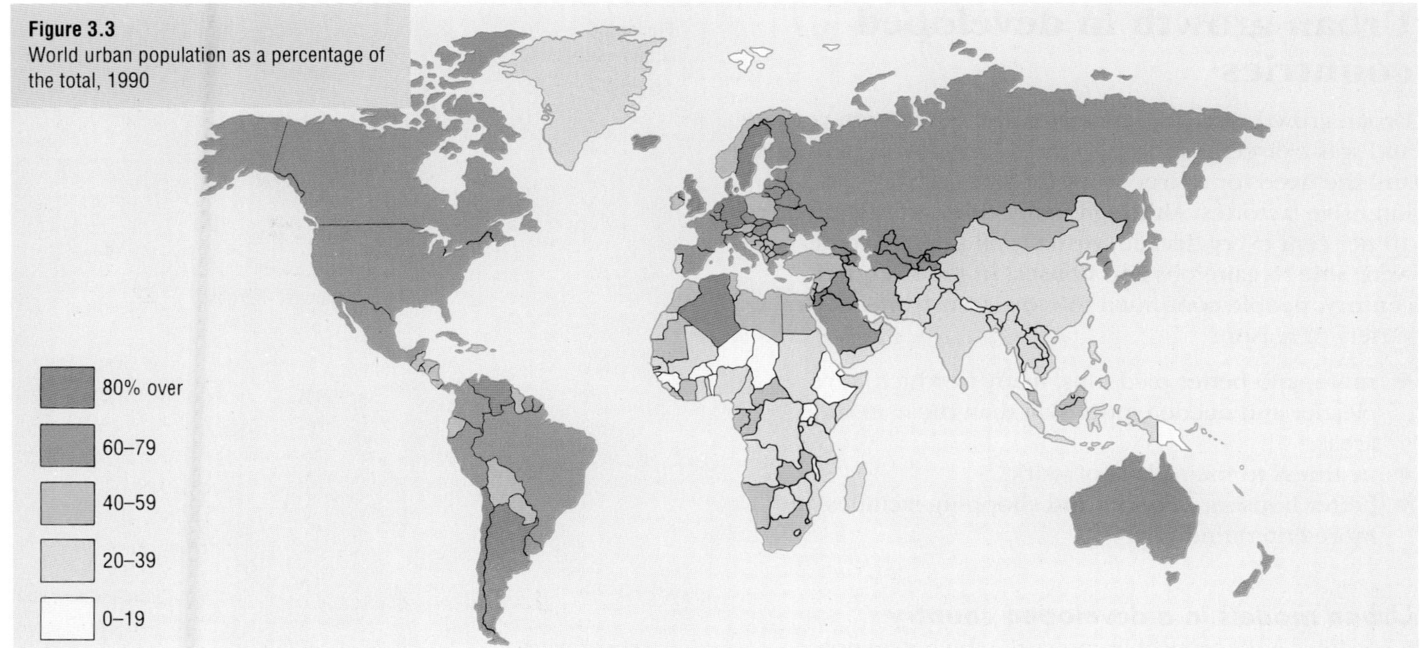

Figure 3.3
World urban population as a percentage of the total, 1990

The process of urbanisation does appear to have slowed down in developed countries; indeed some cities like London have even seen a decline in their total population. Recent information from developing countries suggests that the growth of their cities may also be slowing down. Even so, many of these cities are likely to have doubled their 1980 population by the year 2000.

Figure 3.5 gives two of many quoted estimates for the size of the largest cities in 2000. This discrepancy may be due to several factors:

- Definitions of what is meant by 'urban' and how the size of an 'urban area' is delimited vary widely between countries.
- Countries conduct their census at different times. The actual data collected may not be reliable, and figures given in the years following the census have to be estimated.
- Estimates assume an accuracy in figures for birth and death rates, infant mortality, life expectancy, and rates of migration; and secondly, that rates of change are consistent.

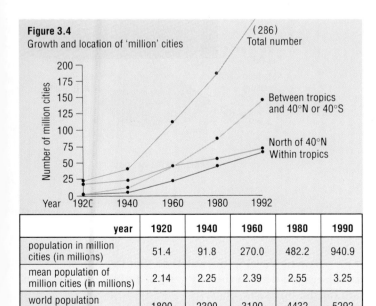

Figure 3.4
Growth and location of 'million' cities

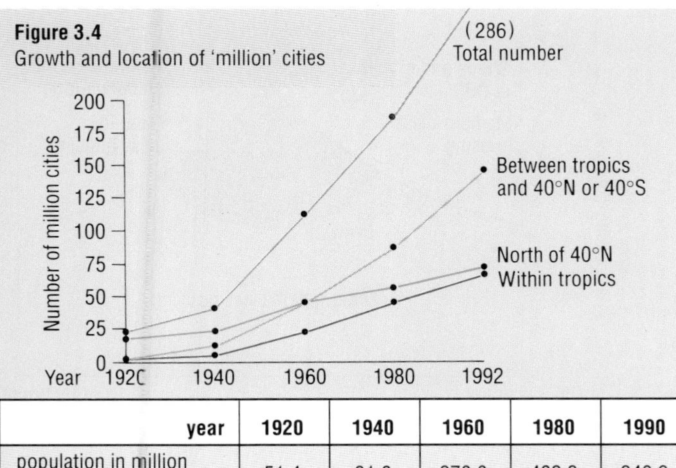

year	1920	1940	1960	1980	1990
population in million cities (in millions)	51.4	91.8	270.0	482.2	940.9
mean population of million cities (in millions)	2.14	2.25	2.39	2.55	3.25
world population (in millions)	1800	2300	3100	4432	5292
% population in million cities	2.86	4.01	8.71	10.88	17.6

Figure 3.5
The world's largest cities

rank order	1970	1985	estimate 2000	(1)	(2)
1	New York 16.5	Tokyo 23.0	Mexico City	31.0	26.0
2	Tokyo 13.4	Mexico City 18.7	São Paulo	25.8	24.1
3	London 10.5	New York 18.2	Tokyo	23.7	17.0
4	Shanghai 10.0	São Paulo 16.8	Shanghai	23.7	13.8
5	Mexico City 8.6	Shanghai 13.3	New York	23.4	15.5
6	Los Angeles 8.4	Los Angeles 12.8	Rio de Janeiro	19.0	13.5
7	Buenos Aires 8.4	Buenos Aires 11.6	Bombay	16.8	16.0
8	Paris 8.4	Rio de Janeiro 11.1	Calcutta	16.4	16.6
9	São Paulo 7.1	Calcutta 9.2	Seoul	13.7	13.5
10	Moscow 7.1	Bombay 8.2	Delhi	11.8	13.3

Figures in millions

Latin America | Europe | North America | Asia

Urban growth in developed countries

Urban growth occurred mainly in the nineteenth century, and was a direct response to the development of industry and the need for a large work force for the labour-intensive factories. Although many cities grew at a rate of 10 per cent every decade, virtually all the newcomers were able to gain jobs and houses. In the twentieth century, people continued to move to urban areas for a variety of reasons:

- more, and better paid jobs, many of which were cleaner and needed more skill than those in rural areas;
- nearness to their place of work;
- better housing, services and shopping facilities and more entertainment.

Urban models in a developed country

A model is a theoretical framework which may not actually exist, but which helps to explain the reality. It has been suggested that towns do not grow in a haphazard way, but that they show certain generalised characteristics. The two simplest models to demonstrate this possible growth are shown in Figure 3.6.

1 Burgess, initially using Chicago as his basis, suggested that most towns grew outwards in a concentric pattern, meaning that buildings are newer the closer one gets to the edge of the city. It is possible that five rings may develop.

2 Hoyt, in contrast, proposed the idea that towns grew as sectors, or in wedge shapes. This means that if, for example, industry grew up in one part of the town in the nineteenth century, later industries would also develop in that sector.

Since then further models have been suggested, but it should be understood that most urban areas are complex and probably show the characteristics of more than one model, and that each city is unique.

Figure 3.6
Urban models

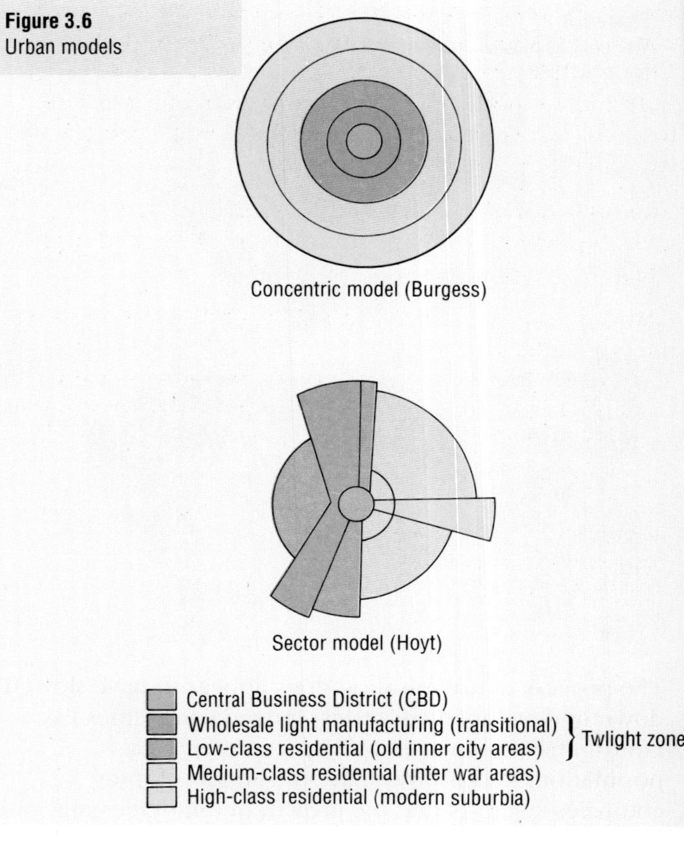

Figure 3.7
Land values across a British city

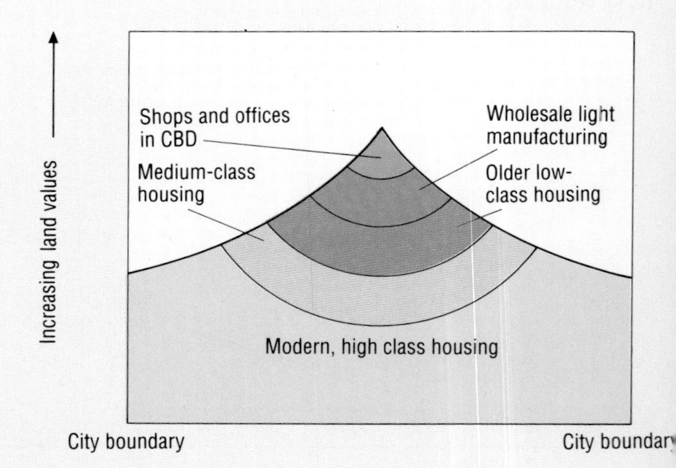

Land use and functional zones in a city

Each of the zones shown in Figure 3.6 has a function and shows a different type of land use. These differences may result from:

Land values Land is expensive in the CBD (Central Business District), where competition is greatest. It becomes increasingly cheaper towards the urban boundary (Figure 3.7).

Space There is very little available space near to the city centre, but this increases towards the outskirts, again partly due to declining land values and improved planning.

Age Towns develop outwards so that the oldest buildings are near to the city centre, and the newest ones are on the outskirts.

Accessibility The CBD is where the main routes from the suburbs meet, and so the area is easier to reach from all parts of the city.

Wealth of the inhabitants The poorer members of the community tend to live in the cheaper houses near to the CBD (with its shops) and the inner city (where most jobs used to be found). These people are less likely to be able to afford transport (private or public) in order to get to work had they lived on the outskirts.

Planning policies These have helped to control the growth of the town (particularly since 1945), and have affected its redevelopment.

Both the land use and the functions of different parts of the town alter with time:

1 Industry in the nineteenth century grew up next to the CBD (inner city area) whereas today most new industries will be on edge-of-town industrial estates or science parks.

2 Terraced nineteenth century housing may have been replaced with high-rise flats or areas of open space.

A typical, present day British town or city may still show several of the characteristics shown in the models in Figure 3.6 and the photograph in Figure 3.9. However, due to changes in land use and functional zones, the modern pattern is likely to be more complex as shown in Figures 3.8 and 3.10.

Figure 3.9
Changing land use in the British city of Peterborough

Figure 3.8
Land use in a modern British city showing a combination of the concentric and sector models

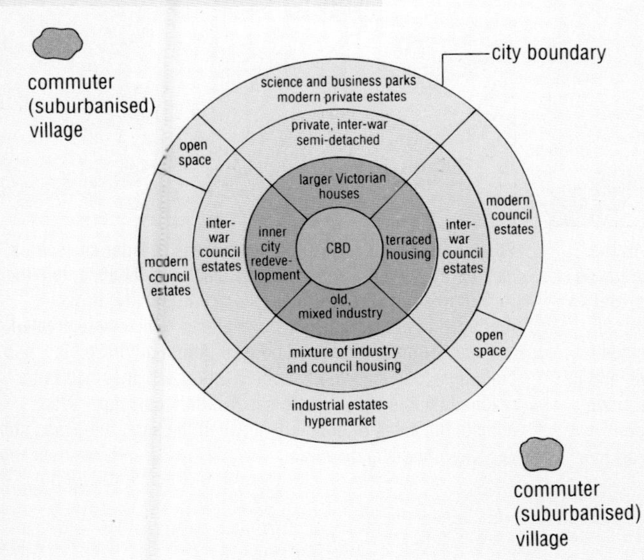

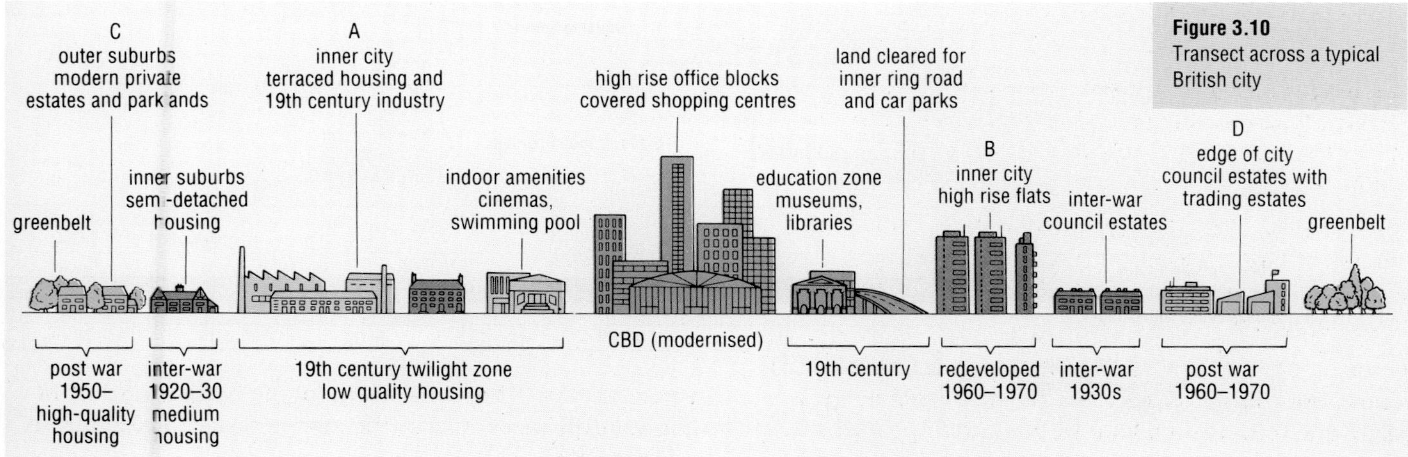

Figure 3.10
Transect across a typical British city

Residential environments in developed cities

A Old inner city area

B Inner city redevelopment

Figure 3.11 Physical appearance

Figure 3.12 Land use

- housing
- open space and gardens
- industry
- transport
- wasteland
- services (schools, shops)

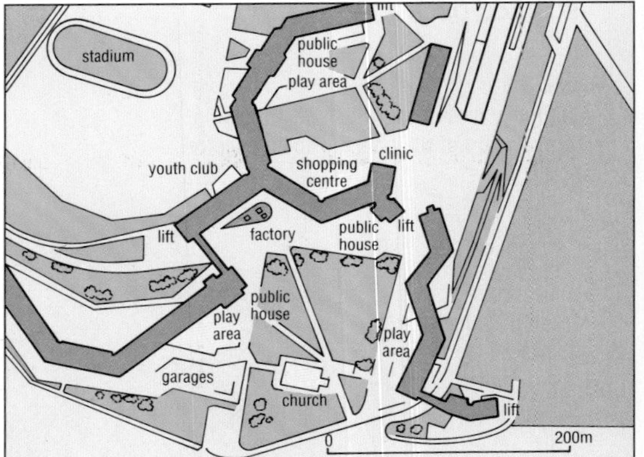

Figure 3.13 Description

The industrial revolution of the nineteenth century led to the growth of towns. The rapid influx of workers into these towns meant a big and immediate demand for cheap housing, and so builders constructed as many houses as possible in a small area, resulting in high density housing with an overcrowded population. The houses were built in long, straight rows and in terraces. In those days of non-planning, few amenities were provided either in the house (e.g. no indoor wc, bathroom, sewerage, electricity) or around it (e.g. no open space and no gardens).

When in the 1950s and 1960s vast areas of inner cities were cleared by bulldozers many of the displaced inhabitants either moved to council estates near the city boundary, or were rehoused in huge high-rise tower blocks which were created on the sites of the old terraced houses. Although these high-rise buildings contained most modern amenities, they had to be reached by lifts which led to narrow, dark corridors. Also, despite the areas of greenery between the flats, there was still a very high housing density.

Figure 3.14 Census data

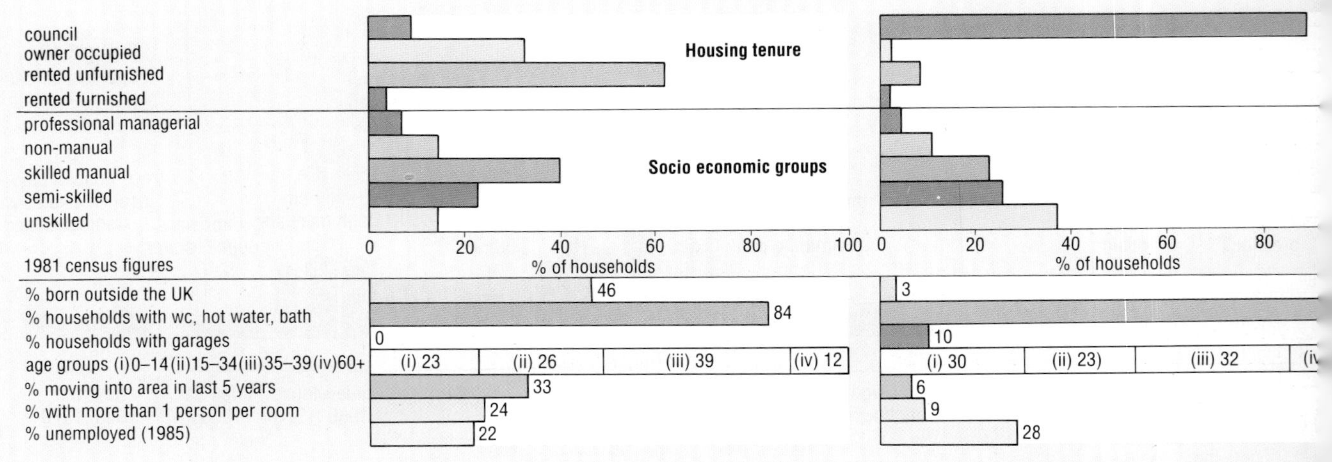

C Suburbia

The rapid outward growth of cities began with the introduction of public transport and accelerated with the popularity of the private car. This outward growth (also known as urban sprawl) led to the construction of numerous private, 'car based' suburbs.

The houses built in the outer suburbs before the Second World War are characterised by their front and back gardens. Usually they have garages and are semi-detached with bay windows. The more recent estates have housing which differs in both style and type, but they remain well planned and spacious.

D Outer city council estate

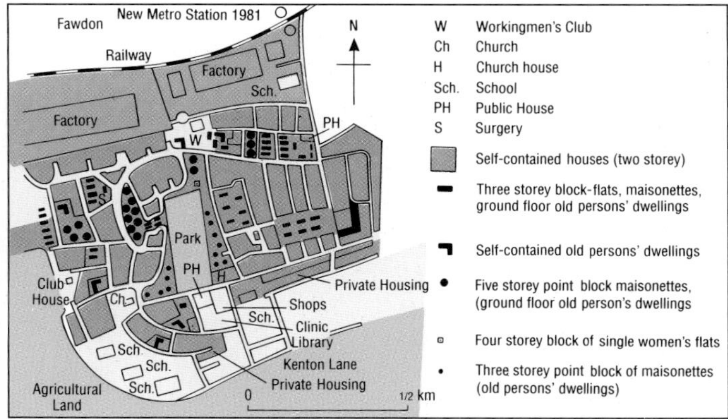

As local councils cleared the worst of the slums from their inner city areas in the 1950s and 1960s many residents were rehoused on large council estates on the fringes of the city. Attempts were made to vary the type and size of accommodation:

- High-rise tower blocks, often of 10–12 storeys.
- Low-rise tower blocks, usually 3–5 storeys high. These were built nearer the city boundaries, where there was more open space.
- Single-storey terraces with some gardens and car parking space.

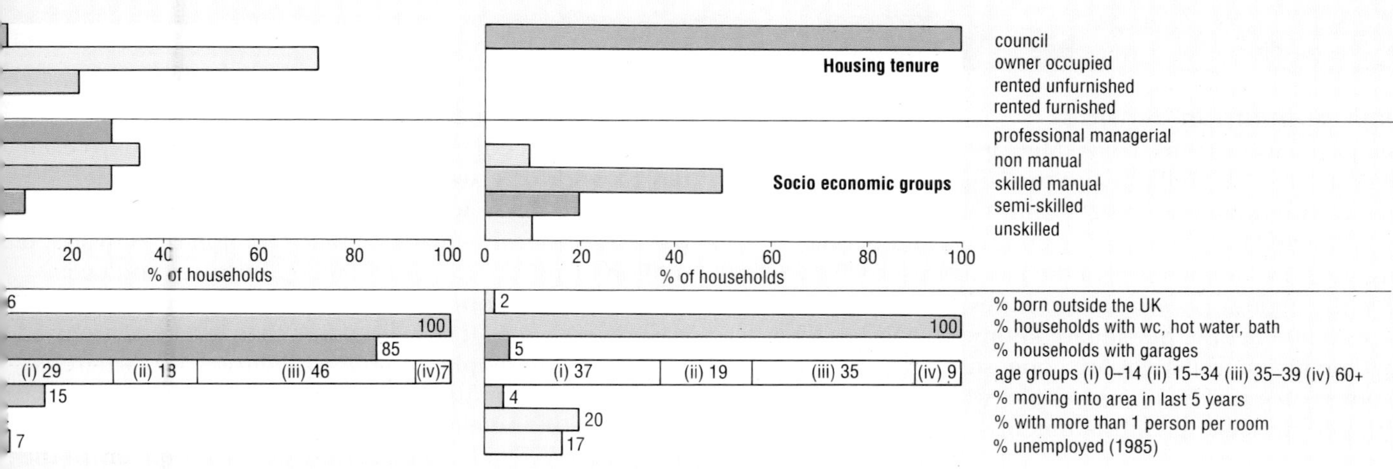

Problems in developed cities

The Japanese capital of Tokyo is the world's richest city in the world's richest country. Indeed in the early 1990s there were only five countries richer than Tokyo. Despite this wealth Tokyo has many of the problems found in other large cities in developed countries.

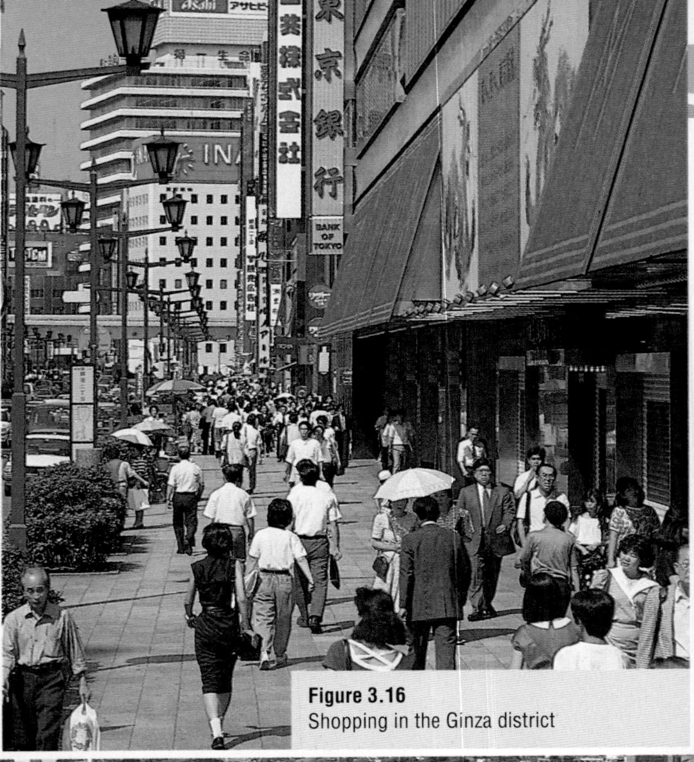

Figure 3.16
Shopping in the Ginza district

Figure 3.15
View across Tokyo showing the high density of building

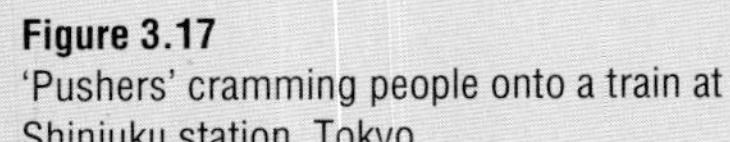

Figure 3.17
'Pushers' cramming people onto a train at Shinjuku station, Tokyo

High population densities

The population of the Tokyo Metropolitan Government Region was 11.93 million and the larger Greater Tokyo region 31.6 million in 1992. Central Tokyo is overcrowded both in terms of buildings and people (Figure 3.15). Some parts of the city nearest to Tokyo Bay have the highest population densities in the world with over 20,000 people per square kilometre. During the daytime the central areas are congested with shoppers (Figure 3.16) and business people, while at night they fill with people seeking entertainment.

Transport problems

Over 2 million commuters travel into central Tokyo each day to work. The average travel time for a commuter is 3 hours a day. Each working day sees 15 million passenger journeys made by rail, 7 million by subways, 6 million by private car and 4 million by buses and taxis. One railway station, Shinjuku, deals with over 4 million passengers a day. It is so crowded that 'pushers' are used to cram more people into trains (Figure 3.17). Where space is at a premium railways run above main roads (Figure 3.19). An elaborate and expensive urban motorway system has been constructed with many of the expressways having four lanes or more in each direction.

Figure 3.18
High density housing in Tokyo

Figure 3.19
A railway line built over a main road in Tokyo

High land values

The demand for a prestige site in one of Tokyo's several CBDs has led to exceptionally high land values and skyscraper development (Figure 3.20). It is claimed that a person wishing to sell even a small plot of land in central Tokyo would become an instant millionaire!

Housing

There are enough houses for each family to have its own home. Most have been built since 1945. The majority are very small with perhaps only one room, are made of wood (risk of fire), do not have gardens and are packed close together (Figure 3.18). In the most crowded housing areas families have to share toilets and sometimes kitchens, but these problems and those of water supply and sewage are far less than in similar parts of cities in other developed countries. Much time and money is being spent on urban renewal schemes.

Pollution

Some of the severe problems of the 1970s have decreased considerably due to stricter controls, but many still remain (pages 224–25). Tokyo's 4 million cars and 80,000 factories cause high levels of noise, vibrations and air pollution. Under extreme conditions people have to wear face-masks as protection against fumes. Companies polluting the air are fined, but penalties are small in value to the large, rich industrial corporations. Sewage has to be collected from those homes not connected to the main sewerage but some, together with industrial discharges, may enter either the many rivers flowing through the city or end up in Tokyo Bay. Rubbish is either incinerated or dumped. Reclaimed land in the bay, needed for port expansion, new industries and housing, has been formed from dumped waste.

Figure 3.20
New Tokyo Metropolitan Government Buildings

Lack of open space

Land prices are too high and the demand for space too great to leave open for many parks or playgrounds.

Crime

The problem is not nearly so acute in Japanese cities as in cities of other countries. New York has 20 murders, 240 muggings and 30 rapes to every one in Tokyo.

Climate

The city becomes extremely hot and humid in summer. Despite being in a sheltered bay, the city lies in the path of autumn typhoons.

Natural disasters

Japan lies on a destructive plate margin (page 212). Tokyo, and its port of Yokohama, were destroyed in 1923 with the loss of 150,000 lives. While larger, modern buildings have been constructed to withstand earth-quakes, houses have not. Coastal areas are vulnerable to flooding caused either by tsunamis (large tidal waves; Figure 16.35) triggered by submarine earth-quakes, swollen rivers following heavy rainfall or high tides.

Urban growth in developing countries

The movement of people to cities in the developing world began in the early twentieth century. Since then it has accelerated so that many places are expanding at a rate of over 25 per cent every decade. The movement, from country areas to towns and cities is called *rural-urban migration*. Figure 3.21 is a quotation from the Brandt Report. It suggests that in developing countries, movement to the city is partly due to *rural push* and partly due to *urban pull* (Figure 3.22).

"The rush to the towns has created the same kind of misery as existed in the nineteenth-century cities of Europe and America. But industrialisation in those days was labour-intensive, so that the cities grew as the jobs expanded. .... The migration in today's developing world is often due to the lack of opportunitiy in the countryside – it is 'rural push' as much as 'urban pull'. The consequences of high birth rates and rapid migration are all too visible in many cities of the Third World, with abysmal living conditions and very high unemployment or underemployment. The strains on families, whose members are often separated, are very heavy. In São Paulo in Brazil, the population was growing at around 6–7 per cent annually in the late sixties and early seventies, in such appalling conditions that infant mortality was actually increasing. The fact that people still migrate to these cities only underlines the desperate situation which they have left behind."

Figure 3.21 Extract from the Brandt Report

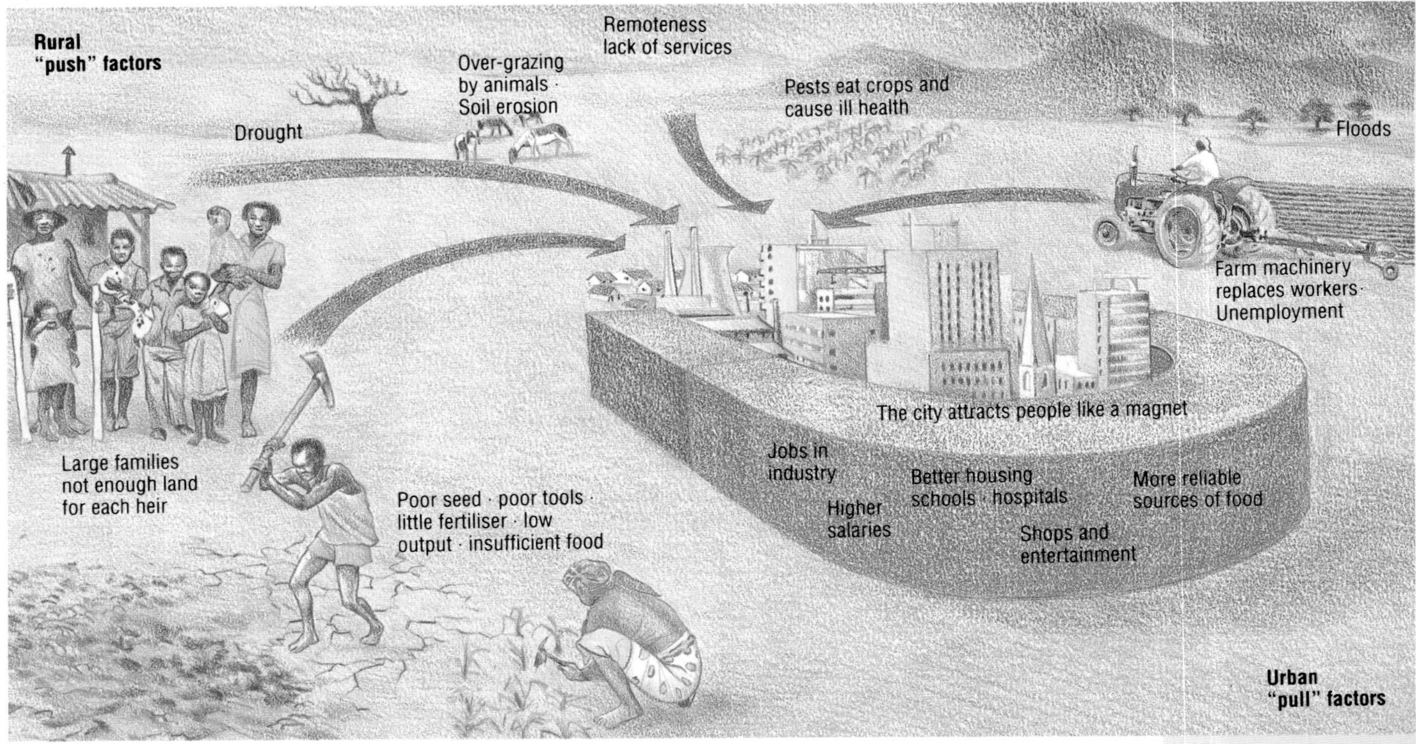

Figure 3.22 Rural 'push' factors and urban 'pull' factors

'Push' factors (why people leave the countryside):

- Pressure on the land, e.g. division of land among sons – each has too little to live on.
- Many families do not own any land.
- Overpopulation, resulting from high birth rates.
- Starvation, resulting from either too little output for the people of the area, or crop failure. Often, it may also be caused by a change in agriculture – from producing crops for local/family consumption to a system that produces cash/plantation crops for consumption in the developed world.
- Limited food production due to overgrazing, or to misuse of the land resulting in soil erosion or exhaustion.
- Mechanisation has caused a reduction in jobs available on the land together with, in many areas, reduced yields.
- Farming is hard work with long hours and little pay. In developing countries a lack of money means a lack of machinery, pesticides and fertilisers.

Figure 3.23
Central Hong Kong

- Natural disasters such as drought (Sahel countries), hurricanes (West Indies), floods (Bangladesh) and volcanic eruptions (Colombia) destroy villages and crops.
- Extreme physical conditions such as aridity, rugged mountains, cold, heat and dense vegetation.
- Local communities (Amazon Amerindians) forced to move.
- Lack of services (schools, hospitals).
- Lack of investment as money available to the government will be spent on urban areas.

'Pull' factors (why people move to the city):

- They are looking for better paid jobs. Factory workers get about three times the wages of farm workers.
- They expect to be housed more comfortably and to have a higher quality of life.
- They have a better chance of services such as schools, medical treatment and entertainment.
- They are attracted to the 'bright lights'.
- More reliable sources of food.
- Religious and political activities can be carried on more safely in larger cities.

Figure 3.22 refers to the family's 'perceptions of the city'. This is what they think, expect or were led to believe the city is like (Figure 3.23). The reality is very different (Figure 3.24). As many new arrivals to the city are unlikely to have much money, they will be unable to buy or rent a house, even if one was available. They will probably have to make a temporary shelter using cheap or waste materials. The gap between the rich and poor is far greater in developing countries than it is in ones which are more developed.

Figure 3.24
New arrivals to developing cities often encounter conditions like these people in the Philippines

Problems in residential areas in developing cities

São Paulo is a notorious example of the ways in which problems are created when cities grow too quickly. Its population is reputed to have grown from 7 million in 1970 to over 17 million in 1990, and is forecast to reach 25 million by 2000.

Just as in the developed world, there are marked differences between the residential areas of cities in the developing world. However, the gulf between the types of residential area in the developing world is greater. São Paulo has:

- Relatively few rich people in comparison with the total population.
- A large proportion of poor inhabitants.
- An increasing number of migrants, most of whom are also very poor.

As a result, the contrast (Figure 3.25) between the well-off areas and the poorest areas shows a great difference in the quality and density of housing, the quality of the environment and the provision of amenities.

Housing for the well off

This group of people will live in expensive housing ranging from elegant apartment complexes, each with its own social and recreational facilities, to Californian-style detached houses with large gardens and individual swimming pools (Figure 3.26). The size of family will probably be limited to two children, with housemaids and security guards. These houses will be located near to the CBD where most of its inhabitants will work – presumably in commercial premises (Figure 3.27). The children, who will be healthy and well educated, will eventually go into well-paid jobs. Such homes will also be near to the shops and amenities in the CBD.

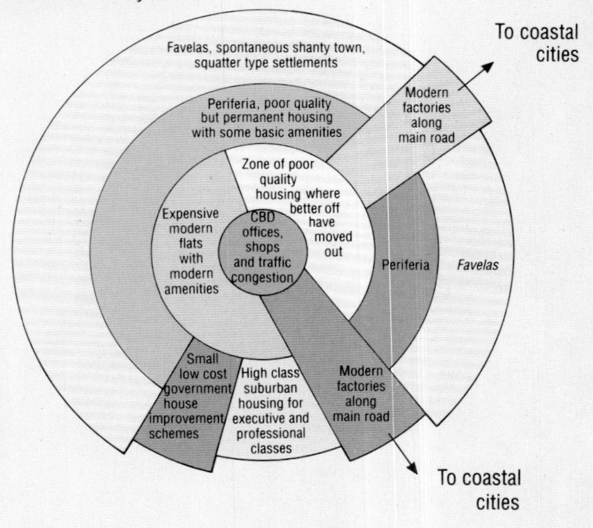

Figure 3.25
Model of land use structures and residential areas in a developing city (based on Brazil)

Figure 3.26
Californian-type housing for the rich in São Paulo

Figure 3.27
Part of São Paulo's CBD. CBDs in developing countries can be as affluent as those in developed countries

Figure 3.28
A favela in São Paulo – a slum of 'despair'

Figure 3.29
Shanty housing in Brazil

Housing for the poor (favelas)

The poor of São Paulo, and the new migrants who amount to half a million people a year, live in temporary accommodation. This is sometimes built on vacant space next to modern factories, alongside main roads leading to the city centre, but usually on the outskirts of the existing urban areas. These people are 'squatters'and have no legal right to the land they occupy. The rapid growth of these spontaneous shanty settlements, or favelas as they are called in Brazil, is common to cities in the developing world (Figures 3.24, 3.28 and 3.29). Favelas are found on land which has little economic value, and which the well off find unsuitable for either farming or housing. Shanty settlements often develop on steep hillsides which are liable to landslides or on badly drained, unhealthy valley floors.

Housing is often a collection of primitive shacks made from any available material – wood, corrugated iron, cardboard or sacking. Some may only have one room in which the family has to live, eat and sleep. Others may have two rooms, one being used to sleep the family which is likely to consist of at least six children. Most houses lack such basic amenities as electricity, gas, clean running water, toilets and main sewerage. Any empty space between houses will soon be filled either with rubbish, as there is no refuse collection, or later migrants. The area becomes overcrowded and has a very high housing density.

Health The twin problems of the disposal of human waste, which is often left to run down the streets, and the lack of clean water lead to disease, especially typhoid and dysentery. There are few, if any, hospitals or doctors and residents are usually unlikely to be able to afford medical care. Infant mortality is high and life expectancy is short.

Education is limited as there are few schools. Children may be left illiterate and lacking in the skills which might have gained them jobs. Many, even by the age of six or seven, are already trying to earn some money (e.g. selling fruit or shoe cleaning, see page 125).

Employment There are relatively few jobs within the favela. Those people with some education and skills may get jobs in São Paulo's many factories, but wages are low and the factories are likely to be a long way off.

Transport The internal roads are frequently only earth tracks. Often they will be full of rubbish or left as open drains. Public transport systems are few and unreliable and this makes it even more difficult for residents to get to work or travel to better shopping areas.

Family life is under constant threat. The factors listed above can lead to break down of marriages, an increase in crime and a drift of teenagers to the CBD where they will swell the large ranks of 'street children' already living there.

Self-help schemes in developing cities

One hundred million people have no shelter of any kind, and over one-third of the inhabitants of developing cities live in squatter settlements – sites only vacant because they are subject to flooding, landslips or industrial pollution. Many local authorities encourage these settlements as it is convenient for them to have a ready pool of cheap labour on their doorsteps even if they fail to take any responsibility for them. Self-help schemes seem the only hope for these squatters to improve their 'homes'. The poor's most immediate needs are often simple – a plot on which to build, a small loan to improve or extend the house, cheap building materials and basic services. There is no need for advanced technology or expensive building schemes (page 123).

Housing improvements in São Paulo

Although most governments would like to remove shanty settlements from their cities, they cannot afford to build the necessary amounts of replacement accommodation. As a result, the favelas become 'permanent'. Two government assisted schemes in São Paulo aimed at improving the quality of life in favela environments are:

1 **Low-cost improvements** (Figure 3.30)
Existing homes may be improved by rebuilding the houses with cheap, and quick and easy to use breeze blocks. A water tank on the roof collects rainwater and is connected to the water supply and in turn to an outside wash basin and an indoor bathroom/toilet. Electricity and main sewerage are added. Most inhabitants of this type of housing, which is found in the peripheral parts of São Paulo (Figure 3.25), will have some type of employment enabling them to pay low rents.

2 **Self-help schemes** (Figure 3.31)
Groups of people are encouraged to help build their new homes. Each group will do basic work such as digging the ditches to take the water and sewage pipes. The local authority will then provide breeze blocks and roofing tiles, and the group will provide the labour. The money which this saves the authorities can be used to provide amenities such as electricity, a clean water supply, tarred roads and a community centre. The advantages of self-help schemes are that they can be done in stages, they can create a community spirit and, as the cost of building is relatively cheap, more houses can be provided.

Unfortunately, despite the introduction of these schemes, local authorities in developing cities like São Paulo cannot keep pace with the continuous and large numbers of new migrants.

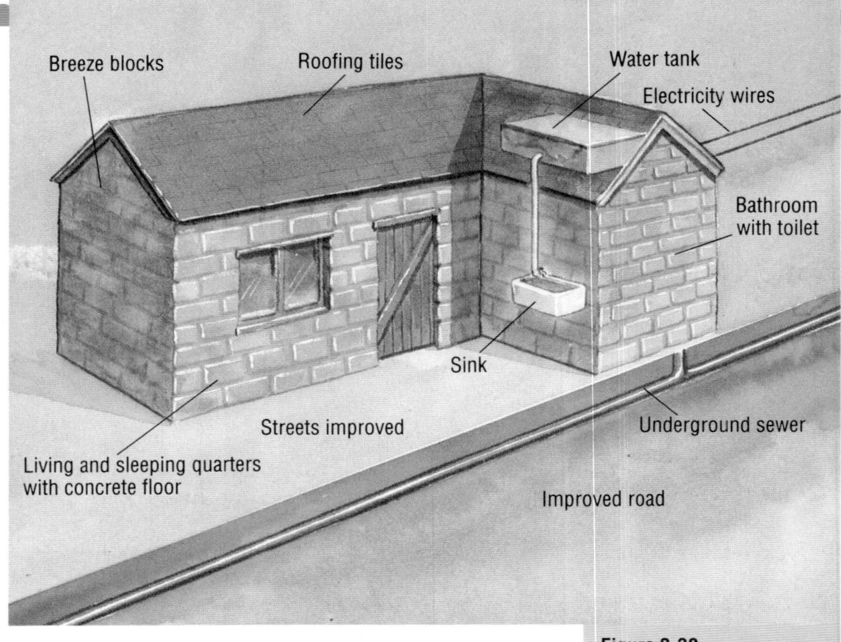

Figure 3.30
A self-help housing scheme in São Paulo

Figure 3.31
A community 'self-help' housing project in São Paulo – a 'slum of hope'

Suburbanised villages in developed countries

In parts of the developed world there has been a reversal of the movement to large urban areas, and groups of people have moved out into surrounding villages. This has led to a change in the character of such settlements and to their being called suburbanised (because they adopt some of the characteristics of the nearby urban areas; Figure 3.33). They are also called *commuter* or *dormitory towns* (because many residents who live and sleep there travel to the nearby towns and cities for work).

Who moves into these villages?

- The more wealthy urban residents and those with improved family status. These groups have the money to afford the larger and often expensive houses, and the cost of travel to work, shops and amenities.
- Those wishing to move into a more attractive environment with less pollution and more space.
- Elderly people who have retired and wish to live in a quieter environment.
- Those seeing a chance to work in or develop a service industry that has resulted from the rising resident population and influx of visitors from nearby urban areas.

Changes in the villages

Braithwaite is a small village on the edge of the Lake District in Cumbria (Figure 3.32). The 1925 map shows the original form of the village which then consisted of tightly grouped farms, outbuildings and terraced cottages along narrow lanes. Most buildings originated during the eighteenth and nineteenth centuries. One was a listed building. The village green gave an open character to the western half.

By 1976 the character had changed due to increased mobility and accessibility. The village lies less than three miles from the tourist centre of Keswick, and next to the improved A66 which links West Cumbria and the M6.

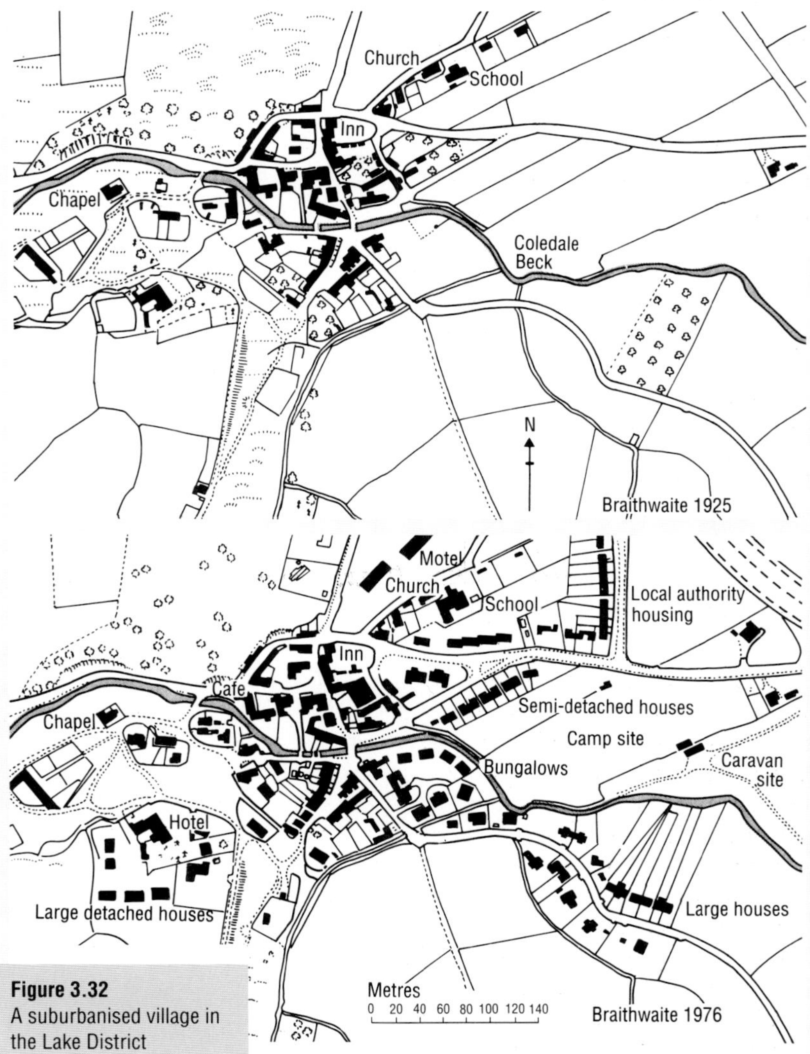

Figure 3.32
A suburbanised village in the Lake District

Figure 3.33
A suburbanised village at Blockley in the Cotswolds

1 *(Page 24)*

a Write out a definition of each of the following:
  i) Urban.
  ii) Urbanisation.
  iii) Million or millionaire cities. *(3)*

b In England and Wales, what percentage of the total population lived in towns in:
  i) 1801?
  ii) 1990? *(2)*

c What caused large scale urbanisation in Britain in the nineteenth century? *(1)*

2 *(Page 24)*

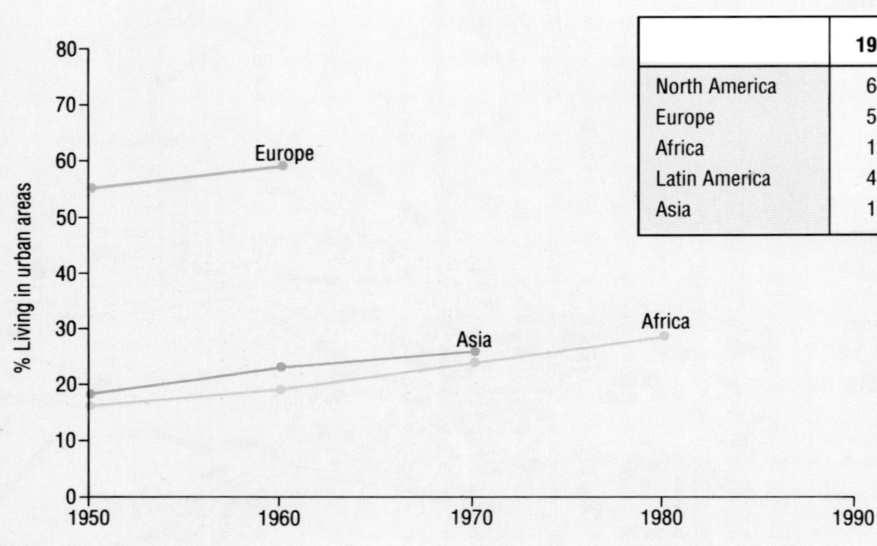

	1950	1960	1970	1980	1990
North America	64	67	70	74	77
Europe	54	58	61	69	73
Africa	15	18	23	28	36
Latin America	41	49	57	65	71
Asia	17	22	25	29	34

Study the graph and table which shows the percentage of population living in urban areas.

a i) Make a copy of the graph outline shown above.
  ii) Plot the information given in the table next to the graph. *(6)*
  iii) Give the graph a suitable title. *(1)*

b Which world region showed the:
  i) Slowest increase in urbanisation between 1950 and 1990?
  ii) Most rapid increase in urbanisation between 1950 and 1990? *(2)*

3 *(Page 25)*

a How many 'million' cities were there in:
  i) 1920?
  ii) 1990? *(2)*

b Approximately what proportion of these were found:
  i) North of 40°N in 1920 and in 1990? *(2)*
  ii) Within the tropics in 1920 and in 1990? *(2)*

c i) Has the average size of 'million' cities increased between 1920 and 1990?
  ii) Has the percentage of people living in these cities increased? *(2)*

d Using Figure 3.2, try to name as many as possible of the
  i) 34 cities with a population of over 5 million in 1990. *(One point per 10 cities)*
  ii) 32 cities with a population between 3 and 5 million in 1990. *(One point per 10 cities)*

e Which was the largest city in the world in 1970? *(1)*

f Which continent contained two of the 12 largest cities in the world in 1970 and yet none in 1985? *(1)*

g By how many millions is Mexico City's population predicted to increase between 1970 and AD 2000? *(1)*

h Give one point to describe the distribution of the 12 largest cities in the world in:
  i) 1970
  ii) AD 2000 *(2)*

4 *(Pages 26 and 27)*

A

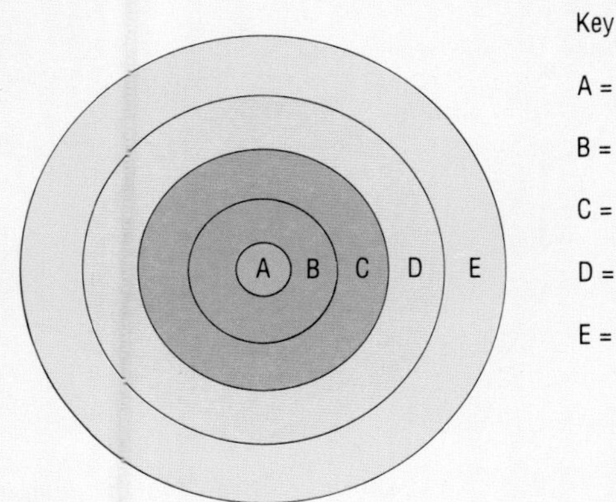

B

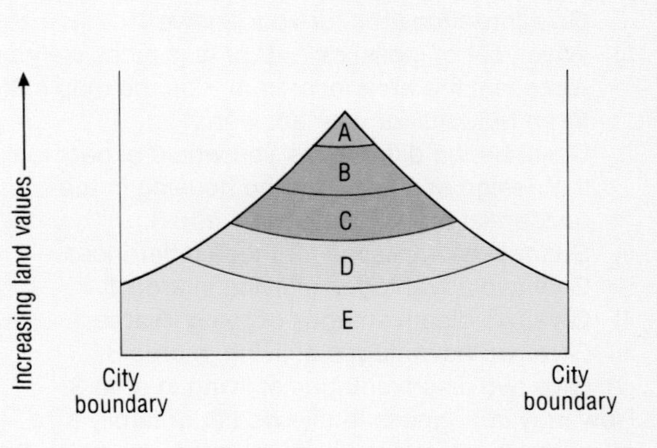

a Figure A is an incomplete model of a city in the developed world. Make a copy of it and complete the key by adding each of the following statements next to the correct letter: *(5)*

- Oldest, poorest quality housing inter-mixed with industry.
- Large shops and office blocks.
- Newest and most expensive housing.
- Traditionally the centre of light manufacturing.
- Mainly interwar medium cost housing.

b Figure B is a transect (section) showing land values across a typical city in a developed country.
- i) Which of the five zones is the central business district? *(1)*
- ii) Why is there very little open space in Zone B? *(1)*
- iii) Which of the five zones is likely to have the largest houses with gardens? *(1)*

5 *(Pages 28 and 29)*

Four residential environments are labelled A to D on pages 28 and 29.

a For each area:
- i) Describe the type, appearance, age and ownership of its housing. *(4)*
- ii) Describe its road pattern. *(2)*
- iii) Give the approximate cost of housing (remembering there will be a difference between the south and the north of Britain). *(1)*
- iv) Describe and give reasons for its land use. *(4)*
- v) Describe its household and neighbourhood amenities. *(4)*
- vi) List the advantages and disadvantages of living in the area. *(4)*

b What is meant by the following terms: socio-economic group; non-manual; housing tenure; owner occupied; suburbia; council estates; redevelopment; housing amenities; and housing density? *(9)*

c Giving a reason for your answer in each case, say which of the four areas is likely to have the:
- i) least and
- ii) most of each of the following:
elderly; young couples; young children; unemployed; immigrants; garages; open space; basic household amenities; housing density; professional and managerial. *(10 x 3)*

d The four maps on pages 28 and 29 show different types of land use in each area.
- i) Take a piece of tracing paper 10cm x 10cm and divide it into 100 squares (1 square to equal 1 per cent). Place the tracing paper over each map in turn, and determine the percentage of land use for each of the following categories:
housing; open space and gardens; industry; transport; wasteland; services (schools, shops). *(4 x 3)*
- ii) Draw a histogram for each area to show your results. *(4)*

e Make a journey along a main road from the CBD to the city boundary. Describe any changes in the housing that you see on your journey. *(4)*

6 *(Pages 28 and 29)*

a i) Which set of statistics, A, B or C is most likely to represent the area located at 1 on the map? Give three reasons for your answer. *(1+3)*

ii) Which set of statistics A, B or C is most likely to represent the area located at 3 on the map? Give three reasons for your answer. *(1+3)*

b i) Describe the differences you would expect to find in the design and layout of the housing in the residential areas located at 1 and 3. *(2)*

ii) Suggest two reasons for these differences. *(2)*

c i) Give two advantages of living in area 1. *(2)*

ii) Give two disadvantages of living in area 1. *(2)*

iii) Give two advantages of living in area 3. *(2)*

iv) Give two disadvantages of living in area 3. *(2)*

d How may changes in family wealth or family size affect the type of area in which people might live? *(4)*

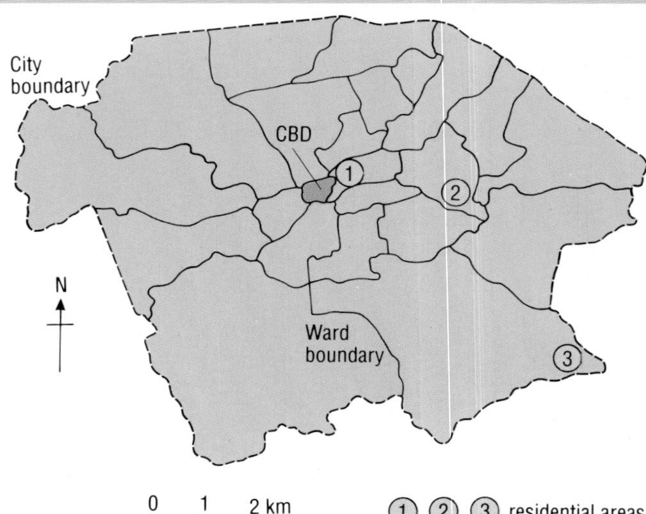

residential areas	housing tenure: % owner occupied	housing tenure: % owned by the council	housing tenure: % rented	housing density: households with over 1.5 persons per room	housing density: households with less than 0.5 persons per room	housing quality: percentage households which share or lack a wc
set of statistics A	98	0	2	1	84	0
set of statistics B	24	34	42	19	35	19
set of statistics C	62	14	24	8	14	10

7 *(Pages 30 and 31)*

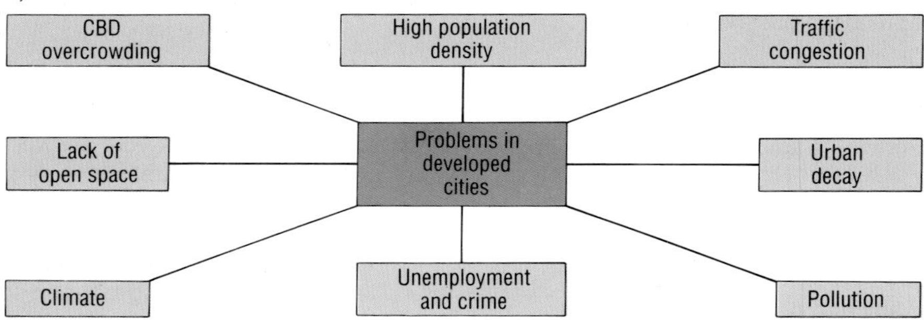

Imagine that you work for an organisation that is interested in improving conditions for people living in large cities in the developed world.

Write a report on the problems facing large cities in the developed world. Consider each of the headings given in the above diagram and give examples from Tokyo to illustrate what you have written. Your report should be about a page to a page and a half in length. *(10)*

8 *(Pages 32 to 35)*

A feature of cities in the developing world is that they are growing very rapidly as people move to them from surrounding rural areas.

a i) What is this movement from the countryside called? *(1)*

ii) Give three reasons why people may wish to move into a city from the surrounding countryside (urban pull factors). *(3)*

iii) Give three reasons why people may have to move away from the countryside (rural push factors). *(3)*

b Name four problems likely to occur in urban areas when large numbers of people move into them. *(4)*

9 *(Pages 34 to 36)*

The diagram (right) is an incomplete model of a city in the developing world.

a Match up the following with letters A to F on the model:
  i) Modern, luxury high-rise flats.
  ii) Squatters who have built shanty towns (favelas).
  iii) A large shopping centre with tall office blocks.
  iv) A suburban luxury estate for professional workers.
  v) Modern factories built alongside main roads leading out of the city.
  vi) An area where some houses have had piped water and electricity added, yet are still of poor quality. *(6)*

b Describe the housing conditions likely to be found in the shanty town (favela). *(4)*

c Describe two different schemes which have been used to try to improve the housing of shanty towns. *(4)*

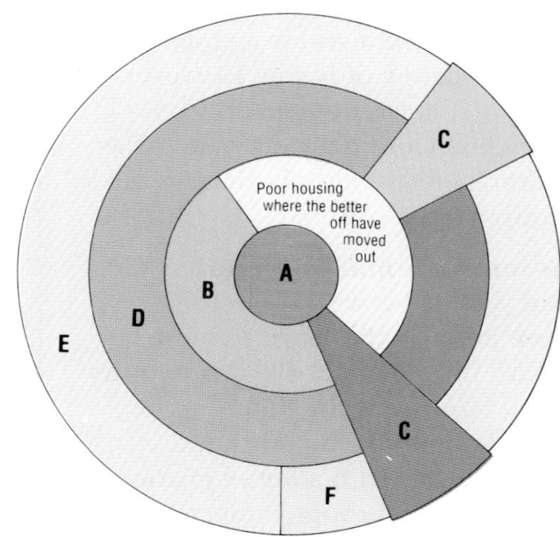

10 *(Page 36)*

Self-help housing schemes are simple, low cost housing projects where, with a little help from government, local people are encouraged to improve their living conditions.

a List four basic things that the poor need to do to improve their housing. *(4)*

b Using Figure 3.30 describe the improvements which have been made in:
  i) the building and
  ii) the provision of services. *(5)*

c What part is played in self-help schemes by:
  i) the local residents and
  ii) the authorities? *(4)*

d Give three advantages and three disadvantages of self-help schemes. *(6)*

11 *(Page 37)*

Using the two maps (Figure 3.32) and your own knowledge, describe the likely changes in the village between 1925 and 1976 in terms of:

a The design and cost of houses. *(2)*

b The age and occupations (socio-economic groups) of the inhabitants. *(2)*

c Public and private transport. *(2)*

d Provision of services. *(2)*

e Quality of life of the original inhabitants. *(2)*

f The land use within and around the original village. *(2)*

g The demands made upon the area by nearby urban settlements. *(2)*

12 *(Page 37)*

Study the diagrams below which show the occupations of people living in the same village in 1880 and 1990.

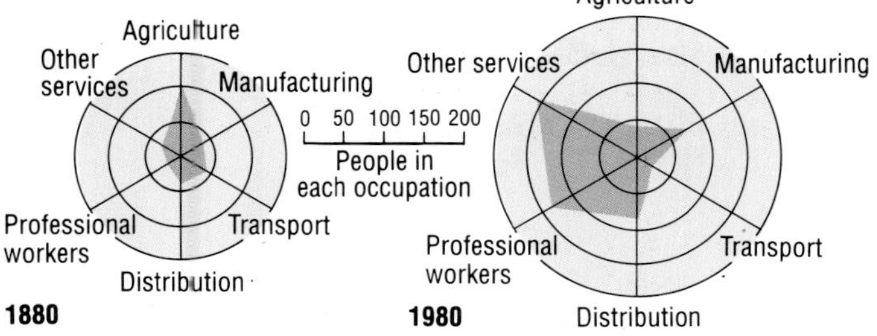

	Agriculture	Manufacturing	Transport	Distribution	Professional workers	Other services
1880	**100**				**20**	
1990	**40**			**80**		

a (i) Make a copy of the table.
  (ii) Complete the table using information from the two diagrams. *(8)*

b (i) In which year were the most jobs available? *(1)*
  (ii) What was the main occupation in 1880 and in 1990? *(2)*

c Write out the following sentences that are **true**: *(3)*

- The greatest increase has been in distribution.
- The number of professional workers has increased by over 100.
- Numbers employed in manufacturing had decreased by around 50.
- Employment in other services has shown the greatest increase.
- Transport is the activity which has shown the greatest decline.
- The village is likely to be a commuter village.

What is migration?

Migration is a movement and in human terms usually means a change of home. However, as seen in Figure 4.1, it can be applied to temporary, seasonal and daily movements as well as to permanent changes both between countries and within a country.

	External (international)	Between countries
Permanent	i) voluntary ii) forced (Refugees)	West Indians to Britain Negro slaves to America, Kurds, Afghans
	Internal	**Within a country**
	i) rural depopulation ii) urban depopulation iii) regional	most developing countries British conurbations North-west to South-east of Britain
Semi-Permanent	for several years	migrant workers in France & West Germany
Seasonal	for several months or several weeks	Mexican harvesters in California Holiday-makers, University students
Daily	commuters	South-east England

Figure 4.1
Types of migration

Permanent international migration is the movement of people between countries. *Emigrants* are people who leave a country; *immigrants* are those who arrive in a country. The *migration balance* is the difference between the numbers of emigrants and immigrants. Countries with a *net migration loss* lose more people through emigration than they gain by immigration and depending on the balance between their birth and death rates (page 8) they may have a declining population. Countries with a *net migration gain* receive more people by immigration than they lose through emigration, and so will have an overall population increase (assuming birth and death rates are evenly balanced). International migration can be divided into two types – voluntary and forced (Figure 4.2):

Voluntary migration is the free movement where the migrants are looking for an improved quality of life and personal freedom, e.g.

- Employment – either to find a job, to earn higher salaries or to avoid paying tax
- Pioneers developing new areas
- Trade and economic expansion
- Territorial expansion
- Better climates, especially on retirement
- Social amenities such as hospitals, schools and entertainment
- To be with friends and relatives

Forced migration is when the migrant has no personal choice but has to move due to natural disasters or to economic or social impositions, e.g.

- Religious and political persecution
- Wars, causing large numbers of refugees
- Forced labour as slaves or prisoners of war
- Racial discrimination
- Lack of food due to famine
- Natural disasters caused by floods, drought, earthquakes, volcanic eruptions or hurricanes
- Overpopulation, when the number of people living in an area exceeds the resources available to them

Figure 4.2
Voluntary and forced migration

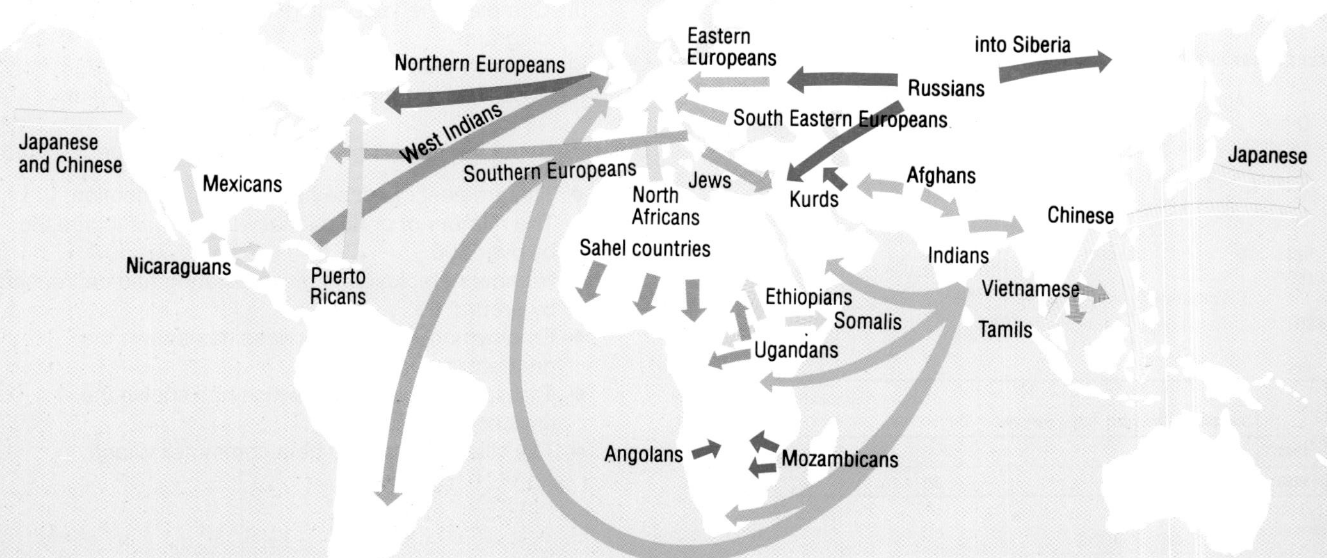

Figure 4.3
Some major twentieth century migrations

Refugees

Refugees are people who have been forced to leave their home country for fear of persecution for reasons of race, religion, politics, internal strife (civil war) or due to environmental disasters. They move to other countries hoping to find help and asylum. Refugees do not include displaced persons who are people who have been forced to move within their own country. By the end of 1992, 600,000 citizens of the former Yugoslavia had become refugees seeking sanctuary in other European countries while over 2 million had become displaced persons mainly due to 'ethnic cleansing'.

The United Nations (UN) suggested that, at the beginning of 1993, there were over 17 million refugees in the world (Figure 4.4). However, as most refugees are illegal immigrants, the UN admit that this figure could be very inaccurate. More than half of the world's refugees are children and most adults are women. Over 80 per cent of refugees are in developing countries – countries which are least able to help. Refugees live in extreme poverty, lacking food, shelter, clothing, education and medical care. They have no citizenship, few, if any rights, virtually no prospects, and are unlikely to return to their homeland (Figure 4.5).

The present problematic refugee situation began over 50 years ago in war-torn Europe, although many of those refugees were later assimilated by their host country. It was the Palestinian Arab refugee camps, set up after the creation of the state of Israel in 1948, that first showed that the problem had become permanent and apparently insoluble. 1.75 million people still live in camps in this part of the Middle East. Trends in the last decade confirm that while the number of refugee movements has continued to increase, most movements are still between developing countries. Those movements include:

- 6 million Afghans forced by war to leave for neighbouring Pakistan and Iran.
- 1.5 million Ethiopians, Sudanese and Somalis driven from their homes in Eastern Africa by drought, famine and civil war.
- Inhabitants from the Southern African states of Angola and Mozambique.
- Movements from several Central American countries including Mexico into the USA.
- People in the Middle East affected by the Gulf War.

Figure 4.4
The increasing number of refugees

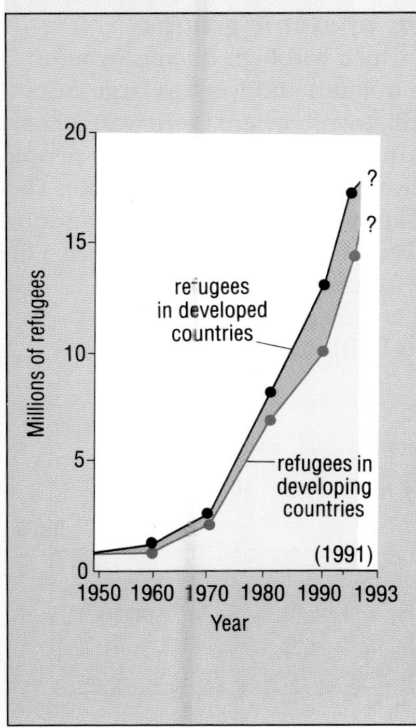

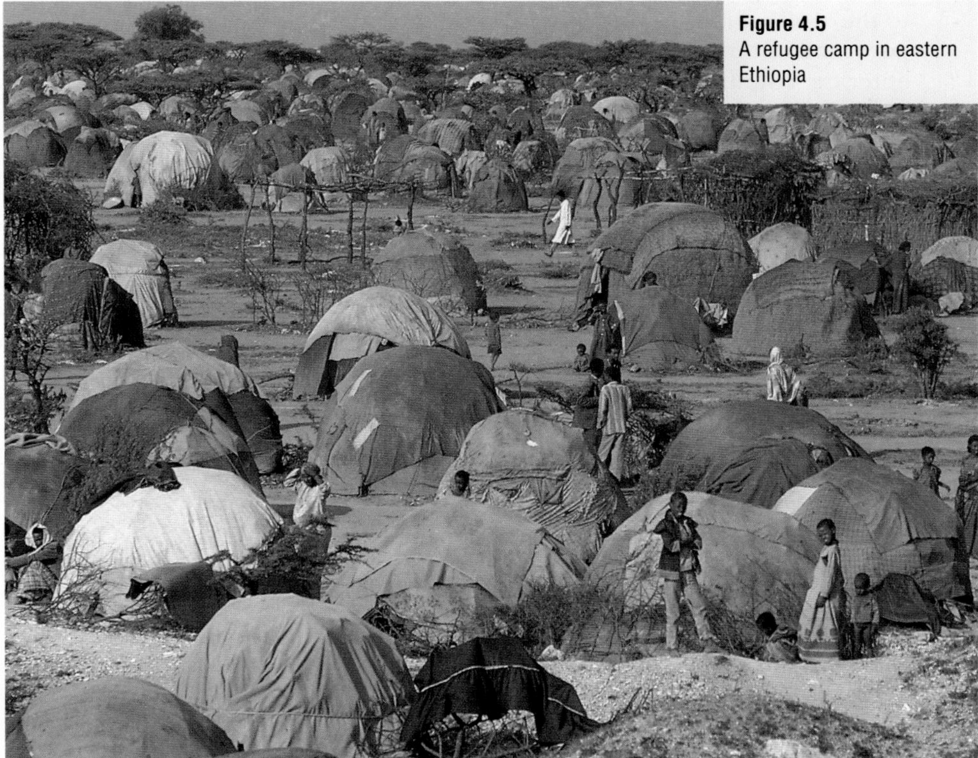

Figure 4.5
A refugee camp in eastern Ethiopia

Migration into the UK

The United Kingdom has experienced many waves of immigrants and our society has always been one of mixed races and cultures. The majority of UK residents are themselves descended from immigrants, from the Romans, Vikings, Angles, Saxons and Normans. The Irish have settled in Britain for several centuries while many Europeans migrated to the UK during and after the Second World War (1939–45). On most occasions the number of immigrants was small enough for them to be easily assimilated into the existing population. Today's racial tensions have followed the larger post-war influx of migrants whose different colour of skin has became an issue for the white population – a problem not easily solved since it is basically a biological rather than a social or cultural difference.

Figure 4.7 shows the sources of immigrants into Britain in 1988:

- Old Commonwealth immigrants are from countries (Australia, New Zealand and Canada) originally settled by British emigrants, and whose descendants have returned.
- New Commonwealth immigrants come from former British Colonies such as India, Pakistan, Bangladesh and Jamaica. Most of these migrants are non-white. Originally they came because:
  1. In the late 1940s and the 1950s Britain was short of labour following the Second World War. Many were West Indians who arrived partly due to overcrowding in their own islands, but mainly due to the 'pull' of jobs in Britain. The British government invited many to apply for permission to enter the country for specific jobs, e.g. with London transport. Many of these immigrants, however, were unskilled and poorly paid.
  2. Several groups of Asians found themselves as either religious or political refugees following the division of India and Pakistan. These groups, which included Hindus, Muslims and Sikhs, came to Britain in the 1950s.

Conurbation	Percentage of total population of Asian or Afro-Caribbean origin
Tyneside	1.0
West Yorkshire	4.4
Greater Manchester	2.7
Merseyside	1.2
East Midlands*	4.8
West Midlands	8.2
Greater London	18.4 (inner London =26%)

**East Midlands (Nottingham, Derby, Leicester) is not usually listed as a conurbation*

Figure 4.6 New Commonwealth immigrants in conurbations (1991)

Successive British governments have, since then, tried to restrict and control the number of non-white immigrants unless they:

- Were dependants of relatives already living in Britain;
- Had specific jobs, especially those involving certain skills which were in short supply in Britain (e.g. doctors);
- Were British passport holders evicted from their home country (e.g. Ugandan Asians);
- Could prove themselves to be genuine refugees (e.g. Vietnamese boat people).

An increasing number of people of Asian or Afro-Caribbean origin have been born in the UK. The 1991 census showed that 5.5 per cent of Britain's population was non-white. Of these over 50 per cent were either second or even third generation British, a figure which could reach 70 per cent by 2000.

Uneven concentrations of ethnic groups

Immigrants avoided areas which had high unemployment levels (Scotland, Northern Ireland) and went to large cities and conurbations (not small towns) where there were greater chances of finding jobs. At the same time, many white people were moving out, making low quality housing available. The greatest concentrations of immigrant groups are in London, the West and East Midlands and West Yorkshire (Figure 4.6). There was also a tendency for one ethnic group to concentrate in a particular area, e.g. Pakistanis in West Yorkshire and West Indians in Birmingham.

Figure 4.7
Sources of immigrants into the UK in 1988

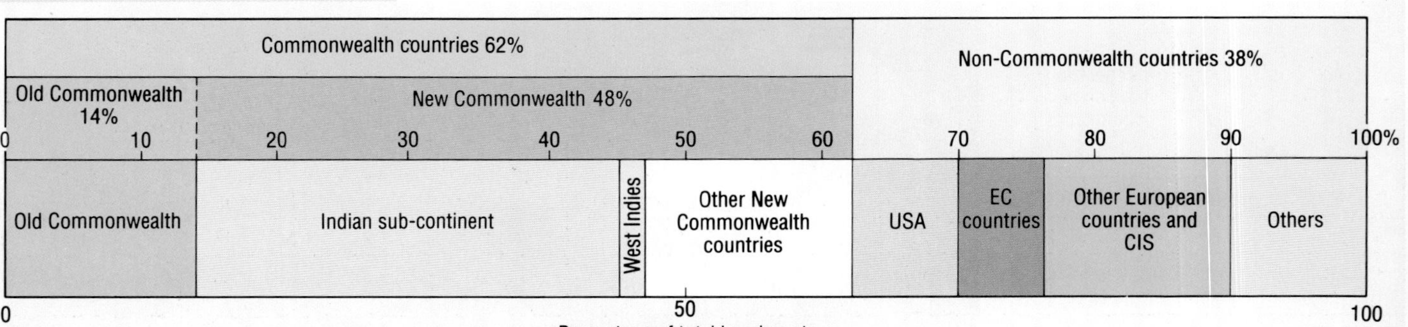

Problems facing immigrants to Britain

The majority of residents in Britain who have come directly as, or who have descended from immigrants from the New Commonwealth, not only live in conurbations, but also tend to group together with members of their own ethnic group in inner city areas (Figure 4.8). The segregation of various ethnic groups in British cities could have resulted from differences in wealth, colour, religion, education and the quality of the environment. Many activities in these communities are positive such as the Notting Hill Carnival. However, we are usually presented with a negative description of ethnic based activities, perhaps because it is considered to be more media worthy.

The major problems confronting immigrants will generally result from difficulties with the English language, cultural differences, and racial prejudices. Many members of ethnic minorities have to live in overcrowded poor quality housing. Overcrowding becomes worse in some groups which have high birth rates and large families. Unemployment often exceeds 70 per cent, much of it long term. Lower education opportunities and, often, lower expectations, mean the inhabitants develop few skills. A lack of money on the part of the inhabitants and the various levels of government means that services which are provided are inadequate. While the authorities speak of the high rate of crime in these areas – violence, drugs and muggings – residents complain of police harassment. The resultant lack of trust leads to further tension. These problems were highlighted during the 1981 and 1985 inner city riots.

Although nowhere have the ghettos of New York developed in Britain, ethnic groups which have a similar religion, language, diet, social organisation and culture tend to concentrate together, e.g. Jamaicans in Brixton, Anguillans in Slough, Sikhs in Southall and Bengalis in East London. Yet, as history has shown in many parts of the world, these concentrations tend to lead to fear, prejudice and jealousy among rival communities.

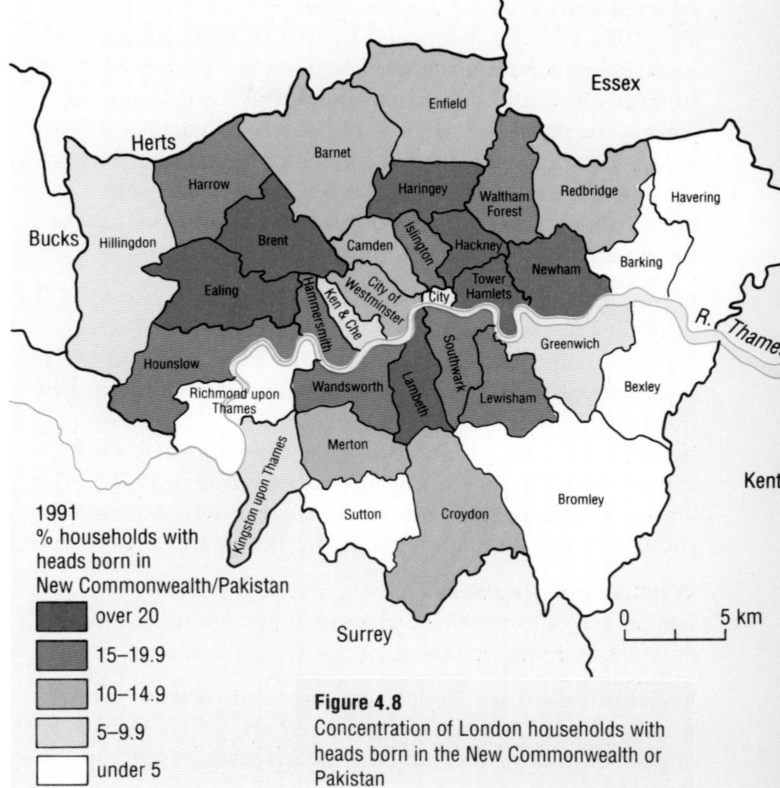

Figure 4.8 Concentration of London households with heads born in the New Commonwealth or Pakistan

The Scarman Report, following the 1981 riots in English cities, identified four main problems (Figure 4.9).

Figure 4.9 Summary of parts of the Scarman Report

Housing Most Blacks and Asians (80 per cent) live in overcrowded buildings which they are able to rent or buy cheaply because the dwellings are sub-standard or in undesirable areas. There is often a reluctance to sell better quality housing to non-whites.

Education Blacks and Asians often experience difficulties with the English language, putting them at a disadvantage. In addition the schools they attend are often old and lack resources.

Jobs These are difficult to find due to fewer skills having been acquired, and to industry moving out of inner city areas. Those with jobs are poorly paid and so cannot afford good housing – a vicious circle. Despite legislation there is still considerable bias against non-white job applicants.

Discrimination This was regarded by Scarman to be (and still is) a major obstacle to assimilation.

Figure 4.10 Inequality in England and Wales

		% of own age group		% of own group			% of own group employed		
Group	% of England's population	under 16	over 60	living in conurbations	given new accommodation	lacking own bath, wc & hot water	professional managerial	semi and unskilled	unemployed 16–29 years old
White	96	24	17	32	64	18	40	18	15
Black and Asian	4	33	4	80	30	35–40	14	37	25

Movement out of large cities

The 1981 census, confirmed by that of 1991, showed an increasing trend among people who had previously lived in large cities and conurbations to move out into new towns, overspill towns and suburbanised villages (Figure 4.11). The biggest outward movement is taking place in the inner cities, and it is because of this movement outwards that newly arrived immigrants and people on low incomes can find accommodation.

Figure 4.12 shows the outward movement in London. The inner city areas, which are often adjacent to the River Thames, suffer the greatest loss. However, until the 1970s, many people initially moved into the outer suburbs. But the 1981 census showed that even these areas were beginning to lose population. The only anomaly (an instance which does not fit the usual pattern) is 'The City' which is still the commercial centre, but which now has such housing developments as the Barbican.

Why do people move?

Figure 4.13 shows which groups of people move out of (and into) inner city areas.

Accommodation People will try to move away from small, terraced houses or high-rise flats. Older houses are of poorer quality, lack amenities, are often rented and are closely packed.

Employment People move either because of promotion, for better prospects or simply to find a job. As industry declines in the cramped, expensive inner city sites, most new jobs are created on the edge-of-city industrial (trading) estates, or in new towns (pages 114–15).

Changing family status This may be the result of an increase in wealth or family size.

Environmental factors These include moving away from noise, air and visual pollution created by traffic or declining industry. People also prefer having access to more open space. In some cases redevelopment schemes force people out (page 134).

Social factors These include prejudice against neighbours and ethnic groups, and an above average crime and vandalism rate. It might mean moving nearer to friends and relatives.

1951	8.2 million
1971	10.5 million
1981	7.2 million
1991	6.4 million

Figure 4.11 London's changing population

Cycle of change Recently there has been a 'reversed' movement by wealthy people moving back into parts of inner London. Derelict property can be bought cheaply, refurbished and transformed into expensive houses and flats. This process is encouraged by property developers and estate agents. Schemes such as those in Islington and along the banks of the Thames (using disused warehouses) do not benefit the local inhabitants (page 133) who cannot afford the high prices of the new properties.

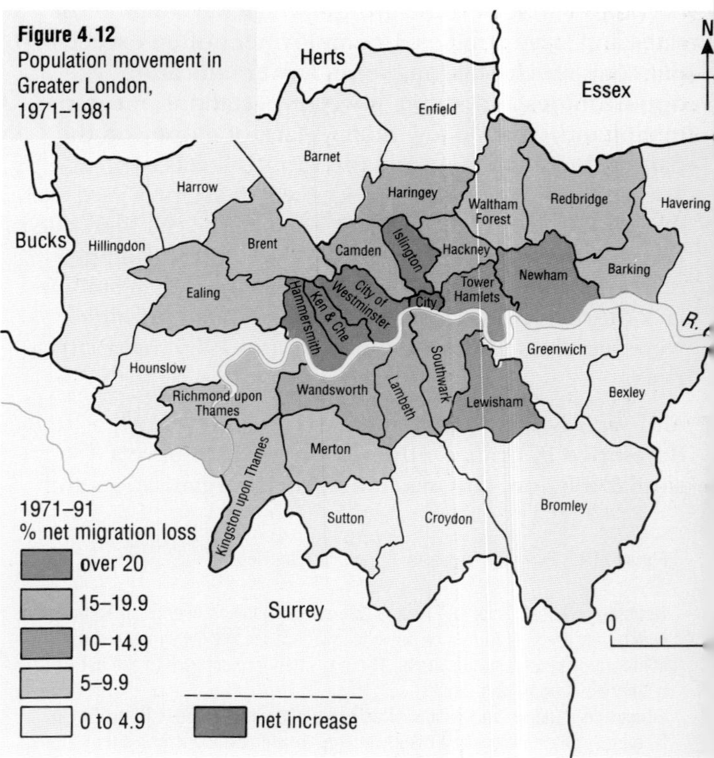

Figure 4.12 Population movement in Greater London, 1971–1981

Figure 4.13 Movement in inner city areas

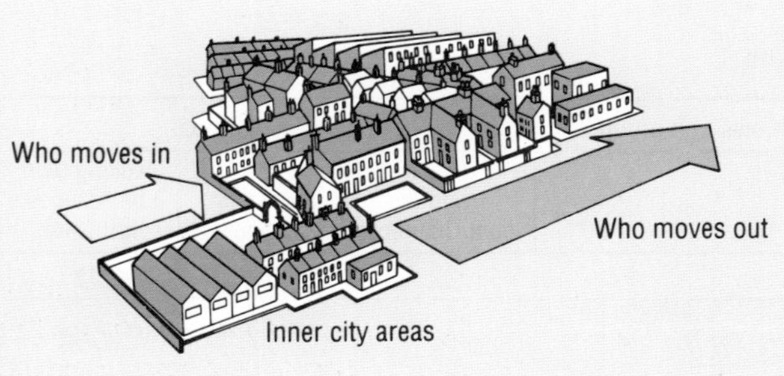

Elderly living on low incomes, no longer with a family, and wishing cheaper housing near to the CBD and other services (shops, library, hospital)

Newly wedded couples with little capital and no family – first time buyers

Poor families with limited resources

Immigrants from overseas especially those with limited money, education and skills

Those with higher incomes now capable of buying their own homes in suburbia

Those with higher skills and qualifications – especially moving to new towns

Parents with a young family wishing for gardens, open space and larger houses

Regional movements

1 From North to South in Great Britain

Why leave the North and West?

- Older, poorer quality housing
- Exhaustion of minerals (coal/iron ore)
- Decline of old heavy industries (ships/steel/textiles)
- Poorly paid jobs, mostly manual.
- Poorer transport links
- Many polluted old industrial environments
- Decline of old ports (Liverpool/Glasgow)
- Fewer cultural amenities, few social/sporting events
- Colder, wetter climate

Why move to the South and East?

- Newer, better quality housing
- Growth of newer/lighter/footloose industries (high-tech/microelectronics)
- Higher skilled and better paid jobs
- Better transport links (air/ports/roads/rail)
- Few old industrial environments
- Ports to EC countries growing
- Better services (shops/schools/hospitals)
- Many cultural amenities, more social/sporting events
- Warmer drier climate. More tourists

During 1992 there were signs that some of the above factors were changing in importance, e.g. house prices falling and unemployment rising in the South whereas both were relatively steady in the North.

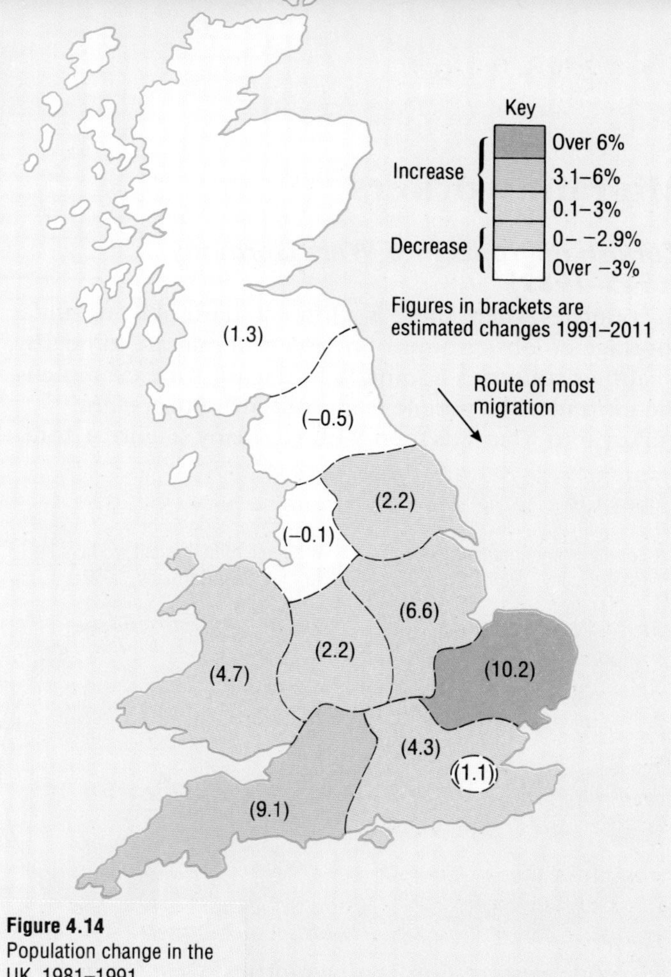

Figure 4.14
Population change in the UK, 1981–1991

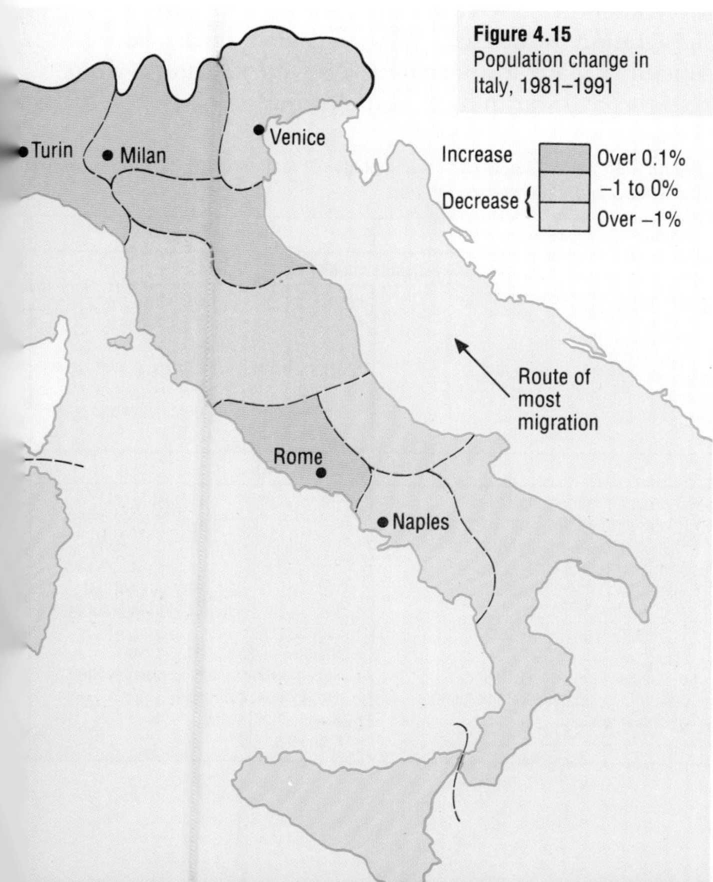

Figure 4.15
Population change in Italy, 1981–1991

2 From South to North in Italy

Why leave the South?

- Relatively few industrial or service jobs
- Poorly paid jobs, mainly manual
- Poorer transport links. More isolated from EC
- Mountainous areas with relatively little soil
- Drought during summer months
- Fewer cultural amenities, few social and sporting events
- Overpopulated. High birth rate/few natural resources
- Little money invested in area

Why move to the North?

- Many industrial and service jobs
- Many highly paid skilled and less skilled jobs (car factories/high-tech/micro-electronics)
- Good transport links. Easier access to rest of EC
- North Italian Plain is flat and soils are fertile
- No water shortage
- Many cultural amenities, more social/sporting events
- Underpopulated. Not enough people to use the resources
- Plenty of money invested in area

There are other reasons, not given, why some people wish to move to the South (tourism) and leave the North (pollution/congestion/ higher prices).

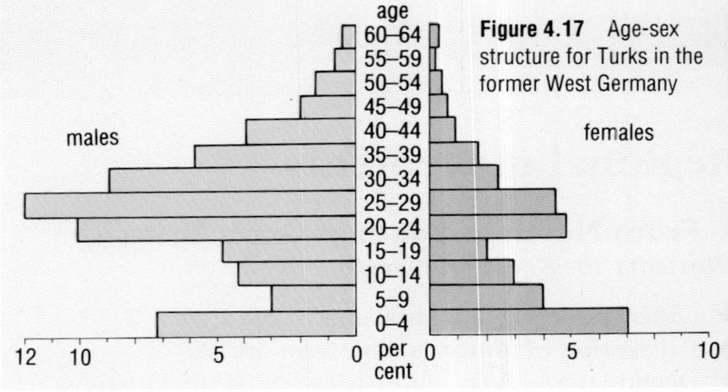

Figure 4.17 Age-sex structure for Turks in the former West Germany

Migrant workers

Turkish migrants into West Germany (1945–1989)

In countries where there is a low standard of living and a shortage of jobs, groups of people will migrate to nearby, wealthier countries hoping to find work. One example is the movement of people from southern Europe and Turkey into what was then West Germany (Figure 4.16(a)).

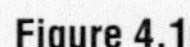

Figure 4.16

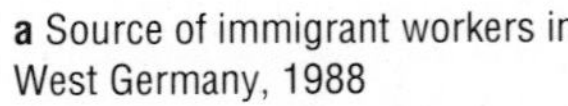

a Source of immigrant workers in West Germany, 1988
b Source of immigrant workers into former West Germany, 1989

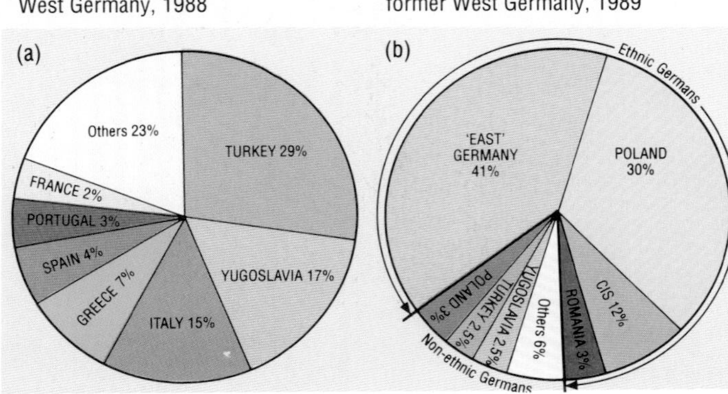

Like other western European countries, West Germany needed rebuilding when the Second World War ended in 1945. There were many more job vacancies than workers and so extra labour was needed. Later, as West Germany became increasingly affluent, it attracted workers from the poorer parts of southern Europe and the Middle East. Many of these migrants initially went into farming, but they soon turned to the relatively better-paid jobs in factories and the construction industry. These jobs were not wanted by the Germans because they were dirty, unskilled, poorly paid and often demanded long and unsociable hours (in 1980, 5000 Turks were employed by Ford's car factory in Cologne). By 1989 West Germany had 4.5 million 'Gastarbeiter' or 'guest workers', accounting for 7.4 per cent of the total workforce. Of these migrants, 29 per cent had come from Turkey. However, although the Turks had found full employment in the 1950s and 1960s, by 1989 nearly 20 per cent were out of work. This was mainly because the manufacturing industry was hardest hit by the recession. Under these conditions it is usually the unskilled jobs which are lost first.

Figure 4.17 shows the imbalance between males and females, and between age groups of Turkish migrant workers into West Germany (this is typical of other countries receiving large numbers of migrant workers). Some of the advantages and disadvantages of this pattern are listed in Figure 4.18.

In common with other western European countries, West Germany imposed a ban on the recruitment of foreign workers after 1973, although Turks still arrived to reunite their families and to seek political asylum. In 1980 new laws reduced the right of asylum and grants were given to Turks wishing to return home. Very few have taken advantage of this offer though even fewer have taken out German citizenship. The Turks have their own 'centres' in most large cities where they have their own food, dress and entertainment. Without the Turks, transport, hospital and electricity services would probably come to a halt.

Migrants into Germany after 1989

The beginnings of a large-scale migration of German-speaking groups living in eastern Europe began in mid-1989. Large numbers made their way to West Germany initially via Hungary and Austria, later through Czechoslovakia and finally, after the dismantling of the Berlin Wall, directly from East Germany (Figure 4.16(b)). Many of these immigrant workers were relatively unskilled and were prepared to accept those types of jobs previously taken by 'guest-workers', especially Turkish workers. Unemployment grew and with it, increased racist attacks on non-German ethnic groups. The German government tried to restrict non-ethnic German immigration in the early 1990s, a decision made more difficult as many former Yugoslavs were seeking asylum from the civil war in their home country.

Figure 4.18 Advantages and disadvantages of migration to the 'losing' and 'receiving' countries

Advantages	Disadvantages
Losing country	
• Reduces pressure on jobs and resources (e.g. food) • Loses people of child-bearing age causing decline in birth rate	• Loses people in working age group • Loses people most likely to have some education and skills • Mainly males leave causing a division in families • Left with an elderly population and so a high death rate
Receiving country	
• Overcomes labour shortage • Prepared to do dirty, unskilled jobs • Prepared to work long hours for low salaries (London Underground) • Cultural advantages and links (e.g. Notting Hill carnival) • Some highly skilled migrants (e.g. Pakistani doctors) • In a developing country these migrants could increase the number of skilled workers	• Pressure on jobs but most likely to be the first unemployed in a recession • Low-quality, overcrowded housing lacking in basic amenities (bidonvilles in France, favelas, inner city slums) • Ethnic groups tend not to integrate • Racial tension • Limited skilled/educated group • Lack of opportunities to practise their own religion, culture etc • Language difficulties • Often less healthy

Mexican workers in California

Hispanics are people from Spanish speaking countries mainly in South and Central America. In recent years many Hispanics, especially those from Mexico, have migrated northwards into the USA. Mexico has a relatively low standard of living (Figure 4.19), a high birth rate and population growth, and insufficient jobs. As a result many Mexicans migrate into the wealthier USA, although often on a temporary rather than on a permanent basis. Many migrants are males who do not possess documents and enter the USA illegally, leaving their families behind. The attraction is earning more during two or three months in the USA than in a full year in Mexico.

Of the 3.5 million Mexicans who took up residence in the USA between 1980 and 1989:

- 1.7 million were legal immigrants;
- 1.2 million were earlier migrants who had set up home in Florida and those American states bordering Mexico (Figure 4.20), and who were granted an amnesty allowing them to remain;
- 0.6 million were illegal immigrants.

In 1990 one million Mexicans were caught by border controls using horses, helicopters and other advanced detective equipment. Even so it was believed that another one million did manage to slip through the controls. As one border guard claimed, "We catch somebody one night, return him to Mexico the next day, for him to try again that night, and the next, and the next until he is successful."

Figure 4.19
Village street in Mexico

Yet these migrants are essential to the American economy where they take the harder, dirtier, seasonal, more monotonous, less skilled and less well paid jobs. In California the vast majority obtain seasonal employment on large agricultural estates at harvest times (Figure 4.21). Many others find employment in either the construction industry or in hotels and restaurants in Los Angeles. One district in Los Angeles, which is only a two hour drive from the Mexican border, has 70 per cent of its residents Hispanic speaking. Migrant labour provides half of California's workforce, yet at times of recession, or at non-harvest time, many are 'returned home'.

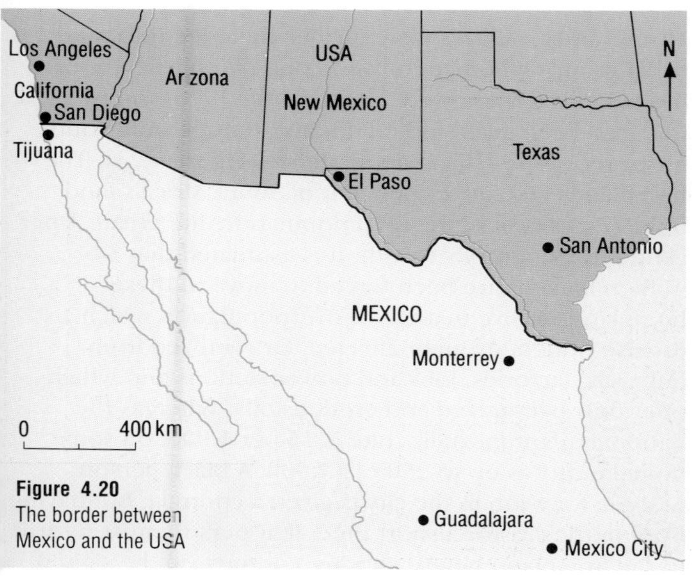

Figure 4.20
The border between Mexico and the USA

Figure 4.21
Tomato picking in central California using Mexican migrant labour

Migrations and apartheid

Voluntary migration

Whites came to South Africa from Europe. The early Dutch settlers (Boers) moved inland when the British arrived in the Cape. The 'Great Trek' led to the creation of the three northern and eastern provinces.

Blacks are Bantu speaking people who moved southwards shortly after the arrival of the Dutch (or Afrikaners as they became known).

Asians came from India and Malaysia during colonial times.

Seasonal migration

Many Bantu from surrounding countries (Figure 4.22) migrate to South Africa to work in factories and in mines. Legally they are only allowed to stay in the country for six months at a time.

Forced migration

Slaves were taken to South Africa, and later political refugees were forced to leave countries such as India, Malaysia, Indonesia and Sri Lanka. White fathers and black, Asian and Khoi (the indigenous people of the western Cape) 'slave' mothers had led to the creation of a new ethnic minority, the Cape coloureds, by the time slavery was abolished in 1834.

Apartheid was legalised in 1948 and the Group Areas Act of 1950 forced many blacks to move. Apartheid means separate development for whites and blacks. It created a system by which the whites had all possible rights and the blacks none (the Asians and coloureds were given very few). There was complete segregation in housing, transport, restaurants, schools, cinemas and at sporting and cultural events. Blacks had to carry passes at all times until 1986 and could be imprisoned without trial.

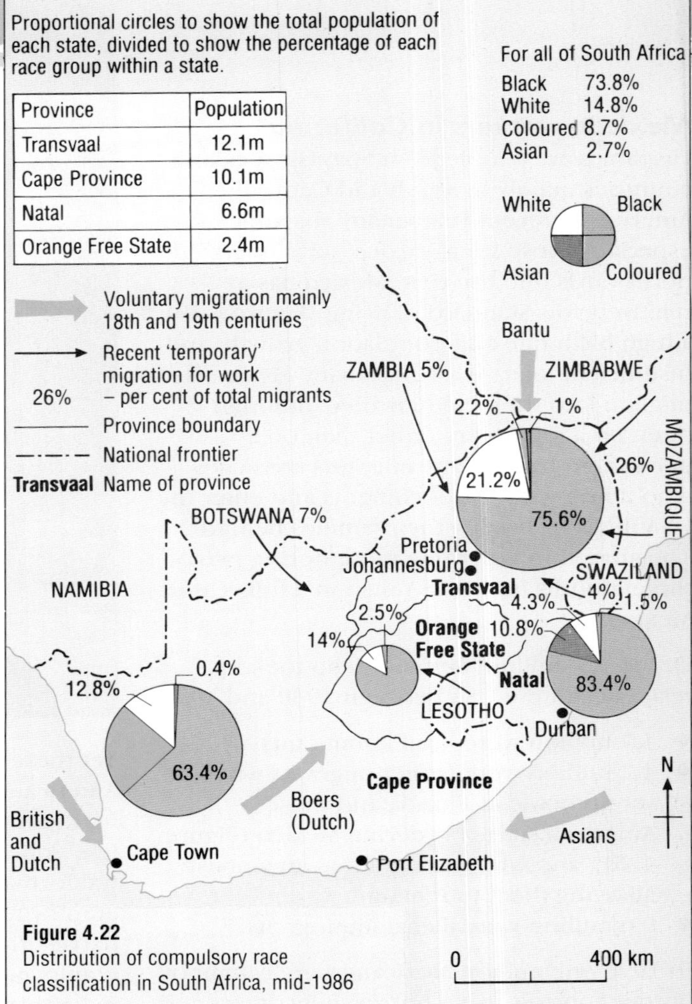

Figure 4.22
Distribution of compulsory race classification in South Africa, mid-1986

They were not allowed any political party, and could only vote in tribal assemblies in their 'homelands'. The white South African government defended this policy by saying that the blacks had only come to work in South Africa and were, therefore, not permanent residents. It seemed logical to this government that only basic necessities needed to be granted to them.

Homelands Blacks were further classified into nine tribal groups who had to live in one of ten reserves or 'homelands'. These were created after 1976, and by 1981 four had been given independence, though only South Africa recognises this independence (Figure 4.23). The homelands take up 13 per cent of South Africa's land, hold 72 per cent of the total population and create 3 per cent of the country's wealth. It is estimated that 3.5 million blacks have been forced to move to these homelands to live in areas of overpopulation which are disease ridden, drought affected, far removed from minerals, factories, jobs and power stations and which offer only overgrazed and eroded soils. Whereas the national infant mortality rate is 15 per 1,000, on some homelands it is up to 250 per 1,000. A black person wishing for a job in the city is given a contract, but having lived in the city for a short time, that person must return to the homeland before another contract can be signed.

Figure 4.23 South Africa's homelands

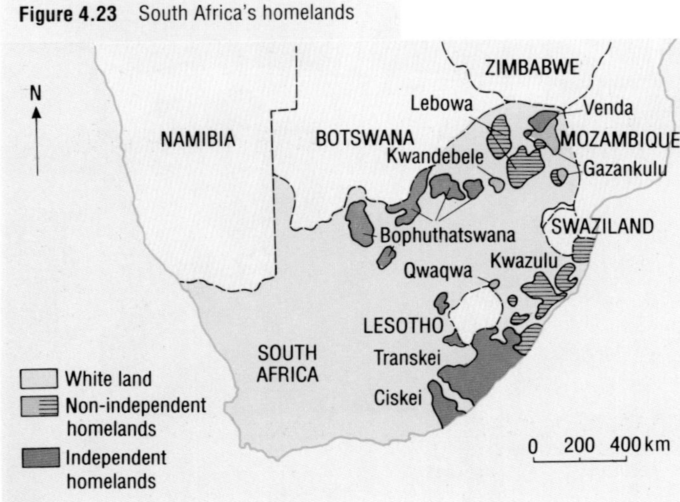

Figure 4.24
Housing in Soweto

Townships have been created for the 'urban blacks'. Townships are away from white residential areas, and the blacks have long and expensive journeys to work. Many of the original shanty settlements have been bulldozed and replaced by rows of similar houses (Figure 4.24). These houses are single storey with four rooms. Toilets are in backyards and only 20 per cent of the houses have electricity. The corrugated roofs make the buildings very hot in summer and very cold in winter. The high natural population increase of blacks already living in the townships, coupled with continued rural–urban migration and a failure by the government to provide sufficient new homes, has led to the resurgence of many new shanty settlements (Figure 4.25). The largest township, Soweto, has a population of over one million people. Of these, one quarter commute, often for several hours a day, to Johannesburg.

In the early 1990s the South African government abolished legalised racial discrimination. The formal ending of apartheid has meant the renewal of international sporting links, and that blacks are allowed to vote and to enter parliament alongside whites. However, the legacy of apartheid is likely to remain for many years as the standard of housing, education and services for black people will not improve overnight (Figure 4.26).

Figure 4.25
Shanty settlement at Crossroads in Cape Town

Figure 4.26
Inequality from cradle to grave

Inequality: from cradle to grave

The difference between the quality of life of white people and black is enormous, and can be measured in every field from child health to average earnings. Merely repealing the racist laws will not eradicate this structural inequality – more fundamental economic change will be required. Compare these figures with those in the box above showing each racial category's percentages of the total South African population.

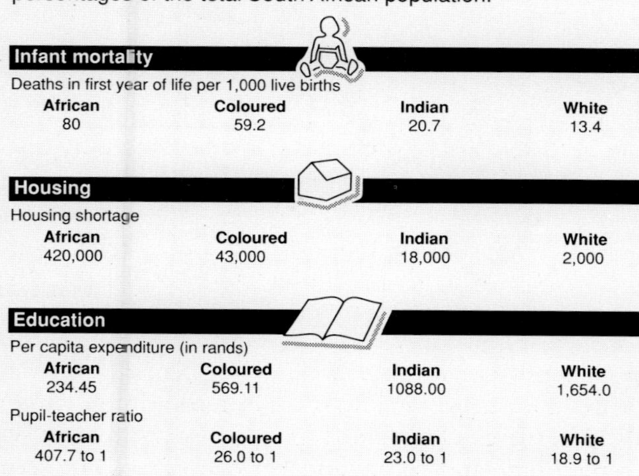

Infant mortality

Deaths in first year of life per 1,000 live births

African	Coloured	Indian	White
80	59.2	20.7	13.4

Housing

Housing shortage

African	Coloured	Indian	White
420,000	43,000	18,000	2,000

Education

Per capita expenditure (in rands)

African	Coloured	Indian	White
234.45	569.11	1088.00	1,654.0

Pupil-teacher ratio

African	Coloured	Indian	White
407.7 to 1	26.0 to 1	23.0 to 1	18.9 to 1

Health

Diseases notification by race

	African	Coloured	Indian	White
Cholera	6,557	8	230	9
Measles	11,734	1,435	20	1,275
Polio	87	4	0	0
Tuberculosis	42,470	10,957	402	660
Typhoid	4,994	67	21	43
Viral hepatitis	644	399	52	732

Nurses per 1,000 people (World Health Organisation minimum 2)

African	Coloured	Indian	White
1.5	1.8	1.4	6

Work

Average monthly household income (in rands)

African	Coloured	Indian	White
273	624	1,072	1,834

Percentage of selected occupations by racial group

	African	Coloured	Indian	White
Managerial/ executive	1.6	1.8	2.0	94.6
Clerical	17.3	10.4	7.7	64.6
Mining/ quarrying	90.6	1.3	0.1	8.0
Service	68.1	10.9	2.1	18.9
Labourers	88.1	11.1	0.7	0.1

Pensions

Percentage of pension budget

African	Coloured	Indian	White
23.5	17.9	3.8	54.7

1 *(Page 42)*

a **Voluntary migration** List possible reasons for the following migrations:

- Bantu into South Africa;
- British doctors to the USA;
- Growth of the Roman Empire;
- Development of British colonies;
- Pop groups to America;
- Elderly, wealthy Americans to Florida;
- West Indians to Britain;
- Europeans into the Prairies;
- Mexicans into California. *(9 x 1)*

b **Forced migration** List possible reasons for the following migrations:

- Africans to the USA;
- Somalis into Kenya;
- Jews from Nazi Germany;
- Chinese into South-east Asia;
- Pilgrims to New England;
- Ugandan Asians;
- Palestinian Arab refugees;
- Colombians from Armero;
- Afghans from Afghanistan. *(9 x 1)*

c i) What is the difference between voluntary and forced migration? *(1)*
ii) What is a refugee? *(1)*
iii) Why have so many refugees recently fled from EITHER the former Yugoslavia OR Somalia OR any other country you have studied? *(3)*

2 *(Pages 44 and 45)*

a i) Explain the meaning of the term 'New Commonwealth immigrants'. *(2)*
ii) Name two New Commonwealth countries. *(2)*

b Four wards have been labelled A, B, J and K below.
i) Which ward has the greatest number of people living in it? *(1)*
ii) Which ward has the highest proportion of New Commonwealth immigrants living in it? Why is this? *(2)*
iii) Which ward has the lowest proportion of New Commonwealth immigrants living in it? Why is this? *(2)*
iv) Why does ward B have an above average number of New Commonwealth immigrants for an edge-of-city ward? *(1)*

c What are the problems any immigrant might face when he or she arrives in a new country as far as the following are concerned? *(5)*
i) Accommodation
ii) Employment
iii) Language
iv) Culture
v) Prejudice

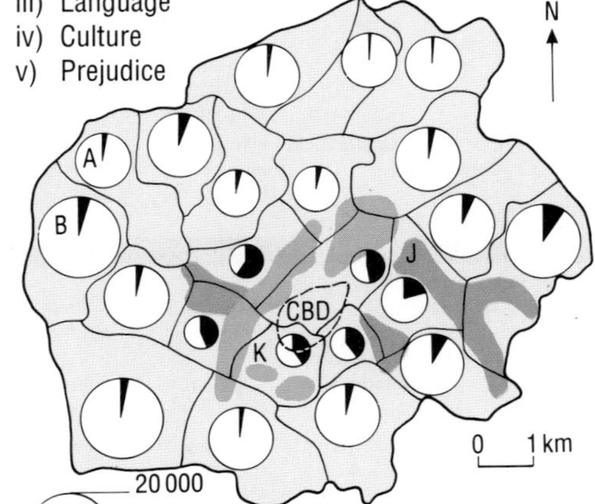

3 *(Page 46)*

a Where was the only part of Belfast to show an increase in population? *(1)*

b i) Describe the location of those districts with the highest percentage of people moving out. *(2)*
ii) Which groups of people were most likely to move out of these districts? *(2)*
iii) Why did these groups of people decide to move out? *(3)*
iv) Which groups of people are likely to have remained living in these districts? *(2)*

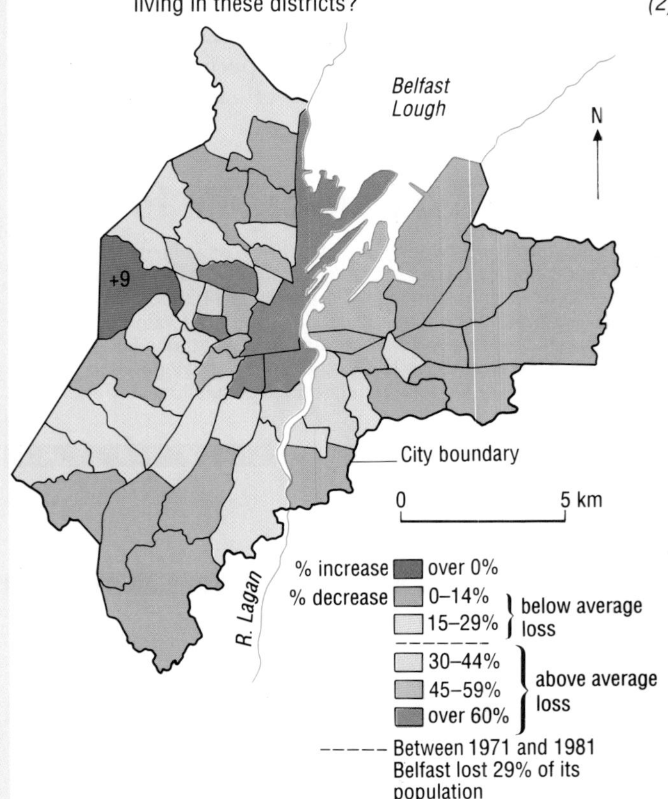

4 *(Page 48)*

a i) Put in rank order (the highest first) the five countries from which most migrant workers to West Germany came in the early 1970s. *(5)*

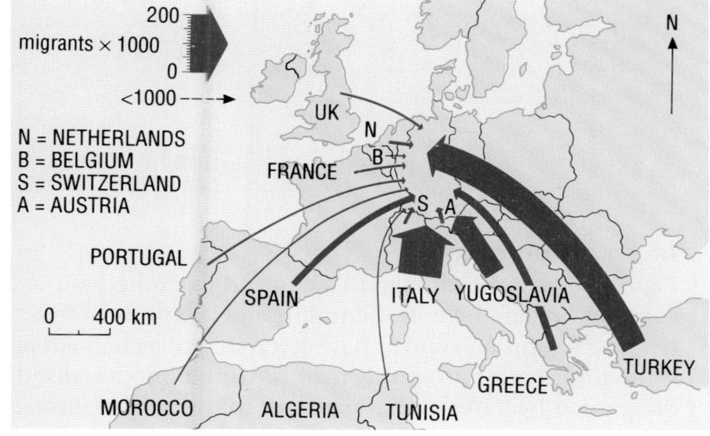

ii) What was the largest number of migrants from any one country (to the nearest 1,000)? *(1)*

b i) Describe and suggest reasons for the pattern shown on the map. *(6)*

ii) State two of the problems which may arise in countries from which large numbers of migrants leave to work elsewhere. *(2)*

c i) Describe and suggest reasons for the types of work foreign workers in West Germany might be engaged in. *(3)*

ii) What problems do migrant workers create for the host country? *(3)*

d By the mid-1980s the West German Government had almost stopped the inflow of migrant workers. Why do you think this was done? *(2)*

e i) Why did many Turkish migrants decide to stay permanently in West Germany? *(2)*

ii) How has the unification of Germany affected the Turkish community? *(2)*

5 *(Page 48)*

Using the population pyramid showing the age-sex structure of the migrant population into West Germany (below):

a What percentage of the migrant population (males and females) is aged between 15 and 19? *(1)*

b i) Which are the four main age groups of immigrants? *(4)*

ii) Are there more male or female immigrants? *(1)*

iii) Suggest three reasons for your answers. *(3)*

c What would be the advantages and disadvantages to a country like West Germany receiving immigrants of those age groups and sex ratio shown in the graph above? *(6)*

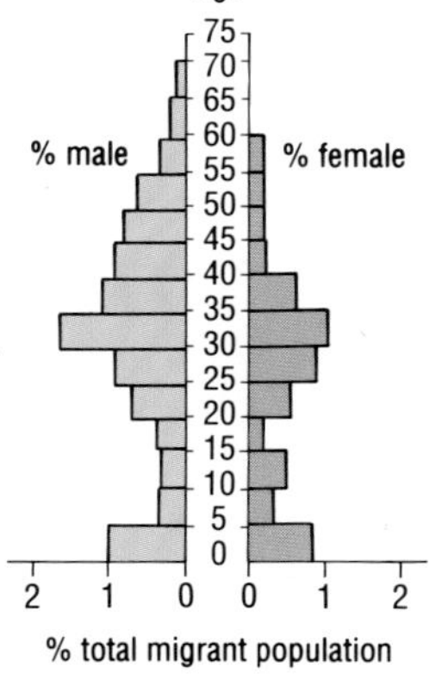

6 *(Page 49)*

a Name a state in the USA which attracts many Mexican migrant workers. *(1)*

b Give two reasons why Mexican workers try to find work in the USA. *(2)*

c Give two reasons why Americans try to restrict Mexican migrant labour entering the USA. *(2)*

d Give one reason why Americans need seasonal Mexican labour. *(1)*

7 *(Pages 50 and 51)*

a What is apartheid? *(1)*

b Draw a pie graph to show the percentages of white, black, coloured and Asian people living in South Africa. *(2)*

c Name one of these groups who were:

i) Voluntary immigrants

ii) Forced immigrants *(2)*

d i) What is meant by the terms 'homelands' and 'townships'? *(2)*

ii) Describe the living conditions on a homeland and in a township. *(6)*

e Give five inequalities between the living conditions of white people and black people in South Africa. *(5)*

5 SHOPPING

Hierarchies

A *hierarchy* is when settlements and shops are put into an order based upon their size (Figure 5.1) or upon the services which they provide (Figure 5.3).

In a region

Each shop or service has a threshold population. The *threshold population* is the number of people needed before a service is either necessary (e.g. a doctor) or can make a profit (a shop). It may also indicate the size and number of shops and services required to serve that population. For example, it is estimated that the threshold population for a branch of Boots is 10,000; a multiple shoe shop 20,000; Marks and Spencer 50,000; and a John Lewis department store 100,000. Other examples are given in Figure 5.1.

Figure 5.1
Shopping hierarchy with threshold populations

Order	Type	Approx. Threshold	Shops and services
1st	village	1000	store, post office
2nd	small town	10 000	small Boots, doctors, Spar, part-time bank
3rd	large town	20 000	Boots, Tesco, Burtons, shoe shop, bank, doctors
4th	regional	50 000	Marks and Spencer, Woolworth, Tesco, Currys Boots, furniture shop, Burtons, banks, shoe shop, department store, accountant, hospital, solicitors

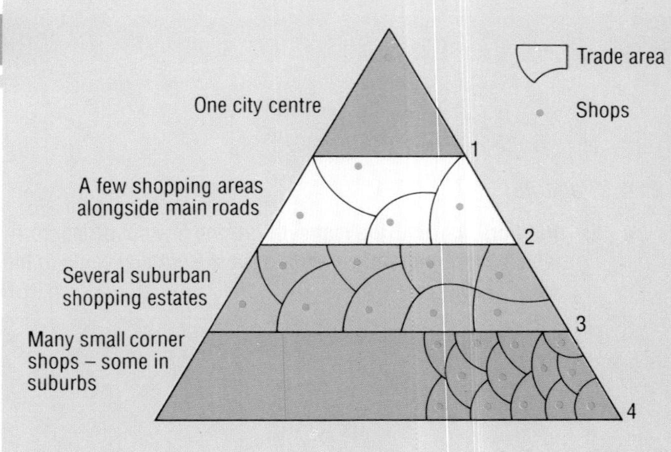

Figure 5.2 A traditional urban shopping hierarchy

In an urban area

Figure 5.3 is a sketch map of a city and its immediate surrounding area. On it the traditional locations of four types of shopping centres have been drawn as half circles. If the information from this map is turned into a stylised diagram, it becomes more apparent that a definite urban shopping hierarchy does exist (Figure 5.2).

It was pointed out that Figure 5.3 showed four traditional shopping centres. How accurate are these locations in your nearest town or city? Places are always changing. For example, it is likely that:

- There are fewer corner shops as they have been priced out by city centre shops, as people have moved away from inner city areas, and as this part of the urban area has been re-developed.
- There has been an increase in the number of edge-of-city/out-of-town hypermarkets and shopping centres.

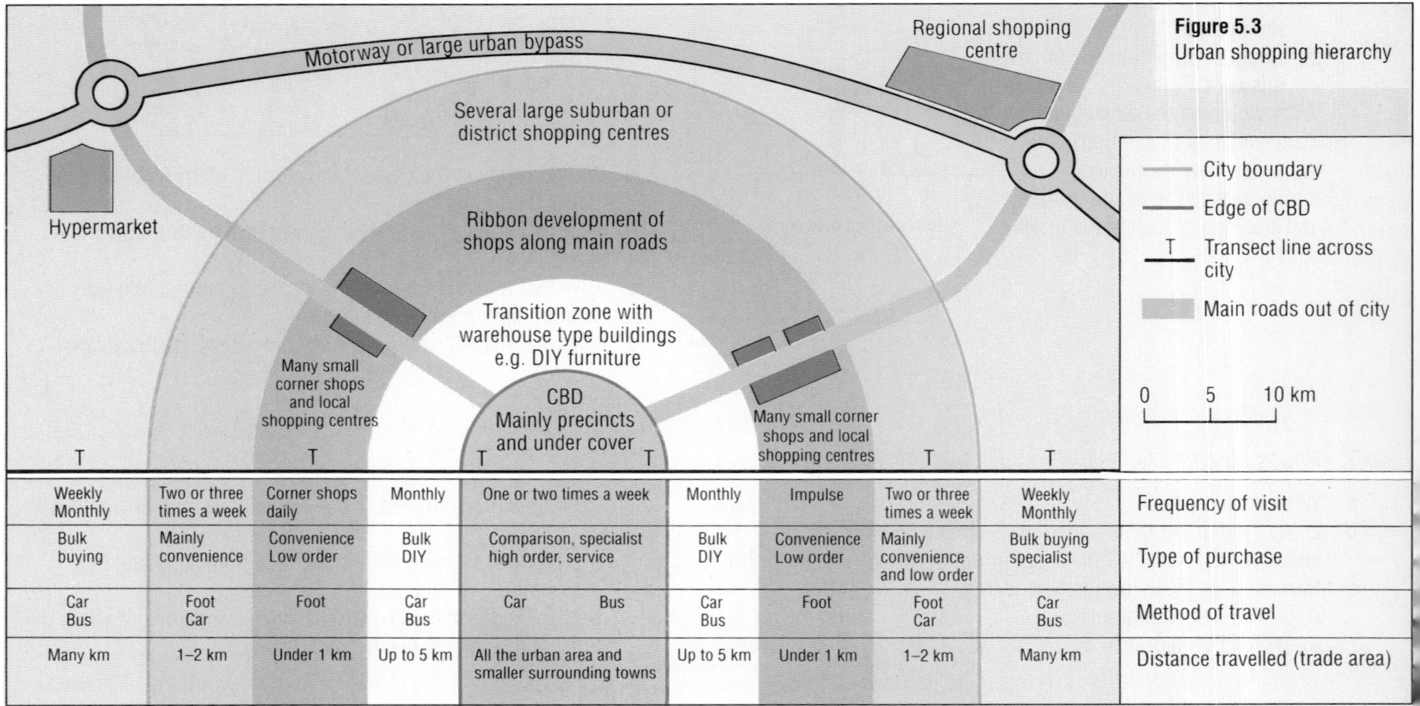

Weekly Monthly	Two or three times a week	Corner shops daily	Monthly	One or two times a week	Monthly	Impulse	Two or three times a week	Weekly Monthly	Frequency of visit
Bulk buying	Mainly convenience	Convenience Low order	Bulk DIY	Comparison, specialist high order, service	Bulk DIY	Convenience Low order	Mainly convenience and low order	Bulk buying specialist	Type of purchase
Car Bus	Foot Car	Foot	Car Bus	Car Bus	Car Bus	Foot	Foot Car	Car Bus	Method of travel
Many km	1–2 km	Under 1 km	Up to 5 km	All the urban area and smaller surrounding towns	Up to 5 km	Under 1 km	1–2 km	Many km	Distance travelled (trade area)

Figure 5.3
Urban shopping hierarchy

Shopping hierarchy in Tokyo

Tokyo has a huge population and covers a large amount of ground. Unlike British cities it has several central business districts. Some of these are important mainly for shopping, others have alternative functions.

The Ginza is one of the most famous and expensive shopping areas in the world (Figures 3.16 and 5.4). It includes many large department stores where everything can be bought under one roof, high-tech showrooms where firms like Sony, Toshiba and Mitsubishi exhibit their latest models and inventions, and exclusive restaurants and nightclubs. On Sundays and Bank Holidays the main streets are closed to traffic allowing Japanese families, many of whom earn high salaries, to wander round in a carnival type atmosphere. However only those people on business accounts are likely to take advantage of the expensive night life.

Shinjuku (Figures 3.20 and 5.5) is the busiest 'centre'. Although it also has department stores, it is better known for its large supermarkets, its discount shopping arcades with their camera and video shops, numerous cafes, restaurants and places for evening entertainment. Prices here are lower than in the Ginza. Outside the railway station, the busiest in the world, is a huge video screen showing advertisements and video clips 24 hours a day.

Suburban shops may include small supermarkets, but the vast majority are minute in size and family owned (Figure 5.6). Most sell convenience goods as most Japanese prefer to buy fresh food daily rather than having to store it in their small homes. These shops remain open 24 hours a day to catch the early and late commuters and to try to make sufficient profit.

Figure 5.4
The Ginza district in Tokyo

The '1990 Report on Tokyo Industry' suggested three recent shopping trends in the city.

- In the city centres more large department stores replacing owner operated stores, specialist shops (clothes and food) and smaller supermarkets.
- An increase in stores owned by a manufacturer or a large company.
- An increase in small suburban shops run by elderly people as younger members of the family were less prepared to work such long hours for relatively little financial reward.

Figure 5.5
The Shinjuku district in Tokyo

Figure 5.6
Local family shops, Tokyo

Figure 5.7
Vending machines selling drinks, as well as snacks and cigarettes, seem to appear every 100 metres

Out-of-town shopping centres

MetroCentre in Gateshead

Family shopping has evolved from the corner shop to the supermarket, and from the hypermarket to the 'out-of-town' shopping centre. Sir John Hall, whose brainchild is the MetroCentres, claims that since the 1960s shopping has evolved in three stages around central malls: the Arndale Centres of the 1960s, the Brent Cross and Eldon Square complexes of the late 1970s, and the MetroCentres of the 1980s. The main concept of the MetroCentre is to create a day out for the family with the emphasis on family shopping and associated leisure activities.

The site for Gateshead's MetroCentre (Figure 5.8) was surveyed in 1980, and at that time received little interest from the city centre 'magnet' (or 'anchor') shops. However, by the time plans were published in 1983, retailing had changed and the success of out-of-town DIY shops led such retailing outlets as Marks & Spencer to reconsider their future policy. Indeed the MetroCentre was Marks & Spencer's first out-of-city location.

Figure 5.8
The site of Gateshead's MetroCentre beside a dual carriageway (foreground), mainline railway and the River Tyne (behind)

The scheme

There is free parking for 10,000 cars with special facilities for the disabled driver and new bus and rail stations for the non-motorist. Inside there are over 300 shops and 40 eating places.

Much attention has been paid to creating a pleasant shopping environment (Figure 5.10) – wide, tree-lined malls, air conditioning, one kilometre of glazed roof to let in natural light (supplemented by modern lighting in 'old world' lamps), numerous seats for relaxing, window boxes, hot air balloons, escalators and lifts for the disabled. A market effect has been created by traders selling goods from decorative street barrows and there is a wide variety of places to eat in. Leisure is a vital part of the scheme. There is a ten-screen cinema, a creche for children, a space city for computer and space enthusiasts, a covered fantasy-land with all the attractions of the fair without the worries of the British climate, and a children's village with children's shops. A one-hundred-and-fifty room luxury hotel has been built as part of the complex.

Advantages of the site (Figure 5.9)

- It was in an enterprise zone (page 118) which initially allowed a relaxation in planning controls and exemption from rates.
- The area was previously marshland and relatively cheap to buy, and the 47 hectare site had possibilities for future expansion.
- It is adjacent to the western bypass (2 km of frontage) which links with the North-east's modern road network – essential for an out-of-town location (Figure 5.9).
- 1.3 million people live within 30 minutes' drive.
- It is adjacent to a main railway line, with its own railway station.

Figure 5.9
The location of the MetroCentre, Gateshead

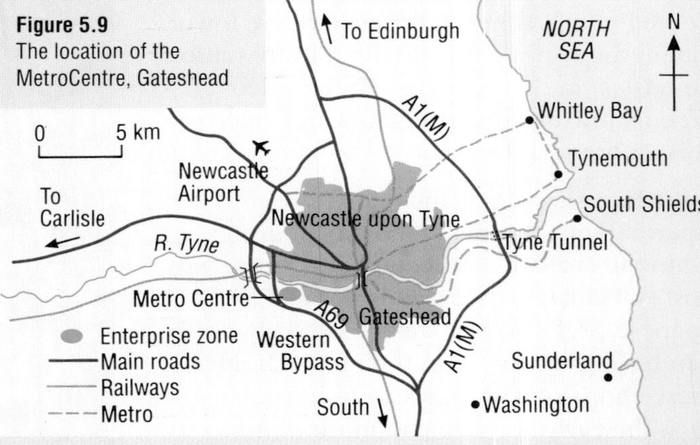

Figure 5.10
The emphasis inside the MetroCentre is on a pleasant, bright layout based on two-tiered malls

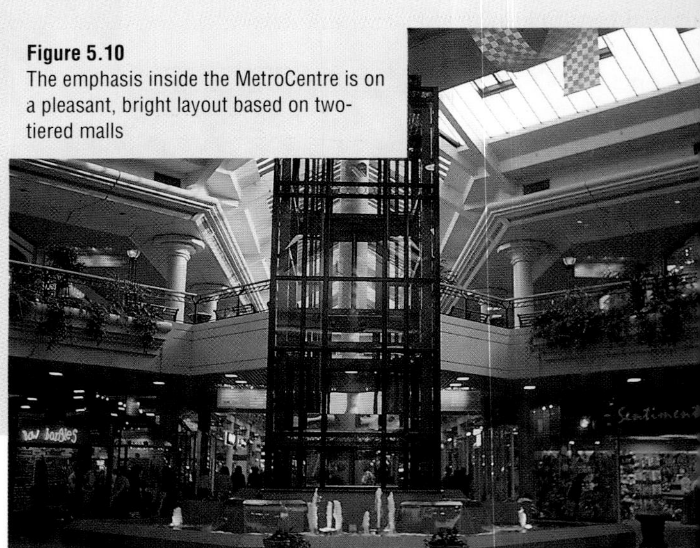

1 *(Page 54)* Refer to Figure 5.3

a Describe carefully the location of the following types of shops:
- i) A corner shop
- ii) A suburban/district shopping centre
- iii) A warehouse-type DIY shop
- iv) A city centre covered precinct
- v) A hypermarket
- vi) An edge-of-town shopping centre *(12)*

b What is meant by the following terms?
- i) Comparison goods
- ii) Convenience goods
- iii) Specialist shops
- iv) Department store
- v) Low and high order goods
- vi) Bulk buying *(12)*

2 *(Page 54)*

	Items to be bought			
Type of shopping centre	**Bread**	**Clothes**	**Furniture**	**Jewellery**
Corner shop (local)	24	0	0	0
Suburban parade (neighbourhood)	28	8	5	0
City centre (CBD)	25	66	75	100
Hypermarket (edge-of-city)	23	26	20	0

The table above shows the percentage of each item bought in each type of shopping centre.

a
- i) Draw a histogram to show where people buy their bread. *(2)*
- ii) Draw a percentage bar graph to show where people buy their clothes. *(2)*
- iii) Draw a pie chart to show where people buy their furniture. *(2)*

b
- i) Which of the four items can be bought only in the city centre?
- ii) Which product can be bought in all four shopping centres? *(2)*

3 *(Page 56)*

a Draw a sketch map to show the location of the MetroCentre. Add 5 labels to show the advantages of its site. *(5)*

b List the factors that make the MetroCentre attractive for:
- i) Shoppers
- ii) A family day out. *(2 x 3)*

4 *(Pages 54 and 56)*

a
- i) Describe the location of the corner shops. *(2)*
- ii) Why are there so many corner shops? *(2)*
- iii) Why have so many corner shops closed in recent years? *(2)*

b
- i) Describe the location of neighbourhood (suburban) shopping parades. *(2)*
- ii) How far are people prepared to travel to these shops? *(1)*
- iii) How often might people shop here? *(1)*
- iv) Give two advantages and two disadvantages of neighbourhood shopping areas. *(4)*

c
- i) What types of shopper use the inner city shops along the main roads? *(1)*
- ii) What types of goods are sold there? *(1)*

d In the CBD of most British cities is a large, modernised, covered, air-conditioned, pedestrianised shopping centre.
- i) Why were such shopping centres built? *(2)*
- ii) What are the advantages of these centres for shoppers and shopkeepers? *(2)*

e In many towns and cities the newest shopping centres are located on the very edge of the urban area. These centres usually include hypermarkets.
- i) What is a hypermarket? *(1)*
- ii) Using the map, give three reasons why site H is a good one for a hypermarket. *(3)*
- iii) What will be the views of the following groups of people to the building of a hypermarket at H:

Town planners • City councillors • People living near to the site • Shopkeepers in the city centre • The elderly and the disabled • Long distance lorry drivers

(6)

- iv) How has the growth of hypermarkets and edge-of-city shopping centres changed the shopping patterns in an area? *(2)*
- v) Draw a sketch map to show the location of a hypermarket or edge-of-city shopping centre that you have studied. *(3)*

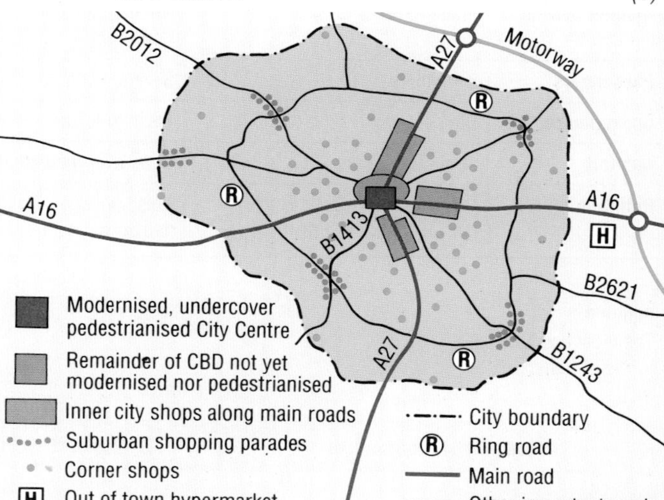

6 Transport

Transport is important to the economy of a country and to the quality of its daily life. It is needed to move goods and people around a country and between countries. It helps to improve the wealth of a country and the standard of living of its inhabitants. There is, however, a realisation that transport is becoming increasingly expensive, causes conflicts, and creates a range of major environmental problems.

There are several types of transport, each with its own advantages and disadvantages (Figure 6.1). Ideally a country needs several of these types of transport so that it can use the benefits of each. Those countries with a range, and therefore a choice, of transport are likely to be the ones which are the more economically developed. Britain was the first country to develop a modern transport system although some parts of it are now out of date while others are either under-used or congested.

When choosing the most appropriate type of transport for the movement of goods or people, the user should consider several factors:

- Time – how long will the journey take and how important is speed?
- Distance – how far is the journey?
- Cost – how much will the journey cost and which type of transport will be cheapest?
- Frequency – how often is the journey to be made?
- What volume and in what state will be the goods or people being carried?

These factors have been summarised in Figure 6.1 so that a comparison can be made between four of the main types of transport.

Figure 6.1
Types of transport – advantages and disadvantages

	Car – Lorry	Train	Air	Water
Speed/Time	Fast over short distances and on motorways	Fast over longer distances	Fastest over long distances	Slowest
Distance/Costs	Cheap over shortest distances	Relatively cheap over longer distances with bulk goods	Relatively cheap over long distances with light goods	Cheapest
Running costs	High costs of building new roads and repairing older ones. Lorries relatively cheap	High cost of maintaining track, new signalling, and new trains	Large airports – expensive use of land and fuel High cost of airports and planes	High cost of port dues and large specialised ships
Number of routes	Numerous – from motorways to minor roads	Mainly limited to Inter-City passengers and freight	Few internal aiports	Few coastal ports Little inland traffic
Congestion	Heavy in towns and on major motorways. Daily and seasonal peaks	No track congestion – limited to commuter trains	Very little	Very little
Weather	Fog and ice cause accidents. Snow causes blockages	Virtually unaffected unless extreme snow, cold and floods	Fog grounds planes	Storms affect coasts
Volume of freight	Small tonnage	Greater tonnage Heavier bulk	Limited to light, high value and perishable goods	Heavy, bulky goods
Passengers	3–4 adults	Several hundred	Up to 200 on internal flights	Very few passengers
Convenience	Door-to-door	Town to town	City to city	Poor
Comfort	Strain for drivers	Good over medium distance	Good over long distance	Good
Pollution	Noise and air pollution, acid rain, Greenhouse Effect	Noise pollution limited to narrow belts	High noise pollution. Some air pollution	Virtually none (unless oil tankers)

Figure 6.2
The most economical forms of transport

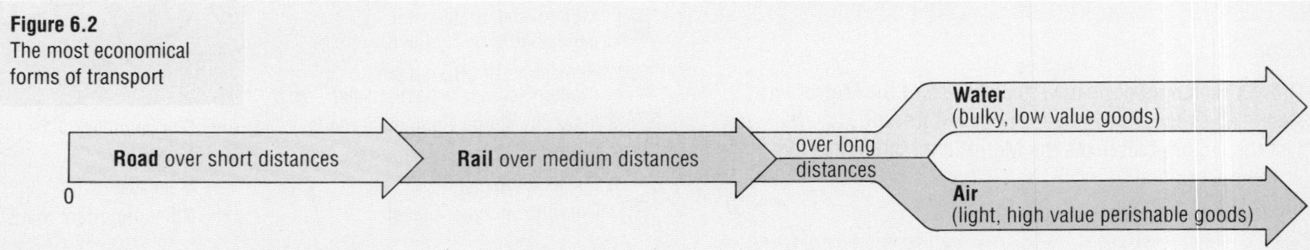

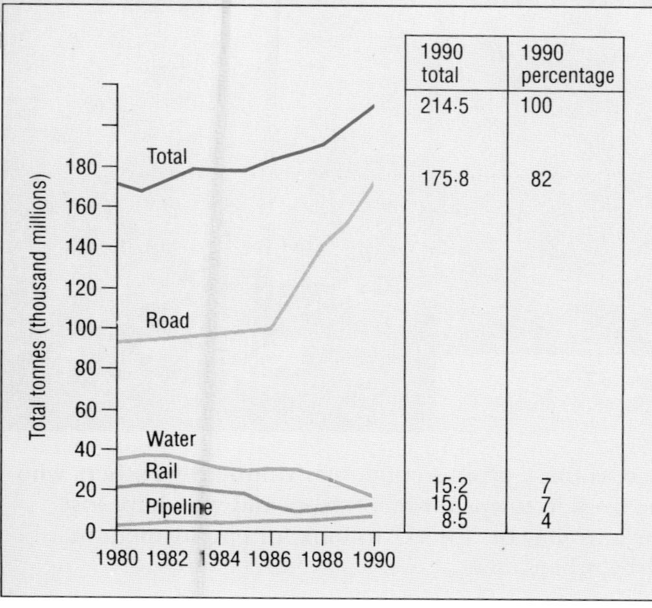

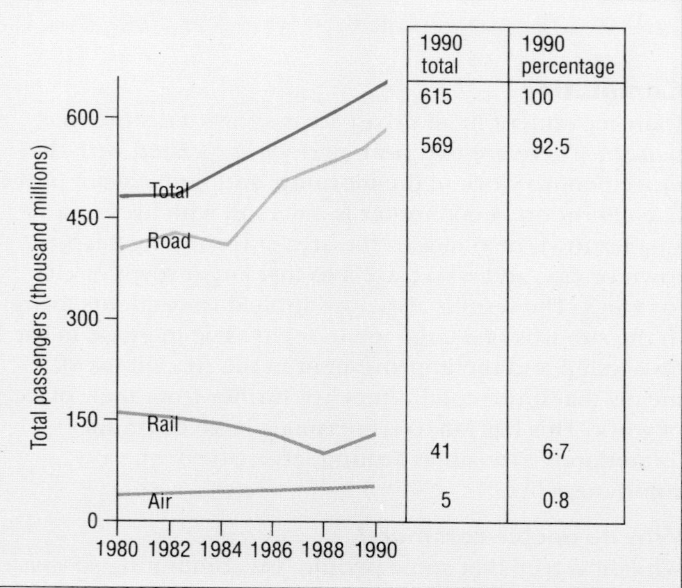

Figure 6.3

Road and rail in Britain

At the beginning of this century virtually all of Britain's goods were moved either by rail or water. By 1990 over 80 per cent of Britain's goods and over 90 per cent of passenger movements were made by road (Figure 6.3).

Road

The biggest advantage is convenience as goods and people can make 'door-to-door' journeys without having to make changes. Cars are increasingly being used for journeys to work, shopping, recreation and holidays as they are relatively cheap to use, especially over short distances (Figure 6.2). Lorries have become more specialised in what they can carry. Goods loaded at a factory in Britain can be sent all over the EC without having to be transferred to other vehicles or other types of transport. The popularity of roads has created many problems including congestion (Figure 6.4), accidents, pollution and a decline in public transport. Certainly people who either cannot afford to own a car or do not have daily access to the 'family' car are disadvantaged.

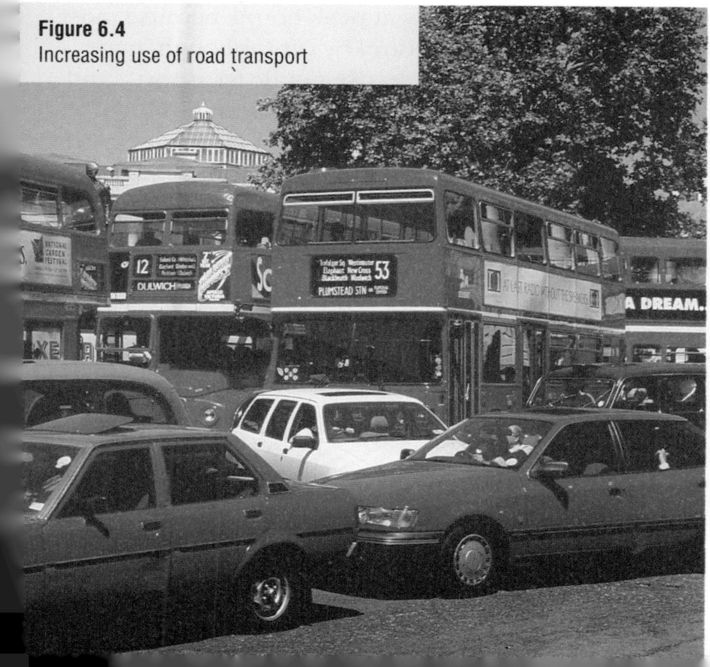

Figure 6.4
Increasing use of road transport

Rail

Compared with road transport, rail travel avoids congestion (apart from in parts of South-east England), causes less pollution, is cheaper and quicker over relatively long distances, and is both safer and more comfortable (Figure 6.5). Despite this, the amount of goods and number of passengers carried by rail continues to decline in comparison to road transport (Figure 6.3). One main reason is the delay in travelling to and from stations and then, often, the need to transfer from one form of transport to another at each end. Rail is ideally suited to carrying heavy, bulky goods such as coal, coke, cement and steel – the very goods which Britain is using in rapidly declining amounts.

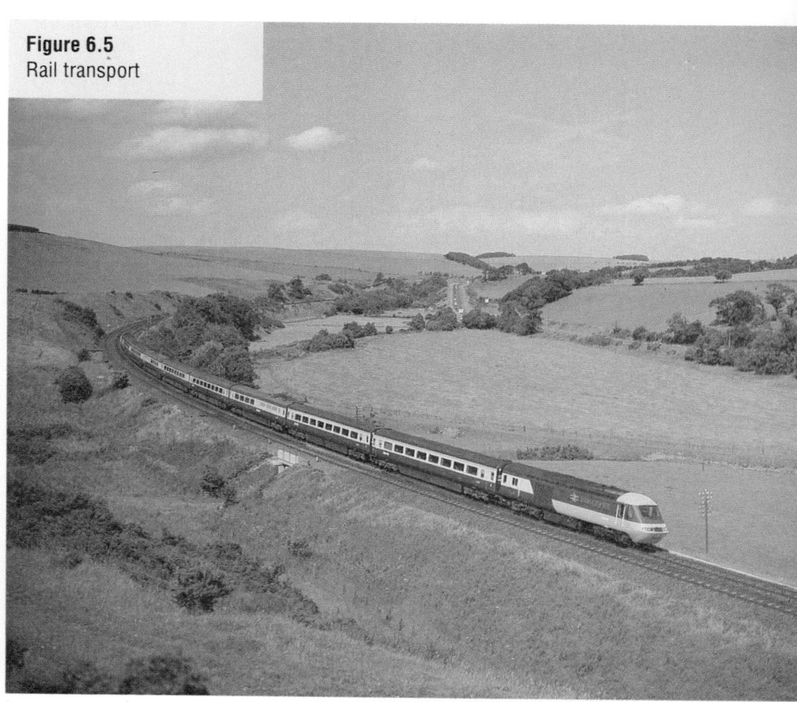

Figure 6.5
Rail transport

Commuting

Daily movement in all urban areas shows a distinctive pattern. There are two peak periods associated with the movement to work in the morning, and home again in the late afternoon. A commuter is a person who lives in a smaller town or village in the area surrounding a larger town or city, and who travels to that larger town or city for work. The term is also now applied to residents living in the suburbs of a large town or city. The increase in car ownership and the improvement in the road network means that more commuters live further from their place of work. This has led to increasingly large commuter 'hinterlands' (the areas around large cities) where commuters live.

Why do people commute?

While it is true that some people like commuting so that they can live away from their place of work, most resent the time and, especially in South-east England, the cost involved. So why commute? Some commuters travel long distances so that they can live in a more pleasant environment. Travel time rather than cost may be a limiting factor for this group. Young people may commute because housing is cheaper in outlying towns and villages. Elderly commuters may have bought property in more rural areas in preparation for their retirement.

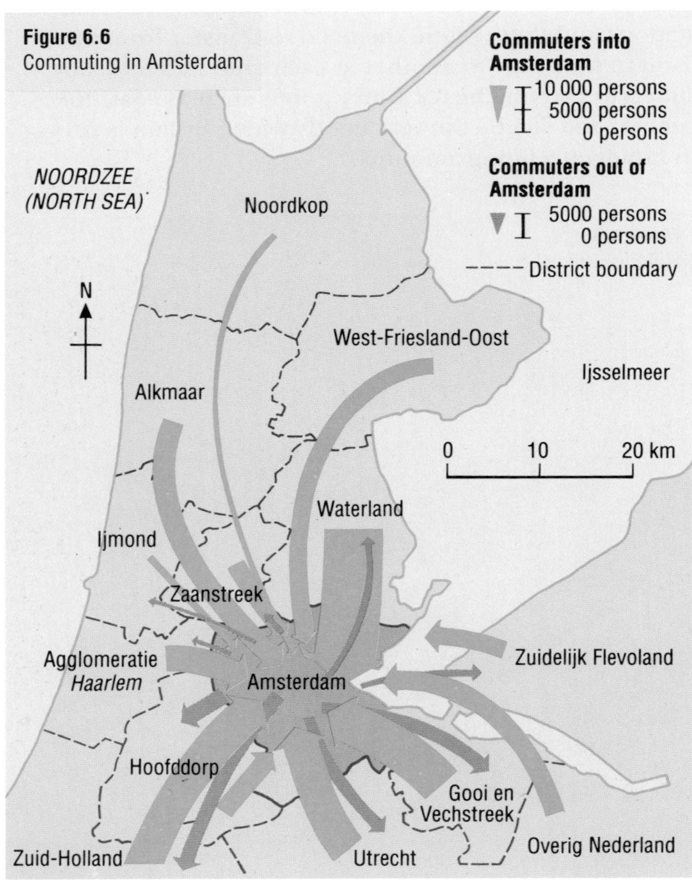

Figure 6.6
Commuting in Amsterdam

Figure 6.7
Traffic in Los Angeles

Whereas these groups commute 'voluntarily', others who have lived in towns for many years and who have lost their jobs may be 'forced' to look for employment in nearby urban areas.

A more recent trend is a 'reversed' flow of commuters. This group tends to include either the less skilled or members of ethnic minorities who both live in low cost inner city housing. As jobs in the inner city decrease, these people have to make long journeys to work on the newer edge-of-city industrial estates (pages 115–117).

Figure 6.6 is a flow line map showing commuters into and out of Amsterdam. Flow lines show the direction and the amount of traffic movement, either people or goods, between set places. The width of the line drawn is proportional to the volume of traffic at points along that route. Usually:

- The greater the distance to travel the fewer the number of commuters.
- Small settlements have a net loss of commuters to surrounding larger settlements while large settlements have a net gain from surrounding smaller settlements.
- People are prepared to commute further if there are good communication links.

Problems caused by commuters in city centres

- **Congestion**, especially at peak hours, because most commuters prefer to travel by car (although, in London, most people do use public transport); and under-use of resources at off-peak times.
- **Air pollution** from car exhausts – a problem especially acute in Los Angeles and Tokyo where smog is a common occurrence (page 31).
- **Noise pollution** from cars and lorries.
- **Visual pollution** of motorways (Figure 6.7).
- **Parking** problems.
- **Increased** risk of accidents.
- **Cost** of building urban freeways, many of which are multi-lane.
- **Destruction** of houses and open spaces to create urban motorways.
- **Increased** cost of energy consumption and the utilisation of oil supplies.

Improved technology – rapid transport systems

Many large urban areas have introduced a rapid transit system of traffic management. The first one in Britain was the Tyne and Wear Metro. It opened in 1980 and integrated public and private transport systems. Its design has since been adopted by cities as far away as Singapore and Hong Kong.

BART – the San Francisco Bay Area Rapid Transit System

Like many other large cities, San Francisco receives thousands of commuters each weekday (Figure 6.8). During the 1960s an increasingly large percentage travelled by car, causing pollution (noise, fumes and visual), accidents and congestion (it could take an hour to cross Oakland Bridge at peak travel times). Increasing demands were made upon the city authorities to construct more freeways into, and car parks within, the CBD. However as this would not have reduced congestion, especially at the bridges, it was decided instead to build a new transport system. Opened in 1974 and completed in 1978, the Bay Area Rapid Transit System (Figure 6.9) is a 120 kilometre electric railway (with underwater, underground, and elevated sections) designed to ease traffic congestion in the CBD. The underwater section was designed to withstand earthquakes by moving as the ground moved. It experienced no problems during the 1989 earthquake whereas several car drivers were killed when part of the Bay Bridge, almost above this section, collapsed.

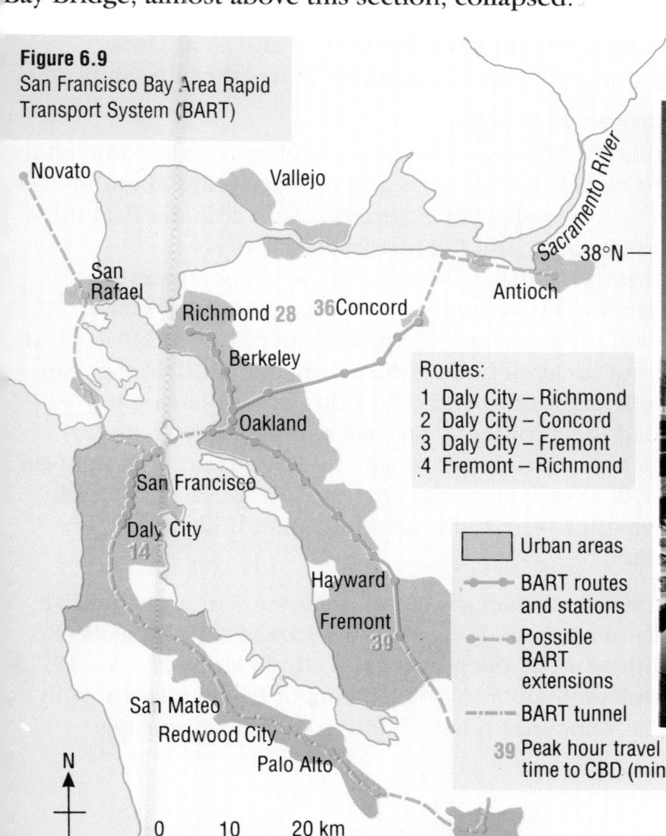

Figure 6.9
San Francisco Bay Area Rapid Transport System (BART)

Figure 6.8
Downtown San Francisco

Advantages

- Electric and so pollution free (Figure 6.10).
- Fast conveyance of 350,000 commuters a day in the early 1990s.
- Trains can travel up to 120 kilometres per hour. Travel time at peak periods over the Bay between Oakland and San Francisco is 9 minutes (11 kilometres) instead of over 40 minutes by road.
- Trains run every 1.5 minutes at peak times and 20 minutes through the night.
- Modern carriages are noiseless, air-conditioned and carpeted.
- The whole system is 'fully automatic and computerised' – drivers only take over in an emergency.
- Long platforms ensure rapid alighting and boarding.
- Lower fares than by bus to attract users.
- Cars left at suburban stations reduce CBD congestion.
- It has helped regenerate commercial life in Downtown San Francisco.

Figure 6.10
BART train

Ports

Traditional British ports

These grew up on the west and south coasts and were linked with the colonial trade. Glasgow, Liverpool and Bristol had connections with the Americas; Southampton and London with Africa and Australasia. However, in the last 40 years these ports have declined considerably due to such factors as the gaining of independence by the former colonies, the increase in rival merchant fleets, an increase in containerisation, the introduction of Ro-Ro (roll on/roll off) loading, and greater links with the EC. These factors, together with an increase in ship size, problems in labour relations and the decrease in world trade resulting from the recession of the early 1980s, have meant a shift in the importance of British ports. London and Liverpool, which still handled 59 per cent of Britain's trade in 1960 handled under 10 per cent in 1990.

Figure 6.11
Loading containers at Felixstowe

Figure 6.12
Aerial view of the port of Felixstowe

Felixstowe

Advantages

From a near-derelict site in 1950, Felixstowe is now Britain's premier container port. This is due to:

- It being a deep water port capable of handling large vessels;
- Being sited on the coast, thus avoiding time-wasting journeys up river estuaries;
- Being on the major trade route between Britain and both the EC and Scandinavia;
- Good industrial relations (it has only one union) which has earned the port a reputation for being efficient and reliable;
- Good road links with its hinterland which pass through mainly non-urban land and so are less congested than the approaches to other British ports.

Improved technology

During the 1960s improved technology was introduced to try to reduce labour costs and the time ships spent in port. Three major developments were containerisation, Ro-Ro facilities and the increased size of ship. *Containerisation* is the use of boxes (containers) of internationally agreed size. Once a cargo has been loaded into containers it can be moved around the world without break-of-bulk. Without break-of-bulk lorries can drive straight onto and off a ship without having to unload their contents. Special 'roll on/roll off' (Ro-Ro) ships were introduced to allow lorries to drive straight on and off. To accommodate the extra large cargoes much larger ships were built including giant bulk oil and ore carriers.

Felixstowe, Britain's largest container port, now has five container terminals (Figures 6.11 and 6.12). It has Ro-Ro facilities and its deep water site allows ships of considerable bulk to dock. Its major trade links are with the EC container ports of Rotterdam and Zeebrugge.

Air

Hong Kong's new airport

Kai Tak Airport in Hong Kong is one of Asia's busiest and one of the world's potentially most dangerous. The approach route to the airport is over one of the world's most densely populated cities (Figure 6.13) and planes seem to 'disappear' behind high rise buildings as they land (Figure 6.15). The runway, although very long, extends out into the one of the world's busiest harbours. What would be the damage and loss of life should the pilot descend too quickly or pull up too slowly? The airport handles 16 million passengers and will be operating at full capacity by 1994.

The Hong Kong government have begun, despite much opposition from China who will take over the colony in 1997, to build a huge new airport and seaport on the island of Lantau (Figure 6.13). The project will include a twin-runway airport with a dozen or more container terminals and cargo berths. These will be linked to Kowloon and Hong Kong Island by a six-lane expressway, a commuter line, a 1.4 kilometre suspension bridge and five tunnels. The first stage, the levelling of a hilly island just off the coast of Lantau, has already begun.

Figure 6.14
The port of Hong Kong

The project is continuing amid considerable political opposition from China. The colony's government claimed that without the new airport Hong Kong could lose 13 billion US dollars a year in trade and tourism. China feels it is an attempt to run down Hong Kong's money reserves before the take over in 1997 and resents the lack of consultation. Unlike other proposed airport developments and extensions elsewhere in the world, such as London, political opposition is greater than environmental protests.

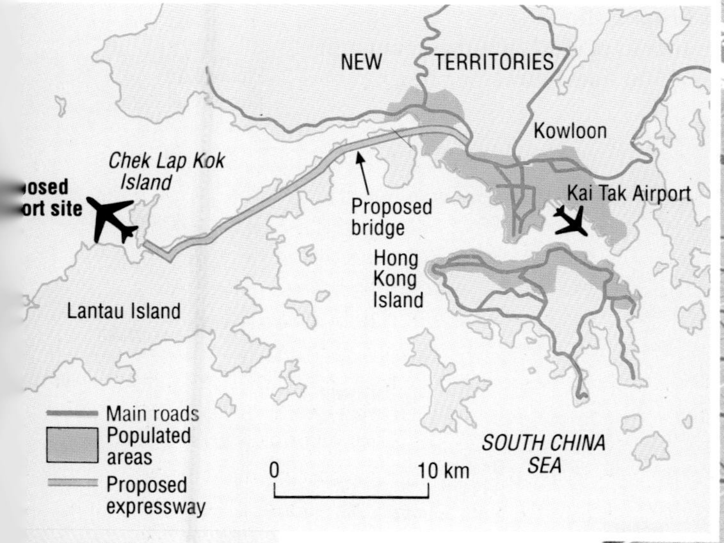

NEW TERRITORIES
Kowloon
Chek Lap Kok Island
Proposed airport site
Proposed bridge
Kai Tak Airport
Hong Kong Island
Lantau Island
Main roads
Populated areas
Proposed expressway
0 10 km
SOUTH CHINA SEA

Figure 6.13
Proposed site of the new Hong Kong airport

Figure 6.15
Cathay Pacific plane 'landing' at Kai Tak airport

Rail

Japan

The Shinkansen, wrongly translated into English as the 'bullet train', provides the most reliable rail service in the world (Figure 6.16). Between 1964 and 1982 three 'new trunk lines' (which is the accurate translation) were built radiating outwards from Tokyo (Figure 6.19). The first section, between Tokyo and Osaka, was opened in time for the 1964 Tokyo Olympic Games. The electrically driven trains run on a specially designed track and at present reach speeds of 240 kilometres per hour (rising to 300 kilometres per hour in the near future). Each train is 16 coaches long, the length of four football pitches, and can carry 1,340 passengers. On several occasions the Shinkansen has carried over 1 million people, in a day. The insides of the coaches are designed to allow passengers to either relax or work in comfort (Figure 6.18). However it is not the speed, nor the comfort, nor the fact that it always arrives on time which pleases the Japanese. Rather, it is that in almost 30 years of operation there has never been one serious accident. As the Japanese say "The Shinkansen has carried over 3 billion passengers (nearly half the world's population) over distances equivalent to 2,000 journeys to the moon and back without the loss of a single life". Although the French TGV travels faster, no other railway can match the reliability and safety of the Shinkansen.

Figure 6.16
The Shinkansen passing in front of Mount Fuji

Figure 6.17
Passengers on the Shinkansen

The Japanese are hoping to have their new 'maglev' train in operation by the beginning of the twenty-first century. This train, initially developed in Britain, 'floats' above a single magnetic rail. It is expected that this train will reach speeds of 500 kilometres per hour.

We bought our tickets at a special counter in Tokyo station. We were travelling first class and were in coach 12. We found a figure 12 painted on the platform and joined the neat queue already waiting behind it. When the train stopped our door was exactly opposite the number 12. The train was on time and there was one minute for people to get off and on. Inside a stewardess showed us to our seat, and we were given a warm towel with which to wipe our hands and face. The seats were reclining and had adjustable footrests, fold up tables and plenty of legroom (Figure 6.17). Later the stewardess, who was responsible for two coaches, brought food and drink. Around us were many commuters, some of whom travel over 200km to work each day, either sleeping, reading or using their lap-top computers and telephones. Eventually a very clear announcement told us we were approaching Osaka. We were, of course, on time.

Figure 6.18
Travelling on the Shinkansen

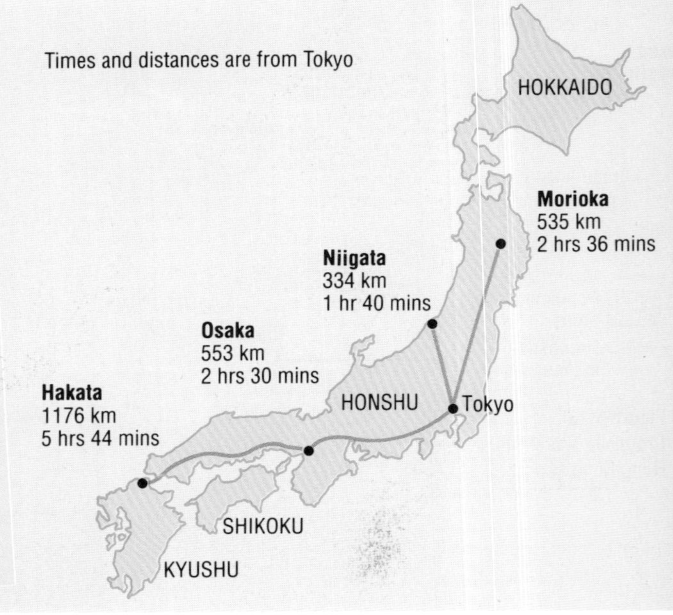

Figure 6.19
Shinkansen routes

Eurotunnel

The British and French governments agreed, in 1986, to accept a scheme which involved building two rail tunnels under the English Channel. The tunnels have a diameter of 7.3 metres and are linked by a central service tunnel. The tunnels connect Cheriton (north-west of Folkestone) with Frethun (south-west of Calais). Of the 50 kilometres of tunnel, 37 are under water. Although early hopes were for the first trains to be running by mid-1991, the actual date was mid-1994.

Use of the tunnel will reduce travel time between Britain and the continent (Figure 6.20). Passengers will be able to travel the 500 km from London to Paris in 3 hours, and the 381 km from London to Brussels in 3 hours 15 minutes. In 1994 trains leaving London will travel along existing track and through the tunnel at 160 kilometres per hour. Once through the tunnel they will travel along new track in France and, after 1996, in Belgium at 300 kilometres per hour. Times will be reduced by a further 30 minutes once Britain's new track is opened.

This is unlikely to be before the year 2000 due to disagreement on economic and environmental grounds as to which will be the preferred route. France (TGV) and Germany (ICE) have both developed new trains running on new track. By the turn of the century Spain and Italy hope to have done the same. The result will be a high-speed network linking the various EC countries (Figure 6.21).

Topological maps

Atlas maps aim to get scale, distances and directions correct. Figure 6.22 is a topological map showing British Rail's routes. A *topological map* is a simplified method of showing geographical data where one aspect of the map is accurate while others, such as distance and direction, are distorted. British Rail passengers are more interested in the number of stops to their destination rather than how far or in which direction their train is travelling.

Other examples of topological maps include those for London's underground, Tyne and Wear's metro and British Airways.

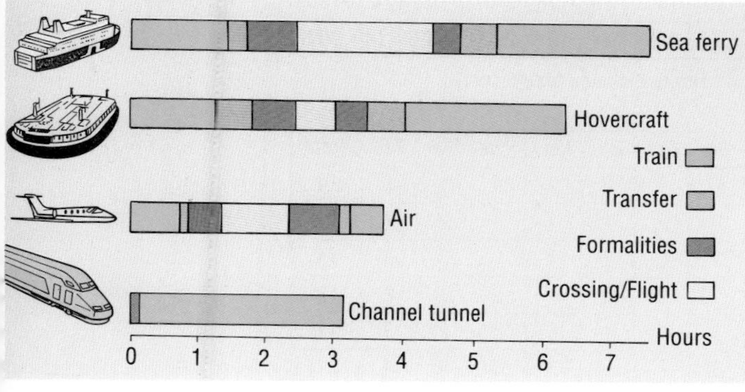

Figure 6.20
Comparative times between London and Paris

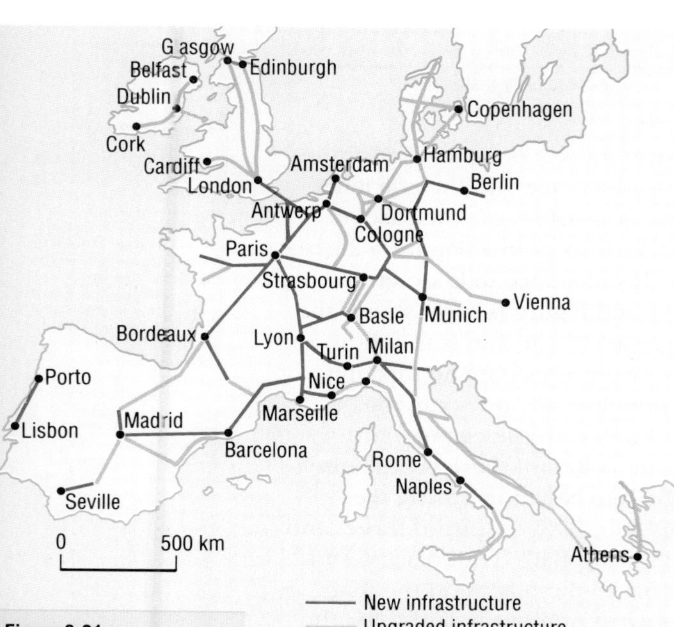

Figure 6.21
High speed EC rail routes

Figure 6.22
Topological map of mainline British Rail routes

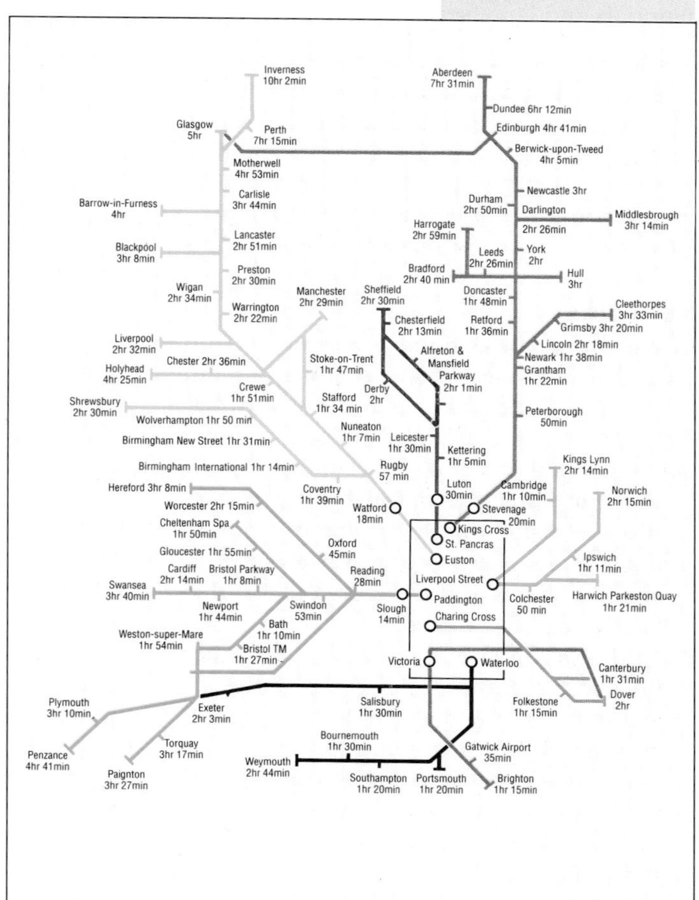

Flows and networks

Flows

We have already seen that the movement of goods and passengers can be shown by a flow map (page 60). Flows of people and goods can be affected by several factors.

Physical The relief of the land can determine both the density of communications (i.e. lengths of road or railways per square kilometre) and the routes taken by those communications. The flatter parts of south-east England have a higher density than upland areas in Wales or Scotland. Routes usually avoid marshy and mountainous regions and concentrate on low lying ground and along coasts and valleys.

Climate Heavy snowfall and flooding can block routes causing considerable delays and detours.

Economic Transport demand and densities are high in industrial and urban areas and in places providing or needing raw materials. They are lower in rural areas lacking raw materials and large settlements.

Wealth Modern communications are expensive to build and to maintain. Often only governments can afford to finance and operate transport systems. Densities and flows are usually greater in countries which are economically more developed than in those which are economically less developed.

Networks

A *network* can be defined as a set of geographical places which are joined together in a system by a number of routes. Networks vary between and within countries. A network can be divided into links and nodes.

1 **Links** are the lines of transport between places. On the topological map (Figure 6.22) these links were converted into straight 'edges' but in Figure 6.23(a) they have been left as 'arcs'.
2 **Nodes** are the points (towns) which the links join together. They can be either:
   a a point of origin or destination
   b a significant town en route
   c a junction of two or more routes
   On Figure 6.23(a) these would be:
   a Swansea
   b Cardiff
   c Bristol

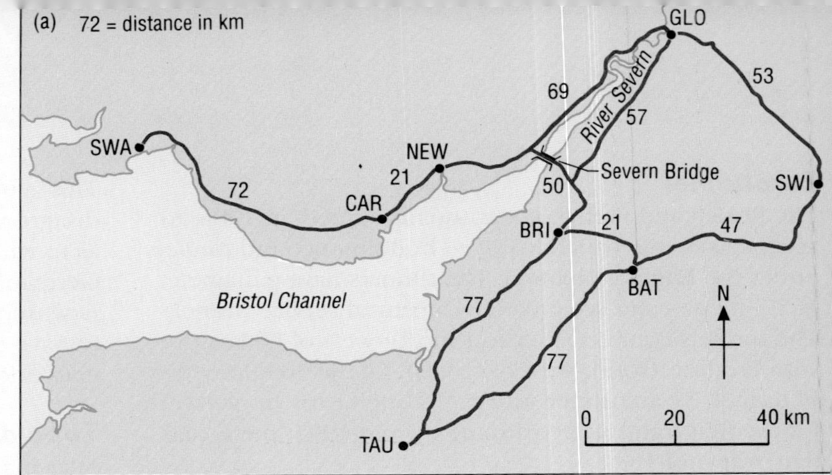

Note: places north and west of the Bristol Channel have (i) a shorter distance to Swindon via the Severn Bridge but (ii) have fewer nodes to Swindon via Gloucester

(b)	Bat	Bri	Car	Glo	New	Swa	Swi	Tau	Total
Bat	0	21	92	78	71	164	47	77	550
Bri	21	0	71	57	50	143	68	77	487
Car	92	71	0	90	21	72	139	148	633
Glo	78	57	90	0	69	162	53	134	643
New	71	50	21	69	0	93	118	127	549
Swa	164	143	72	162	93	0	211	220	1065
Swi	47	68	139	53	118	211	0	124	760
Tau	77	77	148	134	127	220	124	0	907

Route distance matrix (km)

BAT = Bath
BRI = Bristol
CAR = Cardiff
GLO = Gloucester
NEW = Newport
SWA = Swansea
SWI = Swindon
TAU = Taunton
77 Distance in km

(c)	Bat	Bri	Car	Glo	New	Swa	Swi	Tau	Total
Bat	0	1	3	2	2	4	1	1	14
Bri	1	0	2	1	1	3	2	1	11
Car	3	2	0	2	1	1	3	3	15
Glo	2	1	2	0	1	3	1	2	12
New	2	1	1	1	0	2	2	2	11
Swa	4	3	1	3	2	0	4	4	21
Swi	1	2	3	1	2	4	0	2	15
Tau	1	1	3	2	2	4	2	0	15

Accessibility matrix

Figure 6.23
Accessibility matrixes

This division into links and nodes determines the accessibility of a place and the efficiency of the network. *Accessibility* is the ease of travel between various points. Figure 6.23(b) shows the shortest distance in kilometres between places and Figure 6.23(c) shows the 'shortest path matrix'. The aim is to follow a route between two places passing through as few nodes as possible, as nodes can mean congestion and delay. In the example in Figure 6.23 Bath to Bristol there is only one nodal point, Bath to Newport (using the Severn Bridge) two, Bath to Cardiff three, and so on. The total from Bath to all places is 14. After totalling up all the places on the map, that with the lowest number is said to be the most accessible on the network, and the place with the highest total is the least accessible.

None of the routes shown on Figure 6.23(a) take the shortest route. The shortest route would have been shown by a straight line. Routes usually have to make detours either to avoid physical features or to join up places. The *detour index* shows how far a route deviates from the straight line course.

$$\text{Detour Index} = \frac{\text{Shortest possible route distance}}{\text{Direct (straight line) distance}} \times \frac{100}{1}$$

The lowest possible index is 100, whereas an index of 300 would mean that the shortest possible route is three times longer than the straight line path. The higher the index the less efficient the system. A developed country has numerous routes linking many places, making journeys more rapid. Developing countries have fewer routes with many terminal, isolated points, making journeys slow and costly (Figure 6.24).

Transport in developing countries

Transport systems in developing countries tend to be relatively simple and limited in coverage. They tend, in urban areas, to be over-used and, in rural areas, to be outdated. The initial systems were often constructed by colonial powers seeking to obtain primary products for their own consumption, and were built for moving goods rather than passengers. Figure 6.25 attempts to show how transport patterns may have evolved in a developing country. Since independence, few countries have had sufficient money to improve and modernise their communication systems other than those between and within the major urban areas, and the building of a prestigious airport. As a result:

- Few roads are surfaced and tend to become dust tracks in the dry season and quagmires in the wet season;
- Public transport is heavily over-used with passengers hanging onto or riding on top of trains and buses. Relatively few inhabitants can afford private cars;
- Railways, built during colonial days, were not designed for passenger traffic, and their rolling stock is outdated;
- Port development is often hindered by physical problems such as those listed in Stage One in Figure 6.25;
- Airports tend to be built for overseas business persons and tourists rather than for the individual needs of the country.

Figure 6.24
Railway networks for three countries in different stages of economic development

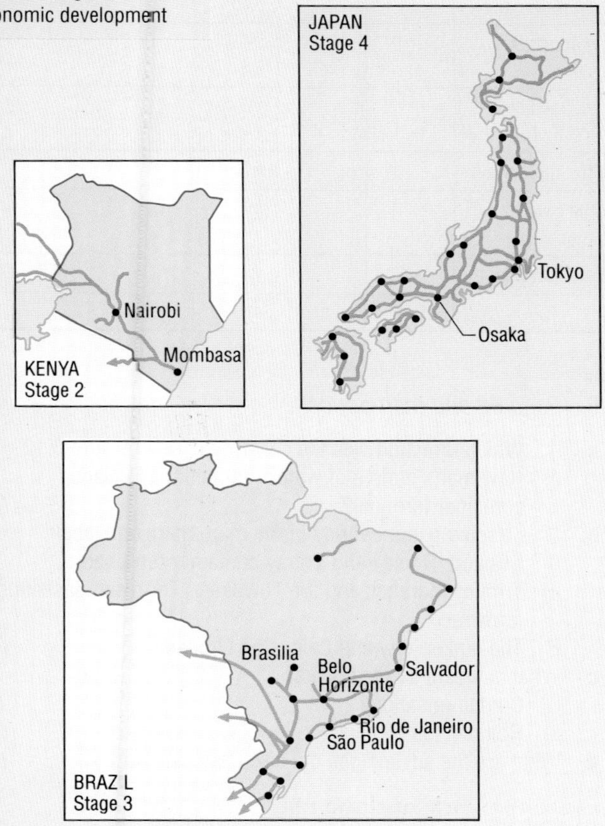

JAPAN Stage 4 — Tokyo, Osaka

KENYA Stage 2 — Nairobi, Mombasa

BRAZIL Stage 3 — Brasilia, Belo Horizonte, Salvador, Rio de Janeiro, São Paulo

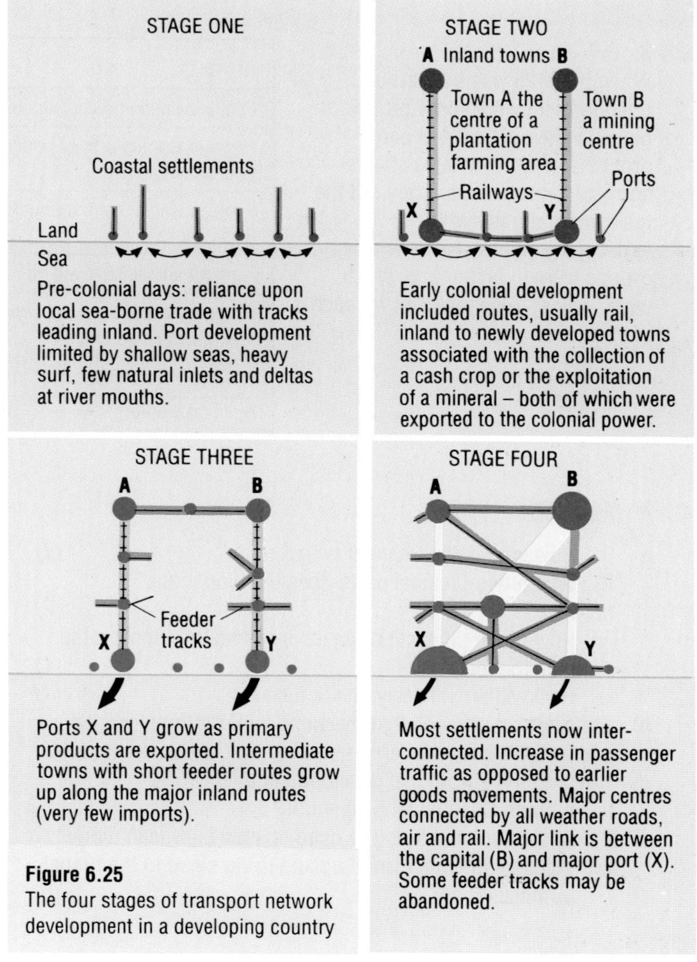

Figure 6.25
The four stages of transport network development in a developing country

QUESTIONS

1 *(Pages 58 and 59)*

a In 1990 what percentage of British goods were sent by
i) Road ii) Rail iii) Water *(3)*

b In 1990 what percentage of passenger movement in Britain was by
i) Road ii) Rail iii) Air *(3)*

c Give two advantages of each of the following compared with other types of transport
i) Road ii) Rail
iii) Water iv) Air *(8)*

2 *(Pages 60 and 61)*

a What is:
i) a commuter?
ii) a commuter hinterland? *(2)*

b i) How many commuters travel into Amsterdam from Zuid-Holland?
ii) How many commuters travel from Amsterdam to Zuid-Holland?
iii) Which district loses most commuters to Amsterdam?
iv) Why do you think so few people commute from Noordkop to Amsterdam? *(4)*

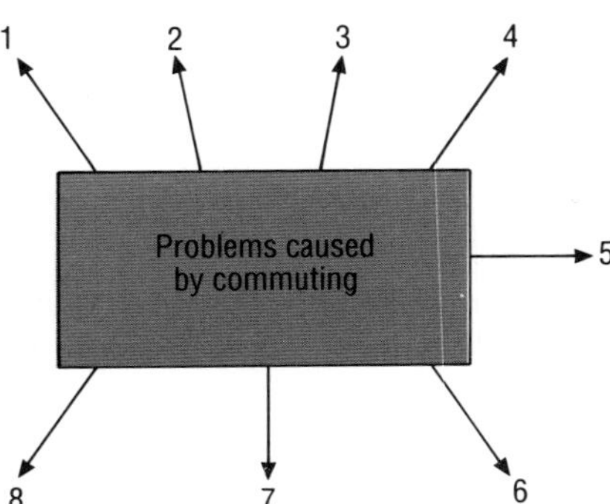

c Why has Amsterdam more incoming than outgoing commuters? *(2)*

d Commuting causes an increase in traffic and produces many problems for cities. Draw a star diagram like the one illustrated to show these problems. Write only three or four words for each problem. *(8)*

e How has the San Francisco Bay Area Rapid Transit System (BART) helped to reduce traffic problems in that city? *(4)*

3
When the M25 was built around London there were some groups of people in favour of it and some groups against. The table shows some of these groups. Copy out the table and put a tick in the appropriate column to show which groups were in favour and which were against. Give a reason for each of your answers. *(7)*

Group	For	Against	Reason
People living in houses alongside the new motorway			
Firms in towns north of London sending goods by road to places south			
People living in central London on streets used by heavy lorries			
Farmers whose land will be crossed by the motorway			
Firms in central London sending goods by road to the rest of Britain and the EC			
Hospitals and traffic police in the middle of London			
Building workers			

4 *(Page 65)*

a i) How long is the Channel tunnel route? *(1)*
ii) Which two Channel ports does the tunnel run between? *(2)*
iii) How much time will be saved by using the tunnel rather than the ferry? *(1)*
iv) How will arrival delays be reduced? *(1)*

b State two advantages that travelling by Eurotunnel will have over travelling by sea ferry. *(2)*

c How will the Eurotunnel development affect:
i) A cross-Channel ferry operator?
ii) An industrialist trying to open up new European markets?
iii) Villagers in France and England living close to the tunnel terminals? *(6)*

5 *(Page 62 and map opposite)*

a i) Which direction was the camera facing in Figure 6.12?
ii) How many metres of waterfront has the Sealand container terminal? *(2)*

b On a tracing paper overlay of the map, mark and label:
i) Sealand, Dooley and Trinity container terminals.
ii) Trimley Marshes and the Townsend Thoresen passenger terminal.
iii) The tanker jetty and Calor Gas Limited. *(4)*

c What is meant by the terms:
i) Containerisation?
ii) Roll on/Roll off? *(2)*

d What are the advantages of Felixstowe as a port? *(4)*

5 Map of the Container terminals

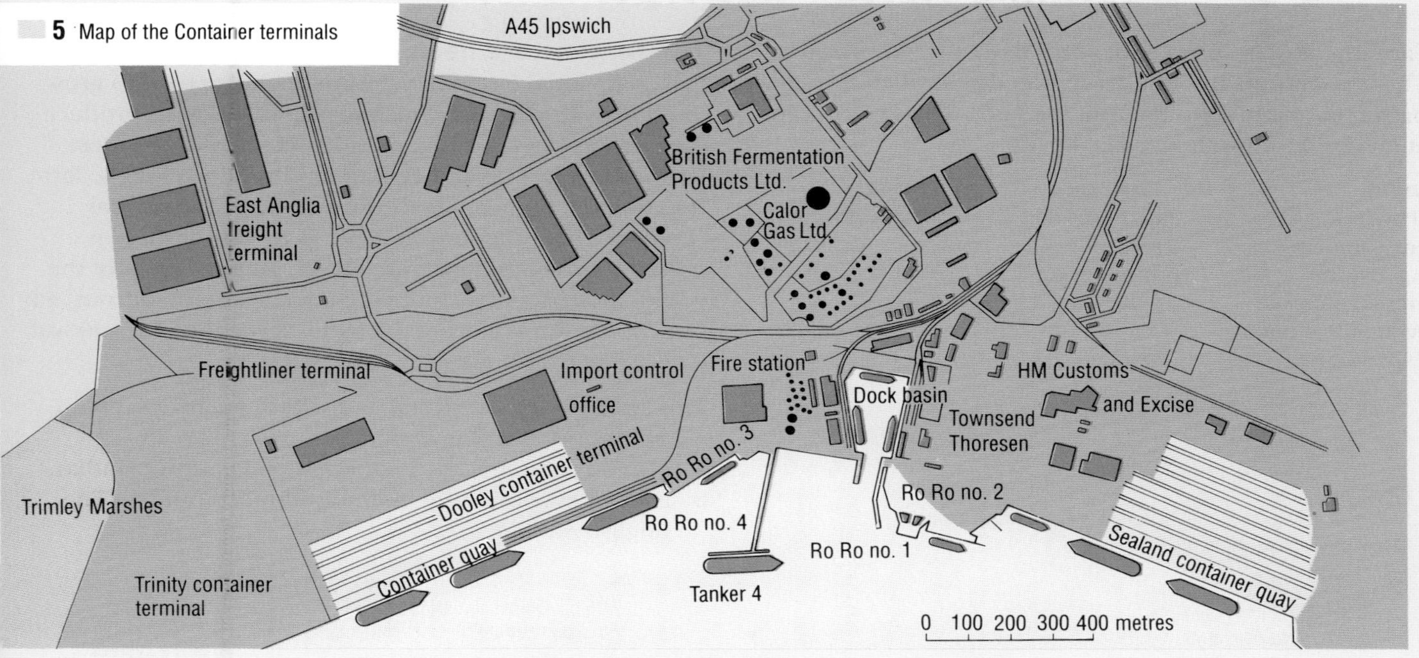

6 *(Page 65)*

a If you lived in London, which stations would you use to catch trains to the following places:
i) Glasgow ii) Edinburgh iii) Cardiff
iv) Plymouth v) Brighton vi) Norwich *(6)*

b i) If you lived in Sheffield and were going on holiday to the Netherlands, which two stations would you pass through in London on your journey from home to the port of Harwich? *(2)*

ii) If you lived in Liverpool and wished to see your football team playing at Southampton, which two London stations would you pass through? *(2)*

c i) How long does it take to travel by fastest train between London and Inverness? *(1)*

ii) How much quicker is the journey between York and Edinburgh than the journey between Rugby and Carlisle? *(1)*

iii) If you left on the fastest train from London Kings Cross to Aberdeen at 0800 hours, what time would you reach York, Newcastle, Edinburgh and Aberdeen? *(4)*

d What are the advantages and disadvantages of a topological map? *(3)*

7 *(Page 66)*

a i) Which two places were the most accessible after the opening of the Severn Bridge? *(2)*

ii) Which place was the least accessible after the opening of the Severn Bridge? *(1)*

b On 24 March 1986 hurricane force winds closed the Severn Bridge to all traffic for the first time since it opened in 1966. Drivers had a choice of either waiting for the winds to subside, or making a detour via Gloucester.

i) Redraw Figure 6.23(b) to show the route distance matrix while the bridge was closed. *(2)*

ii) Redraw Figure 6.23(c) to show the new accessibility matrix assuming drivers went via Gloucester. *(2)*

iii) Which place was the most accessible during the time the bridge was closed? *(1)*

iv) Which place was the least accessible during the time the bridge was closed? *(1)*

c Apart from the extra distance, what other problems faced the driver travelling between Bristol and Cardiff? *(2)*

8 *(Page 67)*
Copy out and complete the table opposite to show some of the differences in the transport network of an economically more developed country and an economically less developed country. *(10)*

Transport network	More economically developed	Less economically developed
Number of links		
Number of nodes		
Density		
Terminals or connections		
Detour index		

Farming systems and types

Farming is an industry and works like other industries. There are inputs into the farm, processes which take place on the farm and outputs from the farm. This system can, at its simplest, be shown as:

Input	➡	**Processes**	➡	**Output**
(Physical environment, e.g. natural inputs, human-economic inputs) Expenditure		(Patterns and methods of farming, e.g. cultivating, rearing and storage)		(Products, e.g. crops, animals) Profits

The farmer as a decision maker

Each individual farmer's decision on what crops to grow or animals to rear and which methods to use to produce the outputs depends on an understanding of the most favourable physical and economic conditions for the farm (Figure 7.1). Sometimes the farmer may have several choices. Where the output exceeds the input there is a profit (commercial farming). Often, in many parts of the world, the farmer has limited choice. Here the output may not exceed input leaving the family struggling for survival (subsistence farming).

This system varies between and within countries. Figure 7.2 shows two farming systems:

a is in an economically less developed country (India).
b is in an economically more developed country (The English Midlands).

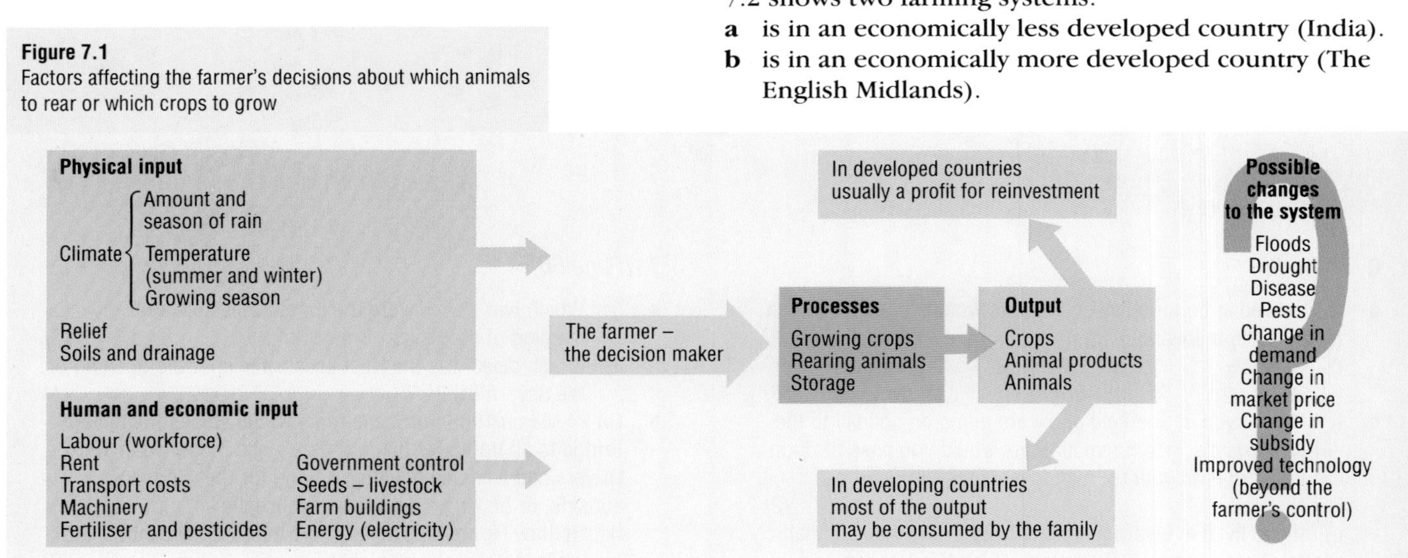

Figure 7.1
Factors affecting the farmer's decisions about which animals to rear or which crops to grow

Figure 7.2 **a** India

A Input		**Processes**	**Output**
Plenty of rain Growing season all year Flat land Rich soils	Much labour Hand tools 2 oxen Rice seed	2 hectares of land 10 chickens 2 cows 2 oxen Rice and wheat cultivation	Rice Some wheat Eggs Chicken
			= **No profit**

b The English Midlands

B Input		**Processes**	**Output**
Skilled labour Electricity Seeds Rain all year Growing season 8 months Machines	Fertiliser Cattle feed Barns for storage Low undulating relief and deep soils	Land 240 hectares Animals 40 calves, 160 cows, 40 pigs Crops Grass, Barley, Potatoes	Milk Pigs Cattle Barley Hay Manure Potatoes
			= **Profit**

Classification of farming systems

No classification can include *all* types of farming, but the classes shown in Figure 7.3 have been based on the following criteria:

1 **Arable** (the growing of crops), **pastoral** (the rearing of animals) or **mixed** (crops and animals).

2 **Subsistence** (growing just enough food for the farmer's family) or **commercial** (the growing of crops or rearing of animals for sale).

3 **Extensive** or **intensive**, depending upon the ratio between land, labour and capital:

  a **Extensive** is where the farm size is very large but either the amount of money spent on it or the numbers working on it are low (e.g. Amazon Basin) or when the numbers working on it are low in comparison with the size of the farm and the capital spent on it (e.g. Prairies).

  b **Intensive** can be either when the numbers working on the land are very high in proportion to the size of the farms (e.g. Ganges Valley) or when a considerable amount of money is used in comparison with the small numbers employed (e.g. the Netherlands).

4 **Shifting cultivation** (where the farmers move from area to area) or **sedentary** (where there is permanent farming and settlement).

A fifth category may also be used based on land tenure when the farm may be:

- **Individually owned** as in most capitalist, developed countries.
- **State owned** as in the centrally planned, socialist economies.
- **Rented** by a tenant or by a sharecropper as in colonial times, and in many economically less developed countries.

	Type of farming	Named example
1	nomadic hunting and collecting	Australian aborigines
2	nomadic herding	Maasai in Kenya
3	shifting cultivation	Amerindians of Amazon Basin
4	intensive subsistence agriculture	rice in the Ganges Valley
5	plantation agriculture	coffee in Brazil
6	livestock ranching (commercial pastoral)	beef on the Pampas
7	cereal cultivation (commercial grain)	Canadian Prairies and Russian Steppes
8	mixed farming	Netherlands
9	'Mediterranean' agriculture	southern Italy
10/I	irrigation	Nile Valley
11	unsuitable for agriculture	Sahara desert

Figure 7.3
World farming types

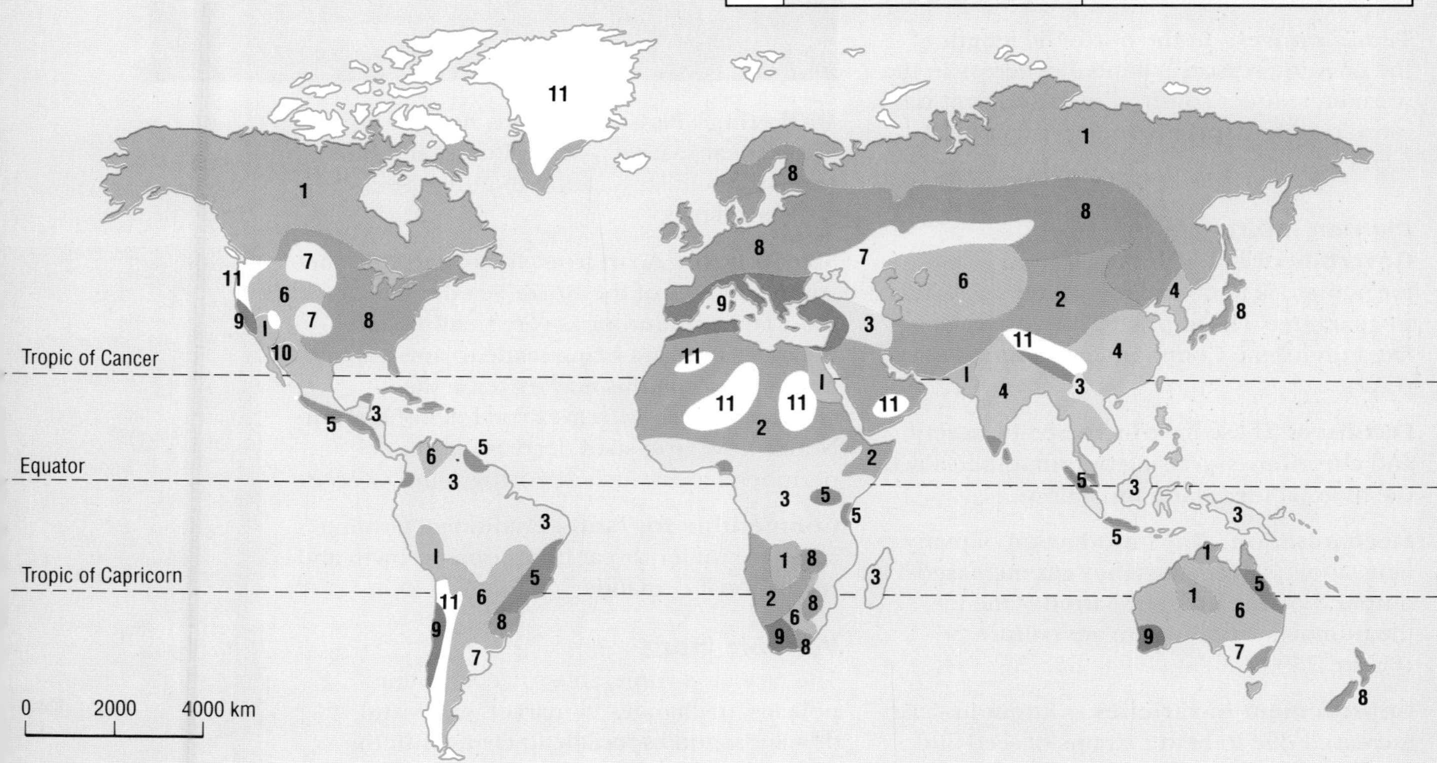

Farming in the EC

Factors affecting farming in the EC

Farmers' decisions on which crops to grow or animals to rear and what methods to use to produce the outputs depend upon an understanding of the most favourable physical and economic conditions of their locations. A simplified map to show the major areas of specialisation is shown in Figure 7.4.

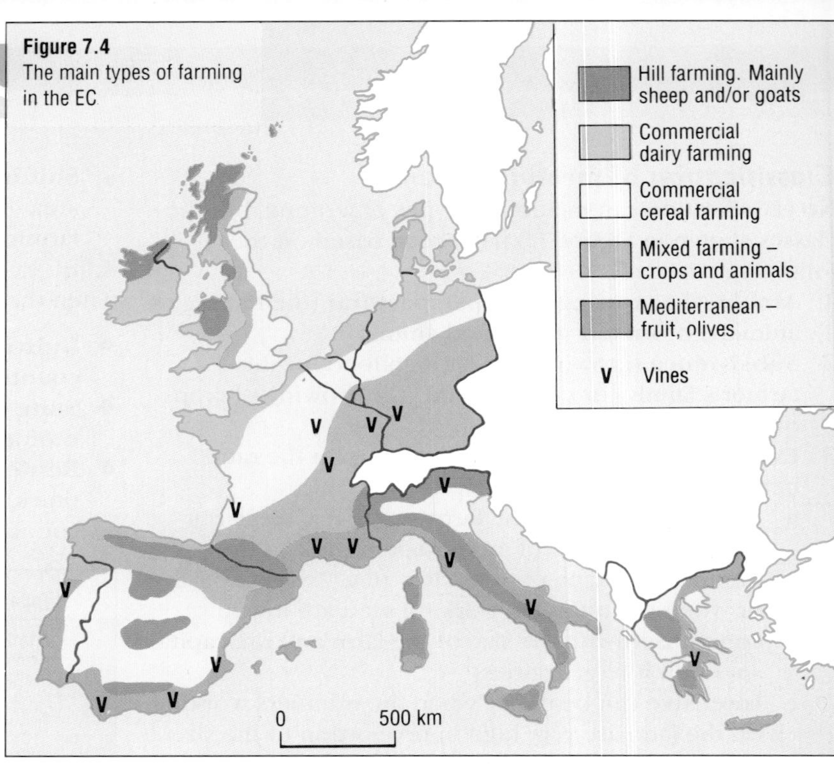

Figure 7.4
The main types of farming in the EC

Physical input

Relief: Usually the flatter the land, the larger and more efficient is the farm (Figure 7.6). Output tends to decline as land gets steeper and higher (Figure 7.5).

Soils: The deeper and richer the soil, the more intensive the farming and higher the output, e.g. limon of the Paris Basin, alluvium of the Po Valley and estuarine deposits in the Netherlands. Soils ideally should be reasonably well drained.

Rainfall: Those areas in the more northern and western parts of the EC with adequate and reliable rainfall throughout the year tend to produce good grass and so rear animals. The drier areas with less reliable rainfall in the south and east are more suited to arable farming.

Temperatures: In the north the length of the growing season is limited, whereas in the warmer, sunnier south, cereals and fruit ripen more readily. Aspect is an important local factor.

Human input

Government aid: Farmers rely on grants for new stock and machinery, and subsidies to guarantee a fixed price. Farm prices are fixed under the Common Agricultural Policy (CAP).

Fertiliser: These have increased in variety and effectiveness, raising output, especially in the more affluent farming regions.

Mechanisation: The introduction of many new labour-saving machines has increased output, but has led to a sharp decline in the numbers employed in agriculture (Figure 7.7).

Improvement in varieties: Output has also increased due to better strains of seed and better quality animals.

Figure 7.5
Mountainous farming landscape – southern Greece

Marketing: Perishable goods need to be grown near markets for freshness, and bulky crops in a similar location to minimise transport costs.

Size of farm: Apart from an area around the southern parts of the North Sea the size of most farms in Europe is very small (Figure 7.7). Attempts are being made to amalgamate farms but while this may increase their efficiency it also increases rural depopulation. Notice how farm sizes decrease in the peripheral areas such as Portugal and Greece.

Competition for land: Traditional farming areas are under threat from urban growth and recreational demands.

Variable input

The farmer is vulnerable to government policies, to changes in market prices and demands, and especially to changes in the weather (flood, drought, frost).

Figure 7.6
Flat farming landscape – Dutch polders

Common Agricultural Policy

The basic aims are to:

- ◆ Increase agricultural productivity
- ◆ Ensure a fair standard of living for farmers
- ◆ Stabilise markets
- ◆ Ensure reasonable consumer prices
- ◆ Maintain jobs on the land

These aims have replaced all existing national policies and have often caused conflict between member states.

Figure 7.7 Agriculture in the EC

	% of economically active population in agriculture		% of total land used for agriculture	Average size of farms (hectares)	% GNP from agriculture
	1960	1990	1990s	1990s	1990s
Netherlands	10	4	59	21	4
Belgium	8	2	46	19	2
Luxembourg	15	4	72	29	3
Germany W	14	3	51	18	2
France	22	6	57	28	3
Italy	30	8	58	11	4
Denmark	16	5	66	32	4
UK	4	2	77	84	2
Republic of Ireland	36	14	82	26	11
Greece	55	25	70	7	16
Spain	42	11	61	18	5
Portugal	44	17	36	9	9

Each member country used its own currency. As exchange rates constantly altered, it was agreed that a new currency be introduced – the ECU (European Currency Unit). This was sometimes called the 'basket of currencies' with each country aligning itself to a set central valuation. A further complication is that farm prices are quoted in 'Green Rates' by which each country fixes its own level of support. Farm prices are fixed in units of account and then translated into national currencies at a certain exchange rate. For Britain, the exchange rate between it and the other EC countries is the 'Green Pound'.

How successful has the Common Agricultural Policy been? In all member countries there are 'pro-marketeers' and 'anti-marketeers' and trying to get a balanced interpretation is difficult. However, Figure 7.8 tries to show some of the arguments used by the 'pro' and 'anti' groups.

Concerns over CAP

- ◆ 70 per cent of the EC's budget is spent supporting farming, yet farming only provides 5 per cent of the EC's total income (GDP).
- ◆ Farmers are given guaranteed prices (subsidies) for their produce, and therefore have produced as much as possible. The resultant surplus in several commodities is referred to as the EC's 'mountains and lakes' (Figure 7.9).

Figure 7.8
A balance sheet showing some of the achievements made and the problems still to be faced by the European Community's Common Agricultural Policy

Achievements

Achieved a larger measure of self-sufficiency. This reduces the costs and unreliability of imports.

Created higher yields due to input of capital for machinery and fertiliser.

In NW Europe the average farm size has increased almost to the recommended level.

Amalgamation of fields – in parts of France the number of fields has been reduced to one-eighth of the 1950 total.

Production has changed according to demands, e.g. less wheat and potatoes and more sugar beet and animal products.

Subsidies to hill farmers have reduced rural depopulation.

Poorer farmers gain an opportunity to receive a second income by working in nearby factories. ('five o'clock farmers') or from tourism.

Higher income for farmers.

Subsidies have reduced the risk of even higher unemployment in such rural areas as the Mezzogiorno.

Reduced reliance on crops imported from developing countries who themselves have a food shortage.

A surplus one year can offset a possible crop failure in another year.

Problems

An increase in food prices, especially in the net importing EC countries of Germany and the UK.

Creation of food surpluses – the so called 'mountains and lakes' (Figure 7.9).

Selling of surplus products at reduced prices to Eastern European countries (causes both political and economic opposition).

Increased gap between the favoured 'core' agriculture regions and the periphery.

Peripheral farm units still very small and often uneconomic.

High costs of subsidies. 'Industrial' countries such as the UK object to 70% of the EC budget being spent on agriculture.

'Five o'clock farmers' spend insufficient time on their farms. In France 15%, and in Germany 30% of farmers have a second income.

Destruction of hedges to create larger fields destroys wild life and increases the risk of soil erosion.

By reducing imports from developing countries the latter's main source of income is lost thus increasing the trade gap between the two areas.

Figure 7.9
'Mountains' and 'lakes'

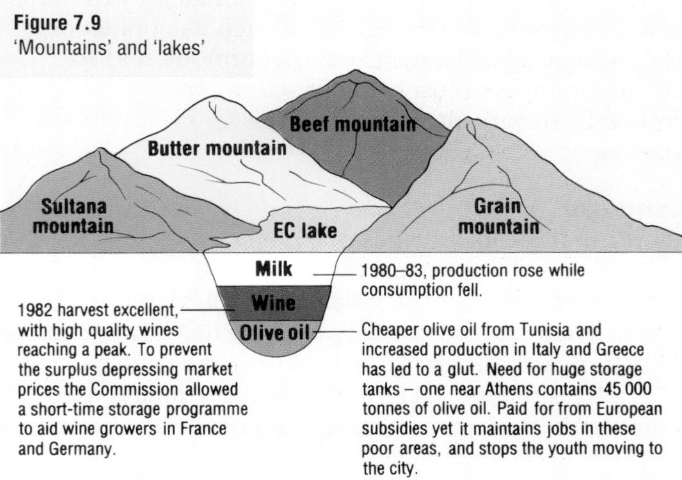

Beef mountain
Butter mountain
Sultana mountain
EC lake
Grain mountain
Milk
Wine
Olive oil
1980–83, production rose while consumption fell.
1982 harvest excellent, with high quality wines reaching a peak. To prevent the surplus depressing market prices the Commission allowed a short-time storage programme to aid wine growers in France and Germany.
Cheaper olive oil from Tunisia and increased production in Italy and Greece has led to a glut. Need for huge storage tanks – one near Athens contains 45 000 tonnes of olive oil. Paid for from European subsidies yet it maintains jobs in these poor areas, and stops the youth moving to the city.

- ◆ Although farms in the EC have become larger and more efficient, this has often been at the expense of the environment, e.g. destruction of hedgerows, draining of wetlands, use of fertiliser and pesticides (pages 54 and 236).
- ◆ The EC pays farmers at above world prices. Various levies, tariffs and quotas have been introduced to stop the import of cheaper products from overseas. This handicaps both rich countries like the USA and the poorer developing countries.
- ◆ GATT (General Agreement on Tariffs and Trade) is the main international trade agreement but, until the latest round of talks, excluded agriculture. The EC fought to protect its own farmers but other countries believed the present arrangements were 'unfair'.

Farming in the EC – The Netherlands

The old polders of the Netherlands

Much of western Netherlands lies below sea level. Most of this area was reclaimed from the sea several centuries ago. The reclaimed areas are called *polders*. A large part of the area between Rotterdam and Amsterdam (Figure 7.10) now lies between two and six metres below present day sea level. The landscape has, in the extreme west, a belt of sand-dunes which act as a natural defence against the sea. Inland lies a perfectly flat area drained by a series of canals, which run between embankments, above the general level of the polders. The fields on the polders are bound by drainage channels and the excess water from the land is pumped, initially by windmills and increasingly by diesel pumps, into the canals. Even now over 20 per cent of the total area is covered in water.

Many areas of these old polders are becoming increasingly urbanised. The Randstad conurbation has helped to raise the density of population in the Netherlands to 366 per km^2 – the highest density in Europe. Extra land is needed for this urban growth (for houses, factories and roads) and to feed its population. The expense of reclaiming land is enormous, and so the maximum use must be made of it to make it profitable. In agricultural terms this is known as *intensive farming*.

Land use

There are three major types of farming:

1 **Dairying** This is most intensive north of Amsterdam and is favoured by the mild winters, flat land, adequate and evenly spread rainfall providing lush grass, and the large nearby urban markets. Most of the cattle are Friesians (Figure 7.11). Although some milk is used fresh, the majority is turned into butter and cheese. The round Dutch cheeses are sold in the cheese-market at Alkmaar.

2 **Horticulture under glass** The area between Rotterdam and The Hague is a mass of glasshouses, with individual holdings making a profit on land averaging only one hectare (Figure 7.12). The costs of production are enormous due to:

- Large, expensive glasshouses.
- Operating oil-fired boilers to maintain high temperatures.
- Sprinkler systems to provide water.
- Computers, on the more modern holdings, to control heating, moisture and ventilation.
- Facilities to cover plants in black plastic to retard growth in order to stagger the period of ripening.
- Annual need to change the soil, and to use large quantities of fertiliser and manure.

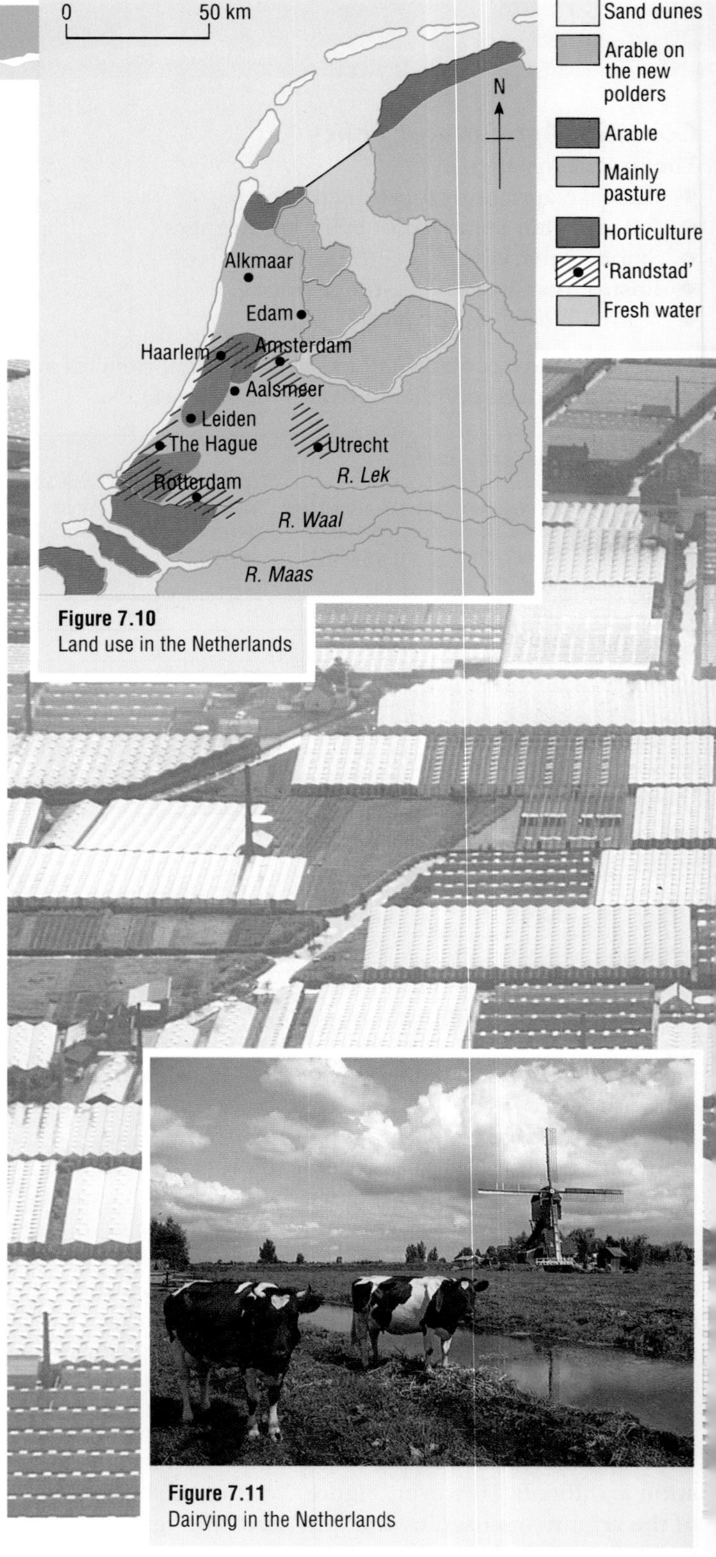

Figure 7.10
Land use in the Netherlands

Figure 7.11
Dairying in the Netherlands

- Machinery to weed and deadhead plants.
- Need for rapid transit to the local markets or for export via Schiphol Airport.

Several crops a year can be grown varying from cut flowers in spring, tomatoes and cucumbers in summer, to lettuce in autumn and winter. In recent years the number of smallholdings has declined as the urban area has expanded.

3 **Bulbs** The sandy soils between Leiden and Haarlem are used to grow bulbs. Tulips, hyacinths and daffodils in particular are grown on farms averaging 6 to 8 hectares in size. The sand dunes offer protection from the prevailing winds. The flowers, which have to be cut early in order to get them to market fresh, also provide a huge seasonal tourist attraction (Figure 7.13).

Figure 7.12
Aalsmeer has approximately 500 hectares of glasshouses

Figure 7.13
Tulip fields between Leiden and Haarlem

Aalsmeer auction mart

This is the largest auction mart in the world. The mart itself covers 45 hectares, and the buildings 30 hectares. Five mornings a week, 4000 growers deliver their produce of flowers, potted plants and roses (Figure 7.14). For every kind of flower there is a special location. The growers place their flowers on awaiting carts which are numbered. By 07.00 hours the prospective buyers have inspected the flowers and go to the two auction halls. Each hall is capable of seating over 300 exporters, wholesalers, shopkeepers and street-traders (Figure 7.15). The buyers have a code disk with a number code on it, and which they use to register on a computer. The auctioneer announces, over a loudspeaker, the name of the nursery from which the flowers come, the specific names of the flowers and details about their quality. The buyers sit with their hands on the pushbuttons. The auctioneer starts the clock and bidding begins. The hand of the auction clock goes from 100 (the highest price) to 1 (the lowest price). The first person to press the button is the buyer of that 'lot' of flowers. The art is not to bid too quickly (or you pay a higher price) or too slowly (for although prices fall, other bidders will get in first). The buyer can also, by microphone, indicate whether he wants the whole lot, or part of it – and bidding begins again. By 10.00 hours all the transactions have been made. The flowers are then prepared for transport by the buyers. Due to efficient organisation, the flowers reach the buyer within 15 minutes of their purchase. Such speed is essential if the flowers are to reach markets as fresh as possible. For overseas buyers, Aalsmeer is within 8 kilometres of Schiphol Airport.

Figure 7.14
Inside the Aalsmeer auction mart

Figure 7.15
Flower auction in progress in Aalsmeer

Farming in the EC – Denmark

Although Denmark today has a high agricultural output , its land was not always fertile. Soils are sandy in the west and clay in the east (Figure 7.16). Since the nineteenth century much money and effort has gone into improving these soils. Modern farms in the west specialise in rearing animals while those in the east concentrate on growing cereals.

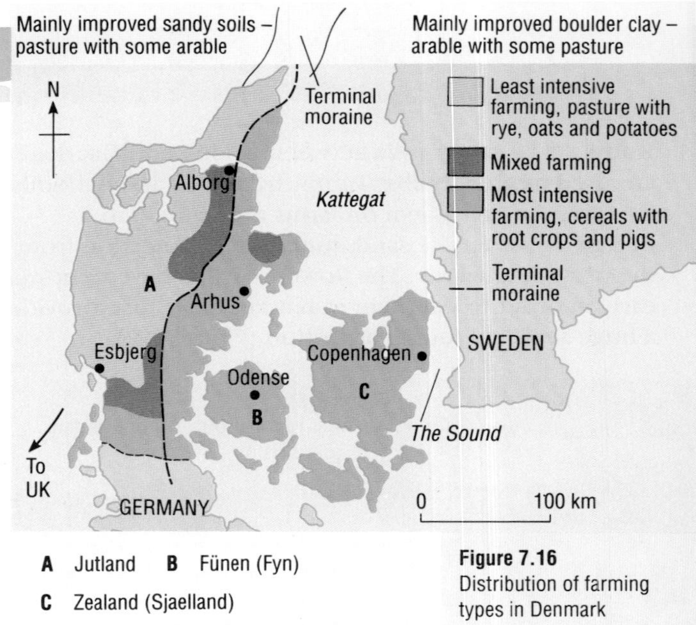

Figure 7.16
Distribution of farming types in Denmark

Danish farming before 1960

The combination of relief (low-lying and relatively flat), soils and climate (winter frosts, warm sunny summers and rainfall below average) meant that Denmark was ideally suited to the growing of cereals. Denmark was a major producer of wheat and barley until, in the 1870s, the building of railways across Canada opened up the Prairies. Denmark could not compete with the flood of cheap wheat but realised that there was a demand for dairy products in the rapidly industrialising countries of Britain and Germany.

Danish farming since 1960

Denmark's climate has always been more suitable for the growing of cereals than for grass. The reliance upon one type of farming is more vulnerable to adverse climatic conditions, changes in market demand and price, and to disease and pests. In mixed farming, on the other hand, the farmers can earn their income from several sources and alternatives. Figure 7.17 shows a modern farming landscape in Denmark. Dairy cattle remain important (they also provide the skimmed milk for the pigs), but in winter they are kept indoors. Pigs and poultry are kept indoors all year (Figure 7.20).

Selective livestock breeding produced:

a the Danish red cow which thrives on relatively poor pasture and gives a high butter fat content;

b the Landrace pig whose long back gives top quality bacon.

Imported Friesian cattle give high milk yields.

Figure 7.17
Danish agricultural landscape

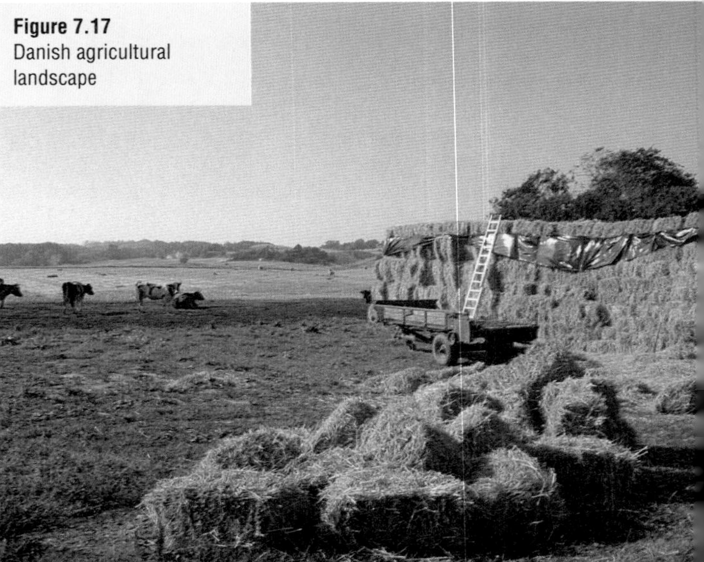

Many farmers have adopted an eight year rotation system which may be wheat – root crops – barley – sugar beet – barley – grass – mixed barley and oats – sugar beet.

The cereals are often cut green for silage, while root crops and sugar beet are not only valuable crops in their own right, but help to replace nitrogen in the soil previously used by the cereal crops.

Figure 7.18 The benefits of the co-operative system

Co-operatives
Most Danish farms are owner-occupied, but the farmers work together to try to get the maximum benefit from buying in bulk and selling on a collective basis. Co-operatives can help individual farmers by:

Bulk buying Co-operatives buy such items as cattle feed, fertiliser and seed in bulk, so reducing the cost to farmers.

Market products 200 or 300 farmers may, among them, own a dairy. The milk is sent to this dairy and the dairy does the processing and selling. The profits are shared according to the amount of milk that each farmer supplies. The dairy will also provide transport, which is a more efficient method than each individual having to do so.

Finance The co-operatives have their own banks which allow cheaper loans for machinery and buildings.

Quality Each farmer is expected to produce goods of the highest quality. The co-operatives help to ensure that goods, such as those branded Lurpak, are equated with top quality.

Back up services These include a veterinary service, free advice on new methods of farming and quality control, research into new techniques, colleges to train young people and to retrain practising farmers, and links with associated agricultural industries (e.g. bacon curing, brewing, milling, the production of butter and cheese, and the manufacture of farm machinery).

Recent changes in Danish farming

- An increase in the average size of Danish farms and a decrease in the number of smaller farms.
- An increase in mechanisation.
- A shift of cattle and milk production from the east to the west (as well as fewer cows overall), and an increase in cereals in the east.
- A decrease in the agricultural workforce and a pronounced movement to the towns for jobs.
- Difficulty in getting labour for the twice-daily milking, leading to an increase in pig farming and cereal growing. In 1980 only 2 per cent of school leavers went into farming.

Since joining the EC

- EC membership has strengthened traditional markets with the UK and Germany, and opened up new ones. 26 per cent of Denmark's exports are agricultural products, and 66 per cent of these go to the EC.
- The EC has provided the subsidies necessary to guarantee fixed prices for farm produce.
- CAP has encouraged an increase in cereal production, especially barley. Barley was also needed to meet the increased demands of the Danish brewing industry.
- CAP has recently cut milk quotas. This has reduced dairy farming and butter production.

Figure 7.19
Layout of a typical Danish farm on Fünen. It has 150 cows (120 Red Danish, 30 Friesian), 240 Landrace pigs and 220 hens

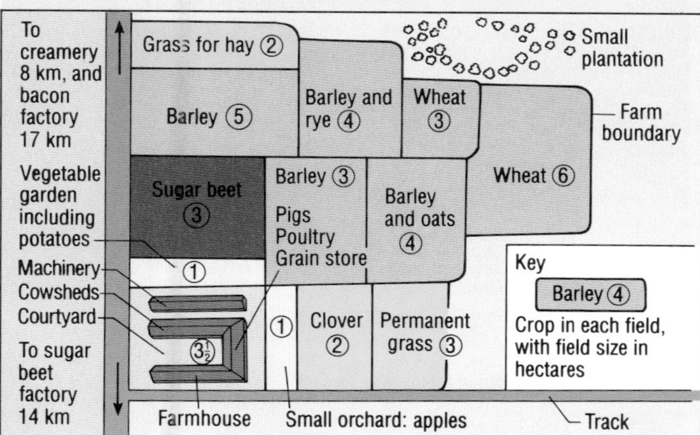

Figure 7.20
Intensive pig farming

Figure 7.21
A typical farm on Fünen

Figure 7.22
Changes in Danish agriculture

	1960	1982	1990
Land use (% of farmland)			
under cereals	47	75	88
under roots	18	8	6
under grass	32	9	6
Animals			
dairy cows (1000s)	1 438	1 063	769
pigs (1000s)	6 147	9 348	9 282
Mechanisation			
number of horses	171	42	24
number of tractors	111 300	176 300	168 000
Number of farms	196 076	107 500	86 000
% of population in agriculture	16	6.1	5.1
average size of farm (hectares)	15.8	26.7	32.4

A typical Danish farm on the island of Fünen

Figure 7.21 shows a view of a farm on Fünen and Figure 7.19 a layout of a typical farm on the island. Despite its emphasis on dairy produce, most of Denmark is arable land (Figure 7.22). The land is divided into large fields, most of which are bordered by wire fences not hedges. Wheat, barley, oats and rye, together with the tops of the sugar beet, are all grown as fodder for the animals, for Danish domestic consumption, or use in industry (e.g. milling, brewing). Only a small proportion of the farm is actually under grass mainly because the grass is not of good enough quality. It is still fairly common to see the Danish red cow tethered, or at least limited to small areas of grazing ground. These animals are usually kept indoors from late September to late April and are fed on fodder crops grown on the farm. Most farms are not large enough to store the large quantities of winter fodder needed. When cereals are harvested they are sent to the co-operatives for storage until they are needed. Root crops and clover are also grown for fodder, although sugar is also obtained from the beet.

Figure 7.19 also shows the farm buildings. Even modern farms are still built around the traditional courtyard. Notice the dwelling house on one side of the yard facing the cowsheds. The third side is usually occupied by accommodation for pigs and poultry and facilities to store some grain.

Farming in the EC – The Mezzogiorno

The Mezzogiorno, which means the *Land of the midday sun*, lies south of Rome and includes the two islands of Sicily and Sardinia (Figure 7.23). It contains the poorest parts of the EC with Basilicata described as 'the most disadvantaged of the 160 regions in the EC' (EC Report). Figure 7.24 gives some of the causes of poverty and high unemployment, and the reasons why so many people have emigrated. To this list can be added the lack of mineral and energy resources, industry, commerce, services and skilled labour. The resultant low standard of living meant that between 1950 and 1975 4.5 million people emigrated to the north of Italy, to the USA and as 'guestworkers' to Germany and Switzerland (page 48).

The following two accounts describe what life was like in Basilicata. The first describes the village of Aliano in the late 1930s, the second, farming in the 1960s.

1 *"The village itself was merely a group of scattered white houses at the summit of the hill* [Figure 7.25].

"The houses were nearly all of one room, with no windows, drawing their light from the door. The one room served as kitchen, bedroom, and usually as quarters for the barnyard animals. On one side was the stove; sticks brought in every day from the fields served as fuel. The walls and ceiling were blackened with smoke. The room was almost entirely filled with an enormous bed; in it slept the whole family, father, mother and children. The smaller children slept in reed cradles hung from the ceiling above the bed, while under the bed slept the animals.

"The second aspect of the trouble is economic, the dilemma of poverty. The land has been gradually impoverished; the forests have been cut down, the rivers have been reduced to mountain streams that often run dry, and livestock has become scarce. Instead of cultivating trees and pasture lands there has been an unfortunate attempt to raise wheat in soil that does not favour it. There is no capital, no industry, no savings, no schools; emigration is no longer possible, taxes are unduly heavy, and malaria is everywhere. All this is in a large part due to the ill-advised intentions and efforts of the State, a State in which the peasants cannot feel they have a share, and which has brought them only poverty and deserts." (Carlo Levi, *Christ stopped at Eboli*)

2 *"To go to the fields is almost a reflex, conditioned by the absolute lack of any other work. You go, even when you might not have to. The donkey needs fodder: you cut it by hand, sometimes just along the verges, and shove it into the sacks that hang from the saddle. While you're about it, you pull up wild greens for a salad – a little sorrel, dandelions, whatever there is. You weed your patch of wheat, you loosen the dirt around the beans, tie up a vine. You look over to see how your neighbour's crops are coming. Not really that you hoped yesterday's hailstorm had beaten them down, but there would be some justice if ... You collect a few twigs for kindling. And finally at some invisible cue of light not yet changed but about to change, the long walk back to town. Five miles, ten – a long way with nothing to think about except how to get a bit more land, a job – how to feed your children. Your children. Will they live like this?"* (Ann Cornelisen, *Women of the Shadows*)

Region		Unemployment 1991	Income per head (100 = average) 1980	1990	Net migration (% per year) 1980	1990
1	North-west	6.7	131	114	+0·8	+1·4
2	Lombardy	3·5	136	131	+0·7	+2·3
3	North-east	4·2	101	112	−0·2	+1·7
4	Emilia-Romagna	4·3	116	123	+0·1	+4·1
5	Centre	7·7	101	103	−0·1	+2·7
6	Lazio	10·4	111	111	+0·6	+1·9
7	Campania	21·0	68	63	−1·0	−0·6
8	Abruzzi	10·9	68	82	−1·3	+2·1
9	South	17·9	62	63	−1·8	−3·7
10	Sicily	22·1	68	65	−1·4	−3·6
11	Sardinia	18·7	78	71	−1·1	−0·8

Milan, Turin, Venice, Genoa, Rome, Naples, Basilicata

'The North'
60% of population
80% of gross national product

'The Mezzogiorno'
40% of population
20% of gross national product

0 200 km

Figure 7.23
Population and wealth distribution in Italy

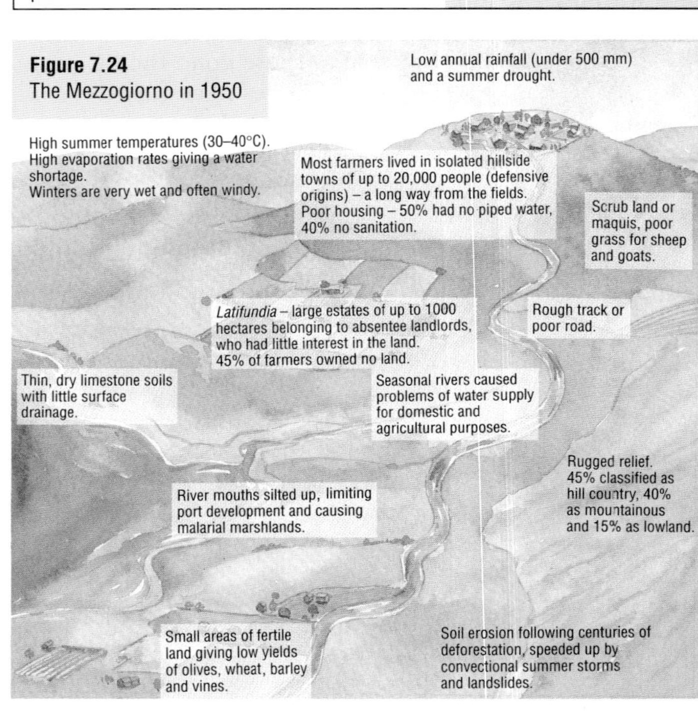

Low annual rainfall (under 500 mm) and a summer drought.
High summer temperatures (30–40°C). High evaporation rates giving a water shortage. Winters are very wet and often windy.
Most farmers lived in isolated hillside towns of up to 20,000 people (defensive origins) – a long way from the fields. Poor housing – 50% had no piped water, 40% no sanitation.
Scrub land or maquis, poor grass for sheep and goats.
Latifundia – large estates of up to 1000 hectares belonging to absentee landlords, who had little interest in the land. 45% of farmers owned no land.
Rough track or poor road.
Thin, dry limestone soils with little surface drainage.
Seasonal rivers caused problems of water supply for domestic and agricultural purposes.
Rugged relief. 45% classified as hill country, 40% as mountainous and 15% as lowland.
River mouths silted up, limiting port development and causing malarial marshlands.
Small areas of fertile land giving low yields of olives, wheat, barley and vines.
Soil erosion following centuries of deforestation, speeded up by convectional summer storms and landslides.

Figure 7.24
The Mezzogiorno in 1950

Figure 7.25
Rivello, a hillside town in Basilicata

Farming in the Mezzogiorno today

Although half the jobs in farming have been lost in the last 30 years, agriculture still employs 25 per cent of the working population. The government, through a scheme called *Cassa per Il Mezzogiorno*, tried to improve agriculture as well as services and industry in the region. Although several coastal areas benefited from a few large-scale developments, the many mountainous areas of the Mezzogiorno saw little improvement. In 1984 the Comunità Montana scheme was introduced with the emphasis on smaller, more practical developments.

Upland subsistence farms

These have hardly changed (Figure 7.26). Wheat is the main crop but yields are low largely due to the soils which are stony, shallow, dry and easily washed away. Olives and vines are still important as they can tolerate the high temperatures, the summer drought and the thin soils. These two crops need a lot of cheap hand labour, especially at harvest time. Much of the higher, poorer areas are left as grazing land for sheep and goats. Most farmers can, through hard work, feed their own families but there is rarely any surplus for sale.

Lowland commercial farms

These are found either where the large estates have been broken up into smaller units or where the malarial marshes have been drained (Figure 7.26). New motorways have been opened and large dams have been built across several rivers. The water stored in the resultant reservoirs is used for both domestic purposes and irrigation. Pipes carry water to coastal farms where large sprinkler systems enable soft fruit (peaches and pears) and citrus fruit (oranges and lemons) to grow commercially. Citrus fruits in particular flourish in the hot summers (their thick skins limit moisture loss), mild winters, alluvial river delta soils and good drainage. Flowers, tomatoes and vines are also grown (Figure 7.27).

Problems

Although wealthier than in the 1950s, most of the Mezzogiorno remains poor by EC standards.

- Farming tends to be done by the older generation and attracts few young people.
- Increased mechanisation has led to increased unemployment (Figure 7.23). There are few alternative jobs and an increasing number of abandoned fields and farms.
- Although many former emigrants have returned home wealthy, the area is receiving numerous immigrants from poorer countries in Africa and the Middle East.
- The ground is unstable with soil erosion, landslides and earthquakes (parts of Aliano and other settlements remain uninhabited after the 1980 'quake).
- This is a peripheral area in the EC, a long way from the main markets, and has received little real help from the CAP (page 164).

Figure 7.26
The Mezzogiorno in the early 1990s

Hill villages, e.g. Aliano. Improved sanitation and piped water to village.
New school
Sheep and goats on poor pasture.
Wheat olives and vines near to village.
Upland subsistence farms.
Improved road to village.
Large estates broken up into individual farms of 5 hectares in irrigated areas, and 25 hectares on more hilly land.
Dam with reservoir giving some HEP and water for irrigation.
Lowland commercial farms.
New motorway 'Autostrada'.
Marshes drained
Afforestation to reduce further soil erosion
More intensive farming with higher yields: citrus fruits, pears, peaches, grapes, tomatoes. 125,000 new farms. Farmers salaries increased by 25%, production by 3%.

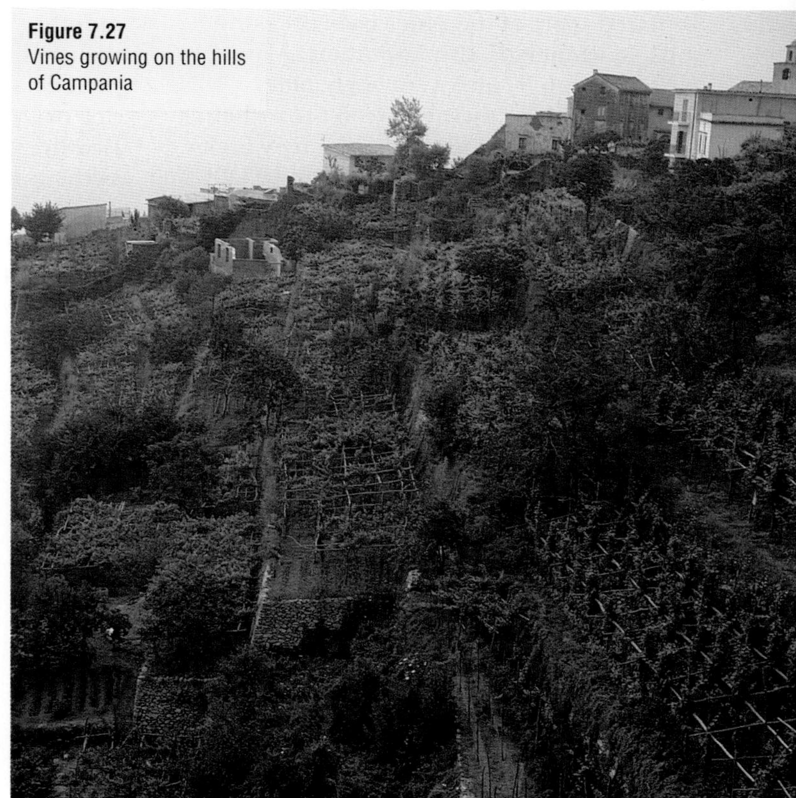

Figure 7.27
Vines growing on the hills of Campania

Farming in Japan

Only 15 per cent of Japan is classed as flat land – the remainder is highland with very steep sides, which hinders economic development. With so little flat land there is great competition for space for housing, industry, communications and farming. Even away from the large cities, such areas as the Obitsu Valley (Figure 7.28) are half urban and half rural. The small, rectangular fields are surrounded by large villages. The average Japanese farm is 1.1 hectares, the equivalent of two football pitches. It has to be carefully looked after and intensively used by the farmer and his family. Just as Japan has become a major industrial country, so too has farming changed rapidly.

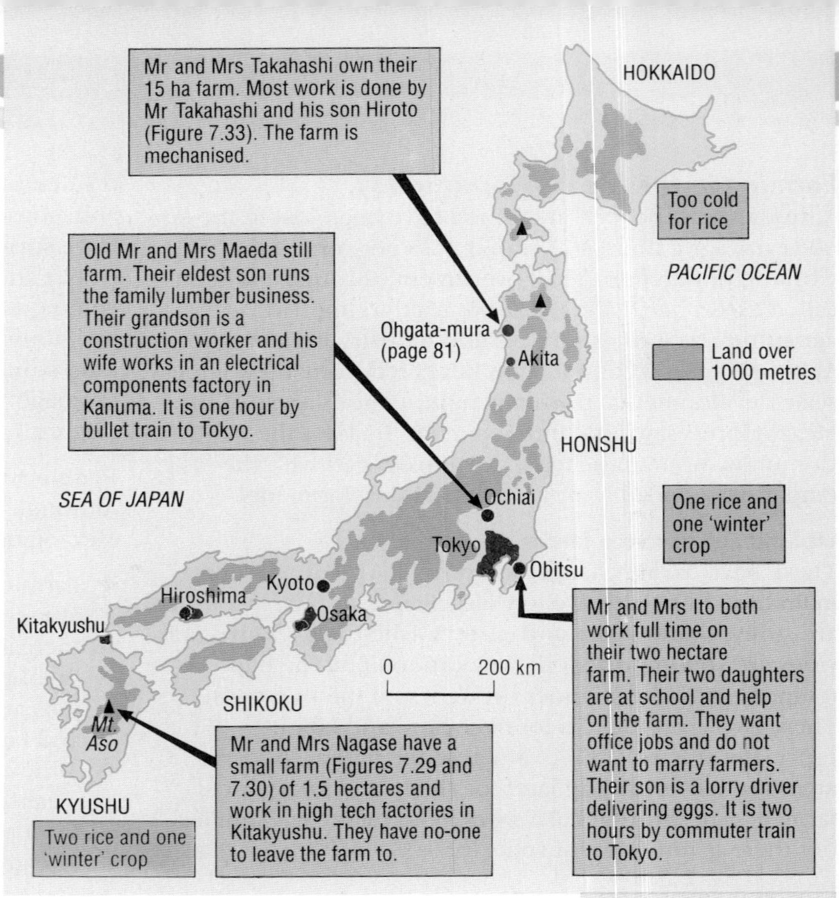

Southern Japan

Rice gives very high yields wherever the land is flat enough for it to be grown. Southern Japan has hot and very wet summers and mild winters. The soils are rich either from volcanic deposits or alluvium brought down from the mountains by fast flowing rivers. No land is wasted, and the lower hillsides are terraced (Figure 7.29). Small machines are used to plough, plant and harvest the crop (Figures 7.30 and 7.31) and these have now replaced most of the older back-breaking jobs. Machinery is also important as most farms are run by an increasingly older workforce, since their children prefer better paid, less demanding jobs in the new high-tech factories in nearby cities (Figure 7.28). Japanese farmers and their wives may work ten hours a day in their fields in order to get two, and in the extreme south, three crops a year from their tiny farms. Vegetables and young rice plants are grown under vinyl sheets or in vinyl greenhouses. The climate is warm enough for crops such as barley, wheat and soya beans to be grown in the winter months. The increase in mechanisation and the use of fertiliser (Japan uses more fertiliser per hectare than any other country) led to rice overproduction and a 'rice mountain'. However, this surplus has declined recently as the number of farms and farmers have decreased because the Japanese have turned more to western type foods. In 1993, Japan had to import rice for the first time.

Mr and Mrs Takahashi own their 15 ha farm. Most work is done by Mr Takahashi and his son Hiroto (Figure 7.33). The farm is mechanised.

Old Mr and Mrs Maeda still farm. Their eldest son runs the family lumber business. Their grandson is a construction worker and his wife works in an electrical components factory in Kanuma. It is one hour by bullet train to Tokyo.

Mr and Mrs Nagase have a small farm (Figures 7.29 and 7.30) of 1.5 hectares and work in high tech factories in Kitakyushu. They have no-one to leave the farm to.

Mr and Mrs Ito both work full time on their two hectare farm. Their two daughters are at school and help on the farm. They want office jobs and do not want to marry farmers. Their son is a lorry driver delivering eggs. It is two hours by commuter train to Tokyo.

HOKKAIDO

Too cold for rice

PACIFIC OCEAN

Land over 1000 metres

Ohgata-mura (page 81)

Akita

HONSHU

SEA OF JAPAN

Ochiai

Tokyo

Obitsu

One rice and one 'winter' crop

Hiroshima

Kyoto

Osaka

Kitakyushu

0 200 km

SHIKOKU

Mt. Aso

KYUSHU

Two rice and one 'winter' crop

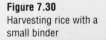

Figure 7.28
Location of four farming families in Japan

Figure 7.29
Rice on terraces ready for harvesting

Figure 7.30
Harvesting rice with a small binder

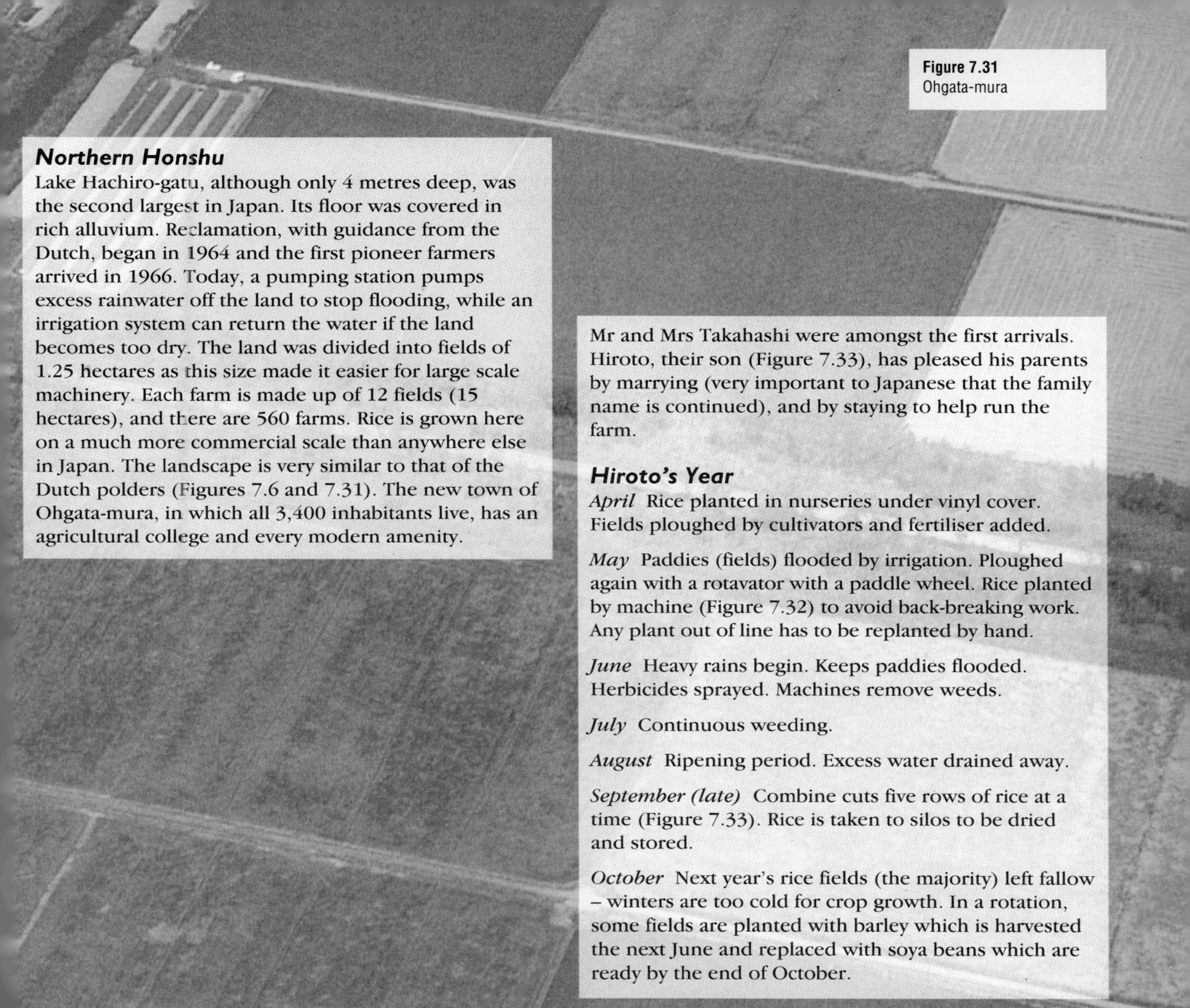

Figure 7.31
Ohgata-mura

Northern Honshu

Lake Hachiro-gatu, although only 4 metres deep, was the second largest in Japan. Its floor was covered in rich alluvium. Reclamation, with guidance from the Dutch, began in 1964 and the first pioneer farmers arrived in 1966. Today, a pumping station pumps excess rainwater off the land to stop flooding, while an irrigation system can return the water if the land becomes too dry. The land was divided into fields of 1.25 hectares as this size made it easier for large scale machinery. Each farm is made up of 12 fields (15 hectares), and there are 560 farms. Rice is grown here on a much more commercial scale than anywhere else in Japan. The landscape is very similar to that of the Dutch polders (Figures 7.6 and 7.31). The new town of Ohgata-mura, in which all 3,400 inhabitants live, has an agricultural college and every modern amenity.

Mr and Mrs Takahashi were amongst the first arrivals. Hiroto, their son (Figure 7.33), has pleased his parents by marrying (very important to Japanese that the family name is continued), and by staying to help run the farm.

Hiroto's Year

April Rice planted in nurseries under vinyl cover. Fields ploughed by cultivators and fertiliser added.

May Paddies (fields) flooded by irrigation. Ploughed again with a rotavator with a paddle wheel. Rice planted by machine (Figure 7.32) to avoid back-breaking work. Any plant out of line has to be replanted by hand.

June Heavy rains begin. Keeps paddies flooded. Herbicides sprayed. Machines remove weeds.

July Continuous weeding.

August Ripening period. Excess water drained away.

September (late) Combine cuts five rows of rice at a time (Figure 7.33). Rice is taken to silos to be dried and stored.

October Next year's rice fields (the majority) left fallow – winters are too cold for crop growth. In a rotation, some fields are planted with barley which is harvested the next June and replaced with soya beans which are ready by the end of October.

Figure 7.32
Planting rice

Figure 7.33
Harvesting rice with a combine, Hiroto can work alone.

Farming in Brazil

Shifting cultivation

Shifting cultivation is a form of subsistence farming, and is a traditional form of agriculture found in many areas of the tropical rainforests. It tends now to be found in only the most inaccessible and least 'exploited' areas. The Amerindians use stone axes and machetes to fell about one hectare of forest, and any undergrowth has to be cleared immediately to prevent it growing rapidly in the hot, wet climate. After a time the felled trees, having been given time to dry, are burned. This burning helps to provide nutrients for the soil as the ash is spread over the ground as a fertiliser. This is also known as 'slash and burn'.

Within the clearings is built the tribal home or *maloca* (Figure 7.34). This usually consists of tree trunks lashed together with lianas, and thatched with leaves. Nearer the rivers the houses are built on stilts (Figure 7.36) as the water level can rise by 15 metres after the rainy season.

The clearings, or gardens, are called *chagras*. Here the women grow virtually all of the tribe's carbohydrate needs. The main crop is manioc, the 'bread of the tropics', which is crushed to produce a flour called *cassava* (Figure 7.35). It can also provide sugar and a local beer. Other crops are yams (though these need a richer soil), beans and pumpkins. The men have to supplement this diet by hunting, mainly for tapirs and monkeys, fishing and collecting fruit. The blow pipe and bow and arrow are still used.

Unfortunately the balance between plants and soil is very delicate. Once the canopy of trees has been removed, the heavy rains associated with afternoon storms can hit the bare soil. This not only causes soil erosion, but it leaches any minerals in the soil downwards. As the source of humus, the trees, has been removed and as there is a lack of fertiliser and animal manure, the soil rapidly loses its fertility (Figure 15.20). Within four or five years yields decline, and the tribe will 'shift' to another part of the forest to begin the cycle all over again.

Shifting cultivation needs a high labour input, and large areas of land to provide enough food for a few people. Although it is a wasteful method of farming, it causes less harm to the environment than permanent agriculture would.

Recently the Amerindians of the Amazon rainforest have been forced to move further into the forest or to live on reservations. Large numbers have died, mainly because they lack immunity to 'western' diseases, and those who survive have the difficult choice of either trying to live in increasingly difficult surroundings, or joining the other homeless and jobless in favelas in the larger urban areas (page 35).

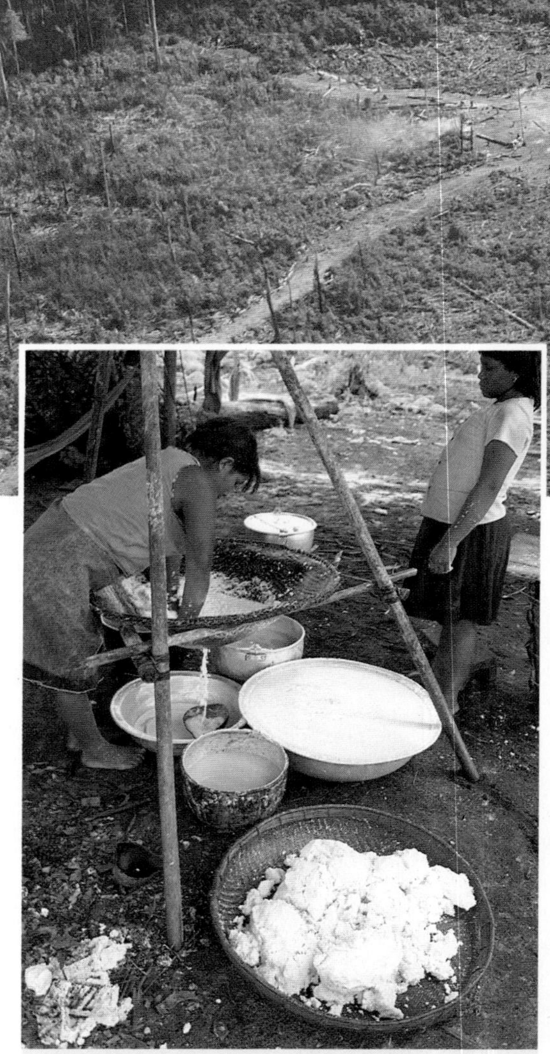

Figure 7.35
Cassava flour being prepared from manioc

Figure 7.36
A maloca, or Indian house, built from materials of the tropical rainforests (near Manaus, Brazil)

Figure 7.34
A clearing in the Amazon forest

Figure 7.37
Ripening coffee cherries

Plantations

Plantations were developed in tropical parts of the world in the eighteenth and nineteenth centuries mainly by European and North American merchants. The natural forest was cleared and a single crop (usually a bush or tree) was planted in rows (Figure 7.38). This so-called 'cash-crop' was grown for export, and was not used or consumed locally. Plantations needed a high capital investment to clear, drain and irrigate the land, to build estate roads, schools and hospitals, and to bridge the several years before the first crop could be harvested. Much manual labour was also needed. The managers were usually European while labourers were either recruited locally or brought in from other countries. Because they were willing to accept lower wages, this workforce secured a greater profit for the recruiting companies. The almost continuous growing season meant that the crop could be harvested virtually throughout the year. Today most plantations are still owned by 'multinational' companies (page 122), with their headquarters in a more economically developed country.

Coffee plantations (fazendas)

Ideal conditions include:

- Gently rolling ground or valley sides at altitudes up to 1,700 metres (Figure 7.39). Valleys which may become waterlogged or act as frost hollows are unfavourable (frost is coffee's worst enemy).
- A deep red soil called *terra rossa*.

The major producing states are Parana, São Paulo and Minas Gerais (Figure 7.39). The tree begins to yield after three years, reaches a maximum between 10 and 15 years and dies after 40. When harvested, the red *cherries* (Figure 7.37), as the ripe coffee is called, are stripped from the branches and cut into halves to expose two 'green beans' which are left in the sun on huge drying yards. They are raked frequently, and large tarpaulins are kept nearby for protection against any rain.

Changes in coffee production

European (mainly Italian) immigrants in the 1870s developed new coffee fazendas. This led to an increase in coffee production. By 1906 Brazil produced 1.2 million tonnes of coffee when world demand was only 0.7 million, and coffee accounted for 70 per cent of Brazil's exports – two major problems! Meanwhile soils on the early plantations had become exhausted and so new fazendas were developed westward in drier but less frosty areas. More immigrants in the 1960s again led to overproduction, but output was soon drastically cut by:

- the government offering incentives for other crops to be grown,
- the spread of disease in coffee trees, and
- several killing frosts.

While Brazil had produced 43 million bags of coffee and 49 per cent of the world's total in 1960, she only produced 20 million bags and 24 per cent of the world's total in 1990.

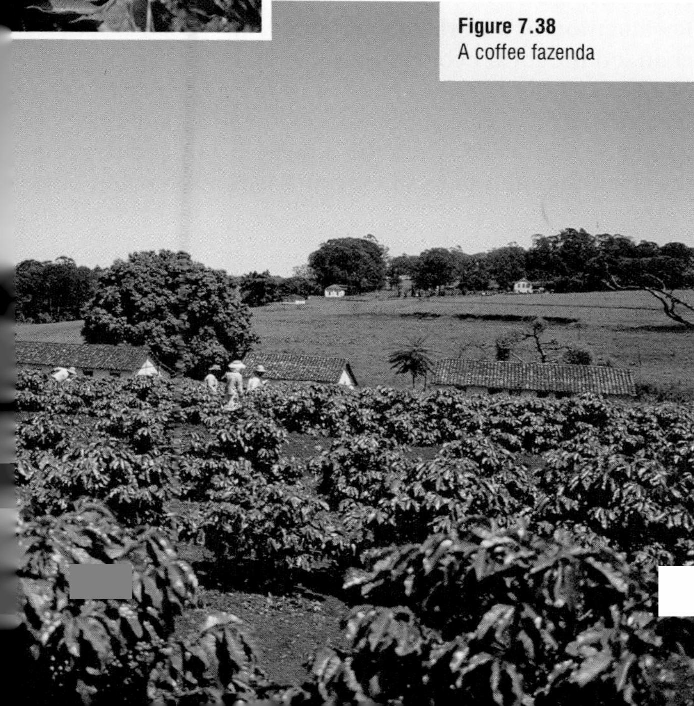

Figure 7.38
A coffee fazenda

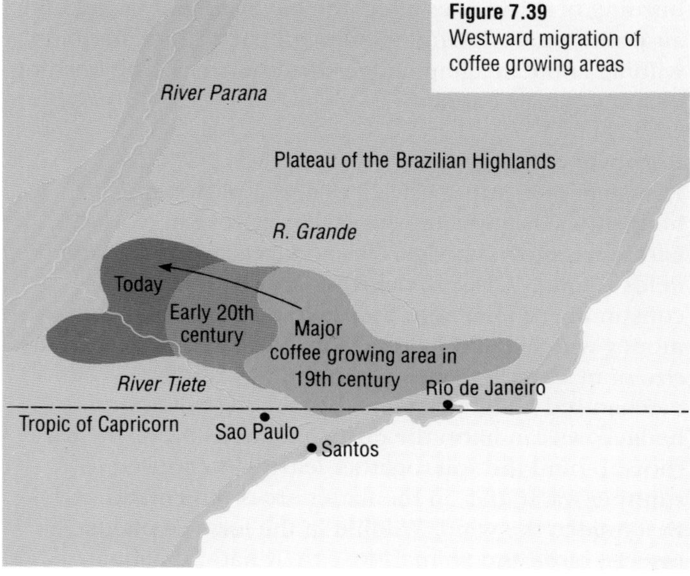

Figure 7.39
Westward migration of coffee growing areas

Farming and the environment

Use of chemicals

a **Pesticide** is defined as all chemicals applied to crops to control pests, disease and weeds (Figure 7.40). The United Nations claimed in the 1960s that 30 to 35 per cent of the world's crops were lost due to pests, disease and weeds. It is claimed that without pesticides yields of cereal crops would be reduced by 25 per cent after one year and 45 per cent after three years.

b **Fertiliser** is a mineral compound containing one or more of the main six elements needed for plant growth. The average soil does not contain sufficient of the essential nutrients (especially nitrogen, phosphorous and potassium) to provide either a healthy crop or an economic yield. There is increasing concern when nitrate is washed (leached) through the soil either into:

i) *Rivers* where, being a fertiliser, it causes rapid growth of algae and other plants which use up oxygen leaving insufficient for fish life;

ii) *Underground water supplies* needed for domestic use.

In 1985 a directive from the EC called for a reduction in the acceptable nitrate levels in water.

Removal of vegetation

Removal of vegetation cover can increase the erosion (loss) of soil by running water and the wind (page 232).

Burning straw

Ploughing straw back into the soil clogs up machinery, increases the cost of labour and can limit root growth of new plants. By burning straw, fungal spores and weed seeds are destroyed to give a cleaner soil. However the burning of straw does affect the environment by creating air pollution, reducing visibility for road users, harming wildlife and damaging hedgerows and trees. The burning of straw is now banned.

Removal of hedgerows

Between 1945 and 1975, 25 per cent of British hedgerows disappeared (over 45 per cent in Norfolk). Farmers removed hedgerows and trees to create larger fields (Figure 7.41). Hedgerows are costly and time-consuming to maintain; they take up both space and money which could be used for crops, and they limit the size of machinery. Trees get in the way of new mechanised hedgetrimmers. Yet the destruction of hedgerows can harm the environment as there are fewer roots to bind the soil together leaving it exposed to running water and, in the flatter areas of Fenland and East Anglia, the wind. Wildlife in the form of plants, insects, birds and animals lose their natural habitat.

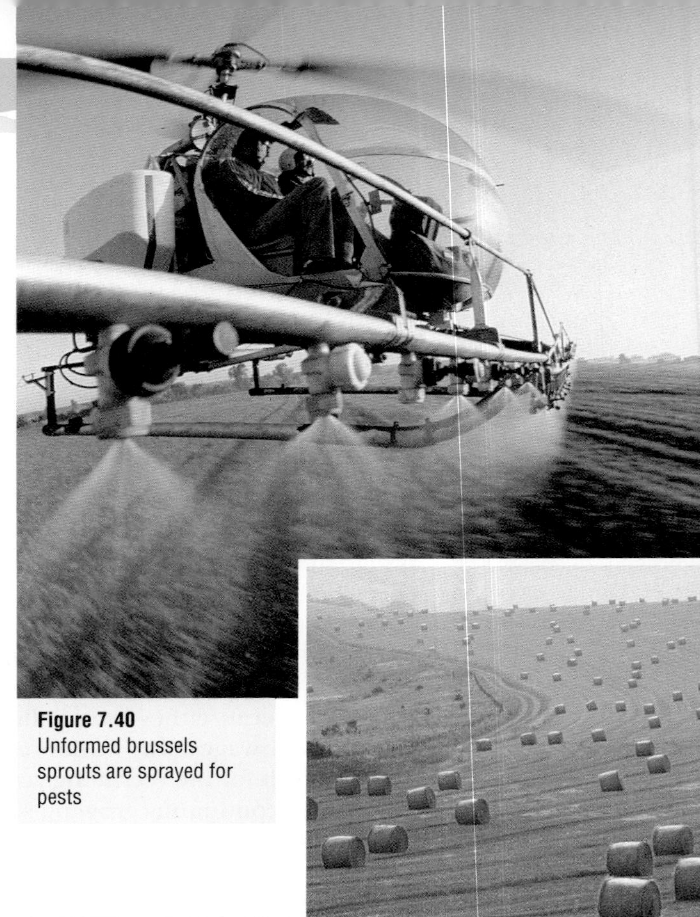

Figure 7.40
Unformed brussels sprouts are sprayed for pests

Figure 7.41
The less acceptable face of modern farming. The removal of hedges and trees during the 1950s and 1960s has left prairie-like scenes such as this one

Many people also feel that the landscape becomes less attractive. Figure 7.42 shows the advantage of well maintained hedgerows.

Reclamation

Reclamation of moorlands and draining wetlands has changed the local ecology (page 232).

Irrigation

Irrigation is needed when the climate is hot and dry but the resultant high rates of evapotranspiration bring salts to the surface.

Trees provide shade and a habitat for wildlife
Bushes are cut and laid almost horizontally. Initially unsightly, these soon produce a thick cover
Hedges reduce wind speed and bind soil together, reducing erosion
Wider base adds to attraction and also provides an environment for wildlife

Figure 7.42
A recent reversal of policy has led to more trimmed hedges which encourage wildlife to flourish

Food supply

"The Food and Agriculture Organisation (FAO) claimed that 1985 saw a satisfactory global cereal harvest. Food production grew faster than the increase in population in all areas, other than in parts of Africa [Figure 7.43]. *In most parts of the world nutritional levels improved, although certain areas still remained critically low. In 1985, 45 nations south of the Sahara had record harvests, and the food emergency crisis was over in 16 of the worst affected 21 countries – although several areas will need food relief for several years.*

"Even so ...

Each year 40 million people, almost half of whom are children, die from hunger and hunger-related diseases. An energy intake of less than 1,600 calories per day is likely to cause severe malnutrition [Figure 7.44]. *Even if malnutrition does not kill, it reduces the capacity to work and increases susceptibility to disease. Among children, a lack of protein can cause a slow mental and physical development. In 1975 there were 435 million people suffering from malnutrition, in 1985 almost 500 million and by 2000 an estimated 600 million".*

(David Waugh, *The World*, 1986)

Recent trends

What has happened since 1986 when the FAO announced that 'there is sufficient food grown in the world to feed everyone – the problem is its uneven distribution and its increasing cost to buy and transport'?

Between 1986 and 1988 the world's food reserves fell from 459 million tonnes (101 days supply) to 240 million tonnes (54 days). This trend has continued due to:

- The EC lowering farm subsidies to reduce its 'mountains and lakes' surpluses (page 73) and to increase land taken out of production.
- Global warming (page 228) which is blamed for increasing drought in the
  - i) marginal rainfall areas, e.g. sub-Saharan Africa
  - ii) major cereal growing areas, e.g. USA and the CIS.
- Increasing world political instability, e.g. several African countries, the breakup of the former USSR.
- The world recession and associated reduction in international trade.

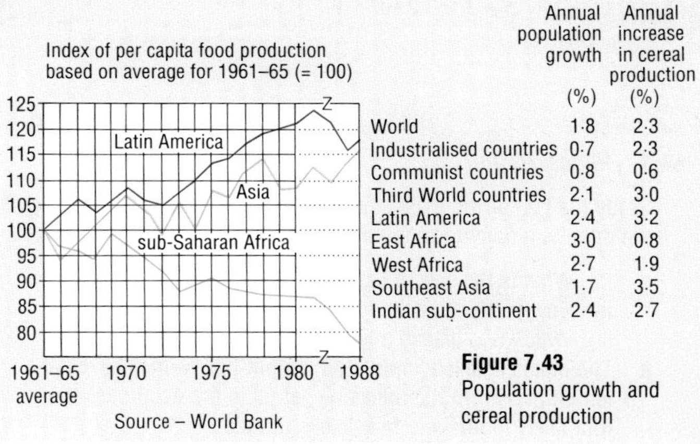

	Annual population growth (%)	Annual increase in cereal production (%)
World	1·8	2·3
Industrialised countries	0·7	2·3
Communist countries	0·8	0·6
Third World countries	2·1	3·0
Latin America	2·4	3·2
East Africa	3·0	0·8
West Africa	2·7	1·9
Southeast Asia	1·7	3·5
Indian sub-continent	2·4	2·7

Figure 7.43
Population growth and cereal production

Why do many parts of Africa suffer from malnutrition?

- The high birth rate and falling death rate means there are many more people to feed.
- The people do not have the money to buy high yielding seeds, fertiliser, pesticides, tools and machinery, nor to implement irrigation schemes.
- The soil has been overused in the past and few nutrients remain. Elsewhere, soil erosion has led to desertification (page 234).
- When food is scarce, these poorer countries cannot buy the surplus due to high prices.
- Many areas suffer from drought. The Sahel (the countries bordering the southern fringes of the Sahara) receives less than 500 mm of rain a year. Amounts are unreliable and vary from year to year (page 217).
- Pests such as the locust and tse-tse fly destroy crops, and storage is inadequate. Much of the crop may be eaten by rats or affected by fungus.
- Governments encourage foreign firms to take over the food-producing land by giving them tax concessions. Multinationals, as in colonial times, grow cash crops for export rather than crops for local consumption.
- There is often a lack of protein in the diet.
- Civil war in several countries affects crop production.

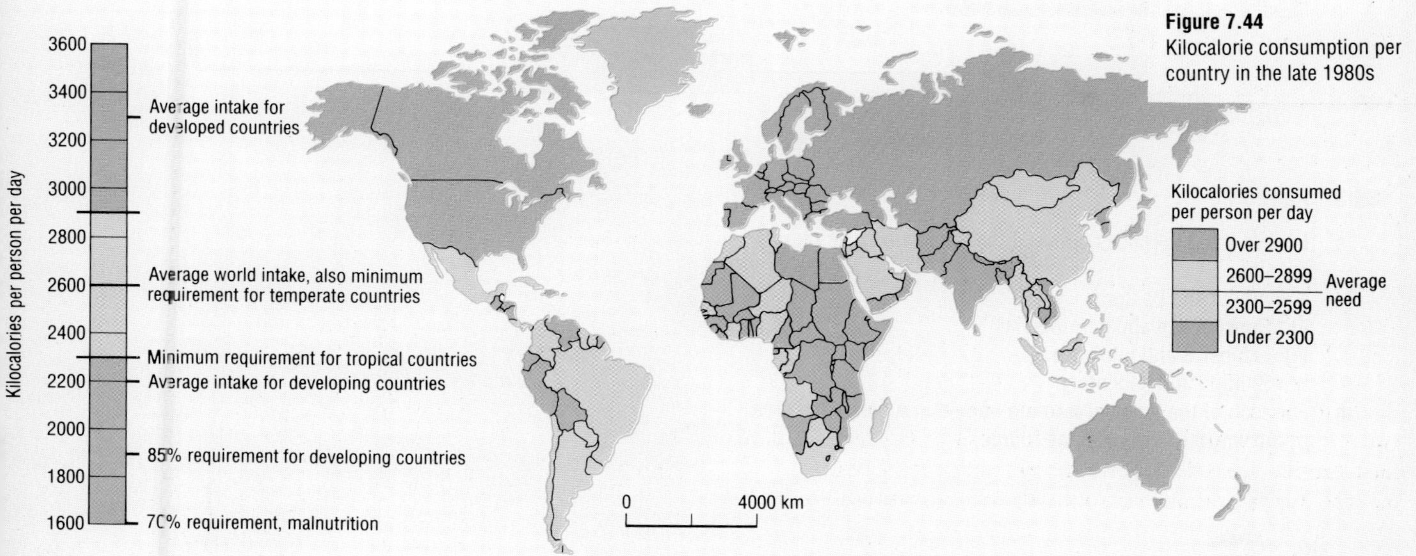

Figure 7.44
Kilocalorie consumption per country in the late 1980s

1 *(Pages 70 and 71)*

Study the two farming systems. One is a subsistence farm in India, the other is a dairy farm in south-west England.

a i) What is the size of Farm A? *(1)*
ii) How many animals are kept on Farm A? *(1)*
iii) Which two places might use the output from Farm A? *(2)*

b The boxes labelled 'input' and 'output' for Farm A have been left empty. From the following list fill in the two boxes to show four likely inputs and four likely outputs: *(8)*
barley, fertiliser, hay, labour, machinery, fattened pigs, manure, milk.

c i) What is meant by the term *subsistence farming*? *(1)*
ii) Explain the differences between the two farms under the following headings:
Land, Labour, Machinery, Animals, Crops. *(5)*

Farm A

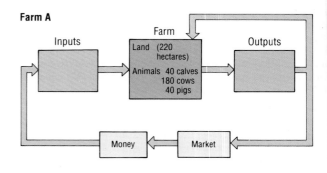

Inputs
Farm
Land (220 hectares)
Animals 40 calves
180 cows
40 pigs
Outputs
Money
Market

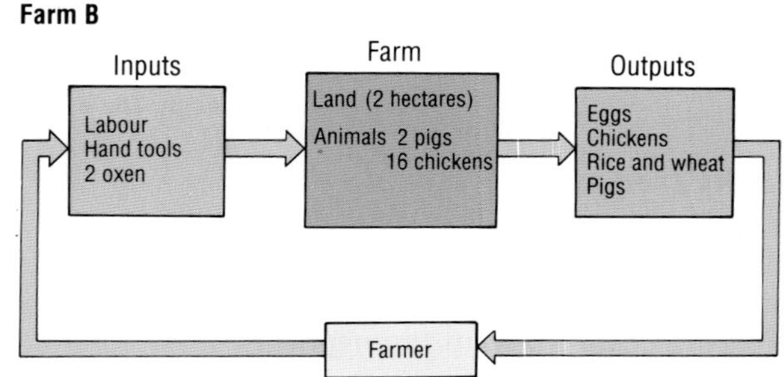

2 *(Page 70)*

The diagram below shows the farming system for a cereal farm in eastern England.

a Make a copy of the systems diagram.

b Complete the diagram by adding the following words or terms in the correct places. *(14)*
Wheat, ploughing and sowing, flat land, fertiliser and seed, deep soil, crop spraying, labour, machinery, market, harvesting, money (profit), barley, sunny summers, re-investment.

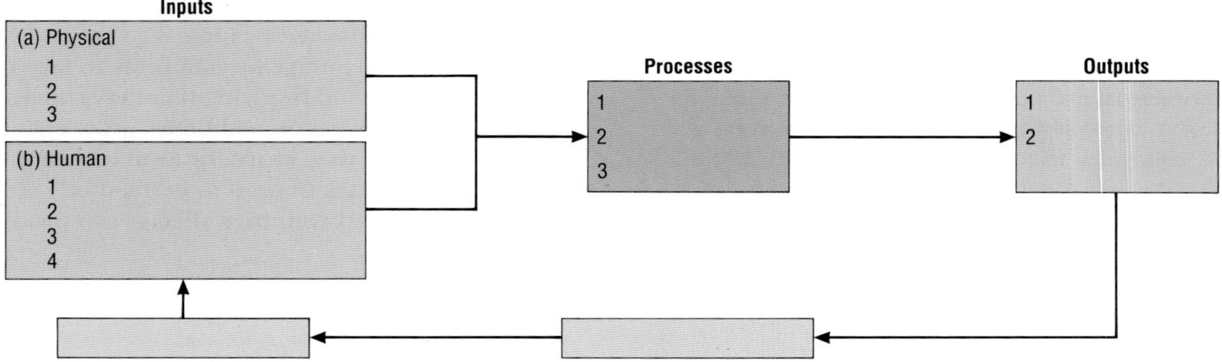

3 *(Page 71)*

a Explain the differences between the following types of farming: *(8)*
i) Arable and pastoral
ii) Subsistence and commercial
iii) Extensive and intensive
iv) Shifting and sedentary

b For each of the types of farming named in **a** name one area of the world where it can be found. *(8)*

4 *(Page 73)*

The diagram below shows surplus food in the European Community (EC).

Europe's food mountains

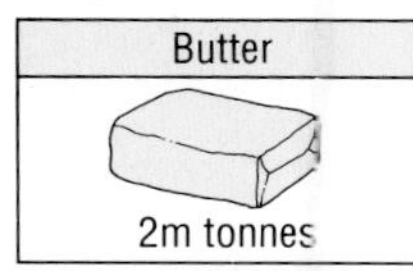

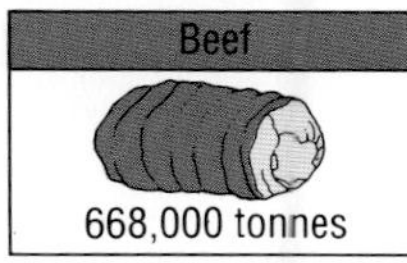

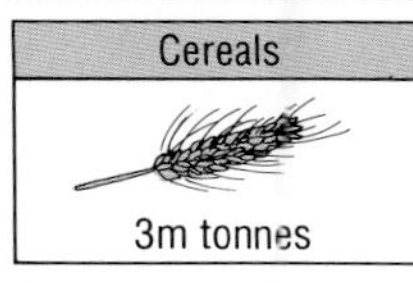

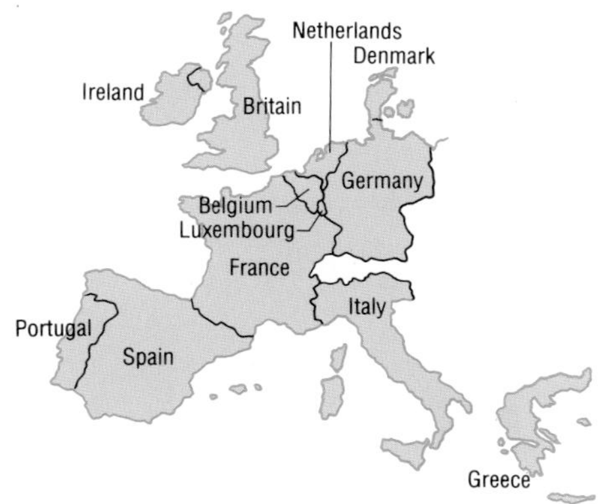

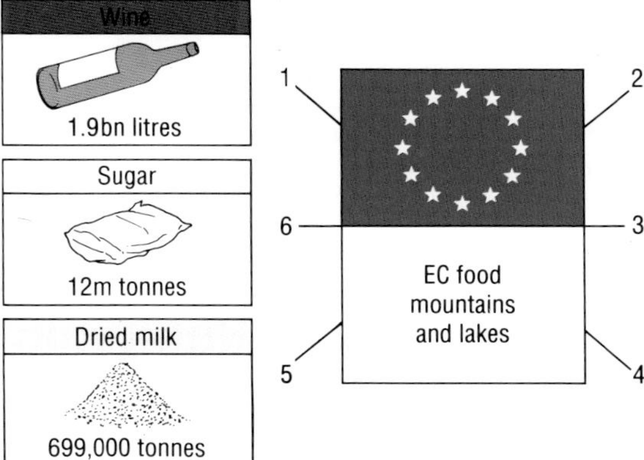

- **a** Draw a star diagram to show surplus food in the EC. *(3)*
- **b** i) What does the term 'food mountain' mean? *(1)*
  ii) Name two surpluses that may be in 'food lakes'. *(2)*
- **c** Write out the sentences below. Unscramble the words in the boxes to fill in the blank spaces. *(6)*

  Food mountains occur mainly:
  - ◆ in the ________ developed areas of the world. EROM
  - ◆ in places like ________ and North America. PEEROU
  - ◆ in some poorer countries like ________ and India. TAANGREIN

  Food mountains grow because:
  - ◆ the food is too ________ PEEEVNISX
  - ◆ people are too ________ to buy it ROPO
  - ◆ it is too difficult to ________ to those in need TTRROPSNA

5 *(Pages 74 to 79)*

Choose **one** of the following – the Netherlands, Denmark or the Mezzogiorno. Then:

- **a** Describe its main type of farming. *(3)*
- **b** Explain how the development of this type of farming has been affected by:
  i) physical ii) economic iii) technological factors. *(6)*
- **c** How has farming been affected by the EC's Common Agricultural Policy (CAP)? *(2)*
- **d** What changes do you think may take place in farming in your chosen area in the next few years? *(2)*

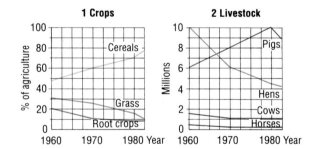

6 *(Pages 76 to 77)*

The graphs give information about recent trends in Danish agriculture.

1 Crops

% of agriculture (0–100); 1960, 1970, 1980 Year; Cereals, Grass, Root crops

2 Livestock

Millions (0–10); 1960, 1970, 1980 Year; Pigs, Hens, Cows, Horses

3 Workers and machinery

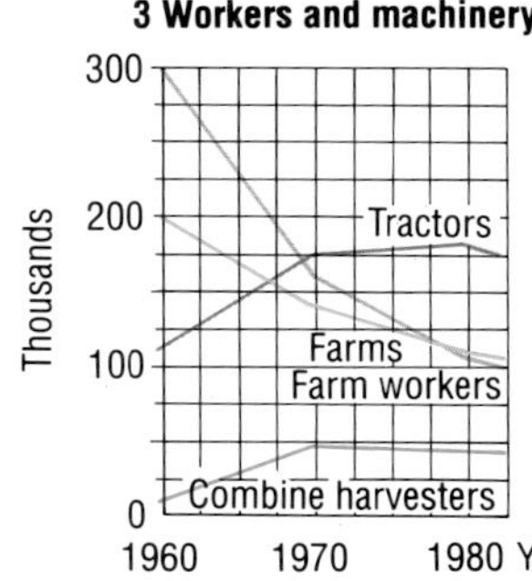

- **a** i) What type of crop covers the largest area? *(1)*
  ii) What percentage of agricultural land did this crop cover in 1980? *(1)*
- **b** i) Between 1960 and 1982 the number of tractors increased and the number of farmworkers decreased. Suggest why this has happened. *(2)*
  ii) Give reasons why the total number of farms decreased between 1960 and 1982 (Hint: think about modern farming methods and how farming in Denmark is now organised). *(2)*
- **c** Most Danish farmers have now joined co-operatives.
  i) What is a co-operative? *(1)*
  ii) Describe **three** ways by which an individual farmer can benefit by being part of a co-operative *(2)*

7 *(Pages 80 and 81)*

The photo opposite was taken at harvest time from a train as it passed through the southern Japanese island of Kyushu.

a i) Describe the size and shape of the fields. *(2)*
ii) What is growing in them? *(1)*
iii) How can you tell that the photo was taken at harvest time? *(2)*

b i) Describe the buildings in the photo. *(2)*
ii) For what do you think they are used? *(2)*

c Name two further uses of the land other than for farming *(2)*

d What percentage of Japan is flat enough for farming and settlement? *(1)*

e Ohgata-mura is towards the north of Japan. Describe the differences between Ohgata-mura and Kyushu using the following headings: *(6)*
i) Relief of the land
ii) Farm size
iii) Field size
iv) Machinery used
v) Summer crops
vi) Winter crops

f Describe the farmer's year in Ohgata-mura. *(3)*

8 *(Page 82)*

Several tribes in Amazonia still practise shifting cultivation.

a Copy and complete the flow chart by putting the correct letter in the appropriate box. *(7)*
A Harvest
B Weed
C Spread ash as fertiliser
D Move to a new area
E Sow crops including manioc
F Burn remaining vegetation
G Select a suitable area
H Fell trees with stone axes
I Soil soon loses fertility

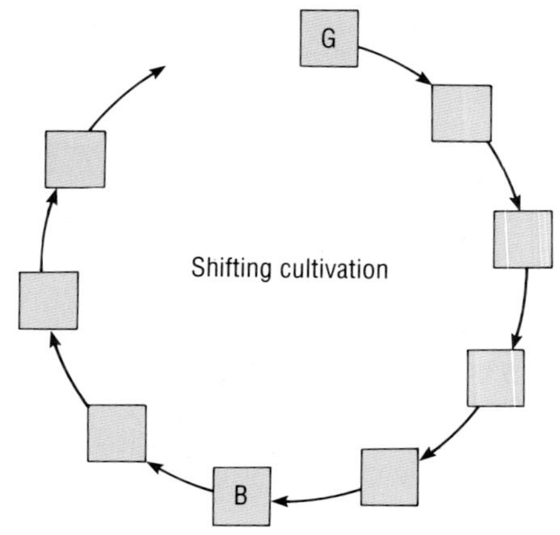

b Describe how clearing the forest may cause:
i) the land to suffer from soil erosion *(2)*
ii) the soil to rapidly lose its fertility *(2)*

c What happens to a system of shifting cultivation if the farming population increases? *(1)*

9 *(Page 83)*

a What is a plantation? *(2)*

b Using your general knowledge, complete the table opposite. *(5)*

c Describe the ideal growing conditions for coffee. *(4)*

d Why has the main area for coffee growing migrated westwards since the nineteenth century? *(2)*

crop	major producing areas
rubber	
bananas	
tea	
sugar	
coffee	
cocoa	
palm oil	
cotton	
tobacco	
cotton	

10 *(Pages 70 to 83)*

a i) Which of the two diagrams fits farming in an economically more developed country? *(1)*

ii) Which of the two diagrams fits farming in an economically less developed country? *(1)*

b Using evidence from the two diagrams give reasons for your answers to part **a**. *(4)*

A

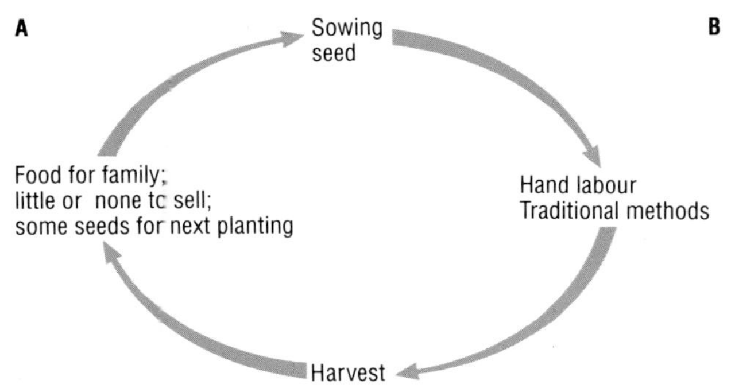
Sowing seed
Hand labour
Traditional methods
Harvest
Food for family;
little or none to sell;
some seeds for next planting

B

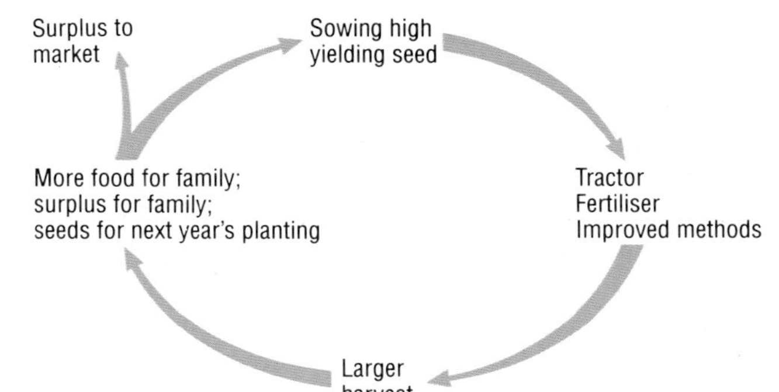
Surplus to market
Sowing high yielding seed
Tractor
Fertiliser
Improved methods
Larger harvest
More food for family;
surplus for family;
seeds for next year's planting

11 *(Page 84)*

The sketch shows a farming landscape in eastern England.

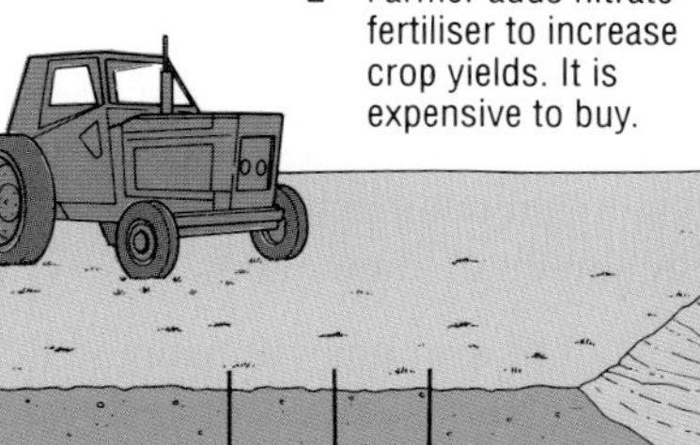
1 Crops use up nutrients in the soil
2 Farmer adds nitrate fertiliser to increase crop yields. It is expensive to buy.
3 Rain washes out (leaches) nitrates
Some enters rivers

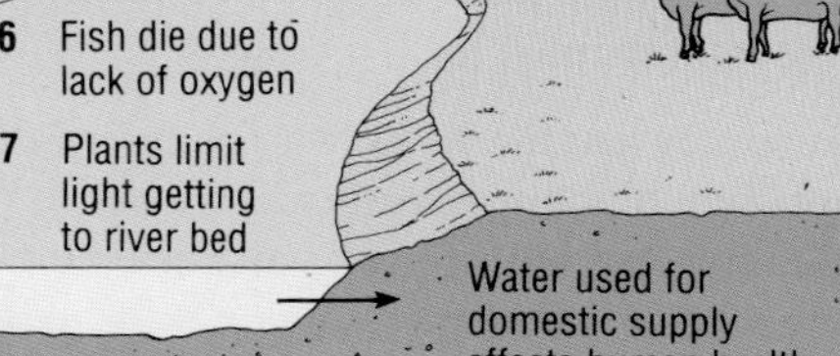
4 Cattle. Their 'manure' becomes nitrogen high slurry, which runs into rivers. Slurry is 200 times more polluting than domestic sewage.
5 Nitrates in rivers encourage growth of algae and larger plants. These use up oxygen.
6 Fish die due to lack of oxygen
7 Plants limit light getting to river bed
Water used for domestic supply affects human health

a What is fertiliser and why do farmers use it? *(2)*

b i) What is one advantage and one disadvantage to the farmer who uses nitrate fertiliser? *(2)*

ii) Describe how nitrate fertiliser reaches rivers. *(1)*

iii) How does an increase in nitrate in rivers affect: **1** fish **2** humans? *(2)*

c Water Authorities claim that in the 1980s the major source of river pollution in Britain was farm slurry.

i) What is farm slurry? *(1)*

ii) Is slurry more or less polluting than domestic sewage? *(1)*

d i) Why is it an advantage to some farmers to clear hedgerows? *(2)*

ii) Give three ways by which this removal can harm the environment. *(3)*

iii) Describe three other aspects of modern farming which it is claimed might harm the environment. *(3)*

12 *(Page 85)*

a Copy and complete the bar graph to show changes in food production between 1961 and 1988 for Latin America, Asia and sub-Saharan Africa. Label the places on the graph. *(3)*

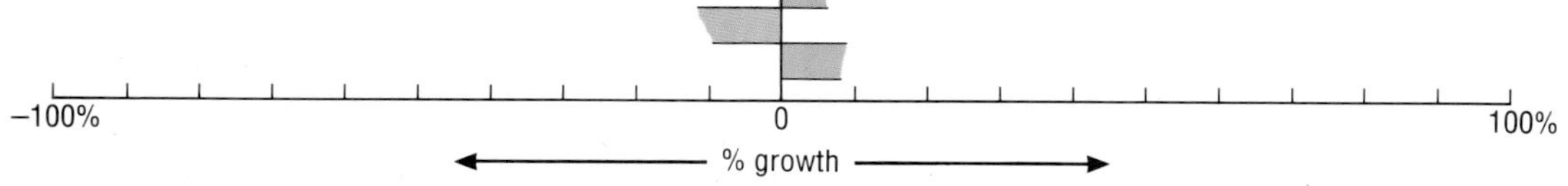
−100%
0
100%
% growth

b Give four reasons why world food reserves have declined since 1986. *(4)*

c Give six reasons why several parts of Africa are suffering from famine. *(6)*

Non-renewable resources

The sun is the source of the earth's energy. Without energy, nothing can live and nothing can be done. Green plants convert the sun's energy into a form which can be used by people. Coal, oil and natural gas, which provide 75 per cent of the world's supply of energy, are mainly used by the economically more developed countries (Figure 8.1). They are forms of stored solar energy produced by photosynthesis in plants over millions of years. Together with fuelwood, which can account for up to 90 per cent of energy consumed in economically less developed countries, these three types of energy are referred to as *fossil fuels*. As fossil fuels need long periods of time to build up and to be replenished, they are classified as a *non-renewable resource*. Once used, their supply is likely to run out. Nuclear energy also uses a non-renewable resource – uranium.

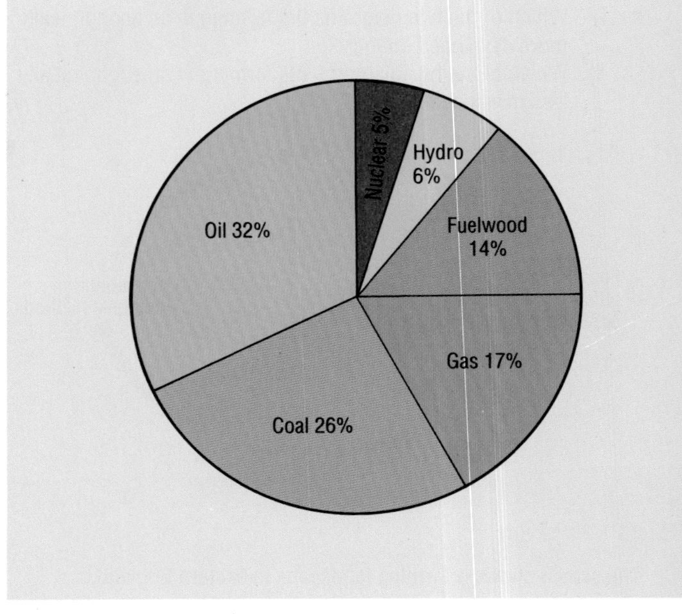

Figure 8.1
The world's supply of energy

Coal

The fortunes of coal in Europe have declined since the 1960s when the cheap price of oil and the exhaustion of the most easily obtainable coal meant a decline in both production and the workforce. Rising oil prices, following the 1974 Middle East war, led to the exploitation of low cost coal resources in the USA, Australia and South Africa. The recessions of the early 1980s and 1990s have sealed the fate of most mining communities.

Advantages Large reserves are likely to last for over 300 years. Improved technology has improved output per worker, allowed deeper mining with fewer workers, and made conversion to electricity more efficient.

Disadvantages The most easily accessible deposits have been used up and production costs have increased rapidly. There is competition from other types of energy. The burning of coal causes air pollution and contributes to the greenhouse effect (page 228) by releasing carbon dioxide into the atmosphere.

Figure 8.2
Open cast coalmine

Oil and natural gas

Most industrialised countries have come to rely upon oil and natural gas as their main sources of energy. Very few of them, the United Kingdom being an exception, have sufficient reserves of their own.

Advantages Oil and gas are more efficient to burn, easier to handle and distribute, and much less harmful to the environment than coal. They are needed for most types of transport and is safer than nuclear energy.

Disadvantages Reserves may only last a few decades. It is expensive to discover and exploit new fields. Both terminals and refineries take up much space and there is danger of spillage and explosions. Reserves are also subject to sudden price changes and vulnerable to political, economic and military pressures.

Figure 8.3
Oil exploration in Alaska

Nuclear power

Few debates generate such heat as that on the merits of nuclear power (Figure 8.5). Many industrialised countries which lack coal and oil have turned increasingly to nuclear power despite grave fears about its safety (Figure 8.4). According to the EC 'coal and nuclear energy are likely to provide the Community with three-quarters of its electricity until the next century. The Community is well aware of the difficulties associated with the public acceptance of nuclear power, and is concerned to help resolve the health, safety and environmental problems associated with it'.

Figure 8.4
Users of nuclear energy, 1990

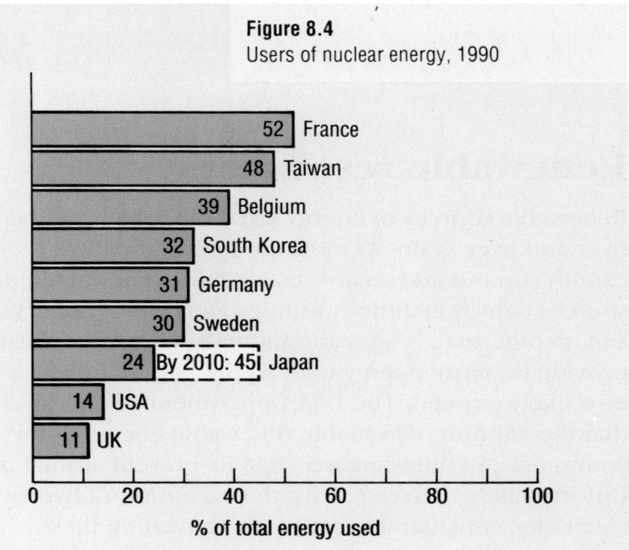

Figure 8.5 The nuclear energy debate

For

- Several independent experts predict that without nuclear power, Britain will face an energy gap by the year 2000, and that this will mean fewer jobs and a lower standard of living. Demand for electricity is predicted to increase by 30 per cent between 1990 and 2000.
- Only very limited raw materials would be needed, e.g. 50 tonnes of uranium per year compared with 540 tonnes of coal per hour needed for coal-fired stations.
- Oil and natural gas could be exhausted by the year 2020. Coal is difficult to obtain and dirty to use.
- Numerous safeguards make the risks of any accident minimal.
- Nuclear waste is limited and can be stored underground.
- Nearly all the money spent in Britain on energy research has been on nuclear power.
- Nuclear energy schemes have the support of large firms and government departments.
- Nuclear power is believed to contribute less than conventional fuels to the greenhouse effect and acid rain.

Against

- It is not clear how safe it is. So far there have been no serious accidents in Britain, as, for example, at Chernobyl in the Ukraine, but there have been several leaks at Sellafield.
- There is a large conservationist lobby which claims that one accident may kill many, and ruin an area of ground for hundreds of years. The Irish Sea is increasingly contaminated.
- Many people think that Britain should concentrate on using renewable forms of energy rather than those that are non-renewable.
- Nuclear power cannot be used for two of industry's major demands, heating and transport, as costs are too high.
- There is less demand for energy by industry as declining industries (such as steel) use more energy than those which are replacing them (such as micro-electronics).
- Potential health risks. The high incidence of leukaemia around Sellafield and Dounreay has been linked to the proximity of the power station.
- Nuclear waste can remain radioactive for many years. There are problems with reprocessing and then storing nuclear waste.
- The cost of decommissioning old power stations, the first of which closed in 1989 at Berkely, is extremely high.

Fuelwood

In Africa, trees have been called the staff of life because of their vital role in preserving the environment and in providing rural communities with their basic necessities (fuel, shade, food and building materials). Yet here, as in other developing continents, trees are being removed at an ever faster rate. Wood is used as a fuel for cooking and heating by over 80 per cent of families. In rural parts of Africa, collecting fuelwood is a time-consuming job for women and children (Figure 8.6). They may have to walk all day to find sufficient wood upon which to cook their meals (women also have to look after large families and the farm). As Africa's population grows the demand for wood increases, more trees are cut down and a cycle of environmental deprivation is created (Figure 8.7).

Figure 8.6
Collecting of wood for fuel, Kenya

Figure 8.7 The cycle of environmental deprivation

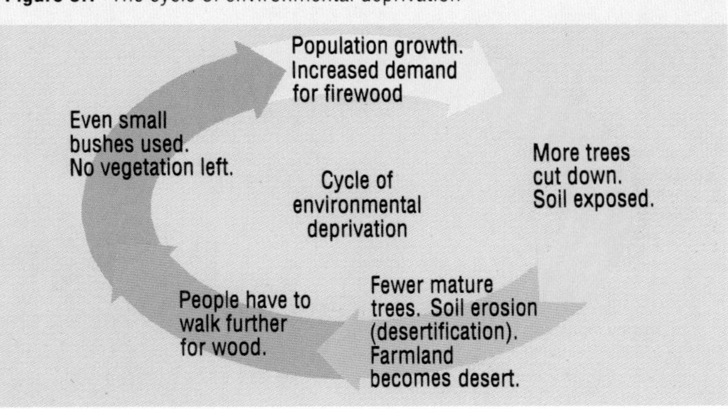

Renewable resources

Renewable sources of energy are those which can be used over and over again. As most are forces of nature they cannot run out and so are sustainable. Renewable energy sources, which include running water, wind, tides, waves, sun, geothermal, biogas and biomass, are vast and can provide far more energy than all the people on earth are ever likely to need. The USA Department of Energy claim that the amount of available renewable energy in the country is 250 times greater than its present annual use. Unfortunately there are, with the exception of hydro-electricity, considerable problems in turning these potential energy sources into forms which can be used. Most are thought to be uneconomic (though their costs are decreasing) in relation to fossil fuels (but their costs are increasing). At some time in the future the world will have to rely much more on renewable energy resources.

Hydro-electric power (HEP)

Hydro-electricity is the most widely used of the renewable types of energy. Although it only accounts for 6 per cent of the world's total energy (Figure 8.1), in many countries it accounts for over 80 per cent, e.g. Paraguay 100 per cent, Norway 96 per cent, Ghana 90 per cent and Brazil 86 per cent. It is, as this list suggests, important in both developed and developing countries – provided they have a constant supply of fast-flowing water.

Heavy precipitation (relief rainfall) over high mountains

Large drainage basin traps more water.

Snow and glaciers provide spring melt water.

Impervious rock prevents water soaking through, and gives solid foundations.

Natural glacial lake or reservoir provides constant supply of water.

Steep sided glaciated valleys help dam construction

Site of former waterfall provides a head of water

Nearby industrial and domestic demand

Figure 8.8
Factors involved in the location of an HEP station

In some cases HEP is generated at a natural waterfall (Niagara Falls), in others it involves building a dam across a valley (the Nile at Aswan), while in a few cases it can be obtained by pumping water down a hillside. Figure 8.8 shows some of the factors ideally needed for the location of an HEP station.

The Itaipu Scheme

In 1982 a dam was completed across the River Parana at Itaipu, on the border between Brazil and Paraguay (Figure 8.9). The lake behind the dam is 180 km long and 5 km wide. The eighteen turbines fitted at the Itaipu power station make this the largest HEP scheme in the world. Although the venture was a joint one between Paraguay and Brazil, Paraguay receives its annual requirements from just one turbine. By agreement, Brazil purchases the remainder of Paraguay's share at a cheap price, and transmits the power to the São Paulo industrial area. As with other HEP schemes there were advantages and disadvantages. The advantages included the jobs created during its construction, the production of a clean and renewable form of energy, and the relatively cheap cost of electricity. The disadvantages included the flooding of farmland and a wildlife environment, the removal and rehousing of 42,000 people, the creation of very few permanent jobs in relation to the huge cost of the scheme, and, now, the slow silting up of the lake. Although the Paraguayan government receives much needed income and São Paulo gets its energy, there has been relatively little benefit to the local residents of Itaipu.

Figure 8.9
The Itaipu dam in Brazil is 190 metres high and is the largest hydro-electricity power station in the world

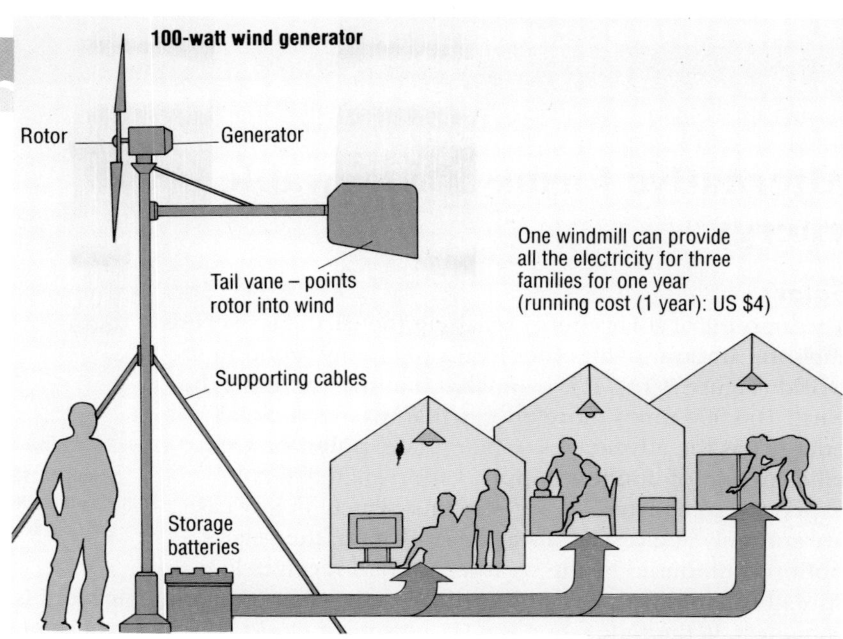

Figure 8.10
Wind generators as used in China

Wind

China first began using the wind to provide power for irrigation 2000 years ago. The mass production of wind power was only started in the late 1960s however, and the experiment with land generators in the late 1970s. China has placed greater emphasis on the development of mini-wind generators (Figure 8.10) which can be used on isolated farms and villages.

Although Britain used windmills in the Middle Ages to grind corn, few attempts were made until recently to generate this form of power. Now, apart from HEP, it is the only renewable option being developed commercially. Wind turbines, to be at their most efficient, need to be in areas with high and regular wind speeds. Such sites are usually found in the more remote parts of western and highland Britain. As the 30 metre high turbines are expensive to build and to maintain, it is an advantage to group about 25 machines together to form a 'windfarm' (Figure 8.11). Britain's first windfarm was opened in December 1991 near Camelford in Cornwall. The farm, on moorland 250 metres above sea-level and where average wind speeds are 27 km/h, generates enough electricity for 3,000 homes. By early 1993 the government had given permission for forty further windfarms to be developed although only a handful were in operation. Future plans include the construction of off-shore windfarms.

Figure 8.11
Wind farm at Camelford, Cornwall

Advantages

- Wind turbines do not cause air pollution and will reduce the use of fossil fuels.
- Winds are much stronger in winter which coincides with the peak demand for electricity.
- After the initial expense of building a windfarm, the production of electricity from this renewable source is relatively cheap.
- Windfarms provide a source of income for farmers and may attract small industries to rural parts of Britain where job opportunities are at present limited.

Disadvantages

- Wind does not blow all the time. At present electricity generated during storms cannot be stored for use during calm periods.
- Groups of 30 metre tall turbines spoil the scenic attraction of the countryside.
- 7000 turbines are needed to produce the same amount of electricity as one nuclear power station. 100,000 windfarms may be needed if Britain is to generate 20 per cent of its total energy supply from the wind.

Alternative forms of renewable energy

Solar

The amount of solar energy reaching the earth far exceeds the total amount of all other forms of energy found in the world (Figure 8.14). It is estimated that the sun gives the earth 100,000 times more energy than we need. Solar energy has the advantages of being safe, pollution free, efficient and of limitless supply. Unfortunately it is expensive to construct solar 'stations' which, in any case, are still only at a research stage. For Britain, the solar option is hindered by the weather. Britain receives less sunlight than most places on earth. Winter, when demand is highest, is the time when the UK gets most cloud, receives shorter hours of daylight and, when it does shine, the sun's angle is low in the sky making it less effective. Whereas solar power is unlikely to provide Britain with more than 1 per cent of its energy requirement, its potential and need is far greater to developing countries, especially as most of these countries are found in warmer, sunnier latitudes. In developing countries solar energy can be used in isolated, rural areas where mains electricity is too expensive to be practical. The 'solar village' concept was first adopted in Mali (West Africa) in 1978 and is beginning to spread more rapidly. The fastest growth is in India.

Geothermal

Holes are bored into hotter areas of the earth's crust. Cold water is pumped downwards and is heated by contact with underlying rocks, where it is turned to steam. It is then returned to power stations on the surface where, at temperatures of about 100°C, it can drive turbines to produce electricity (Figures 8.12 and 8.13).

Figure 8.13
How geothermal energy is produced

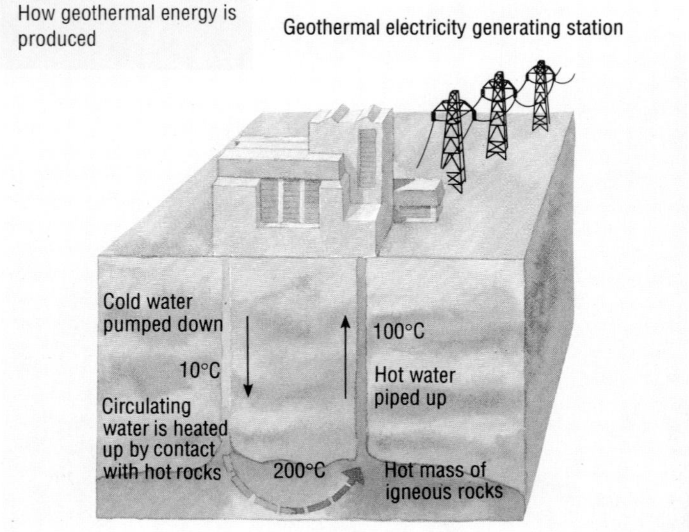

Geothermal electricity generating station

Cold water pumped down

10°C

Circulating water is heated up by contact with hot rocks

200°C

100°C

Hot water piped up

Hot mass of igneous rocks

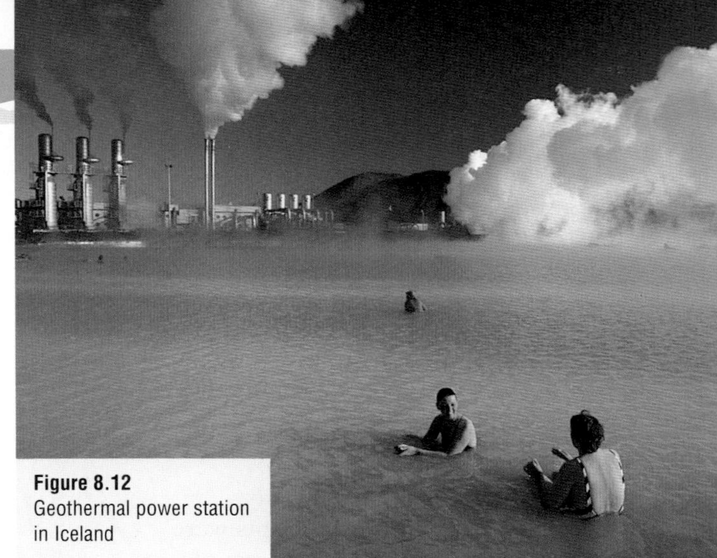

Figure 8.12
Geothermal power station in Iceland

Iceland is ideally situated on the Mid-Atlantic Ridge, where new rock is being formed at a point where the American plate is moving away from the Eurasian plate (page 211). Geothermal power has for some time been used in Reykjavik for central (space) heating, open-air swimming pools, and greenhouses. A controversial new power station has been drilled near Krafla in the north of the island, the site of an active volcano. Early tests ended after lava was seen erupting from one of the trial boreholes. This scheme had numerous problems which included:

- Possible damage to the power station by earthquakes and volcanic eruptions.
- The high temperatures, over 300°C at production levels, and acidity of the water damaging concrete casings, and corroding and blocking the boreholes at depths.
- High costs of developing and then producing energy.

Geothermal power is also important in Central America where it supplies 14 per cent of El Salvador's and 10 per cent of Nicaragua's energy demands.

Figure 8.14
Solar roof panels

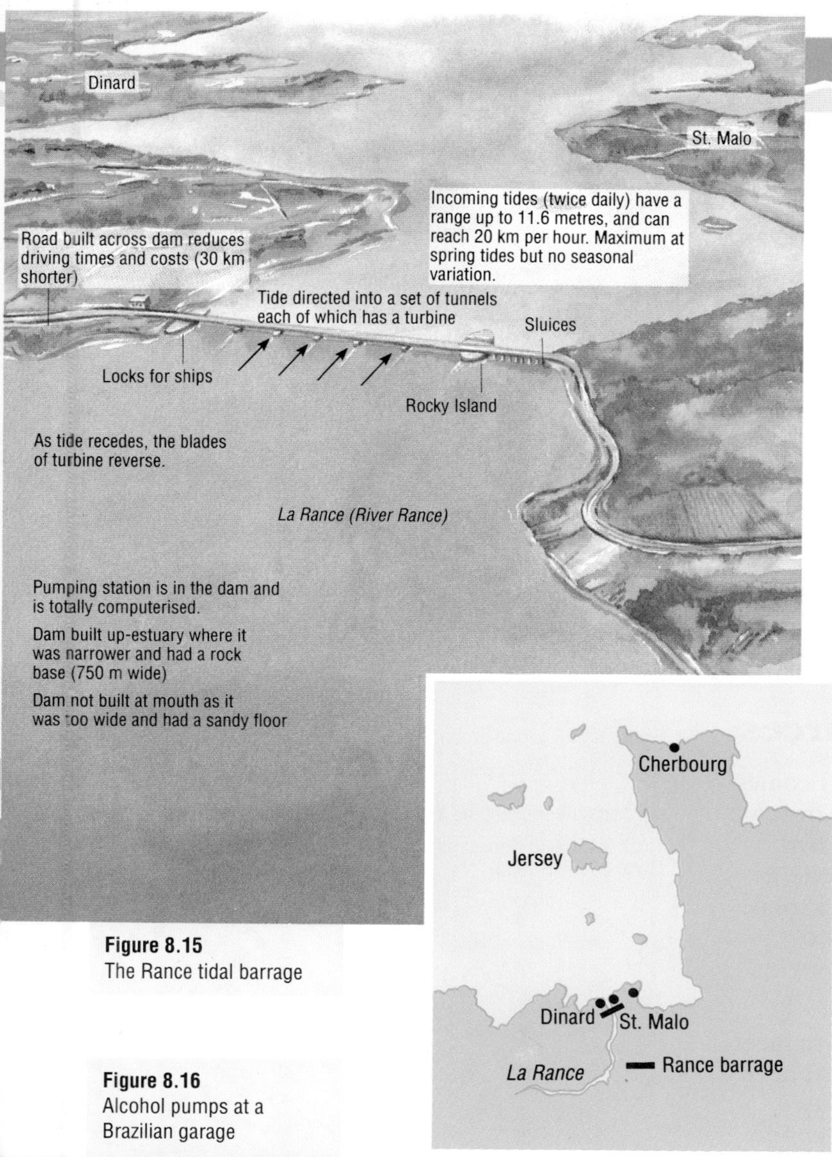
Dinard
St. Malo
Incoming tides (twice daily) have a range up to 11.6 metres, and can reach 20 km per hour. Maximum at spring tides but no seasonal variation.
Road built across dam reduces driving times and costs (30 km shorter)
Tide directed into a set of tunnels each of which has a turbine
Sluices
Locks for ships
Rocky Island
As tide recedes, the blades of turbine reverse.
La Rance (River Rance)
Pumping station is in the dam and is totally computerised.
Dam built up-estuary where it was narrower and had a rock base (750 m wide)
Dam not built at mouth as it was too wide and had a sandy floor
Cherbourg
Jersey
Dinard
St. Malo
La Rance
Rance barrage

Figure 8.15
The Rance tidal barrage

Figure 8.16
Alcohol pumps at a Brazilian garage

COOL HIDRATADO:
1-Não misturar à gasolina.
2-Não utilizar em motores não adaptados.
do Alcoo
LCOOL BR
BR

Figure 8.17
Wave power in Norway

Tidal

River estuaries with large tidal ranges have the potential to generate large amounts of electricity. The Rance Barrage in Brittany (France) was the first to be built (Figure 8.15). Tides in the Rance estuary have a range of over eleven metres and can enter and leave the estuary at speeds of 20 km/h. The incoming tide turns turbines, the blades of which can be reversed to harness the receding tide. In Britain the Severn Barrage, under discussion since the 1920s, is one of several suggested schemes. Apart from the huge building cost, barrages destroy inter-tidal environments and can disrupt shipping.

Waves

Waves approaching Britain from the Atlantic, especially during winter storms, have exceptionally high energy levels. The problem is designing machinery which can withstand the power of large waves and at the same time convert the energy into electricity. The world's first commercial wave power station is in Norway (Figure 8.17). Waves enter a narrowing channel, increase in height and spill over into a reservoir. As the water is allowed to fall from the reservoir it operates the power station generators.

Biogas

Fermenting animal dung produces a methane type gas which is used in some developing countries instead of fuelwood. Although cheap to run, the installation of a fermenting system may be expensive and the dung can no longer be used as a fertiliser.

Biomass

Crops like sugar cane, cassava and maize contain enough starch to produce ethanol (a type of alcohol) when fermented. Brazil began, in 1975, to convert vehicles so that they could run on ethanol instead of petrol (Figure 8.16). By 1990, 5 per cent of Brazil's energy requirements came from alcohol, and 75 per cent of vehicles were dependent upon it. Its advantages include its cheapness compared to imported oil, the creation of employment in new sugar cane growing areas and a large reduction in air pollution. Its disadvantages include the clearing of vast areas of tropical rainforest to plant the cane, the low wages paid to plantation workers, and the reduction in crops previously grown for home consumption.

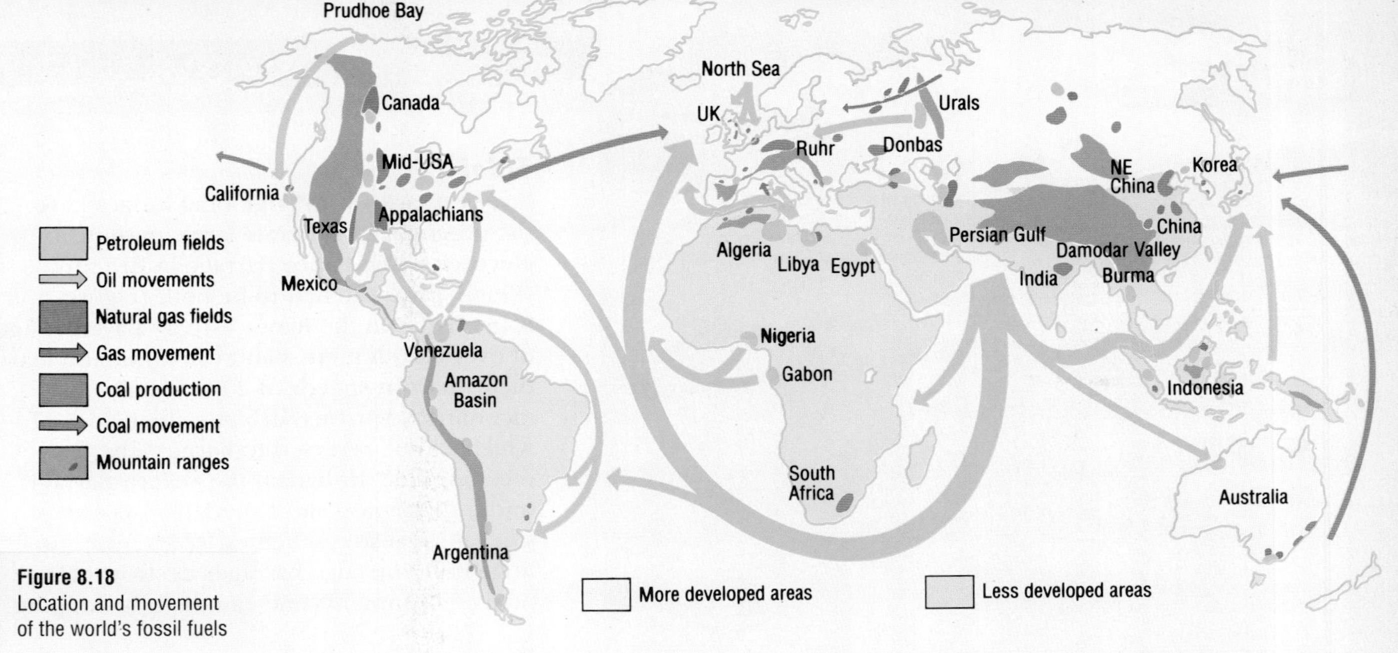

Figure 8.18
Location and movement of the world's fossil fuels

Distribution of energy resources

About 75 per cent of the world's supply of energy comes from three fossil fuels – coal, oil and natural gas. In some areas electricity generated by nuclear power and hydro-electricity is important. Although other forms of energy account for only a small percentage of the world's total, they can account for 90 per cent in some of the less developed countries. Figure 8.18 shows the uneven distribution of the three fossil fuels.

Developed countries usually have insufficient oil to meet their demands (except the UK and Norway) and so need to import vast quantities. Even the USA, the world's second major producer (Figure 8.19 (a)), had to import nearly half of its requirements in 1990. Several developing countries produce oil, but few refine and use it.

Coal, which gave the impetus to the industrial revolution of the nineteenth century, is mined largely in the developed countries and the former communist bloc (Figure 8.19(b)). Few developing countries have reserves of coal and this has been partly the cause of their delayed industrial development.

Nuclear power has become increasingly important since the 1970s, yet, again, only developed countries and the former communist bloc have had the money to invest in this controversial form of energy (Figure 8.20 (a)).

Hydro-electric power, the only major renewable form of energy, is more widespread though developing countries (Figure 8.20 (b)) tend to have large prestige schemes not always suitable to their particular stage of development.

The unevenness in distribution, the fact that developed countries use, on average, 15 times more coal, oil and gas than developing countries and technological improvements in transport mean that energy is moved great distances (Figure 8.18).

Figure 8.19 World production of crude oil and coal

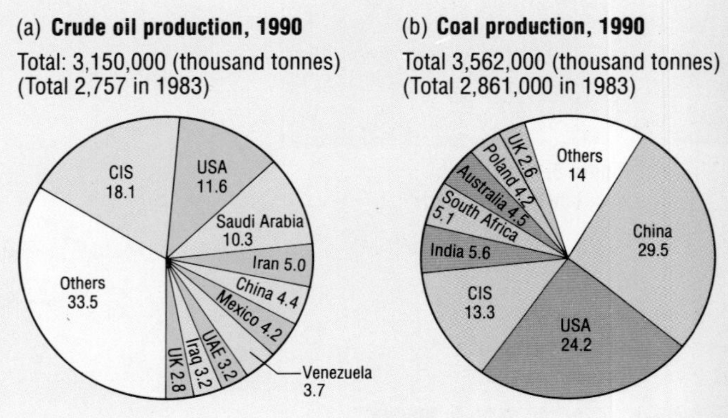

Figure 8.20 Importance of nuclear and hydro-electricity

a Reliance upon nuclear power, 1990 (% of country's energy from nuclear power)

40% and over	30–39%	20–29%	10–19%
France 52	Belgium 39	Bulgaria 25	Switzerland 19
Taiwan 48	South Korea 32	Japan 24	Czechoslovakia 19
	Germany 31	Hungary 24	Finland 18
	Sweden 30		Spain 17
			USA 14
			CIS 11
			UK 11

b Reliance upon hydro-electric power, 1990 (% of country's energy from HEP)

75% and over	50–74%	45–49%
Paraguay 100	Colombia 74	Bolivia 47
Norway 99	Uruguay 71	Nigeria 47
Zaire 98	Kenya 69	Ecuador 47
Uganda 96	Ethiopia 67	Haiti 46
Zambia 92	Angola 67	Honduras 45
Ghana 90	Austria 64	Portugal 45
Laos 89	New Zealand 62	
Mozambique 88	Panama 61	
Brazil 86	Canada 59	
Cameroon 86	Peru 57	
Costa Rica 80	Chile 56	
Malawi 79		
Nepal 79		
Sri Lanka 78		
Iceland 76		

Distribution of energy resources in Britain

Britain has always been fortunate in its energy supplies. In the Middle Ages the many fast-flowing rivers, resulting from heavy rainfall in hilly areas, were used to drive waterwheels. The invention of the steam engine, which enabled Britain to become the first industrialised country in the world, was dependent upon heat derived from coal. During the nineteenth century coalmining regions saw the most rapid growth in towns and in jobs. When, by the mid-twentieth century, the most accessible reserves had been exhausted, new forms of energy were discovered. In 1965 natural gas was found in the North Sea, off the coast of Norfolk, and in 1970 oil was discovered off the east coast of Scotland. At a time when world oil prices reached their maximum, Britain became self-sufficient in this form of energy. At the same time, Britain took a lead in the development of nuclear power, although in the 1980s, fears over its safety and the availability of other fuels meant that the industry grew less quickly than in other developed countries (Figure 8.20 (a)).

Oil and gas were only expected to last until about 2000 AD, but now, due to a falling demand for energy and the discovery of new fields, these two forms of energy should last until 2035 AD. However, after 2000 AD, oil at least may have to be imported in increasingly large amounts. Although coal reserves are expected to last for another 300 years, their exploitation is becoming increasingly limited due to cheaper imports, arguably cheaper alternative types of domestic energy, difficult working conditions, and a strong environmental lobby. Deep coalmining is becoming restricted to parts of East Yorkshire, East Nottinghamshire and Leicestershire.

Yet even when fossil fuels become less available, Britain's seas and weather provide the potential to produce 'alternative' or renewable sources of energy based on waves, tides and wind (pages 93 and 95). Tentative experiments have been made to produce geothermal (SW England) and biomass (Western Isles) energy. Although many individual properties have added solar panels, solar power is unlikely to become a major source of energy in 'cloudy' Britain. Perhaps what is surprising, considering the amount of highland and rainfall in western Britain, is the relative unimportance of hydro-electricity.

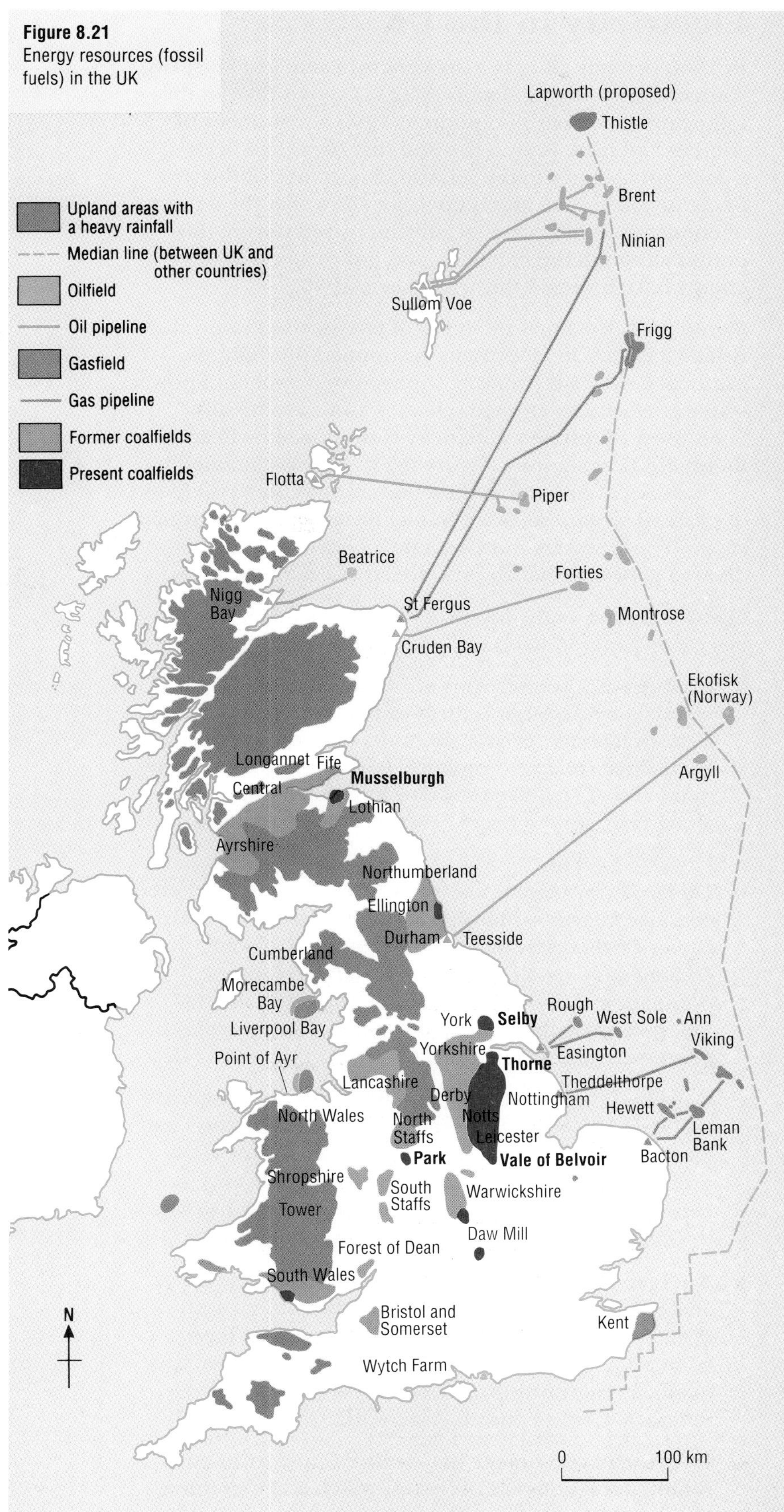

Figure 8.21
Energy resources (fossil fuels) in the UK

Electricity in the UK

In 1960 virtually all of Britain's energy came from just two sources – coal and oil. Figure 8.22 (a) shows that, in the following thirty year period up to 1990, the number of sources had increased to five and that there had been significant changes in the relative importance of the type of energy used. The graph does not show that the amount of energy used in Britain steadily increased during this period although the recession and increasing cost of energy have reversed this trend since 1990.

Figure 8.22 (b) shows the types of energy used to produce Britain's electricity. Electricity is supplied through the National Grid – a technically sophisticated system of power stations, electricity storage schemes and transmission lines. Most of Britain's electricity is produced by heat in thermal power stations (Figure 8.23). Heat is obtained by the burning of one of the three non-renewable fossil fuels of coal, oil or natural gas. The fuel heats water to produce steam. The steam then drives a turbine which in turn drives a generator which produces the electricity.

Figure 8.24 shows the location of Britain's major electricity generating power stations in the early 1990s.

a **Coal-fired** power stations are ideally located on or near coalfields, large centres of population and older industrial areas. As large amounts of water are needed to cool the steam to condense it back into water many more recent coal-fired stations have been built either along main inland rivers (Trent) or on coastal estuaries (Thames).

b **Oil-fired** power stations are located on deep, sheltered coastal estuaries which can accommodate large tankers. Estuaries also provide the large amounts of water for cooling and, ideally, are away from large centres of population (Milford Haven). Present British and EC fuel policies make it unlikely that any further oil-fired power stations will be built.

c **Gas-fired** power stations have become the fashion in the early 1990s, partly because of their lower costs and partly because they produce a smaller amount of greenhouse gases (page 228). Unfortunately any increase in gas-fired power will be at the expense of the coal-fired stations and the coal mining industry.

d **Nuclear power** stations tend to be located on coasts and estuaries where there is water for cooling and cheap, easily reclaimable land. Although they have been built away from large centres of population, they need a good transport system for fuel input and radioactive waste output (Sizewell).

e **Hydro-electric power** stations are found in some remote, upland areas of Britain which receive large and reliable amounts of rain.

	1960	1970	1980	1990
Coal	76.5	50.7	35.2	30.6
Oil	22.6	42.7	39.7	34.7
Natural gas	0.1	2.7	20.1	25.6
Nuclear	0.2	3.3	4.5	8.0
Hydro-electric	0.6	0.6	0.6	0.5

Figure 8.22a
The UK's total energy consumption (%)

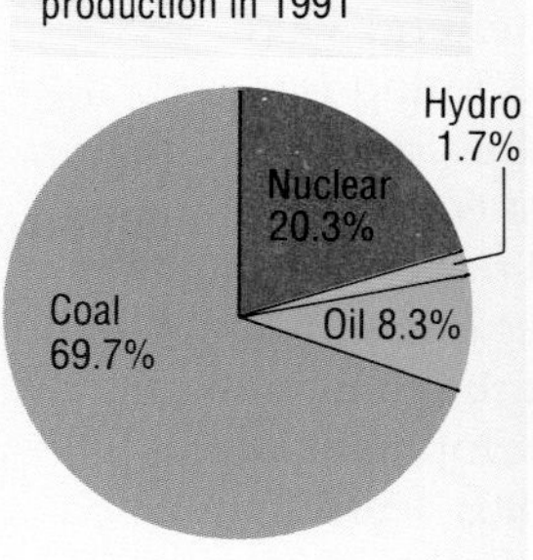

Figure 8.22b
Fuel used for electricity production in 1991

Figure 8.23
DRAX power station, Thorpe Marsh near Doncaster

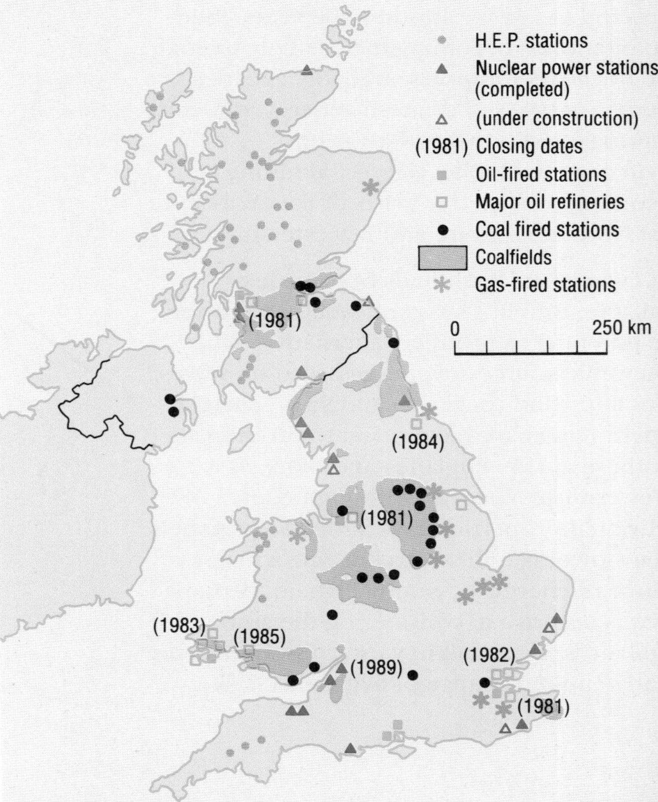

Figure 8.24
Location of Britain's main power stations

New technology and the Shetlands oilfields

As soon as the explorers began to search for oil off the north-east coast of Scotland it became obvious that they would be faced with considerable and new problems. They realised that the weather was worse, the sea deeper and rougher and the supply distances greater than anything they had previously experienced. Even before oil was discovered it was accepted that a new technology was needed to explore and, once oil was located, to exploit the resource.

The depth of the North Sea varies between 80 to 180 metres. This in itself called for the development of a complete new technology. Large concrete platforms (Figure 8.25) had to be designed and constructed. These had to be able to withstand the severe storms and winter ice of the area. Each production platform had to be large enough to accommodate a drilling rig, process plant, power plant, pump and a helicopter landing pad as well as living and sleeping quarters for the crew. Each platform consists of a base which supports four towers. Some towers may be used to store oil, others are filled with ballast to provide extra anchorage and stability.

It was soon realised that the amount of oil likely to be produced was far in excess of the amount which could be taken ashore by tanker. It was decided to lay two 36-inch trunk pipelines to an oil terminal which would be built at Sullom Voe. However the uneven sea bed made pipe-laying difficult. A giant pipe-laying barge was designed to weld and coat the pipe before it was fed over a laying arm (Figure 8.26). Improvements in transport were needed to fly both workers and supplies between the Shetlands and the mainland (very few employees were local Shetlanders) and then to and from the oil platforms.

Meanwhile, new techniques in oil safety and in protecting the environment were necessary. The Alpha Piper explosion in 1988 and the running aground of the ***Braer*** oiltanker in 1993 are constant reminders of the potential dangers in the oil industry. At Sullom Voe the storage tanks are built on heated ground to prevent freezing and possible fracturing in winter. The tanks are surrounded by concrete 'ditches' which could contain the oil should a tank leak. To deal with possible spillages at sea, sea booms are in place to limit the spread of oil. Both skimmers, to collect surface oil, and oil dispersant chemicals are also available.

Figure 8.25
The Thistle platform with drilling derricks in place on the left

Figure 8.26
The giant pipe-laying barge Viking Piper laying the submarine pipeline from the Ninian field

Energy supplies in Japan

Japan has become the world's leading industrial country (page 120). Industry needs lots of energy and yet Japan has very limited energy resources of its own (Figure 8.28). It is this lack of energy resource which has made Japan's industrial achievements even more remarkable.

Japan's industry grew rapidly after 1945. Like other industrialised countries Japan became reliant upon coal and later oil and natural gas. Japan had some coal reserves (Figure 8.27) but most of these have been used up leaving, by 1990, only seven coalmines still in use. Oil and natural gas are found in even smaller amounts. As a result most of these costly fossil fuels have to be imported. To try to reduce this dependence on imported fuels, Japan has turned increasingly to nuclear power. By 2010 Japan hopes to obtain 45 per cent of its energy requirements from this source (Figure 8.5). There is, however, a strong anti-nuclear lobby in Japan. This is hardly surprising as the Japanese are more sensitive than most people to the dangers of nuclear accidents having experienced the results of two atomic explosions in 1945.

Japan also appears to have the widest possible range of options regarding the use of renewable forms of energy. With 83 per cent of the country being mountainous and rain falling throughout the year, especially during the summer monsoon, Japan has been able to use the resultant fast flowing rivers to generate hydro-electricity. Production from this source is not expected to increase as most of the ideal sites have already been used. Japan, being a group of islands, is surrounded by the sea, receives strong winds (typhoons), has an above average amount of sunlight and has over 40 active volcanoes. Unfortunately no-one has, as yet, developed an economic method of harnessing these potential sources of energy.

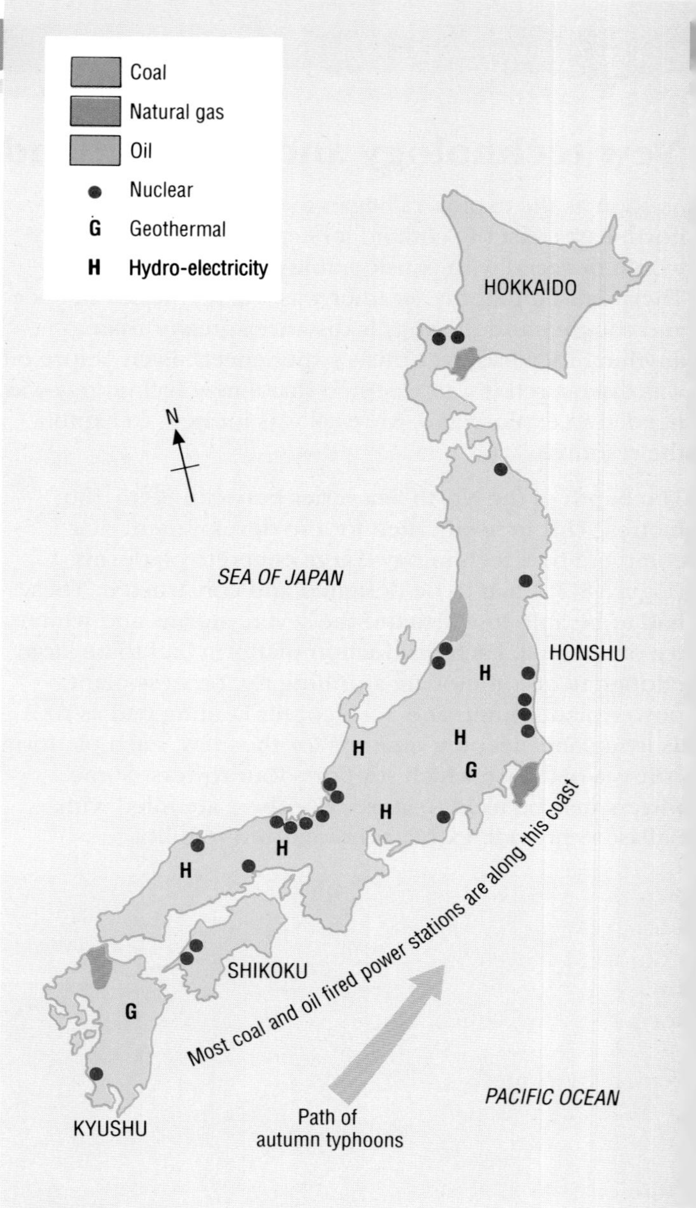

Figure 8.27
Energy resources in Japan

Figure 8.28 Sources of energy in Japan (1992)

		% of Japan's total energy	% found in Japan	Locations in Japan	% imported	Major source of imports
Non-renewable fossil fuels	A Coal	15	12	A little in Hokkaido & N.W. Kyushu	88	Australia, Canada, USA
	B Oil	29	0.2	Very little in N. Honshu	99.8	United Arab Emirates, Saudi Arabia, Indonesia
	C Natural Gas	19	0.5	A little east of Tokyo	99.5	Indonesia
Non-renewable	D Nuclear	24	–	–	100	Uranium from Canada and Australia
Renewable	E Hydro-electricity	7	100	Mountains throughout Japan	0	–
	F Geothermal	5	100	Mainly Kyushu	0	–
	G Solar	1	100	Mainly southern Japan	0	–

Energy in Ghana

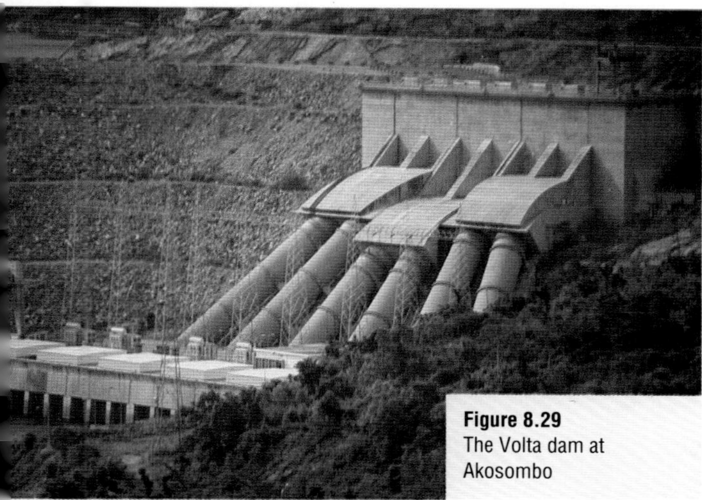

Figure 8.29 The Volta dam at Akosombo

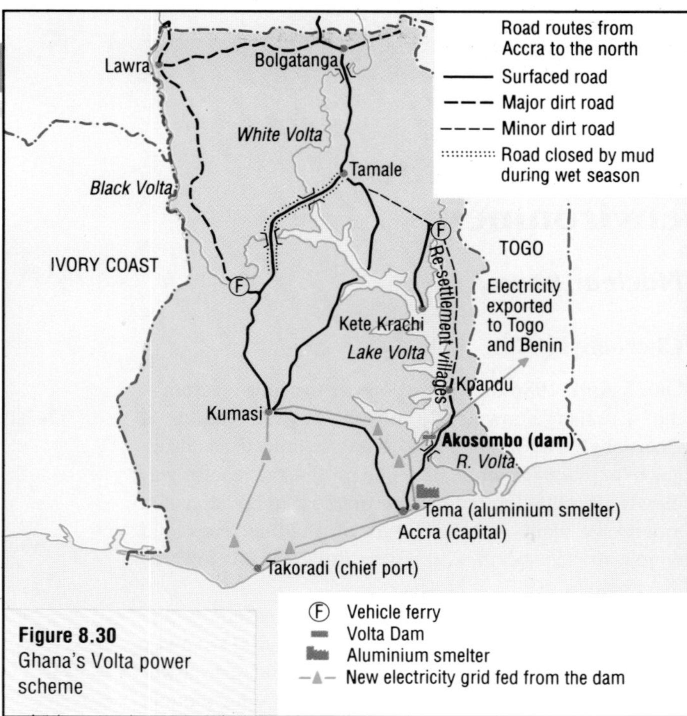

Figure 8.30 Ghana's Volta power scheme

In the mid-1950s, Ghana's first President, Dr Kwame Nkrumah, saw the River Volta as his country's chance to improve its economy. Before then, Ghana had been a British colony, the Gold Coast, relying mainly on the export of one crop, cocoa, for its income. Dr Nkrumah believed that with a limitless supply of cheap electricity his country could develop – but, as in all developing countries, the problem was how to obtain sufficient money for the scheme. The solution appeared in the form of a multinational (page 122) called Valco (Volta Aluminium Company). It agreed to build a smelter in return for duty and tax exemptions on the import of bauxite and the export of aluminium, and for the purchase of cheap electricity.

In order to supply the energy necessary for the creation of jobs, the development of secondary and service industries, and the money needed to create large, often prestigious schemes, a developing country often has to rely upon a multinational company. In return the developing country is expected to grant favours to that firm.

The Volta scheme (Figure 8.29) included the building of a dam at Akosombo in a gorge on the River Volta. This created a huge lake. A power station provided electricity for the newly built aluminium smelter, situated on the coast at Tema (Figure 8.30). Although the scheme has brought many advantages to Ghana, it has also created many problems (Figure 8.31).

The project in the early 1990s

Just as 40 years earlier, Ghana had suffered from having only one main export, cocoa, by 1990 its economy was again affected by its reliance on one main project. The drought, which led to the famine in Ethiopia, Somalia and Sudan, also caused the drying up of rivers which fed Lake Volta. Power supplies from Akosombo to Togo and Benin were cut by half (each country had received 95 per cent of its electricity from Ghana), the Valco Aluminium Smelter had to close making its workforce redundant, and all other factories were restricted to a three-day week in an attempt to conserve energy. So, until the rains come in sufficient quantity to refill Lake Volta, Ghana will be unable to repay loans to the World Bank and will use up more of its dwindling wood supply as an alternative form of energy.

Figure 8.31 Advantages and disadvantages of the Volta scheme

Advantages
- Prestigious project for Ghana.
- Long term cheap electricity and a new electricity grid.
- Created a pool of skilled Ghanaian technicians.
- Ghanaians obtained top jobs.
- Growth of industry, i.e. aluminium, boat-building, construction.
- New jobs in fishing on Lake Volta and refrigerator plants.
- Fish from the lake improved the local diet.
- The lake provided an assured water supply for domestic use, farming and industry.
- Development of water transport on the lake.
- Electricity exported to Togo and Benin.

Disadvantages
- Much land, even if poor quality, was flooded.
- Seasonal variations in lake levels leave swampy areas around its edges.
- 80,000 people had to be rehoused.
- Loss of wildlife to the lake.
- The main north-south road was flooded.
- Relatively few jobs, only 2500 at Tema, in return for the huge amount of money spent on the scheme.
- All profits went overseas – not to Ghana.
- None of Ghana's bauxite used – imported from the Americas, just as all the aluminium is exported.
- 65–70 per cent of Akosombo's power goes to Valco.
- Electricity is only available for towns in the south, not for the north.

Energy and the environment

Nuclear power

Chernobyl (CIS)

On 25 April 1986 the core of one of the four reactors at the Russian showpiece nuclear power station at Chernobyl, 100 km north of Kiev, overheated causing gas to explode (Figure 8.32). The roof of the reactor was blown off, allowing radioactive material to be deposited around the plant, and the release of a radioactive cloud which drifted north-west over Poland and towards Scandinavia.

No news of this explosion was released by the Soviet Union until three days later, when 1,500 km away in Sweden, alarm signals were set off at a nuclear power station south of Stockholm. At first the Swedes thought that their reactor was leaking and they evacuated the site – only to realise later that it was the radioactivity from Chernobyl which had activated their alarms. Radioactivity readings soon rose ten times in Sweden and five times in Denmark and Finland, though experts said these levels were well below those which would threaten human life. It took two weeks for the fire at Chernobyl to be put out – a task achieved by dropping sand and lead from helicopters. Action was taken just in time to stop radioactivity contaminating underground water supplies which drained into Kiev's main reservoir. The explosion killed only two people, though within four months this total had risen to 31, following the deaths of several who had been most severely exposed to radiation. Four settlements, including the new town of Pripyat (built to house the workers at Chernobyl), were evacuated.

In Britain where levels of radioactivity rose 12 days after the accident, the transportation of sheep was restricted for several years in North Wales, the Lake District and parts of south-west Scotland.

Assessments of the impact of the accident differ. In 1992 the International Atomic Energy Agency stated:

'no health disorders could be attributed directly to radiation exposure. The incidence of leukaemia and cancer and the contamination of the local environment are both less than had been feared.'

However, a group of doctors declared that 66 per cent of children had thyroid disorders and 35 per cent of 17 year old boys had no puberty development. Whichever is true, Chernobyl continues to cause grave concern, especially since its reopening for the winter of 1992–3 due to the acute shortage of energy in the CIS.

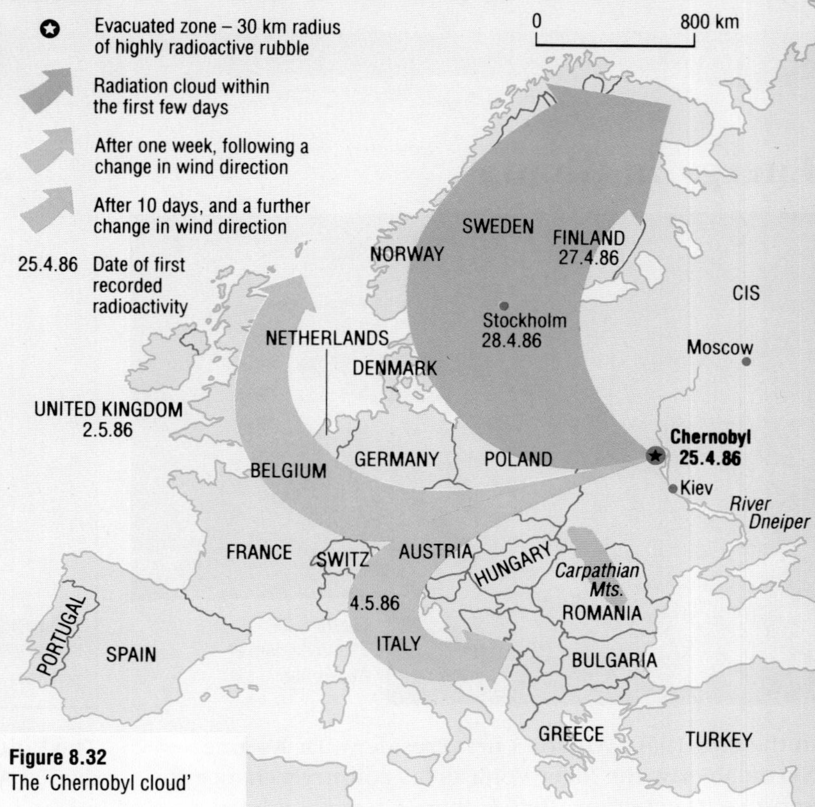

Figure 8.32
The 'Chernobyl cloud'

Sellafield (Cumbria)

A series of leaks and discharges from Sellafield, and the question of the disposal and storage of nuclear waste has become a major environmental concern in Britain. An independent authority claimed, after Chernobyl, that 'radioactivity released from coal burning power stations is twice that released at nuclear stations' (and it only made up 0.15 per cent of radiation in the atmosphere). He also said that 'a winkle at Seascale (the beach next to Sellafield) contained less radiation than that present naturally in a Brazil nut'. Anti-nuclear campaigners point to increases in radiation in the Irish Sea and on Cumbrian beaches and ask what would happen in Britain if one of our reactors exploded (Figures 8.4 and 8.33).

Figure 8.33 The Sellafield saga

DANGER

DO NOT LOITER! RADIATION HAZARD

This beach is contaminated with radioactivity from the Windscale Nuclear Fuel Reprocessing Plant which has caused high concentrations of radionuclides to be present on this beach.

DO NOT allow children to play here. Whilst reading this notice you may inhale PLUTONIUM – a known cancer causing agent.

DO NOT bathe from this beach. The Irish Sea is the most radioactive sea in the world.

DO NOT catch or consume fish as they contain high concentrations of radionuclides.

DO NOT touch or pick up items on this beach.

IF YOU MUST USE THIS BEACH, WEAR HEAVY RUBBER BOOTS AND GLOVES. WEAR A FILTER MASK AND LEAVE AS QUICKLY AS POSSIBLE.

For further advice or information ring British Nuclear Fuels Limited, Seascale (0940) 28333.

The Sellafield saga

The chattering classes in this country have never shown much interest in the creation of new wealth. That is seen at its starkest today in their attitude towards the nuclear power industry. Somebody only has to sneeze at the Sellafield nuclear waste reprocessing plant these days to get on to the front page of the nation's press. An alliance of anti-nuke environmentalists, opportunist politicians and a media establishment which cannot tell the difference between press vigilance and press vendetta seems determined to have Sellafield closed down, despite the fact that it employs 15,500 people, invests £1m a day and has won international orders worth £2.7 billion to keep it in work into the next century. Of course, nuclear safety is of crucial importance and Sellafield has to be held to account when its safety procedures are not up to scratch, and when it tries to cover up past mistakes. This paper will continue to subject Sellafield to the utmost scrutiny. But its safety record must be seen in perspective. As far as we know, nobody has died because of Sellafield. Yet every year during this decade about 40 people have died in coal, oil and gas, with barely a footnote in the newspapers or television. Much urgent research remains to be done, of course, on the possibility of any link between radiation leaks at Sellafield and the incidence of forms of cancer in the surrounding area. But even if such a link is ever established it again has to be seen in perspective. All the evidence suggests that, even on the very worst assumptions, nuclear power is far less dangerous to your health than most types of mass-produced energy. Since it is an international industry that Britain happens to be rather good at we should not be in such a rush to destroy it.

Oil and transcontinental pipelines – Alaska

The Alaskan oilfield, discovered in 1968, is the largest in North America. The oil is essential to the economy of the USA and now provides 33 per cent of that country's oil and 12 per cent of its natural gas. However, before the oil could be used, it had to be transported south. Two routes were suggested:

1 By tanker from Prudhoe Bay (Figure 8.34). But the Beaufort Sea is frozen for most of the year; the route is dangerous and would require too many tankers; and the risk of spillage was too great.

2 A pipeline 1300 km southwards to the ice-free port of Valdez (Figure 8.35). This would have to be built in the face of great difficulties and to the satisfaction of a highly organised lobby of conservationists.

The pipeline was selected and opened in 1977.

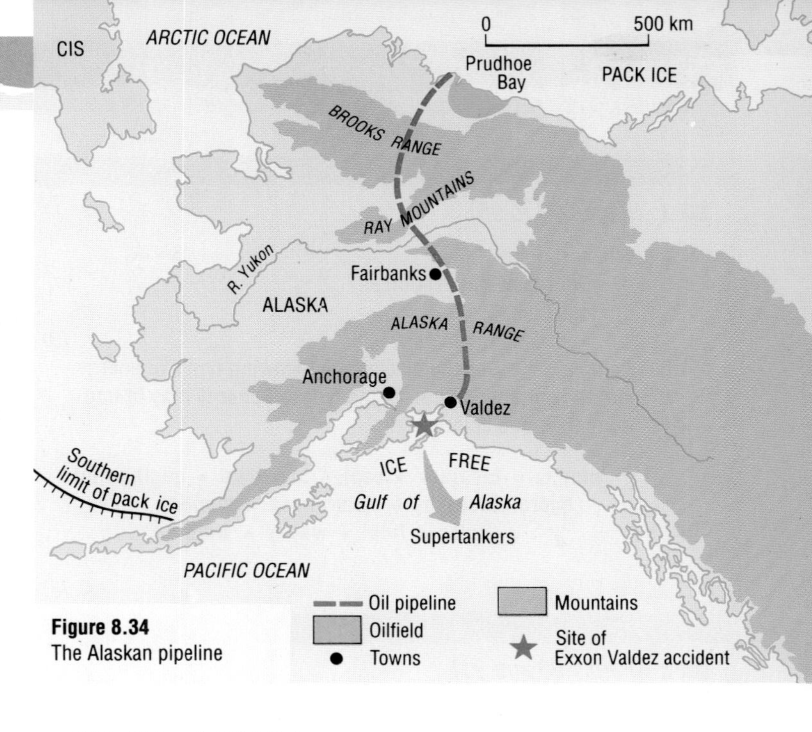

CIS
ARCTIC OCEAN
0
500 km
Prudhoe Bay
PACK ICE
BROOKS RANGE
RAY MOUNTAINS
R. Yukon
Fairbanks
ALASKA
ALASKA RANGE
Anchorage
Valdez
Southern limit of pack ice
ICE FREE
Gulf of Alaska
Supertankers
PACIFIC OCEAN
Oil pipeline
Oilfield
Towns
Mountains
Site of Exxon Valdez accident

Figure 8.34
The Alaskan pipeline

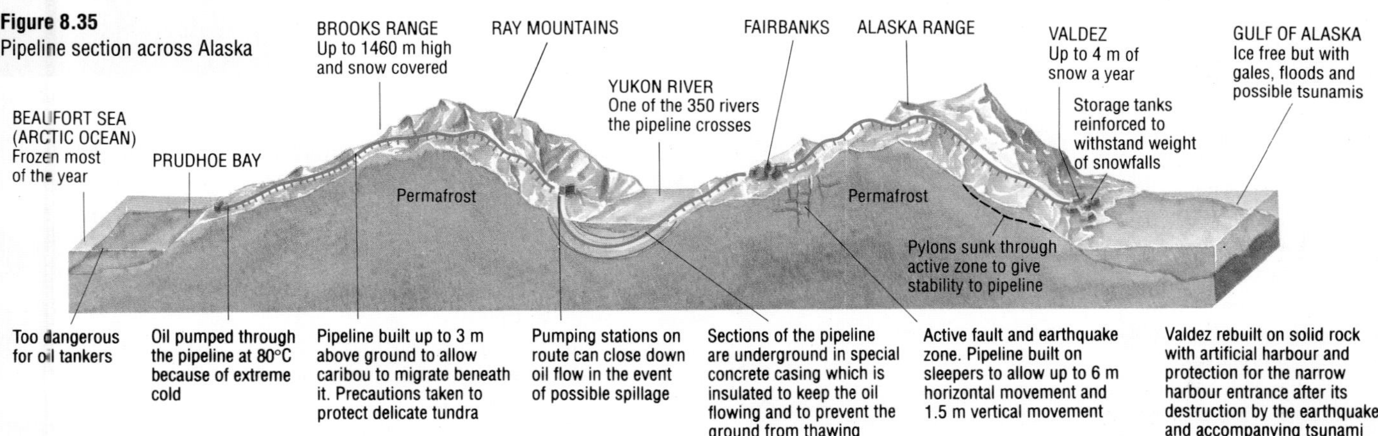

BROOKS RANGE
Up to 1460 m high and snow covered
RAY MOUNTAINS
FAIRBANKS
ALASKA RANGE
VALDEZ
Up to 4 m of snow a year
GULF OF ALASKA
Ice free but with gales, floods and possible tsunamis
YUKON RIVER
One of the 350 rivers the pipeline crosses
Storage tanks reinforced to withstand weight of snowfalls
BEAUFORT SEA (ARCTIC OCEAN)
Frozen most of the year
PRUDHOE BAY
Permafrost
Permafrost
Pylons sunk through active zone to give stability to pipeline
Too dangerous for oil tankers
Oil pumped through the pipeline at 80°C because of extreme cold
Pipeline built up to 3 m above ground to allow caribou to migrate beneath it. Precautions taken to protect delicate tundra
Pumping stations on route can close down oil flow in the event of possible spillage
Sections of the pipeline are underground in special concrete casing which is insulated to keep the oil flowing and to prevent the ground from thawing
Active fault and earthquake zone. Pipeline built on sleepers to allow up to 6 m horizontal movement and 1.5 m vertical movement
Valdez rebuilt on solid rock with artificial harbour and protection for the narrow harbour entrance after its destruction by the earthquake and accompanying tsunami of 1964

Figure 8.35
Pipeline section across Alaska

Threats to the environment included:

- Concern that, once the tundra vegetation was removed, regeneration would be very slow – a fear partly confirmed by some of the destruction caused in the early days of oil exploration.

Figure 8.36
The pipeline cannot pass through the frozen ground; it has to be suspended above Alaskan rivers.

- The pipeline had to cross the caribou migration routes; a problem overcome by raising the pipe on stilts.
- The change to the habitat of foxes, wolves, bears and moose.
- Fears that as the pipeline had to cross an earthquake zone, a major earth movement might break the pipe causing a massive spillage. The oil companies claim that the pipeline is built to bend rather than break. In addition several pumping stations were built to close down sections in the event of any spillage.
- Fears that the storms and tsunamis (tidal waves) in the Gulf of Alaska might cause coastal flooding and, together with fogs, cause a major hazard to oil tankers. The worst of these fears were realised in 1989 when the supertanker 'Exxon Valdez' ran aground and released its contents into Prince William Sound (Figure 8.34). In the worst environmental disaster of its kind many birds, sea otters and fish died, schools of whales and dolphins had to move, and hundreds of kilometres of coastline were covered in black slime.

QUESTIONS

1 *(Pages 90 to 95)*

a What are
i) non-renewable resources?
ii) fossil fuels?
iii) renewable resources? *(3)*

b Complete the table by placing the following types of energy into the correct column. Some types of energy may fit into more than one column:

biogas • biomass • coal • fuelwood • geothermal
hydro-electricity • natural gas • nuclear • oil
solar • tidal • waves • wind

(6)

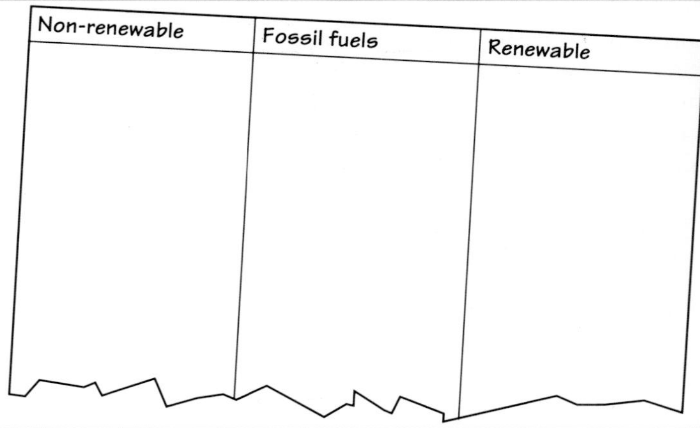

Non-renewable	Fossil fuels	Renewable

2 *(Pages 90 and 91)*

a Give two advantages and two disadvantages of each of the following types of energy:
coal; oil and natural gas; nuclear *(3 x 4)*

b About 2,500 million people, nearly half the world's total, rely on fuelwood as their source of fuel. About 50 per cent of these find difficulty in collecting sufficient fuelwood to cook their daily meal.
i) Name three countries in which most of the inhabitants have to rely upon fuelwood for cooking. *(3)*
ii) Why is fuelwood becoming very scarce in some countries? *(2)*
iii) Give two problems of collecting fuelwood in these countries. *(2)*

3 *(Pages 92 to 94)*

Four types of renewable energy are hydro-electricity, wind, solar and geothermal.

a i) What is hydro-electricity? *(1)*
ii) Draw an annotated (labelled) sketch to show what makes the ideal site for a hydro-electric power station. *(4)*

b The photograph below shows a windfarm and statements linked to the use of wind and the introduction of wind farms.
i) The Central Electricity Generating Board believes wind power to be the most promising source of renewable energy. Give three reasons for this statement. *(3)*
ii) Describe the problems of using wind as a source of energy. *(3)*

c i) What is solar energy? *(1)*
ii) Draw a star diagram to show the advantages of solar energy. *(4)*
iii) What is the disadvantage of solar energy in Britain? *(1)*
iv) Why have so few tropical countries developed solar energy? *(2)*

d i) Draw a simple diagram to show how geothermal energy is obtained. *(4)*
ii) Why is a country like Iceland able to use geothermal power? *(2)*

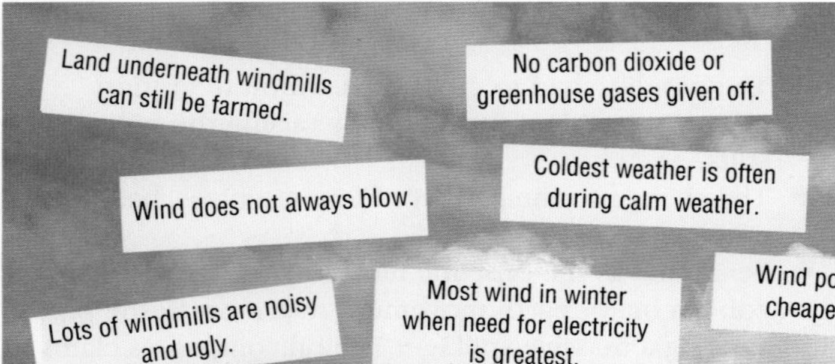

Land underneath windmills can still be farmed.
No carbon dioxide or greenhouse gases given off.
Wind does not always blow.
Coldest weather is often during calm weather.
Lots of windmills are noisy and ugly.
Most wind in winter when need for electricity is greatest.
Wind power is getting cheaper to develop.

4 (Page 96)

a i) Which three countries produced most crude oil in 1990? *(3)*
ii) What percentage of the world's crude oil did they produce? *(1)*
iii) Which was the only European country to be an important oil producer? *(1)*
iv) Describe the two most important routes for the movement of crude oil. *(2)*

b i) Which three countries produced most coal in 1990? *(3)*
ii) What percentage of the world's coal did they produce? *(1)*
iii) Describe the two most important routes for the movement of coal. *(2)*

5 (Page 98)

a i) What percentage of Britain's energy came from fossil fuels in
1. 1960? 2. 1990? *(2)*
ii) Between 1960 and 1990 which fuels increased in importance and which decreased in importance? *(2)*
iii) Which was the main fuel used to produce electricity in 1991? *(1)*

b The graphs below show energy statistics for the EC. Which country
i) Produced most energy?
ii) Produced no energy?
iii) Consumed most energy?
iv) Consumed least energy? *(4)*

c i) Rank in order the five main types of energy produced by the EC in 1990. *(2)*
ii) In which of those types of energy did consumption exceed production? *(2)*

Primary energy production and consumption 1990

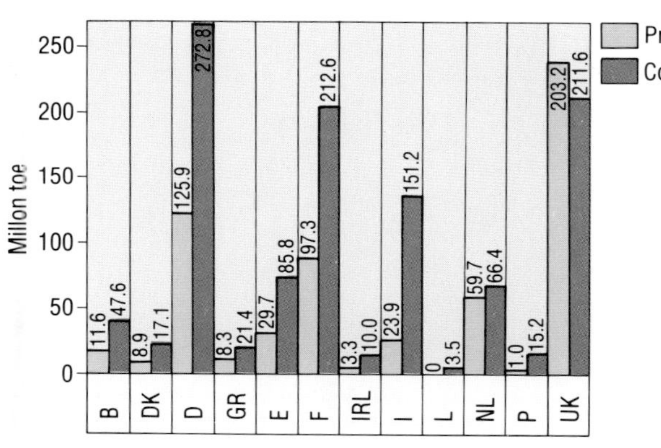

Production and consumption of primary energy EC 1990

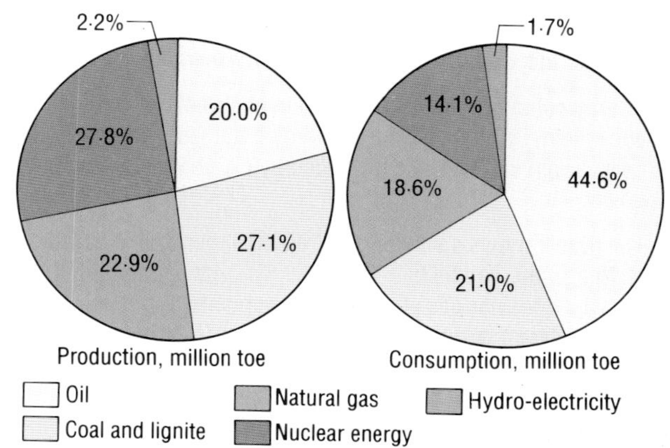

6 (Page 98)

Figure 8.24 shows the location of coal-fired, oil-fired, nuclear and hydro-electric power stations in Britain. For each of the four types of power station

a Give two points to describe their location. *(8)*
b Give two reasons for their location. *(8)*

7 (Page 99)

The following headlines are related to the exploitation of oil in the North Sea. Divide them into the following two lists: *(10)*

a Problems in exploitation.
b Technological improvements.

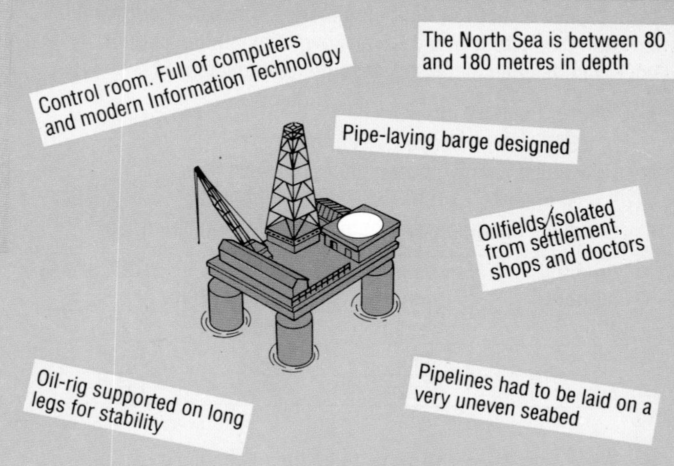

Control room. Full of computers and modern Information Technology
The North Sea is between 80 and 180 metres in depth
Pipe-laying barge designed
Oilfields isolated from settlement, shops and doctors
Oil-rig supported on long legs for stability
Pipelines had to be laid on a very uneven seabed

Severe storms and large waves

Oil discovered a long way from land

Helipad. Helicopters can bring in daily supplies of food and mail. Needed in case of emergencies (storms and illness).

Dangers of explosions and spillages

8 *(Page 100)*

a The growth of Japan's industry depended upon the use of fossil fuels. What percentage of Japan's energy requirements came from fossil fuels in 1992? *(1)*

b Japan has very few deposits of fossil fuels and so has to import large amounts. Name one country from which Japan obtains
i) Coal. ii) Oil. iii) Natural gas. *(3)*

c i) Which type of energy has Japan developed to try to reduce the cost of imports? *(1)*
ii) Why are many Japanese not in favour of this type of energy? *(1)*

d What types of renewable energy are available to Japan? *(3)*

10 Energy and development

The graph attempts to illustrate any link between the wealth of a country and the amount of energy it uses.

GNP (Gross National Product) per capita is the amount of money earned by a country divided by the number of people living in that country. It is expressed in American dollars.

Energy consumption is measured in kilograms of coal (or oil) equivalent, i.e. the amount of energy obtained from a kilogram of coal (or oil) whether it is produced by oil, coal, gas, nuclear power, etc.

The graph shows a scatter of 21 points – hence it is called a *scattergraph.* To this has been added a *best fit line.* Notice that this line does not pass through all the points, but is the line drawn nearest to most of the points. Occasionally one or two points, in this case countries 18 and 21, lie a long way from this best fit line. These are *anomalies* in that they do not fit in with the pattern. If, as in this case, the best fit line goes from bottom left to top right there is a *positive correlation,* i.e. the amount of energy consumed does increase as the GNP increases. If it goes from top left to bottom right then there is a *negative correlation* – for example, here it would have shown that, as the amount of energy consumed increased, then the GNP decreased.

a What is the GNP for
i) USA? ii) Mexico? iii) India? *(3)*

b How much energy is used per person in:
i) Germany? ii) Venezuela? iii) Egypt? *(3)*

c Complete the graph by plotting the following countries:

Country number	Country name	Energy consumption	GNP (US $)
17	Japan	3,800	7,200
15	Italy	3,400	3,800
10	Brazil	800	1,600

(3)

d What does the graph show to be the relationship between energy consumption per head and GNP? *(1)*

e Why do Saudi Arabia (18) and the USA (21) not fit the general pattern? *(2)*

9 *(Page 101)*

The Volta scheme was part of an attempt by Ghana to improve its economy.

a i) Make a good copy of the map below.
ii) In pencil, make the map clearer by lightly shading the water blue, the national boundary red, and the country of Ghana green.
iii) Print the following labels in the correct places:
- ◆ Lake Volta
- ◆ River Volta
- ◆ Accra
- ◆ capital
- ◆ Akosombo dam
- ◆ Tema
- ◆ aluminium smelter

iv) Add a key and title. *(10)*

b i) Briefly describe how Ghana intended to improve its economy. *(2)*
ii) Give five benefits that the scheme has brought to Ghana. *(5)*
iii) Give five problems or disadvantages of the scheme. *(5)*

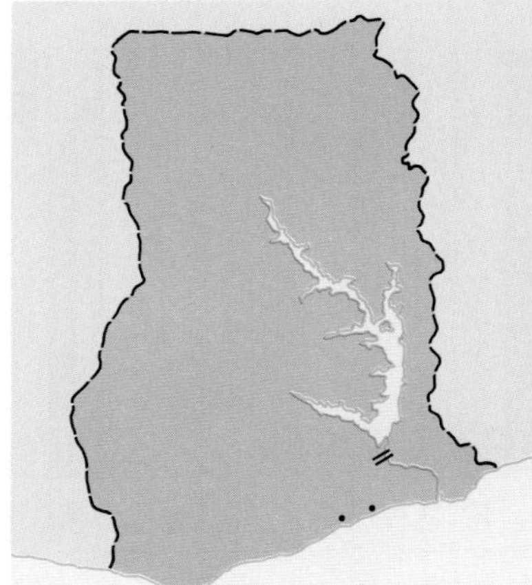

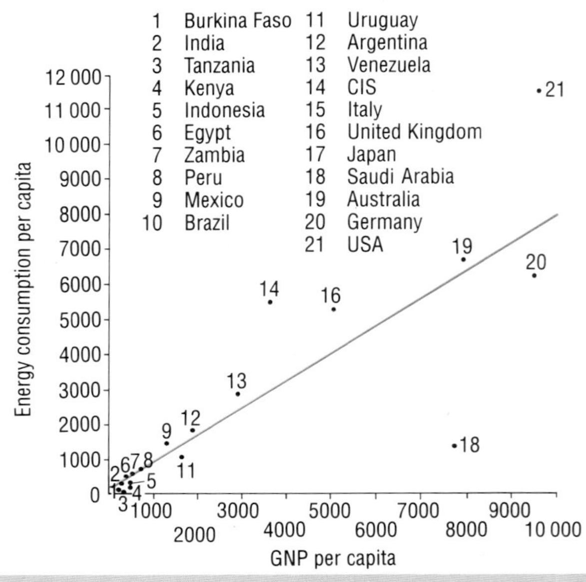

11 *(Page 103)*

a i) Name the oilfield in Alaska. *(1)*
ii) Why is this oilfield important to the USA? *(1)*

b The left column in the table below lists six problems which had to be overcome before oil could be transported from Alaska to the rest of the USA. The right column lists six solutions to these problems. Make a copy of the table matching each problem with the appropriate solution. *(6)*

Problem	Attempted solution
◆ Beaufort Seas frozen for most of the year	◆ Pipeline built on stilts 3 metres above ground
◆ Air temperature down to minus 50°C	◆ Pipelines encased in concrete to reduce ground thawing
◆ Surface thawing and movement in summer	◆ Pipelines on sleepers to allow sideways movement
◆ Pipeline crosses earthquake belt	◆ Oil pumped at 80°C
◆ Pipeline crosses caribou migrating route	◆ Pipelines built across Alaska to ice-free port of Valdez
◆ Underground pipeline may thaw ground	◆ Pylons sunk through active zone to give stability

c The map below shows some of the dangers to oiltankers using the Alaskan port of Valdez. Draw a star diagram to show six dangers to oiltankers using Prince William Sound and the port of Valdez. *(6)*

Columbia and other glaciers melt as they reach the sea. Ice breaks off into icebergs
Prince William Sound sheltered but full of rocky islands and submerged reefs
Earthquake 'destroyed' original port of Valdez in 1964. Danger of flooding from tidal waves
Valdez
Pipeline
ACCIDENT
Prince William Sound
Dangerous narrow outlet into open sea
N
Sea ice
Pipeline
ALASKA
CANADA
Valdez
Area of map
0 500 1000 km
0 50 km
Open sea: subject to severe gales and dense fogs

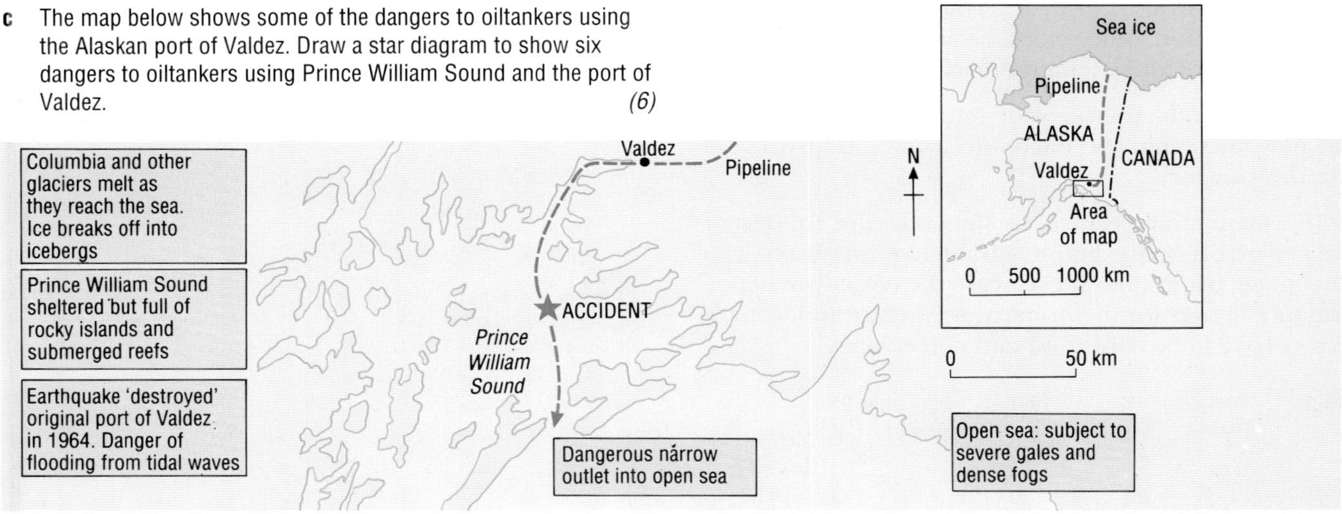

d On 24 May 1989 the fully laden tanker Exxon Valdez ran aground and released its contents into Prince William Sound. With the help of the diagram below describe what effect the accident had upon:
i) fish and sea animals
ii) birds
iii) land animals
iv) plants (vegetation) *(8)*

e The impact of industrial activity such as oil extraction can be very damaging to the environment. Do you think that these activities should go on in difficult and dangerous places like Alaska? Give reasons for and against your answer. *(4)*

Some effects of the oil slick on Prince William Sound

Land animals
Caribou poisoned by eating seaweed. Bears' diet reduced as fewer salmon
Sea otter
Dies because fur coat gets clogged by oil
Birds
Ducks and geese covered in oil. Wading birds can't reach food because of oil on beaches
Fish
Less plankton so less food for herring and salmon
Sunlight
Oil prevents most of sun's light getting through water
Sea mammals
Whales and dolphins driven elsewhere
Oil slick
Water plants
Seaweed becomes poisonous and inedible
Crustacea and molluscs
Shrimps and other small shell fish suffocated by oil
Micro-organisms
Plankton reduced in numbers due to less photosynthesis

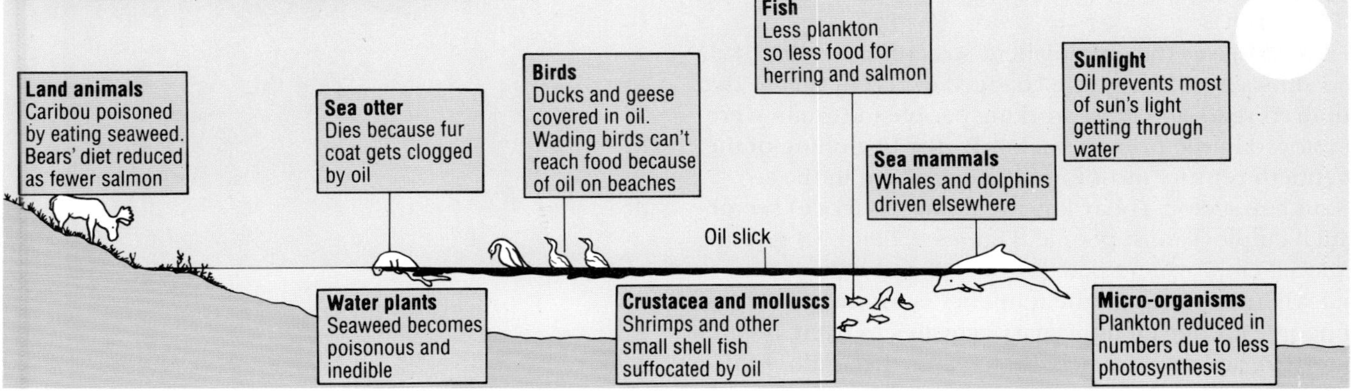

9 INDUSTRY

Employment structures

Classification of industries

Traditionally, industry has been broken down into three groups (primary, secondary and tertiary), although during the 1980s a fourth group was added (quaternary).

Primary industries extract raw materials directly from the earth or sea. Examples are farming, fishing, forestry and mining.

Secondary industries process and manufacture the primary products (e.g. steel, shipbuilding or furniture-making). They include the construction industry and the assembly of components made by other secondary industries.

Tertiary industries provide a service. These include health, education, office work, local and national government, retailing, entertainment and transport.

Quaternary industries provide information and expertise. The new microchip and micro-electronics industries fall into this category.

Employment structures can be shown by three different types of graph – a pie graph, a triangular graph and a percentage bar graph. In each case the employment structure figures for the primary, secondary and tertiary sectors have to be converted into percentages.

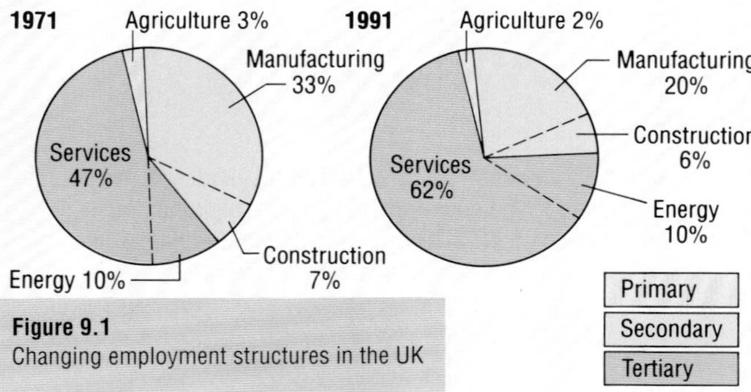

Figure 9.1
Changing employment structures in the UK

I Pie graph

Figure 9.1 gives the employment structures for the UK and shows how these have changed in recent times. Two hundred years ago most working people in Britain were employed in the primary sector. By the beginning of the twentieth century most found employment in the secondary sector. Today it is the tertiary (service) sector which employs most people. Figures 9.2 and 9.3 give the regional employment data for the UK and Italy. Notice that whereas in Britain the tendency is for the percentage of people employed in primary activities to decrease and in tertiary activities to increase towards the south, in Italy the position is reversed. Generally it is those places, either regions or countries, with a higher percentage in tertiary activities which have the higher standard of living.

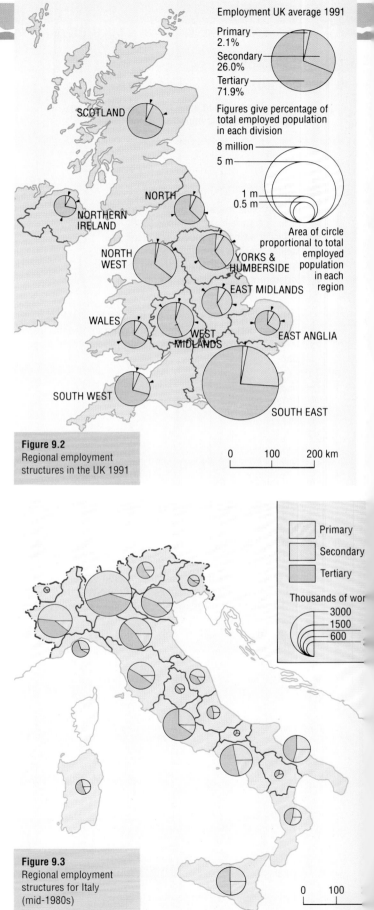

Figure 9.2
Regional employment structures in the UK 1991

Figure 9.3
Regional employment structures for Italy (mid-1980s)

2 Triangular graph

A second method of illustrating the percentages employed in primary, secondary and tertiary industries is to present these three variables on a triangular graph (Figure 9.4). This is an equilateral triangle with each 'base' divided into percentage scales to represent each variable. It may be more convenient, though not essential, to have the sides of the triangle 10 centimetres in length. Figure 9.4 shows how the three variables are plotted for the employment structure of Town A. The figure for primary is found by using the left hand scale (see 'green' graph), for secondary by using the right hand scale (see 'blue' graph) and for tertiary the base (see 'orange' graph). The answer for Town A is given in the table underneath the graph. Complete this table (Figure 9.4) for Towns B and C. These three towns represent, but not necessarily in this order, a small market town, a holiday resort and an industrial town. Which figures do you think fit each letter? Give reasons for your answers.

Figure 9.4
Triangular graphs showing the structure of industry

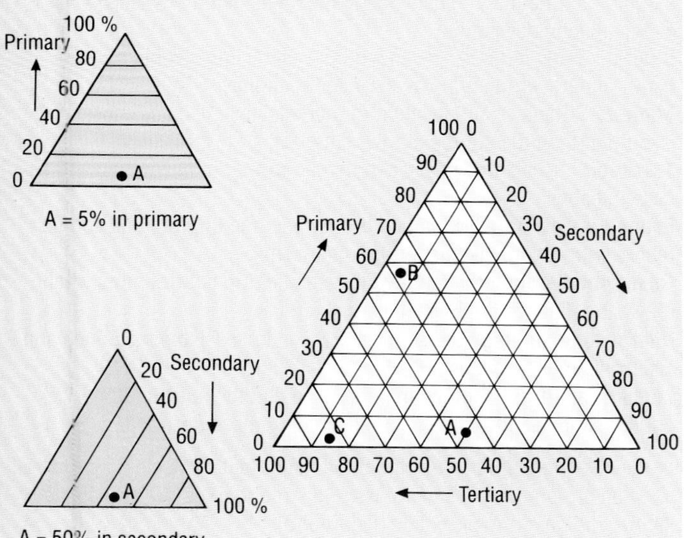

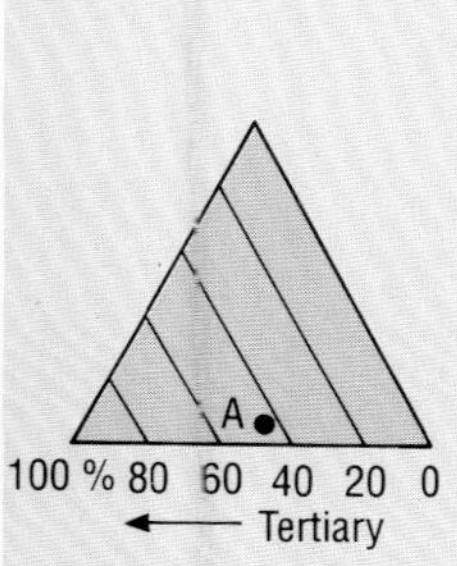

Town	Primary	Secondary	Tertiary
A	5	50	45
B			
C			

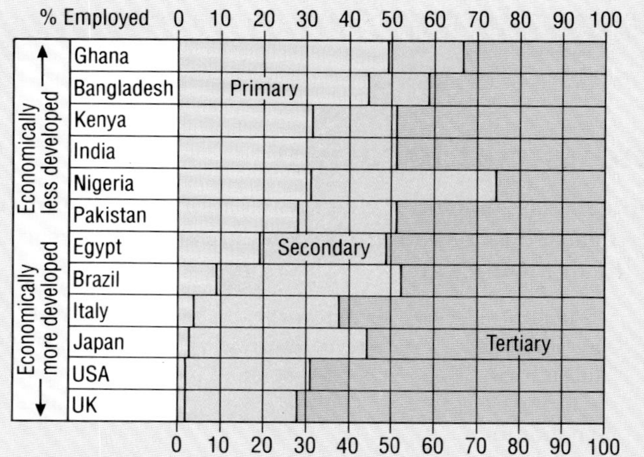

Figure 9.5
Employment structures in economically more and less developed countries

3 Percentage bar graph

Figure 9.5, a percentage bar graph, shows the differences in employment structures between several countries which are at different stages of economic development.

As can be seen, economically less developed countries have a high percentage of their workforce in the primary sector (e.g. Ghana 49 per cent, Bangladesh 45 per cent). Most of these workers will be employed in mining, forestry, fishing or farming, which are all labour intensive. Countries in an early stage of economic development have a concentration in subsistence agriculture (page 71). As countries reach a more intermediate stage of development (e.g. Brazil) and as mechanisation increases, the numbers in primary occupations fall until in an economically more developed country, they are very small. The UK and USA each have a primary activity level of 2 per cent.

Economically less developed countries have a relatively low percentage engaged in secondary industries. This may be due to reasons such as a lack of capital to establish industry, a more limited education system leaving a less skilled workforce, a lack of technological knowledge, a lack of mechanisation, the export of most primary products, a lack of energy supply to operate factories and a limited local market not wealthy enough to buy manufactured goods. At a more intermediate level, the numbers in the secondary sector increase (e.g. Brazil 43 per cent, Nigeria 44 per cent) although there does seem to be a point in development beyond which numbers begin to decrease (e.g. USA 29 per cent).

Economically less developed countries have relatively small numbers in the tertiary sector (e.g. Ghana 34 per cent, Nigeria 25 per cent) due to limited developments in education, health, commerce, transport, recreation and tourism. In the economically more developed countries the numbers employed in service industries are greater than in both the primary and secondary industries combined (e.g. UK 72 per cent, USA 69 per cent).

Industrial location

Industry as a whole, or a factory as an individual unit, can be regarded as a system. This system can be represented in the following way:

Input	➡	**Factory**	➡	**Output**
(Raw materials and human input) Expenditure		(Manufacturing processes)		(End products) Income

In this model, output (income) minus input (expenditure) will give the industry a profit or a loss. For a firm to remain profitable, some of the income must be re-invested to modernise the factory.

Before building a factory, the manufacturer should consider the major elements in the system diagram. It is unlikely that the manufacturer will find all the elements available at one site. A decision must be made as to which site has the greatest advantages.

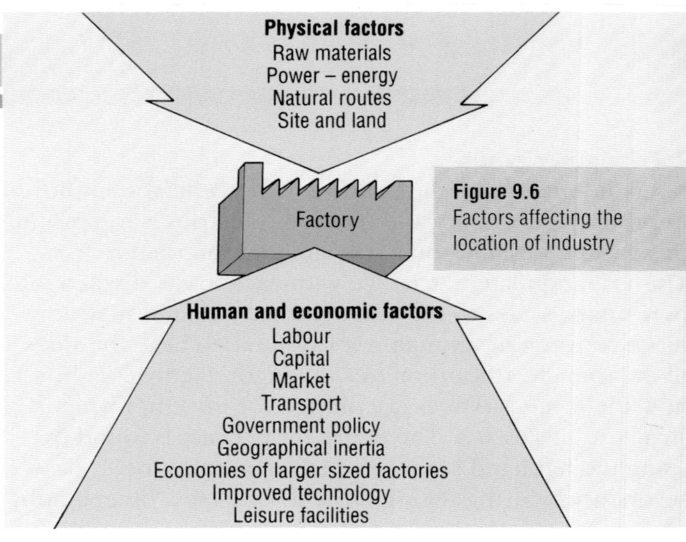

Figure 9.6 Factors affecting the location of industry

Where many sites are available, the firm or company will choose the most profitable one. This will be the site where the costs of raw materials, fuel and power, labour, land and transport are minimised, and where there is a large market for the product. These factors are summarised in Figure 9.6 where they have been divided into (a) physical factors and (b) human and economic factors.

(a) **Physical factors**

Raw materials The bulkier and heavier these are to transport, the nearer the factory should be located to the raw materials. This was even more important in times when transport was less developed.

Power – energy This is needed to work the machines in the factory. Early industry needed to be sited near to fast-flowing rivers or coal reserves, but today electricity can be transported long distances.

Natural routes River valleys and flat areas were essential in the days before the railway, car or lorry.

Site and land Although early industry did not at first take up much land, it did need flat land. As the size of plant increased (e.g. steelworks), more land was needed. Ideally such sites should be on low quality farmland where the cost of purchase is lower. Last century many sites were in today's 'inner city' areas whereas now they tend to be on edge-of-city 'greenfield' locations.

In the nineteenth century it was physical factors such as the source of raw materials (e.g. iron ore) and sources of energy (e.g. coal) which determined industrial locations

(b) **Human and economic factors**

Labour This includes both quantity (large numbers in nineteenth century factories) and quality (as some areas demand special skills as technology develops).

Capital Early industry depended on wealthy entrepreneurs. Now banks and governments may provide the money.

Markets The size and location of markets have become more important than the source of raw materials.

Transport Costs increase when items moved are bulky, fragile, heavy or perishable.

Economies of scale Small units may become unprofitable and so merge with, or are taken over by, other firms.

Government policies As governments tend to control most wealth, they can influence industrial location.

Improved technology Examples are Facsimile ('Fax') machines and electronic mail.

Leisure facilities Both within the town and the surrounding countryside, leisure activities are becoming more desirable.

In the late twentieth century the three major factors deciding industrial location are possibly the nearness to a large market, the availability of labour and government policy (Figure 9.8).

Figure 9.7 Shipyard on the Clyde in the early 1920s

Figure 9.8 New industry at Woodlands, Bristol

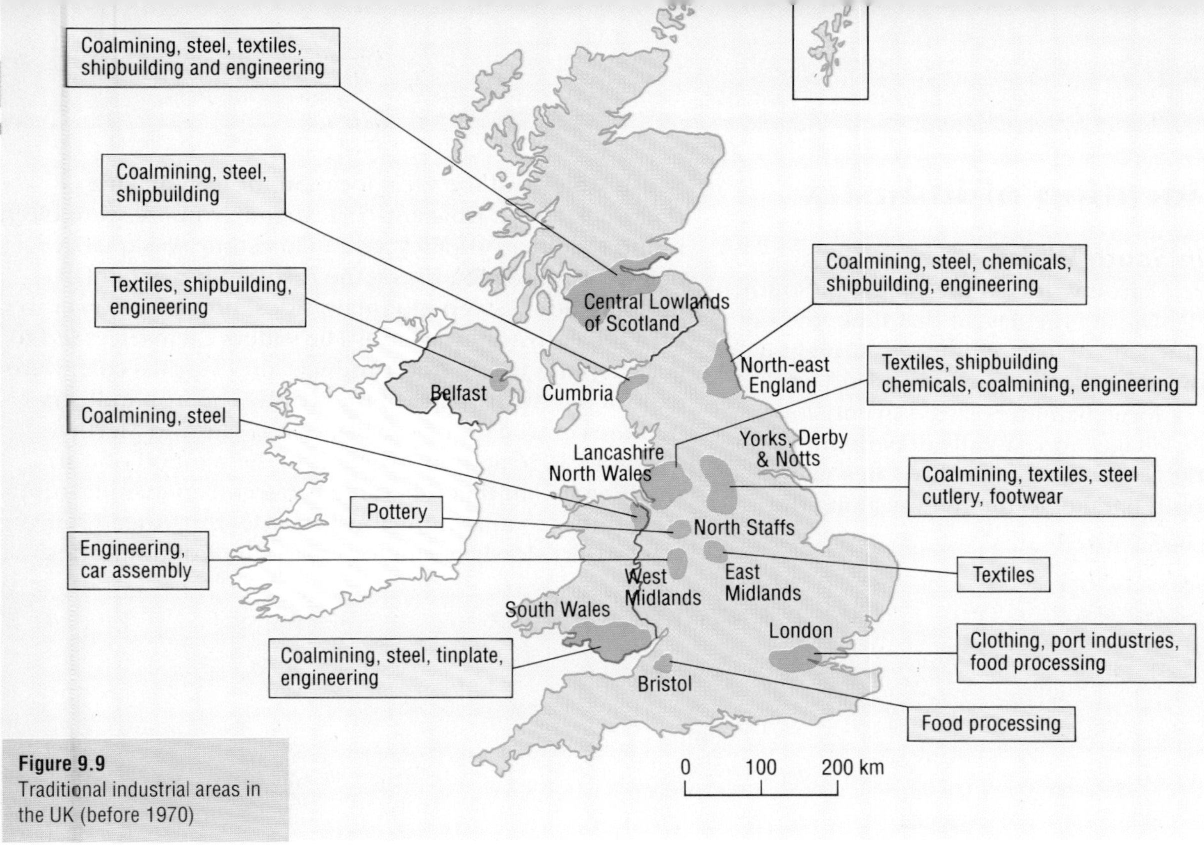

Coalmining, steel, textiles, shipbuilding and engineering
Coalmining, steel, shipbuilding
Textiles, shipbuilding, engineering
Coalmining, steel
Pottery
Engineering, car assembly
Coalmining, steel, tinplate, engineering
Central Lowlands of Scotland
Belfast
Cumbria
Lancashire North Wales
North Staffs
West Midlands
South Wales
Bristol
North-east England
Yorks, Derby & Notts
East Midlands
London
Coalmining, steel, chemicals, shipbuilding, engineering
Textiles, shipbuilding chemicals, coalmining, engineering
Coalmining, textiles, steel cutlery, footwear
Textiles
Clothing, port industries, food processing
Food processing
0 100 200 km

Figure 9.9
Traditional industrial areas in the UK (before 1970)

Distribution of industry in the UK

Figure 9.9 shows the location and distribution of Britain's traditional, heavy industry. Most of these industries were established in the nineteenth century. Their growth was based upon the use of coal, the creativity of the people, the development of technology to process imported raw materials, and the ability to export manufactured goods. Consequently the major industrial areas were either on Britain's coalfields or in coastal ports located on deep-water estuaries. The location, importance and type of Britain's present day manufacturing industry have changed considerably. Coalmines began to close in the 1920s, textile mills in the 1960s, shipyards in the 1970s, and steelworks and car assembly plants in the 1980s. The relatively few new industries, mainly high-technology and electronics, are fewer in number and are often located well away from the traditional areas (Figure 9.10).

Location quotient

The *location quotient* (LQ) measures the concentration of a specific industry. It shows whether an industry is spread out evenly across all the regions of a country or whether it is concentrated within a few parts of that country. The LQ is found by comparing the proportion of workers in an industry in one part of a country with the proportion of workers in that industry for the country as a whole. For example, textiles employ 5.33 per cent of Britain's working population. The corresponding figures for the East Midlands and East Anglia are 16.0 per cent and 1.4 per cent respectively. This means that the LQ for:

i) East Midlands is

$$\frac{16.0}{5.33} = 3.00$$

ii) East Anglia is

$$\frac{1.4}{5.33} = 0.26$$

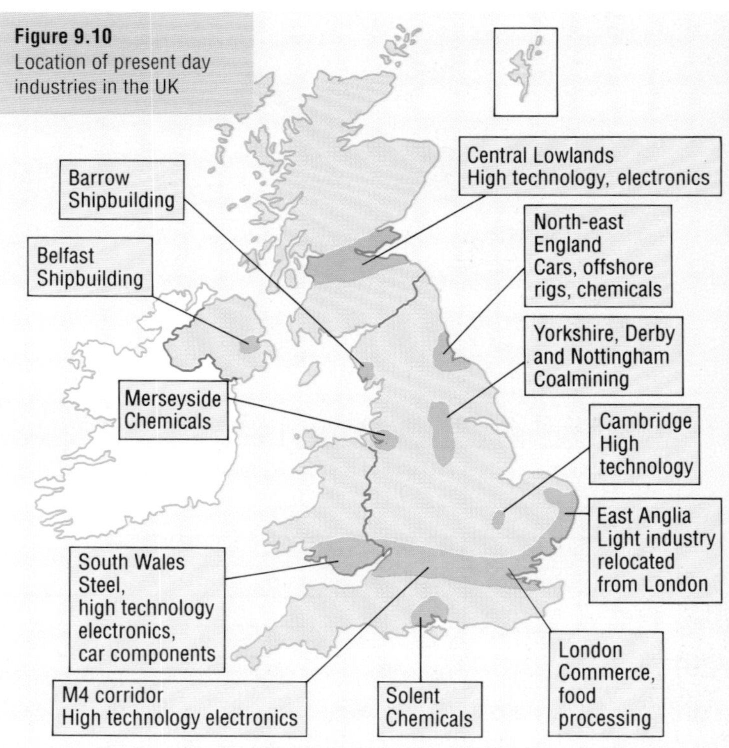

Figure 9.10
Location of present day industries in the UK

Barrow Shipbuilding
Belfast Shipbuilding
Merseyside Chemicals
South Wales Steel, high technology electronics, car components
M4 corridor High technology electronics
Solent Chemicals
Central Lowlands High technology, electronics
North-east England Cars, offshore rigs, chemicals
Yorkshire, Derby and Nottingham Coalmining
Cambridge High technology
East Anglia Light industry relocated from London
London Commerce, food processing

If an industry was spread evenly across a country it would have an LQ of 1.00. The higher the LQ above 1.00 the greater the concentration of that industry in a region (e.g. textiles in the East Midlands). Where the LQ is below 1.00 it means that the industry is not concentrated in that region (e.g. textiles in East Anglia). Britain's older, heavier industries tended to be more concentrated; the newer, lighter industries tend to be more dispersed.

Changing location of industry

Iron and steel in South Wales

In 1860 there were 35 iron works in the valleys of South Wales (Figure 9.11). During the day, at that time, the sky was blackened by the smoke from chimneys. At night it turned red from the glare of the many furnaces. The shuddering noise of forge hammers lasted twenty-four hours a day. Whole villages were totally dependent upon the local iron works. Their inhabitants lived in small terraced houses, built parallel to the railway along the valley floor in a linear pattern.

South Wales had the ideal location for iron making (Figure 9.12(a)). Coal and 'blackband' iron ore were often found together on valley sides. Limestone was quarried nearby. Fast flowing rivers, the result of heavy rainfall draining down steep mountain sides, provided power to turn the early water wheels. The valleys themselves led to coastal ports where iron products, and surplus coal, were exported to many parts of the world. The iron industry became centred on places like Ebbw Vale and Merthyr Tydfil. In 1856 an improvement in the method of iron smelting meant that it became economic to manufacture steel rather than the previously brittle iron. After 1860, steel works slowly began to replace the iron foundries.

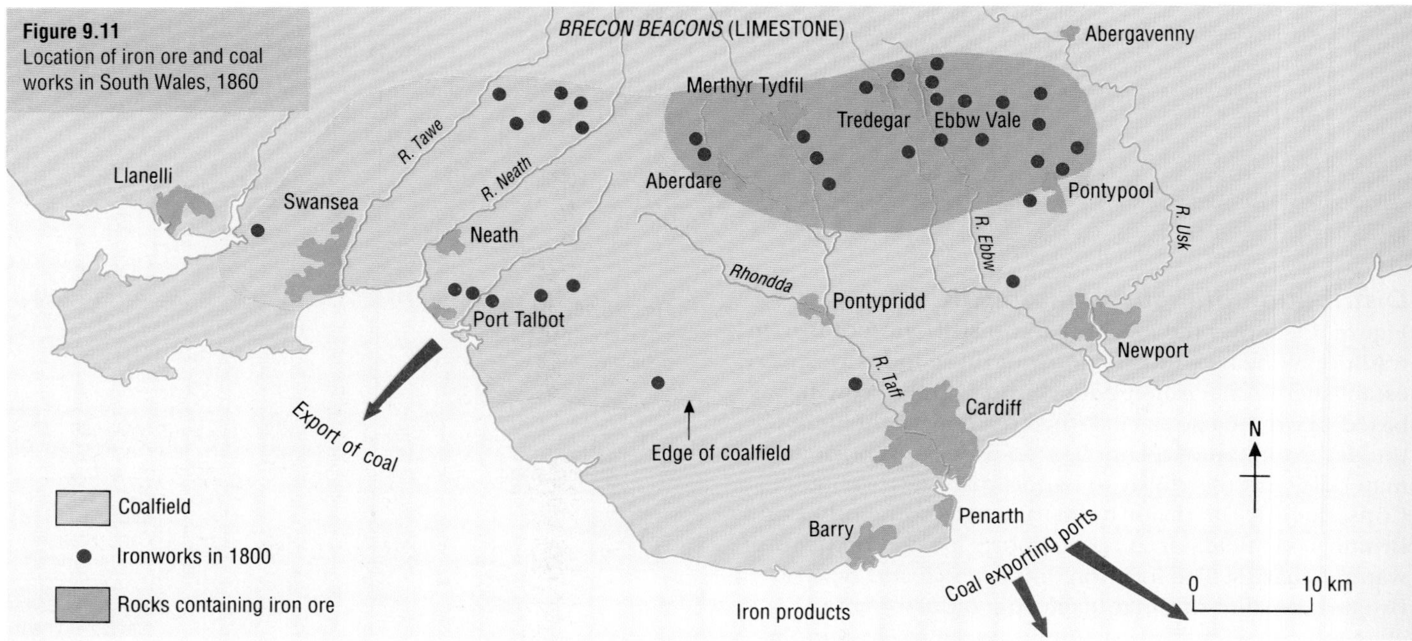

Figure 9.11 Location of iron ore and coal works in South Wales, 1860

Figure 9.12 Changing reasons for location of iron industry in South Wales

Period of time		(a) Location of early 19th century foundries in South Wales (e.g. Ebbw Vale)	(b) Location of integrated steelworks of the 1990s at Port Talbot and Llanwern (Newport)
Physical			
Raw Materials	Coal	Mined locally in valleys	Only one coal mine open, most of coal imported
	Iron ore	Found within the coal measures	Imported from North Africa and North America
	Limestone	Found locally	Found locally
	Water	For power and effluent – local rivers	For cooling – coastal site
Energy – fuel		Charcoal for early smelting, later rivers to drive machinery and then coal	Electricity from national grid (using coal, oil,. natural gas and nuclear)
Natural routes		Materials mainly on hand. 'Export' routes via the valleys	Coastal sites
Site and land		Small valley floor locations	Large areas of flat, low capacity farmland
Human and economic			
Labour		Large numbers of unskilled labour	Still relatively large numbers but with a higher level of skill. Fewer due to high tech
Capital		Local entrepreneurs	Government. E.C.
Markets		Local	The car industry
Transport		Little needed, some canals	M4. Purpose-built ports
Geographical inertia		Not applicable	Tradition of high quality goods
Economies of scale		Not applicable	Two large steelworks more economical than numerous small iron foundries
Government policy			Having the capital they can determine locations and closures
Technology		Small scale – mainly manual	High technology – computers, lasers etc.

By the 1990s there were only two steelworks left in Wales. These were not, however, located in the valleys but on the coast at Port Talbot and Llanwern (Figure 9.13). This was because many of the initial advantages of the area for steel-making had disappeared (Figure 9.12(b)). By 1993 only one coal mine remained open in the area, while high quality iron ore deposits had long since been exhausted. As both of these raw materials had now to be imported, it was logical to build any modern steelworks on the coast at a *break of bulk* location. Break of bulk is when a transported product has to be transferred from one form of transport to another – a process which takes up time and money. It was easier, therefore to have the steelworks where the raw materials were unloaded, rather than transporting the coal and iron ore to the older, inland works.

Port Talbot, Figure 9.14, has its own harbour and docks for the import of coal and iron ore. These are, with limestone, fed into a blast furnace where the iron ore is smelted and most of the impurities are removed. This produces pig iron to which oxygen is later added. Oxygen reduces the carbon content to give steel. The introduction of the oxygen furnace has reduced the amount of coal needed. The steel is then usually rolled into thin sheets which may be used to make, among other things, car bodies. Port Talbot is one of Britain's four remaining integrated steelworks each using advanced technology. An *integrated works* is where all the stages in the manufacture of steel take place on the same site. The decision to locate at Port Talbot was made by the British government. Whether the works remain open or not is likely to depend on an EC decision. Market demand and government decisions are now more important than nineteenth century natural physical advantages.

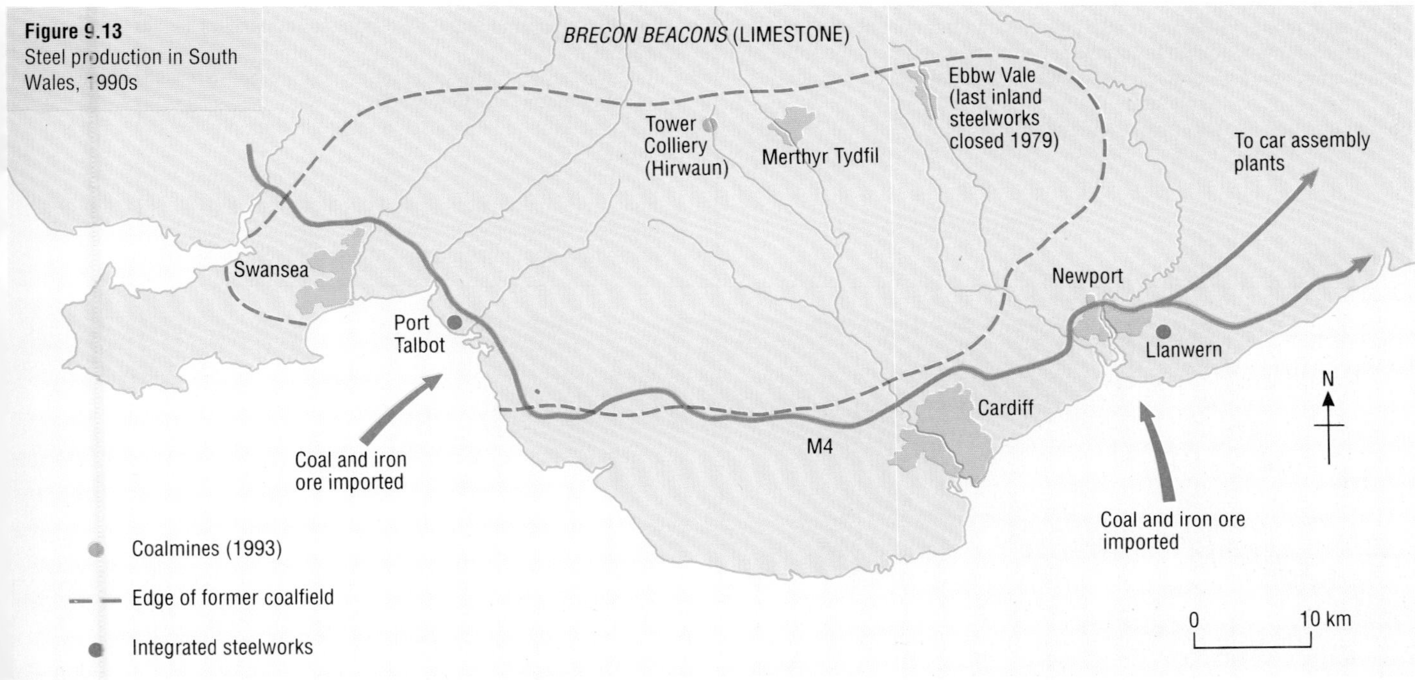

Figure 9.13
Steel production in South Wales, 1990s

Figure 9.14
Port Talbot steelworks

Changing industrial locations

Nineteenth century industry

When the Industrial Revolution began in Britain in the early nineteenth century most towns were still relatively small in size. As new industries grew, so too did the demand for workers. As people moved in increasingly large numbers from rural areas to the towns for work, they needed houses in which to live. As, at that time, there was neither public nor private transport, people wanted to live as close as possible to their place of work. More and more factories and houses were built on what were then edge-of-town sites. Since then these early industries and older houses have been surrounded by newer buildings. As a result these original growth areas are now referred to as Britain's 'old inner cities'. Until fairly recently many industries still found several advantages in having an inner city location (Figure 9.15(a)).

The present day needs of industry, and people, are very different to those of nearly two hundred years ago. Many of the early advantages of an inner city location have now become disadvantages (Figure 9.15(b) and 9.16). Modern industry finds it more beneficial to move from these inner city areas to new 'edge-of-city, greenfield sites'.

a Advantages of an inner city location	**b** Disadvantages of an inner city location
◆ Houses and factories were close together so that workers did not have far to walk to work. ◆ Poorly paid factory workers could afford the low cost terraced housing. ◆ Nearby railways (after the 1840s) and, often, a canal were needed to transport the heavy and bulky raw materials and manufactured goods. ◆ Nearby rivers and canals provided water for washing and cooling, and a means of disposing of waste. ◆ Near to jobs and shops in the town centre.	◆ Cramped sites had little or no room for expansion. ◆ Old out-dated nineteenth century buildings and services made firms less efficient. ◆ Competition for land near to CBD increased land values and therefore rates and rent. ◆ Traffic congestion increased as the narrow, unplanned roads were built before the invention of the car and lorry. ◆ Labour tends to be unskilled or, as people move out of the area, in short supply. ◆ Higher than average levels of noise, air and visual pollution. Many properties have either been pulled down or left derelict. Some parts may have been redeveloped, others left as wasteland. ◆ People have been forced to move due to redevelopment schemes.

Figure 9.15

Figure 9.16
Nineteenth century industries located near the centre of town

Edge-of-city locations and footloose industries

The term *footloose* is applied to those firms which have a relatively free choice of location. Many of these newer industries provide services for people and are therefore market orientated. The raw materials are often component goods made elsewhere, and the finished product is usually light and easily transportable by road or air.

Location

Two prime sites for these footloose industries are:

1 On large trading or industrial estates built on former greenfield sites on the edges of towns and cities (Figure 9.17).

2 Alongside major motorways to capitalise upon efficient transport links (e.g. M4 in Figure 9.19).

Advantages of an edge-of-city location (Figure 9.17)

- Cheaper land values away from the CBD as competition for land is lower near to the city boundary (lower rents and rates).
- Ample space for the construction of large buildings, car parks and lorry unloading bays, together with room for possible future expansion.
- Well planned, modern estates, often with local roads, services and factory units built in advance.
- A good internal road system linked by main roads to motorway intersections.
- Adjacent to modern, suburban housing estates, both private and council, as well as access to commuter villages which provide a local labour force – an increasing proportion of which is female.
- A pleasant working environment. These new industries give off very little air or noise pollution.
- Access to urban markets.

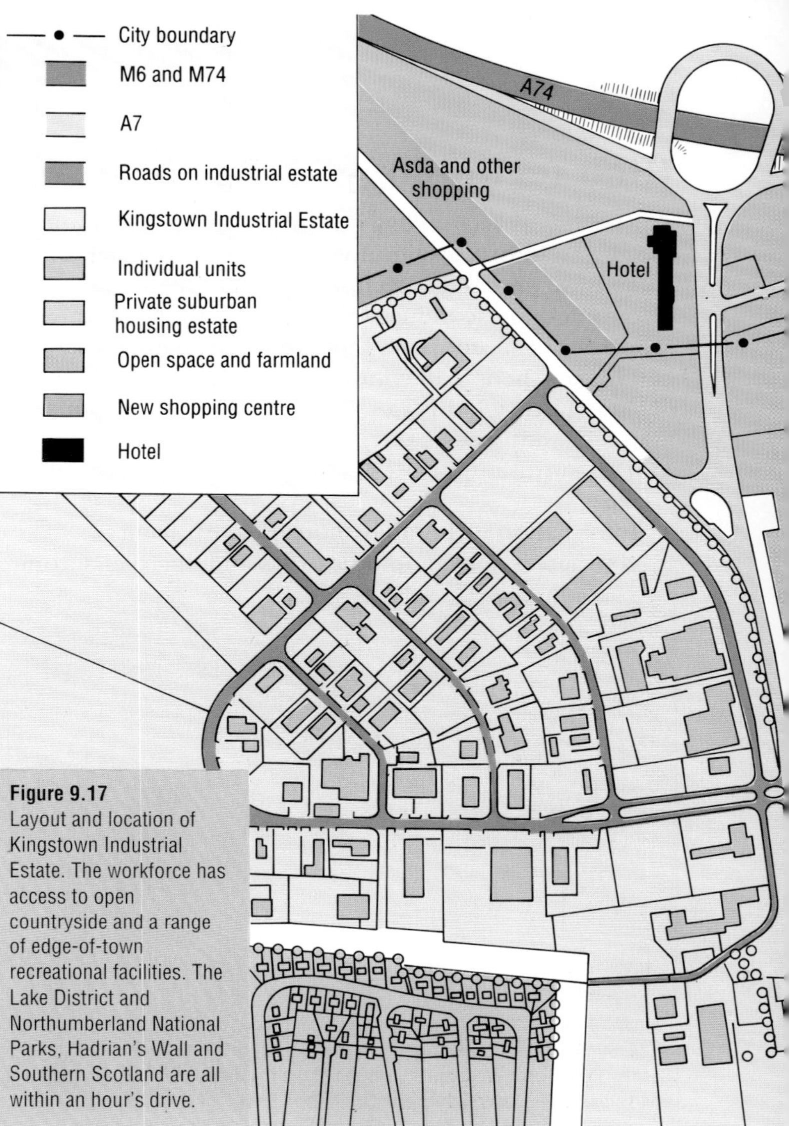

Figure 9.17 Layout and location of Kingstown Industrial Estate. The workforce has access to open countryside and a range of edge-of-town recreational facilities. The Lake District and Northumberland National Parks, Hadrian's Wall and Southern Scotland are all within an hour's drive.

Figure 9.18 The layout of Euroway Industrial Estate, Swindon

Layout of estates (Figure 9.18)

- Roads are usually wide and straight, or gently curving, to allow easy access and turning for large delivery lorries.
- Each factory unit is in its own relatively large area of land with room for expansion, and has its own car and lorry park.
- Some vacant sites have been designated to try to attract firms in future years.

Types of firm

- Distributive firms which can warehouse their goods either for dispatch by motorways to other parts of the country or for later delivery to the CBD (e.g. food, drink, car parts).
- Food processing firms.
- Light, small scale, manufacturing industries.
- High technology firms.
- The more recent addition of offices, hotels and hypermarkets (Figure 9.17).

The demand for leisure and social activities is now an important consideration in locating new firms.

High technology industries

The term *high technology industry* (or high-tech) refers, usually, to industries developed within the last 25 years and whose processing techniques often involve micro-electronics. These industries have been the 'growth' industries of recent years though unfortunately they employ few people in comparison with the older, declining heavy industries. Two possible subdivisions of high-tech industries are:

1 The 'sunrise industries' which have a high technology base.
2 Information technology industries involving computers, telecommunications and micro-electronics.

As a highly skilled, inventive, intelligent workforce is essential, and as access to raw materials is relatively unimportant, these high-tech footloose industries tend to become attracted to areas which the researchers and operators find attractive – from a climatic, scenic, health and social point of view. Such areas include:

- Silicon Glen in central Scotland.
- Silicon Valley in California.
- Sunrise Strip which follows the route of the M4 from London westwards towards Newbury (locally known as Video Valley), Bristol (Aztec West) and into South Wales (Figure 9.19).

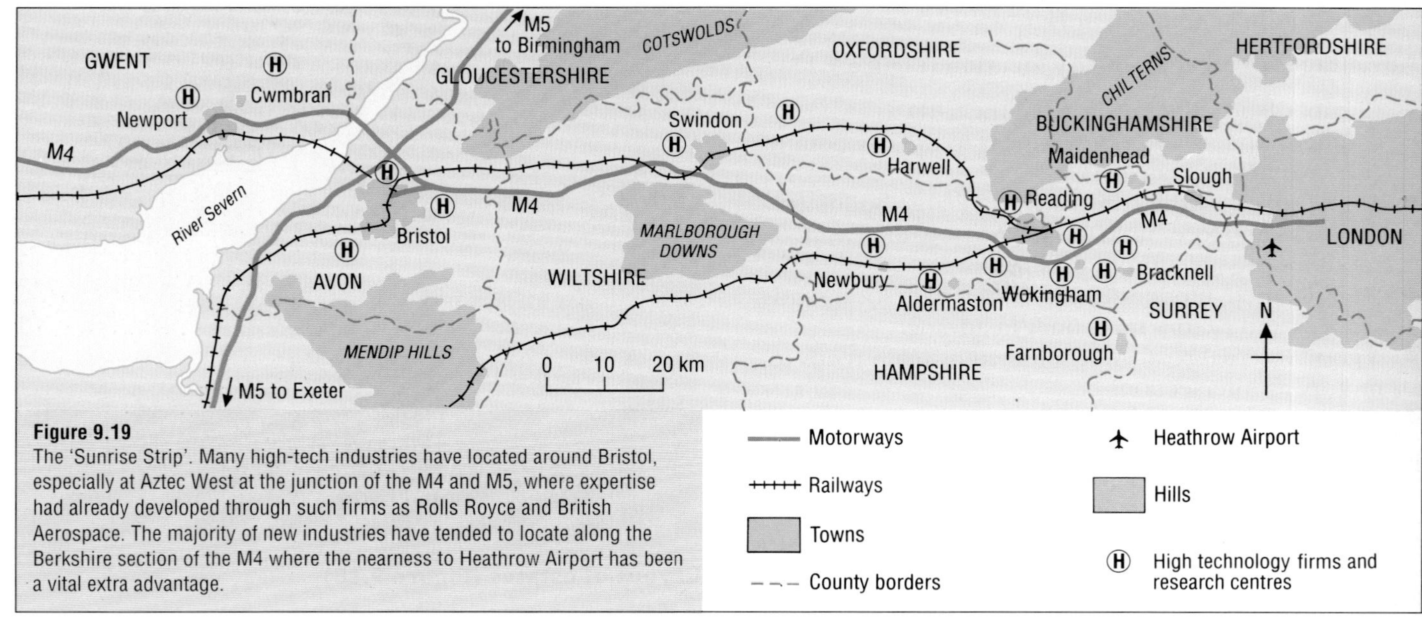

Figure 9.19
The 'Sunrise Strip'. Many high-tech industries have located around Bristol, especially at Aztec West at the junction of the M4 and M5, where expertise had already developed through such firms as Rolls Royce and British Aerospace. The majority of new industries have tended to locate along the Berkshire section of the M4 where the nearness to Heathrow Airport has been a vital extra advantage.

Figure 9.20
Windmill Hill Business Park, Swindon. In all, three large business parks have been developed, each offering facilities and accommodation in a landscaped, parkland environment.

Sunrise Strip

The advantages of this area for spontaneous, unplanned growth of micro-electronics industries include:

- The proximity of the M4 and main line railways.
- The presence of Heathrow airport.
- The previous location and existence of government and other research centres.
- A large labour force, many of whom have moved out of London into new towns and overspill towns.
- The proximity of other associated industries with which ideas and information can be exchanged.
- Nearness to universities with expertise and research facilities available. A science park is located near to a university so that high-tech firms can work closely with that campus.
- An attractive environment. Figure 9.19 names the Cotswolds, Mendips, Chilterns and Marlborough Downs. Nearby are the North Downs, three National Parks (Brecon Beacons, Dartmoor and Exmoor) and, through the centre of the area, the Thames Valley.

Business and science parks

Most business parks have grown up on edge-of-city greenfield sites, the remainder as part of inner city redevelopment schemes. The major attractions of greenfield sites are the relative low cost of land and a pleasant working environment with a low density of buildings. Usually over 70 per cent of the land in business parks is left under grass and trees or converted into ornamental gardens and lakes (Figures 9.20 and 9.21). Business parks form an ideal location for high-tech industries such as electronics, and research institutions. Science parks are similar but with the addition of direct links with universities (Figure 9.22). Some business parks include offices, hypermarkets and leisure complexes.

Why do similar industries locate together?

By locating near to each other, high-tech firms have the advantages of being able to exchange ideas and information with neighbouring companies, sharing maintenance and support services, sharing basic amenities such as connecting roads, and building up a pool of highly skilled, increasingly female labour.

Figure 9.21
Tsukuba Science City

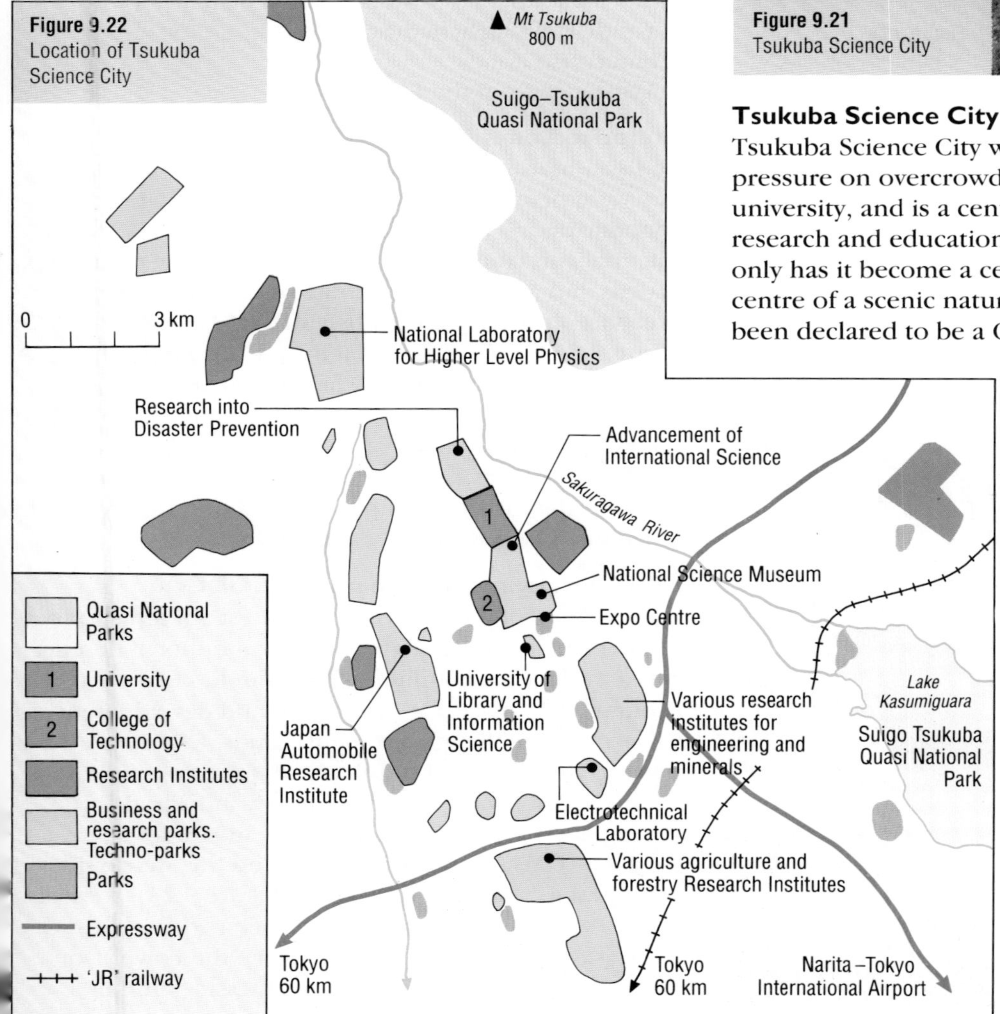

Figure 9.22
Location of Tsukuba Science City

Tsukuba Science City

Tsukuba Science City was specifically created to relieve pressure on overcrowded, overexpensive Tokyo. It has a university, and is a centre for many public and private research and educational institutions (Figure 9.22). Not only has it become a centre of science, it is also in the centre of a scenic natural environment, part of which has been declared to be a Quasi National Park.

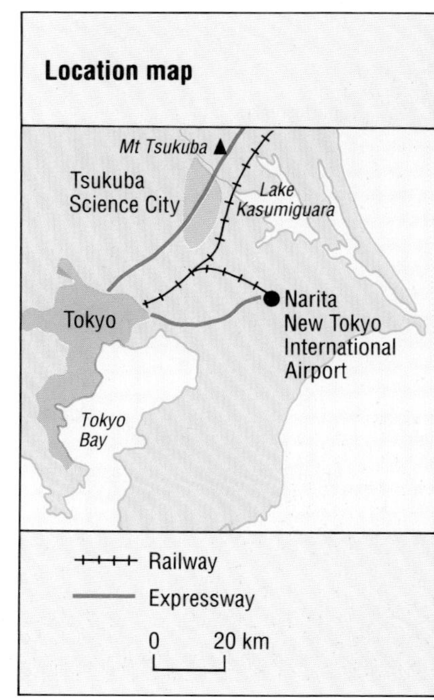

Government aid

I In the UK

Successive British governments have tried, since 1945, to encourage industry to move to areas of high unemployment. The size and location of these areas of high unemployment has changed over time. Figure 9.24 shows the areas which were regarded as needing the most assistance in 1993. Over the years governments have tried to encourage new industries to reduce unemployment by:

- Industrial development certificates which control where a firm can locate. These were first issued by the British government in 1947.
- The creation of new towns in order to take work to the unemployed.
- Providing 'advanced factories' and industrial estates with services already present (e.g. roads, electricity).
- Financial aid in the form of removal grants, rent-free periods, tax relief on new machinery, and reduced interest rates.

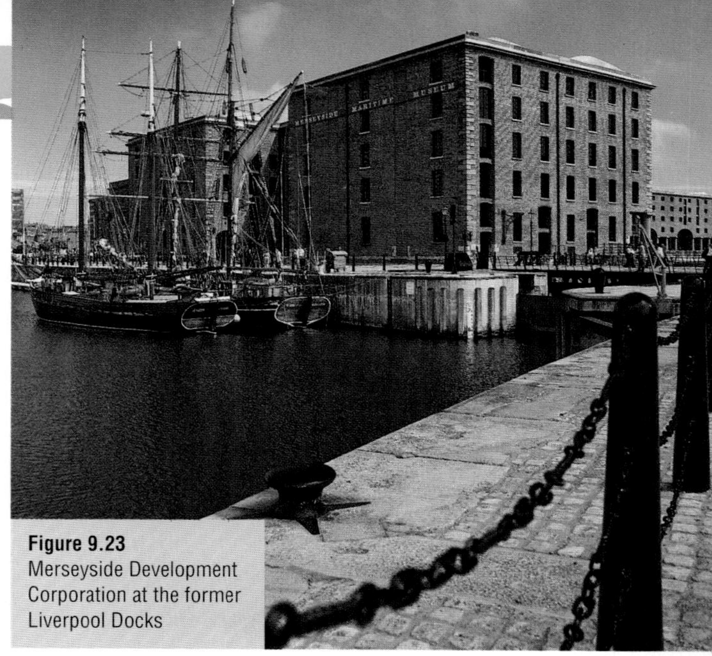
Figure 9.23
Merseyside Development Corporation at the former Liverpool Docks

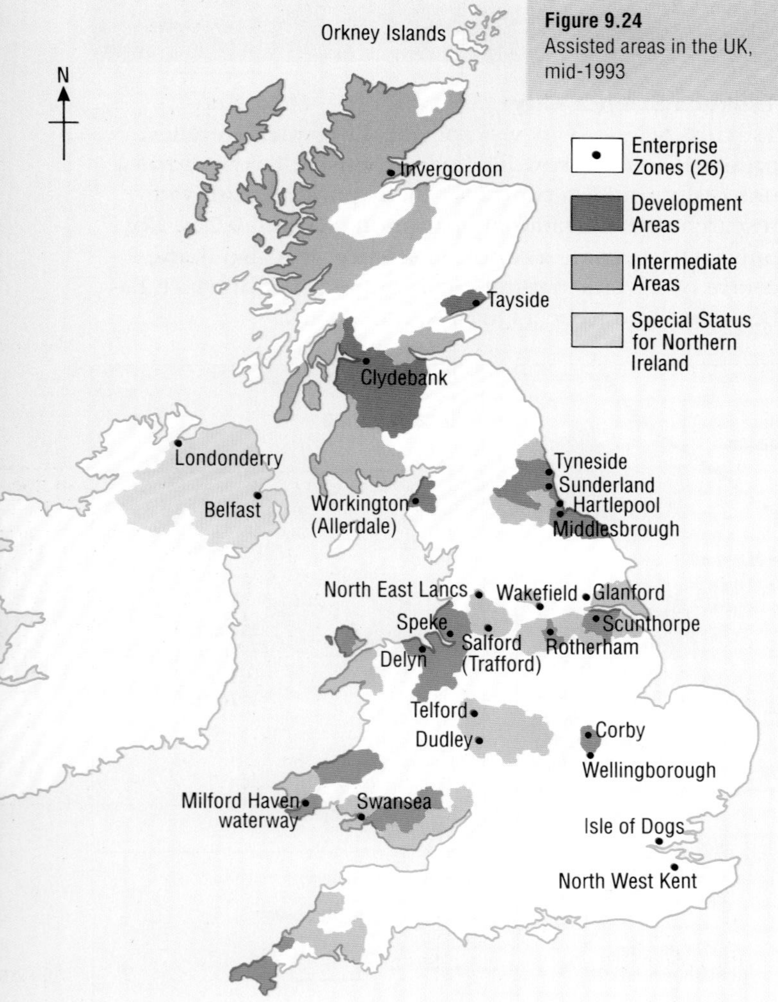

Figure 9.24
Assisted areas in the UK, mid-1993

- Decentralising government offices.
- Improving communications and accessibility.
- Subsidies to keep firms going which otherwise would close down.
- Retraining schemes.
- Job Creation, Manpower Creation Schemes (MCS) and Youth Training Schemes (YTS).
- Enterprise Zones.
- Assistance from the EC.

Enterprise Zones (EZs)

The first Enterprise Zones came into operation in 1981. They were planned for areas in acute physical and economic decay, with the aim of creating conditions for industrial and commercial revival by removing certain tax burdens and administrative controls. Initially eleven Enterprise Zones were established. By 1993 there were 26 (Figure 9.24). They tend to fall into two main groups:

1 Old inner city areas where factories had closed, causing high unemployment, and where old houses had been pulled down and the land left derelict, e.g. Isle of Dogs (pages 132 and 133).
2 Towns that had relied upon one major industry which had been forced to close, e.g. Corby.

Urban Development Corporations (UDCs)

These are one of the government's latest attempts to try to rejuvenate areas which have large amounts of derelict or unused land and buildings. One aim has been to encourage private sector investment and development as well as using public (government) funds. UDCs have power to purchase and reclaim land, to restore buildings to effective use, and to encourage new industrial and housing developments. The first two, in London's Dockland (LDDC – pages 132–133) and the Merseyside Development Corporation (MDC – Figure 9.23), were set up in 1981. Since 1986 others have been created in such places as Salford (Greater Manchester), the Lower Don Valley (Sheffield), on Tyneside and Teesside, and in Bristol, Leeds and the West Midlands.

2 The Mezzogiorno – Southern Italy

Italy is one of the richer countries in the EC. However this wealth is not spread evenly across the country (Figure 9.26). The north has a high standard of living and is the country's core for economic development. In comparison the extreme south, forming the periphery, is much poorer. It was pointed out earlier (page 78) that the south, or Mezzogiorno, is the poorest region in the EC. Indeed in 1950 the Mezzogiorno shared many characteristics normally associated with economically less developed countries.

In 1950, the Mezzogiorno had a very high birth rate, a short life expectancy (42 years), a low standard of living, most of its workforce engaged in agriculture (53 per cent), very few industries or services, a low level of education (24 per cent illiterate), poor housing conditions (40 per cent without sanitation, 50 per cent without water supply), poor transport links and a high rate of outward migration (4.5 million between 1950 and 1975).

The Cassa per il Mezzogiorno (1950–1984) was set up in 1950 by the Italian government to try to develop the Mezzogiorno. Initially most of the money allocated to the region was spent on improving and diversifying farming, improving roads and water supplies, and draining malarial marshes. After 1957 greater attempts were made to attract industry. Several places were designated as growth poles where several large companies, based in the North of Italy, built new factories. Fiat, Alfa-Romeo, Olivetti and Pirelli all located in the Naples area. A large steelworks together with oil-refining, chemicals and cement factories were built in Sicily, the Taranto, Bari and Brindisi districts. After the sharp rise in oil prices after 1974, the Cassa began to concentrate more on introducing smaller, labour intensive projects and developing tourism.

The Cassa ceased to exist in 1984. Despite many successes and a marked improvement in its standard of living, the Mezzogiorno still lagged a long way behind the North. The large multinational companies (page 120) which located here did so for similar reasons and with similar effects as in developing countries. To the parent company land values and salaries were lower than in the North; to the local inhabitants the prestigious, heavily mechanised projects employed relatively few people, were too limited in their distribution, and any profit was sent back to the North. Since then two government agencies have been created:

1 **The Comunità Montana** is a rural planning agency whose main aim is to encourage farmers, especially in the more remote, mountainous areas, to diversify and to remain on the land. It provides grants for new farm buildings, improved livestock and small irrigation schemes. It has planted trees to reduce soil erosion and has set up farmer co-operatives.
2 **The Agency for the Promotion of the Development of the Mezzogiorno**, while encouraging small scale industry, has concentrated upon developing the region's varied tourist potential – the hot, dry and sunny climate; warm, clear seas; sandy, unspoilt beaches; volcanoes (e.g. Vesuvius), and historic sites (e.g. Pompeii).

Today, despite government and EC aid, the gap in prosperity between the two halves of Italy remains as wide as it was in 1950. There has been an almost total elimination of poverty and a reversal in migration where many families who had previously moved out of the area to earn money are now returning with their hard earned capital.

Figure 9.25
Liguria, a hill town in Italy

Figure 9.26
The North/South divide in Italian industrial production

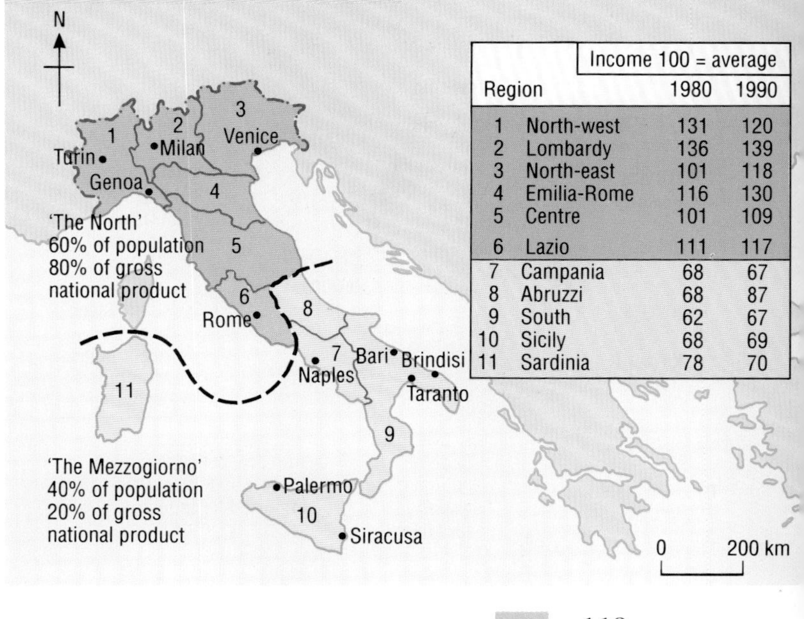

Region		Income 100 = average 1980	1990
1	North-west	131	120
2	Lombardy	136	139
3	North-east	101	118
4	Emilia-Rome	116	130
5	Centre	101	109
6	Lazio	111	117
7	Campania	68	67
8	Abruzzi	68	87
9	South	62	67
10	Sicily	68	69
11	Sardinia	78	70

Industry in a developed country – Japan

In 1945 Japan's industry lay in ruins after World War II. By 1989 Japan had become the world's richest industrialised country, an achievement even more remarkable considering that:

- Only 17 per cent of the country is flat enough for farming, industry and settlement.
- The country has very limited energy resources (page 100), and now has to import virtually all the oil, natural gas and coal which it needs.
- The country lacks most of the basic raw materials needed by industry. It no longer has workable supplies of iron ore and coking coal (yet it is the world's second largest steel producer), nor has minerals of any significance.
- It had lost its overseas territories and its world markets.

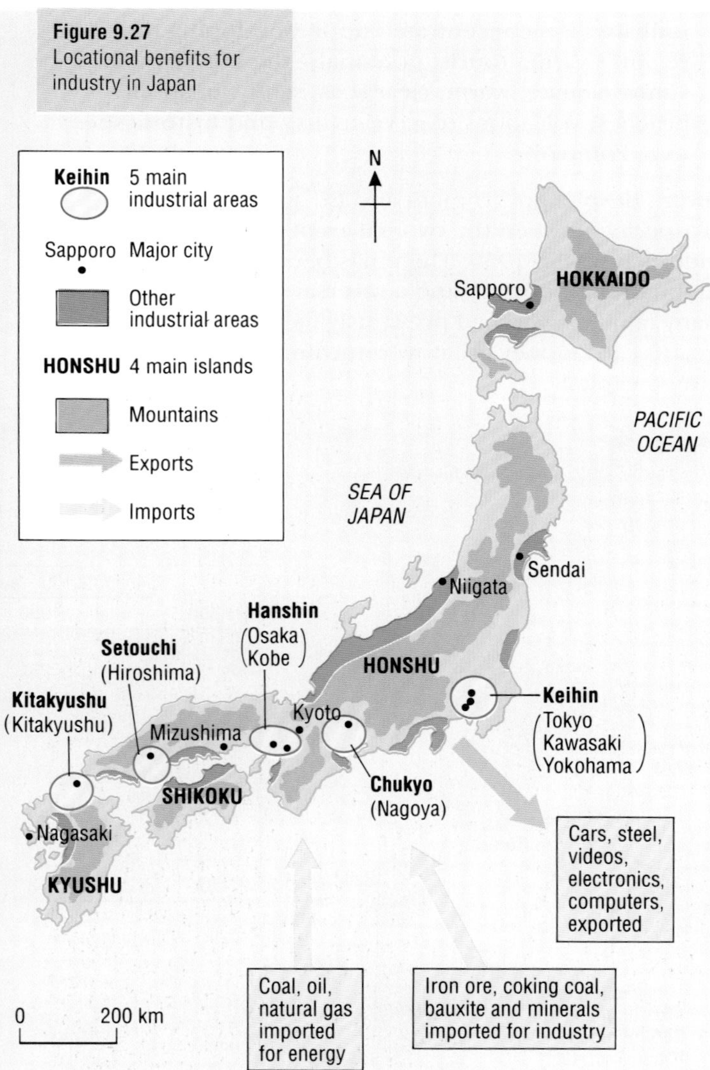

Figure 9.27 Locational benefits for industry in Japan

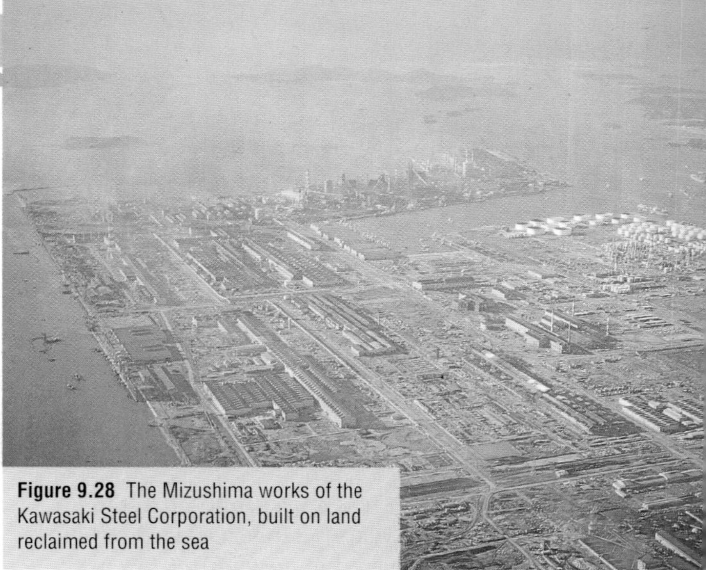

Figure 9.28 The Mizushima works of the Kawasaki Steel Corporation, built on land reclaimed from the sea

How was Japan's economic miracle achieved?

- Postwar demilitarisation meant money could be invested into the economy rather than spent on armaments.
- It has political stability and a government committed to industrialisation.
- Modern machinery and technology has been introduced and the profits re-invested into research.
- The workforce is prepared to work long hours, to become better educated and trained, to work as a team, and to give total loyalty to their company.
- The country had, especially along its Pacific coastline, many deep and sheltered harbours which facilitated the import of energy and raw materials and the export of manufactured goods (Figure 9.27).
- The development of transport is based upon a first class rail network (page 64), motorway expressways and the use of coastal shipping.
- The domestic demand (market) for high quality goods increased rapidly as Japan's population and standard of living increased.
- Japan has the wealth and the technology to reclaim land from the sea (Figure 9.28).

These factors have led to the concentration of industry around five main coastal areas (Figure 9.27). The Japanese themselves consider the most important industrial location factors to be the distribution of lowland, the distribution of people, and the availability of sheltered deep-water ports.

Japan began to improve its economy by using its limited supplies of iron ore and coal to produce steel. The steel was used to make ships specifically designed to carry the necessary raw materials (oil tankers and ore carriers). Attention was then turned to making cars and, later, developing electronics and high-technology industries. Although most of the world's largest car and electronic multinationals are Japanese, the vast majority of local firms are still small family units, many of which make component parts for their multinational neighbours.

The Mazda car factory, Hiroshima

Hiroshima is one of many large cities lying in a discontinuous coastal zone of 1,200 kilometres between Tokyo and northern Kyushu (Figure 9.27). Its growth resulted from a location on the flat delta of the Ota River, at the head of an inlet of the sheltered, navigable Inland Sea. Hiroshima developed its own technology for the manufacture of iron, ships and engineering. The Mazda Motor Corporation began, in 1920, as a small cork manufacturing company. It rapidly diversified into making machine tools and three wheel trucks. Today, with a workforce of 20,000, it is by far the largest employer in the city, having produced 1.1 million cars in 1991 (Figure 9.29). Mazda cars are listed at the top end of the Japanese market and make up 61 per cent of the total export.

	1972	1982	1992
USA	8.6	9.2	6.1
Japan	3.7	6.9	9.9
Germany	3.7	3.7	4.6
France	2.7	2.7	3.2
Italy	1.7	1.3	1.3
UK (8th)	1.7	0.9	1.3

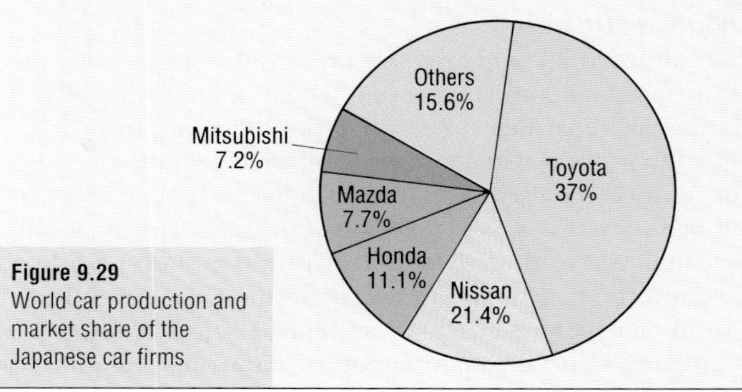

Figure 9.29
World car production and market share of the Japanese car firms

What are the advantages to Mazda of Hiroshima for a car assembly plant when its main competitors are located near to Tokyo (Nissan and Honda) and Nagoya (Toyota)?

- The older parts of the factory were built on a flat site on the Ota delta (A on Figure 9.30). The latest production line requires much space as it is three kilometres in length. This space was obtained by reclaiming land from the sea (B). More land is reclaimed as the demand for Mazda cars increases (C).
- The Inland Sea provides a deep-water access for ships bringing in semi-processed materials for car assembly (D) and exporting the completed cars (E). Hiroshima is sheltered from typhoons and heavy seas by the island of Shikoku.
- A large, highly skilled labour force lives nearby (F). The 1.1 million inhabitants of Hiroshima also form part of Japan's 125 million domestic market for car sales.
- Hiroshima lies on the Shinkansen (bullet train) route (G). The railway is built on stilts as it passes through the city before disappearing into tunnels in the surrounding mountains.
- The environment surrounding Hiroshima is scenic and, unlike the larger Japanese cities, is pollution free (H). One of Japan's most popular tourist attractions, the Shinto shrine on the island of Miyajima, is in Hiroshima Bay. This area is also far less vulnerable to earthquakes than the car assembly centres to the east (Page 210)

Labour shortages in the 1960s led to the introduction of labour-saving machines and robots. The latest assembly line, opened in 1992, shows technology at its most advanced level of development (Figure 9.31). It takes only 12 hours from the first stage of assembly to the end of testing, to ensure that all parts of the vehicle are safe and working correctly. Assembly begins by welding the four main parts of the frame at the same time (the latest technology). 187 robots do 2,100 welding jobs leaving just 12 to be done manually. The cars are rotated on a spit when painted to allow even coverage and drying. The computer controlled assembly line can cope with several different models in several different colours at the same time – a red door always goes onto a red frame! Most improvements to the assembly line have been suggested by the workers themselves as they try to make their jobs easier and quicker.

Figure 9.30
Location of the Mazda car plant in Hiroshima

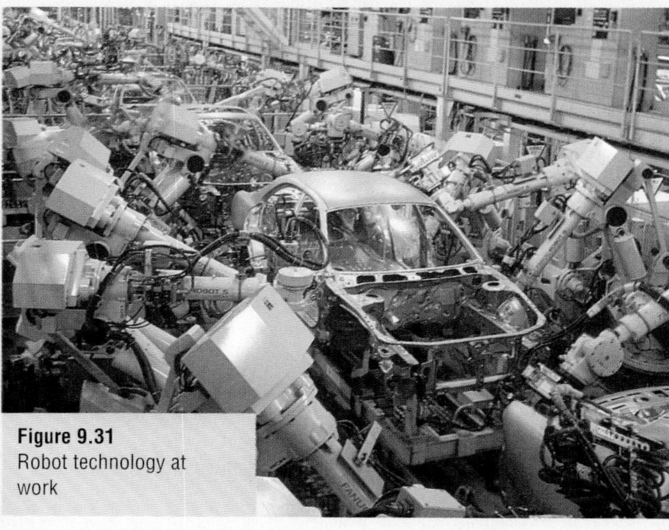

Figure 9.31
Robot technology at work

Industry in economically less developed countries

Multinationals

A multinational company, also referred to as a transnational company, is one which operates in many countries regardless of national boundaries. The headquarters is usually in an economically more developed country with, increasingly, its branch factories in economically less developed countries. Multinationals are believed to directly employ over 30 million people around the world, and indirectly influence an even larger number. The largest 100 multinationals, led by oil companies and car manufacturers, controlled one-fifth of the world's manufacturing in 1966 and nearly one-half in 1988. Several of the largest multinationals have a higher turnover than all of Africa's GNP in total (Figure 9.33). Recently some multinationals have centred their operations in economically less developed countries. Many organisations in developed countries attack multinationals as exploiters of poor people in less well off countries. Yet talking to workers in several parts of Brazil and Kenya, their attitude is rather "perhaps, but it is more important to us to have jobs". Do you think, after studying Figure 9.32, that multinationals are, on balance, a blessing or a curse to an economically less developed country?

Advantages to the country	Disadvantages to the country
Brings work to the country and uses local labour	Numbers employed small in comparison with amount of investment
Local workforce receives a guaranteed income	Local labour force usually poorly paid
Improves the levels of education and technical skill of the people	Very few local skilled workers employed
Brings welcome investment and foreign currency to the country	Most of the profits go overseas (outflow of wealth)
Companies provide expensive machinery and modern technology	Mechanisation reduces the size of the labour force
Increased gross national product/personal income can lead to an increased demand for consumer goods and the growth of new industries	GNP grows less quickly than that of the parent company's headquarters, widening the gap between developed and developing countries
Leads to the development of mineral wealth and new energy resources	Minerals are usually exported rather than manufactured and energy costs may lead to a national debt
Improvements in roads, airports and services	Money possibly better spent on improving housing, diet and sanitation
Prestige value (e.g. Volta project)	Big schemes can increase national debt (e.g. Brazil)
Widens economic base of country	Decisions are made outside the country, and the firm could pull out at any time
Some improvement in standards of production, health control, and recently in environmental control	Insufficient attention to safety and health factors and the protection of the environment

Figure 9.32 Advantages and disadvantages of multinational companies

Figure 9.33 Importance of multi-nationals

Multinational	Sales in million US$ (1990)
1 General Motors	126,974
2 Ford Motor Company	96,933
3 Exxon Oil	88,652
4 Royal Dutch/Shell	85,527
5 IBM	63,438
6 Toyota Cars	60,433
Country	**GNP in million US$ (1990)**
1 Ghana	5,503
2 Kenya	8,785
3 Bangladesh	19,913
4 Peru	23,009
5 Nigeria	28,314
6 Egypt	32,501

Figure 9.34 The worldwide production and assembly of Ford cars

By the 1990s the Ford Motor Company was:

- Manufacturing and/or assembling its cars worldwide although the bulk of the parts were still produced in the more industrialised parts of North America, Japan and the EC.
- Increasingly locating its new factories which either manufactured cars (e.g. São Paulo) or assembled parts made elsewhere (e.g. Malaysia, the Philippines) in economically less developed countries.
- Increasingly making parts in several countries (reducing the risk of strikes) so that each particular model is no longer made in one country.
- Facing increased competition, especially from Japanese manufacturers, at a time of economic recession. Any resultant factory closures are more likely in the economically less developed countries where the local market is smaller and where redundancies are of less concern to the parent company.

Appropriate (intermediate) technology

In most economically less developed countries, not only are high-tech industries too expensive to develop, they are also usually inappropriate to the needs of the local people and the environment in which they live. Appropriate technology, which concentrates on the needs of the people and the environment, has a useful role to play in the economically developed countries of the north, as well as in the south. It can contribute to a more sustainable way of life for rich and poor alike. Examples of appropriate technology include:

- Labour intensive projects as, with so many people already unemployed or underemployed, it is of little value to replace existing workers by machines.
- Encouraging technology which is sustainable and fully utilises the existing skills of the local people.
- To use tools and techniques designed to take advantage of local resources of knowledge and skills.
- To develop local industries, farming and natural resources rather than to replace them by expensive, imported technologies.
- Low cost schemes using technologies which ordinary people can afford, manage and control.
- Developing projects which are in harmony with the environment.

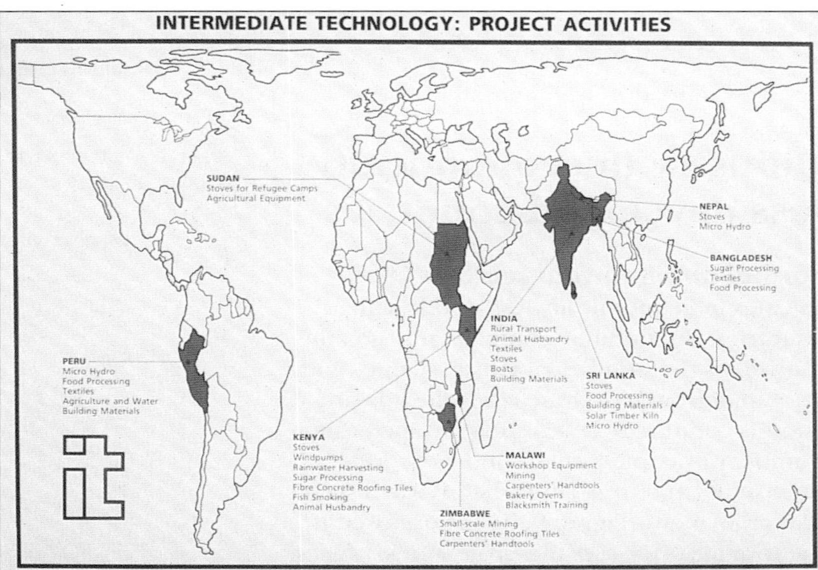

Figure 9.35 Location of Intermediate Technology activity around the world

Intermediate Technology (IT)

IT is a British charitable organisation which works with people in economically less developed countries, especially in rural areas, to acquire the tools and techniques needed if they are to work themselves out of poverty. IT helps people to meet their needs of food, clothes, housing, farm equipment, energy and employment. IT uses and adds to local knowledge by providing technical advice, training, equipment and financial support so that people can become more self-sufficient and independent. Ideally the aim is for people to create a surplus which can then be invested into their small farms, businesses and communities (Figure 9.35).

ITDG's projects in Kenya

Most projects (Figure 9.36) are in response to requests from local groups, often women, who need assistance in one or more stages of their planned work.

Figure 9.36

Housing materials Improved building materials using locally available resources. Locally-made roofing tiles (Figure 9.37). Building houses for the Maasai, and improving the ventilation and lighting in existing houses.

Farming Growing more indigenous crops. Improved methods of food storage. Training a member of a village to become a *wasaidizi* or animal care-worker capable of recognising and treating basic animal illnesses.

Industry and energy Training potters in the production of fuel efficient cooking stoves (Figure 9.38) reducing the time needed to collect fuelwood and creating income for producers. Assessing rural transport needs.

Figure 9.37 Production of low cost roofing tiles in Kenya

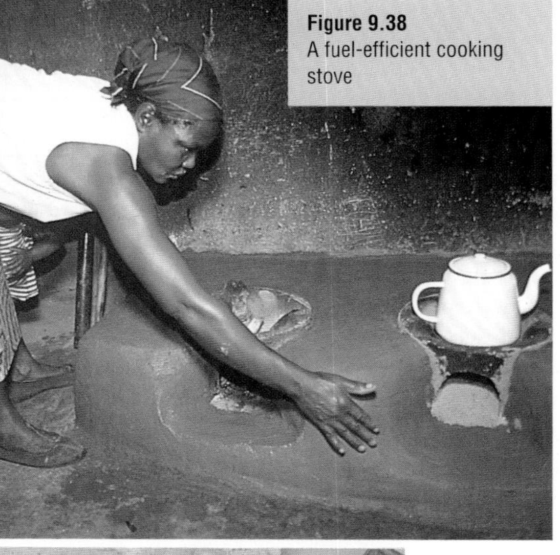

Figure 9.38 A fuel-efficient cooking stove

Industry in economically less developed countries

Formal and informal sectors

In cities in economically less developed countries, the number of inhabitants greatly outweighs the number of jobs available. With the rapid growth of these cities the job situation is continually worsening. An increasing number of people have to find work for themselves and thus enter the informal sector of employment (Figure 9.40), as opposed to the formal sector (i.e. the professions, offices, shops and organised modern industry). The differences between the formal and informal sectors are given in Figure 9.41.

In many cities there are now publicly and privately promoted schemes to support these self-help efforts. In Nairobi, for example, there are several *jua kali* (meaning 'under the hot sun') with metal workshops. In one area little more than the size of three football pitches, 1,000 workers hammer scrap metal into an assortment of products. (Figure 9.39).

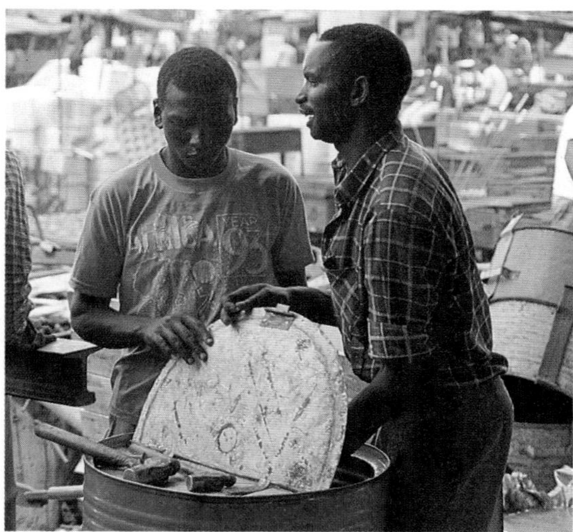

Figure 9.39

Role of children

Children, many of whom are under ten years old, make up a large proportion of the informal sector workers. Very few of them have schools to go to, and from an early age go out onto the streets to try to supplement the family income. One such 'worker', who has become well known in British schools, was a shoe-shine boy called Mauru who lived in São Paulo, and was seen in a TV programme *Skyscrapers and Slums*. He would try to earn money during the day, and study to become an airline pilot, at night.

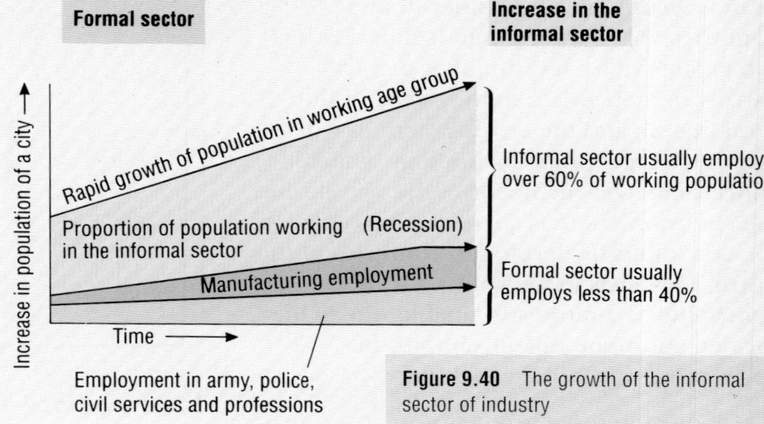
COMPETITION FOR JOBS
Inhabitants of the city
Migrants into the city
Perhaps some education and skills
Usually no education and very few skills
May get one of the few relatively regular paid jobs, possibly with a multinational company
Unlikely to get a regular or a paid job – they need to create their own jobs in order to survive
Formal sector
Increase in the informal sector
Increase in population of a city
Rapid growth of population in working age group
Proportion of population working in the informal sector
(Recession)
Manufacturing employment
Time
Employment in army, police, civil services and professions
Informal sector usually employs over 60% of working population
Formal sector usually employs less than 40%

Figure 9.40 The growth of the informal sector of industry

Differences between the formal and informal sectors	
Formal	**Informal**
Description	
Employee of a large firm	Self employed
Often a multinational	Small scale/family enterprise
Much capital employed	Little capital involved
Capital-intensive with relatively few workers. Mechanised	Labour-intensive with the use of very few tools
Expensive raw materials	Using cheap or recycled waste materials
A guaranteed standard in the final product	Often a low standard in quality of goods
Regular hours (often long) and wages (often low)	Irregular hours and uncertain wages
Fixed prices	Prices rarely fixed and so negotiable (bartering)
Jobs done in factories	Jobs often done in the home (cottage industry) or on the streets
Government and multinational help	No government assistance
Legal	Often outside the law (illegal)
Usually males	Often children and females
Type of job	
Manufacturing – both local and multinational industries Government-created jobs such as the police, army and civil service	Distributive, e.g. street pedlars and small stalls Services, e.g. shoecleaners, selling clothes and fruit Small scale industry, e.g. food processing, dress repairs, furniture repairs
Advantages	
Uses some skilled and many unskilled workers	Employs many thousands of unskilled workers
Provides permanent jobs and regular wages	Jobs may provide some training and skills which might lead to better jobs in the future
Produces goods for the more wealthy (cars, food) within their *own* country so that profits may remain within the country	Any profit will be used within the city The products will be for local use by the lower paid people
Waste materials provide raw materials for the informal sector	Uses local and waste materials

Figure 9.41

Figure 9.42
Main photo: Copacabana beach and Sugarloaf Mountain.
Inset: shoe-shine boys, Mexico; girl selling shuttlecocks in Rio de Janeiro; beach vendors on Copacabana beach

"Our small group of 11 tourists from Britain was staying at the Rio Palace, a five star hotel overlooking the famous Copacabana beach in Rio de Janeiro. Walking along the beach one afternoon, I noticed numerous beach vendors. These form part of Rio's large informal sector. Several vendors carried large umbrellas from which dangled an assortment of sun hats, suntan lotion or tangas (bikinis). One vendor carried pineapples in a basket perched on his head and, in his hand, a large knife with which to cut the fruit. Some vendors carried cooler boxes in which were ice cream, Coca Cola, coconut water and other drinks, while others carried large metal drums which contained maté (a local drink). These people drew attention to themselves by shouting, blowing whistles, beating metal drums or whirling a metal ratchet that clattered loudly. On the pavement next to the beach were small children trying to sell sweets and chocolate, and numerous kiosks with fruit and drink available.

Returning to the hotel, several of us were tempted to buy a brightly feathered shuttlecock from a girl who had a most enchanting smile (Figure 8.34) but we resisted other sellers of cheap jewellery and Copacabana T-shirts. That evening as our group ate in a restaurant next to the Rio Palace, other pedlars poked their heads through the open door and windows trying to sell not very musical instruments, monkey-puppets and T-shirts. As we left the restaurant at 9.30 pm to visit one of Rio's famous Samba shows, we saw a small boy of four or five years with sad, appealing eyes trying to sell roses individually wrapped in cellophane. How could one fail to buy a rose which, he indicated by his fingers, were only 15 crusadas (about 50p)? However by the time the money was produced, he had raised his price to 20 crusadas – and shown us that his eyes had been trained and his brain sharpened for business. When we returned at 1.00 am, he was still outside the hotel with the remainder of his roses."

1 *(Page 108)*

Employment (jobs) can be divided into three main groups – primary, secondary and tertiary.

a What is meant by each of the terms primary, secondary and tertiary? *(3)*

b Which of the jobs/industries shown below are primary, secondary and tertiary? *(5)*

2 *(Pages 108 and 109)*

a Copy out the four pie graphs showing employment structures. Using the information given in the table, complete the graphs by adding the figures for Kenya and the UK. *(6)*

b Which two countries have the largest workforce employed in primary occupations? *(2)*

c What percentage of the workforce is employed in primary occupations in:
i) India?
ii) the USA? *(2)*

d i) Give three differences in the employment structures of the economically more developed and the economically less developed countries. *(3)*
ii) Give one reason for each difference. *(3)*

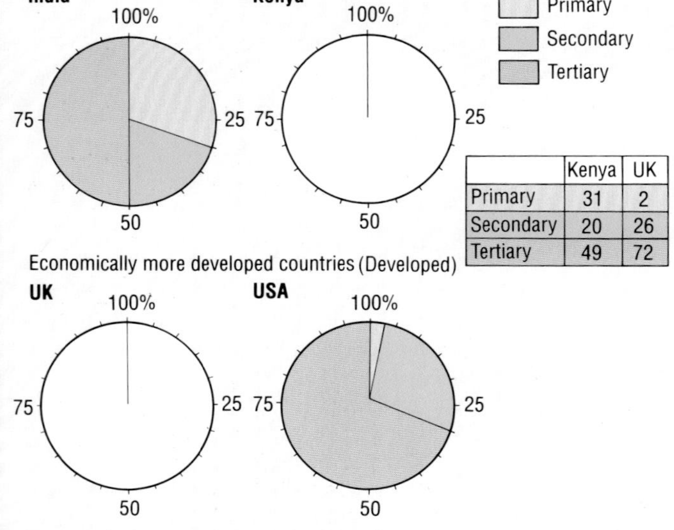

	Kenya	UK
Primary	31	2
Secondary	20	26
Tertiary	49	72

3 *(Page 109)*

The triangular graph shows the percentage of the working population in each of the three main sectors of industry in ten selected countries.

a Complete the following table: *(5)*

	Japan	Brazil	Ghana
% Primary industry	3		49
% Secondary industry		43	
% Tertiary industry	56		

b Which country has 44 per cent in primary, 15 per cent in secondary and 41 per cent in tertiary? *(1)*

c Using evidence on the graph:
i) Name the four economically least developed countries *(4)*
ii) Name the four economically most developed countries. *(4)*
iii) Give three differences between the figures of these two sets of countries. *(3)*

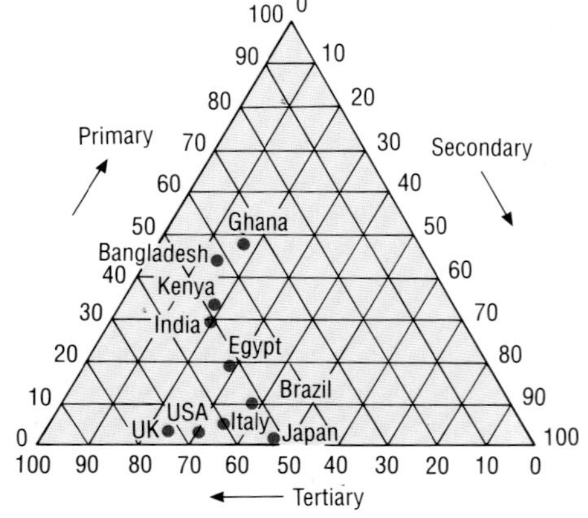

4 *(Page 110)*

a Complete the star diagram to show some of the factors affecting the location of industry. Add four physical factors and four human and economic factors. *(8)*

b Why were physical factors more important than human and economic factors in locating nineteenth century industry? *(3)*

c Give three reasons why human and economic factors are more important than physical factors when considering the location of a modern factory. *(3)*

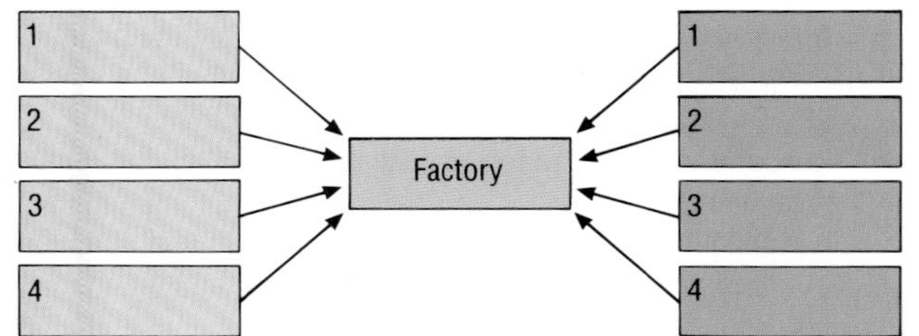

5 *(Page 110)*

For any industry that you have studied:

a Name an area where it is located. *(1)*

b Draw a labelled sketch map to show its location. *(4)*

c Give three reasons why that industry has either grown or declined in the area named. *(3)*

d What effects has this growth or decline had upon the local economy? *(3)*

6 *(Page 111)*

a What does the location quotient show? *(2)*

b The table below gives employment figures by region in the UK for printing and publishing.

GREAT BRITAIN	509.7
REGION:	
South East	225.4
East Anglia	19.7
South West	32.6
West Midlands	30.7
East Midlands	30.6
Yorks and Humberside	33.2
North West	63.7
North	21.3
Wales	13.3
Scotland	39.2

What is the location quotient for printing and publishing for
i) the South-east?
ii) Wales? *(4)*

7 *(Pages 112 and 113)*

a i) Give four reasons why Town X became important for the manufacture of iron in the nineteenth century. *(4)*
ii) Why did Town Y become an important exporting port? *(2)*

b i) Give four reasons why a large modern steelworks has been built at town A. *(4)*
ii) Why was the steelworks not built at Town B? *(2)*

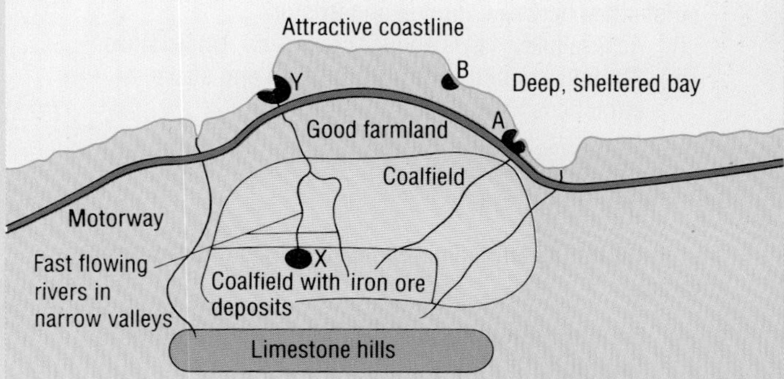

8 *(Page 115)*

Many of Britain's newer industries are said to be 'footloose' and are located on industrial estates which have been built on the outskirts of urban areas.

a i) What is meant by the terms: a footloose industry; an industrial estate? *(2)*
ii) Give three reasons why industrial estates are found on the outskirts of urban areas. *(3)*
iii) List four factors describing industrial estates. *(4)*
iv) Why are footloose industries found on industrial estates? *(1)*
v) What types of industry are found on industrial estates? *(2)*

b A firm which has a factory in an old inner city area wishes to move to an industrial estate.
i) Suggest three advantages of the proposed move. *(3)*
ii) Suggest two disadvantages of the proposed move. *(2)*

c The sketch shows Figure 9.18. Complete the labelling by choosing the correct six labels from the following list: nearby motorway; access via interchange; near to city centre; cheap land on edge-of-city; nearby housing estate for workforce; nearby city provides a large market; attractive greenfield site; space for car parking and future expansion. *(6)*

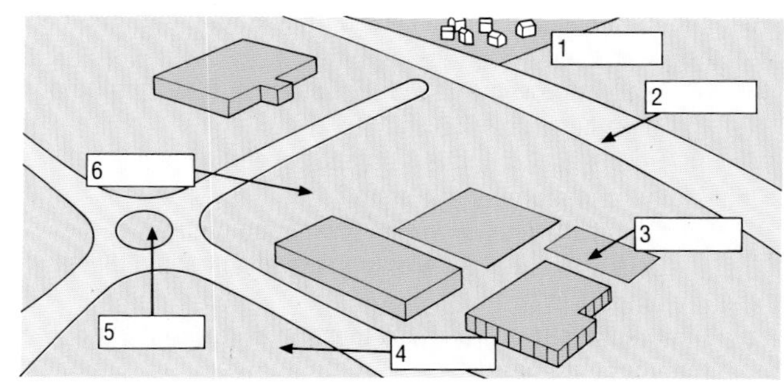

9 *(Pages 116 and 117)*

In recent years there has been a rapid growth of high-technology (high-tech) industries in the area between London and Bristol.

a i) What is meant by a 'high-tech' industry?
ii) Give two examples of high-tech industries.
iii) What is a science park? *(3)*

b How have the following encouraged the location of high-tech industries between London and Bristol?
i) Accessibility ii) Labour supply iii) Universities
iv) Attractive countryside v) Cultural and social attractions. *(5)*

10 *(Pages 115 to 117)*

If a town wants to attract more industry it has to advertise its advantages.

a i) Give four advantages listed in the advertisement for Swindon. *(4)*
ii) Explain why each would be good for a company seeking a new industrial site. *(4)*

b Compose an advertisement to put into a national newspaper to show the advantages of locating a new factory in your nearest town or city. *(6)*

££'s LOWER OVERHEADS – AROUND ONE FIFTH CENTRAL LONDON'S ✈ HEATHROW 60 MINS – GATWICK 1 HR 30 MINS LONDON 50 MINS BY HIGH SPEED TRAIN PRIME M4 CORRIDOR LOCATION – LONDON 90 MINS EXCELLENT ADVANCED COMMUNICATIONS OUTSTANDING QUALITY OF LIFE YOUNG, DYNAMIC AND VERSATILE WORKFORCE

THAMESDOWN BOROUGH COUNCIL HAS A RANGE OF SITES AVAILABLE

12 *(Page 119)*

a i) Where is the Mezzogiorno? *(1)*
ii) Give 10 points to show how it was one of the poorest parts of Europe in 1950. *(10)*

b The Italian government has tried three ways, since 1950, to help the region.
i) What improvements did the Cassa per il Mezzogiorno make between 1950 and 1984? *(5)*
ii) How is the Comunità Montana benefitting people living in more remote areas? *(3)*
iii) How is the Agency for the Promotion of the Development of the Mezzogiorno encouraging the growth of tourism? *(3)*

c How successful do you think these three government schemes have been? *(3)*

11 *(Pages 116 and 117)*

Study the information for the Cambridge Science Park below.

a i) What is a science park? *(1)*
ii) Name three types of companies which have located in the Cambridge Science Park. *(3)*
iii) How many companies have located here? *(1)*
iv) How many of these companies employ less than 10 people? *(1)*
v) Why do most companies only employ a few people? *(1)*
vi) What type of people are likely to be employed in the science park? *(2)*

b i) Why has the science park been built beside the A45 Northern Bypass which leads to the M11? *(1)*
ii) Why have so many car parks been provided? *(2)*

c Describe the layout of the science park under the following headings:
i) buildings
ii) road pattern
iii) landscaped areas. *(6)*

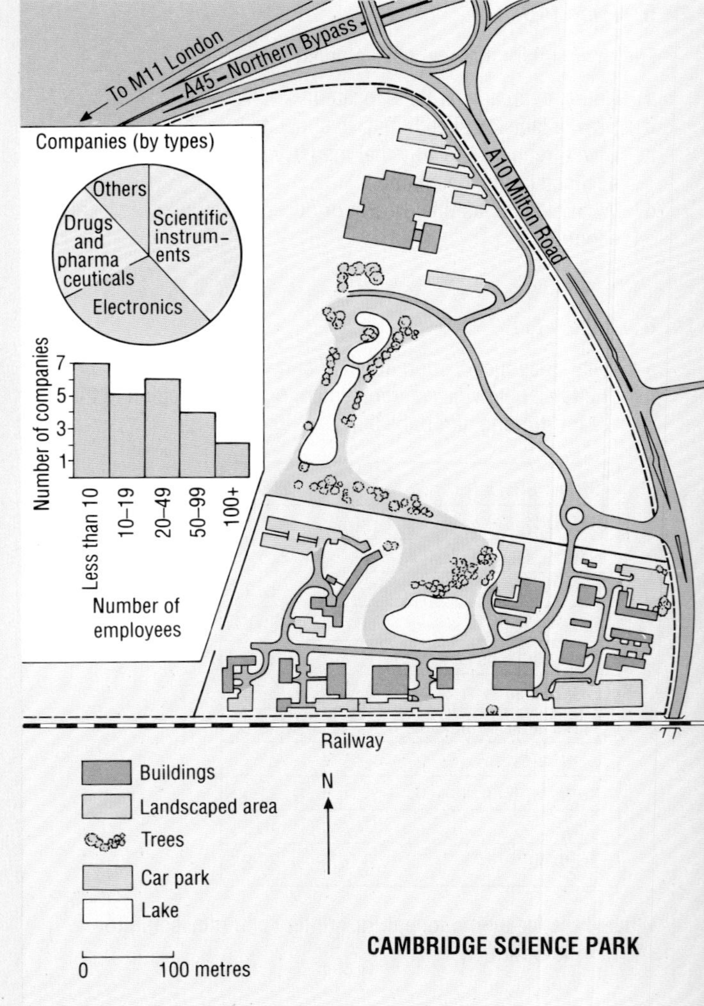

CAMBRIDGE SCIENCE PARK

13 *(Pages 120 and 121)*

a On a larger copy of the map of Japan, name:
- i) The islands numbered 1 to 4. *(4)*
- ii) The towns numbered 5 to 8. *(4)*
- iii) Two imported types of energy. *(2)*
- iv) Two imported minerals. *(2)*
- v) Three major exports. *(3)*

b
- i) Japan's industry developed despite three major physical disadvantages. What were these three disadvantages? *(3)*
- ii) Give five reasons why Japan has become the world's richest industrial country. *(5)*

c
- i) Name, in order, the four largest Japanese car companies. *(2)*
- ii) The Mazda Motor Corporation is located at Hiroshima. With the help of the star diagram, explain why this is a good site for a car factory. *(5)*

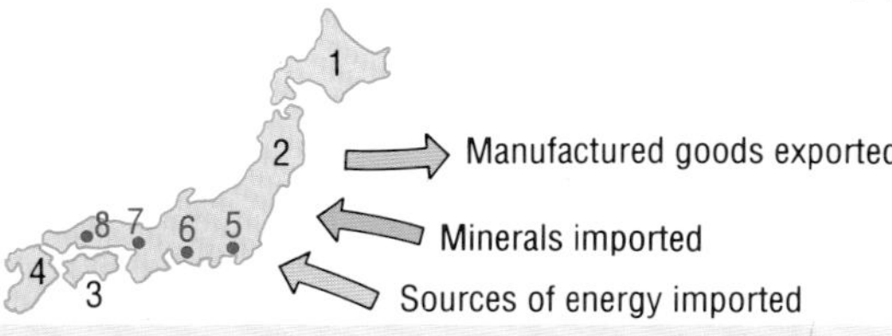

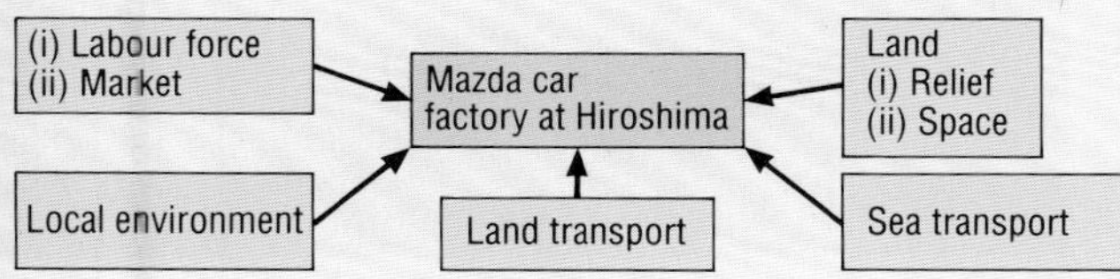

16 *(Pages 124 and 125)*

a Give four differences between the formal and informal sectors of employment. *(4)*

b Rearrange the jobs listed below, which were noted during a study of a city in the economically less developed world, into:
- i) primary, secondary and tertiary occupations and
- ii) formal and informal occupations

by completing the accompanying table.

Shoe-shiner • maker of sandals from old wood and tyres • policeman • bus driver • tinsmith using old beer cans • soldier • self-employed fisherman with a fish stall • car-factory worker • snake-charmer • bottler at a Coca-Cola works • hotel waitress • tour guide • smallholder with a few goats • worker on a coffee plantation • cool-drink vendor • gardener in a city park

	Formal	Informal
Primary		
Secondary		
Tertiary		

14 *(Page 122)*

a List four features of a multinational company. *(4)*

b Governments of economically less developed countries have encouraged multinationals to open up factories in their countries.
- i) Give three reasons why these governments want multinationals. *(3)*
- ii) Give three disadvantages of multinationals to the countries in which they have opened factories. *(3)*

c Give three reasons why the Ford Motor Corporation has factories in several different countries. *(3)*

15 *(Page 123)*

a What is meant by the term 'appropriate technology'? *(1)*

b The following extract and photo describe an Intermediate Technology project in Kenya.
- i) Describe four ways in which IT is helping the Maasai to upgrade their houses. *(3)*
- ii) Why are these improvements more appropriate than building western style houses? *(3)*

The Kenya Shelter and Building Materials Programme – The Maasai Housing Project

"The Maasai are slowly being forced to live in permanent homes, but many cannot afford a new house. IT is helping them to find affordable ways to upgrade their existing houses. Women have told us that their primary concern is a leaky roof; they dread being woken up by their husbands and ordered to climb up in the middle of the night to smear more cow-dung over a crack in the roof. One answer, is a thin layer of cement reinforced with chicken wire laid over the old flat mud roof. Roof plastering is a job the women can do themselves. By incorporating a gutter and a water-jar women should be spared another tiresome chore – collecting water from a spring or river possibly several miles away. By adding small windows and a chimney cowl, the inside of the house can be made lighter, less smoky and more healthy." (IT – Nairobi).

New towns

New towns have been built in many parts of the world for a variety of reasons. In the United Kingdom they were created mainly to:

- Take the overspill from expanding conurbations or from inner city clearances.
- Attract new industries to areas of high unemployment.
- Try to create a more pleasant environment in areas of old, declining industry.

Elsewhere in the world, new towns serve a variety of purposes. For example in South Africa new townships were established to house and to segregate black workers (page 51), while in Israel new communes, called Kibbutz, were built to try to colonise former desert areas and to house the influx of Jewish migrants.

The main aim when planning new towns is to make them self-contained and balanced communities in which to live and work. Apart from creating housing and jobs (to limit the time, distance and cost of the journey to work) they provide services such as schools, shops, hospitals and leisure amenities, good internal communications, and an attractive environment.

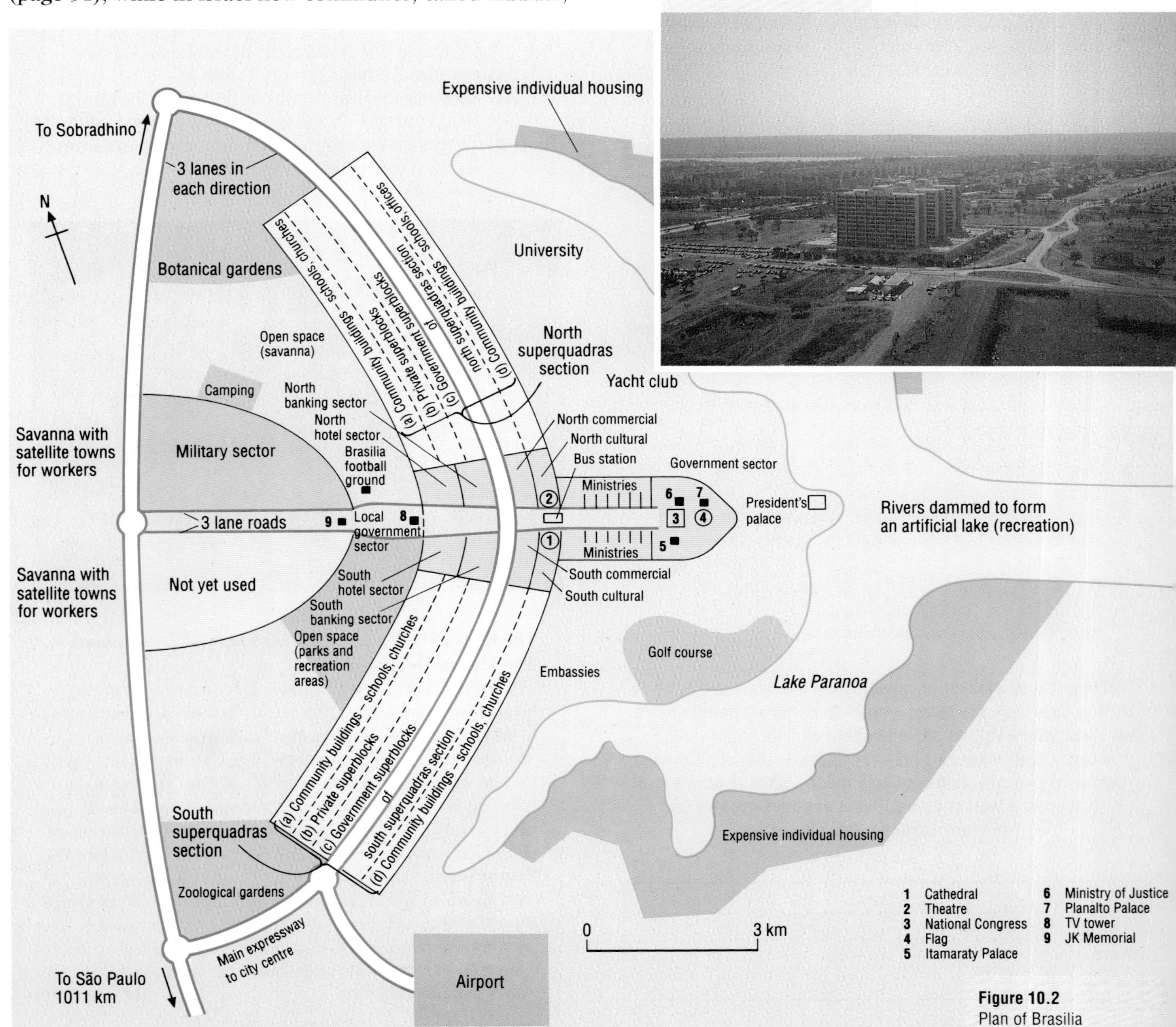

Figure 10.1
A view of the superblocks

Figure 10.2
Plan of Brasilia

Figure 10.3
Inside one of the superblocks, Brasilia

Brasilia

This is perhaps the most famous example of an elaborately planned new town. For decades, concern had been expressed at the relative richness and overpopulation of the south-east of Brazil (São Paulo and Rio de Janeiro) compared with the rest of the country. In 1952 Congress approved, by only three votes, the move of the capital from Rio de Janeiro (where most politicians preferred to live) inland to Brasilia to try to open up the more central parts of the country. Building began in 1957.

Brasilia was built in the shape of an aeroplane. The two wings, each 6.5 kilometres long, were used for housing (superblocks); the fuselage, 9 kilometres long, has been divided into sections for local government, hotels, commerce, culture and national government (Figure 10.2). Each section is paired along the length of the fuselage. Many of the cultural and civic buildings are noted for their futuristic architecture.

Brasilia was built for the motorist. The idea was to have a road network enabling people to get to work and shops without having to use traffic lights and in safety. The result has been great distances between places (often too far to walk), adding danger to those wishing to walk (as they have to cross three-lane expressways), and an increasing number of accidents. Traffic lights eventually had to be introduced.

Several local rivers have been dammed to form a large artificial lake (mainly used for recreation). Around this lake are the very expensive, individual houses, and foreign embassies. By 1985 the city had already reached one million inhabitants – a figure initially planned for the year 2000 – and 1.7 million by 1990. Brasilia is a bureaucratic city with little industry.

The Superblocks (superquadras)

The wings of the 'aeroplane' are used for housing and are divided into superblocks (superquadras), each of which is meant to be a complete unit in itself (Figure 10.4), similar to a neighbourhood unit in a British new town. Each superblock is approached by a slip road, and at each entrance is a post box, public telephone and a newspaper kiosk. Inside the superblock are nine to eleven apartment blocks, each ten storeys high, and housing about 2500 people. The apartments are luxurious, unlike most British high rise flats, and are well looked after. The apartments shown in Figures 10.1 and 10.3 belong to the Bank of Brazil and are occupied by its employees. Almost all the other apartments are inhabited by local or national government workers, all of whom have well paid jobs. The apartments' rear windows are covered by a grid for privacy, and the fronts have shutters which can be opened or closed. The whole area is very clean and well maintained. Many flowering trees and shrubs have been planted (Brasilia has 30,000 new trees planted each year). The inhabitants favour living in these apartments as it gives them security (although Brasilia's crime rate is well below the national average), the environment is attractive, services are nearby, and those working in the town centre can easily travel home at lunch time (unlike other Brazilian cities). Each superblock has its own kindergarten, to save the children crossing roads. Each pair of superblocks has a play area and a self contained shopping area. On the edge of the housing area are community buildings with a Catholic church, a senior school and a community centre for each set of four superblocks.

Figure 10.4
Plan of part of the south superquadras (residential) section

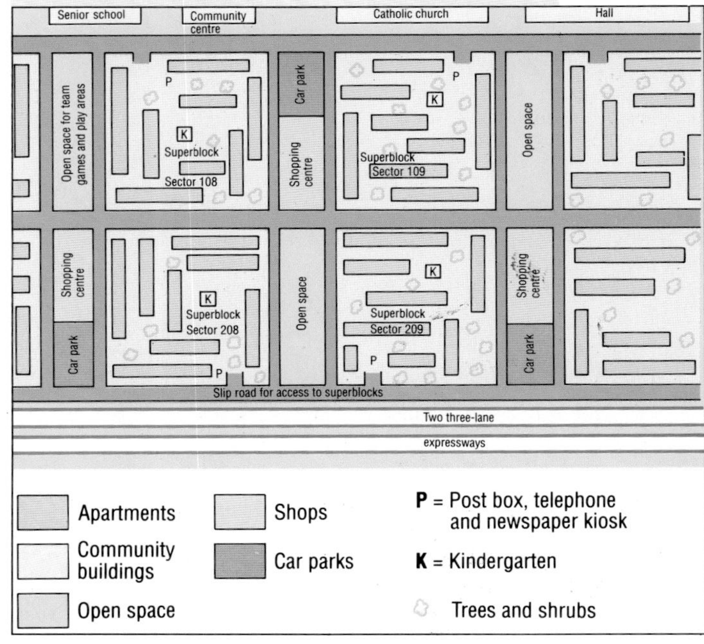

Inner city redevelopment

London's Dockland

During the nineteenth century and up to the early 1950s, London was the busiest port in the world. Because of a series of changes after that, many of them due to improvements in technology, the docks had virtually become abandoned and derelict. By 1981 (page 62), larger ships could no longer reach the port of London and containerisation did away with the need for large numbers of dockers. One of the first enterprise zones to be created in 1981 (page 118) was the Isle of Dogs in the heart of London's dockland. By that time the area had very few jobs, the docks had closed, over half the land was derelict, many of the nineteenth century terraced houses needed urgent repair, transport was poorly developed, and there was a lack of basic services, leisure amenities and open space (Figure 10.5). The London Dockland's Development Corporation (LDDC) was set up to try to improve the economic, social and environmental conditions of the area.

Many changes took place during 1981–1992 (Figure 10.6). These included:

Employment Financial and high-tech firms were among the first to be attracted by the low rates of the enterprise zone, e.g. the Stock Exchange, Limehouse ITV studios, and the printing plants for the Guardian and Daily Telegraph newspapers. These were followed by firms wishing to relocate in new office blocks, and especially in the prestigious Canary Wharf business complex with its dominating 245 metre tower (Figure 10.7).

Transport Improved links meant that central London could now be reached within ten minutes. The Dockland Light Railway (Figure 10.6), running above ground, connects with Bank and Monument underground stations. The Jubilee underground extension will give improved access to London's mainline stations, including a direct link with Waterloo and London Bridge. The new City Airport was built on land between two docks. Improvements have been made to roads leading to, and within, dockland.

Housing Over 20,000 new homes have been created, many of them in former warehouses which have been converted into luxury flats. More recently Newham Council has either built low-cost housing or upgraded existing older property.

Services and Recreation A large, modern shopping complex has been built near to Canary Wharf. A national indoor sports centre and a marina for water sports have opened. Several areas have been cleared and converted into parks and areas of open space. The area boasts the largest urban tree planting scheme in the UK.

Figure 10.5

a The first stages of London dockland development

b The London Docklands area in the late 1980s

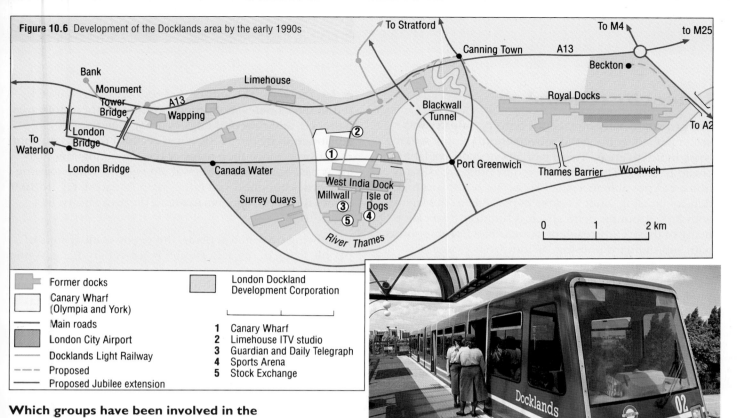

Figure 10.6 Development of the Docklands area by the early 1990s

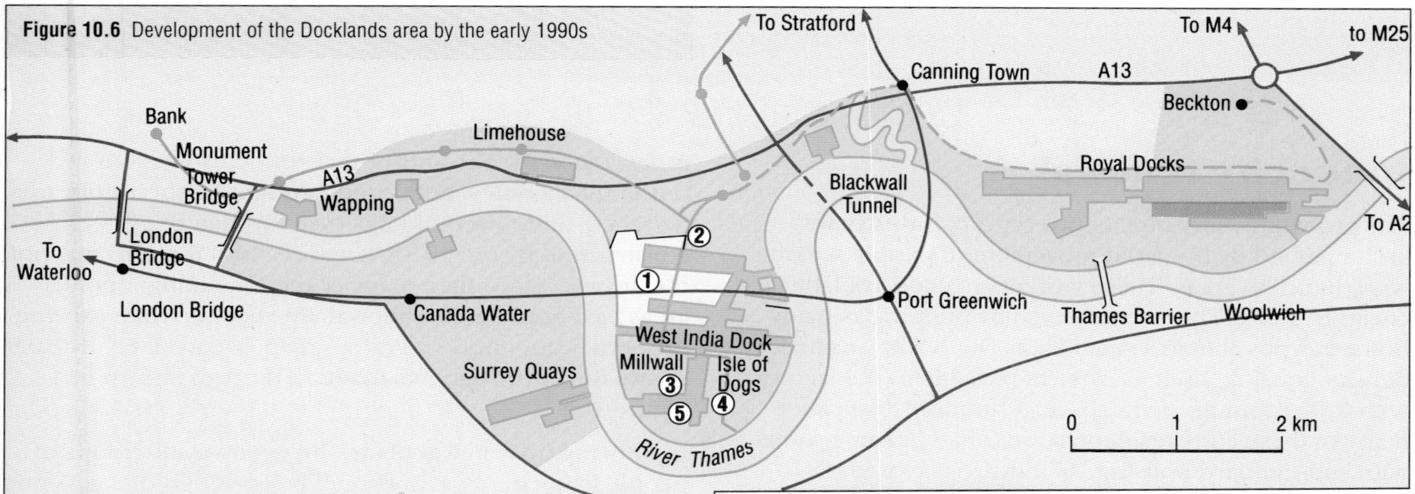

To Stratford
To M4
to M25
Canning Town
A13
Beckton
Bank
Monument
Limehouse
Royal Docks
Tower Bridge
A13
Wapping
Blackwall Tunnel
To A2
London Bridge
To Waterloo
London Bridge
Canada Water
Port Greenwich
Thames Barrier
Woolwich
West India Dock
Millwall
Isle of Dogs
Surrey Quays
River Thames
0 1 2 km

Former docks
Canary Wharf (Olympia and York)
Main roads
London City Airport
Docklands Light Railway
Proposed
Proposed Jubilee extension
London Dockland Development Corporation

1 Canary Wharf
2 Limehouse ITV studio
3 Guardian and Daily Telegraph
4 Sports Arena
5 Stock Exchange

Docklands 02

The Docklands light railway

Which groups have been involved in the redevelopment of Dockland?

- **Local housing associations** have helped by gaining home improvement grants.
- **The local Newham Council** have built, when they had sufficient money, low cost, affordable houses and upgraded older properties. They have also tried to improve local services.
- **The LDDC** have been responsible for planning and redeveloping dockland.
- **The national government** created the enterprise zone with its reduced rates. It encouraged private investment and has given financial help towards improving transport systems.
- **Property developers** have been responsible for building the large office blocks (e.g Canary Wharf by Olympia and York – Figure 10.7) and converting derelict warehouses into luxury flats.
- **Conservation groups** have supported tree planting and other schemes aimed at improving the quality of the environment.

:onflicting opinions

;ome groups of people will have benefitted from the ıbove changes and so will be in favour of the scheme.)thers will feel disadvantaged and so will be against it. .ocal residents cannot afford the expensive flats built by peculative property developers and there is a shortage of ɔw cost housing. Jobs in the new high-tech industries are elatively few in number and they demand skills not ›ossessed by former dockers. The 'yuppie' newcomers arely mix with the original 'Eastenders' who find that heir close-knit community has been broken up. Property evelopers have not provided sufficient services, e.g. ospitals, care for the elderly.

Problems in the early 1990s

The recession came before Canary Wharf could be completed. The result was that parts were left vacant and the property developers had insufficient capital to continue. The government, also short of money, delayed the decision to finance the Jubilee Line extension until late 1993. Without this link the future of London's Docklands had been left in doubt. What is certain, however, is that the situation will have changed by the time you read this! As a geographer you must be aware of recent changes.

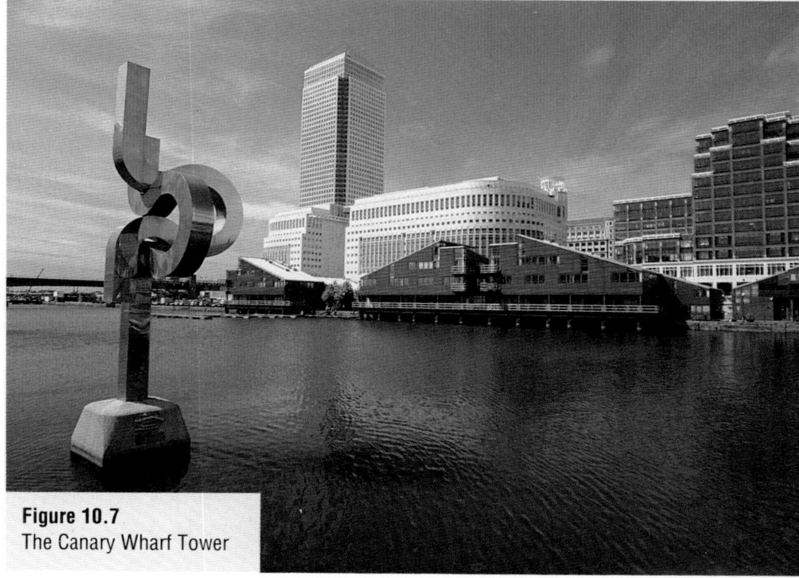

Figure 10.7
The Canary Wharf Tower

Inner city renewal

The growth of early nineteenth century industry was accompanied by the rapid movement of people seeking work in urban areas. These workers needed available and cheap housing. This was achieved by building as many houses as possible in a small area. The result was high density housing, built as close as possible to the factories, with little room for open space. A hundred years later many of these early residential areas had become slums with sub-standard housing. As industries closed or relocated there were increases in unemployment and derelict land and buildings. There was often a lack of modern services, a spoilt environment and, in general, a low quality of life. A typical inner city area of that time is shown in Figure 10.8. The letter P marks the spot from which the photo in Figure 3.11a was taken.

During the 1950s and 1960s it was thought that the only solution to the problem of inner cities was total *redevelopment*. This meant that residents were moved out of their homes, bulldozers brought in, the whole area flattened, and new buildings (usually high rise) constructed. By the 1970s it was realised that this was not the answer. Since then many of the remaining inner city areas have undergone renewal. *Renewal* is when existing properties are improved rather than replaced. Figure 10.9 shows the improvements made to the area shown in Figure 10.8.

In drawing up renewal plans, the needs of all groups of people living in the area should be considered, e.g. young children, teenagers, young married couples, the elderly, the disabled, etc. The most successful schemes have been where the local community has been consulted and has become involved. Local community groups can help by providing accommodation for people in need of housing, supervising grants for home improvements, encouraging small industries to move into the area, and improving the range of services and the quality of the environment.

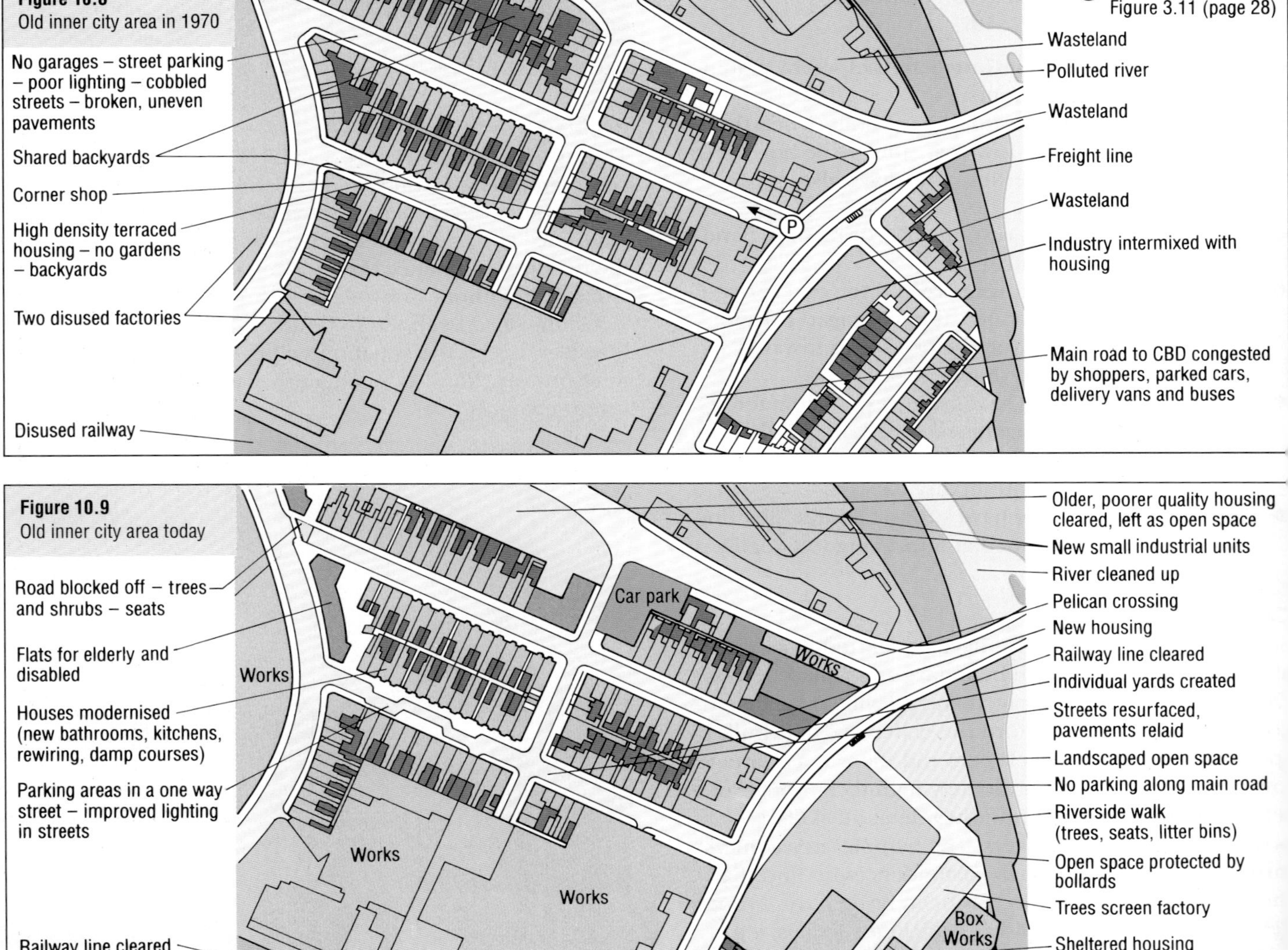

Figure 10.8 Old inner city area in 1970

Figure 10.9 Old inner city area today

1 *(Pages 130 and 131)*

a i) Give three reasons why new towns were built in the UK. *(3)*
ii) What should be the main aims when planning a new town? *(4)*

b How far do you think that the planners of Brasilia achieved the aims which you listed in part a ii)? *(6)*

2 *(Pages 132 and 133)*

a i) Give two reasons why the London docks lost their trade? *(2)*
ii) By 1981 London's dockland faced severe social, economic and environmental problems. List six of these problems. *(6)*

b Between 1981 and 1992 many changes took place.
i) What changes took place in the number of people employed and the types of jobs they did? The graph below will help you to answer this question. *(2)*
ii) Why were new companies and businesses attracted to London's Dockland? *(2)*
iii) Briefly describe the main changes in transport; housing; and the environment. *(6)*

c The advert for Hermitage Court appeared in a national newspaper in the early 1990s.
i) On which street is Hermitage Court located? *(1)*
ii) What was the price of a three bedroom apartment? *(1)*
iii) Give four advantages of living in Hermitage Court. *(4)*
iv) Which groups of people can afford to live here? *(2)*

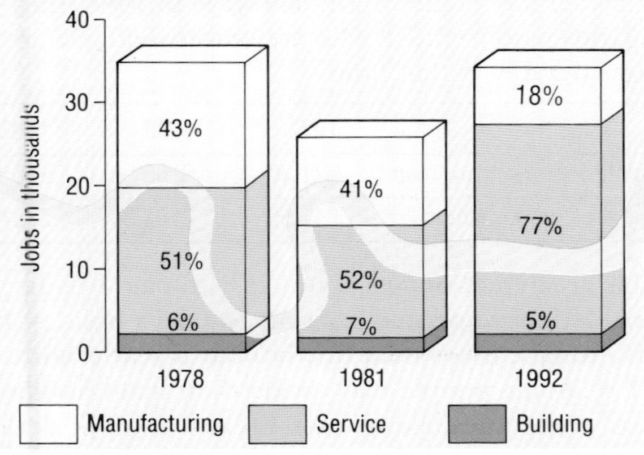

d Name *four* groups who have helped in the redevelopment of Dockland. For each give one way in which they have improved the area. *(4)*

e How do you think each of the following will answer the question 'Do you think the changes to London's dockland has improved the area or made it worse?'

a school-leaver • local shopkeeper • a local retired couple • a former docker • a bank manager who lives in Dockland but who works in central London

(5)

Hermitage Court. Tranquility next door to the City's bustle.

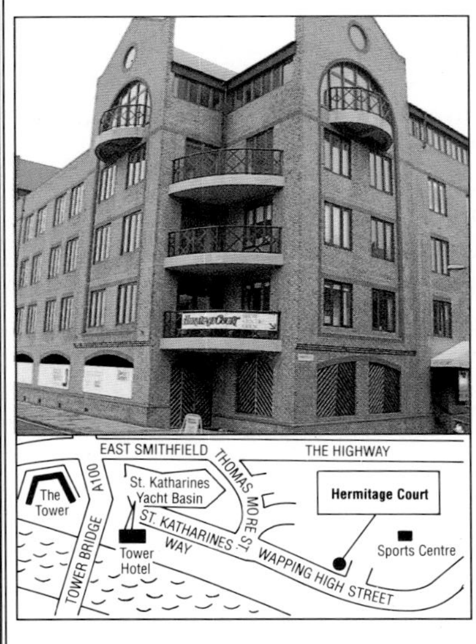

Hermitage Court offers a range of one, two, and three bedroom apartments of individual character combining the height of modern luxury with the period charm of Wapping's historic riverside, and the tranquility of its own landscaped, sunny courtyard. Some have conservatories or balconies, too.Whether you choose a one bedroom apartment from £117,500 or a spacious three bedroom apartment at £275,000 you'll enjoy secure underground parking, porterage service and easy access to the City just a short walk away.

3 *(Page 134)*

a List some of the:
i) social
ii) environmental
iii) economic problems found on the map in Figure 10.8. *(6)*

b How is urban renewal different from urban redevelopment? *(2)*

c In drawing up any new plan for an area, all groups living there should be considered, e.g. young children, teenagers, couples, the elderly, the disabled, pedestrians, car-drivers, etc. Study Figure 10.9 which shows the changes that have been made to this area.
i) Which of the groups in the community do you think have been catered for, and which have not? *(4)*
ii) How successful do you think the planners have been in trying to overcome the social, environmental and economic problems of the area? *(6)*
iii) If you were on the local housing association, what further ideas would you put forward to improve the area – bearing in mind that inner city areas are usually short of money? *(3)*

11 TOURISM

Recent trends

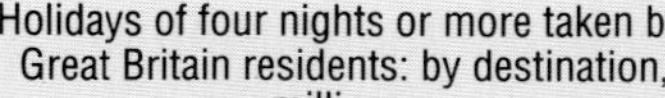

Holidays of four nights or more taken by Great Britain residents: by destination, millions

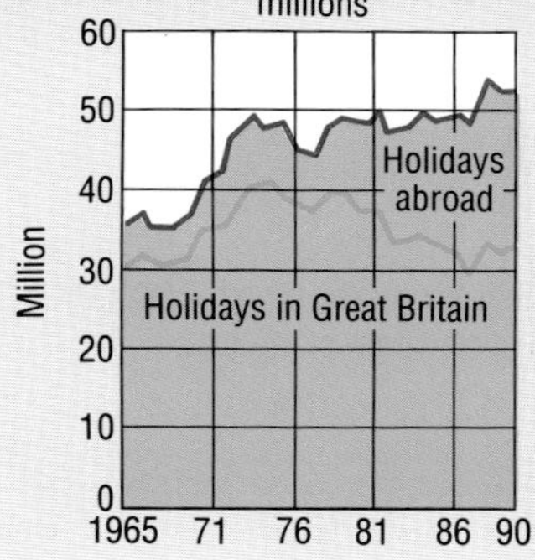

Figure 11.1
Holidays taken by British residents

Tourism is one of the fastest growing industries in the world today. It is an important factor in the economy of most developed countries, while it is seen by many developing countries as the one possible way to obtain income and to create jobs. In Britain in the eighteenth century, spa towns developed for the wealthy to 'take the waters'. By the late nineteenth or early twentieth centuries, many industrial workers enjoyed a day or even a few days by the seaside. The annual holiday has become part of most families' way of life. As seen in Figure 11.1, an increasing number of British people are now travelling abroad. The British Tourist Authority defines a short-term holiday as being one to three nights away, and a long-term holiday as four nights or more.

Figure 11.2
Increase in Britain's elderly population

Year	Total population (million)	Over 65 years old (million)
1951	50.3	5.5
1961	52.8	6.2
1971	55.9	7.3
1981	56.3	8.5
1989	56.9	9.0
1991	57.2	9.1
2001	est. 59.2	est. 9.3

Growth in tourism in Britain

More leisure time

1 **An ageing population**
The number of elderly people is rising rapidly (Figure 11.2), and while some may not be fit or wealthy enough to take holidays, many are – even if their holiday is spent staying with friends and relations. As many people are taking either voluntary or enforced early retirement, they are then able to take advantage of their greater fitness.

2 **Shorter working week**
The number of contractual hours which the average British person works in paid employment has continued to decrease.

Contractual hours	1973	1983	1991
Full time working woman	37.5	37.2	36.3
Full time working man	44.7	41.5	38.4

Recently, many companies, especially in retailing, have been laying-off people in full time employment, and replacing them with people who work part time.

3 **Longer holidays with pay**
Earlier this century those people who did take holidays forfeited their salary for the time spent away from work. It is now usual for most employees to be granted either several days or, and in some cases, three or four weeks' paid holiday each year. This has greatly increased the number of people who are able to take holidays.

4 **Greater affluence**
Although Britain's unemployment figures are considerably higher than they were in 1980, the salaries paid to those who are employed have grown considerably in that time.

	1973	1983	1993
Full time working woman	£21.20	£106.90	£253
Full time working man	£41.50	£163.80	£354

This greater affluence, coupled with paid holidays, has enabled more people not only to take a holiday, but also to take more than one holiday a year (Figure 11.3). Some people may divide their main holiday into two, sometimes taking 'mini-breaks' at off-peak times. Others feel the need to have more breaks to escape increased pressures at work.

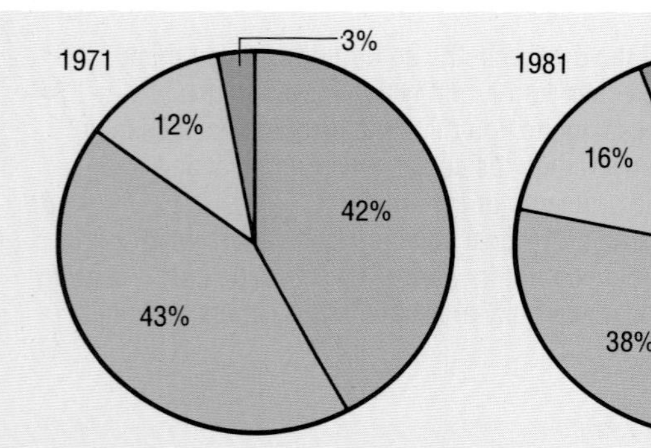

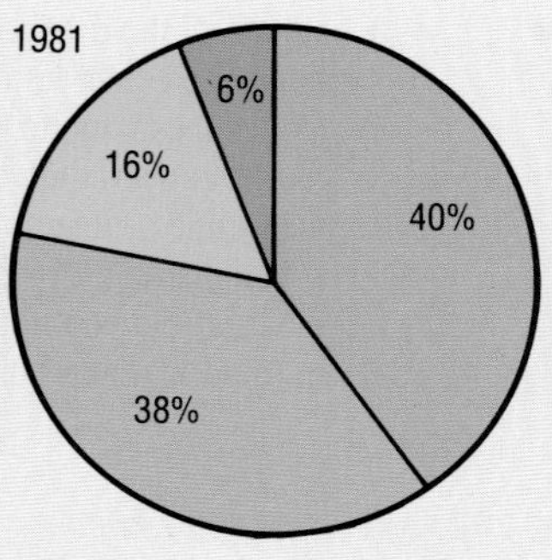

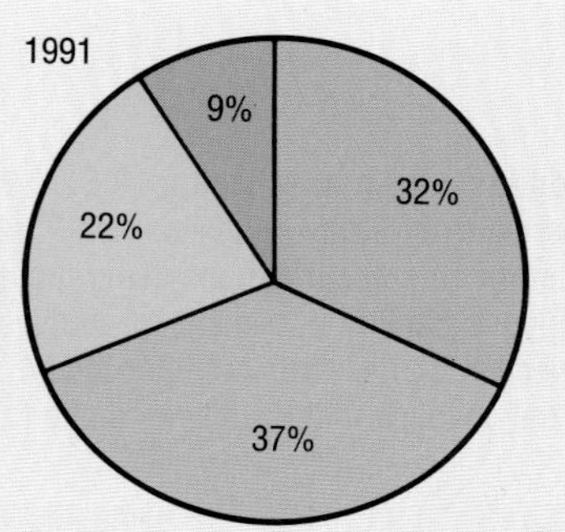

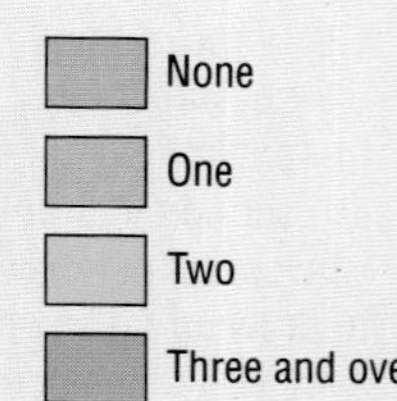

Figure 11.3
Number of holidays in a year

	1961	1971	1981	1991
2 cars	3	8	17	22
1 car	33	48	44	42
No car	64	44	39	36

Figure 11.5 Car ownership per family (%)

Greater mobility and accessibility

The increase in car ownership has given people much greater freedom to choose where and when they go for the day or for a longer period of time. Added to this is the convenience of loading the boot (or roof-rack) with luggage, and being able to drive from door to door. In 1951 only one family in twenty had a car, whereas by 1990 almost two in every three had their own vehicle (Figure 11.5).

During the same period the number of motorways had increased (Britain had none in 1951), as had the quality of roads and the number of by-passes built to avoid bottlenecks and steep gradients. This has led to a reduction in driving time between places, which has encouraged more people to travel greater distances. Figure 11.4 shows how the reduction in driving time from the Dartmoor National Park, mainly due to the building of the M5, has meant that many more people from London, Birmingham and South Wales are likely to visit the park. This is one reason why the West Country is the most popular region in Britain for domestic holidays (Figure 11.7).

Also, before the 1950s, air travel for a holiday was beyond the means of most British families. Since then the use of charter aircraft has reduced fares, and the building of international airports near to large holiday resorts has enabled tourists to travel in larger numbers and greater distances than before. This trend has recently been reversed due to the recession of the early 1990s and during the Gulf War in 1991.

Package holidays

These are holidays for a set period of time in which travel, accommodation and predetermined meals (full board or half board) are all included in the price. Tour operators can charter flights and make block bookings at holiday resorts at prices well within the range of most British people. The most popular overseas destinations for British tourists in 1991 are shown in Figure 11.8.

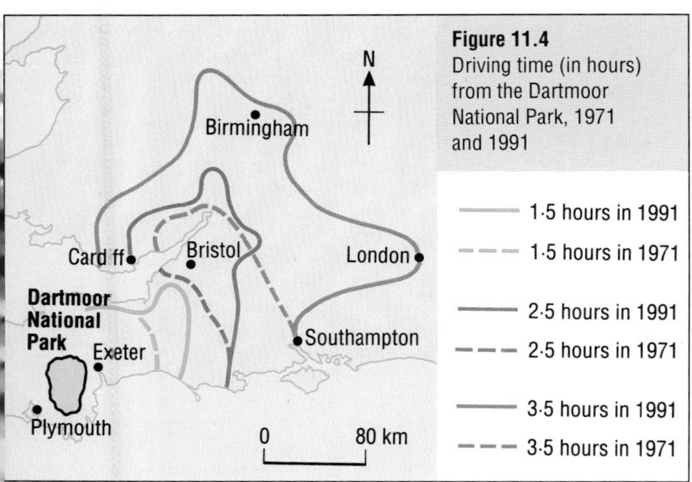

Figure 11.4 Driving time (in hours) from the Dartmoor National Park, 1971 and 1991

Self-catering holidays

The increase in camping, caravans and rented holiday flats has further lowered the cost of holidays. This allows families with young children to enjoy a holiday and to stay away from home for longer periods.

Advertising has made people even more aware of the range of holidays and recreational activities available to them. **Other factors** include:

- the increasing pressure of modern life and, for many, an unattractive local environment which encourages people to 'get away from it all';
- times of advantageous foreign exchange rates which make certain overseas holidays cheaper;
- increased education;
- a desire to experience other cultures (long haul holidays);
- the unreliable British weather and the desire to find places with a hot, dry, sunny climate.

	1968	1978	1988
Money spent in UK by overseas residents (£m)	282	2507	6193
Money spent abroad by UK residents (£m)	271	1549	8228
Balance	+11	+958	–2035

Figure 11.6 Revenue from tourism

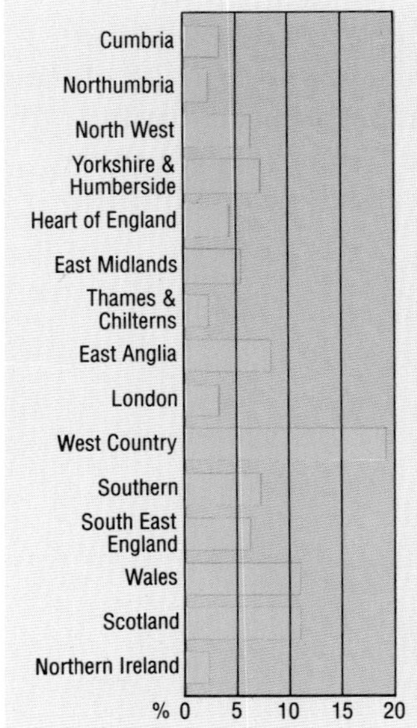

Figure 11.7 Domestic holidays taken by UK residents by region

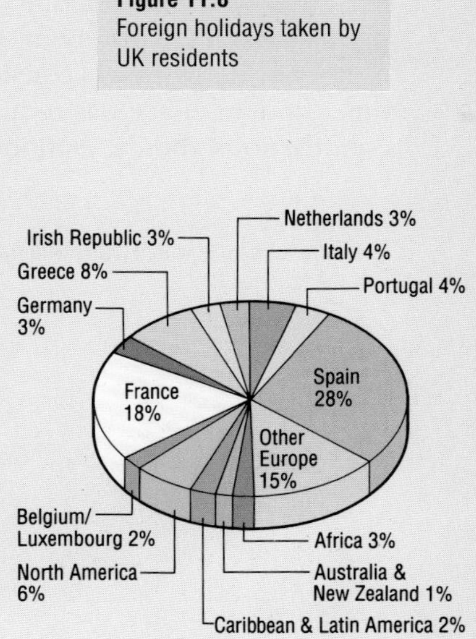

Figure 11.8 Foreign holidays taken by UK residents

National Parks

These are defined by Act of Parliament (1949) as *'areas of great natural beauty giving opportunity for open-air recreation, established so that natural beauty can be preserved and enhanced, and so that the enjoyment of the scenery by the public can be promoted'.*

- They contain some of the most diverse and spectacular upland scenery in England and Wales (Pembrokeshire Coast National Park, being coastal, is the exception).
- They are mainly in private ownership, though bodies such as the National Trust, Forestry Commission and water authorities are important landowners (these parks are not owned by the nation).
- Public access is encouraged, but is restricted to footpaths, bridleways, open fells and mountains (with the exceptions of military training areas and grouse moors).
- They support local populations who are dependent on primary (farming, forestry and mining) and tertiary (tourism) forms of employment.
- The ten National Parks contain a variety of scenery which in turn provides a wide range of recreational activities (Figure 11.11). All the parks provide basic opportunities for walking, riding and fishing but some provide specialist attractions, e.g. caving and potholing in the limestone areas of the Brecon Beacons and the Peak District (Figure 11.11). The Norfolk Broads and the New Forest are now National Parks in all but name.

Time and distance to National Parks

The National Parks were usually located within easy reach of the major conurbations (Figure 11.11). This enabled the maximum number of people, including those who lived in large urban areas, to escape to a quieter, more pleasant rural environment. Since then the growth of the motorway network has considerably reduced driving times and, in effect, has reduced distances between the conurbations and the National Parks (Figure 11.9).

Figure 11.9
Number of people within a three-hour drive of the National Parks

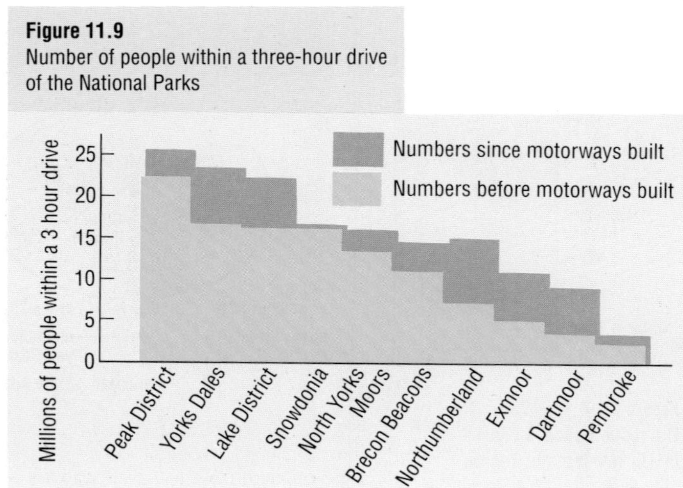

Figure 11.10
Gunnerside, Swaledale

Figure 11.11
National Parks, conurbations and motorways in the UK

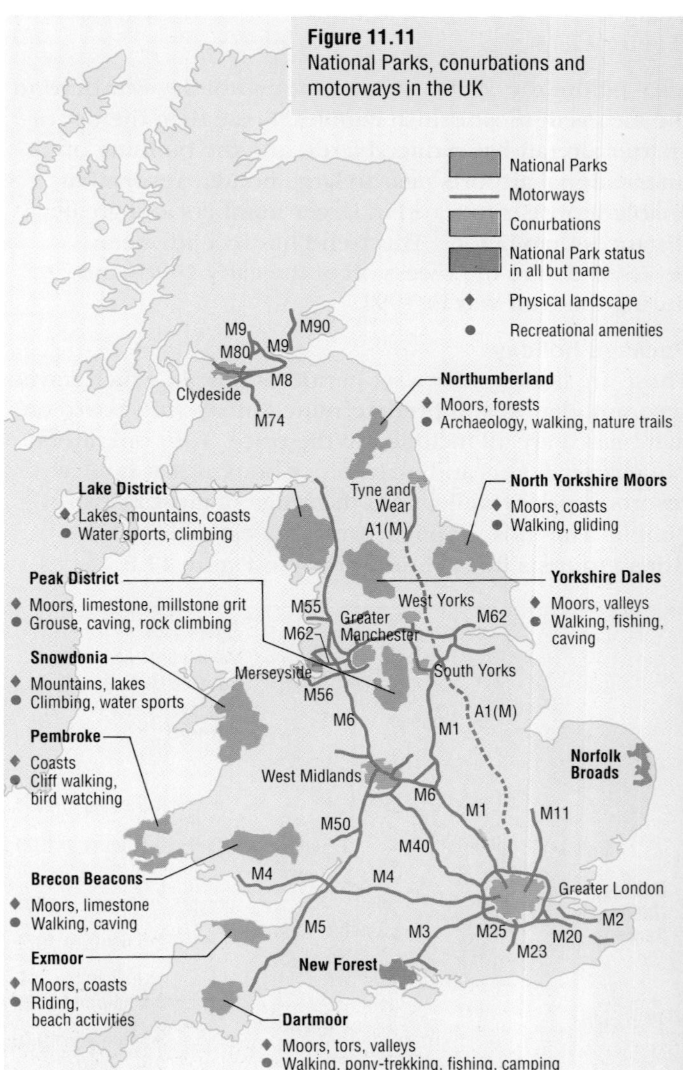

Who owns the National Parks?

In total, 81 per cent of the land is owned privately, mainly by farmers, with 6 per cent belonging to the Forestry Commission, 5 per cent to the National Trust (a charitable organisation earning revenue from membership, admission fees and souvenirs), 3 per cent to water authorities, 3 per cent to the Ministry of Defence, 1 per cent to county councils and 1 per cent to the National Parks themselves.

Conflict of users in National Parks

With over two people per hectare, the UK is one of the most densely populated countries in the world, and so there is considerable competition for land. This competition is also seen within the National Parks.

- Town dwellers wish to use the countryside for recreation and relaxation.
- Farmers wish to protect their land and in areas such as Exmoor are ploughing to a higher altitude by using government grants.
- The Forestry Commission has planted many hectares of trees in the poorer soils of Northumberland, the North Yorkshire Moors and the Snowdonia Parks.
- The mining and quarrying of slate (Lake District and Snowdonia) and limestone (Peak District) creates local jobs but ruins the environment (Figure 11.12).
- Water authorities have created reservoirs in the Lake and Peak Districts.
- The Ministry of Defence owns nearly a quarter of the Northumberland Park.
- Walkers and climbers wish for free access to all parts of the parks, and campers and caravanners seek more sites for accommodation.
- Despite planning controls, the demand for housing has led to an increased suburbanisation of villages (page 37) and the use of property as 'second homes' for town dwellers.
- Nature lovers wish to create nature reserves and to protect birds, animals and plants from the invading tourists.

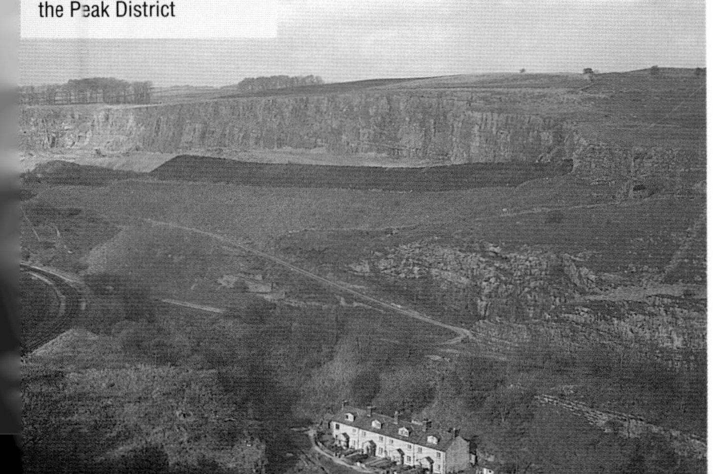

Figure 11.12
The scars of quarrying in the Peak District

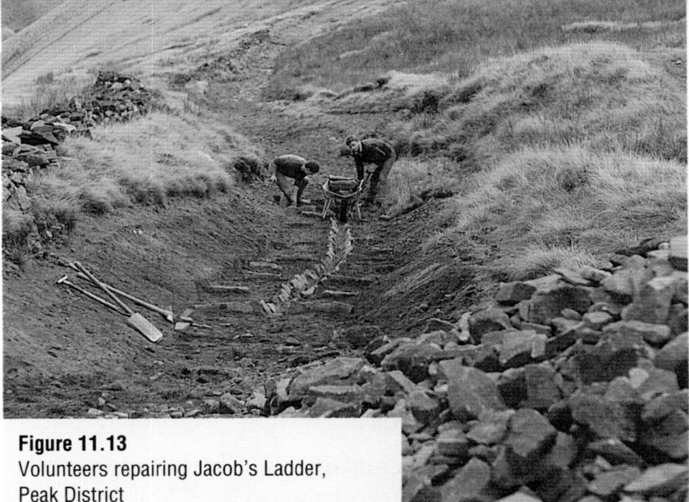

Figure 11.13
Volunteers repairing Jacob's Ladder, Peak District

Honeypots

The National Parks include many of the nation's *honeypots* – areas of attractive scenery (Malham Cove in the Yorkshire Dales), or of historic interest (the Roman Wall in the Northumberland Park), to which tourists swarm in large numbers. The problem is how to preserve the honeypots' natural beauty and their unspoilt quality (the essence of their appeal), while providing facilities for the hordes who arrive at peak summer periods. At Malham Cove steps have been cut into the limestone to safeguard paths. It is estimated that £1.5 million is needed to repair the six paths leading to the top of Snowdon where, on a summer's day, 2500 people might reach the summit. Parts of the 400 kilometre Pennine Way have had to have artificial surfaces laid as the tracks of walkers have penetrated over a metre into the peat in certain places (Figure 11.13). The footpaths on the Roman Wall are being eroded and, as soil is washed away, the foundations of the wall are being exposed.

Figure 11.14
How planning in a National Park can help to solve problems such as over-use, congestion and conflicts of use

Problems	Attempted solutions
Footpaths worn away (See Figure 11.13)	New routes planned; signposted routes; artificial surfaces laid
Destruction of vegetation	Areas fenced off; education of visitors
Litter, vandalism, trespassing	Provision of picnic areas with litter bins; park wardens
Cars parked on grass verges or in narrow lanes	Car parks; one-way systems; park and ride schemes
Congestion on narrow roads	Roads closed to traffic in tourist season/ weekends; park and ride; encouragement to use minibuses, to cycle or to walk
Heavy lorries, local traffic and tourist traffic	Scenic routes separating local and tourist traffic
'Honeypots' (views, cafés) cause crowding	Develop alternative honeypots, direct visitors to other attractions
Conflict of users, e.g. a) local farmers/tourists b) between tourists	Restricting tourist access to footpaths and bridleways. Separating activities, e.g. water skiing and angling
Unsightly new cafés, car parks and caravan parks	Screened behind trees. Only certain natural colours allowed in paint schemes

Tourism in the EC

Tourism is a labour intensive industry. An EC estimate, made for 1990, suggested that over 8.5 million people found employment in tourism within the community. Despite the fact that tourism is likely to become the largest single employer by the year 2000, it is not seen as a priority by EC ministers. Indeed the Community has no real overall policy towards it.

Europe can satisfy the needs of most types of tourist. The majority of people who travel abroad for a holiday tend to look for places with either a specific type of climate, spectacular scenery, opportunities for active pastimes and cultural pursuits, or facilities which promote health. The major types of resort and holiday areas within the EC are shown in Figure 11.16.

- Countries with a Mediterranean coastline attract many tourists partly because of spectacular scenery, but mainly because of their hot, dry, sunny summers and mild winters. Italy, Spain, Greece and the south of France tend to become congested with 'sun-worshippers' in summer. Spain also attracts retired people in the winter.
- Many, but not all, coastal areas in Portugal and around the Mediterranean Sea, have large expanses of sandy beaches with warm, clear seas.
- Mountainous regions such as the Pyrenees and Alpine Italy and France attract skiers in winter and walkers and climbers in summer. Alpine areas often include health resorts and offer spectacular scenery.
- Each country offers a range of cultural and historical holidays.

N
Ireland
United Kingdom
Netherlands
Denmark
Belgium
Luxembourg
Germany
France
Italy
Portugal
Spain
Greece
20
10
0
Tourist arrivals
Tourist departures
(millions)

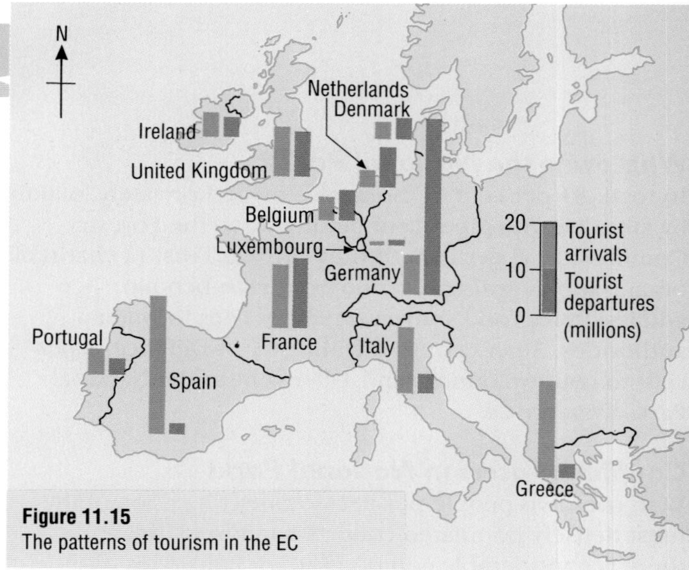

Figure 11.15
The patterns of tourism in the EC

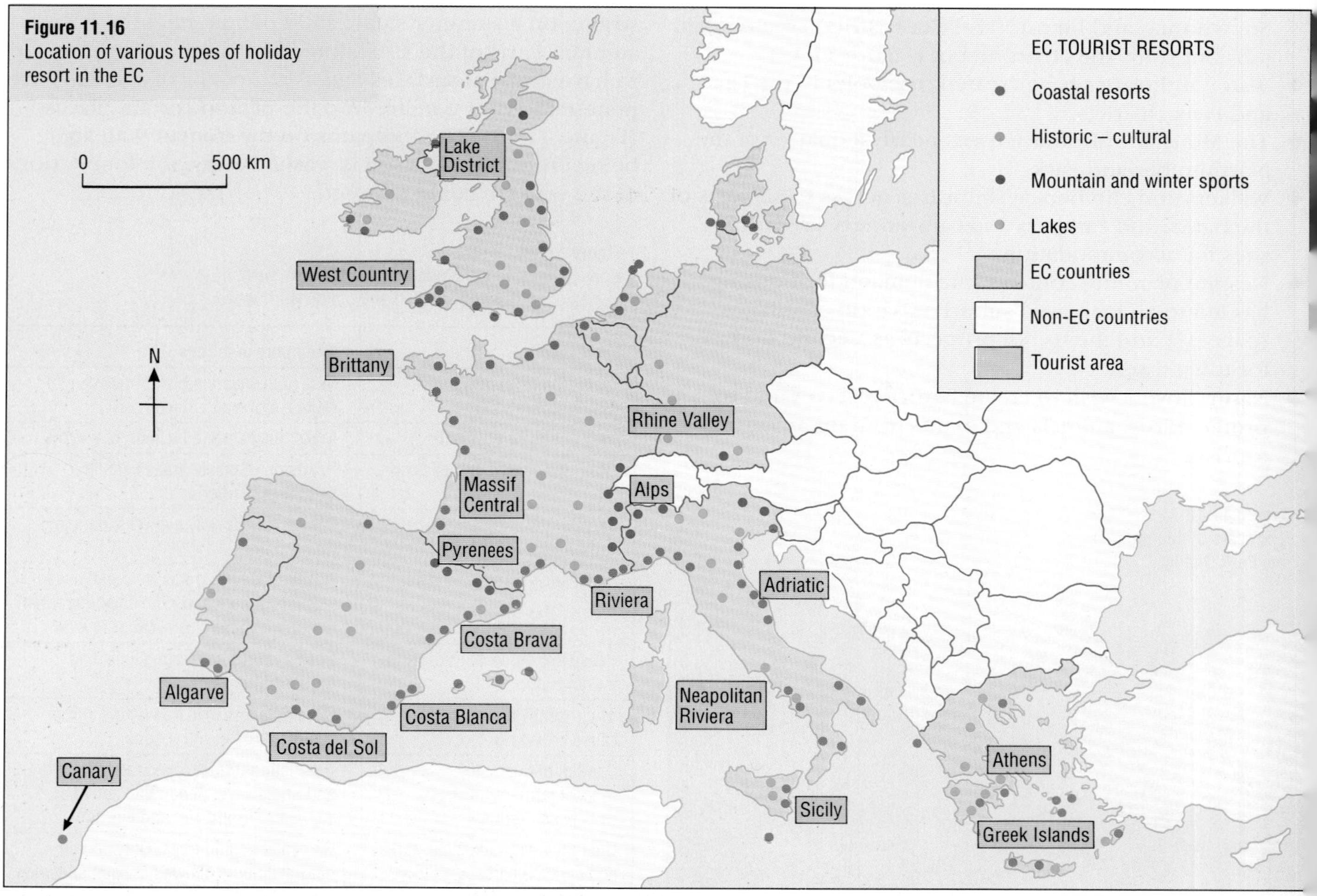

0
500 km
N
EC TOURIST RESORTS
Coastal resorts
Historic – cultural
Mountain and winter sports
Lakes
EC countries
Non-EC countries
Tourist area
Lake District
West Country
Brittany
Rhine Valley
Massif Central
Alps
Pyrenees
Riviera
Adriatic
Costa Brava
Algarve
Costa Blanca
Costa del Sol
Neapolitan Riviera
Athens
Sicily
Greek Islands
Canary

Figure 11.16
Location of various types of holiday resort in the EC

The pattern of tourism in the EC (Figures 11.15 and 11.17)

The most obvious pattern is the movement of large numbers of tourists from the more northerly countries in the EC to the south. This is because the north:

- Is much cooler and wetter than the south.
- Includes the more affluent countries (Germany, the Netherlands and France) whose inhabitants can afford to travel abroad for holidays.
- Has been more industrialised (Germany, Belgium and the UK) and is perceived to be less attractive.
- Has fewer of its own residents involved in tourism unlike countries like Spain, Portugal, southern Italy and Greece where people are either too busy in their own tourist industry, are too poor, or see little need to leave their own attractive climate and scenery to holiday abroad.

Figure 11.17 shows that several EC countries earn more from tourism than their residents spend overseas. Each year more people visit Greece than actually live there. The net beneficiaries tend to be in the poorer south of the EC. Without tourism those countries would be even poorer. Greece earns 20 per cent of its annual income from tourism. It is only the relatively low cost of holidays in these southern countries that keeps their net gain relatively low in comparison to the great numbers of people who visit them.

Despite the lack of a coherent tourist policy, the EC does aim to:

- Stimulate trade and business.
- Provide money from the Regional Development Fund to promote tourism (southern Italy, page 109).

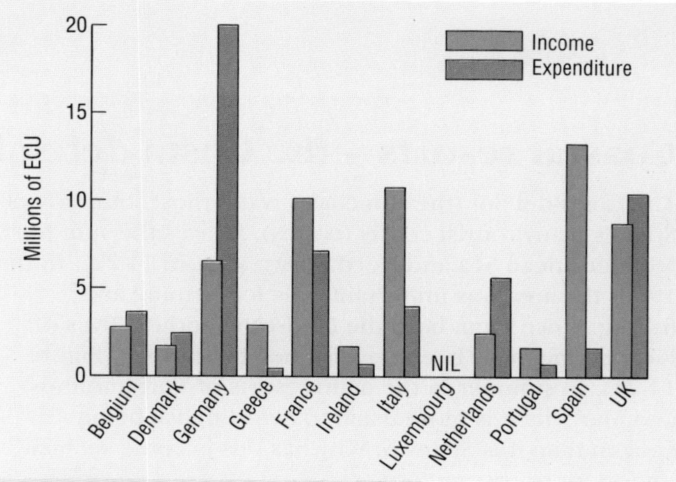

Figure 11.17
Revenue from overseas tourists and expenditure on visiting other countries (1990)

- Improve services such as water supply, electricity and accommodation.
- Improve and integrate transport routes, e.g. Eurorail and 'E' roads.
- Protect the environment – both natural (beaches, seas, wildlife) and cultural.
- Make journeys between countries easier by, in 1993, removing passport and customs controls, and eventually to have common passports and driving licences.
- Help the balance of payments of the poorer EC countries.

What is disturbing, as highlighted in *Holiday Which*, is the lack of EC directives and a common policy on important issues such as fire precautions in hotels, safety in swimming pools, standards of hotel hygiene, insurance policies on lost property, procedures following muggings or theft, and health care.

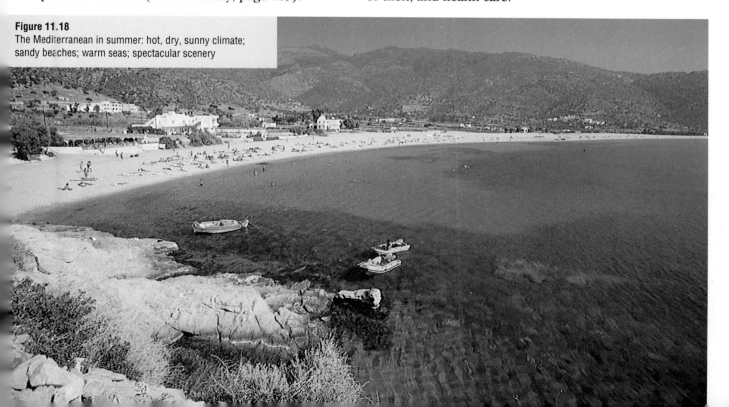

Figure 11.18
The Mediterranean in summer: hot, dry, sunny climate; sandy beaches; warm seas; spectacular scenery

Coastal resorts – the Costa del Sol

The Costa del Sol (the sun coast) is the most southerly of Spain's many tourist coasts (costas). It faces the sun, the Mediterranean Sea and North Africa (Figure 11.22). In the 1950s the area was important only for farming and fishing. Since then, both the landscape and the lives of local people have been transformed by tourism (Figure 11.21). In summer in the main resorts of Torremolinos and Marbella it is more usual to hear English being spoken than it is Spanish. Why has this become such an important tourist region?

Climate (Figure 11.20) Summers are hot, sunny and dry. Although winters are wet, it rarely rains all day and it is usually mild enough for people to sit out of doors.

Landscape There are long stretches of sandy beaches along the warm, blue Mediterranean Sea. Some beaches consist of shingle; others are artificial. Inland are the spectacular Sierra Nevada Mountains.

Accommodation Torremolinos consists of high density, low priced, high-rise hotels and apartments (Figure 11.19). Fuengirola's hotels provide the cheapest accommodation along the coast. Marbella has the most modern and luxurious of the hotels, and the hills behind are dotted with many time-share apartments. There are numerous campsites near to the N340 road.

Nightlife and shopping Illuminated shops attract tourists after dark. Numerous restaurants, cafés and bars provide flamenco and disco music, wine and beer, and Spanish, British and other European food. Most resorts have nightclubs. Shops range from the cheaper local bazaars and souvenir shops (mainly Torremolinos area) to chic boutiques with designer clothes (more likely in Marbella). Leather goods, ceramics and perfume can be bought in most places.

Average hours of sunshine

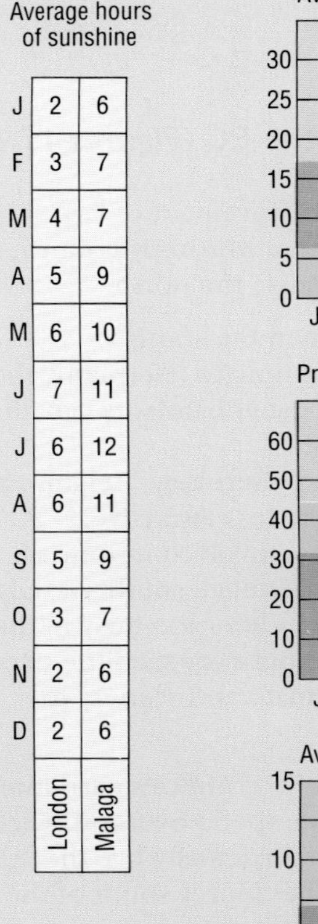

	London	Malaga
J	2	6
F	3	7
M	4	7
A	5	9
M	6	10
J	7	11
J	6	12
A	6	11
S	5	9
O	3	7
N	2	6
D	2	6

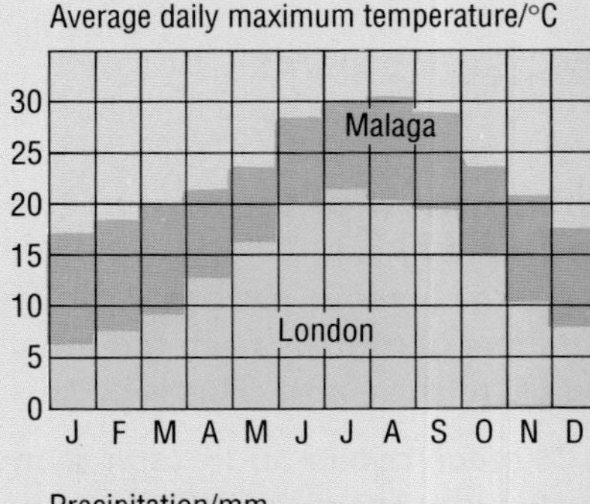

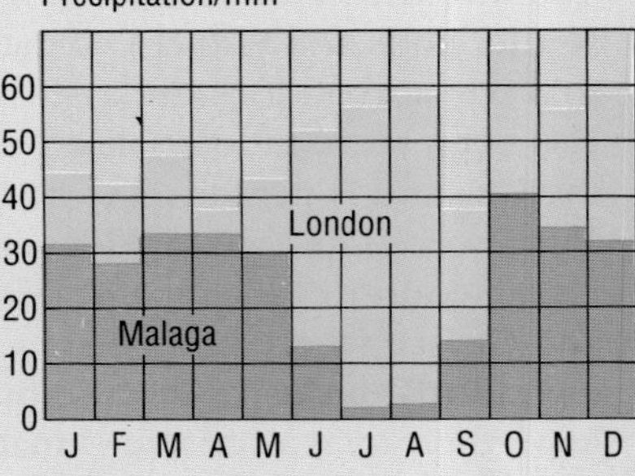

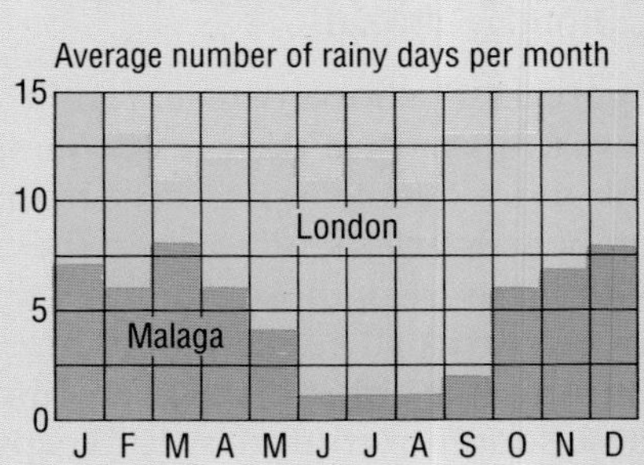

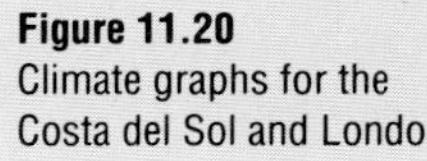

Figure 11.20 Climate graphs for the Costa del Sol and London

Things to do Many activities are linked to the sea, e.g. watersports and Aquapark at Torremolinos, and yachting marinas and harbours at Benalmadena, Puerto Banus and Estepona (Figure 11.23). There are also many golf courses, especially near Marbella. Day visits can be made to the whitewashed village of Mijas (perhaps the only 'real Spain' seen by tourists), to Ronda in the higher mountains, or to the historic centres of Granada and Seville.

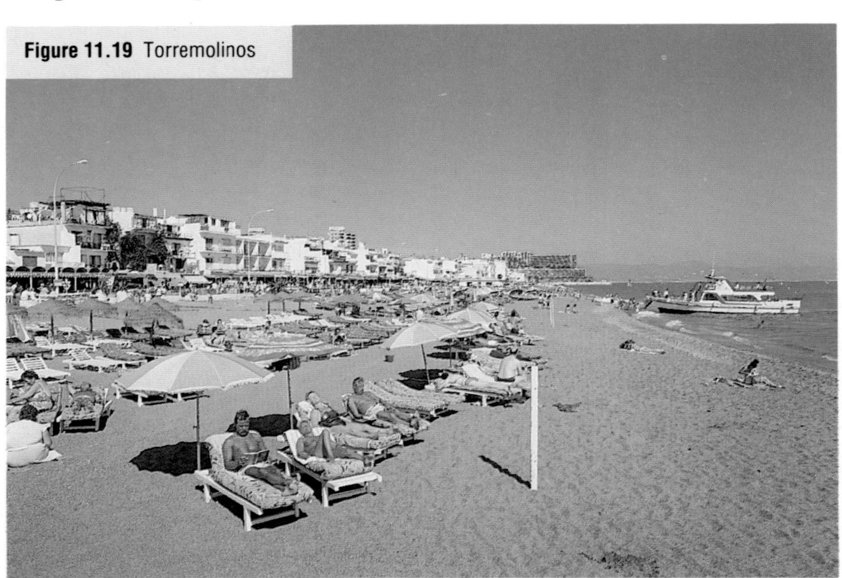

Figure 11.19 Torremolinos

Figure 11.21

"Sun-drenched southern Spain has always been one of the most popular holiday destinations and there's a very good reason for it. This wonderful stretch of coastline, fringed by long sandy beaches and backed by dramatic mountain ranges, has so much to offer. Variety is the key to the coast's success. Dedicate your days to that all-important tan, taking an occasional, refreshing dip in the western Mediterranean. Explore this fascinating part of Spain by visiting romantic Seville, British Gibraltar, stylish Puerto Banus and historic Granada. Once the sun goes down, enjoy a range of nightspots, bars and restaurants from the sophisticated to the informal."

Thomson

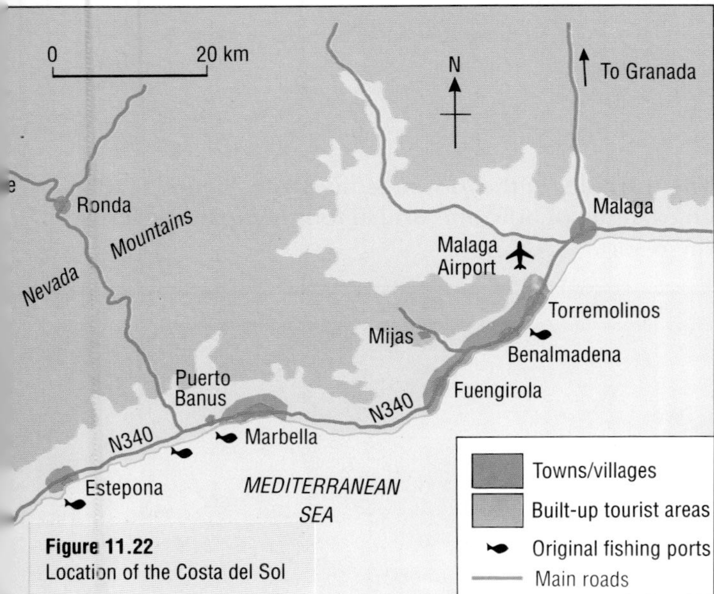

Figure 11.22
Location of the Costa del Sol

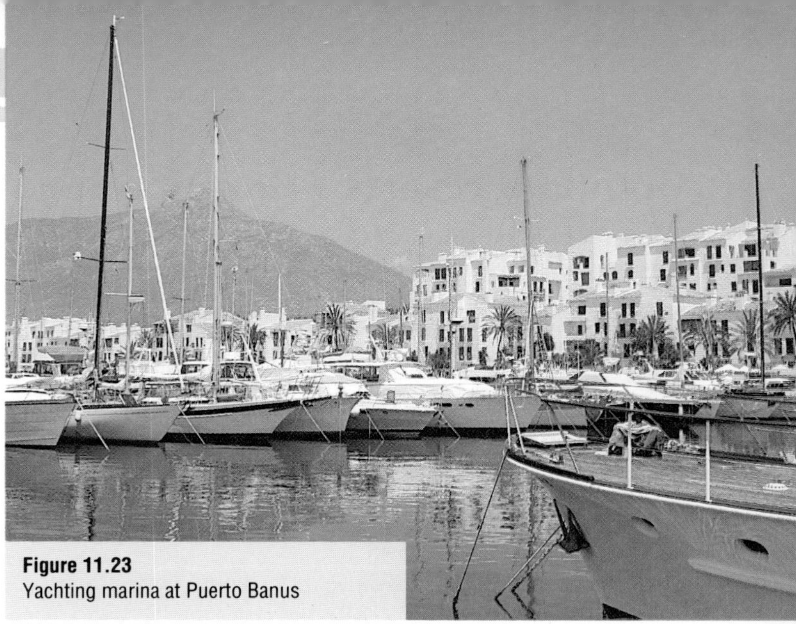

Figure 11.23
Yachting marina at Puerto Banus

Changes in tourism and to the environment

Places with pleasant climates and spectacular scenery attract tourists. Tourists demand amenities to make their visit more comfortable (e.g. accommodation, car parks) and activities to fill their leisure time (e.g. water sports). As more amenities are added and more leisure activities become available, the environment which first attracted people to these areas either deteriorates or becomes congested. Tourists will therefore seek alternative places to visit. This is happening on the Costa del Sol (Figure 11.24).

Role of the Spanish government

The Spanish government saw tourism as one way to provide jobs and to raise the country's standard of living. In places like the Costa del Sol it encouraged the construction of new hotels and apartment blocks and the provision of leisure amenities such as swimming pools, marinas and entertainment. More recently it has reduced VAT to 6 per cent in luxury hotels to try to maintain cheap holidays. It has also introduced stricter controls to improve the quality of the environment, which include cleaner beaches and reducing sea pollution (Spain now has the most 'Blue Flag' beaches in the EC).

Figure 11.24 Changes in tourism

Growth in tourism ↑ — Stage 1 — Stage 2 — Stage 3 — Stage 4 — ?

Date	1960s	1970s	1980s	1990s
Tourists from UK to Spain	1960 = 0.4 million	1971 = 3.0 m.	1984 = 6.2m. 1988 = 7.5m.	1990 = 7.0m.
State of, and changes in, tourism	Very few tourists	Rapid increase in tourism. Government encouragement	Carrying capacity reached – tourists outstrip resources, e.g. water supply and sewage	Decline – world recession, prices too high – cheaper upper market hotels elsewhere
Local employment	Mainly in farming and fishing	Construction workers. Jobs in hotels, cafés, shops. Decline in farming and fishing	Mainly in tourism – up to 70% in some areas	Unemployment increases as tourism declines (20%). Farmers use irrigation
Holiday accommodation	Limited accommodation, very few hotels and apartments, some holiday cottages	Large hotels built (using breeze block and concrete), more apartment blocks and villas	More large hotels built, also apartments and time share, luxury villas	Older hotels looking dirty and run down. Fall in house prices. Only high class hotels allowed to be built
Infrastructure (amenities and activities)	Limited access and few amenities. Poor roads. Limited streetlighting and electricity	Some road improvements but congestion in towns. Bars, discos, restaurants and shops added	E340 opened – 'The Highway of Death'. More congestion in towns. Marinas and golf courses built	Bars/cafés closing, Malaga bypass and new air terminal opened
Landscape and environment	Clean, unspoilt beaches. Warm sea with relatively little pollution Pleasant villages. Quiet. Little visual pollution	Farmland built upon. Wildlife frightened away. Beaches and sea less clean	Mountains hidden behind hotels. Litter on beaches. Polluted seas (sewage). Crime (drugs, vandalism and mugging). Noise from traffic and tourism	Attempts to clean up beaches and seas (EC Blue Flag beaches) New public parks and gardens opened. Nature reserves

Mountain resorts – Courmayeur

The winter sports resort of Courmayeur is located in the extreme north-western corner of Italy (Figure 11.25). The town lies at the foot of Mont Blanc. Figure 11.25 is an example of how one British tour company advertises the resort.

COURMAYEUR 4,016 - 11,385ft (1,224 - 3,470m)

Nestling beneath Mont Blanc, Courmayeur is a bustling market town, full of character with a marvellous Italian atmosphere. The main skiing area with 100km of marked piste is reached by cable car which is just 150m from the Hotel Pavilion

***Skiing**: Excellent for intermediates and advanced; famous Vallée Blanche run to Chamonix; tree-lined slopes; under Mont Blanc.*

***Resort**: Traditional country town; twisting streets; market; lively nightlife; great cuisine; varied shopping.*

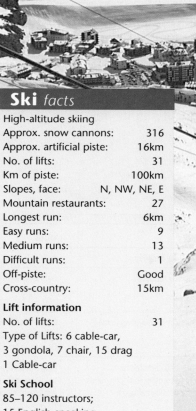

SKI RANGE: The high-altitude resort of Courmayeur has a super past snow record. Mont Blanc towers over this impressive region, which takes in 100km of mainly intermediate pistes. The main ski areas are the massive, sunny plateaux of the Checrouit slopes to the northeast, the Val Veny slopes and Mont Blanc, all served by elaborate and extremely well-run lift networks. From Courmayeur, a cable-car (No 1) takes you across the valley to Plan Checrouit, then a gondola and a series of drag and chair-lifts ascend further to Colle Checrouit. The Mont Blanc area offers fabulous late-season skiing from the Helbronner peak, including the well-known 20km Vallée Blanche to Chamonix.

Included in a special six-day pass is 4 days skiing in the Chamonix area, including Argentière, and one day in Pila, the Aosta ski area. Snow cannons are available to provide extra cover on 16km of pistes. Cross-country enthusiasts have 15km of trails.

APRES-SKI: In the evening you can sample some local Aosta specialities such as fontina cheese or beef steak Valdostan. You can also enjoy the many wines from northern Italy, such as Barolo or Prosecco. Check out the best bars – Roma or Steve's Cocktail Bar among them – then go dancing at one of the clubs, like Le Clochard or Abat Jour.

Ski *facts*

High-altitude skiing

Approx. snow cannons:	316
Approx. artificial piste:	16km
No. of lifts:	31
Km of piste:	100km
Slopes, face:	N, NW, NE, E
Mountain restaurants:	27
Longest run:	6km
Easy runs:	9
Medium runs:	13
Difficult runs:	1
Off-piste:	Good
Cross-country:	15km

Lift information

No. of lifts: 31

Type of Lifts: 6 cable-car, 3 gondola, 7 chair, 15 drag

1 Cable-car

Ski School

85–120 instructors;
15 English-speaking

Figure 11.25 Courmayeur

Within Courmayeur there is a weekly market, an ice rink and a swimming pool as well as opportunities for walking and horseriding. There are buses to Chamonix (40 minutes) and Aosta (1 hour).

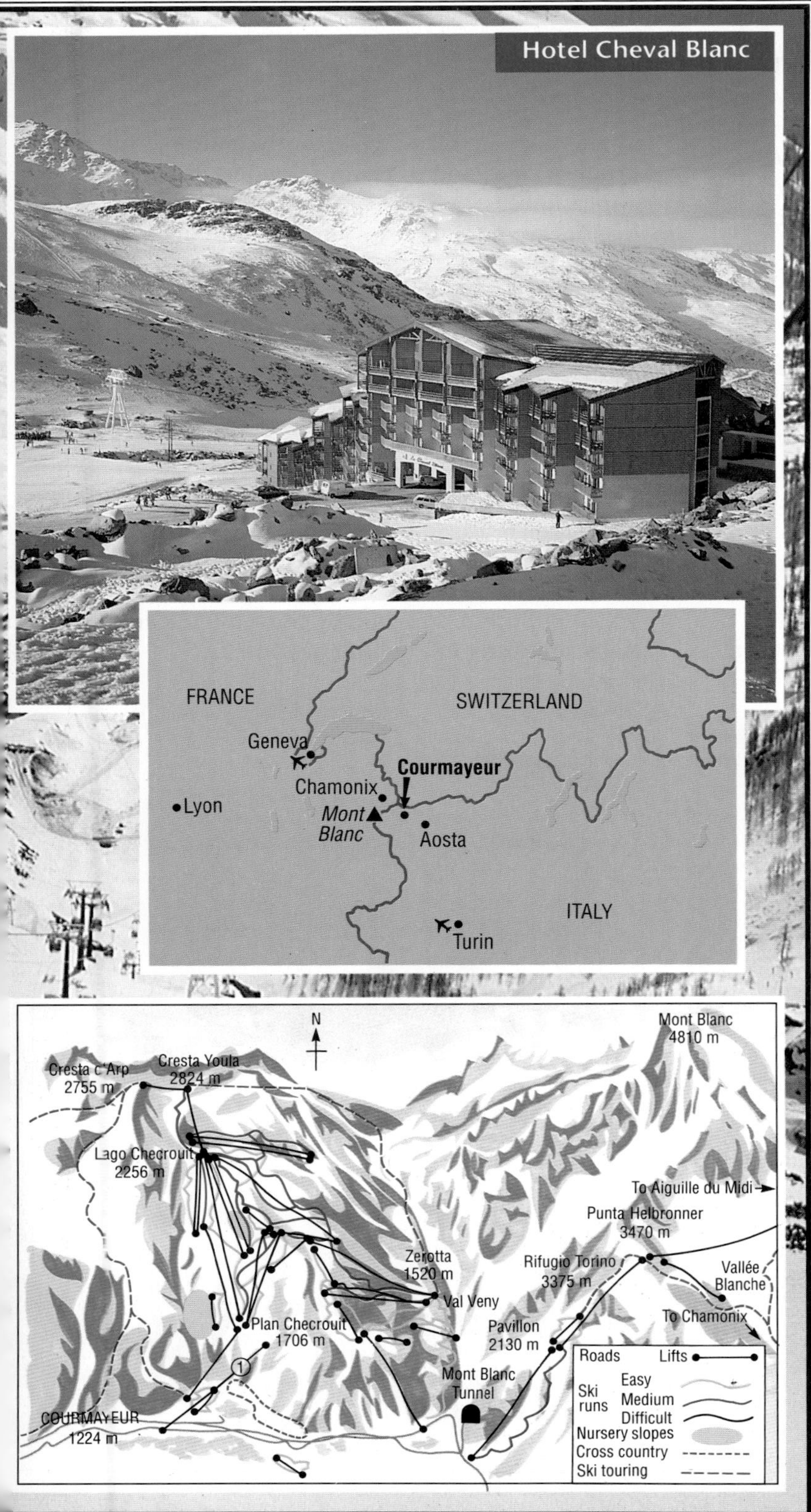

Benefits and problems of winter sports at Courmayeur

Benefits

There has been an increase in employment, especially among younger people, which has reduced the rate of migration away from the area. The standard of living of local people has risen as most jobs in the tourist industry are better paid than the traditional ones in farming and forestry. Roads, water supplies and sewage have all been improved. The ice rink and swimming pool are available to local residents.

Problems

Alp Action, a conservation group, launched a campaign in 1991 to alert people to the devastating effects of tourism on mountain habitats. The group claimed:

> *'Every year, 50 million people visit the Alps, two-thirds of them on winter skiing holidays, serviced by 40,000 ski runs. This has resulted in widespread deforestation of mountain slopes to make way for new and enlarged ski resorts and ski runs, while the huge increase in winter sports activities has added to serious erosion of mountain topsoil and a loss of Alpine vegetation. As a result, the danger of floods and avalanches has substantially increased during summer thunderstorms or following snow melt in spring. Likewise several hundred animal, insect and plant species are threatened with extinction. The several million vehicles which cross the Alps each year are partly blamed for the increase in incidence of Acid Rain* [Page 226] *which has affected 60 per cent of trees in Alpine Europe'.*

The report could have added the problems of visual pollution caused by the construction of unsightly buildings, as not all have been built to blend in with the natural environment, and ski-lifts. It could also have pointed out that many of the new jobs are seasonal, and have only replaced those in farming and forestry. The change in type of employment, together with the large influx of tourists, has destroyed the community's traditional way of life. The last few winters have been mild, and snowfalls have been light, late in arriving and not lying long at low altitudes. This has increased skiing at higher levels where the environment is most fragile. Artificial snow is being used in some places to prolong the winter season, but this can upset growth and hibernation cycles for plants and animals.

Cultural centres – Athens and a classical tour

Culture, in this sense, means learning about a country's civilisation and way of life. Travel programmes on television have made people in economically more developed countries aware of the intellectually satisfying holiday spent in countries and cities where the life style is different to their own (e.g. Thailand). Added to this is the holiday to 'historic' places where tourists can gain an insight into former civilisations (e.g. Egypt). An increasing number of tourists wish to combine a cultural-historic holiday with the more traditional beach holiday. Such visits have become possible due to increases in wealth, longer paid holidays from work, package holidays, and cheaper air flights. Cultural centres tend to attract short-stay visitors and people on touring holidays rather than long-stay tourists. These visits tend to be less seasonal than at coastal or winter resorts.

Although the largest group of tourists to Greece go there to relax on its many islands, an increasing number now visit sites associated with ancient Greece. The main centre for these visitors is Athens, with the most popular attraction being the Acropolis (Figure 11.26a). From Athens tourists can either make day excursions to the surrounding ancient sites, or join one of several 'classical tours' (Figure 11.27).

The Acropolis

While the increase in tourism is good for local economies, the extra pressure on such sites does create many problems. Many of these can be seen on a visit to Athens' most famous site, the Acropolis:

- Individual buildings like the Parthenon have to be roped off to prevent people climbing over them.
- Several buildings are usually hidden behind scaffolding as attempts are made to repair them from a safety point of view, and to restore them to their original appearance.
- Visitors are not admitted after 1500 hours partly to give the site 'time to recover'.
- The steps up to the Acropolis and some rocky paths on its summit have become polished and slippery after centuries of use, and dangerous to walk upon.
- Guides, who must be authorised, have whistles to keep people to well-defined paths.
- The many tourist coaches and cars have led to major parking problems and can cause vibrations which affect the foundations of buildings.
- Chemicals released by traffic and local industry are eroding buildings and statues causing them to crumble away (Figure 11.26b).
- Visual pollution is caused by souvenir and refreshment stalls, and litter left behind by tourists.

Figure 11.26a Acropolis

b Caryatids

c Theatre of Herodus Atticus

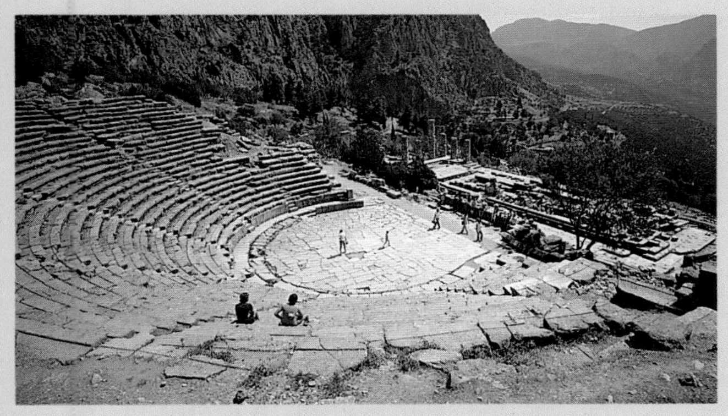

Delphi was famous in classical Greece for its oracle which gave advice and prophecies (although both were ambiguous). The Temple of Apollo and a well-preserved theatre and athletics stadium cling to a mountain side and overlook an olive-forested valley. The museum contains many outstanding works of art.

Sounion has a cliff-top temple and gets spectacular sunsets.

Figure 11.27 The classical tour route around Athens

Delphi
Corinth
Athens
Mycenae
Olympia
Epidauros
Sounion
······· Classical tour

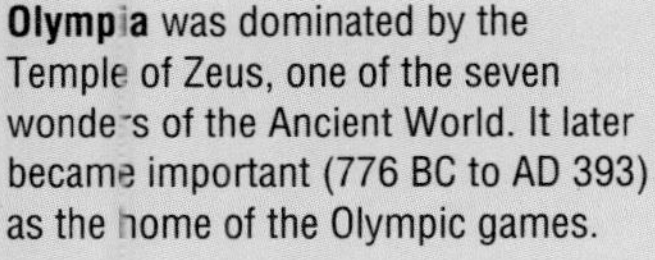

Olympia was dominated by the Temple of Zeus, one of the seven wonders of the Ancient World. It later became important (776 BC to AD 393) as the home of the Olympic games.

Corinth has well-excavated remains and is near to the Corinth canal.

Mycenae was the centre of one of Europe's first civilisations. It is noted for the Lion Gate and the discovery of a gold death mask believed to have belonged to Agamemnon, the most famous king of Mycenae.

A classical tour

The most popular tour takes place in Delphi and parts of the Peloponnese (Figure 11.27) However, as on the Acropolis, the increasing number of tourists can spoil the environment that is the source of attraction. The impact of tourists is harming both the Greek landscape and the historic buildings. At Delphi, for example, which is built on a steep hillside:

- Footpaths are worn away as tourists walk uphill from the coach park to the temple, theatre and stadium.
- Authorised guides have whistles which are needed to keep people to set paths.
- The guides have to keep a constant watch to ensure that a minority of tourists do not remove parts of buildings to take home as souvenirs.
- The narrow access roads, with their hairpin bends, were not built for large tourist coaches, nor for the increasing volume of cars.
- The small but attractively designed museum is exceptionally congested in summer when each room is likely to be packed with a coach load of visitors. Guides usually have to shout to make themselves heard over 'rival' guides.
- Flash photography is not allowed in the museum as the bright light destroys the natural colours of the exhibits.
- Video cameras are only allowed on payment of an exorbitant price (over £30 in 1992). Other sites have banned the use of video cameras altogether.

Tourism and the environment – Kenya

Few countries in the world can offer the traveller the variety of landscapes that Kenya can. It has mountains, grassy plains, sandy beaches, coral reefs and an abundance of wildlife. Kenya appreciates these natural resources and has set up over 50 National Parks and game reserves to protect and manage its environment. Tourism has become Kenya's major source of overseas income. *Safaris*, meaning 'a journey', are organised so that tourists can be driven around, usually in seven or nine-seater minibuses with adjustable roofs to allow easier viewing . Unlike on early safaris, today's tourists are only allowed to shoot with cameras. An advertisement for one safari is given in Figure 11.28.

Day 1 Nairobi/Samburu (310km)

After breakfast drive north, cross the Equator and pass Mt Kenya, to Samburu Lodge. After lunch there will be a game drive when you should see elephant, buffalo, lion, reticulated giraffe, zebra, crocodile and many species of bird.

Day 2 Samburu

Early morning game drive. Relax at mid-day around the swimming pool or watch the Samburu perform traditional dances. Late afternoon game drive.

Day 3 Samburu/Treetops (200 km)

Drive south for lunch at the Outspan Hotel. A short journey takes you into the Anberdare Mountains where you will spend the night at Treetops, the world famous tree hotel. As evening approaches buffalo, elephant and rhino join other animals at the waterhole.

Day 4 Treetops/Nakuru/Naivasha (240 km)

Transfer to Outspan for breakfast. Drive to the Thomson's Falls, and down into the Rift Valley to Nakuru for lunch. A short drive will let you see vast flocks of flamingos and the endangered Rothschild giraffe. Continue to Lake Naivasha Hotel for overnight.

Day 5 Naivasha/Maasai Mara (240 km)

Leisurely morning by the lakeside. After lunch drive to Keekorok Lodge in the Maasai Mara.

Day 6 Maasai Mara

The huge Mara plain provides some of the best game-viewing in East Africa. During early morning and late afternoon game drives you are likely to see huge herds of wildebeest and zebra, as well as lion, elephant, cheetah, leopard, Maasai giraffe, and hippo. An option is the early morning Balloon Safari .

Day 7 Maasai Mara/Nairobi (260 km)

Early morning departure arriving at Nairobi for lunch. Afternoon flight to Mombasa to continue your holiday at a beach hotel.

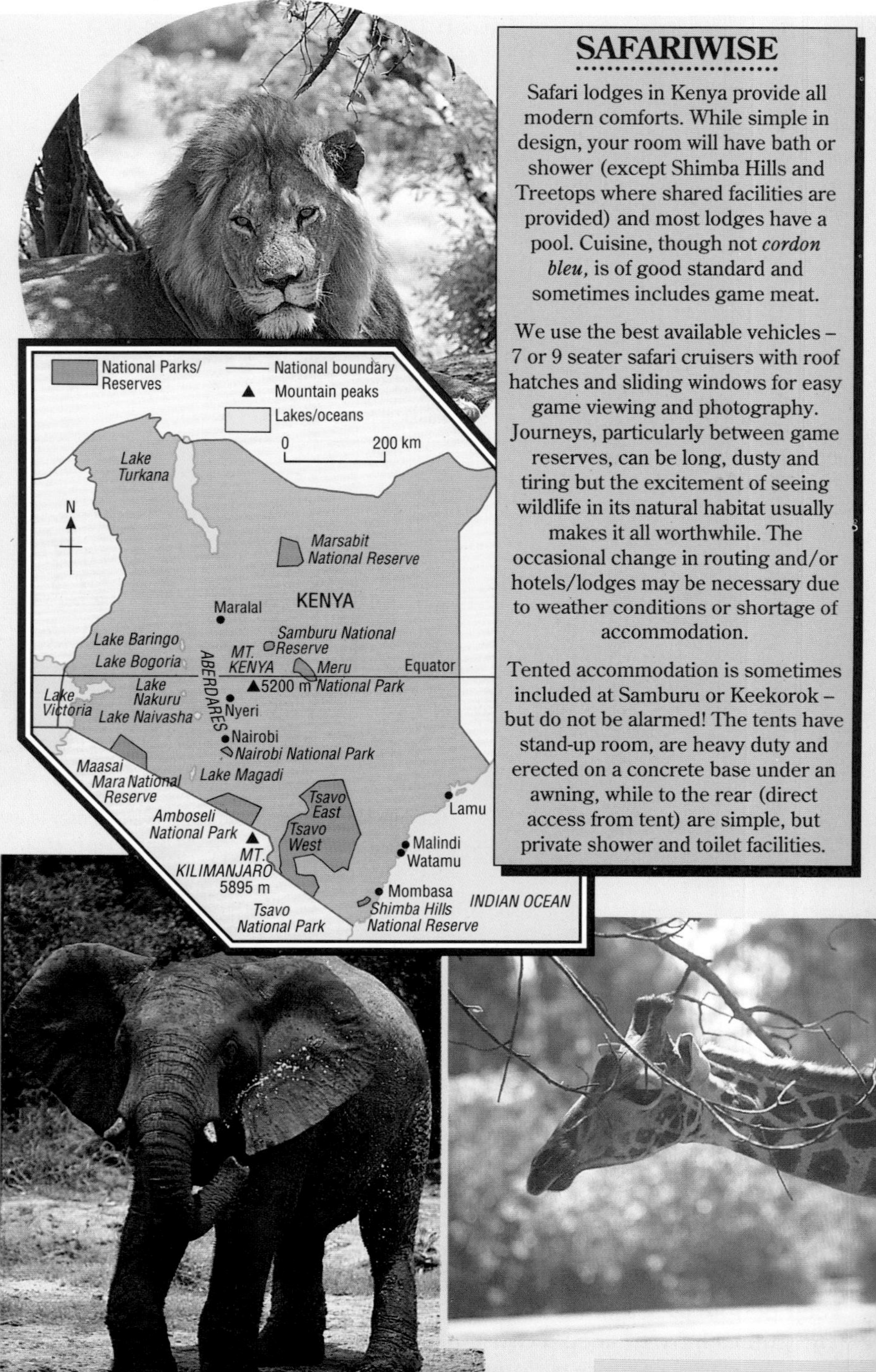

Figure 11.28 Safari in Kenya

Figure 11.29
Erosion by minibuses

Figure 11.30
Dust track in Amboseli

Figure 11.31
A dust storm causing soil erosion

Figure 11.32
Balloon safari

BALLOON SAFARI

No visit to Maasai Mara could be complete without a trip in a hot air balloon. The excursion operates on a daily basis (subject to weather conditions). After an early start, drift above the browsing game for about an hour (ideal for keen photographers). After the flight a champagne style breakfast is served.

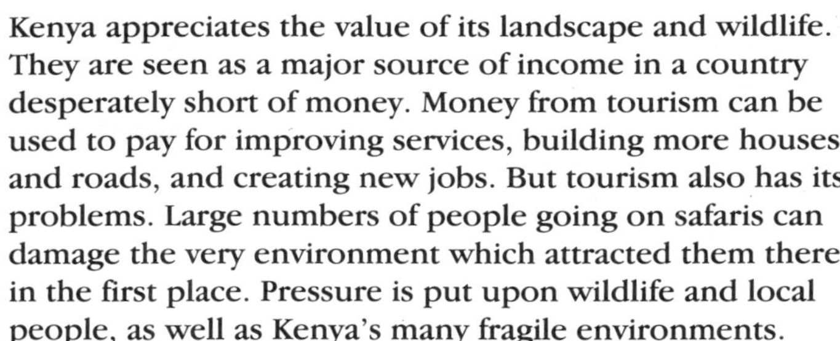

Kenya appreciates the value of its landscape and wildlife. They are seen as a major source of income in a country desperately short of money. Money from tourism can be used to pay for improving services, building more houses and roads, and creating new jobs. But tourism also has its problems. Large numbers of people going on safaris can damage the very environment which attracted them there in the first place. Pressure is put upon wildlife and local people, as well as Kenya's many fragile environments.

The environment Safari minibuses are meant to keep to well-defined tracks in National Parks and game reserves. However drivers often form new routes, either to enable their passengers to get as close as possible to wildlife, or to avoid wet season marshy areas. Minibuses can get stuck in the mud, ruining vegetation (Figure 11.29), or widening existing tracks (Figure 11.30). In Amboseli, as in other parks, the wind, minibuses and herds of animals all cause mini dust storms which increase the rate of soil erosion (Figure 11.31).

Wildlife Minibuses are not meant to go within 25 metres of animals, but their drivers often ignore this as they are unlikely to get good tips from their passengers if the best close-up views of wildlife are not obtained. Animals may be prevented from mating, making a kill, or forced to move to less favourable areas. Balloon Safaris (Figure 11.32) cause controversy as conservationists claim that the intermittent release of hot air and the shadow of passing balloons disturb wildlife.

People Today, apart from employees at safari lodges, nobody is allowed to live in National Parks. Even game reserves only permit a limited number of herders and their cattle. The setting up of National Parks meant that nomadic tribes, such as the Maasai, had to be moved away from their traditional grazing grounds. Many now have to live a more permanent life (Question 16 page 129), earning money by selling small artefacts to, or performing traditional dances for, the tourist (Figure 11.33). Recently the government has begun to work with the Maasai, allocating them a share of the wealth obtained from tourism towards improving their education, housing and water supply (page 129).

Figure 11.33 Maasai selling artefacts to tourists

Tourism in developing countries – a West Indies beach village

During the 1980s tourists became less satisfied with package tours to European coastal resorts and sought holidays further afield, in places with different environments and cultures. Long-haul holidays benefited from travel programmes on television. The chief beneficiaries from this change in holiday fashion were developing countries such as Kenya, Egypt, Sri Lanka, Thailand, Malaysia and Jamaica. The attractions of earning money from tourism are considerable to economically less developed countries, many of whom see its development as the only way to prosperity. Even so, only a limited number of developing countries profit from tourists on long-haul holidays, and to those limited countries the damage to their culture and environment can, at times, outweigh the benefits.

Attractions of the West Indies

- Winters (25°C) are much warmer than those in North America and Europe. Summers are hot (28°C) but not oppressive.
- Most days have over eight hours of sun.
- The scenery is attractive, usually either volcanic mountains covered in forest or coral islands with sandy beaches.
- The warm, clear, blue seas are ideal for water sports (sailing and water skiing).
- There is varied wild life.
- Customs are different (calypsos, steel bands, food, festivals and carnivals).
- There are many cultural resorts.
- They are situated a relatively short flight time from North America.

The beach village is a recent attempt to try to disperse accommodation and amenities so that they merge with the natural environment (Figure 11.34), and to avoid spoiling the advantages which originally attracted tourists to the islands. The advantages and disadvantages are summarised in the table.

Disadvantages of tourism

1. Hotels, airports and roads spoil the visual appearance and create noise, air pollution and litter.
2. Usually only 10% – 20% of the income received from tourists stays in the country. Most hotels are foreign owned and profits go overseas. Tourists spend most of their money in the hotels.
3. Much employment is seasonal. Overseas labour may be brought in to fill the better-paying jobs.
4. Local craft industries may be destroyed in order to provide mass-produced, cheap souvenirs.
5. Farming economy is damaged as land is sold to developers. Much of the food eaten by tourists is imported either because local production is insufficient or to meet the demands for European type foods (but sold at the developing country's prices).
6. Locals cannot afford tourist facilities.
7. Borrowed money increases national debt.
8. Tourists expect unlimited water. Many areas may be short of water for domestic and farming use.
9. Local cultures and traditions are destroyed. New social problems of prostitution, crime, drugs and drunkenness. Lack of respect for local customs and religious beliefs (e.g. semi-naked tourists into mosques and temples).

..... Tourism is a form of economic colonialism

Advantages of tourism

1. The natural environment (sun, sand, sea and scenery) is used to attract tourists and their much-needed money.
2. Income from tourism is usually greater than the income from the export of a few raw materials.
3. Creates domestic employment, e.g. hotels, entertainment and guides. It is labour intensive.
4. Encourages the production of souvenirs.
5. Creates a market for local farm produce.
6. Overseas investment in airports, roads and hotels.
7. Profits can be used to improve local housing, schools, hospitals, electricity and water supplies.
8. Increased cultural links with foreign countries, and the preservation of local customs and heritage.
9. Reduces migration.

..... Tourism raises the standard of living

Figure 11.34 A beach village in Barbados

Figure 11.35 A beach village merging with the natural environment

1 *(Pages 136, 138 and 139)*

a What is a National Park? *(2)*

b i) Is it true that the National Parks are owned by the government? *(1)*

ii) The graph shows the different land owners in the National Parks. Match up each segment of the graph with its correct land owner. *(6)*

c 'National Parks contain a variety of scenery which in turn provides a wide range of recreational activities'. Copy and complete the following two tables. *(10)*

d i) Which conurbation is not near to a National Park? *(1)*

ii) Which National Park is surrounded by most motorways and conurbations? *(1)*

iii) Which two parks have been least affected by the construction of motorways? *(2)*

e Many more people now visit National Parks than in 1950. Give four reasons (other than the building of motorways) for the increase in numbers. *(4)*

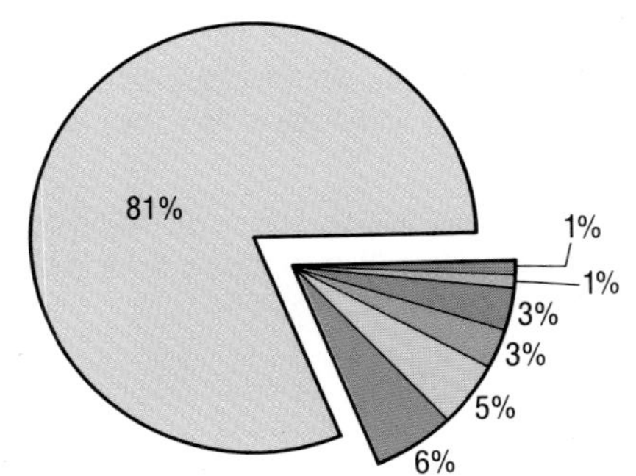

a Scenery	National Park
Coasts	Pembroke
Forests	
Lakes	
Limestone	
Moors	
Mountains	

b Activity	National Park
Archaeology	Northumberland
Bird-watching	
Caving	
Climbing	
Gliding	
Riding	

2 *(Pages 138 and 139)*

a Name two towns within a short distance of the Peak District. *(2)*

b List three different physical attractions referred to on the map. *(3)*

c Giving map evidence, list three different types of summer activity which can take place in this National Park. *(3)*

d Give two separate pieces of evidence to show that the Peak District also attracts visitors on cultural (historical) trips. *(2)*

e i) Give reasons why the Peak District National Park is likely to be very busy on a sunny Sunday in August. *(4)*

ii) Why might some visitors be attracted to the Peak District in winter? *(2)*

f Choose the correct word from each pair of words given in brackets:
'Most visitors to the Peak District National Park will go in (summer/winter). They will tend to visit mainly (in the week/at weekends) and stay there for (a week/a day). Most will travel for less than (1 hour/3 hours)'. *(4)*

g Castleton is said to be a 'honeypot'.

i) What is meant by the term 'honeypot'? *(1)*

ii) Give three problems that may result from the increased numbers of visitors to a honeypot. *(3)*

iii) Describe and explain three ways in which these problems may be solved by the National Park planners. *(3)*

iv) Give three ways in which the pressure on a honeypot may be reduced. *(3)*

v) From your general knowledge, can you name any two famous buildings in Britain and any two places of national beauty which have become honeypots? *(4)*

h Visitors to a National Park may come into conflict with the local inhabitants. Suggest three conflicts which might occur between the visitors and different groups of residents in the park. *(3)*

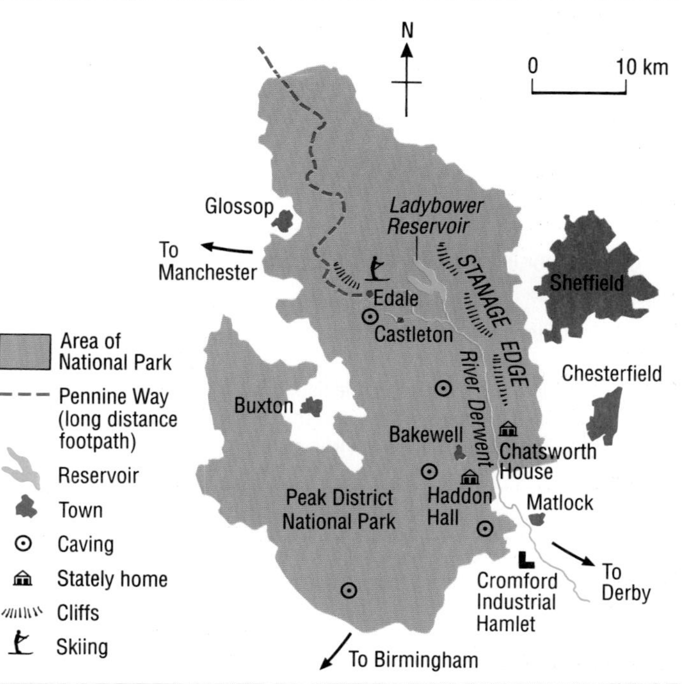

3 *(Figure 11.12 on page 139)*

Conflicts occur between tourists visiting a National Park for recreation and residents who have to earn their living in the National Park.

a Name the economic activity shown on the photograph. *(1)*

b i) Name two groups of people likely to be in favour of this activity. *(2)*

ii) For each group give one reason why they may be in favour. *(2)*

c i) Name two groups of people likely to be against this activity. *(2)*

ii) For each group give one reason for their opposition. *(2)*

4 *(Page 140)*

Eighteen holiday resorts/areas are named on Figure 11.16. Complete the table below by:

a Putting each resort/area into its correct column (some resorts could appear in more than one column).

b Naming the country in which each resort/area is located. *(18)*

Coastal resort	Country	Mountain resort	Country	Historic/cultural	Country	Lakes	Country

5 *(Pages 142 and 143)*

The landsketch shows part of the Costa del Sol.

a Why does the climate of the Costa del Sol attract tourists throughout the year? *(4)*

b What other natural attractions does the Costa del Sol possess? *(3)*

c Name five amenities, shown on the landsketch, added for the benefit of tourists. *(5)*

d It is proposed to build a new hotel and leisure complex at location A on the sketch. Why might this development be:

i) Opposed by environmentalists and some local residents?

ii) Welcomed by many local residents? *(4)*

6 *(Pages 144 and 145)*

Courmayeur in the Italian Alps is increasingly dependent upon tourism.

a Describe its natural environment and its traditional way of life. *(4)*

b Complete the following table listing ways in which tourism may have harmed or benefited the local economy, local community and natural environment. *(6)*

	harmed	benefited
Local economy		
Local community		
Natural environment		

7 *(Pages 146 and 147)*

a i) What is meant by the term 'cultural holiday'? *(1)*

ii) Why do some people take cultural holidays in Athens and southern Greece (Peloponnese)? *(3)*

b i) What problems can tourists create at cultural sites such as Athens and Delphi? *(5)*

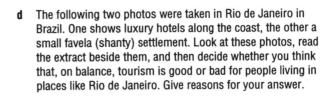

8 (Pages 148, 149 and 150)

a Why is tourism important to economically less developed countries like Kenya? (4)

b Give three reasons why tourists are attracted to Kenya. (3)

c How has the success of tourism in Kenya affected the i) landscape? ii) wildlife? iii) local people? (6)

d The following two photos were taken in Rio de Janeiro in Brazil. One shows luxury hotels along the coast, the other a small favela (shanty) settlement. Look at these photos, read the extract beside them, and then decide whether you think that, on balance, tourism is good or bad for people living in places like Rio de Janeiro. Give reasons for your answer.

Tourism – benefits and costs

A conference held in 1985 concluded that *'International tourism is causing severe damage to the culture and economies of many developing countries and contributes little to their development'*. Yet to many developing countries tourism appears as their only hope of escape from the vicious circle of poverty. Figures A and B are intended to help you to draw your own conclusion.

9 (Page 150)

a Using the climate graph of Montego Bay, Jamaica (West Indies),
- i) What is the maximum temperature? (1)
- ii) What is the annual range of temperature? (1)
- iii) Which month has both the lowest rainfall and most hours of sunshine? (1)
- iv) Which month has both the highest rainfall and the fewest hours of sunshine? (1)

b Draw a star diagram to show the main features of climate and scenery in the West Indies. (6)

c
- i) At which two airports in Jamaica do tourists arrive? (2)
- ii) Do most visitors to Jamaica stay in hotels or resort cottages? (1)
- iii) Name three physical attractions of the area around Montego Bay. (3)

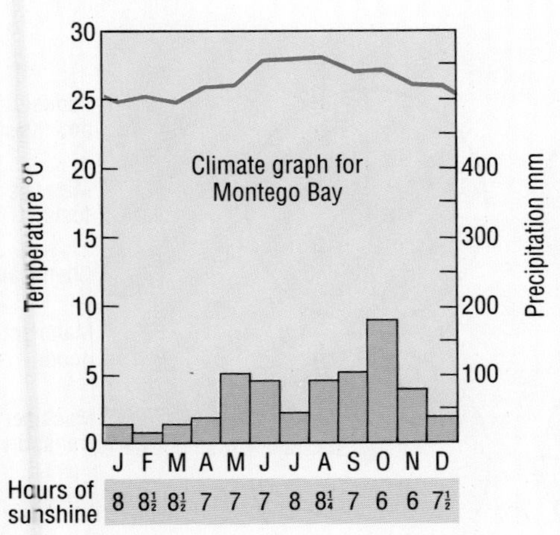

d It is proposed to build a beach village between Montego Bay and Negril.
- i) What is a beach village? (1)
- ii) How may the building of this beach village benefit and harm the natural environment, the local economy, and the local community? (6)
- iii) Who else might benefit from the building of the beach village? Give a reason for your answer. (2)

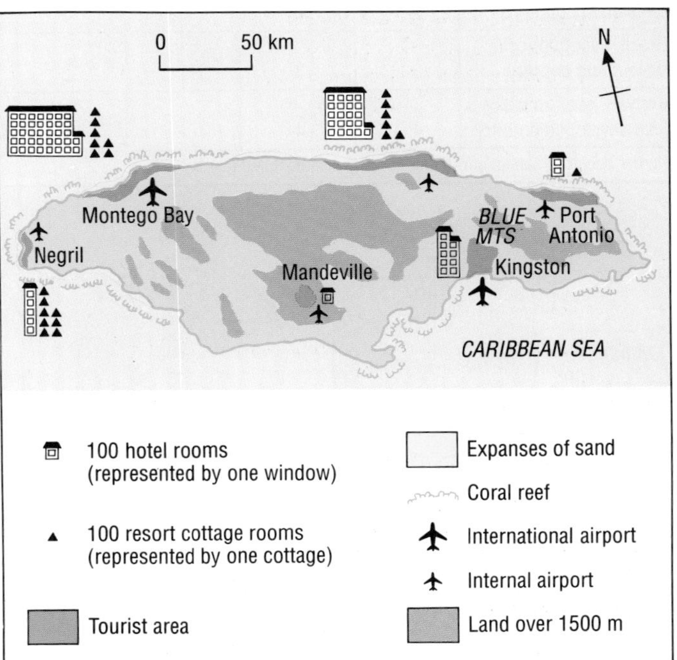

12 TRADE

No country is self-sufficient in the full range of raw materials (food, minerals and energy) and manufactured goods which are needed by its inhabitants. To try to achieve sufficiency countries must trade with each other. *Trade* is the flow of commodities from producers to consumers, and is important in the development of a country. One way for a country to improve its standard of living and to grow more wealthy is to sell more goods than it buys. Unfortunately, for every country that exports more than it imports, at least one other country will have to import more than it exports. The result is that some countries will have a *trade surplus* allowing them to become richer, while others will have a *trade deficit* making them poorer.

Most of the world's population live in economically less developed countries. They produce many of the primary products (agricultural and mineral) which are needed by the economically more developed countries. The developed countries then process many of these primary products into manufactured goods which are needed by themselves and the developing countries.

Trade of developing countries	Trade of developed countries
A legacy of former colonial economies where a mineral once mined, or a crop once grown is exported in its 'raw state'. Most exports are primary products	Mainly manufactured goods are traded, as these countries have become industrialised. Cereals also exported
Often only two or three items are exported	A wide range of items are exported
Prices of, and demand for, these products fluctuate annually. Prices rise less quickly than for manufactured goods	Prices of, and demand for, these products tend to be steady. Prices have risen considerably in comparison to raw materials
The total trade of these countries is small	The total trade of these countries is large
Most exports come from multi-national companies which tend to send profits back to the parent company	Profits are retained by the exporting country
Trade is hindered by poor internal transport networks	Trade is helped by good internal transport networks
Trade is severely hit at times of world economic recession	Trade is badly affected at times of world economic recession

Figure 12.1 Differences between the trade of developing and developed countries

	% World's population	% World's exports of primary products	% World's exports of manufactured goods
Developed (EMDC)	25	24	61
Developing (ELDC)	75	76	39

However, although prices of raw materials have increased over the years, the prices of manufactured goods have increased much more. This means that a developed country exporting manufactured goods earns increasingly more than a developing country selling raw materials. The result is a widening trade gap between the developed and developing countries. The differences in the type of trade between four countries at different stages of economic development are given in Figures 12.2 and 12.3, and the effect of these differences, in Figure 12.1.

Country and stage of economic development	Rank order: Wealth (GDP)	Import of raw material	Export of raw material	Export of manufactured goods
Japan – most wealthy industrialised country	1	1	4	1
UK – economically developed country	2	2	3	2
Brazil – economically developing country	3	3	2	3
Kenya – economically less developed country	4	4	1	4
Poorer countries cannot afford to buy many manufactured goods				

Figure 12.2 Stages of economic development

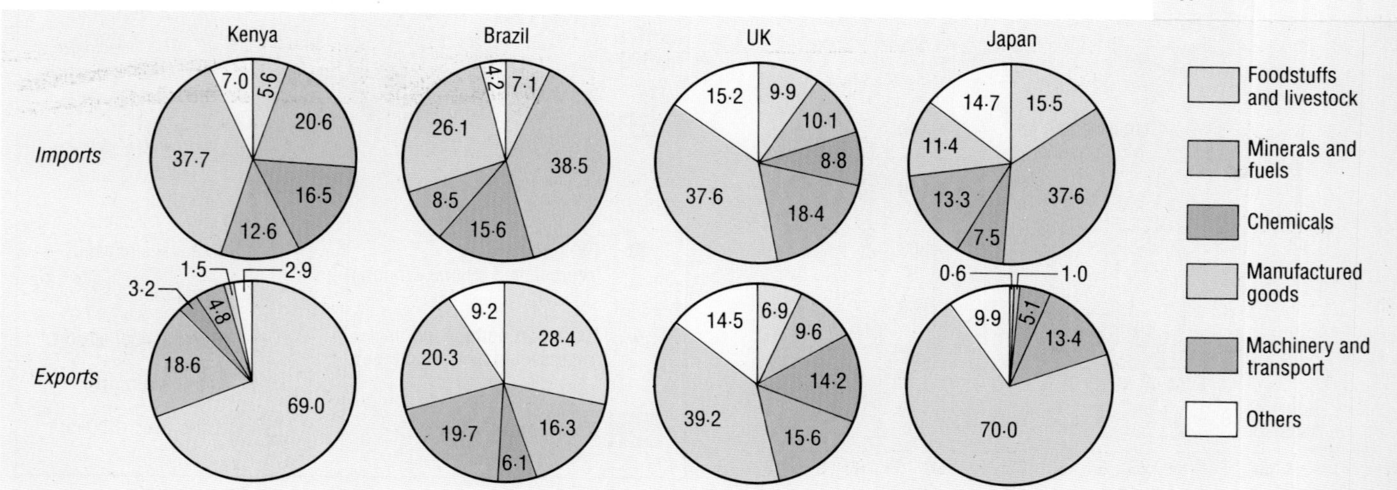

Figure 12.3 Types of trade

Many developing countries rely heavily upon the export of only one or two major commodities (Figure 12.4). The price paid for these commodities is fixed by the developed countries. If there is a world recession, an overproduction of a crop or mineral, a change or a fall in demand for a product, or a crop failure, then the economy of the producing country can be seriously affected. The developed countries try to depress the prices of raw materials which they have to buy from developing countries. They also try to protect their own manufacturing industries by suppressing industrial development and limiting the imports of processed goods from developing countries.

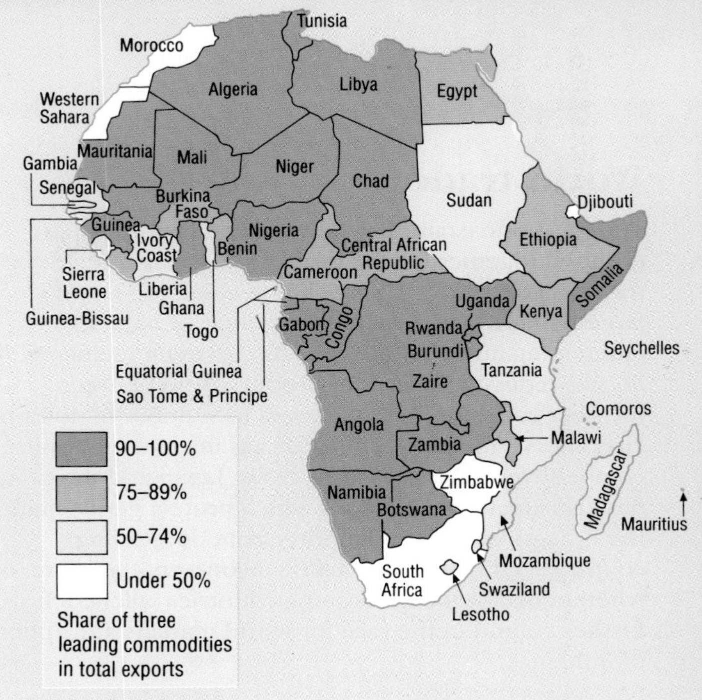

Dependence upon: (a) a single commodity	(b) two or three commodities
NIGERIA 90% oil	KENYA 52% coffee and tea
GHANA 68% coal	EGYPT 83% oil, cotton and textile
ZAMBIA 88% copper	MAURITANIA 84% iron ore and fresh fish
UGANDA 86% coffee	ALGERIA 98% oil, oil products and natural gas

Figure 12.4
Africa – the reliance upon one, two or three commodities

Changes in Britain's Trade

Figure 12.5 shows how Britain's trading partners have changed since 1973.

- The biggest increase has been with countries in the EC. Whether we like being in the EC or not, the graph shows just how dependent we have become upon it for trade.
- By 1992, 82.5 per cent of Britain's trade was with economically more developed countries (North America, Japan and the EC) – an increase of 8.5 per cent since 1973.
- Despite our need for raw materials there has been a decline in trade between ourselves and the economically less developed countries. Many of these trade links were formed during colonial times, e.g. cocoa from Ghana, tea from Sri Lanka, and bananas from Jamaica.
- Britain's links with oil producing countries (OPEC) have declined since the exploitation of North Sea oil.
- There has always been minimal trade between Britain and the former centrally planned economies of the CIS and Eastern Europe.

Despite Britain's position as an economically more developed country, we have developed a trade deficit which is proving to be increasingly hard to reduce (Figure 12.6).

Figure 12.6 Britain's trade balance

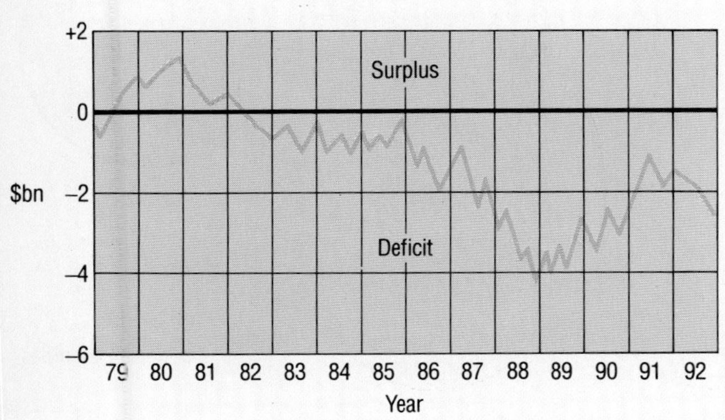

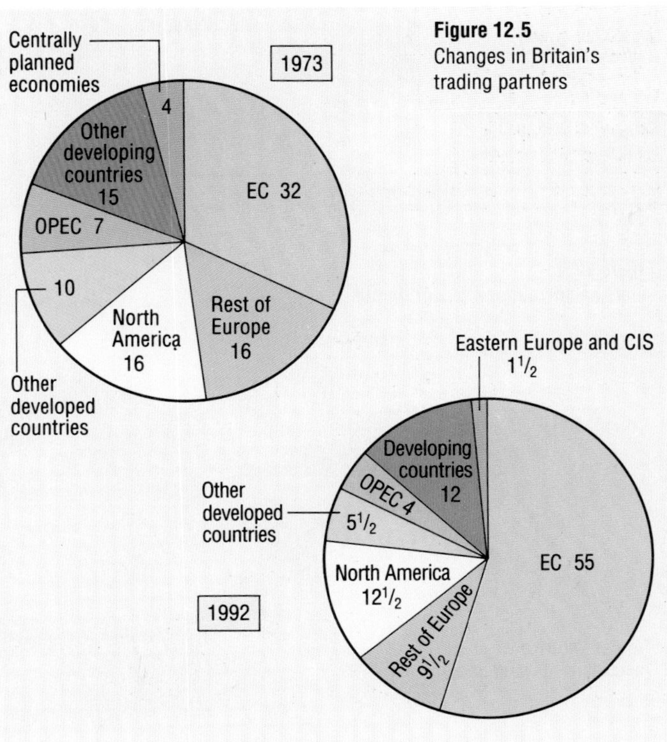

Figure 12.5
Changes in Britain's trading partners

World trade

The EC is one example where several countries have grouped together for the purpose of trying to increase trade (Figure 12.7). The EC has become the world's largest single market with 320 million people. By eliminating import duties (tariffs) between members, the EC has reduced the cost of products sold between member countries and increased its number of potential customers. However, while this has made the EC more competitive against its major rivals, Japan and the USA, it has also created restrictions which protect goods made in the EC against cheaper imports from developing countries. Of major international concern, therefore, is whether or not the developing countries will be left further behind in the race for world markets and spheres of influence.

Direction and volume of world trade

- Despite the growing number of global trading groups, most of the world's trade is dominated by the relatively few 'market economies' of the industrialised countries in the developed world (Figure 12.8). In 1992 the EC's share of world trade was 44 per cent, the USA 13 per cent, Japan 9 per cent and EFTA 6 per cent. Japan had a large and growing trade surplus; the EC and the USA an increasingly large trade deficit (Figure 12.9).
- In recent years the older industrialised countries of Europe and North America have faced increasing competition not only from Japan but from other newly industrialising 'Pacific Rim' countries in eastern Asia (e.g. South Korea, Singapore, Hong Kong and Taiwan). The amount of trade between the USA and eastern Asia now exceeds that between the USA and Europe.

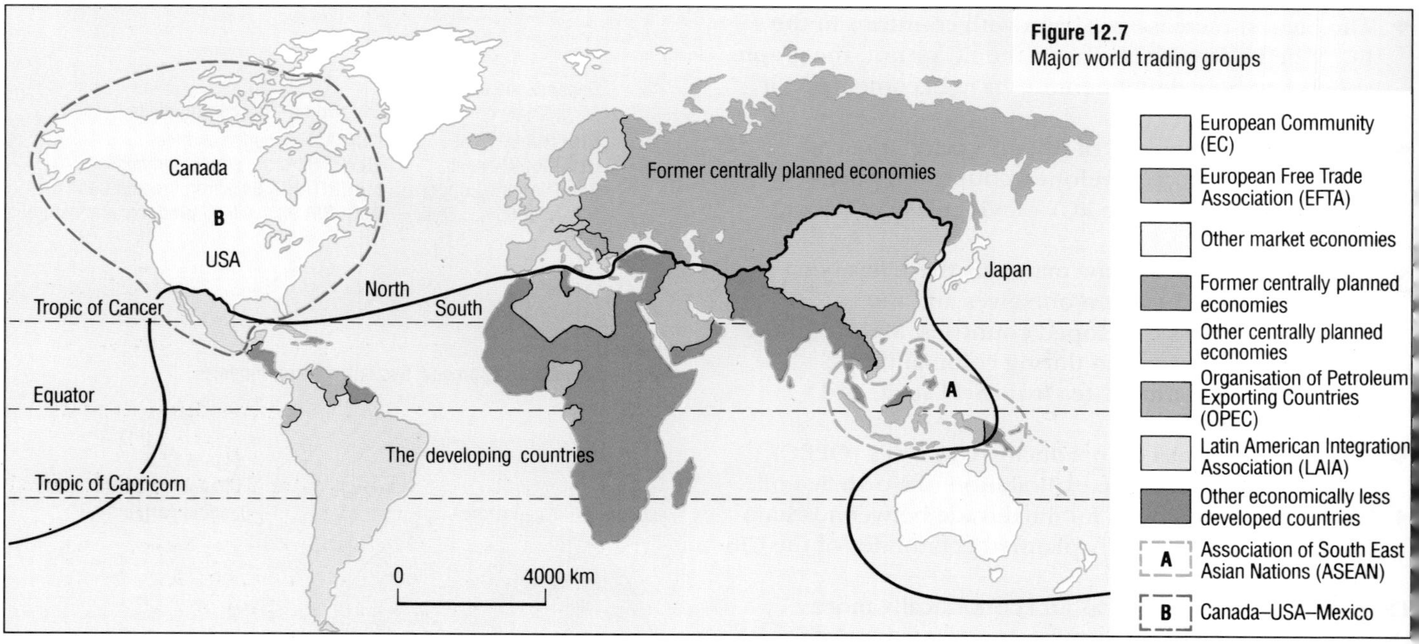

Figure 12.7
Major world trading groups

European Community (EC)
European Free Trade Association (EFTA)
Other market economies
Former centrally planned economies
Other centrally planned economies
Organisation of Petroleum Exporting Countries (OPEC)
Latin American Integration Association (LAIA)
Other economically less developed countries
A Association of South East Asian Nations (ASEAN)
B Canada–USA–Mexico

Canada
B
USA
Former centrally planned economies
Japan
North
South
Tropic of Cancer
Equator
Tropic of Capricorn
The developing countries
A
0 4000 km

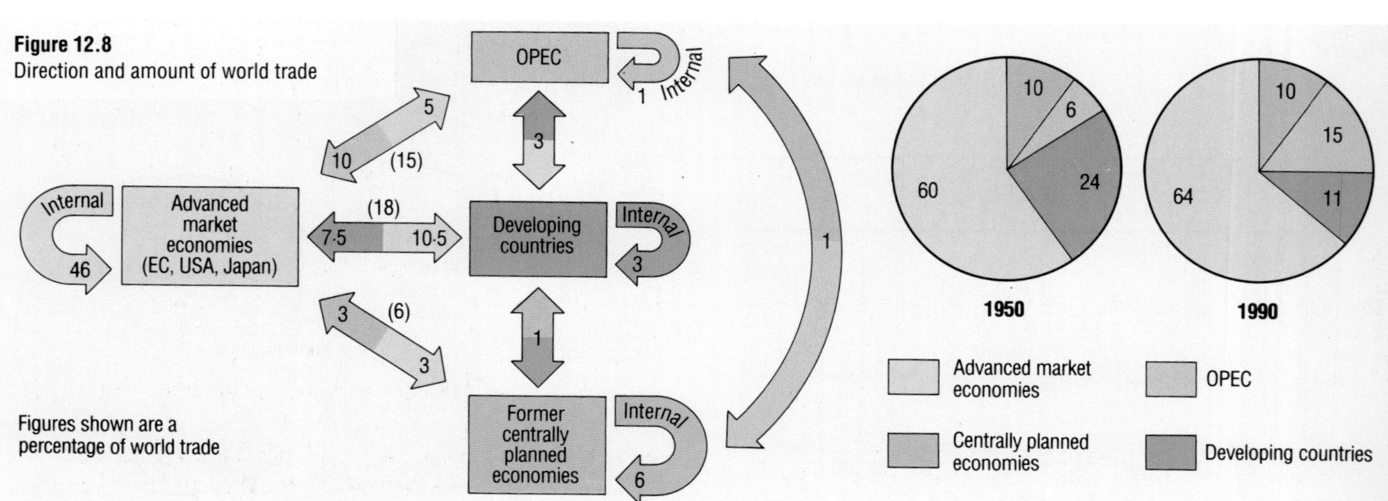

Figure 12.8
Direction and amount of world trade

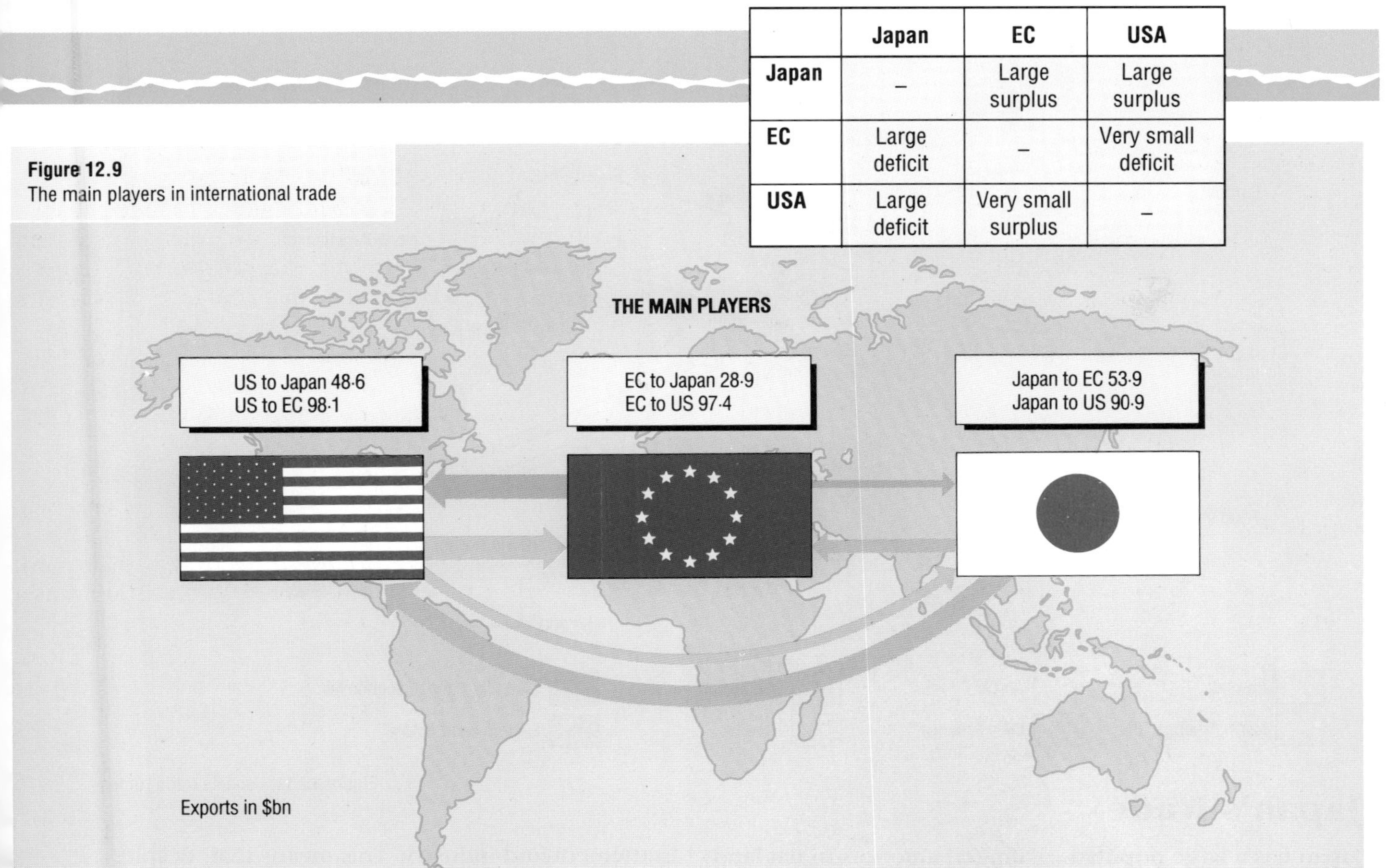

	Japan	EC	USA
Japan	–	Large surplus	Large surplus
EC	Large deficit	–	Very small deficit
USA	Large deficit	Very small surplus	–

Figure 12.9
The main players in international trade

- Although trade between economically less developed countries has increased slowly, nevertheless in 1990 only eight of the developing countries accounted for over 60 per cent of this trade (e.g. Brazil and Mexico). The trade gap for most developing countries is increasing as they continue to export unprocessed raw materials and to import manufactured goods. The recession has made primary products even more vulnerable to changes in market price and market demand. As the trade gap of developing countries widens, they fall deeper into debt. They cannot, therefore, afford to buy as many overseas goods and so the volume of world trade is now decreasing (Figure 12.10).

Figure 12.10 Changes in volume of world trade

- The oil producing countries (OPEC) increased their share of world trade during the 1980s, but this has declined in the early 1990s due to the Gulf War and the world recession.
- World trade is becoming increasingly dominated by the large multinational companies (page 120).

GATT (General Agreement on Trade and Tariffs)

The present round of GATT talks began in 1986. It took until December 1993 before the 105 negotiating countries agreed to ways by which they hoped to increase international trade in agricultural and industrial products and services..Although tariffs (import duties) were reduced on many manufactured goods, strong farming lobbies in the EC and the USA delayed similar success on agricultural products. Farmers in those two areas receive large subsidies which have led to overproduction and food surpluses (page 73). Tariffs were imposed by industrialised countries to try to protect their own products from competition from poorer countries. In Britain, for example, we complain about losing jobs due to cheap imports from overseas, yet without being able to sell their goods how else can overseas countries earn sufficient money to buy our goods? With the world economy in an unhealthy state, it was in everyone's best self-interest to accept the GATT proposals. Many people believe that this acceptance will stimulate world trade and, certainly in the industrialised countries, reduce the level of unemployment.

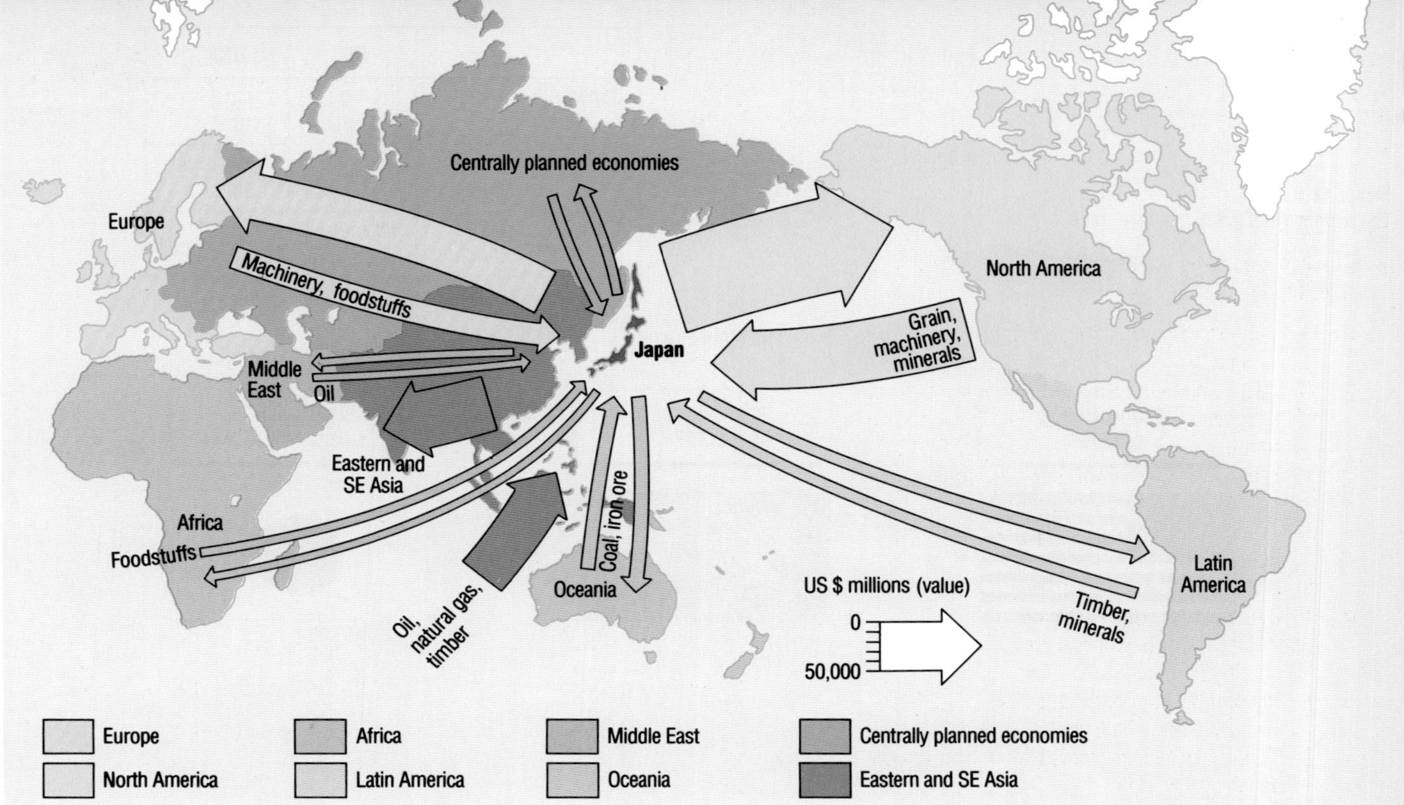

Figure 12.11 Japan's trade routes

Japan's trade

Japan has a large population, limited amounts of flat land and very few natural resources of its own (page 120). It has to import virtually all of its energy supplies, which are expensive, as well as various minerals required by its industries (Figure 12.3). Most of the flat land is used for settlement and industry. This means that, despite farming being intensive and mechanised (page 80), Japan is not self-sufficient in foodstuffs, and large quantities have to be imported. As well as working long hours, the Japanese have introduced modern machinery and developed high levels of technology in their industries. Japanese cars, electrical goods, office equipment and high-technology products, exported across the world, are known for their high quality and reliability.

Figure 12.12 Japan's trade surplus

Top Exports (1990)	Top Imports (1990)
1 Machinery and transport equipment	1 Oil
2 Electrical and electronic machinery	2 Foodstuffs and livestock
3 Iron and steel	3 Machinery and transport equipment
4 Chemicals	4 Minerals
5 Textiles	5 Timber

Exports
Imports
Value (US $ million)
200 000
100 000
1980
1985
1990

Japan is the world's third largest trader, after the USA and the EC (page 156). Indeed, 45 per cent of Japan's total trade is with the USA and the EC (Figure 12.11). Almost every year since the mid-1960s Japan has exported more than it has imported, and since 1983 it has had the world's largest trade surplus (Figure 12.12). This healthy trade surplus is due to Japan:

- Reducing its previously high energy bill by changing from expensive imports of oil to the more controversial use of nuclear power (page 100).
- Importing relatively cheap raw materials, especially from poorer, economically less developed countries, and exporting expensive processed goods to richer, economically more developed countries.
- Protecting certain domestic industries by imposing high duties (tariffs) on many imported goods, and gaining markets in overseas countries through investment and building new factories (e.g. Nissan, Toyota and Honda car factories in the UK). This Japanese 'protectionist' policy has been a major issue at GATT and other international trade meetings.

1 *(Page 154)*

The two pie charts show the trade pattern for a typical developing country.

a i) Which two items appear as both imports and exports? *(1)*
ii) Name, in rank order, the three main exports. *(1)*
iii) Are these exports raw materials or manufactured goods? *(1)*
iv) Why is this typical for a developing country? *(1)*

b i) Name, in rank order, the three main imports. *(1)*
ii) Are these imports raw materials or manufactured goods? *(1)*
iii) Why is this typical for a developing country? *(1)*

c i) By how many US dollars do imports exceed exports? *(1)*
ii) What problems will this create in the developing country? *(2)*

d i) How might industrialisation help to improve the country's trade balance? *(2)*
ii) How might this industrialisation affect countries in the developed world? *(2)*

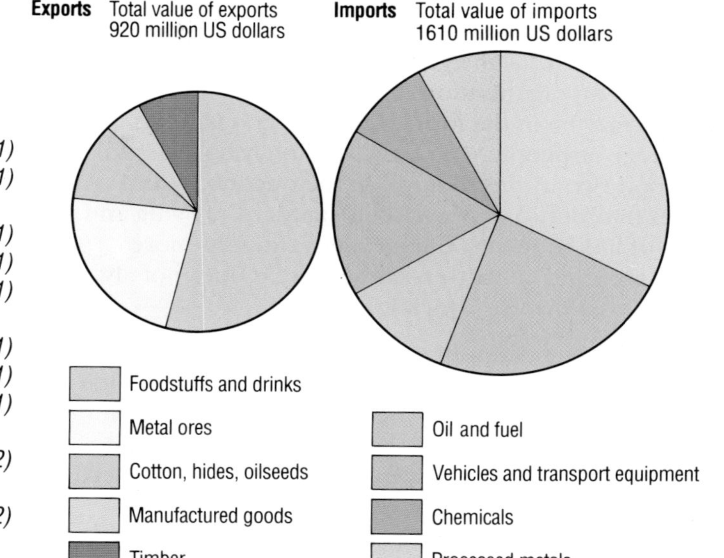

2 *(Pages 155 and 156)*

a i) Name Britain's main trading partner. *(1)*
ii) With whom did Britain have the least trade in 1992? *(1)*
iii) What was the approximate value of Britain's exports to North America in 1992? *(1)*

b i) Imports are goods brought into a country. What are exports? *(1)*
ii) What is meant by the balance of trade? *(1)*
iii) Why should countries try to export more than they import? *(1)*

c i) Make a copy of the balance of trade diagram and add the following information:
Exports £104,816 million;
Imports £118,867 million; 1991. *(2)*
ii) Was Britain's balance of trade in 1991 good or bad for the country? *(1)*
iii) Give two ways by which Britain might improve its balance of trade. *(2)*

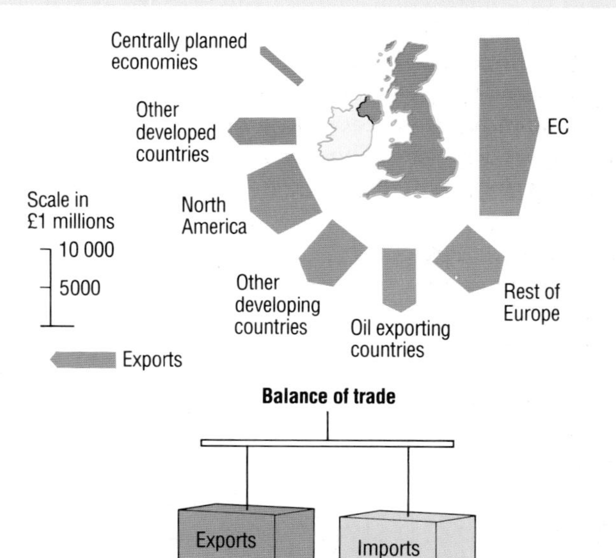

3 *(Pages 154 and 158)*

a i) What type of import accounted for 37.6 per cent of Japan's total (Figure 12.3)? *(1)*
ii) Name two sources of this type of import. *(2)*
iii) Why is it Japan's main type of import? *(2)*
iv) Give three reasons why foodstuffs and livestock was Japan's second largest import. *(3)*
v) What percentage of Japan's exports was machinery and transport (Figure 12.3)? *(1)*
vi) Which two parts of the world were most likely to have bought these goods? *(2)*

b i) How much of Japan's trade is with the USA and the EC? *(1)*
ii) With which part of the world does Japan have a large trade deficit? Give one reason for this trade deficit. *(2)*
iii) Give three reasons why Japan has a large trade surplus. *(3)*
iv) Why do you think Japan was reluctant to accept the GATT proposals? *(2)*

c What products, made by Japanese firms, have you got in your home? Give the name of the firm for each product. *(6)*

13 WORLD DEVELOPMENT

Aid

Many economically developing countries have come to rely upon aid. *Aid* is the giving of resources by one country, or an organisation, to another country. The resource may be in the form of money, goods, food, technology or people. The basic aim in giving aid is to help poorer countries to develop their economy and services in order to improve their standard of living and quality of life. In reality, the giving of aid is far more complicated and controversial, because it does not always benefit the country to which it is given.

Why do many developing countries need aid?

- Many countries have large and often increasing trade deficits (page 154). They need to borrow money in order to buy goods from the richer industrialised countries. Unfortunately, by borrowing money, these countries fall further into debt (Figure 13.1).
- Aid is needed to try to improve their standard of living. This often involves borrowing money for large prestigious schemes, e.g. improving an international airport or constructing a large hydro-electricity scheme which, in reality, benefits relatively few people.
- Many are prone to either natural disasters (e.g. drought, flooding, earthquakes), or suffer as a result of human induced disasters (e.g. desertification (page 234), civil war). This aid is often only needed for a short period of time.

Types of aid

1 **Bilateral aid** This type of aid is between two countries. Resources are 'given' directly by a rich 'donor' country to a poor 'recipient' country. In reality the aid is not 'given' but is often 'tied', i.e. there are 'strings attached'. This means that the donor imposes conditions upon the recipient country. For example, building contracts are given to the donor country, or goods and services can only be bought from the donor country. The donor country benefits by increasing its trade and extending its economic influence. The recipient country falls further into debt as it has, eventually, to repay the loan at a relatively high rate of interest. Developing countries regard this form of aid as 'economic colonialism'.

2 **Multilateral aid** This is when the richer countries give money to international organisations such as the World Bank, the IMF (International Monetary Fund), or the EC Development Fund. These organisations then redistribute the money to poorer countries. Although, theoretically, there should be no political ties, recently these organisations have taken upon themselves to withhold aid if they disagree with the economic and political system within a recipient country. Aid is unlikely to be given to countries which do not have a market economy or a democratically elected government. The UN recommend that rich countries spend 0.7 per cent of their GNP on aid – a figure which is rarely reached (Figure 13.2).

3 **Voluntary aid** Voluntary organisations such as Oxfam, Christian Aid, Save the Children and Intermediate Technology, raise money from the general public in rich countries and send it for use on specific projects in poorer countries. There are no political ties. Projects are on a smaller scale and use a more appropriate type of technology (page 123). These organisations are usually the first to provide food, clothing and shelter following a major disaster within a country.

Figure 13.1 Foreign debts in 1988

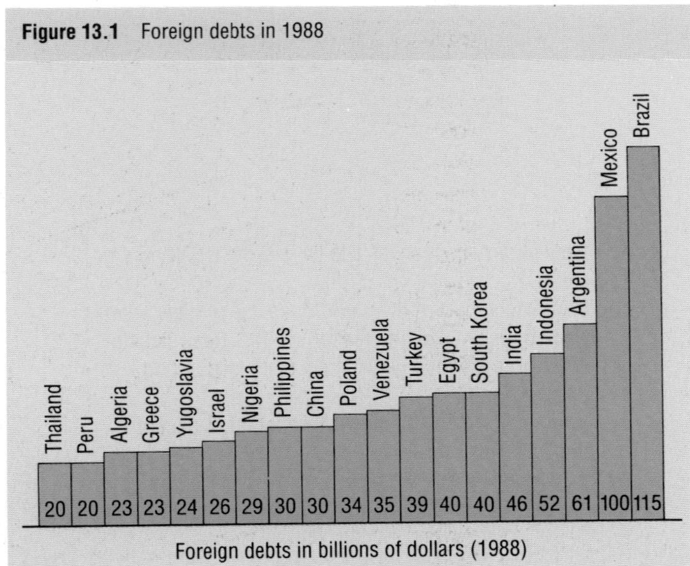

Figure 13.2 Percentage of GNP spent on aid 1988

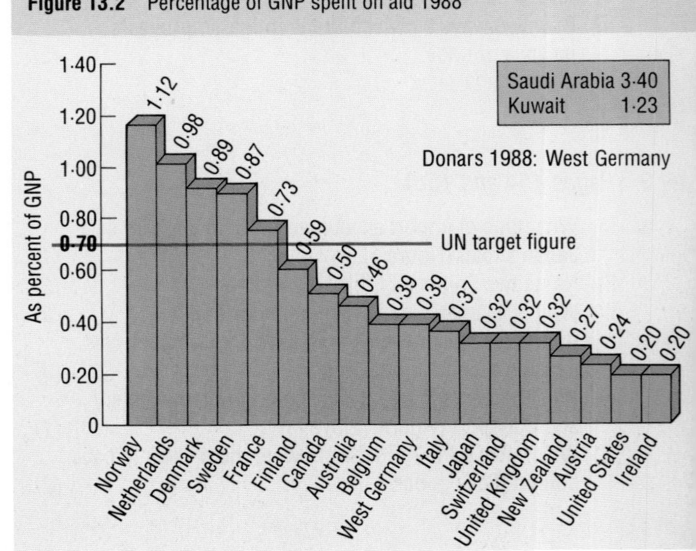

The disadvantages to a recipient country

Aid rarely reaches the poorest people who live in the rural areas. Inefficient and corrupt officials direct it to themselves and the urban areas where many of them live. The gap between the wealthier town dweller and the poorer rural dweller increases. Aid also forces countries to produce raw materials for richer countries rather than growing food or developing industries for themselves. In time these countries come to rely upon aid. As aid comes in the form of loans upon which interest has to be paid, the poorer countries get into permanent and ever increasing debt (Figure 13.3 and 13.4A).

Figure 13.4 The trade–aid cycle

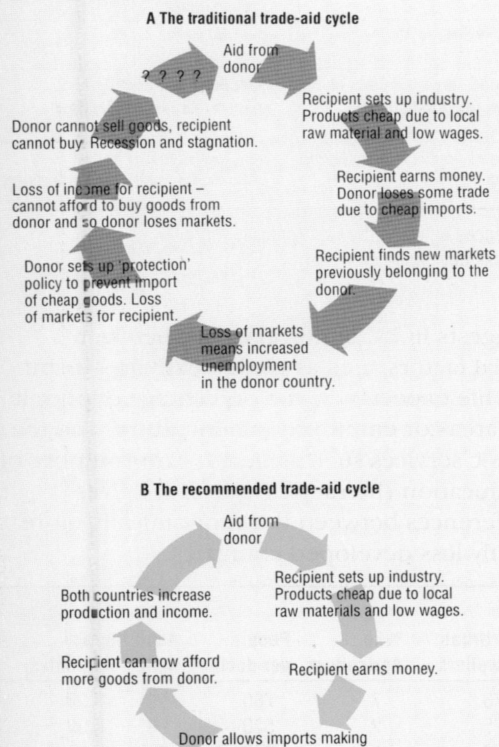
A The traditional trade-aid cycle
Aid from donor
? ? ? ?
Recipient sets up industry. Products cheap due to local raw material and low wages.
Recipient earns money. Donor loses some trade due to cheap imports.
Recipient finds new markets previously belonging to the donor.
Loss of markets means increased unemployment in the donor country.
Donor sets up 'protection' policy to prevent import of cheap goods. Loss of markets for recipient.
Loss of income for recipient – cannot afford to buy goods from donor and so donor loses markets.
Donor cannot sell goods, recipient cannot buy. Recession and stagnation.
B The recommended trade-aid cycle
Aid from donor
Recipient sets up industry. Products cheap due to local raw materials and low wages.
Recipient earns money.
Donor allows imports making recipient better off.
Recipient can now afford more goods from donor.
Both countries increase production and income.

There might have been some justification for the steady increases from year to year in external aid if there was evidence that the battle against poverty was being won. All the evidence, however, clearly demonstrates that the poor are getting poorer.

The reason why there is little effect on poverty is that most aid is spent on heavily capitalised infrastructure projects such as railways, bridges and roads. These may have some indirect effect on the lives of poor people, but what people really want is better health and education services, improvements in village roads rather than highways and access to proper credit facilities to help them improve agriculture and raise their incomes. Although there are some enlightened donors. most big western government and UN agencies find these types of projects too small-scale and difficult to measure and administer; they would rather give money for power stations and fertiliser plants since such things can be seen and their performance measured. They also look impressive in glossy magazines telling the tax payers back home how the government is spending their money. **'OXFAM'**

'Aid is primarily a mechanism for transferring money from poor people in rich countries into the pockets of rich people in poor countries.'

THE CUMULATIVE effect of the way in which the developing world is portrayed by charitable organisations and the media is grossly misleading. And it results in deeply held public misconceptions that are ultimately damaging to the understanding they seek to promote.

Ninety per cent of people's knowledge and impressions of the developing world come from two sources: the news media and fund-raising agencies. Both are responsible for distorting the public's perception of the developing world – the one because it is in the business of reporting the exceptional; the other because it is in the business of raising money.

One of the worst examples of a distorted message came during the massive campaign mounted in response to the African emergency in the mid-Eighties. The public in the industrialised world donated roughly half a billion dollars in one 12-month period – one of the greatest fund-raising responses of all time. At the same time, the industrialised world's governments gave $2bn in extra emergency aid to Africa. However, almost three times that sum was paid to the industrialised world by Africa in debt and interest repayments. The net flow of finance in that year was therefore *out* of Africa. This year the outflow is at least $10bn in interest repayments alone – more than Africa spends on its health and education services. **UNESCO**

Figure 13.3 The aid/debt relationship

How might aid benefit a recipient country?

Short term aid can include food, clothing, shelter and medical care after a natural disaster or a civil war. Long term aid should encourage poorer countries to become increasingly self-sufficient and independent. This can be achieved (Figure 13.5) by helping to improve education standards and to develop skills, to grow higher yielding crops for their own consumption rather than for export, to develop small scale, sustainable industries using appropriate technology, and to improve water supplies as one method of improving health standards. The rich countries can also help by buying products rather than setting up tariffs to protect their own industries (Figure 13.4B).

Figure 13.5 Aid to help self-sufficiency and independence

Differences in world development

Geographers are interested in the differences in levels of development between places across the world. However, they find considerable difficulty in finding acceptable and accurate methods of measuring levels of development. This book has, so far, taken just one measure – that of wealth. Based on wealth the world can be divided into the:

1 Economically more developed countries which include the richer, industrialised nations of the developed 'North'.
2 Economically less developed countries which include the poorer, less industrialised nations of the developing 'South'.

The wealth of a country is measured in terms of its GNP per capita (*Gross National Product* per person). The *GNP* per capita is the total value of goods produced and services provided by a country in a year divided by the number of people living in that country. Figure 13.6 shows the GNP per capita for 13 selected countries at different levels of development, expressed in US dollars. It shows that, in 1990, every person in the UK would have received US$ 14,570 had the wealth created in the UK that year been shared out evenly. While GNP is a good measure to compare differences in wealth between countries, it does not show differences in wealth between people and regions within a country. Often linked to GNP are various other social factors which are used to measure human welfare and differences in the standard of living between places.

	Economically more developed countries	Economically less developed countries
Gross National Product	majority over US$5000 per person per year; 80% of world's total income	majority under US$2000 per person per year; 20% of world's total income
population growth	relatively slow partly due to family planning; 25% of world's population; population doubles in 80 years	extremely fast, little or no family planning; 75% of world's population; population doubles in 30 years
housing	high standard of permanent housing; indoor amenities, e.g. electricity, water supply and sewerage	low standard, mainly temporary housing; very rarely any amenities
types of jobs	manufacturing and service industries (75% of world's manufacturing industry)	mainly in primary industries (25% of world's manufacturing industry)
levels of mechanisation	highly mechanised with new techniques; 96% of world spending on development projects and research	mainly hand labour or the use of animals
exports	manufactured goods	unprocessed raw materials
energy	high level of consumption; main sources are coal, oil, HEP and nuclear power. Use 80% world's energy	low level of consumption; wood still a major source. Use 20% world's energy
communications	motorways, railways and airports	road, rail and airports only near main cities, rural areas have little development
diet	balanced diet; several meals per day; high protein intake	unbalanced diet; 20% of population suffers from malnutrition; low protein intake
life expectancy	over 75 years	over 60 years
health	very good, large numbers of doctors and good hospital facilities	very poor, few doctors and inadequate hospital facilities
education	majority have full time secondary education (16+)	very few have any formal education; females disadvantaged

Figure 13.7 Differences between the economically more and economically less developed countries

Figure 13.6 suggests links, or correlations, between wealth and social factors such as birth, death and infant mortality rates, life expectancy, the percentage of people living in urban areas or employed in agriculture, and the provision of basic services such as health care (number of doctors) and education (literacy). Figure 13.7 gives generalised differences between the economically more and economically less developed countries.

Figure 13.6
Differences in world development 1990

1990	Country	GNP– US$ per capita	Birth Rate	Death Rate	Infant Mortality (per 1000)	Life Expectancy	% Urban Dwellers	% in Agriculture	People per doctor	Adult literacy males	Adult literacy females
Market Economies – the rich or developed world	Japan	23,730	12	8	5	79	78	7	780	99	99
	USA	21,000	14	9	8	76	75	2	520	99	99
	Italy	15,150	11	11	9	76	72	8	340	98	96
	UK	14,570	14	12	8	76	94	2	650	99	99
OPEC	Kuwait	16,380	26	6	15	74	97	2	930	76	63
	Saudi Arabia	6,230	42	7	58	66	82	40	1,670	71	31
former centrally planned economies	CIS	3,800	17	10	20	71	71	14	270	99	99
'middle' income developing countries	Brazil	2,550	26	8	57	66	83	25	1,660	79	77
	Mexico	1,990	27	5	36	70	77	31	2,010	92	88
'low' income developing countries	Egypt	630	31	11	57	61	55	41	970	59	30
	Kenya	380	47	10	64	61	32	77	7,890	70	49
	India	350	31	12	88	60	34	67	3,690	58	57
	Bangladesh	180	41	14	108	53	18	69	7,810	43	22

To people living in a western, industrialised society, economic development tends to mean a growth in wealth. This suggests that the GNP of a country must increase if the standard of living of its inhabitants is to improve. Recently, other criteria have been suggested which concentrate more upon the quality of life, rather than the level of wealth.

1 The *physical quality of life index* (PQLI) was introduced by the Overseas Development Council (ODC). The PQLI is the average of three variables – literacy, life expectancy and infant mortality. Each characteristic is given an index scale ranging from 0 to 100.

- Literacy rates of zero and 100 per cent are scaled as 0 and 100 respectively.
- Sierra Leone, which has the world's shortest life expectancy of only 36 years, is scaled 0. Japan, with the longest life expectancy of 79 years, has an index of 100.
- Afghanistan, with the world's highest infant mortality rate of 162 per 1000, has an index of 0. Denmark, Iceland and Japan, with only 5 per 1000, have an index of 100.

Figure 13.8 is a PLQI map of the world. Notice how the countries with the highest PQLI lie in the 'North' as defined by the Brandt Report, and how most countries with the lower indices lie in Africa and parts of South-east Asia.

2 An organisation in the USA widened the PQLI to include political freedom and civil rights. Their resultant *League of Human Suffering* is given in Figure 13.9.

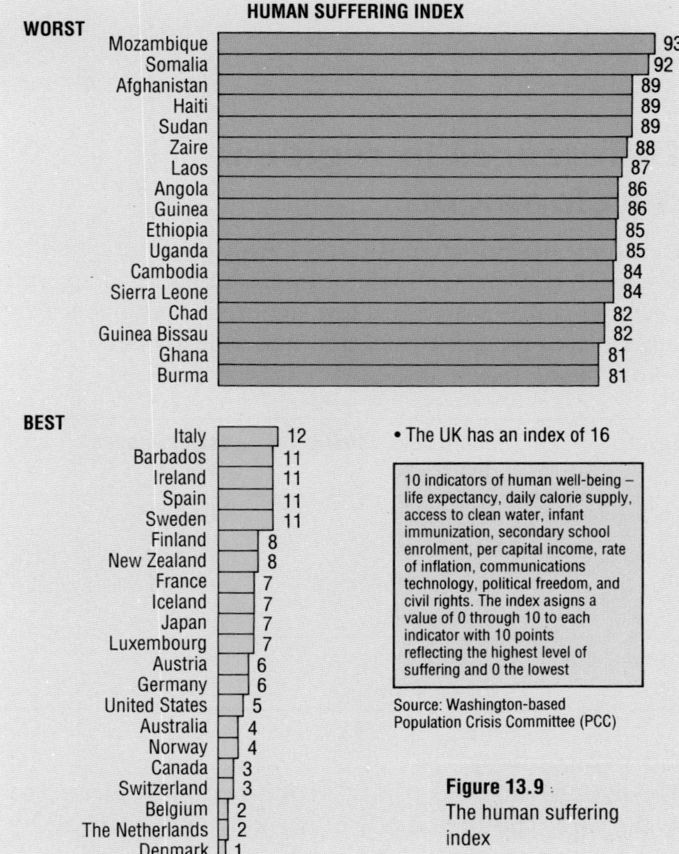

Figure 13.9 The human suffering index

3 More recently other quality of life factors have been introduced, especially those relating to culture and the environment. For example, are people living in the economically more developed world more content (Figure 13.10), do they live in a more pleasant and less polluted environment, and is their culture (e.g. music) more developed than people living in the economically less developed countries?

Figure 13.8 PLQI map of the world

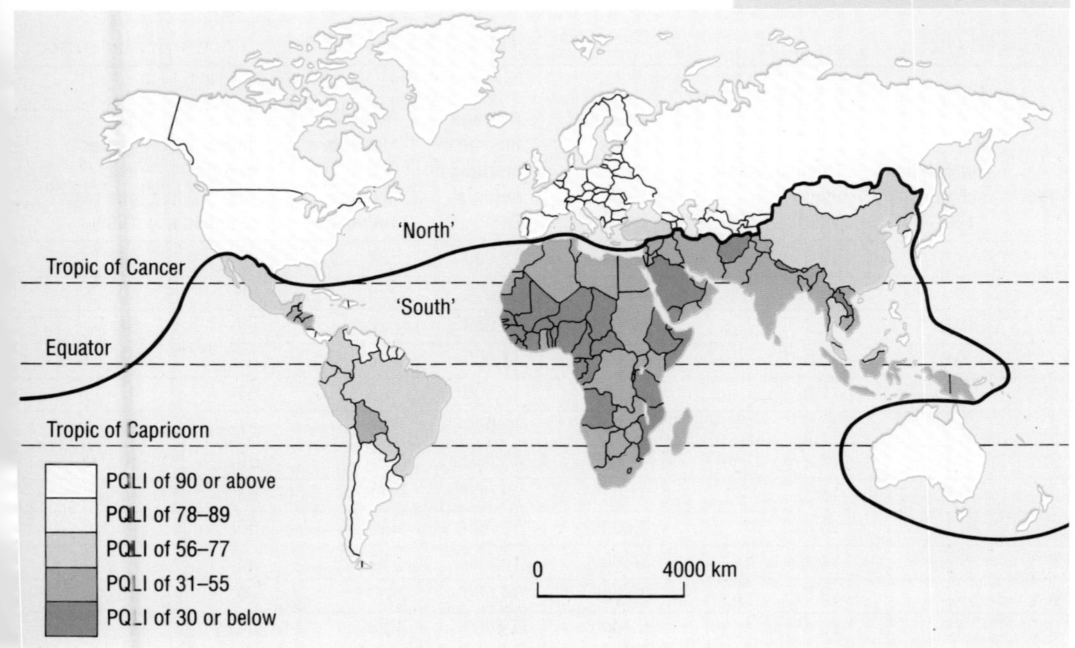

A personal view on quality of life:
"People walking along a street in a western city rarely seem to smile. They look harassed and under pressure. Perhaps it is the strain of work or trying to find a job, of paying the mortgage or finding a home. In contrast, people in the developing countries which I have visited, such as Kenya, Thailand and Malaysia always seem to be very much more cheerful, laid back and relaxed, and always prepared to help the visitor. Socially and culturally they are in no way 'less developed'." Which society appears to have the more preferable quality of life?

Differences in regional development

Economic development is rarely evenly distributed, either at a local, regional, national or international level. Growth becomes concentrated in a few favoured locations, leaving other places relatively poor and under-developed in comparison.

Level	More developed/ better off	Less developed/ worse off
Local/British city	Suburbia	Old inner city
Regional/National	Capital city South-east England North of Italy	Isolated, rural village North and west Britain South of Italy
International	EC – Germany, Netherlands	EC – Portugal and Ireland

Core-periphery

The most prosperous part of a country can be referred to as the *core*. This region is likely to contain the capital city and the country's major industrial areas. These will provide a large local market, and will attract other industries and services such as banking, insurance and government offices, a process known as *cumulative causation*. As levels of capital, technology and skilled labour increase, the region becomes more wealthy. It can afford to provide schools, hospitals, shopping centres, modern transport networks and better quality housing. These pull factors encourage the in-migration of people from surrounding areas.

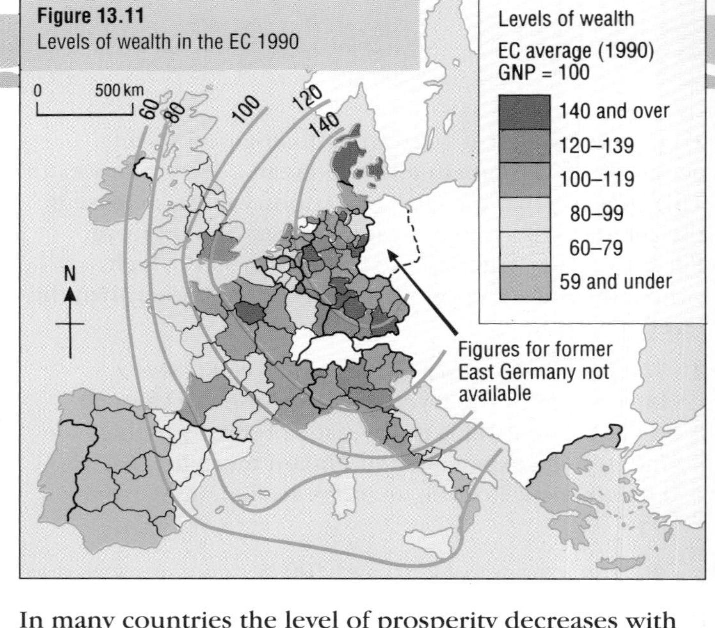

Figure 13.11
Levels of wealth in the EC 1990

In many countries the level of prosperity decreases with distance from the core region. The poorest places are therefore found towards the *periphery* of a country. Here jobs will be fewer in number, poorly paid and, probably, mainly in the primary sector. There is often a lack of opportunity, poor service provision and insufficient government investment. These push factors force many people to migrate to the core region.

It is about 150 years since a former British Prime Minister, Disraeli, wrote a book in which he described Britain as being 'two nations' – the North and the South. In recent years this 'North–South' divide has become increasingly pronounced. The south-east, including London, has become the core, while places furthest from this region form the periphery (Figure 13.10). Similarly in the EC, there is a wealthy core nearer to its centre in Brussels (although parts of Belgium are relatively poor). Generally, although there are exceptions, prosperity declines towards the fringe regions of the community (Figure 13.11).

Figure 13.10 Uneven regional development in the UK

Uneven regional development in the UK	GNP EC average 100	% population change 1981–91	Unemployment June 1993	Average house prices 1990 £s	Average income of mortgage holders £s	% school leavers going into higher education	% home owners with telephone	% homes with one car 1990
South-east	120.2	4.3	10.2	90,000	18,000	33	76	52
South-west	93.6	9.1	10.2	78,000	15,000	29	66	55
East Anglia	96.9	10.2	8.4	67,000	15,000	26	68	54
East Midlands	92.2	6.6	9.5	51,000	13,500	28	61	55
West Midlands	89.9	2.2	11.0	52,000	13,500	23	64	47
Yorks & Humberside	88.5	2.2	10.3	42,000	13,000	28	61	47
Wales	81.7	4.7	10.2	41,000	13,000	26	59	51
North	85.0	-0.5	12.2	31,000	13,000	21	53	46
North-west	90.6	-0.1	10.8	39,000	13,000	22	66	46
Northern Ireland	73.4	-3.1	14.4	34,000	13,500	31	46	44
Scotland	92.5	1.3	9.6	36,000	14,500	30	70	46
UK	98.9	2.9	10.4	57,000	15,000	28	64	49

Core-periphery in Japan

The Core – Tokyo It has already been pointed out (page 30) that land values in Tokyo are the highest in the world, and that Japan is the world's leading industrialised country. The area around Tokyo Bay is the centre of Japan's industry (page 120 and Figure 13.13), commerce and services. Tokyo Bay is sheltered, allowing large ships to bring in energy supplies (page 100) and raw materials (pages 120 and 158). Land is constantly being reclaimed from the sea for the building of new factories, houses and port facilities. The Shinkansen (page 64) and other rail and road routes meet in Tokyo. The promise of jobs and the perception of Tokyo's 'bright lights' still act as a magnet to many younger people living in the surrounding rural areas (page 81), despite Tokyo's already high population density (Figure 13.12) and high cost of accommodation.

The Periphery – Hokkaido Hokkaido is much poorer than Tokyo, although it is still as well off as the UK and many other economically more developed countries. Nevertheless, by Japanese standards, and to Japanese perception, it is a periphery region. The island used to be important in providing primary products such as food, fish, timber and coal. The latter led to the development of a steel and shipbuilding industry. There has been a recent decline in both fishing and forestry. Due to the closing of all but one coal mine, and the distance from Japan's major ports and internal markets, steel and shipbuilding have also declined. Hokkaido tends not to attract new industries as Japanese industrialists perceive the island to be too cold, prone to earthquakes and isolated, despite the building of a rail tunnel linking the island with the mainland. Although Hokkaido already has the lowest population density in Japan (Figure 13.12), and has wages which are high by world standards, many younger people choose to move away to live and work in Japan's core regions.

Figure 13.13
Location of major industries in Japan

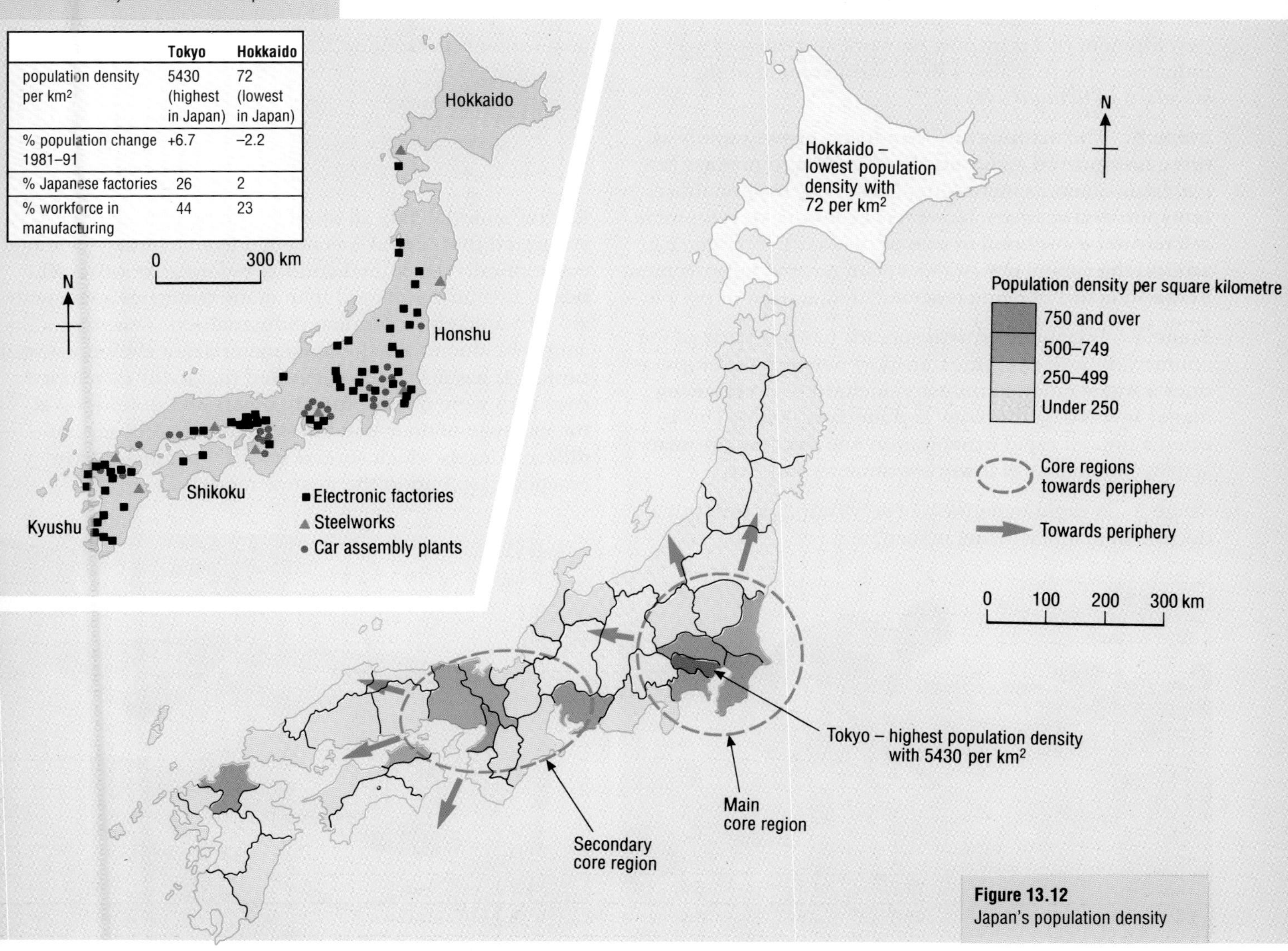

	Tokyo	Hokkaido
population density per km²	5430 (highest in Japan)	72 (lowest in Japan)
% population change 1981–91	+6.7	–2.2
% Japanese factories	26	2
% workforce in manufacturing	44	23

Figure 13.12
Japan's population density

Stages in economic development

The Rostow model

Walt Rostow was an economist. After studying several economically more developed countries, he suggested a model for economic growth. Remember that a *model* (page 26) is a theoretical framework which may not actually exist, but which helps to explain reality in a more simplified way. Rostow suggested that all countries had the potential to pass through a series of stages of growth until they became fully industrialised and economically developed (Figure 13.14).

Stage 1 This is usually a subsistence economy based mainly upon farming. There is insufficient technology and capital to process raw materials or to develop industries and services.

Stage 2 A country usually needs external help to move into this stage, e.g. a colony. Primary activities are developed although most products are exported. There are some technological improvements, and the development of a transport network and one or two industries. There is also a slow improvement in the standard of living (GNP).

Stage 3 The manufacturing industry grows rapidly as there is improved technology and capital to process raw materials. There is increasing investment in agriculture, transport and services. However, economic development is likely to be confined to one or two 'core' regions, e.g. around the capital city or chief port. A rapid improvement in the standard of living is seen.

Stage 4 Economic growth spreads to most parts of the country. A more complex transport network develops, as does a wider range of industry, including several using higher levels of technology and mechanisation. This is often a time of rapid urbanisation and declining primary activity. Standards of living continue to improve.

Stage 5 A rapid expansion of service industries, but a decline in manufacturing is seen.

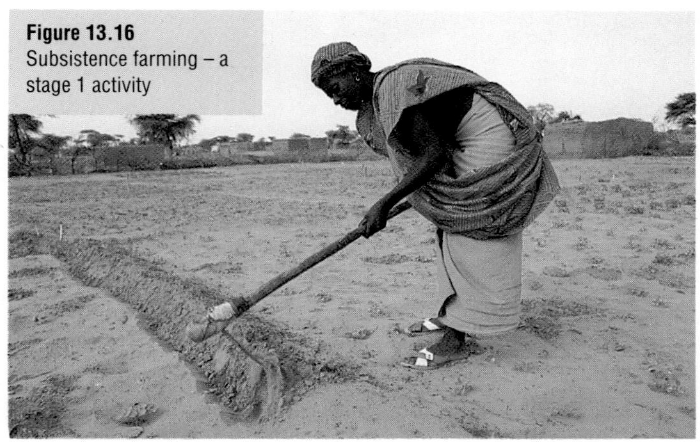

Figure 13.16
Subsistence farming – a stage 1 activity

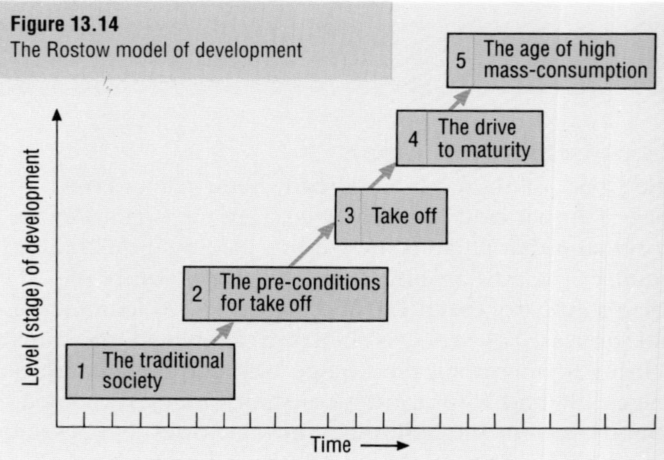

Figure 13.14
The Rostow model of development

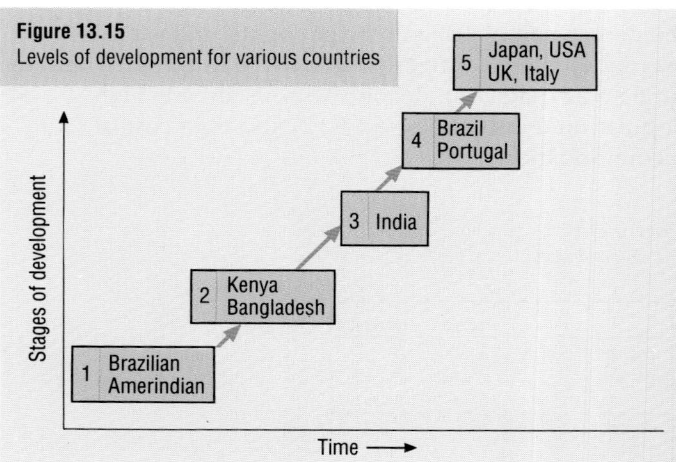

Figure 13.15
Levels of development for various countries

Rostow's model, like all models, can be criticised. He suggested that capital was needed from a more economically developed country before 'take off' could begin. It is now accepted than many countries, even with aid, are unlikely to become industrialised. This may simply be due to a lack of raw materials or the necessary capital. It has also been suggested that many developed countries were once colonial powers and developed at the expense of their 'satellites'. Figure 13.15 suggests different levels which several selected countries have reached based upon the Rostow model.

Figure 13.17
Analysing serum – a stage 5 activity

1 *(Pages 160 and 161)*

a i) What are the differences between bilateral, multilateral and voluntary aid? *(6)*
ii) Which type of aid do you think is best for the recipient country? *(1)*
iii) Give two reasons for your answer. *(2)*

b i) Give four reasons why some countries need aid. *(4)*
ii) Give three problems which might arise in a country which receives aid. *(3)*

c Some people criticise Britain for giving relatively little aid. Others say that if we stopped giving aid then every person in Britain would be £50 a year better off. Do you think we should give more aid or less aid? *(4)*

3 *(Pages 164 and 165)*

a What is meant by the terms *core* and *periphery*? *(2)*

b For any country which you have studied (UK, Japan, Brazil, Kenya, Italy, etc)
i) Draw a map to show its core region and its periphery regions. *(4)*
ii) Give reasons why the core region has had the most rapid development. *(3)*
iii) Give reasons why the periphery regions have developed less rapidly. *(3)*

2 *(Pages 162 and 163)*

a i) Name three continents lying in the 'North' and three lying in the 'South'. *(6)*
ii) Which continent lies partly in the 'North' and partly in the 'South'? *(1)*

b i) State how the five basic indicators on the map show that Africa is less well off compared with other parts of the world. *(5)*
ii) Suggest three other indicators which may be used to measure living standards. *(3)*

c Make a copy of the table right, and add the information given in the correct columns. *(7)*

d i) What is the PQLI? *(1)*
ii) Why is GNP not always a good measure of development? *(3)*

High GNP • Low GNP • High birth rate • Low birth rate
Long life expectancy • Short life expectancy
High percentage in agriculture
Low percentage in agriculture
High percentage in services • Low percentage in services
High percentage urban dwellers
Low percentage urban dwellers
High literacy levels • Low literacy levels

Economically more developed	Economically less developed

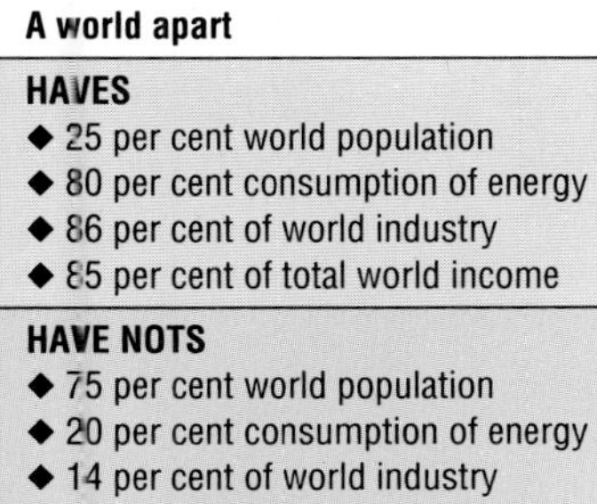
A world apart

HAVES
- 25 per cent world population
- 80 per cent consumption of energy
- 86 per cent of world industry
- 85 per cent of total world income

HAVE NOTS
- 75 per cent world population
- 20 per cent consumption of energy
- 14 per cent of world industry
- 15 per cent of total world income

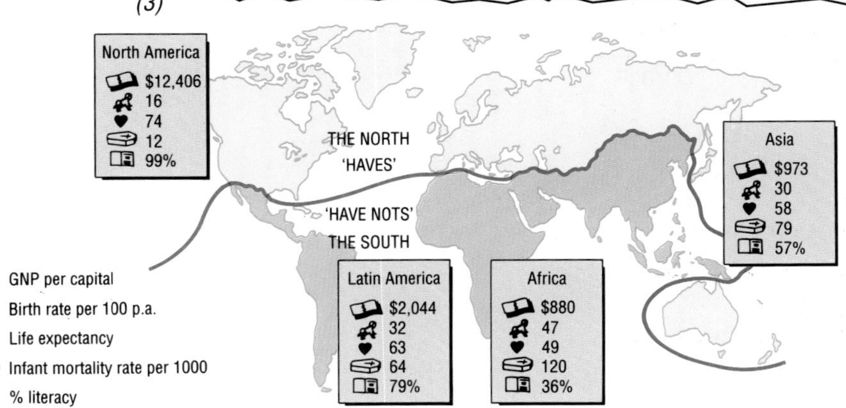

4 *(Page 166)*

The diagram shows the levels of development reached by three groups of countries. The three groups of countries are:
i) Kenya and Bangladesh.
ii) the UK, USA and Japan.
iii) Brazil.

Match up the groups of countries with the three parts of the diagram. *(3)*
Give reasons for your answer. *(6)*

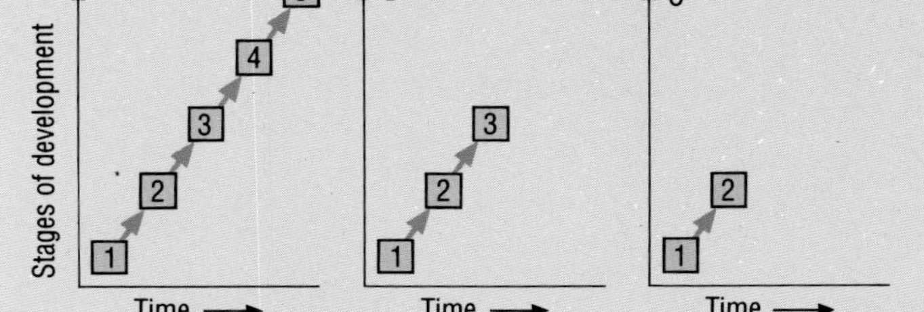

Drainage basins

A *drainage* or *river basin* is an area of land drained by a main river and its tributaries (Figure 14.1). Its boundary, marked by a ridge of higher land, is called a watershed. A *watershed*, therefore, separates one drainage basin from neighbouring drainage basins. Some basins, like the Mississippi which drains over one-third of the USA, are enormous. Others, possibly that of your local river, can be small. However, size is less important than the drainage density. The drainage density is:

$$\frac{\text{the total length of all the streams in the drainage basin}}{\text{the total area of the drainage basin}}$$

The drainage basin of the River Exe (Figure 14.2) has a much higher density than the basin in Figure 14.1. The density is highest on impermeable rocks and clays, and lowest on permeable rocks and sands. The higher the density the greater the risk of flooding, especially a flash flood (page 218).

Drainage basins can store rainwater, either within the river channel itself, or in lakes and in the ground. Excess water is carried back to the sea by rivers. Rivers form part of the hydrological (water) cycle (Figure 14.3). The seas and oceans contain 97 per cent of the world's water, but being salty it is not suitable for use by terrestrial plants, animals and people.

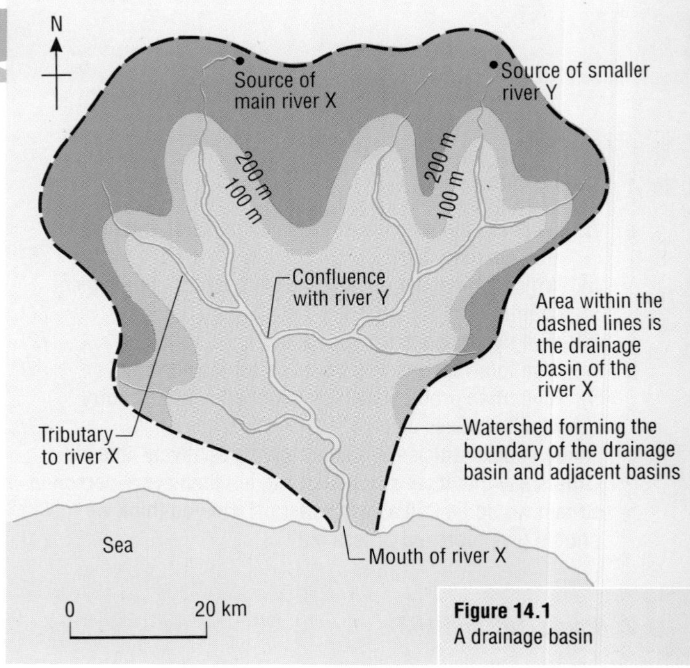

Figure 14.1
A drainage basin

Two per cent of the world's water is stored as ice and snow in arctic and alpine areas. That leaves 1 per cent which is either fresh water on land or water vapour in the atmosphere. As the amount of fresh water and vapour is limited, it has to be recycled over and over again. It is this constant recycling of water between the sea, air and land which is known as the ***hydrological cycle***. As no water is added to or lost from the hydrological cycle, it is said to be a *closed system*.

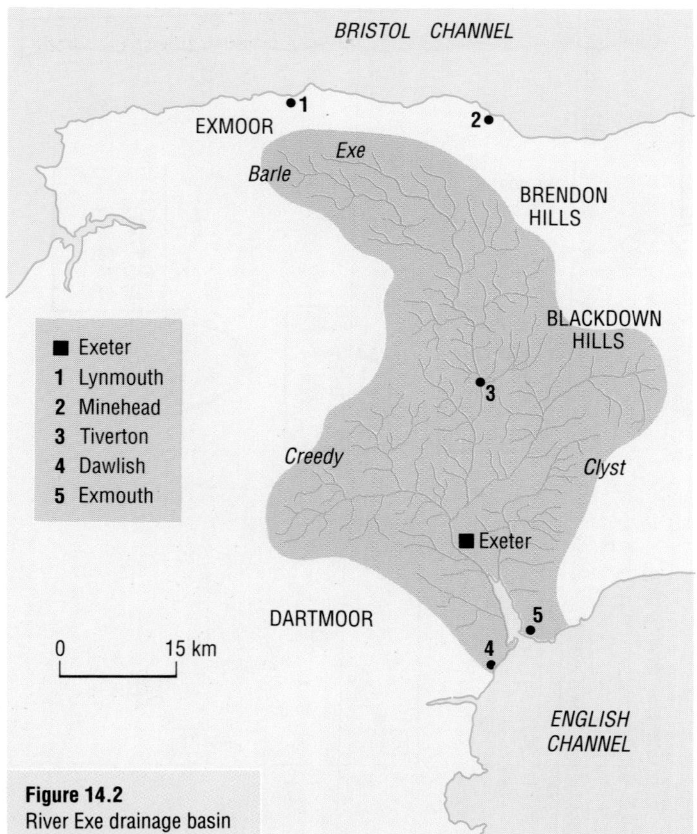

Figure 14.2
River Exe drainage basin

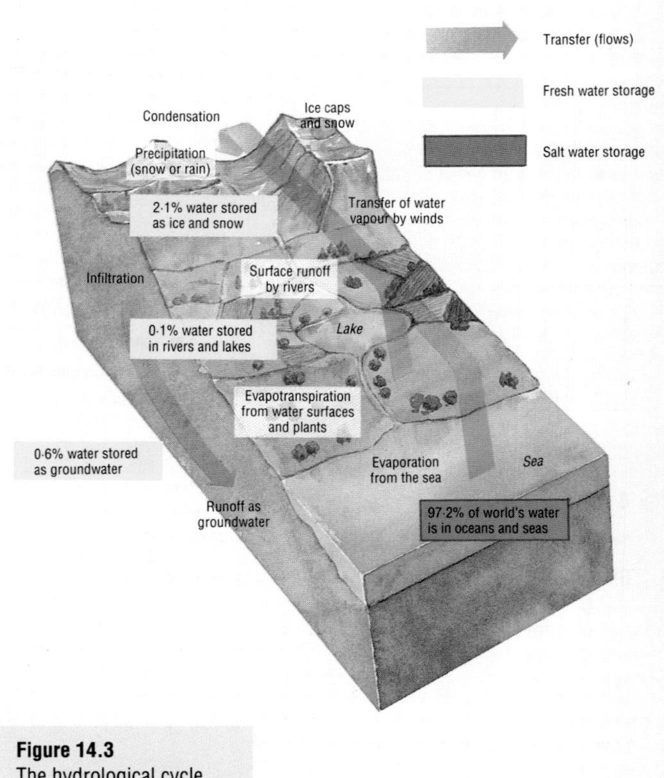

Figure 14.3
The hydrological cycle

The drainage basin system

A drainage basin forms part of the hydrological cycle but, unlike the hydrological cycle, it is an *open system*.

INPUTS → flows → STORES → flows → STORES → flows → OUTPUTS

It is an open system because it has:

- Inputs where water enters the system through precipitation (rain and snow).
- Outputs where water is lost to the system either by rivers carrying it to the sea or through evapotranspiration. *Evapotranspiration* is the loss of moisture directly from rivers or lakes (evaporation) or from vegetation (transpiration).

Within the system are *stores* and *transfers* (flows).

- *Stores* are places where water is held, e.g. in pools and lakes on the surface or in soil and rocks underground.
- *Transfers* are processes by which water flows, or moves, through the system, e.g. infiltration, surface run-off, throughflow.

A typical drainage basin system is shown in Figure 14.4.

When it rains, most water droplets are intercepted by trees and plants. Interception is greatest in summer. If the rain falls as a short, light shower then little water will reach the ground. It will be stored on leaves and then lost to the system through evaporation.

When the rain is heavier and lasts longer, water will drip from the vegetation on to the ground. At first it may form pools (*surface storage*) but as the ground becomes increasingly wet and soft, it will begin to infiltrate. *Infiltration* is the downward movement of water through tiny pores in the soil. This downward transfer will be greatest in porous rock or soil such as chalk or sand, and least in impermeable rock or soil like granite or clay. The water will then either be stored in the soil or slowly transferred sideways or downwards. The movement of water sideways is called *throughflow* and it is likely to form, eventually, a spring on a valley side. When the movement of water is downwards it is called *percolation*. Percolation forms *groundwater*, which is water stored at a depth in rocks. Groundwater flow is the slowest form of water transfer. The fastest process of water movement is surface run-off. *Surface run-off*, sometimes referred to as *overland flow*, occurs when either the storm is too heavy for water to infiltrate into the soil, where the soil is impermeable, or when the soil has become saturated. The level of *saturation*, i.e. when all the pores have been filled with water, is known as the *water table*. Although some rain may fall directly into the river, most water reaches it by a combination of surface run-off, throughflow and groundwater flow. Rivers carry water to the sea where it is lost to the system.

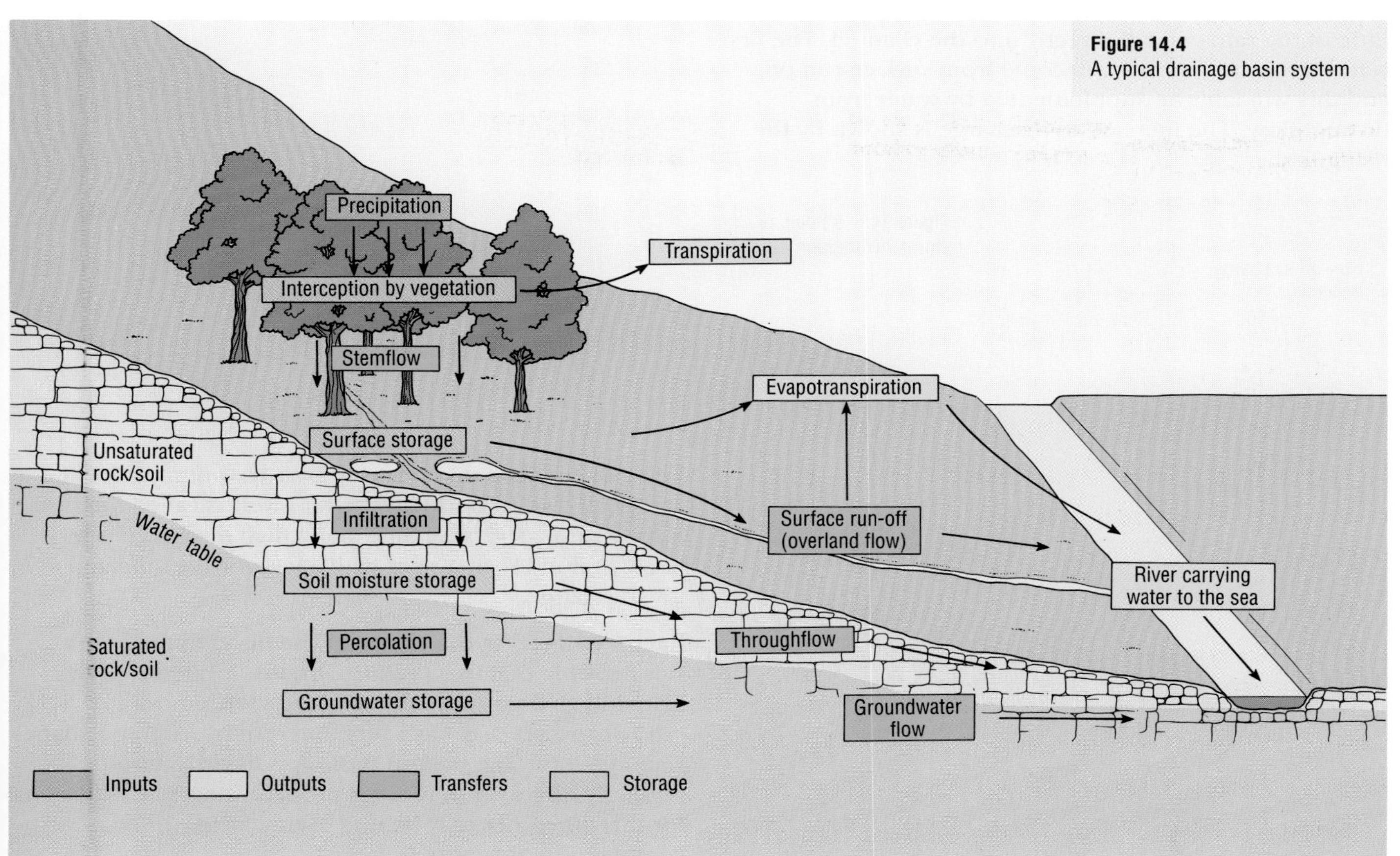

Figure 14.4
A typical drainage basin system

River discharge and flood hydrographs

Discharge depends upon the river's velocity and volume.
Velocity is the speed of the river. It is measured in metres per second.
Volume is the amount of water in the river. It is the cross-sectional area of the river's channel measured in square metres.
Discharge is the velocity of the river times its volume. It is the amount of water in the river passing a given point at a given time, measured in cumecs (cubic metres per second).

In some drainage basins, discharge and river levels rise very quickly after a storm. This can cause frequent, and occasionally serious, flooding. Following a storm in these basins, both discharge and river levels fall almost as rapidly, and after dry spells, become very low. In other drainage basins, rivers seem to maintain a more even flow.

The flood (storm) hydrograph

A *hydrograph* is a graph showing the discharge of a river at a given point (a gauging station) over a period of time. A flood or storm hydrograph shows how a river responds to one particular storm (Figure 14.5). When a storm begins, discharge does not increase immediately as only a little of the rain will fall directly into the channel. The first water to reach the river will come from surface run-off, and this will later be supplemented by water from throughflow. The increase in discharge is shown by the rising limb.

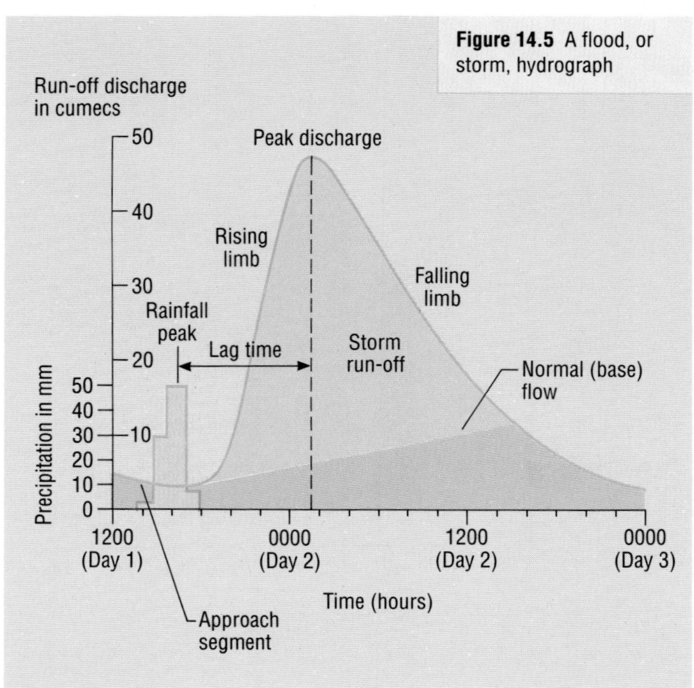

Figure 14.5 A flood, or storm, hydrograph

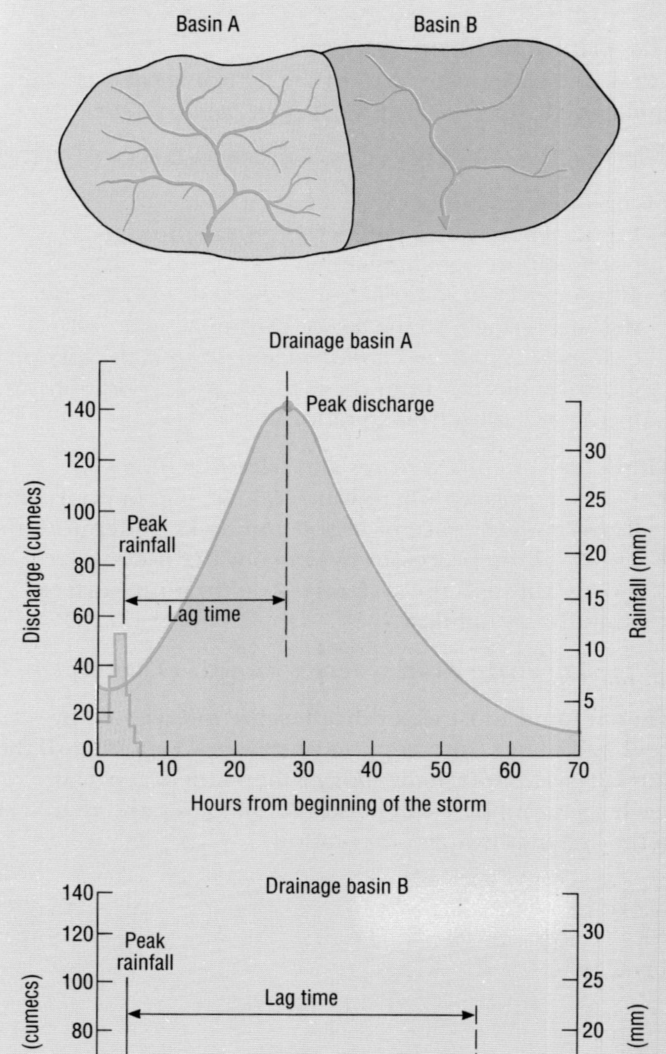

Figure 14.6 Differences between drainage basins

The gap between the time of peak (maximum) rainfall and peak discharge (highest river level) is called *lag time*. A river with a short lag time and a high discharge is more likely to flood than a river with a lengthy lag time and a low discharge.

Factors affecting the shape of the flood hydrograph
It is possible that two drainage basins, located side by side, can receive approximately the same amount of rainfall and yet may have very different hydrograph shapes (Figure 14.6). The river in Basin A is likely to flood regularly, the river in Basin B probably never. The reasons for this difference may be due to one factor, or a combination of factors (Figure 14.7).

Factor	Drainage Basin A	Drainage Basin B
Relief	Faster run-off on steep slopes	Slower run-off on more gentle slopes
Rock type	Surface run-off on impermeable rock	Throughflow and groundwater flow as rainfall infiltrates into permeable (porous) rock
Soil	Very thin soil; less infiltration	Deeper soil; more infiltration
Natural vegetation	Thin grass and moorland; less interception	Forest; most interception. Roots delay throughflow and absorb moisture. Evapotranspiration reduces chances of water reaching river
Land use	Urbanisation; increased tarmac (impermeable layer) and drains (increased run-off). Arable land expose more soil	Rural area with little tarmac, concrete or drains. Tree crops and arable farming increase interception
Use of river	Limited use	Water extracted for industry, domestic use and irrigation. Dam built to store water
Drainage density	Higher density means more streams to collect water quickly	Lower density; fewer streams to collect water

Figure 14.7
Differences in flood hydrographs for two adjacent river basins

Extreme weather conditions are often the major cause of a river flooding. A torrential thunderstorm, continuous rainfall for several days, or a heavy snowfall melting while it rains all increase the discharge of a river. Although high summer temperatures increase evapotranspiration and reduce the amount of water available to reach a river, they can make the ground hard, reducing infiltration when it does rain. Freezing conditions in winter can make the ground impermeable.

Hydrographs can also be drawn for longer periods of time. The National Rivers Authority (NRA) produce hydrographs to show, among other things, if there is a relationship between the two variables of rainfall and discharge. Figure 14.8 was provided by the NRA for the River Torridge in North Devon. It covers a very wet month in late 1992.

Notice that:

- Discharge is dependent upon rainfall, but rainfall does not depend upon discharge.
- Most of the discharge peaks are a half or full day after the rainfall peak (lag time).
- The highest discharge peak came after several very wet days during which river levels had no time to drop, rather than after the wettest day which followed a relatively dry spell when the river level had fallen.
- The River Torridge responds very quickly to rainfall and so would appear to pose a flood risk.

Figure 14.8
Hydrograph for the River Torridge at Torrington (Devon)

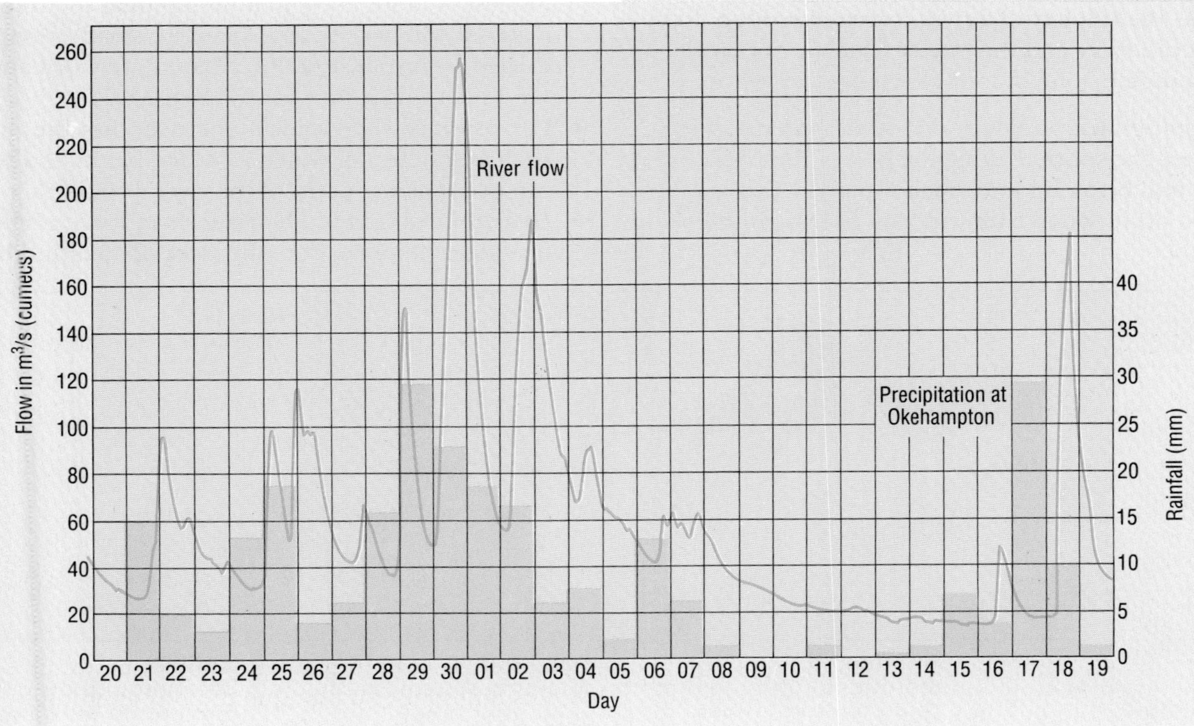

River processes and landforms

Energy is needed in any system, not just the drainage basin, for transfers to take place.

In the case of a river most of this energy, an estimated 95 per cent under normal conditions, is needed to overcome friction. Most friction occurs at the *wetted perimeter*, i.e. where the water comes into contact with the river's banks and bed. The channel of a mountain stream, often filled with boulders, creates much friction (Figure 14.9). As a result, water flows less quickly here than in the lowlands where the channel becomes wider and deeper (Figure 14.10).

Following a period of heavy rain, or after the confluence with a major tributary, the volume of the river will increase. As less water will be in contact with the wetted perimeter then friction will be reduced and the river will increase its velocity. The surplus energy, resulting from the decrease in friction, can now be used to pick up and transport material. The greater the velocity of a river the greater the amount of material, both in quantity and size, that can be carried. The material which is transported by a river is called its *load*.

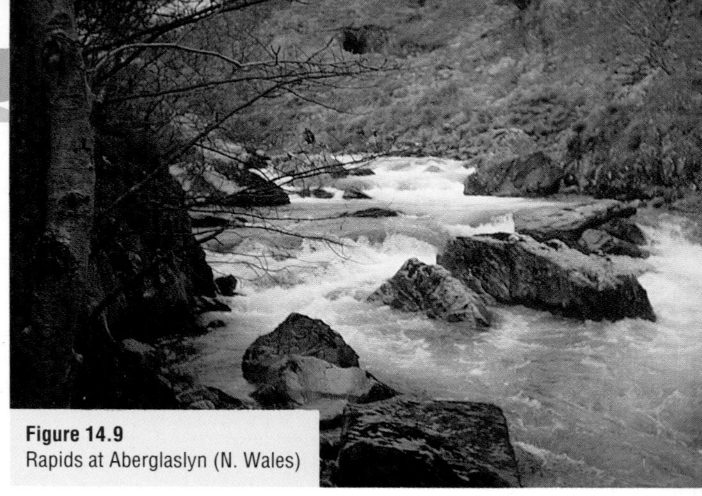

Figure 14.9
Rapids at Aberglaslyn (N. Wales)

Figure 14.10
Velocity and discharge in the upper and lower course of a highland stream

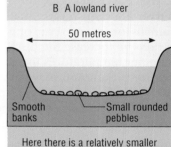

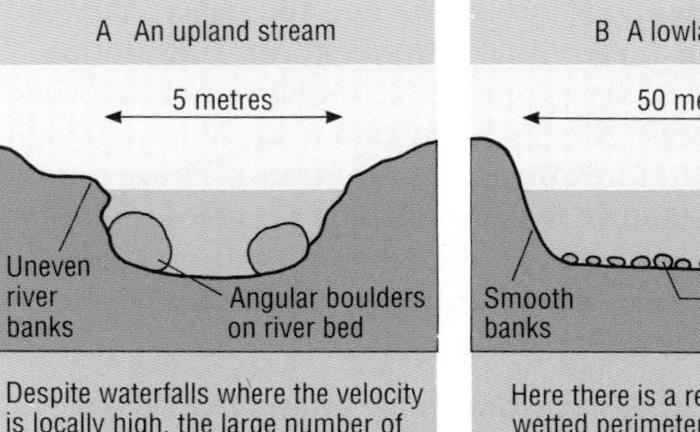

Transportation

A river can transport its load by one of four processes: traction and saltation, along its bed; suspension and solution, within the river itself (Figure 14.11).

Erosion

A river uses the transported material to erode its banks and bed. As the velocity of a river increases, so too does the load it can carry and the rate at which it can erode. A river may erode by one of four processes:

- *Attrition* is when boulders and other material, which are being transported along the bed of the river, collide and break up into smaller pieces. This is more likely to occur when rivers are still flowing in highland areas.
- *Corrasion* occurs when smaller material, carried in suspension, rubs against the banks of the river. This process is more likely in lowland areas by which time material will have been broken up small enough to be carried in suspension. River banks are worn away by a sand-papering action called *abrasion*.
- *Corrosion* is when acids in the river dissolve rocks, such as limestone, which form the banks and bed. This can occur at any point of the river's course.
- *Hydraulic action* is when the sheer force of the river dislodges particles from the river's banks and bed.

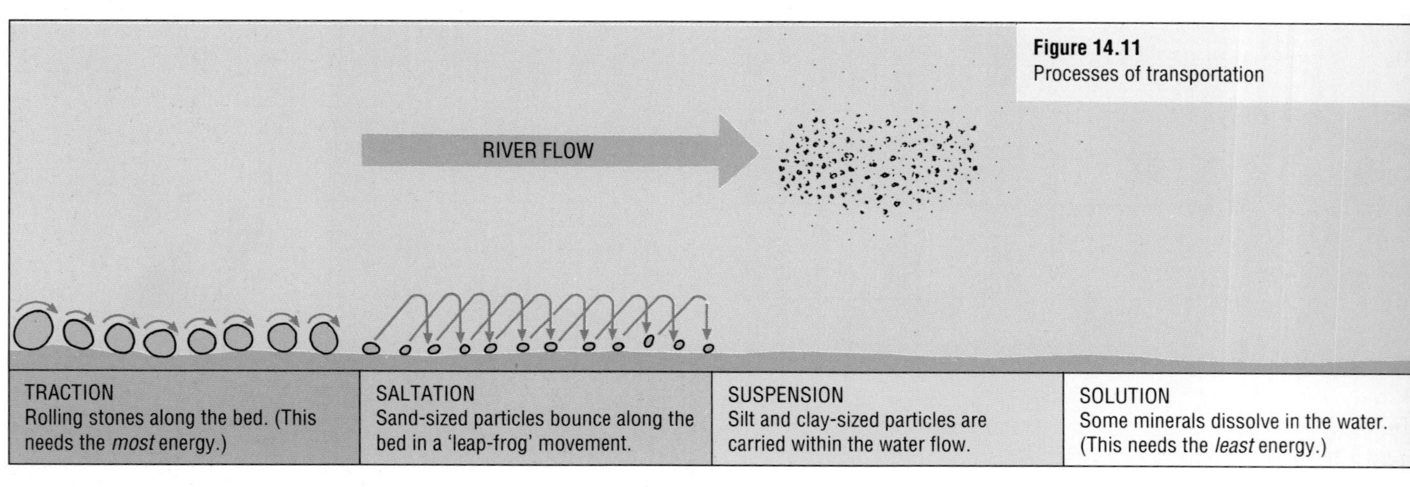

RIVER FLOW
TRACTION
Rolling stones along the bed. (This needs the *most* energy.)
SALTATION
Sand-sized particles bounce along the bed in a 'leap-frog' movement.
SUSPENSION
Silt and clay-sized particles are carried within the water flow.
SOLUTION
Some minerals dissolve in the water. (This needs the *least* energy.)

Figure 14.11
Processes of transportation

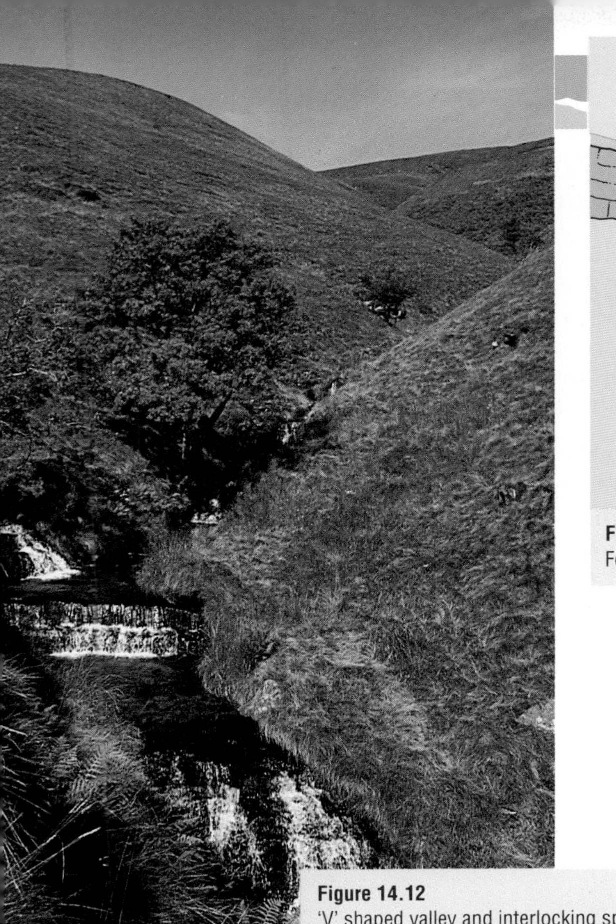

Figure 14.12
'V' shaped valley and interlocking spurs

Deposition

Deposition occurs when a river lacks enough energy to carry its load. Deposition, beginning with the heaviest material first, can occur following a dry spell when the discharge and velocity of the river drop, or where the current slows down (the inside of a meander bend or where the river enters the sea).

River landforms in a highland area

'V' shaped valleys and interlocking spurs

Any spare energy possessed by a river near to its source will be used to transport large boulders along its bed. This results in the river cutting rapidly downwards, a process called *vertical erosion*. Vertical erosion leads to the development of steep-sided, narrow valleys shaped like the letter 'V' (Figure 14.12). The valley sides are steep due to soil and loose rock being washed downhill following periods of heavy rainfall. The material is then added to the load of the river. The river itself is forced to wind its way around protruding hillsides. These hillsides, known as interlocking spurs, restrict the view up or down the valley.

Waterfalls and rapids

Waterfalls form when there is a sudden interruption in the course of a river. They may result from erosion by ice (page 182), changes in sea-level, and earth movements.

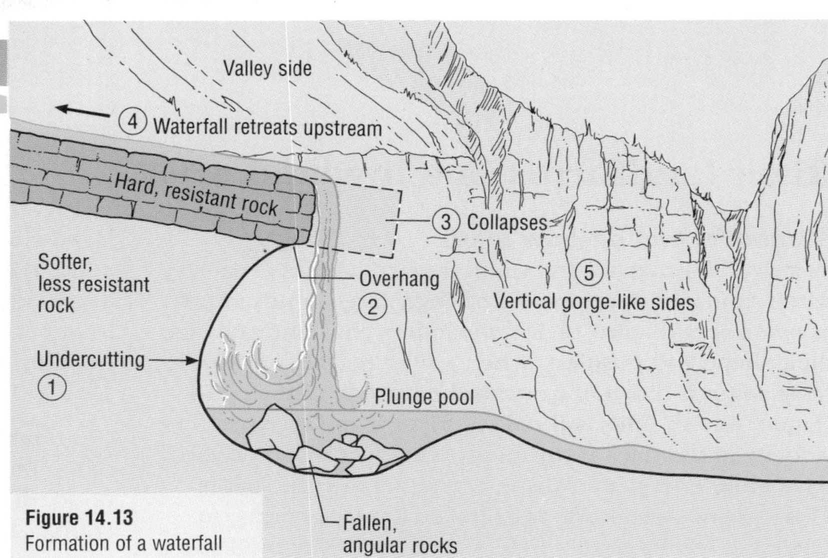

Figure 14.13
Formation of a waterfall

However, many waterfalls form when rivers meet a band of softer, less resistant rock after flowing over a relatively hard, resistant rock (Figure 14.13). The underlying softer rock is worn away more quickly, and the harder rock is undercut. In time the overlying harder rock will become unsupported and will collapse. After its collapse, some of the rock will be swirled around by the river, especially during times of high discharge, to form a deep plunge pool. This process is likely to be repeated many times causing the waterfall to retreat upstream and leave a steep-sided gorge (Figure 14.14). The Niagara Falls are retreating by one metre a year. *Rapids* occur where the layers of hard and soft rock are very thin, and so no obvious break of slope develops as in a waterfall .

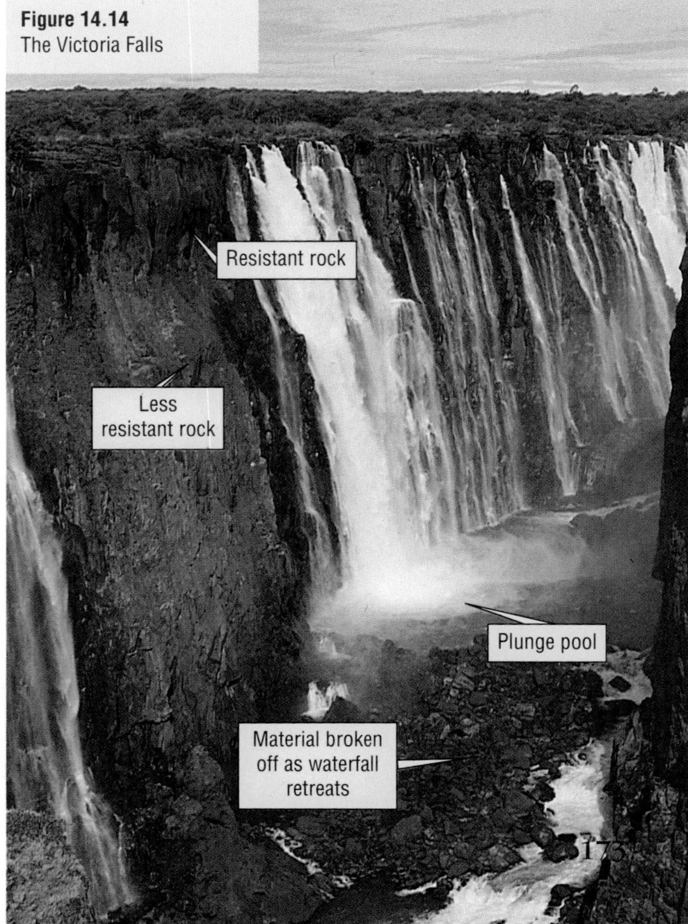

Figure 14.14
The Victoria Falls

River landforms in a lowland area

Meanders and ox-bow lakes

As a river approaches its mouth it usually flows over flatter land and develops increasingly large bends known as *meanders* (Figure 14.15). Meanders constantly change their shape and position. When a river reaches a meander most water is directed towards the outside of the bend (Figure 14.16). This will reduce friction and increase the velocity of the river at this point. The river will therefore have more energy to transport material in suspension. This material will erode the outside bank by corrasion. The bank will be undercut, collapse and retreat to leave a small river cliff. The river is now eroding through *lateral*, not vertical, *erosion*.

Meanwhile, as there will be less water on the inside of the bend, there will also be an increase in friction and a decrease in velocity. As the river loses energy it will begin to deposit some of its load. The deposited material will build up to form a gently sloping slip-off slope (Figure 14.17).

Continual erosion on the outside bends result in the neck of the meander getting narrower until, usually at a time of flood, the river cuts through the neck and shortens its course. The fastest current will now be flowing in the centre of the channel and deposition is more likely next to the banks. The original meander will be blocked off to leave a crescent shaped *ox-bow lake*. This lake will slowly dry up, apart from during periods of heavy rain.

Figure 14.15 River Ouse – a meandering river

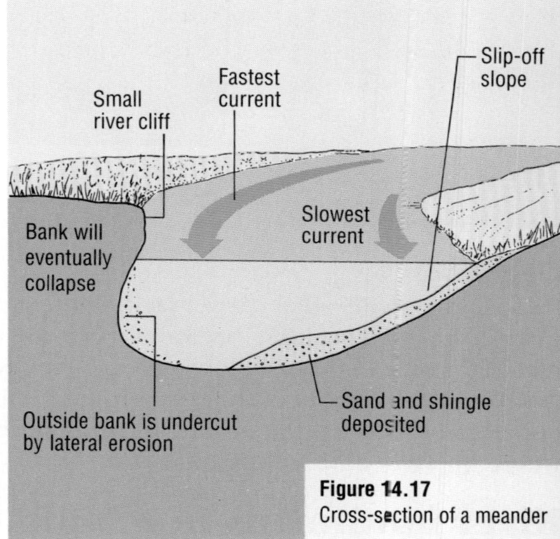

Figure 14.17
Cross-section of a meander

Figure 14.16
Formation of an ox-bow lake

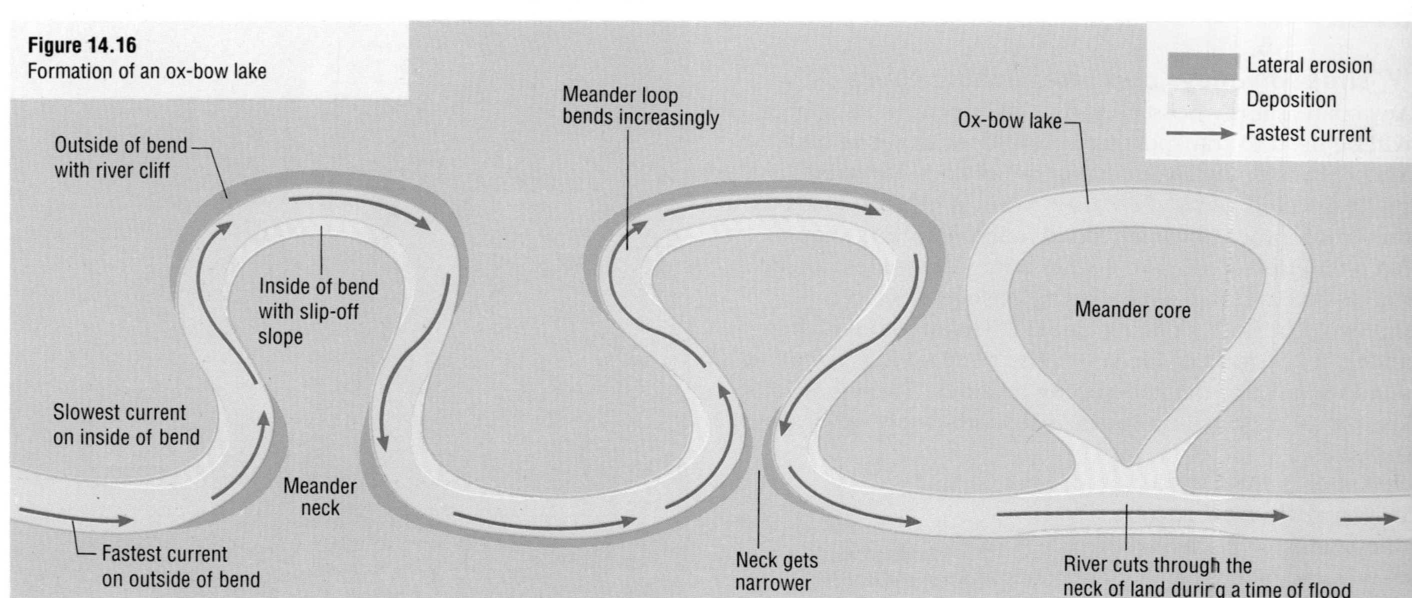

Flood plain and levées

The river widens its valley by lateral erosion. At times of high discharge, the river has considerable amounts of energy which it uses to transport large amounts of material in suspension. When the river overflows its banks it will spread out across any surrounding flat land. The sudden increase in friction will reduce the water's velocity and fine silt will be deposited. Each time the river floods another layer of silt is added and a flat *flood plain* is formed (Figure 14.18). The coarsest material will be dropped first and this can form a natural embankment, called a *levée*, next to the river. Sometimes levées are artificially strengthened to act as flood banks. Some rivers, like the Mississippi, flow between levées at a height well above their flood plain. If, during a later flood, the river breaks through its levées, then widespread flooding may occur.

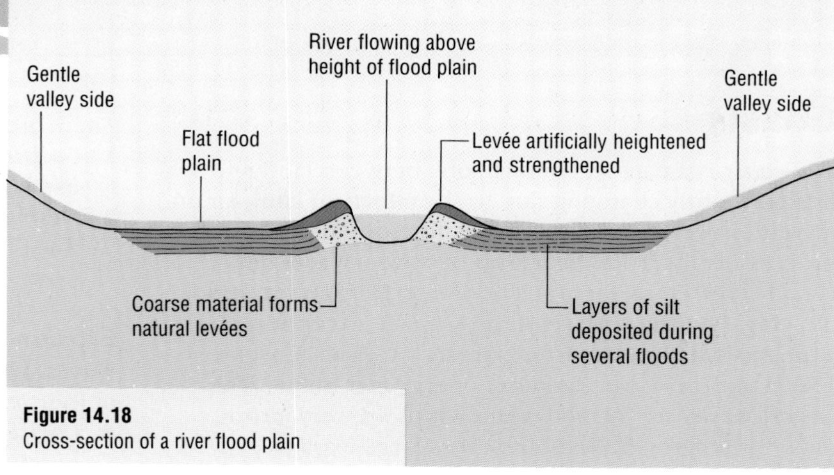

Figure 14.18
Cross-section of a river flood plain

Figure 14.19
The Mississippi Delta

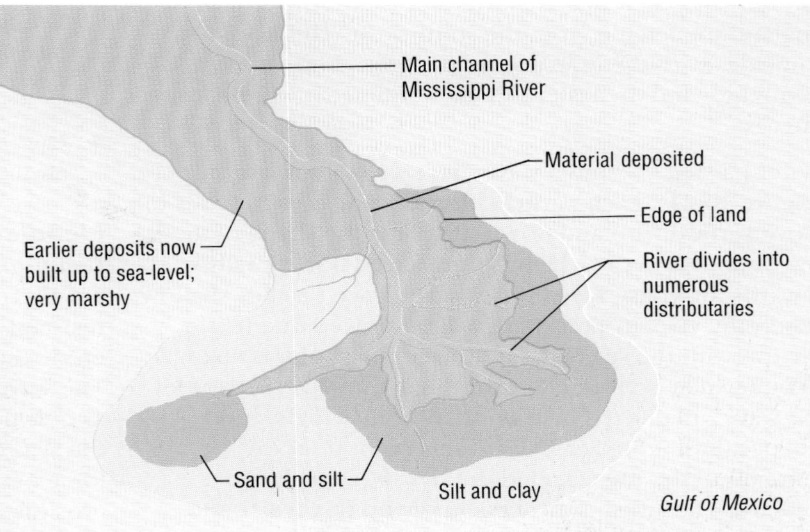

Figure 14.20
Formation of the Mississippi Delta

Deltas

As large rivers approach the sea, they have the energy to carry large amounts of fine material in suspension. On reaching the sea, the river current may suddenly be reduced and the material deposited (Figure 14.19). Sometimes deposition occurs in the main channel, and blocks it. The river has then to divide into a series of channels, called *distributaries*, in order to find its way into the sea. Over a period of time the deposited materials of sand and silt may build upwards and outwards to form a *delta* (Figure 14.20). Deltas are only likely to form where the material brought down by a river is too much for sea currents to remove it (e.g. Mississippi and Ganges) or in seas which are virtually tideless (the Nile and the Rhone in the Mediterranean Sea). Deltas can also form when a river flows into the gentle waters of a lake.

Coasts

The *coast* is a narrow contact zone between land and sea. It is constantly changing due to the effects of land, air and marine processes. On many coastlines the dominant process results from the action of waves. Waves are usually created by the transfer of energy from the wind blowing over the surface of the sea (the exceptions are tsunamis which result from submarine earth movements). The larger the wave, the more energy it contains. The largest waves are formed when winds are very strong, blow for lengthy periods and cross large expanses of water. The maximum distance of water over which winds can blow is called the *fetch*. In the case of south-west England the fetch is from the south-west. This also coincides with the direction of the prevailing, or most frequent, wind. In eastern England the fetch will be from the east.

Water particles within a wave move in a circular orbit (Figure 14.21). Each particle, or a floating object, tends to move vertically up and down. It is only the shape of the wave and its energy which is transferred horizontally towards the coast. However, when a wave reaches shallow water, the velocity at its base will be slowed due to friction with the sea-bed, and the circular orbit is changed to one which is more elliptical (Figure 14.21). The top of the wave, unaffected by friction, becomes higher and steeper until it breaks. Only at this point does the remnant of the wave, called the *swash*, actually move forward. The swash transfers energy up the beach, the *backwash* returns energy down the beach.

There are two types of wave (Figure 14.22).

1 *Constructive waves* have limited energy. Most of this is used by the swash to transport material up the beach.
2 *Destructive waves* have much more energy. Most of this is used by the backwash to transport material back down the beach.

Erosion

Waves, like rivers (page 172), can erode the land by one of four processes.

- *Corrasion* (abrasion) is caused by large waves hurling beach material against a cliff.
- *Attrition* is when waves cause rocks and boulders on the beach to bump into each other and to break up into small particles.
- *Corrosion* (solution) is when salts and other acids in seawater slowly dissolve a cliff.
- *Hydraulic pressure* is the force of waves compressing air in cracks in a cliff.

Headlands and bays

Headlands and *bays* form along coastlines where there are alternating outcrops of resistant (harder) and less resistant (softer) rock (Figure 14.23). Destructive waves erode the areas of softer rock more rapidly to form bays. The waves cannot, however, wear away the resistant rock as quickly and so headlands are left protruding out into the sea. The headlands will now be exposed to the full force of the waves, and will become more vulnerable to erosion. At the same time they will protect the adjacent bays from destructive waves.

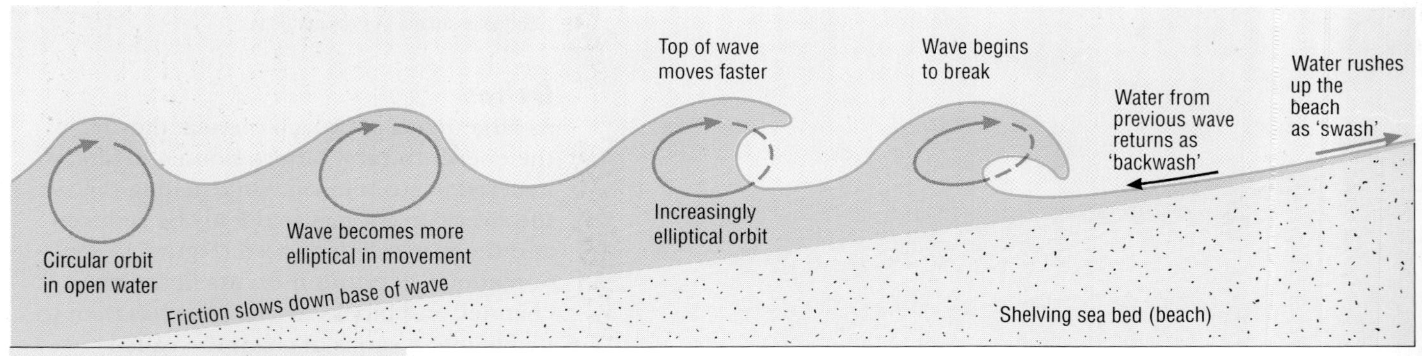

Figure 14.21 Formation of a wave

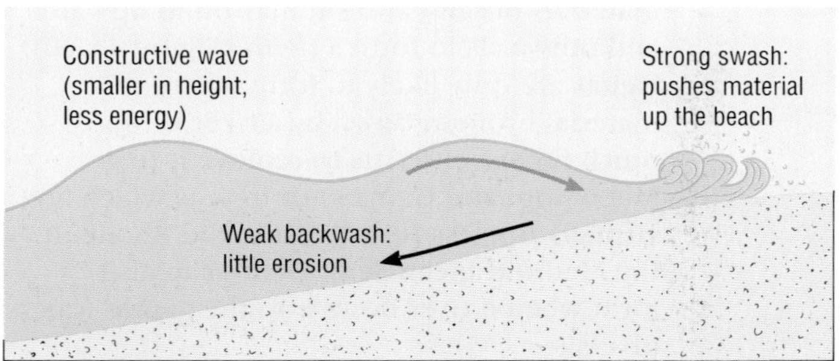

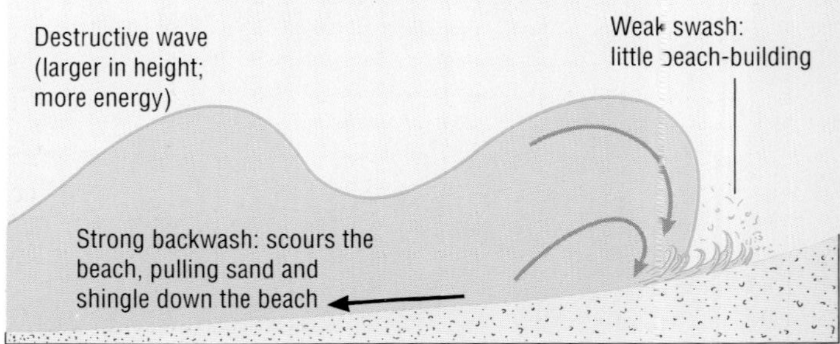

Figure 14.22 Constructive and destructive waves

Cliffs, wave-cut notches and wave-cut platforms

Wave erosion is greatest when large waves break against the foot of the cliff. With wave energy at its maximum, the waves will undercut the foot of the cliff to form a *wave-cut notch* (Figure 14.24). Over a period of time the notch will enlarge until the cliff above it, left unsupported, collapses. As this process is repeated, the cliff will retreat and, often, will increase in height. The gently sloping expanse of rock marking the foot of the retreating cliff is called a *wave-cut platform* (Figure 14.25). Wave-cut platforms are exposed at low tide but covered at high tide.

Caves, arches and stacks

Cliffs are more likely to form where the coastline consists of resistant rock. However, within resistant rocks there are usually places of weakness, such as a joint or a fault (Figure 14.26). Corrasion, corrosion and hydraulic action by the waves will widen any weakness to form, initially, a *cave*. If a cave forms at a headland, the cave might be widened and deepened until the sea cuts through to form a *natural arch* (Figure 14.27). Waves will continue to erode the foot of the arch until its roof becomes too heavy to be supported. When the roof collapses it will leave part of the former cliff isolated as a *stack* (Figure 14.28). In time, further wave action will result in the stack collapsing to leave a *stump*.

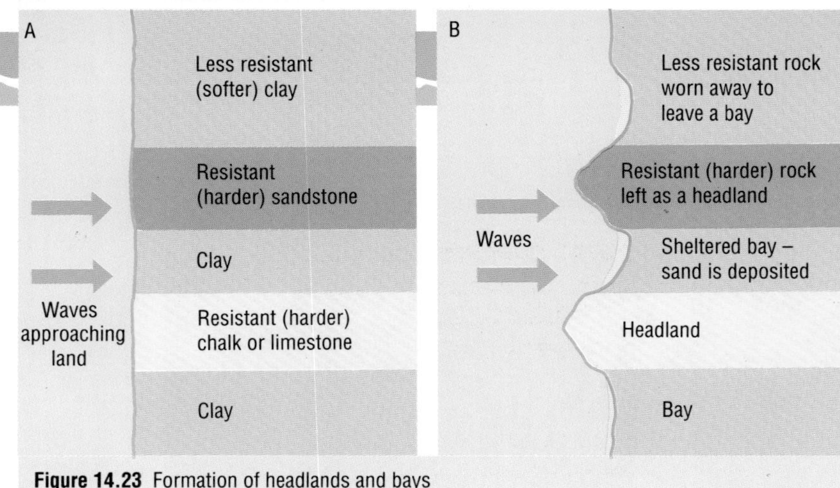

Figure 14.23 Formation of headlands and bays

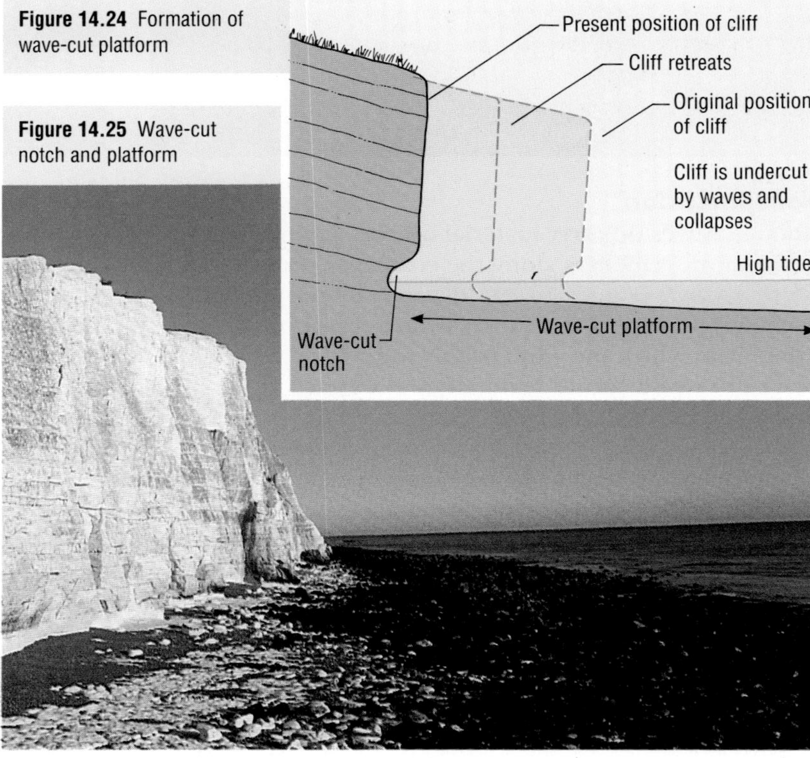

Figure 14.24 Formation of wave-cut platform

Figure 14.25 Wave-cut notch and platform

Figure 14.26 Formation of caves, arches and stacks

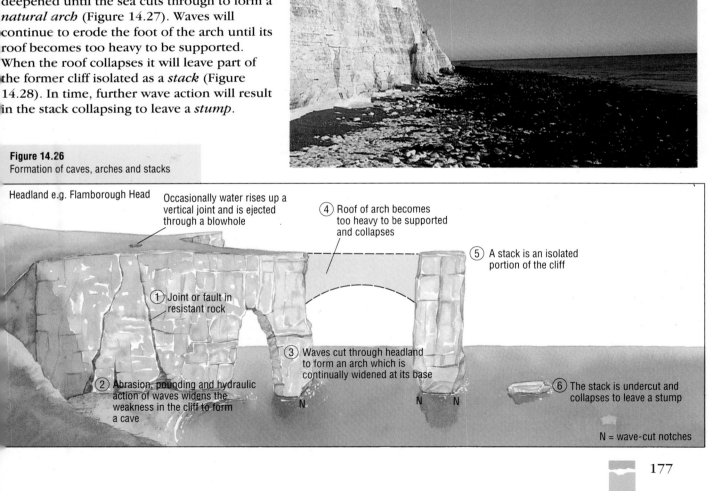

Figure 14.28
A stack on the island of Hoy, Orkney Islands

Figure 14.27
A natural arch and stack at Pembroke, Wales

Transportation

Although waves do carry material up and down a beach, the major movement is along the coast by a process called *longshore drift* (Figure 14.29). Waves rarely approach a beach at right angles, but rather from a direction similar to that from which the wind is blowing. When a wave breaks the swash carries material up the beach at the same angle at which the wave approached the shore. As the swash dies away, the backwash returns material straight down the beach, at right angles to the water, under the influence of gravity. Material is slowly moved along the coast in a zig-zag course. The effect of longshore drift can best be seen when wooden groynes have been built to prevent material from being moved along the beach (Figure 14.30).

Deposition

Sand and shingle being transported along the coast by longshore drift will, in time, reach an area where the water is sheltered and the waves lack energy, e.g. a bay. The material may be temporarily deposited to form a beach. Beaches are not permanent features as their shape can be altered by waves every time the tide comes in and goes out. Shingle beaches have a steeper gradient than sandy beaches.

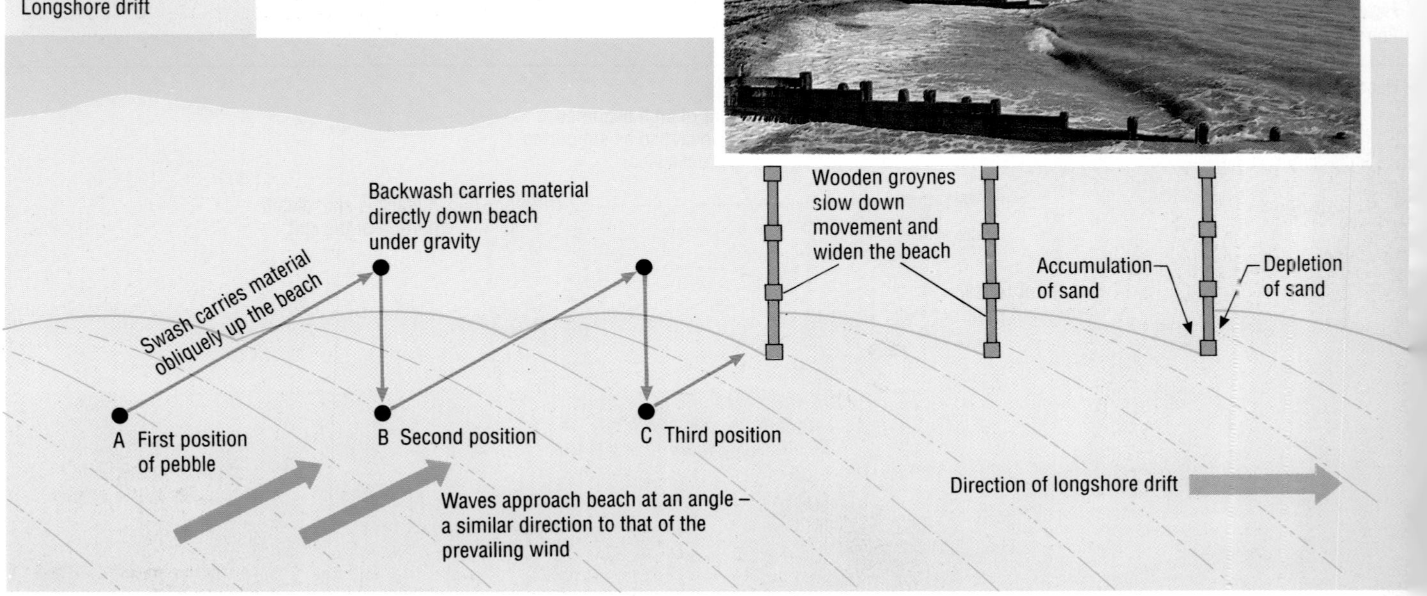

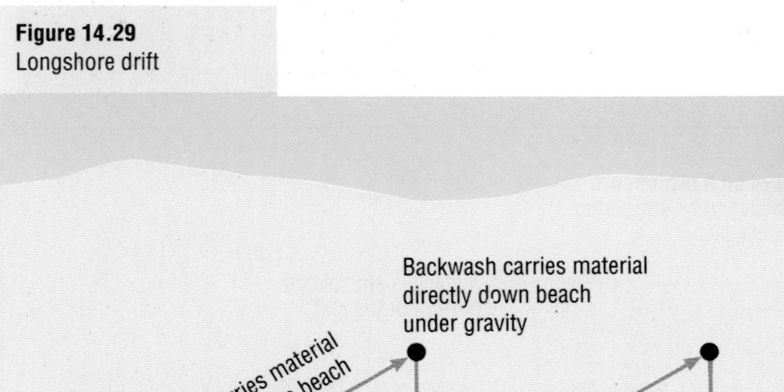
Backwash carries material directly down beach under gravity
Swash carries material obliquely up the beach
A First position of pebble
B Second position
C Third position
Waves approach beach at an angle – a similar direction to that of the prevailing wind
Wooden groynes slow down movement and widen the beach
Accumulation of sand
Depletion of sand
Direction of longshore drift
Figure 14.29
Longshore drift

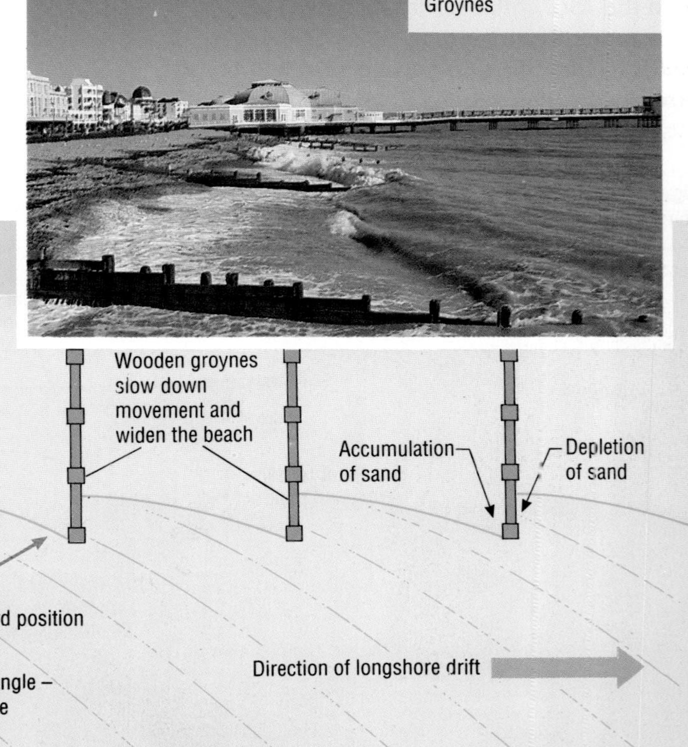
Figure 14.30
Groynes

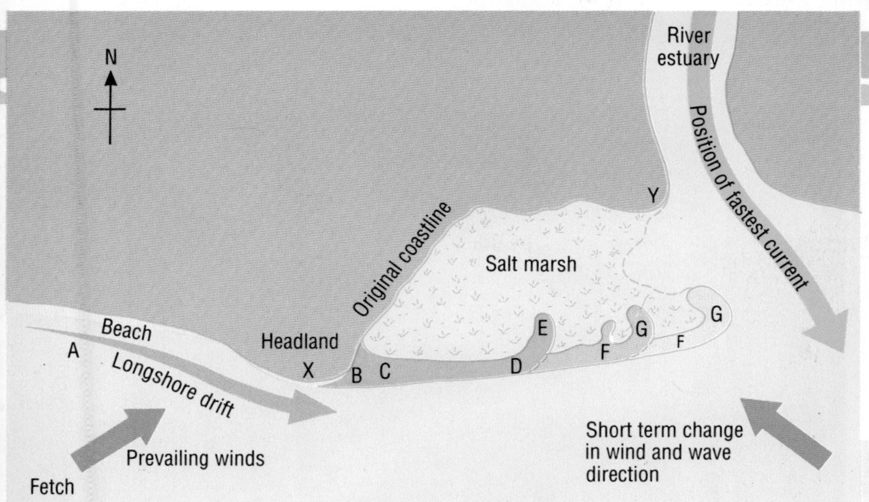

Figure 14.32
Formation of a spit

Figure 14.31
A spit

Spits

A spit is a permanent landform resulting from marine deposition. A *spit* is a long, narrow accumulation of sand or shingle, with one end attached to the land, and the other projecting at a narrow angle either into the sea or across a river estuary. Many spits have a hooked or curved end (Figure 14.31). They form where longshore drift moves large amounts of sand and shingle along the coast, and where the coastline suddenly changes direction to leave a shallow, sheltered area of water. In Figure 14.32 line X to Y marks the position of the original coastline. As the fetch and prevailing winds are, in this example, from the south-west, material will be moved eastwards along the coast by longshore drift. After headland X the direction of the original coastline changes and larger material (shingle) is deposited in water sheltered by the headland (B). Further deposition of finer material (sand) enables the feature to build up slowly to sea-level (C) and to extend its length (D). Occasionally the wind changes its direction (e.g. comes from the east). This in turn causes the waves to alter their direction (e.g. approach from the south-east).

Figure 14.33
Geiranger Fiord, Norway

During this time some material at the end of the spit may be pushed inland to form a curved end (E). When the wind returns to its usual direction the spit resumes its growth eastwards (F). Spits become permanent when sand is blown up the beach, by the prevailing wind, to form *sand-dunes*. *Salt marsh* is likely to develop in the sheltered water behind the spit. The spit is unable to grow across the estuary as the river current carries material out to sea. Should there be no river, the spit may grow across the bay to form a *bar*.

Sea-level changes

During the ice age large amounts of water were held in storage as ice and snow. This interruption in the hydrological cycle (page 168) caused the world's sea-level to fall. After the ice age sea-level rose as the ice and snow melted. Many coastal areas were drowned creating landforms such as fiords and rias. Both *fiords* and *rias* are drowned valleys. Fiords are found where glaciers overdeepened valleys until they were below sea-level (Figure 14.33) while rias occur in valleys which were formed by rivers (Figure 14.34). Fiords are long, narrow inlets with high, cliff-like sides. They are very deep, apart from a shallow entrance. Rias are more winding with relatively low, gentle sides. The depth of a ria increases towards the sea.

Figure 14.34
A ria

Glaciation

Although it is too warm for glaciers to be found in Britain today, much of the spectacular highland scenery of Scotland, Wales and northern England owes its attractiveness to the work of ice in earlier times. At the height of the ice age, northern Britain was covered by a large ice sheet. At other times glaciers extended down valleys leading from the higher mountains.

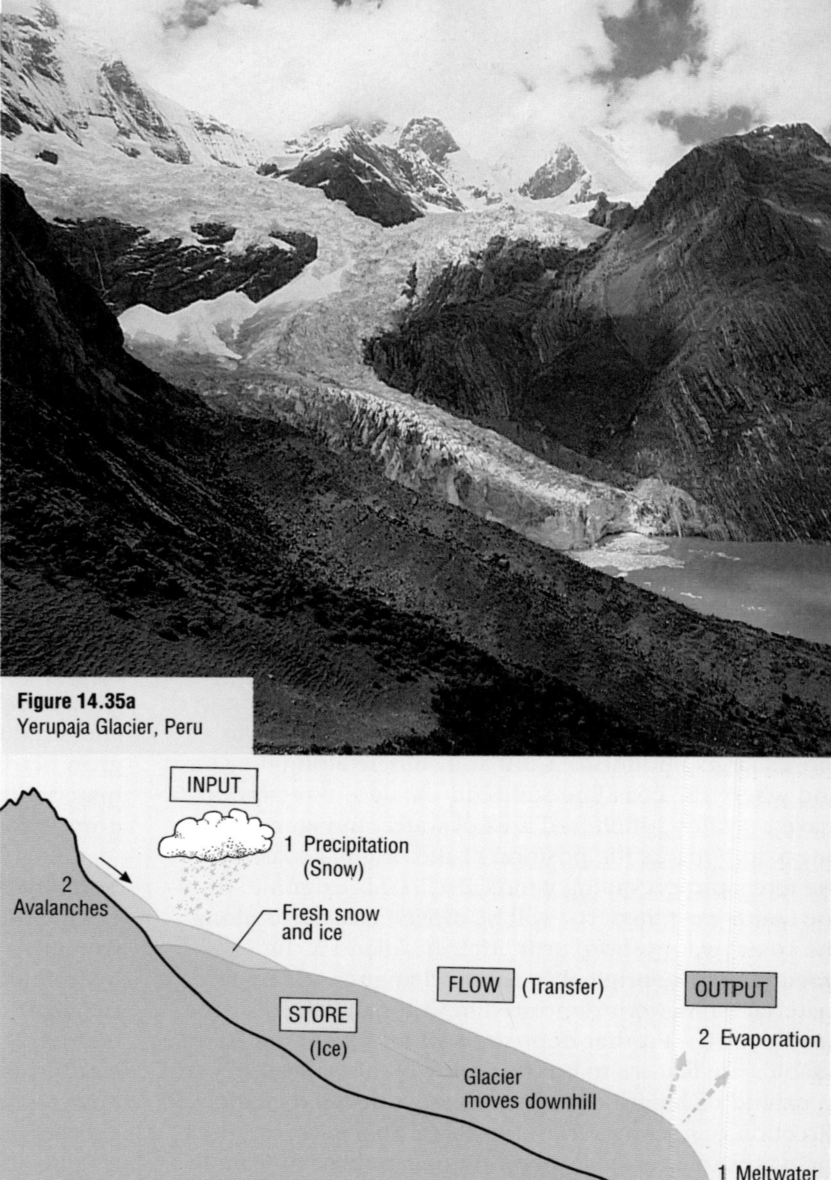

Figure 14.35a Yerupaja Glacier, Peru

Figure 14.35b The glacier system

The glacier system

A glacier, like a river, behaves as a system with input, stores, flows and output (Figure 14.35). Input comes from precipitation in the form of snow falling directly onto the glacier, or from avalanches along the glacier sides. Input mainly occurs near to the head of a glacier in the *zone of accumulation*. During fresh falls of snow, air is trapped between the flakes. As more snow falls the underlying layers are compressed, the air is squeezed out and the snow becomes firmer (like making a snowball). As more snow accumulates, the underlying layers are compressed into ice. Ice without any air (oxygen) left in it turns blue. The glacier itself is water held in storage and, as ice, flows (transfers) downhill under the force of gravity.

Output from the system are mainly meltwater with a limited amount of evaporation. When a glacier melts it is called *ablation*. Input (accumulation) is likely to exceed output (ablation) near to the head of a glacier and in winter. Ablation will exceed accumulation in summer and in lower altitudes where temperatures are warmer. If, over a period of time, the annual rate of accumulation exceeds ablation, then the glacier will advance. If ablation exceeds accumulation, the glacier will retreat. At present most of the world's remaining glaciers are retreating.

Erosion

A glacier can erode much faster than a river, but like a river, it can only erode if it has a continuous supply of material. The main source of material for a glacier results from the process of freeze-thaw weathering (or frost shattering). Freeze-thaw occurs in rocks which have many joints and cracks in them, and where temperatures are frequently around freezing point. Water, which gets into the cracks during the day, freezes at night. As it freezes it expands and puts pressure on the surrounding rock. When the ice melts, pressure is released. Repeated freezing and thawing widens the cracks and causes jagged pieces of rock to break off. The glacier uses this material, called *moraine*, to widen and deepen its valley.

There are two main processes of glacial erosion:

1 *Abrasion* is when the material carried by a glacier rubs against and, like sandpaper, wears away the sides and floor of the valley. It is similar to corrasion by a river, but on a much larger scale.
2 *Plucking* results from glacial ice freezing onto solid rock. As the glacier moves away it pulls with it large pieces of rock.

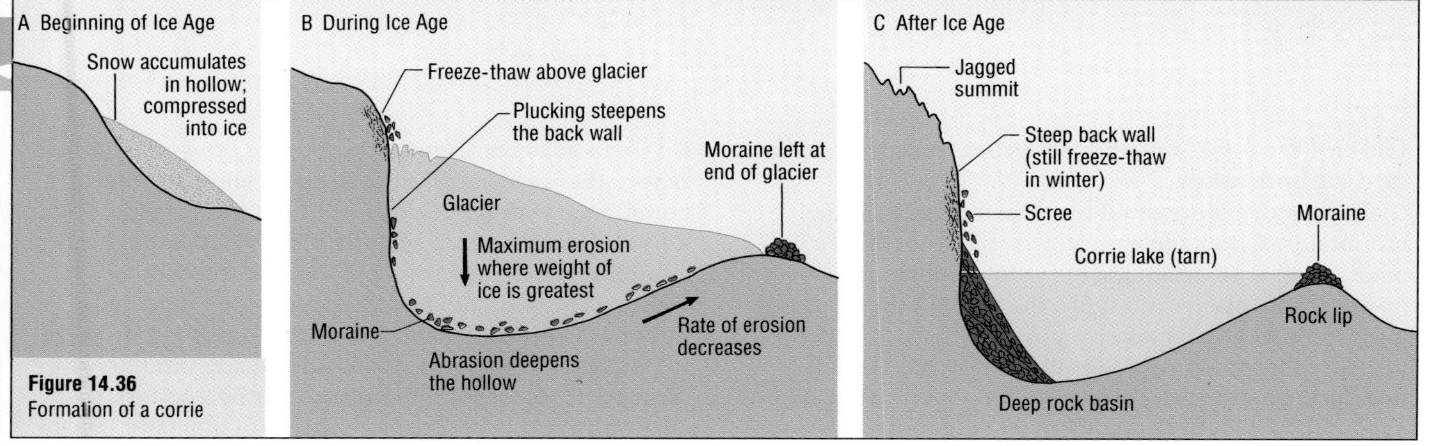

Figure 14.36
Formation of a corrie

Glacial landforms

Corries

Corries, which are also known as *cirques* and *cwms*, are deep, rounded hollows with a steep back wall and a rock basin (Figure 14.36). They began to form at the beginning of the ice age when snow accumulated in hollows on hillsides, especially in hollows with a less sunny north and east facing aspect. Snow turned into ice, and the ice moved downhill. Freeze-thaw and plucking loosened and removed material from the back of the hollow creating a steep back wall (Figure 14.36). Moraine, dragged along the base of the glacier, deepened the floor of the hollow by abrasion, and formed a rock basin. *A rock lip* was left where the rate of erosion decreased. This lip was often heightened by the deposition of moraine. After the ice age the rock lip and moraine acted as a natural dam to meltwater, and many rock basins are now occupied by a deep, round *corrie lake* or *tarn*.

Figure 14.37
A pyramidal peak in Norway

Arêtes and pyramidal peaks

When two or more corries developed back-to-back (or side-by-side) they cut backwards (or sideways) towards each other. The land between them got narrower until a knife-edged ridge, called an *arête*, was formed (Figure 14.40). Where three or more corries cut backwards into the same mountain, a *pyramidal peak*, or *horn*, was formed (Figure 14.37). Arêtes radiate from the central peak (Figure 14.38).

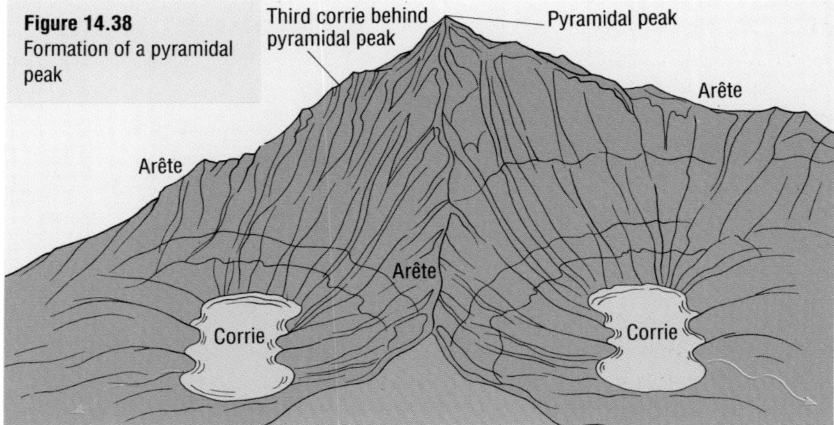

Figure 14.38
Formation of a pyramidal peak

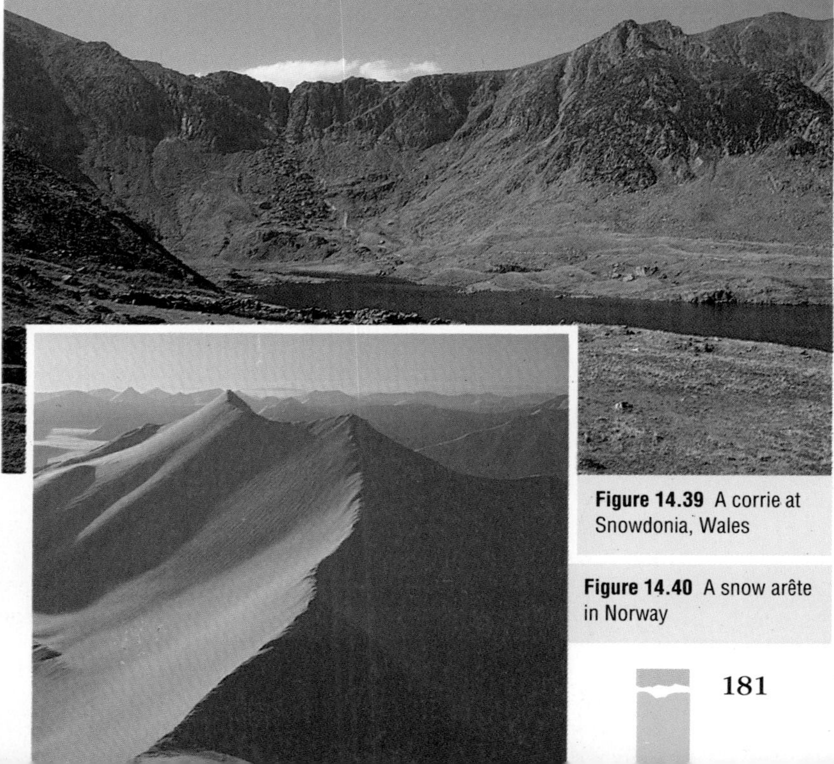

Figure 14.39 A corrie at Snowdonia, Wales

Figure 14.40 A snow arête in Norway

Glacial troughs, truncated spurs, hanging valleys and ribbon lakes

Glaciers, moving downhill from their source in the mountains, follow the easiest possible route which, in most cases, is an existing river valley. Unlike a river, however, the glacier often fills the whole valley and this gives it much greater erosive power. This means that, instead of having to wind around obstacles, such as interlocking spurs, the glacier is able, mainly through abrasion, to widen, deepen and straighten its valley (Figure 14.41). The result is that the characteristic 'V' shape of a river valley in a highland area is converted into the equally characteristic 'U' shape of a *glacial trough* (Figure 14.42). As the glacier moves downvalley it removes the ends of interlocking spurs to leave steep, cliff-like, *truncated spurs*.

Between adjacent truncated spurs are *hanging valleys*. Before the ice age, tributary rivers would have their confluence with the main river at the same height (Figure 14.41). During the ice age, the glacier in the main valley would be much larger than glaciers in the tributary valleys, and so it could erode downwards much more rapidly. When the ice melted, the tributary valleys were left 'hanging' above the main valley. Each tributary river has now to descend to the main river by a waterfall (Figure 14.43). Many glacial troughs in highland Britain contain long, narrow, ribbon lakes. *Ribbon lakes* are partly the result of erosion when a glacier over-deepens part of its valley, perhaps in an area of softer rock or due to increased erosion after being joined by a tributary glacier. They may also be partly created by deposition of moraine across the main valley (Figure 14.42).

Figure 14.41 Formation of a glacial trough

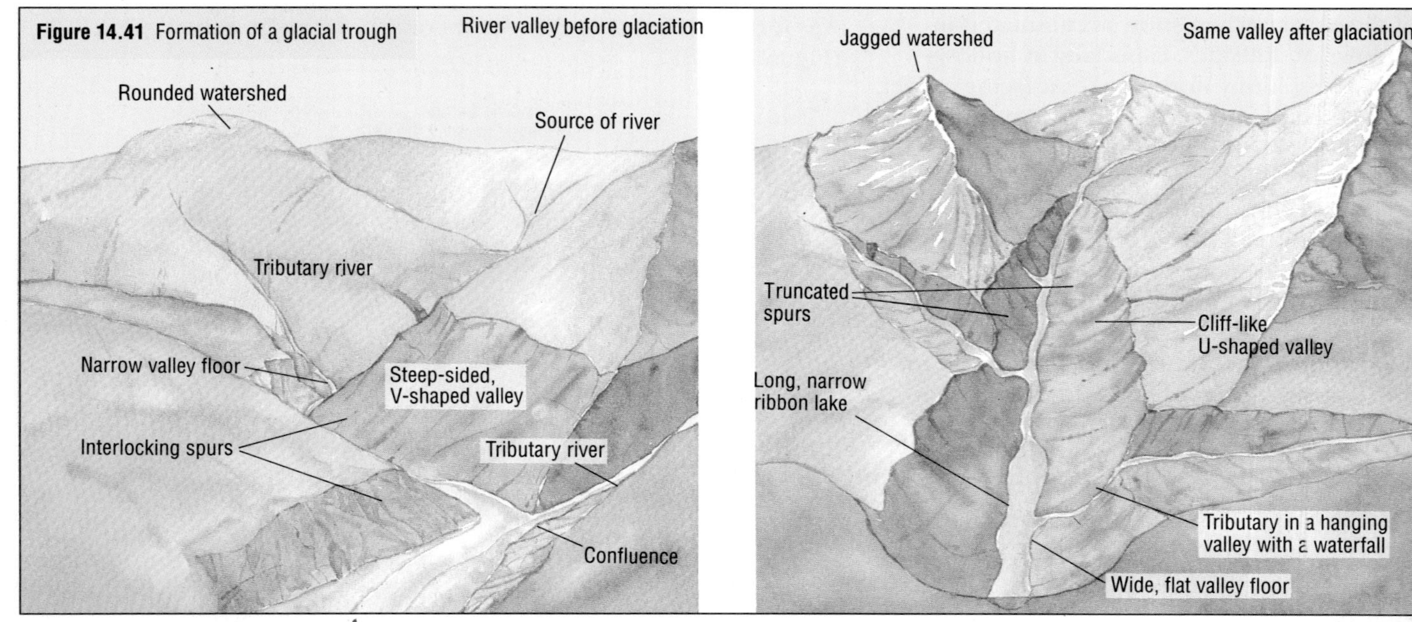

Figure 14.42
A glacial trough with ribbon lake in Austria

Figure 14.43
Hanging valley with waterfall in California

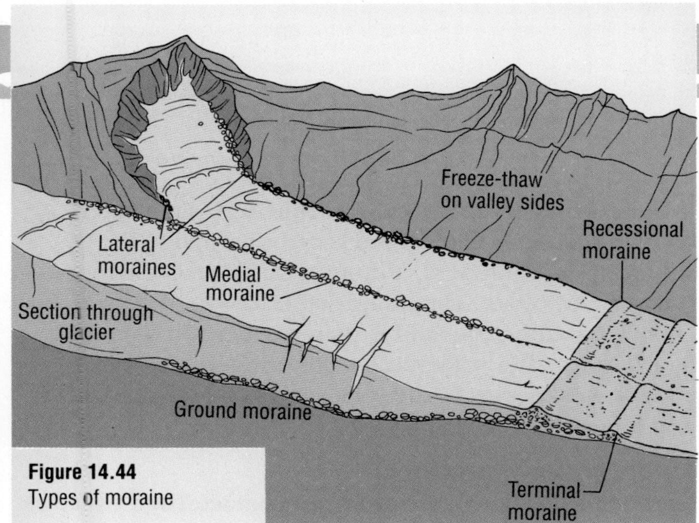

Figure 14.44
Types of moraine

Figure 14.45
Terminal moraine in Norway

Transportation and deposition

Moraine is material, mainly angular rock, which is transported and later deposited by a glacier. It is deposited when there is a rise in temperature. As the glacier begins to melt, it cannot carry as much material. There are several types of moraine (Figure 14.44):

- *Lateral moraine* is material derived from freeze-thaw weathering of valley sides and which is carried at the sides of a glacier.
- *Medial moraine* is found in the centre of a glacier and results from two lateral moraines joining together.
- *Ground moraine* is material dragged underneath a glacier which, when deposited, forms the flat valley floor. Ground moraine is also referred to as *till* or *boulder clay*.
- *Terminal moraine* marks the maximum advance of a glacier. It is material deposited at the snout, or end, of a glacier (Figure 14.45). If a glacier remains stationary for a lengthy period then a sizeable mound of material, extending across the valley, can build up.
- *Recessional moraines* form behind, and parallel to, the terminal moraine. They mark interruptions in the retreat of a glacier when it remained stationary for long enough for further ridges to develop across the valley. Both terminal and recessional moraines can act as natural dams behind which ribbon lakes can form.

Figure 14.46 An erratic in County Clare, Ireland

Glaciers can transport material many kilometres. *Erratics* are rocks and boulders carried by the ice and deposited in an area of totally different rock (Figure 14.46). Material from Norway can be found on parts of England's east coast, and Lake District rock on Anglesey.

Drumlins are smooth, elongated mounds of material formed parallel to the direction of ice movement. They often consist of stones and clay, and are believed to result from the load, carried by a glacier, becoming too heavy and being deposited. They owe their streamlined shape to later ice movement (Figure 14.47)

Figure 14.47
Drumlins in Cumbria

Limestone

Limestone consists mainly of calcium carbonate. There are several types of limestone including Chalk, and Jurassic and Carboniferous limestone. Carboniferous limestone contains many fossils, including coral, indicating that it was formed on the bed of warm, clear seas.

Since its emergence from the sea, Carboniferous limestone has developed its own distinctive type of scenery, known as *karst*. The development of karst landforms is greatly influenced by three factors: the rock's structure, its permeability and its vulnerability to chemical weathering.

Structure Carboniferous limestone is a hard, grey sedimentary rock which was laid down in layers on the sea-bed. The horizontal junctions between the layers are called *bedding planes*. *Joints* are lines of weakness at right angles to the bedding planes (Figure 14.48).

Permeability *Permeability* is the rate at which water can either be stored in a rock or is able to pass through it. Chalk, which consists of many pore spaces, can store water and is an example of a *porous rock*. Carboniferous limestone, which lacks pore spaces, allows water to flow along the bedding planes and down the joints, and is an example of a *pervious rock*.

Vulnerability to chemical weathering Rainwater contains carbonic acid which is carbon dioxide in solution. Carbonic acid, although weak, reacts with calcium carbonate. The limestone is slowly dissolved, by chemical weathering, and is then removed in solution by running water. Chemical weathering, therefore, widens weaknesses in the rock such as bedding planes and joints.

Underground landforms

Carboniferous limestone areas are characterised by a lack of surface drainage. A river which has its source and headwaters on nearby impermeable rock will flow over the surface until its reaches an area of limestone (Figure 14.48). Various acids in the water, including carbonic acid derived from rainfall, begin to dissolve and widen surface joints to form *swallow holes*, or *sinks* (Figure 14.49). The river will, in time, disappear down one of these swallow holes. Once underground, the river will continue to widen joints and bedding planes through solution. Where solution is more active, underground caverns may form. The river will abandon these caverns as it tries to find a lower level. Should the river meet an underlying impermeable rock, it will have to flow over this rock until it reaches the surface at a *spring*, or *resurgence* (Figure 14.50).

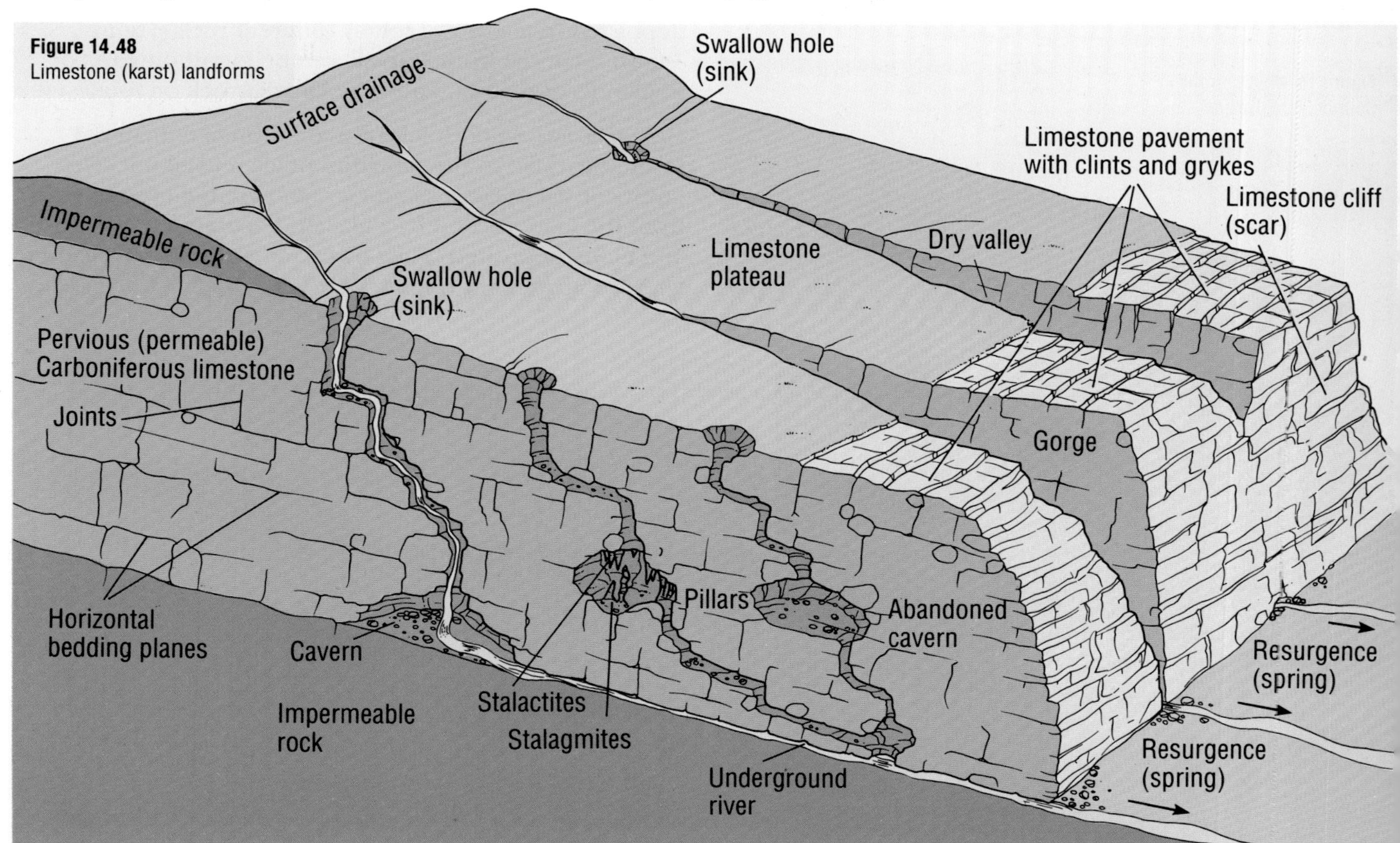

Figure 14.48
Limestone (karst) landforms

Surface landforms

Dry valleys are evidence that rivers once flowed on top of limestone (Figure 14.51). This might have occurred during the ice age when the ground was frozen and acted as an impermeable rock. The dry valleys are usually very steep-sided. Limestone areas often have a flat, plateau-like appearance. The flatness is due to the underlying horizontal bedding planes. Where there is no soil, the top bedding plane will be exposed as a limestone pavement (Figure 14.52). Many joints reach the surface along this pavement. They are widened and deepened by solution to form grooves known as *grykes*. The flat-topped blocks between grykes are called *clints*. Other surface landforms, often more developed in areas outside of Britain, result from limestone having collapsed. Where limestone collapses over an underground river it creates a gorge. If it collapses over a small cave then it forms a small depression called a *doline*; if over a series of caves, it produces a much larger depression known as a *polje*.

Deposition landforms

Water, containing calcium carbonate in solution, continually drips from the ceilings of underground caves. Although it is cold in these caves, some evaporation does take place allowing the formation of icicle-shaped *stalactites* (Figure 14.50). In caves in northern England stalactites only grow about 7.5 mm a year. As water drips onto the floor beneath the stalactite, further deposits of calcium carbonate produce the more rounded *stalagmites*. *Pillars* are the result of stalactites and stalagmites joining together.

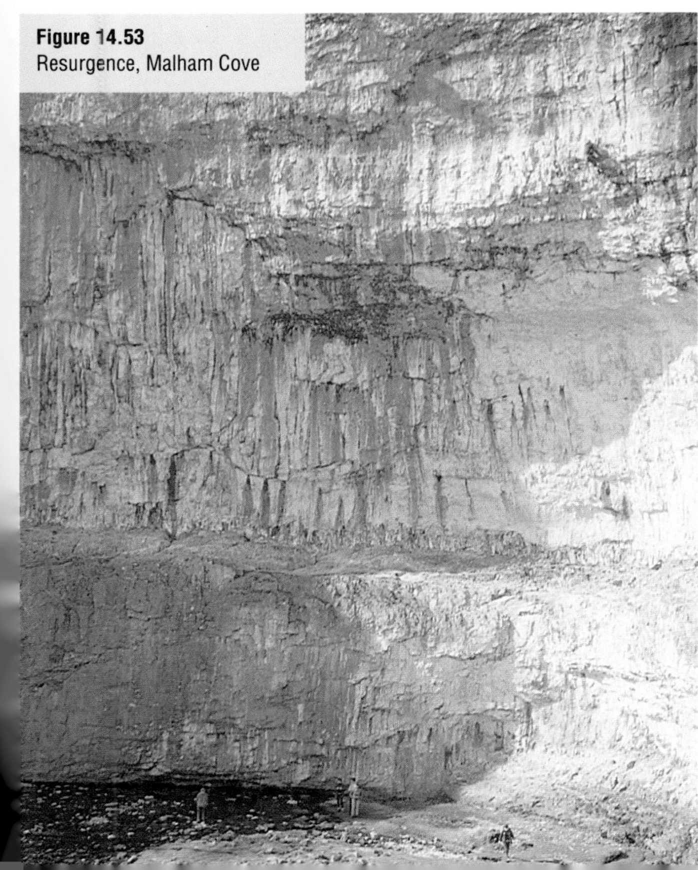

Figure 14.53
Resurgence, Malham Cove

Figure 14.49
Swallow hole, Malham

Figure 14.50
Stalactites and stalagmites

Figure 14.51
Watlowes dry valley, Malham

Figure 14.52
Limestone pavement, Malham

QUESTIONS

1 (Page 168)

a Name the features labelled **a** to **e** on drainage basin B. *(5)*
b Does basin A or B have the higher drainage density? *(1)*
c Will basin A or basin B have the higher flood risk? *(1)*
d Give a reason for your answer to **c**. *(1)*

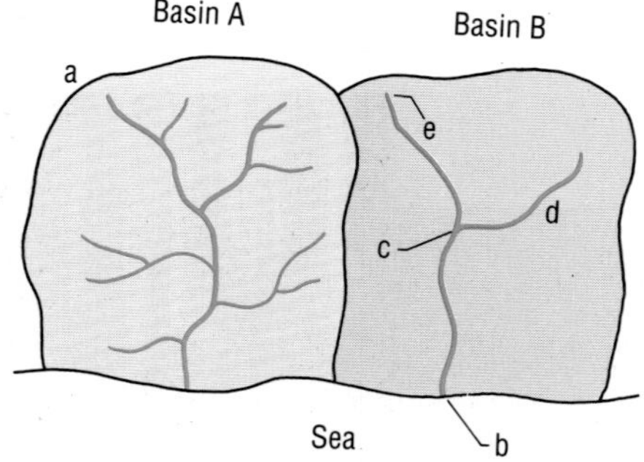

3 (Page 170)

a What is a flood hydrograph? *(1)*
b What is meant by peak rainfall, peak discharge, and lag time? *(3)*
c On the hydrograph below:
i) What time was peak rainfall?
ii) How many hours was lag time? *(2)*
d i) Why was there a slight rise in discharge at point X?
ii) What was the cause of the steep rising limb at Y?
iii) Why was the falling limb at Z less steep than the rising limb? *(3)*

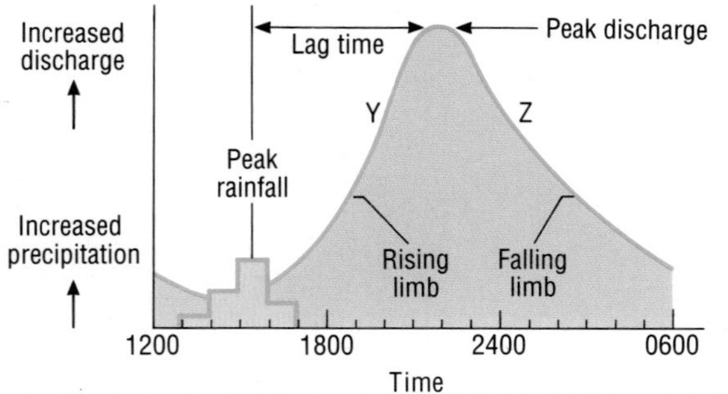

4 (Pages 170 and 171)

The diagram shows two hydrographs. Which graph, A or B, is more likely to correspond to each of the pairs in the following situations:
i) A long period of gentle rain and a short, heavy thunderstorm?
ii) A basin with steep valley sides and a basin with gently sloping sides?
iii) An area of impermeable rock and an area of permeable rock?
iv) An area of forest and an area of moorland and little vegetation?
v) A mainly urbanised basin and a mainly rural basin?
vi) A river with a dam built across it and a river with no dam? *(6)*

2 (Page 169)

a The diagram below shows a partly completed drainage basin system. Complete it by matching the following terms with the appropriate numbered boxes:
evaporation; groundwater; infiltration; interception; surface run-off; throughflow; transpiration. *(7)*
b Draw a table with four columns. Head these columns Inputs; Stores; Flows; and Outputs.
Fill in the table by adding the 14 labels from the drainage basin system which you completed in part **a**. *(14)*
c What is the difference between:
i) Evaporation and transpiration?
ii) Infiltration and interception?
iii) Surface run-off and throughflow? *(6)*

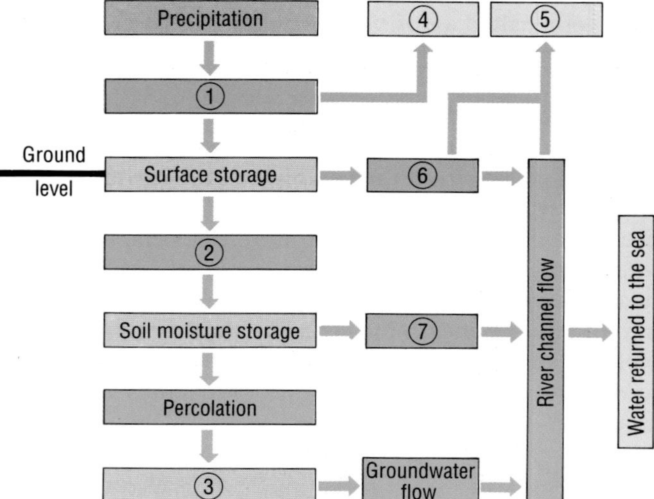

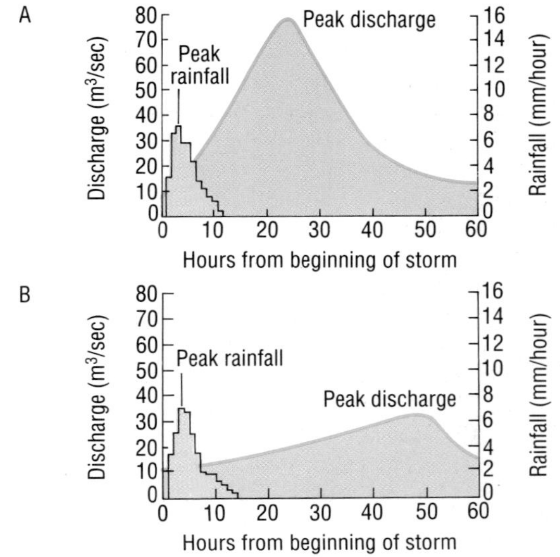

5 *(Pages 170 and 171)*

The hydrograph opposite is for the River Camel in Cornwall. It covered one of the wettest days ever recorded in the area.

a i) Why do you think discharge hardly increased after the rain of 8 June? *(1)*

ii) 11 June was an exceptionally wet day. How did this affect the hydrograph? *(1)*

iii) 16 June was not as wet as 8 June yet the hydrograph shows it to have caused a larger discharge. How do you account for this? *(1)*

b What does the hydrograph suggest about the rock types, steepness of slope and land use of the basin of the River Camel? *(3)*

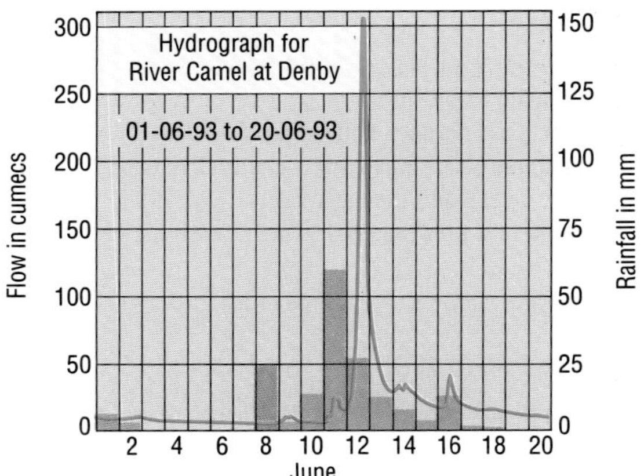

6 *(Pages 172 and 173)*

a Describe four processes by which a river can transport material. *(4)*

b Describe four processes by which a river can erode its banks and bed. *(4)*

c What is the difference between vertical and lateral erosion? *(2)*

7 *(Pages 172 to 175)*

a Fifteen river features have been labelled 'a' to 'o' on the sketch opposite. Match up the correct letter with the features named in the following list:

delta; flood plain; gorge; interlocking spurs; levees; meander; mouth; ox-bow; plunge pool; rapids; river cliff; slip-off slope; source; 'V' shaped valley; waterfall. *(15)*

b The sketch has also divided the river valley into two sections labelled **A** and **B**. For each pair of terms below, say which is more likely to occur in Zone A and which in Zone B. In each case give a reason for your answer:

i) vertical erosion and lateral erosion

ii) attrition and corrasion

iii) traction and suspension *(9)*

c With the help of labelled sketches, describe the formation of each of the following river landforms:

i) 'V' shaped valley

ii) waterfall

iii) ox-bow lake

iv) delta *(12)*

d i) Draw a large labelled diagram of a meander. On it mark areas of erosion, areas of deposition, and the position of the fastest current. *(5)*

ii) Draw a cross section of a meander. Label the river cliff and slip-off slope. Explain carefully why erosion occurs on the outside bend and deposition on the inside. Your answer should include the terms: energy, friction, velocity, and volume *(7)*

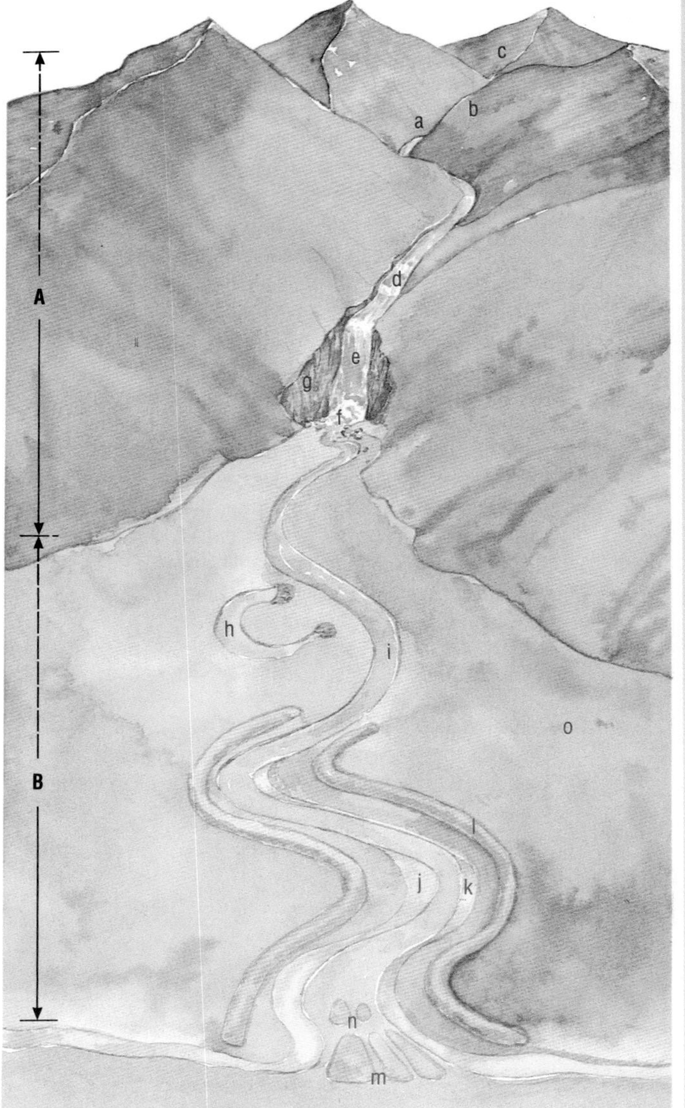

8 *(Page 176)*

a i) How do large waves form? *(1)*
ii) Why do waves break? *(1)*

b What is the difference between:
i) A constructive wave and a destructive wave?
ii) The swash and the backwash? *(4)*

c Describe four processes by which waves can erode the land. *(4)*

9 *(Pages 177 to 179)*

With the help of labelled diagrams

a Explain the process of longshore drift. *(4)*

b Describe the formation of:
i) headlands and bays
ii) a wave-cut platform
iii) a stack
iv) a spit *(16)*

10 *(Pages 176 to 179)*

The map opposite shows part of the Yorkshire coast. The landforms found here are the result of erosion, deposition and differences in rock structure (strength).

a Why have cliffs formed at Scarborough, Filey Brigg and Flamborough Head? *(1)*

b Why have bays formed at Filey and Bridlington? *(1)*

c Why can caves, arches, stacks and wave-cut platforms be found at Flamborough Head? *(2)*

d i) What has happened to the coastline at Holderness since Roman times?
ii) Why has this change taken place? *(2)*

e Why have groynes been built along the Holderness coast? *(1)*

f Spurn Head is a spit.
i) What material is likely to be found at Spurn Head?
ii) From which direction must this material have come?
iii) Why was this material deposited here?
iv) Why has Spurn Head a curved (hooked) end?
v) Why is it unlikely that Spurn Head will grow across the Humber Estuary? *(5)*

g Make a large copy of the map. On it label the following coastal features:
three headlands; three bays; three areas with resistant cliffs; caves, arches and stacks; one area with easily eroded cliffs; groynes; longshore drift (with an arrow to show its direction); spit; sand-dunes. *(15)*

h Re-draw the map to show the possible shape of this stretch of coastline in several thousand years time. *(3)*

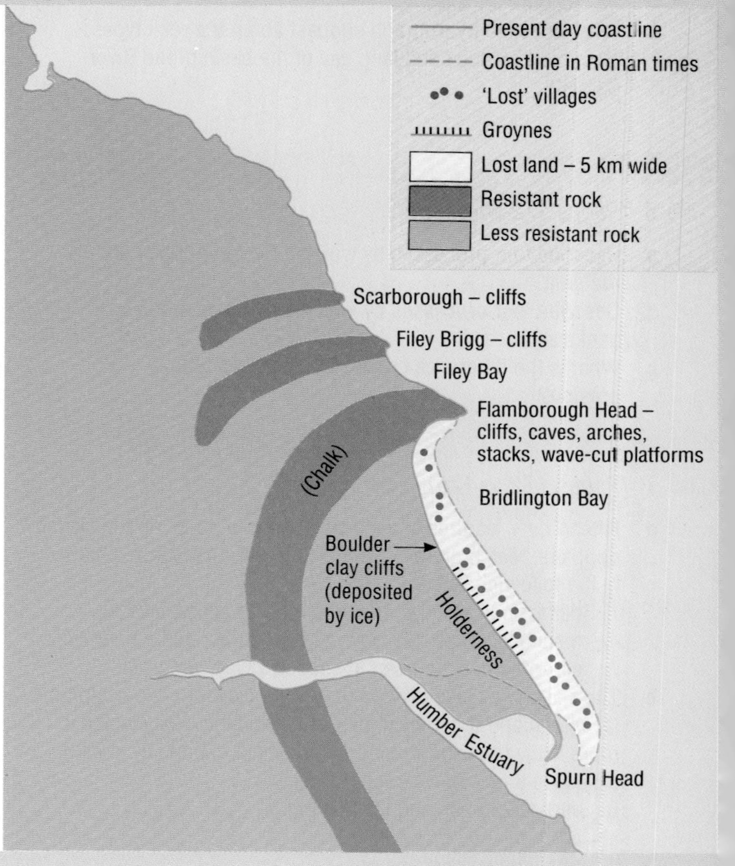

11 *(Page 180)*

a Complete the diagram below to show a glacier system. *(8)*

b i) Describe the process of freeze-thaw weathering. *(2)*
ii) Describe two processes by which a glacier can erode the land. *(4)*

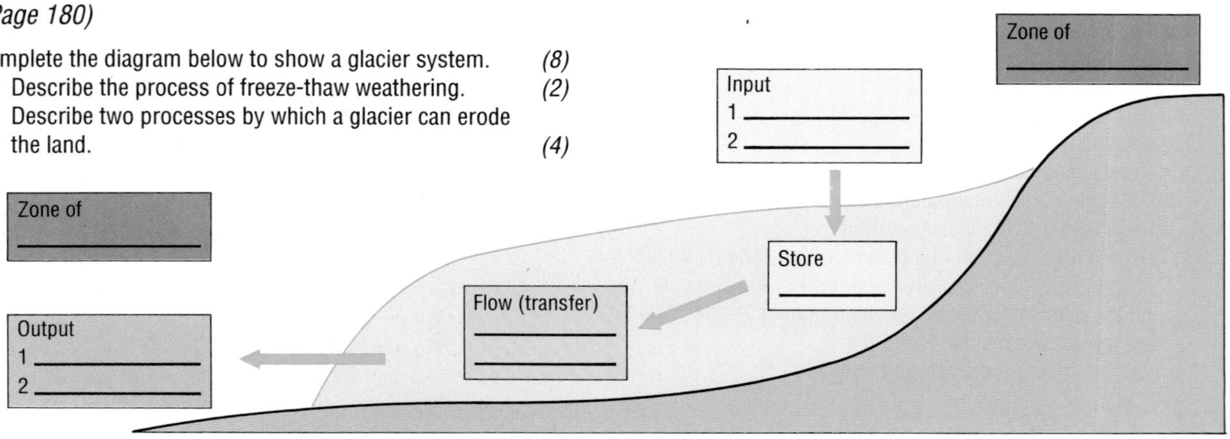

12 *(Pages 180 and 181)*

Rearrange the following eleven statements to give a description of the formation of a corrie (cirque or cwm): *(11)*

ice melts to leave a corrie lake;
snow collects in north facing hollows;
freeze-thaw still continues producing scree;
moraine left at the end of the glacier;
decrease in erosion leaves a rock lip;
freeze-thaw weathering loosens rock;
glacier moves downhill under gravity;
snow is compressed until it becomes ice;
corrie floor is overdeepened by abrasion;
ice with all air (oxygen) squeezed out turns blue;
plucking removes rocks from the backwall.

13 *(Pages 181 to 183)*

The fieldsketch shows ten glacial landforms found in the Snowdon area of North Wales. These ten features, numbered **a** to **j** (but not in that order), include two corries, two arêtes, a pyramidal peak, a glacial trough, two hanging valleys, a truncated spur, and a ribbon lake.

Either

i) Make a copy of the sketch and add the names of the ten glacial landforms

or

ii) Make a list matching the landforms with their appropriate letter. *(10)*

14 *(Pages 181 to 183)*

With the help of well-labelled diagrams describe the formation of a:

i) pyramidal peak.
ii) hanging valley.
iii) glacial trough.
iv) terminal moraine. *(12)*

15 *(Page 183)*

a What is the difference between:

i) lateral moraine and medial moraine?
ii) terminal moraine and recessional moraine?
iii) erratics and drumlins? *(6)*

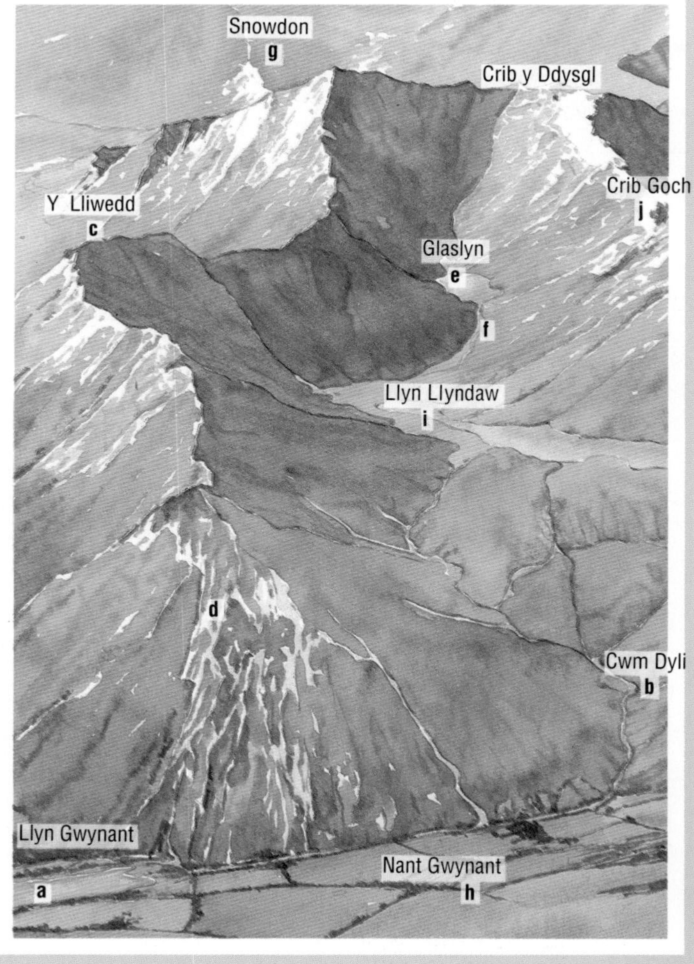

16 *(Page 184)*

a How does each of the following affect the development of the characteristic landforms found on Carboniferous limestone (karst)?

i) rock structure
ii) permeability
iii) vulnerability to chemical weathering *(9)*

b Re-arrange the following ten statements to give a description of landforms in a Carboniferous limestone area:

stalactites and stalagmites join to form pillars;
water seeks a lower level until it reaches an impermeable rock;
rivers have their source on impermeable rocks;
rivers re-appear on the surface at a resurgence;
water drips onto the floor of caves to form stalagmites;
some joints and bedding planes are widened to form caves;
once underground, rivers widen joints and bedding planes through solution;
rivers disappearing underground leave dry valleys on the surface;
water dripping from the ceiling of caves forms stalactites;
on reaching a limestone surface rivers disappear down swallow holes (sinks). *(10)*

c Describe, with the help of diagrams, how each of the following forms:

i) clints and grykes.
ii) dry valleys.
iii) pillars. *(9)*

15 WEATHER, CLIMATE AND VEGETATION

Weather

Weather is the hour to hour, day to day state of the atmosphere. It includes temperature, sunshine, precipitation and wind. It is short term and is often localised in area.

Climate is the average weather conditions for a place taken over a period of time, usually 30 years. It is the expected, rather than the actual, conditions for a place. It is long term and is often applied to sizeable parts of the globe (e.g. the equatorial or Mediterranean climate).

Britain's climate

Britain has:

- A variable climate, which means that the weather changes from day to day, and this makes it difficult to forecast.
- An equable climate, which means that extremes of heat or cold, or of drought or prolonged rainfall, are rarely experienced.

If we wish to generalise about Britain's climate, we can say that it has cool summers, mild winters, and a steady, reliable rainfall which is spread fairly evenly throughout the year. However, there are, even across an area as small on a global scale as the British Isles, significant differences:

- Seasonally, between summer and winter.
- Between places in the extreme north and south, and places on the east and west coasts (Figure 15.1).

Why is it:

- That places in the south are warmer and sunnier than places to the north in summer (page 191)?
- That places in the west are milder and cloudier than places to the east in winter (page 191)?
- That places in the west are wetter, with a winter maximum of rainfall, than places in the east which are drier, and have a summer maximum of rainfall (pages 192 and 193)?

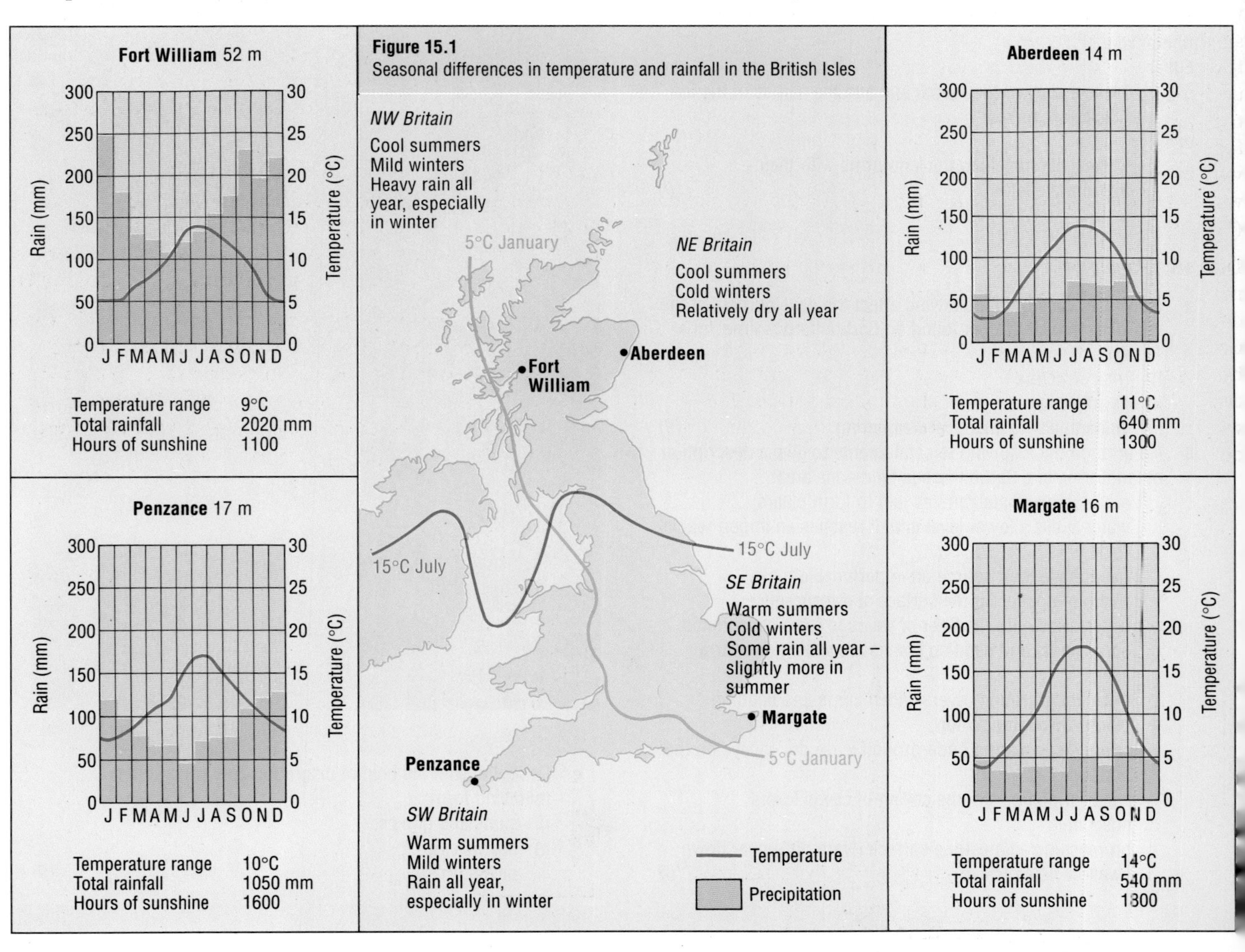

Figure 15.1
Seasonal differences in temperature and rainfall in the British Isles

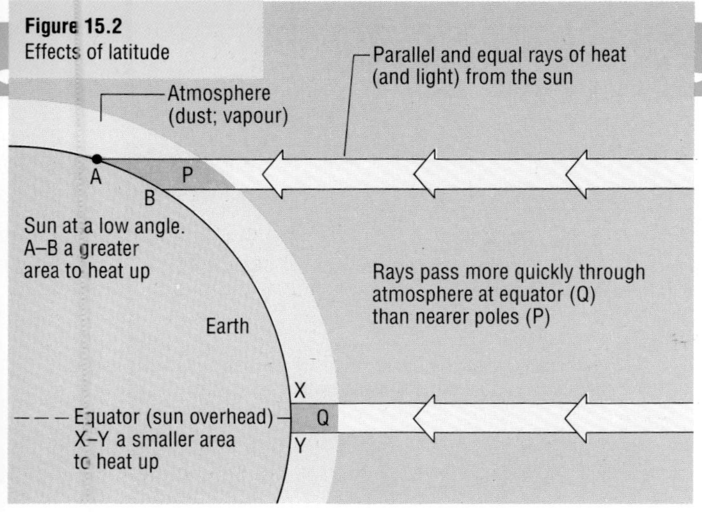

Figure 15.2
Effects of latitude

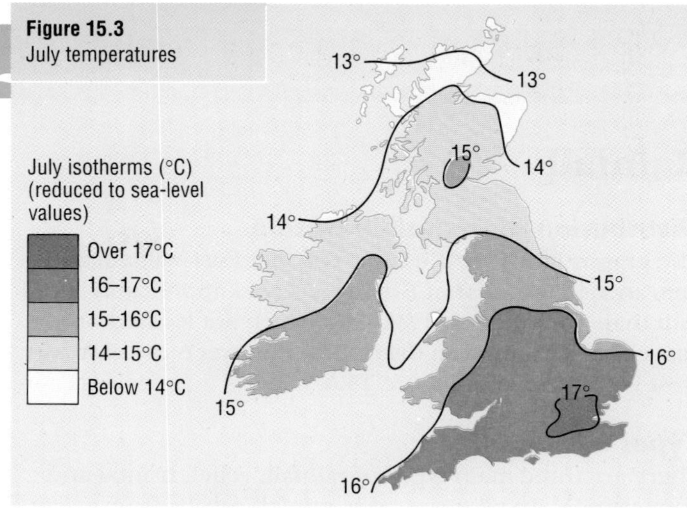

Figure 15.3
July temperatures

Factors affecting temperature

Latitude Places nearer to the Equator are much warmer than places nearer to the poles. This is due to the curvature of the earth and the angle of the sun (Figure 15.2). At the Equator the sun is always high in the sky. When it is overhead it shines directly downwards, concentrating its heat into a small area which will become very hot. In contrast, the sun is always low in the sky towards the poles. This means that its heat is spread over a wide area, and so temperatures remain lower. Notice also that the lower the angle of the sun, the greater the amount of atmosphere through which the rays have to pass. This means that more heat will be lost to gases, dust and cloud in the atmosphere. This is why places in the south of Britain can expect to be warmer, especially in summer, than places further north (Figure 15.3).

Distance from the sea The sea (a liquid) is less dense than the land (a solid) and can be heated to a greater depth. This means that the sea takes much longer to heat up in summer than does the land. Once warmed, however, the sea retains its heat for much longer, and cools down more slowly than the land in winter. This is why places which are inland are warmer in summer but colder in winter than places on the coast. As Britain is surrounded by the sea, it tends to get cool summers and mild winters. The largest reservoir of heat in winter is the Atlantic Ocean, even though it is still cold enough to die from hypothermia within a few minutes should you fall into it. This explains why western parts of Britain are warmer than places to the east in winter (Figure 15.4).

Prevailing winds Prevailing winds will bring warm weather if they pass over warm surfaces (the land in summer, the sea in winter) and cold weather if they blow across cold surfaces (the land in winter, the sea in summer). As Britain's prevailing winds are from the south-west, they will be cool in summer but warm (mild) in winter.

Ocean currents Many coastal areas are affected by ocean currents (page 204). The North Atlantic Drift is a warm current of water which originates in the Gulf of Mexico. It keeps the west coast of Britain much warmer in winter than other places in similar latitudes (Figure 15.43).

Altitude Temperatures decrease, on average, by 1°C for every 100 metres in height. As many parts of the Scottish Highlands are over 1000 metres, they will be at least 10°C cooler than coastal places. In fact, the windchill factor will make them even colder, and enables snow to lie for long periods during winter (Figure 15.5).

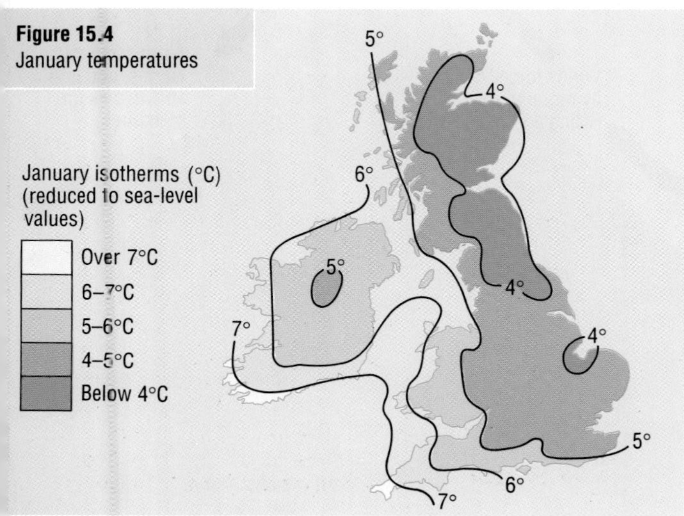

Figure 15.4
January temperatures

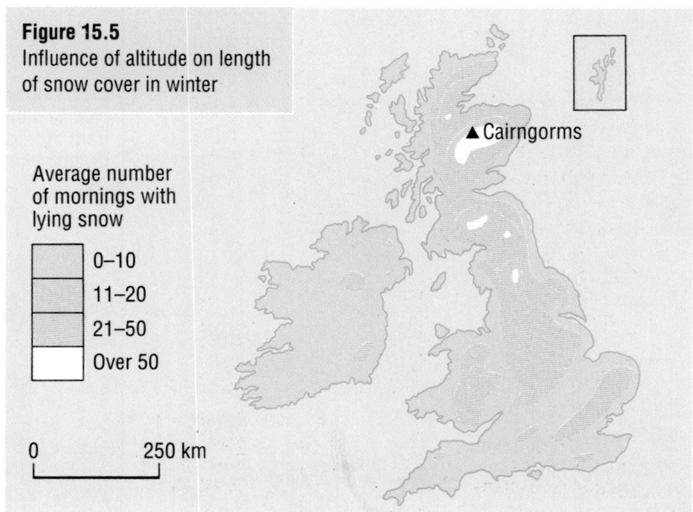

Figure 15.5
Influence of altitude on length of snow cover in winter

Rainfall

Distribution of rainfall in Britain

The graphs in Figure 15.1 showed that Fort William and Penzance in the west of Britain received appreciably more rain than Aberdeen and Margate which are located on the east coast. This uneven distribution between the east and west is confirmed in Figure 15.6.

Types of rainfall

There are three main types of rainfall: relief, frontal and convectional. In all three cases rainfall results from warm air, which contains water vapour, being forced to rise until it cools sufficiently for condensation to take place (Figure 15.7). Condensation can only occur when two conditions are met:

i) Cold air cannot hold as much moisture as warm air. As the warm air and water vapour rises, it will cool until a critical temperature is reached at which point the air becomes saturated. This critical temperature is called *dew point*. If air continues to rise and cool, some of the water vapour in it will condense back into minute droplets of water.

ii) Condensation requires the presence of large numbers of microscopic particles known as *hygroscopic nuclei*. This is because condensation can only take place on solid surfaces such as volcanic dust, salt or smoke (or on windows and walls in a bathroom or kitchen).

The difference between the three types of rainfall is the condition which forces the warm air to rise in the first place.

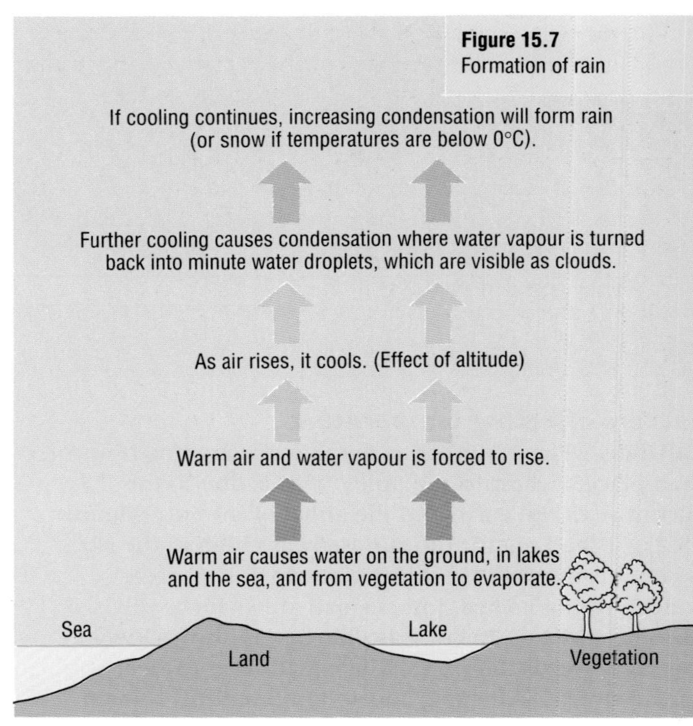

If cooling continues, increasing condensation will form rain (or snow if temperatures are below 0°C).
Further cooling causes condensation where water vapour is turned back into minute water droplets, which are visible as clouds.
As air rises, it cools. (Effect of altitude)
Warm air and water vapour is forced to rise.
Warm air causes water on the ground, in lakes and the sea, and from vegetation to evaporate.
Sea
Land
Lake
Vegetation

Figure 15.7
Formation of rain

1 Relief rainfall (Figure 15.8)

Relief rain occurs when warm, almost saturated air from the sea is blown inland by the wind. Where there is a coastal mountain barrier, the air will be forced to rise over it. The rising air will cool and, if dew point is reached, condensation will take place. Once over the mountains the air will descend, warm and therefore, the rain is likely to stop.

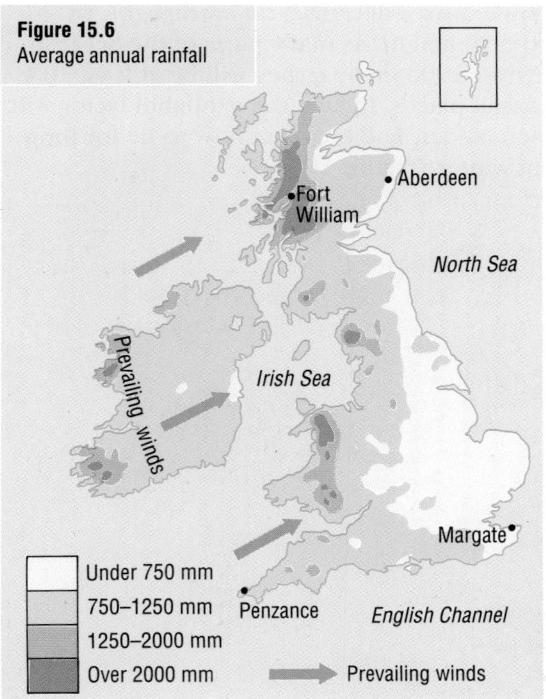

Figure 15.6
Average annual rainfall

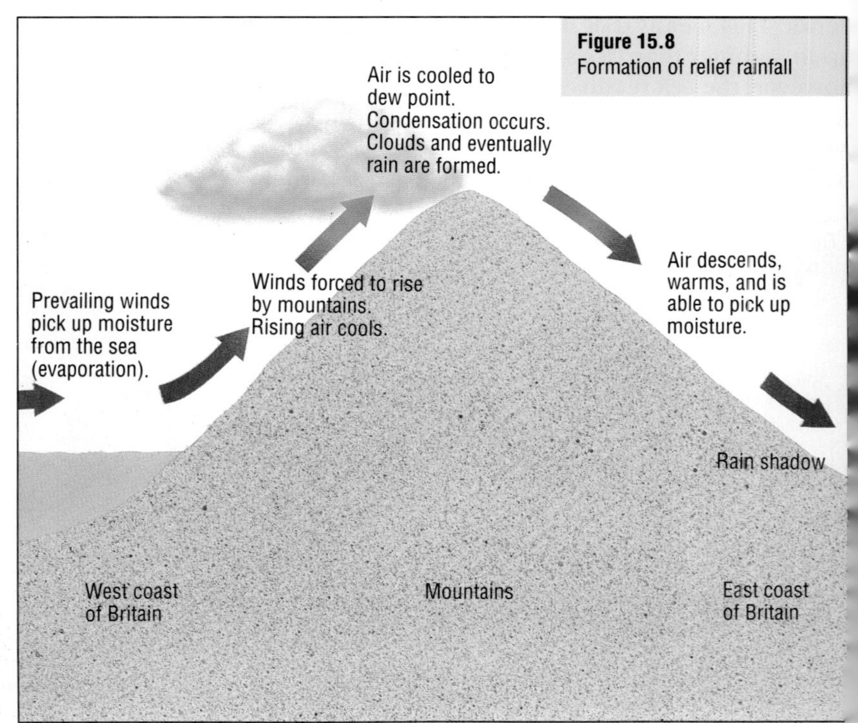

Figure 15.8
Formation of relief rainfall

The protected side of a mountain range is the *rain shadow*. In Britain the prevailing winds come from the south-west collecting moisture as they cross the Atlantic Ocean. They bring heavy rainfall to western parts as they cross the mountains of Scotland, Wales and northern England. Eastern areas receive much less rain as they are in the rain shadow area. Places like Fort William and Penzance get heavy rainfall in late autumn when the sea is at its warmest, and winds blowing over it can pick up most moisture.

2 **Frontal rainfall (Figure 15.9)**
Frontal rain is associated with depressions (page 194) and results from warm, moist air from the tropics meeting colder, drier air from polar areas. As the two air masses have different densities, they cannot merge. Instead the warmer, moister and lighter air is forced to rise over the colder, denser air, setting the condensation process into motion. The boundary between the warm and cold air is called a *front*. Most depressions have two fronts, a warm and a cold front, giving two periods of rainfall (Figure 15.11). Britain receives many depressions and their associated fronts each year. Depressions usually come from the Atlantic Ocean, increasing rainfall on the west coasts. Depressions are more common in winter, as illustrated by the winter rainfall maximum.

3 **Convectional rainfall (Figure 15.10)**
Convectional rain occurs where the ground surface is heated by the sun. As the air adjacent to the ground is heated, it expands and begins to rise. If the ground surface is wet and heavily vegetated, as in equatorial areas (page 196), there will be rapid evaporation. As the air rises, it cools and water vapour condenses to form towering cumulonimbus clouds and, later, heavy thunderstorms. Equatorial areas, where the sun is constantly at a high angle in the sky, experience convectional storms most afternoons. Convectional rain is less frequent in cooler Britain, and is most likely in South-east England in summer when temperatures are at their highest (Figure 15.1). This also accounts for the summer rainfall maximum in this region.

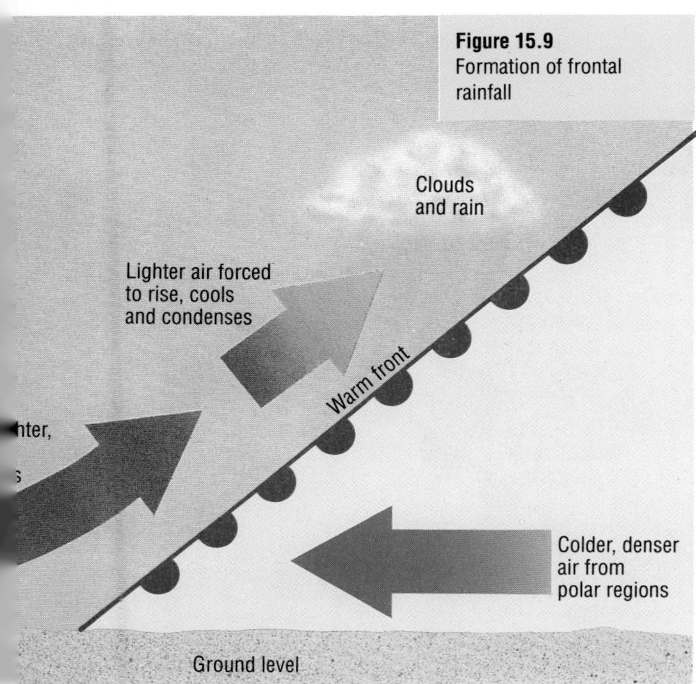
Clouds and rain
Lighter air forced to rise, cools and condenses
Warm front
Colder, denser air from polar regions
Ground level

Figure 15.9
Formation of frontal rainfall

Figure 15.10
Formation of convectional rainfall

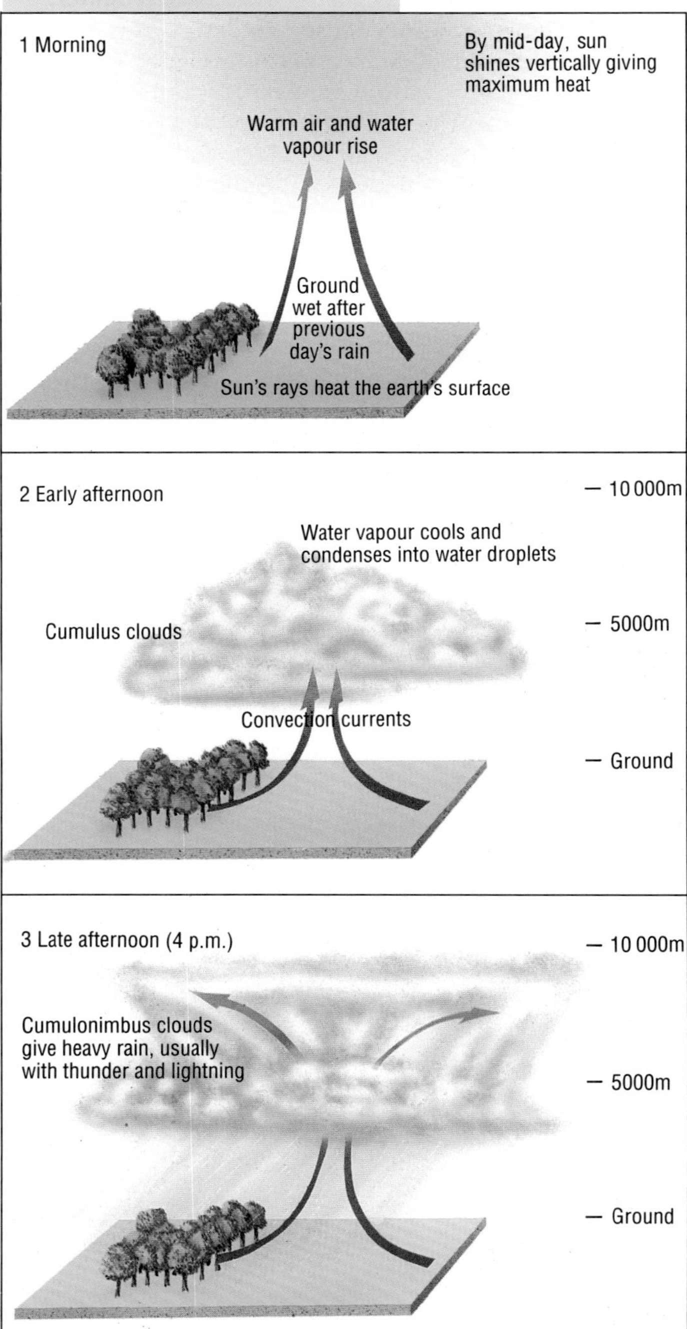
1 Morning
By mid-day, sun shines vertically giving maximum heat
Warm air and water vapour rise
Ground wet after previous day's rain
Sun's rays heat the earth's surface
2 Early afternoon
— 10 000m
Water vapour cools and condenses into water droplets
Cumulus clouds
— 5000m
Convection currents
— Ground
3 Late afternoon (4 p.m.)
— 10 000m
Cumulonimbus clouds give heavy rain, usually with thunder and lightning
— 5000m
— Ground

Depressions and anticyclones

Depressions

Britain's weather changes from day to day. For much of the year our climate is dominated by the passing of depressions. *Depressions* are areas of low pressure which bring rain, cloud and wind. They form over the Atlantic Ocean when a mass of warm, moist tropical air from the south meets a mass of colder, drier, heavier polar air from the north. The two masses of air do not easily mix due to differences in temperature and density. The boundary between two air masses is called a *front*. When lighter, warmer air moves towards denser, colder air, it is forced to rise over the cold air at a warm front (Figure 15.11). When denser, colder air moves towards warm air, it undercuts the warm air forcing it to rise at a cold front. In both cases the rising warm air is cooled and some of its water vapour content condenses, producing cloud and frontal rain (page 193). The cold front travels faster than the warm front, catching it up to form an *occluded front*. Although each depression is unique, the weather they bring to Britain as they travel eastwards tends to have an easily recognisable pattern.

As a warm front approaches clouds begin to form. They get lower, and thicken (Figure 15.11). Winds blow from the south-east, in an anticlockwise direction, and slowly increase in strength. As the air rises, atmospheric pressure drops. The passing of the warm front is usually characterised by a lengthy period of steady rainfall, low cloud and strong winds. As the warm front passes there is a sudden rise in temperature and the wind turns to a south-westerly direction. The warm sector of a depression is usually a time of low and sometimes broken cloud, decreasing winds, and drizzle or even dry weather. As a cold front passes the weather deteriorates rapidly. Winds often reach gale force and swing round to the north-west. Rainfall is very heavy, though of relatively short duration, and temperatures fall rapidly. After the cold front passes, the weather slowly improves as pressure increases. The heavy rain gives way to heavy showers and eventually to sunny intervals. Winds are cold and slowly moderate, but still come from the north-west. Most depressions take between one and three days to pass over the British Isles.

Depressions can be seen on satellite images as masses of swirling cloud (Figure 15.12). Satellite images are photos taken from space and sent back to earth. They are invaluable when trying to produce a weather forecast or predicting short-term changes in the weather. The state of the weather at any one given time is shown on a *synoptic chart* (a weather map). The two synoptic charts in Figure 15.13 match the satellite images in Figure 15.12. The daily weather map as shown on television or in a newspaper aims to give a clear, but very simplified, forecast. Synoptic maps produced by the Meteorological Office use official symbols to show conditions at specific weather stations (Figure 15.14). The weather stations on Figure 15.13 show five elements: temperature, wind speed, wind direction, amount of cloud cover and type of precipitation, while a sixth, atmospheric pressure, can be obtained by interpreting the isobars.

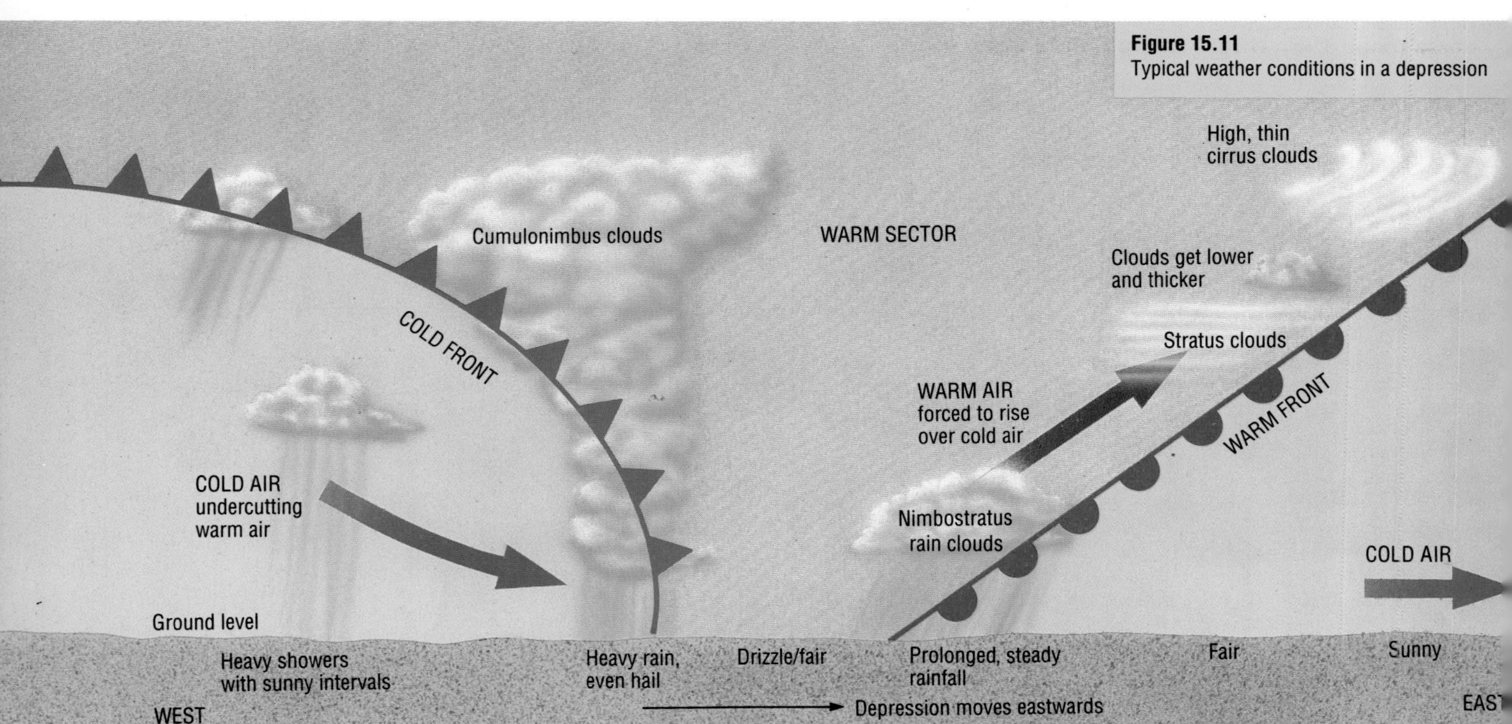

Figure 15.11
Typical weather conditions in a depression

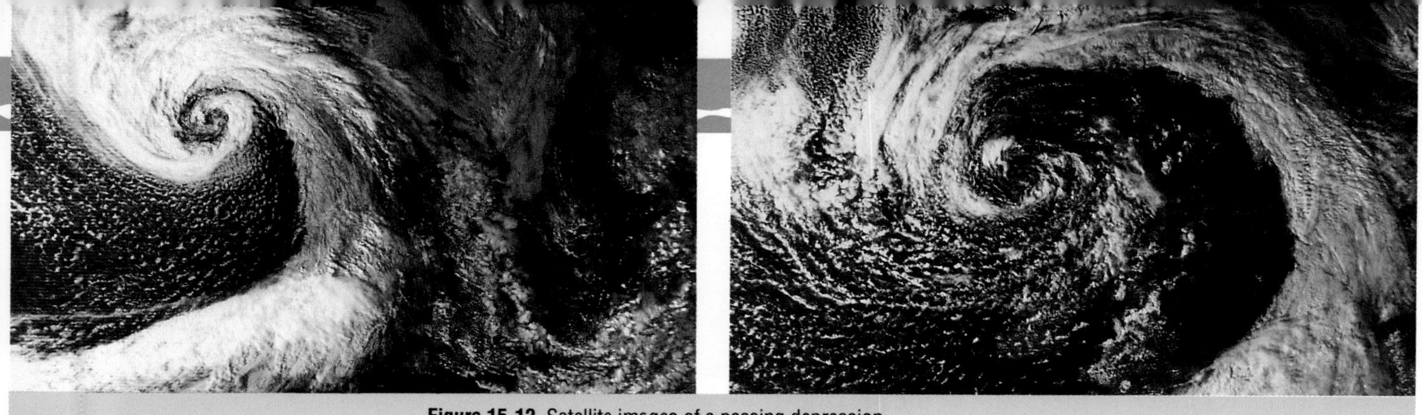

Figure 15.12 Satellite images of a passing depression

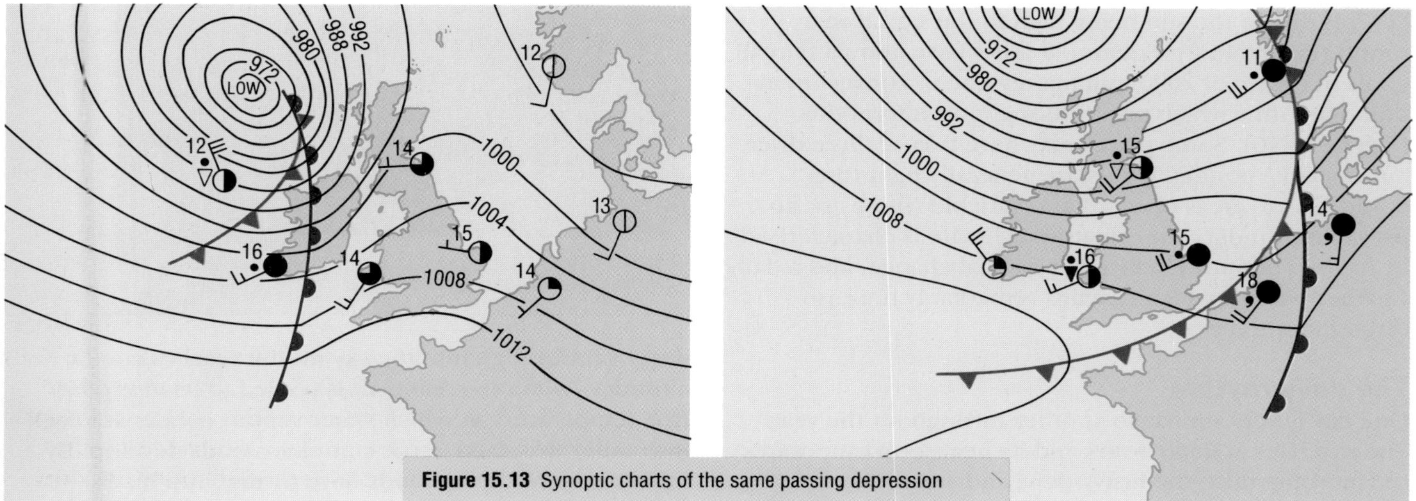

Figure 15.13 Synoptic charts of the same passing depression

Anticyclones

In Britain anticyclones are experienced far less frequently than depressions. Their main characteristics are the opposite to those of depressions (Figure 15.15). In an anticyclone, air descends and pressure increases. Winds are very light, at times non-existent, blowing in a clockwise direction. As the air descends it warms and picks up moisture. This results in clear skies which give very warm conditions in summer and very cold conditions in winter. Although it is unusual for it to rain in anticyclones, conditions are ideal for mist and dew to form in summer and fog and frost in winter. Once an anticyclone is established over the British Isles it can remain stationary for several days.

Figure 15.14 Weather map symbols

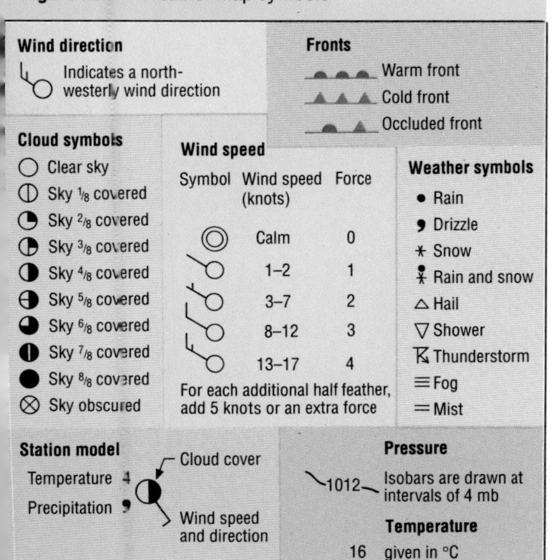

Wind direction
Indicates a north-westerly wind direction
Fronts
Warm front
Cold front
Occluded front
Cloud symbols
Clear sky
Sky 1/8 covered
Sky 2/8 covered
Sky 3/8 covered
Sky 4/8 covered
Sky 5/8 covered
Sky 6/8 covered
Sky 7/8 covered
Sky 8/8 covered
Sky obscured
Wind speed
Symbol Wind speed (knots) Force
Calm 0
1–2 1
3–7 2
8–12 3
13–17 4
For each additional half feather, add 5 knots or an extra force
Weather symbols
Rain
Drizzle
Snow
Rain and snow
Hail
Shower
Thunderstorm
Fog
Mist
Station model
Temperature 4
Precipitation
Cloud cover
Wind speed and direction
Pressure
1012
Isobars are drawn at intervals of 4 mb
Temperature
16 given in °C

Figure 15.15 Satellite image and synoptic chart of an anticyclone

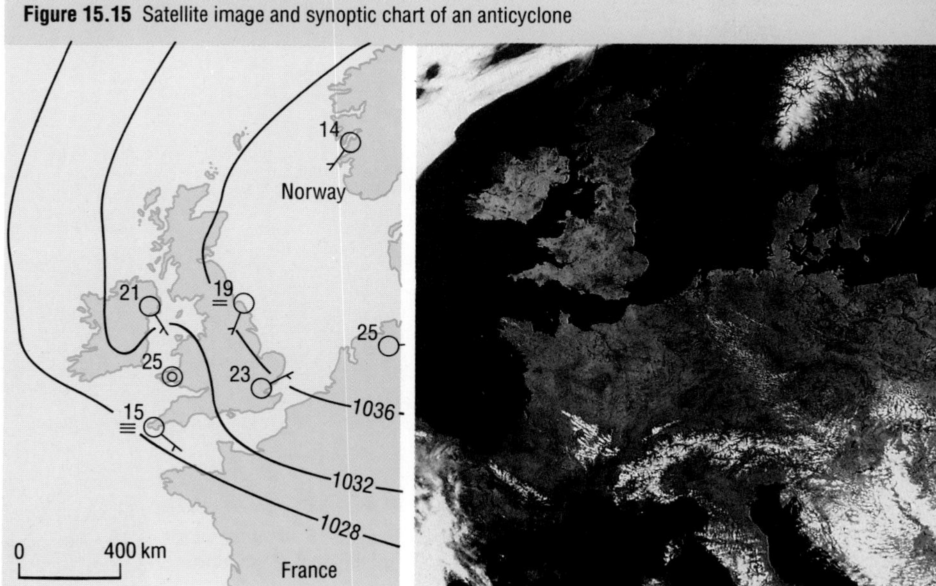

Equatorial climate and vegetation

Climate

Places with an equatorial climate lie within 5° either side of the Equator. The two main areas are the large drainage basins of the Amazon, in South America, and the Zaire in Africa (page 204). Figure 15.17 is a climate graph for Manaus which is located in the centre of the Amazon basin in Brazil. It shows temperatures to be high and constant throughout the year. The small annual range (2°C) is due to the sun being high in the sky all year round (Figure 15.2). Equatorial areas have annual rainfall totals in excess of 2000 mm mainly due to convectional thunderstorms which occur during most afternoons (Figure 15.10). Some places may have two or three drier, but not dry, months. Winds are generally light (the doldrums are areas of calm) and variable (there are no prevailing winds). The equatorial climate is characterised by its high humidity, a lack of seasonal change, and a daily weather pattern which remains remarkably uniform throughout the year.

emergents 40 m
main canopy 30 m
under canopy 20 m
shrub layer 10 m

Figure 15.16
Vegetation layers in the tropical rainforest

The daily rhythm

One day is very similar to another throughout the year. The sun rises at 0600 hours and its heat soon evaporates the morning mist, the heavy dew, and any moisture remaining from the previous afternoon's storm. Even by 0800 hours temperatures are as high as 25°C. As the sun rises to a near vertical position, temperatures reach 33°C. Water from swamps, the numerous rivers and the rainforest is evaporated (evapotranspiration). Strong upward convection currents (Figure 15.10) carry the water vapour high into the sky until it reaches cooler altitudes. When the rising air is cooled to its *dew point* (the temperature at which water vapour condenses back into water droplets), large cumulus clouds develop. By mid-afternoon these clouds have turned into black, towering cumulonimbus. These produce torrential downpours which are accompanied by thunder and lightning. The storms soon cease leaving the air calm and humid. By sunset, always about 1800 hours, the clouds have already broken up. Such conditions are similar throughout the year, seemingly one long tropical day.

Figure 15.17
Climate graph for Manaus

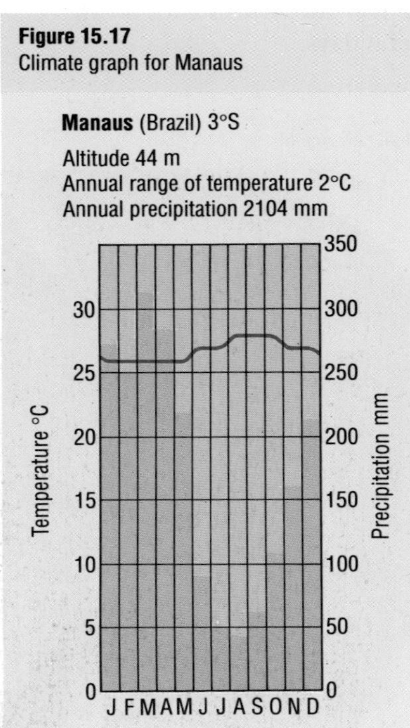

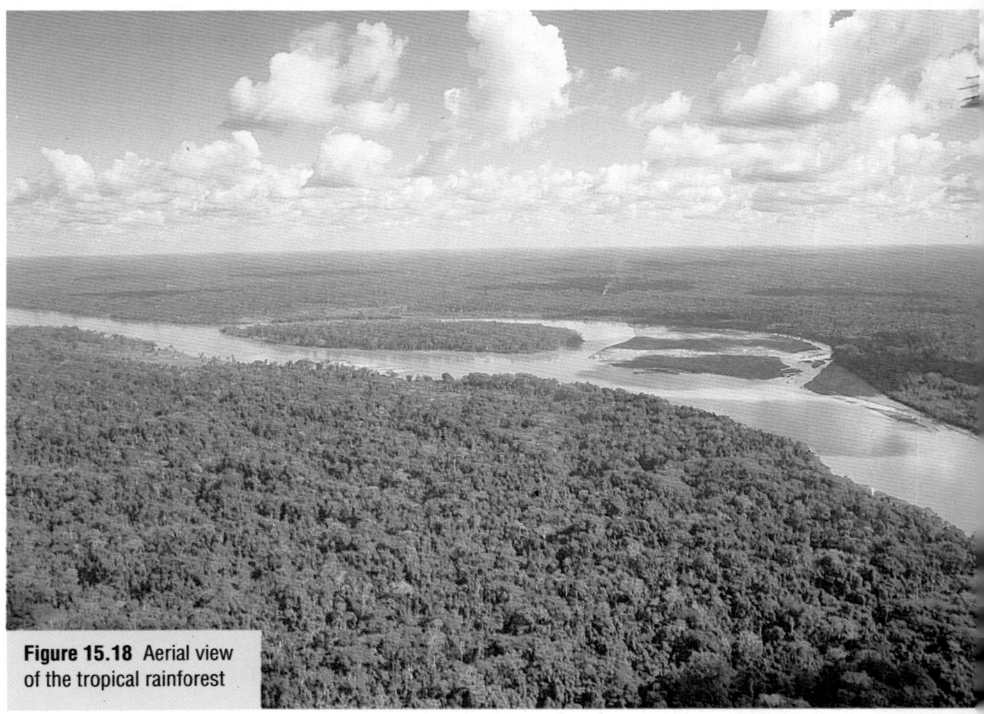

Figure 15.18 Aerial view of the tropical rainforest

Vegetation

- Tropical rainforests grow in places which have an equatorial climate. The rainforest is the most luxuriant vegetation system in the world although its trees have had to adapt to the constant high temperatures, the heavy rainfall and the continuous growing season. Over one-third of the world's trees grow here.
- Although the trees are deciduous, the rainforest has an evergreen appearance as the continuous growing season allows trees to shed their leaves at any time (Figure 15.18).
- Vegetation grows in distinct layers (Figure 15.16). The lowest layer consists of shrubs. Above this is the under canopy, the main canopy and, rising above, the emergents, which can grow to 50 metres in height. Trees have to grow rapidly in order to reach the life-giving sunlight.
- Tree trunks are straight and, in their lower parts, branchless in their efforts to grow tall.
- Large buttress roots stand above the ground to give support to the trees.
- Lianas, which are vine-like plants, use the large trees as a support in their efforts to reach the canopy and sunlight.
- As only about 1 per cent of the incoming sunlight reaches the forest floor, there is little undergrowth. Shrubs and other plants which grow here have had to adapt to the lack of light.
- During the wetter months, large areas of land near to the main rivers are flooded (Figure 15.19).
- Leaves have drip tips to shed the heavy rainfall.
- Fallen leaves soon decay in the hot, wet climate.
- There are over 1000 different species of tree, including such hardwoods as mahogany, rosewood and greenheart.
- Dense undergrowth occurs near to rivers and forest clearings where sunlight is able to penetrate the canopy.

Despite its luxuriant appearance, the rainforest is a fragile environment whose existence relies upon the rapid and unbroken recycling of nutrients (Figure 15.20). Once the forest is cleared (deforestation page 230), then the nutrient cycle is broken. Humus is not replaced and the underlying soils will soon become infertile and eroded. Not only will the rainforest not be able to re-establish itself, but the land will become too poor to be used for farming (page 82).

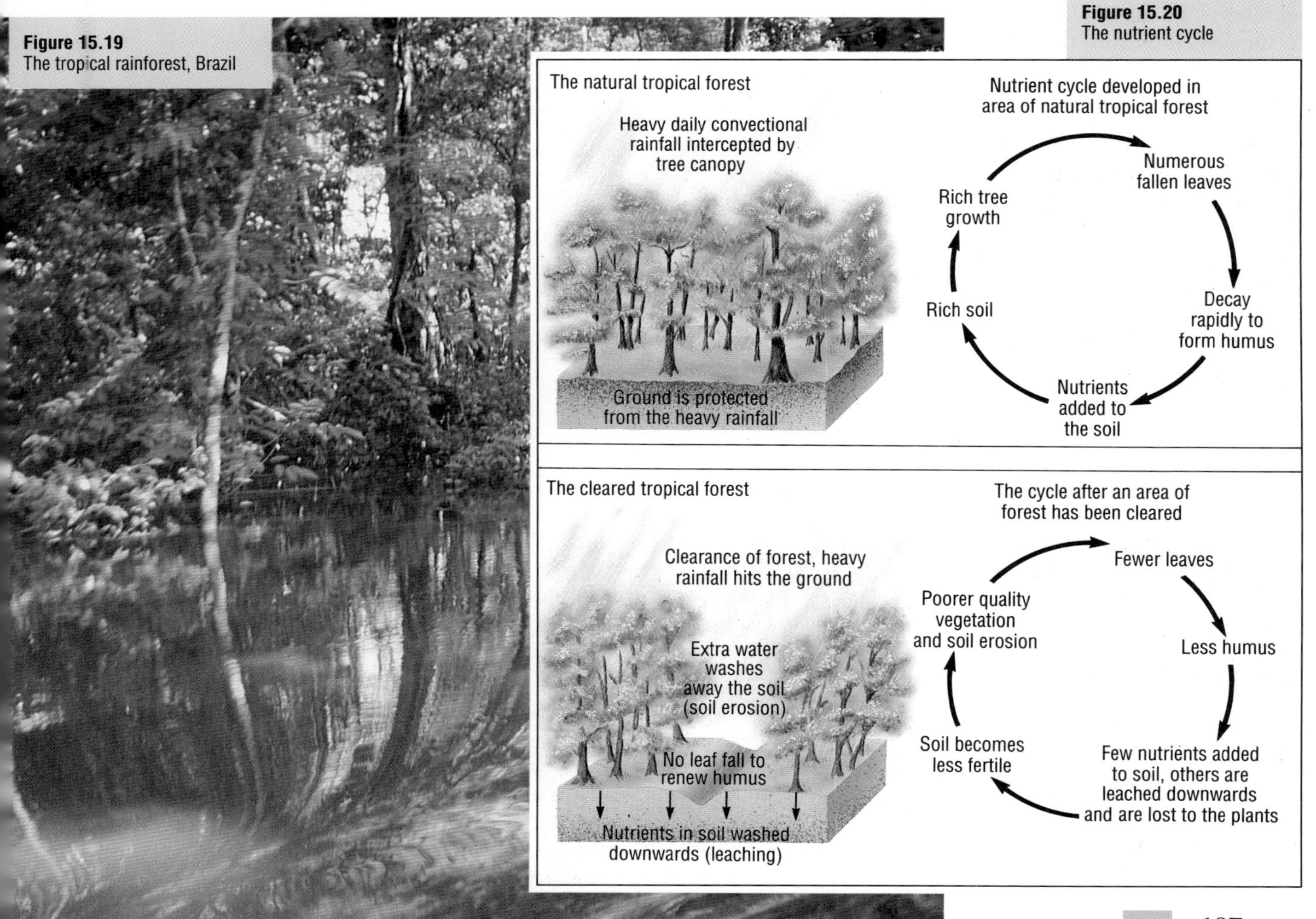
The natural tropical forest
Heavy daily convectional rainfall intercepted by tree canopy
Ground is protected from the heavy rainfall
Nutrient cycle developed in area of natural tropical forest
Numerous fallen leaves
Decay rapidly to form humus
Nutrients added to the soil
Rich soil
Rich tree growth
The cleared tropical forest
Clearance of forest, heavy rainfall hits the ground
Extra water washes away the soil (soil erosion)
No leaf fall to renew humus
Nutrients in soil washed downwards (leaching)
The cycle after an area of forest has been cleared
Fewer leaves
Less humus
Few nutrients added to soil, others are leached downwards and are lost to the plants
Soil becomes less fertile
Poorer quality vegetation and soil erosion

Figure 15.19 The tropical rainforest, Brazil

Figure 15.20 The nutrient cycle

Mediterranean climate and vegetation

Figure 15.21
Mediterranean scrub, Crete

Figure 15.22
Climate graph for Malta

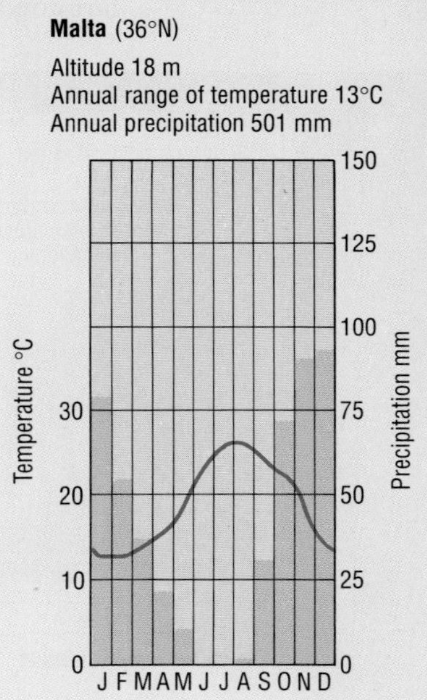

Figure 15.23
Mediterranean woodland, Tuscany

Climate

Places with a Mediterranean climate are usually found on the west coast of continents between latitudes 30° and 40° north and south of the Equator (page 204). Apart from the area surrounding the Mediterranean Sea in Europe, where the climate does extend inland from the west coast, this climate is also found in California, Central Chile, around Cape Town in South Africa and in parts of southern Australia. The climate, as shown by the graph for Malta (Figure 15.22), is characterised by hot, dry summers and warm, wet winters.

Summers are hot, for although the sun never shines directly from overhead, it does reach a high angle in the sky. Also during summer, the prevailing wind blows from the land. As the land is hot at this time of the year, the prevailing wind will bring with it very warm weather. The exception is places actually next to the sea (therefore not applicable to Europe) where the cooler sea lowers temperatures appreciably (San Francisco is no warmer than southern England). As the wind also blows across a dry land surface it cannot pick up much moisture. Apart from an occasional thunderstorm, most places are therefore dry, cloudless and sunny for several months.

Winters are warm for although the sun is now at a lower angle in the sky, it is still higher than places further from the Equator like Britain. The nearby sea, which remains relatively warm at this time of year, also helps to keep coastal places warm. However, the prevailing wind has reversed its summer direction and now blows from the sea. It brings with it warm, moist air which, as it is forced to rise over the many coastal mountains, gives large amounts of relief rainfall and, at higher altitudes, snow. Even so, wet days are usually separated by several which are warm and sunny.

Vegetation

The natural vegetation of the Mediterranean lands is woodland and scrub (Figures 15.21 and 15.23). At one time most Mediterranean hillsides were extensively wooded. Where this is still so, they are dominated by evergreen oaks (e.g. the cork oak) and conifers (e.g. the Corsican pine and, in California, the giant sequoia (redwood), Figure 15.25). Elsewhere, where forests have been destroyed by natural fires or cut down for human needs, a scrub type of vegetation has developed. In Europe there are two major types of scrub:

- *Maquis*, which is a dense, tangled undergrowth more typical on granite and other impermeable rocks.
- *Garigue*, which is a much sparser, lower-lying scrub with many aromatic plants such as rosemary and lavender, and which develops on limestone and other permeable rocks. In California, a similar type of sagebrush scrub is called *chaparral*.

All these types of vegetation have had to adapt to the summer drought. The vegetation often has:

- Either small, waxy, glossy leaves or sharp thorns in order to reduce the amount of moisture lost by transpiration. Rosemary can achieve this by curling up its leaves.
- A protective bark which acts as a seal against the heat as well as transpiration loss.
- Long tap roots to reach underground water supplies.
- A short life cycle which avoids times of drought. Aromatic herbs and other plants germinate during winter rains, flower in spring, and lie dormant (inactive) during the summer drought.

Due to various human activities over many centuries, little of the natural Mediterranean vegetation remains, especially in Europe. Vegetation has been affected by:

- Deforestation. Trees have been cut down either to create space for farming or settlement, to use for fuel, or for the construction of ships and buildings. Much of the natural forest was cleared long ago in the time of the ancient Greek and Roman Empires. Once deforested, the hillsides become vulnerable to soil erosion during the heavy winter rains (Figure 15.24).
- Grazing animals. Herds of sheep and, especially, goats eat leaves of young trees before the plants have time to re-establish themselves.
- Fire. Forest fires, sometimes started deliberately, have added to the destruction of vegetation (Figure 15.26).

Figure 15.24
Soil erosion in the Apennines

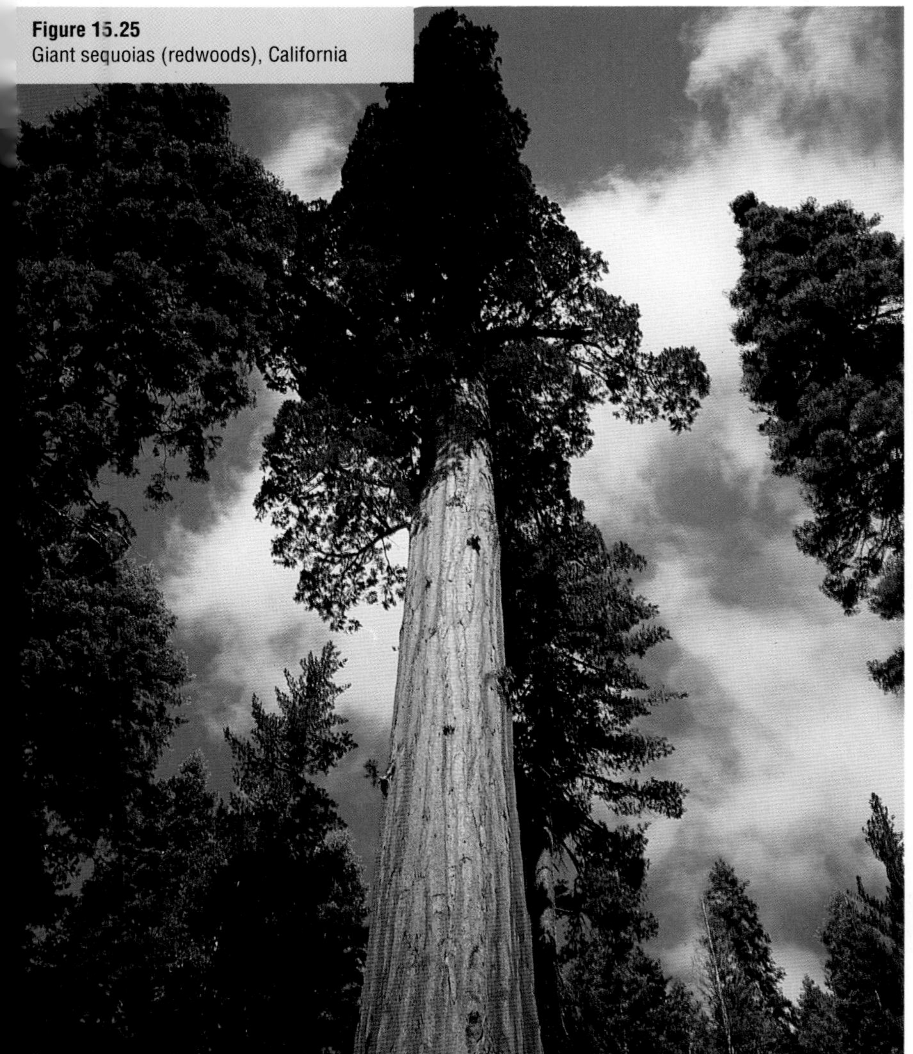

Figure 15.25
Giant sequoias (redwoods), California

Figure 15.26 Fires destroy vegetation

Tourists flee fires raging in Capri

STRONG winds yesterday foiled a frantic battle by US marines, Italian troops, firemen, and an army of volunteers backed by tanker-planes and helicopters to control vast brush fires which have turned much of the island of Capri into an inferno.

As they struggled against the blaze, fire broke out on the island of Ischia on the other side of the Gulf of Naples and swept through the island's loveliest woods, full of pines, ilexes and rare plants. Firefighters were hampered by a shortage of water and tanker-planes.

In Capri, many residents and holiday-makers fled from their villas as the fires raging since Friday on Monte Solaro, the mountain which dominates the island, came dangerously close. Troops and volunteers, who have been in action non-stop for four days and three nights, dug trenches to try and stop the fire, but flying sparks often made their efforts futile.

The authorities are investigating the possibility of arson, after a pensioner reported hearing someone on the mountainside tell a companion to "burn it and throw it down". But the Mayor of Anacapri, Rino di Pietro, dismissed the idea. "It has not rained here for four months," he pointed out. The environmental association Legambiente has launched an appeal for funds to reforest the devastated areas and create an efficient fire-spotting system.

Tropical continental climate and savanna grasslands

Climate

This climate is found in central parts of continents, away from coasts, which lie approximately between latitudes 5° and 15° north and south of the Equator (page 204). This includes parts of Venezuela and Brazil in South America, northern Australia, and a large semi-circle surrounding the Zaire basin in Africa. The latter includes Kenya which, although straddling the Equator, lies at an altitude too high to support rainforest. The main characteristic of this climate, as illustrated by the graph for Kano in northern Nigeria (Figure 15.27), is the alternate wet and dry season. This seasonal variation is due to the apparent movement of the overhead sun (Figure 15.28).

The dry, slightly cooler season occurs when the sun is overhead in the opposite hemisphere (21 December on Figure 15.28). The sun still reaches a high enough angle in the sky to generate very warm conditions but, being inland, there is no additional warming influence from the sea. As the prevailing winds, the trades, blow from the east they will have shed any moisture long before they reach these areas. Indeed the climate at this time of year is very similar to that of the hot deserts (page 202).

The hot, wet season coincides with the sun having returned to an overhead position (21 June on Figure 15.28), and the trade winds having died away. Temperatures rise as the sun takes a more vertical position and because these places are too far inland to be affected by any moderating influence of the sea. However, temperatures do fall as cloud cover and rainfall increase. The frequent afternoon convectional thunderstorms mean that the climate now resembles that of equatorial areas (page 196). Unfortunately, the length of the rainy season and the total amounts of rain are both unreliable (page 206) and many areas, especially in Africa, have experienced several severe droughts in recent years.

The length of the dry season increases and the amounts of rainfall decrease with distance from the Equator (less convectional rain) and the east coast (less rain from the trade winds).

Figure 15.27
Climate graph for Kano, Nigeria

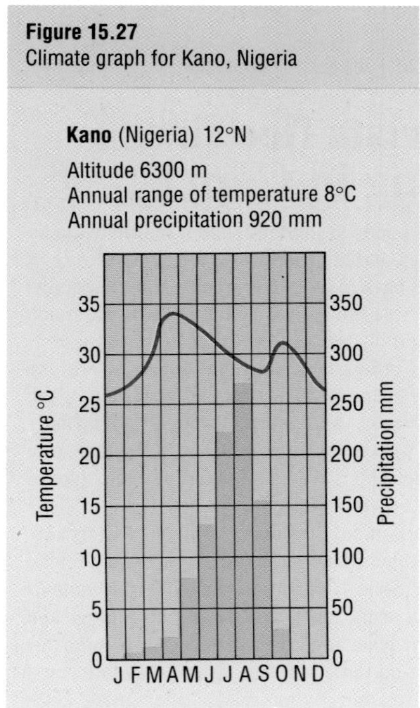

(1) March 21
Overhead sun
Kano
Dry
Wet
Dry
Tropic of Cancer 23½°N
Equator 0°
Tropic of Capricorn 23½°S

(3) September 21
Overhead sun

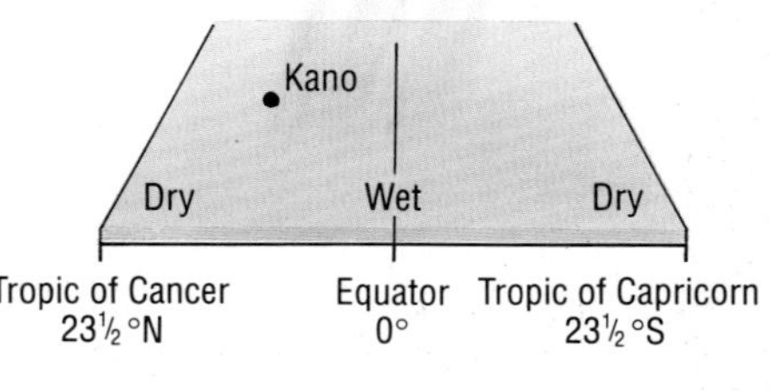

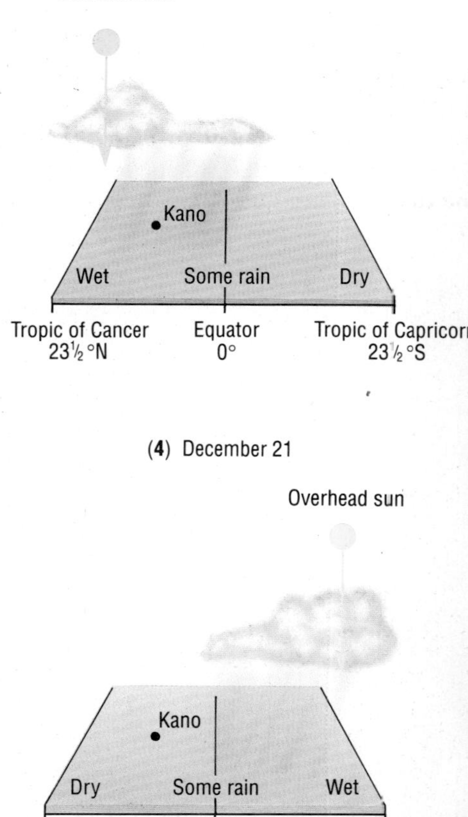

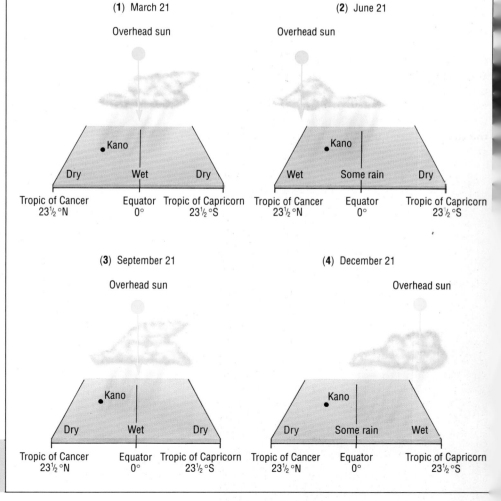

Figure 15.28
Causes of seasonal rainfall in a tropical continental climate

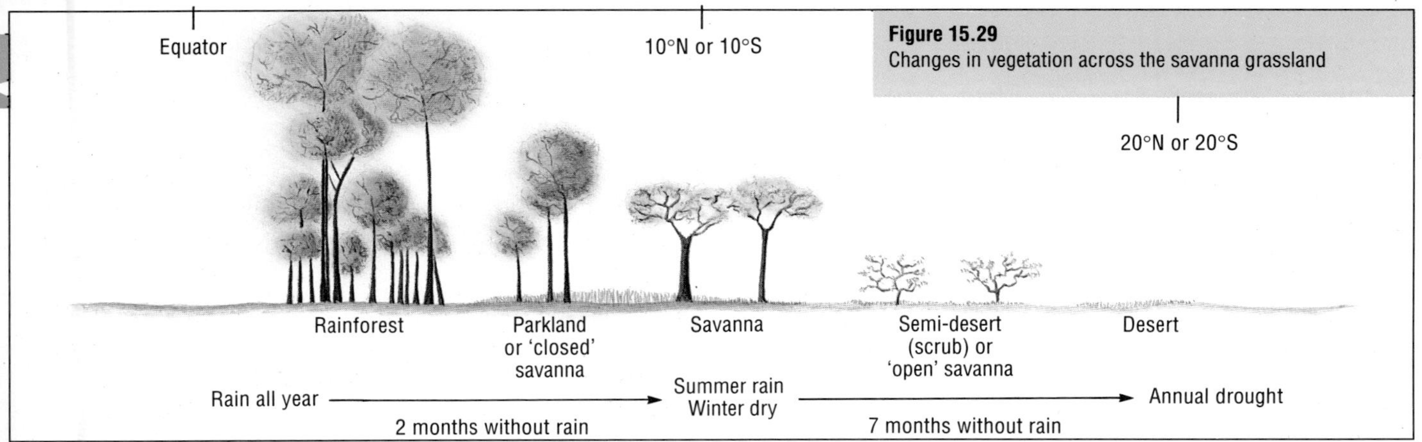

Figure 15.29
Changes in vegetation across the savanna grassland

Vegetation

A transect (section) across the savanna grasslands shows how the natural vegetation changes in response to the climate (Figure 15.29). Where the savanna merges with the tropical rainforest (rain all year), the vegetation is dense woodland with patches of tall grass. Moving away from these margins, the vegetation slowly changes to typical savanna grasslands with scattered trees (rain for half the year), and eventually to the drought-resistant bushes and odd clumps of grass on the desert margins (hardly any rain).

The dry season

The scattered deciduous trees lose their leaves, grasses turn yellow and dry up, and the ground assumes a dusty, reddish-brown colour. Some trees shed their leaves while others produce thin, waxy and even thornlike leaves to try to keep transpiration to a minimum. Most plants are ***xerophytic*** (drought-resistant) with very long roots to tap underground water supplies or with thick bark to store water in the trunk, like the baobab tree (Figure 15.30). Grasses grow in tufts, separated by patches of bare soil. As the dry season progresses, their stalks become stiff, yellow and straw-like, and in time, the plants wither.

The wet season

After the first rains, the grass seeds germinate and trees produce new leaves. Under the hot, wet conditions the grasses grow quickly and can reach a height of three or four metres before flowering and producing new seeds. The seemingly endless plains of the Serengeti (Tanzania) and Maasai Mara (Kenya) resemble a vast green sea occasionally interrupted by acacia trees (Figure 15.31). The acacias, with their crowns flattened by the trade winds, provide welcome shelter for wildlife.

The vegetation of these areas has been altered over a period of time by fire, either started deliberately or as a result of electrical storms. More recently, areas nearer the desert margins have experienced desertification (page 234) mainly from pressures resulting from rapid population growth. Trees and shrubs have been removed for fuelwood. As settlements and cultivated areas increase, many nomadic herders, like the Fulani in West Africa and the Maasai in East Africa, find their traditional grazing grounds reduced in size. This leads to overgrazing and soil erosion in the areas to which they are restricted.

Figure 15.30
Baobab tree

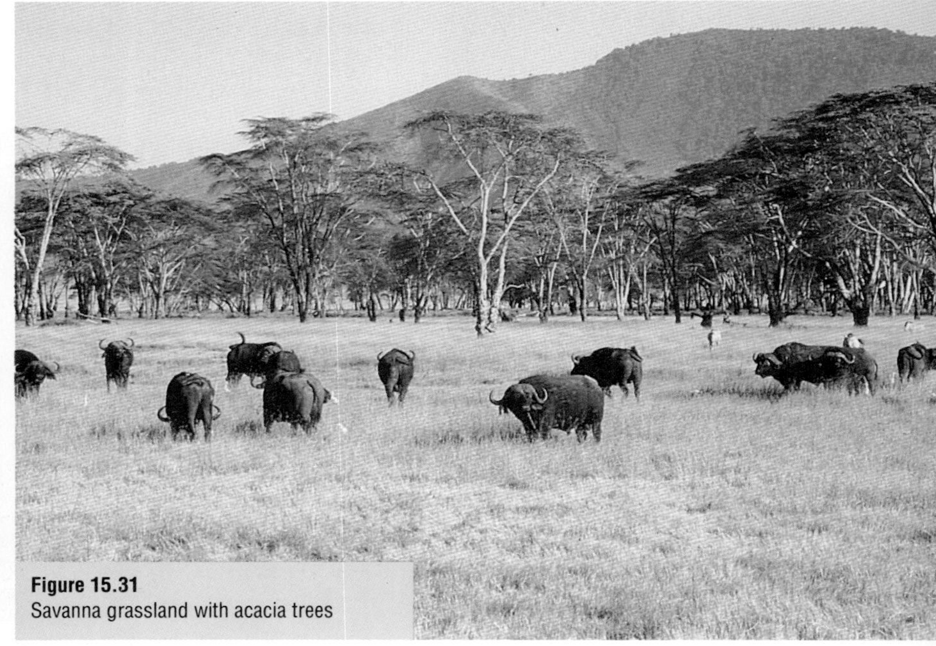
Figure 15.31
Savanna grassland with acacia trees

Hot deserts

Climate

Hot deserts are places with high annual temperatures, less than 250 mm of rain a year, and high evaporation rates (Figure 15.33). Apart from the Sahara, which extends across Africa, most deserts are located on west coasts of continents between latitudes 5° and 30° north and south of the Equator. They include the Kalahari-Namib in southern Africa, the Atacama in South America, and the Australian and Mexican deserts (page 204).

Temperatures are highest when the sun is directly overhead, but cooler when it is in the opposite hemisphere. Coastal areas are also much cooler, partly because of the influence of the sea and partly because of off-shore cold ocean currents (page 207). Inland, and away from the influence of the sea, cloudless skies allow day temperatures to rise to 50°C and night temperatures to fall to below freezing. Although deserts are very dry, none are completely rainless. The lack of rain is due to a combination of reasons:

- ◆ Prevailing winds blow from the dry land and cannot pick up moisture.
- ◆ Prevailing winds have to cross mountain barriers which create rain shadows.
- ◆ Air which rose into the atmosphere as convection currents on the Equator descends in these latitudes (page 205). As it descends it warms, creates areas of high pressure, and gives clear skies (compare anticyclones in Britain – page 195).
- ◆ When winds do blow from the sea, they are cool and unable to pick up much moisture.

Figure 15.33
Climate graph for Ain Salah, Algeria

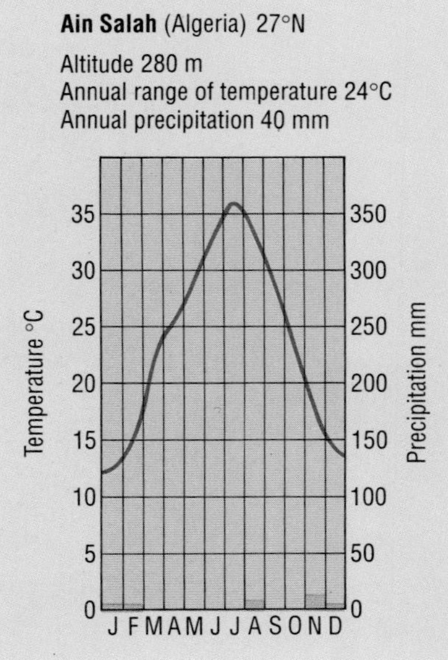

Ain Salah (Algeria) 27°N
Altitude 280 m
Annual range of temperature 24°C
Annual precipitation 40 mm

Temperature °C: 0, 5, 10, 15, 20, 25, 30, 35
Precipitation mm: 0, 50, 100, 150, 200, 250, 300, 350
J F M A M J J A S O N D

Figure 15.32
Saguaro cacti

Vegetation

- ◆ Plants such as cacti have thick, waxy skins to reduce transpiration, and fleshy stems in which to store water (Figure 15.32).
- ◆ Many plants have thin, spiky or glossy leaves, also to reduce transpiration.
- ◆ Plants have long roots to tap underground supplies of water.
- ◆ Seeds can lie dormant for several years. After a heavy shower they germinate rapidly. The plants complete their life-cycle within two or three weeks. After a period of rain the desert literally 'blooms' with flowering plants (Figure 15.34).

Figure 15.34
The desert in 'bloom'

Figure 15.35
Desert landscape

Cold climates and coniferous forests

Climate

Cold climates extend across northern North America and northern Eurasia (page 204) and occur at higher altitudes in mountainous areas. Winters are very long and cold (Figure 15.37). As most places are inland, they are a long way from any warming influence of the sea. Places within the Arctic Circle have a period when the sun never rises above the horizon. The wind-chill factor is high with strong winds which evaporate moisture, freeze the skin and cause frostbite. Summers are short. Although the hours of daylight are long, days remain relatively cool due to the low angle of the sun in the sky. Precipitation is light. It falls as snow in winter and in short convectional showers in summer. However, precipitation amounts are not as critical to vegetation as are temperatures and the short growing season.

Vegetation

Vegetation consists of vast stands of coniferous forest (Figure 15.36). The most common tree is the spruce and this, like other conifers such as the Scots pine and fir, has had to adapt itself to the severe climatic conditions (Figure 15.38). Coniferous trees are softwoods, and are valuable for timber as well as pulp and paper. Often, unlike in deciduous forests, there may be extensive stands of a single species. In colder areas, like Siberia, the larch tends to dominate. Although the larch is cone-bearing, it is deciduous and sheds its needles in winter.

Figure 15.37
Climate graph for Dawson, Canada

Dawson
(Yukon Territory, Canada)
Latitude 64°N
Altitude 324 m
Annual range of temperature 44°C
Annual precipitation 319 mm

Temperature °C: 20, 10, 0, –10, –20, –30, –40
Precipitation mm: 150, 125, 100, 75, 50, 25, 0
J F M A M J J A S O N D

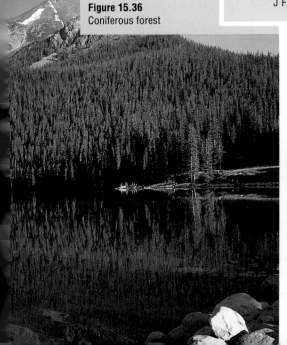

Figure 15.36
Coniferous forest

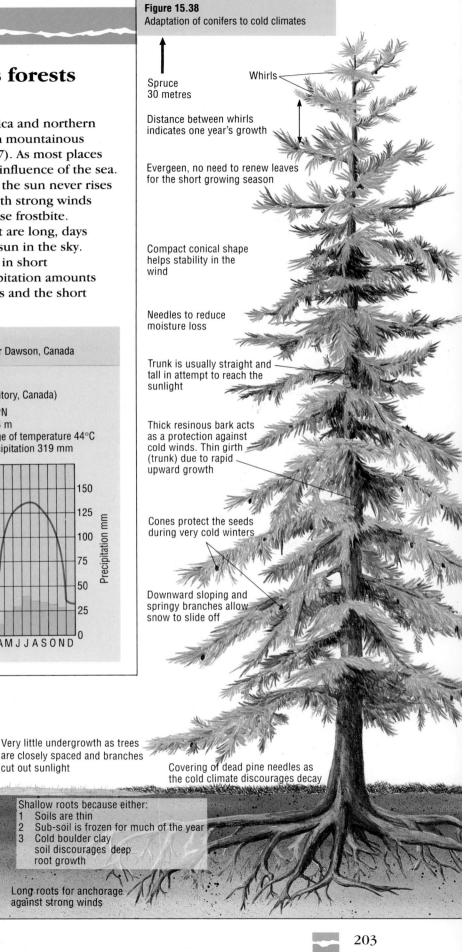

Figure 15.38
Adaptation of conifers to cold climates

World climates and atmospheric circulation

Figure 15.39 shows the location of the six types of world climate and vegetation described in this chapter. Maps which show the location and distribution of the world's climatic and vegetation types are very generalised (simplified). Due to their scale they cannot show local variations. They also, unintentionally, imply that the boundary between two climatic and vegetation types is a thin line. In reality, as was seen in the transect across the savanna (Figure 15.29), any change is often gradual and extends across a wide transition zone.

Although it may not be obvious to you at first glance, the map does show distinct patterns in the location of the major climatic and vegetation types. Take the British type as an example. Notice that it tends to appear on the west coast of continents between latitudes 40° and 60° north and south of the Equator. Try to identify patterns for the other types before referring back to their general locations as given between pages 196 and 203. The pattern which you should have been able to identify is mainly the result of the circulation of air within the atmosphere (Figure 15.40). In order to try to understand the circulation within the atmosphere, you should be aware of three processes.

1 If air next to the ground is heated, it expands, gets lighter and rises. This will lead to a decrease in the amount of air at ground level and the creation of an area of low pressure.

2 If air in the atmosphere is cooled, it will become denser and descends. This will lead to an increase in the amount of air at ground level and the formation of a high pressure area.

3 Wind, which is air in motion, blows from areas of high pressure to areas of low pressure. (In reality other factors, including the earth's rotation, prevent air from moving directly from high pressure to low – otherwise the prevailing wind in Britain would be from the south.)

Figure 15.40 shows the major areas of high and low pressure, and the general circulation of air. The circulation is controlled by the build-up of heat on the Equator. Air is forced to rise (convection currents) creating low pressure. As the rising air cools it condenses to give daily afternoon thunderstorms. As the upper air spreads out away from the Equator, it cools, becomes denser and descends back to earth forming a high pressure belt near to the tropics. As the descending air gets warmer and drier, hot deserts develop. On reaching the ground some of the warm air will return to the Equator (the trade winds) replacing air which had previously risen, while the remainder will move away from the Equator (the westerlies) towards places like Britain. When this warm tropical air meets with colder polar air, it is forced to rise (creating low pressure) and produces rain (frontal rain in depressions).

Figure 15.39
Location of world climate and vegetation types described in this chapter

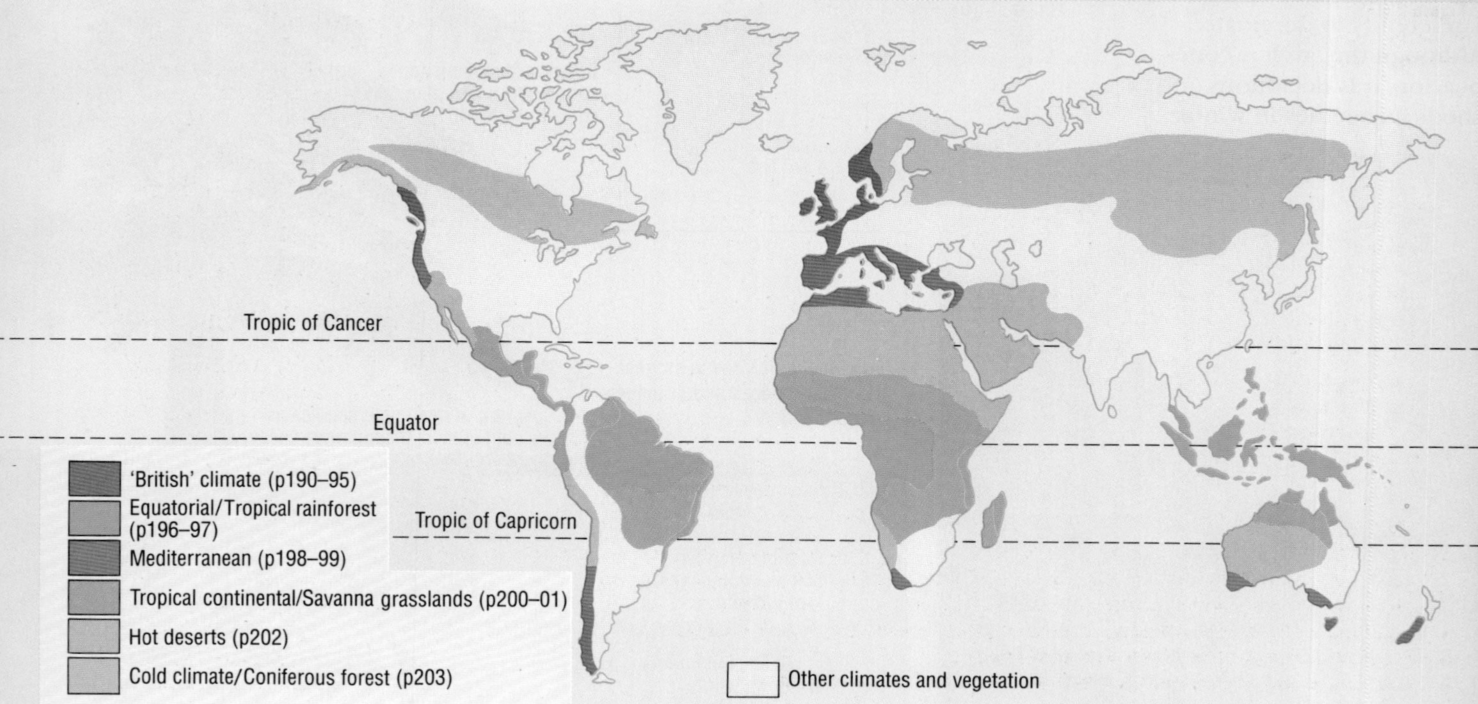

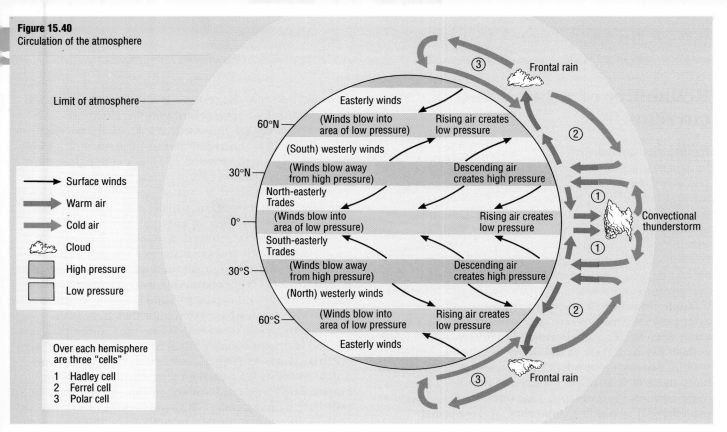

Figure 15.40
Circulation of the atmosphere

Limit of atmosphere

Surface winds
Warm air
Cold air
Cloud
High pressure
Low pressure

Over each hemisphere are three "cells"
1 Hadley cell
2 Ferrel cell
3 Polar cell

Easterly winds
60°N
(Winds blow into area of low pressure)
Rising air creates low pressure
(South) westerly winds
30°N
(Winds blow away from high pressure)
Descending air creates high pressure
North-easterly Trades
0°
(Winds blow into area of low pressure)
Rising air creates low pressure
South-easterly Trades
30°S
(Winds blow away from high pressure)
Descending air creates high pressure
(North) westerly winds
60°S
(Winds blow into area of low pressure)
Rising air creates low pressure
Easterly winds
Frontal rain
Convectional thunderstorm
Frontal rain

In reality, an explanation of the circulation of the atmosphere is not so simple; if it was then weather forecasting would be easy! Due to the tilt and the rotation of the earth, the position of the overhead sun appears to change. The southern hemisphere is hottest when the sun appears to be overhead at the Tropic of Capricorn (21 December). At this time of year, the pressure and wind belts move southwards (Figure 15.41). The northern hemisphere is hottest when the sun appears to be overhead at the Tropic of Cancer (21 June), by which time the pressure and wind belts have also moved northwards (Figure 15.41). The resultant changes in pressure and wind are responsible for the seasonal contrasts in climates such as the Mediterranean and the Tropical Continental. Notice the changes in wind direction for the Mediterranean climate (marked M on Figure 15.41).

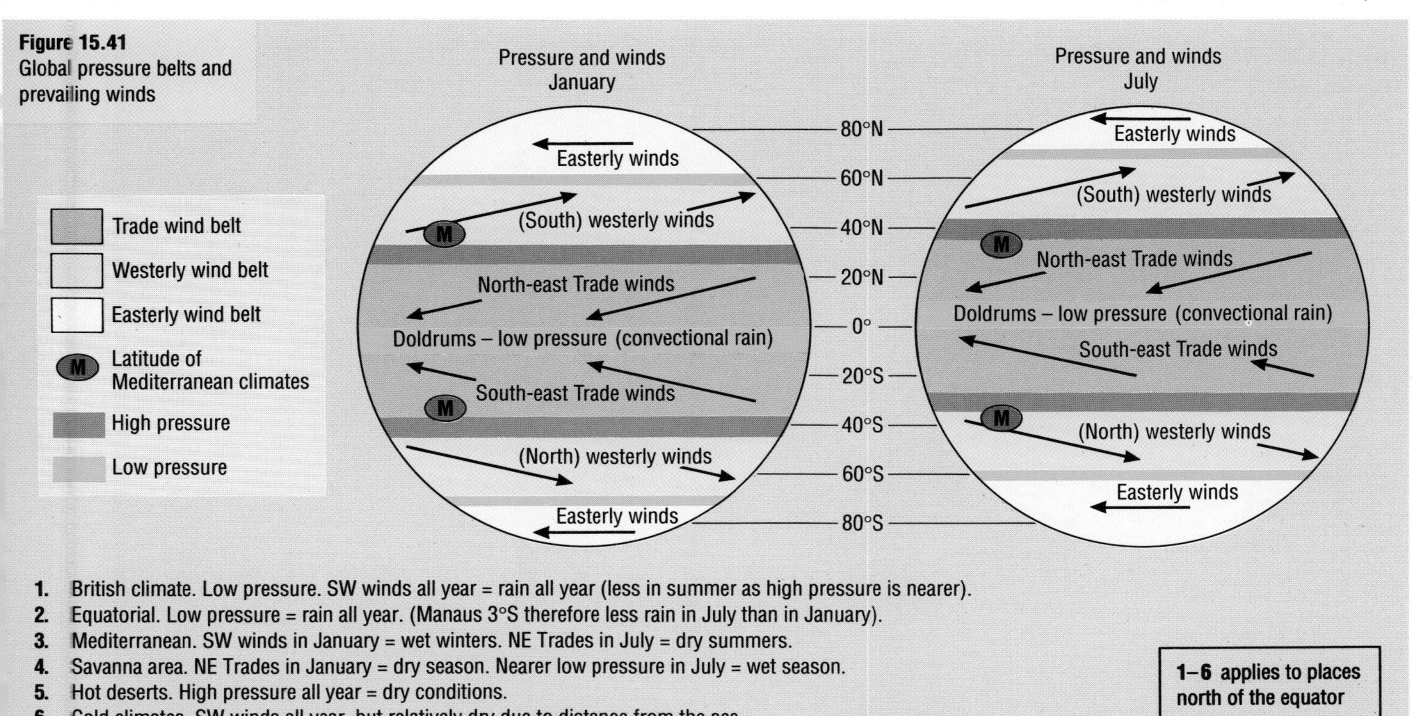

Figure 15.41
Global pressure belts and prevailing winds

1. British climate. Low pressure. SW winds all year = rain all year (less in summer as high pressure is nearer).
2. Equatorial. Low pressure = rain all year. (Manaus 3°S therefore less rain in July than in January).
3. Mediterranean. SW winds in January = wet winters. NE Trades in July = dry summers.
4. Savanna area. NE Trades in January = dry season. Nearer low pressure in July = wet season.
5. Hot deserts. High pressure all year = dry conditions.
6. Cold climates. SW winds all year, but relatively dry due to distance from the sea.

Reliability of rainfall and ocean currents

Reliability of rainfall

In Britain it is more or less taken for granted that it will rain every few days. As rainfall is spread out evenly throughout the year, Britain is rarely short of water. Even if there is the occasional summer drought, supplies are usually replenished the following winter. Only in exceptional circumstances, as in 1976, do parts of Britain receive less than 70 per cent of their expected rainfall. Moreover, when it does rain in Britain, it is likely to fall steadily for several hours. This allows the water time to infiltrate into the soil where it can be stored for use in drier periods. Only on rare occasions (5 per cent of the total) does Britain get torrential downpours which result in flash floods and the water being rapidly lost to the system. Britain has also had the technology and capital to build dams so that surplus water can be stored in reservoirs until it is needed. This water is then piped (transferred) to our homes so that, under normal conditions, all we need to do is to turn on a tap. The fact that Britain's population is growing very slowly and it has been a time of economic recession means that there is limited demand for extra water supplies. For most British people, a permanent water supply is usually guaranteed.

The situation in many economically less developed countries is very different. Instead of rain falling throughout the year, many countries experience a pronounced wet and dry season. Consequently, if the rains fail one year the result is disastrous for crops, and possibly also for livestock and people. The most vulnerable areas are those with a low annual average rainfall, e.g. desert margins and tropical savannas. Here, where even a small variation of 10 per cent below the average rainfall can be critical, many countries often experience a variation of over 30 per cent (Figure 15.42). The rain, when it does fall, usually comes in torrential downpours (40 per cent of the total) which give insufficient time for infiltration. Rapid surface run-off causes flash floods and the water is soon lost to the system. Although the rainfall total may appear to be high, its effectiveness is very limited. Few countries have had the technology and capital to build dams in which to store water. Where dams have been built they have been financed by overseas aid which has, more often than not, put the recipient country further into debt, e.g. the Volta (Ghana), Turkwel (Kenya) and Aswan (Egypt) dams in Africa. In countries with high temperatures and high evaporation rates, large surface storage reservoirs may only have a limited value. Relatively few people have piped water and, especially in rural areas, the daily walk to the local well can be very time consuming. Where animals gather around a well, the land becomes overgrazed. As many of these countries also have high birth rates (page 12), there is a rapidly increasing demand for water for domestic purposes, as well as for the extra crops and animals needed to feed the growing population. It has been claimed that the most serious single climatic hazard in the least economically developed countries is the high variability and uncertainty of rainfall.

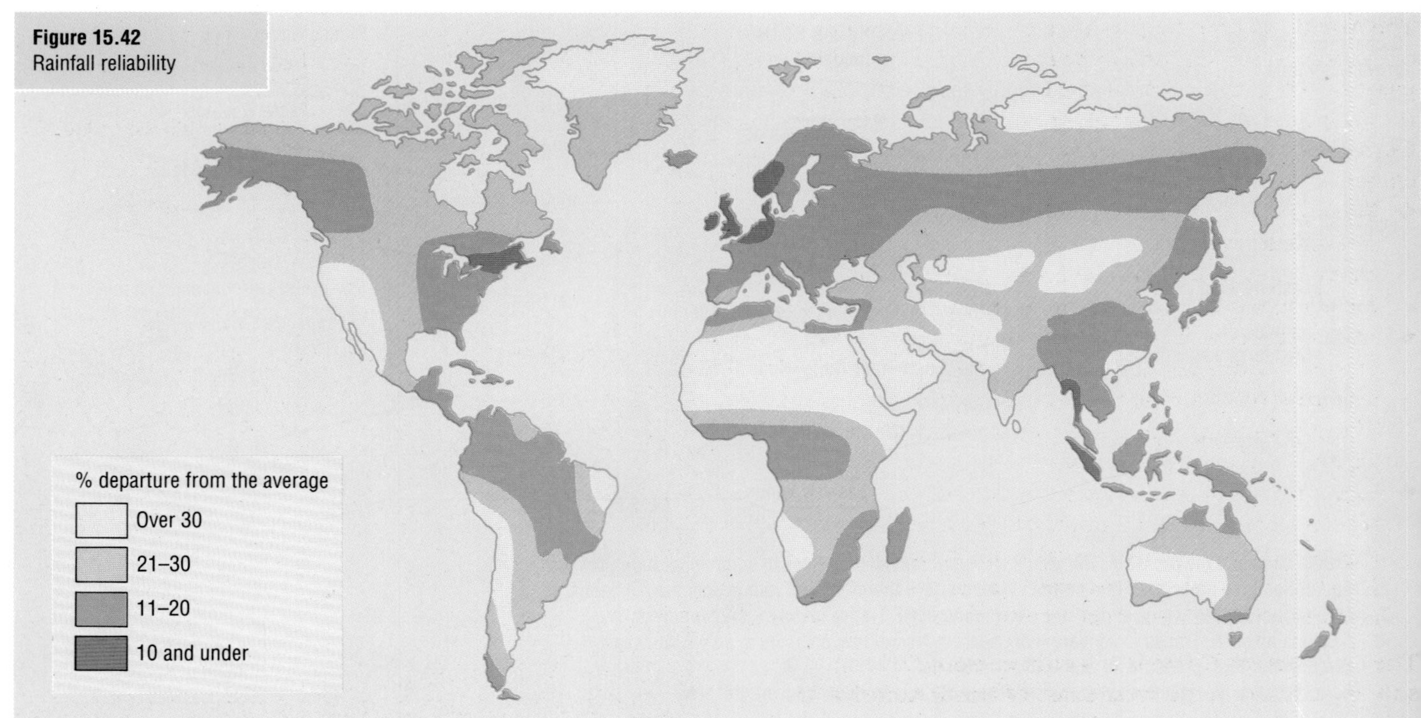

Figure 15.42
Rainfall reliability

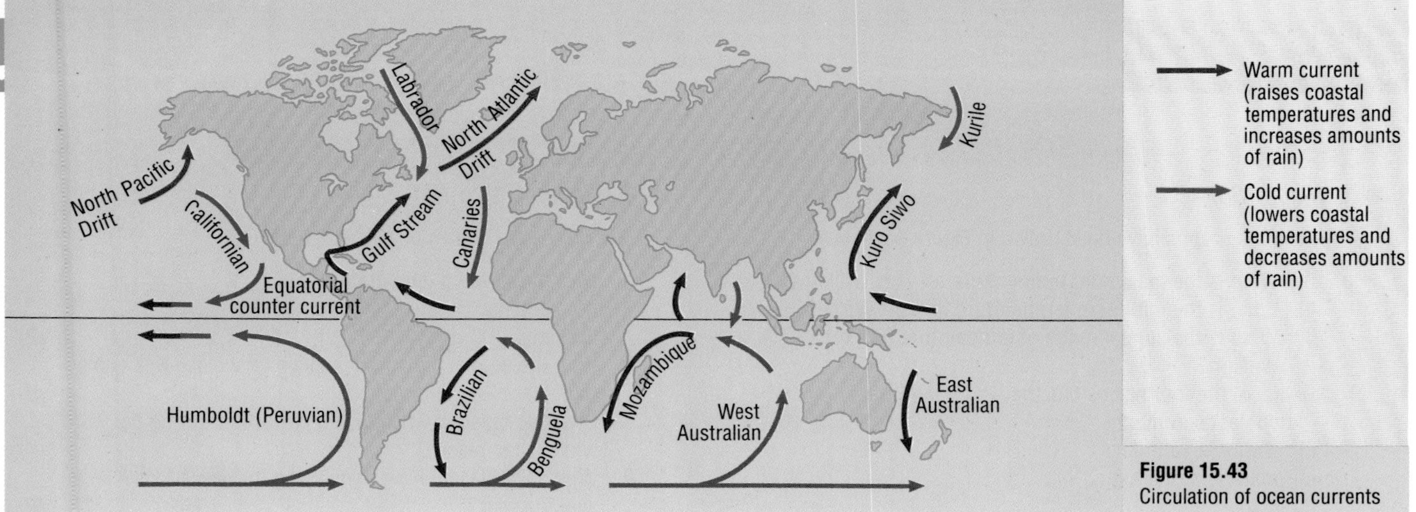

Figure 15.43
Circulation of ocean currents

Ocean currents

Ocean currents are movements of surface water. They are set in motion by prevailing winds associated with the circulation of the atmosphere. The main ocean currents follow a clockwise circulation in the northern hemisphere and an anticlockwise circulation in the southern hemisphere (Figure 15.44). Ocean currents often exert a considerable influence upon the climate of adjacent coastal areas. This influence largely depends upon whether the current is classified as a warm or a cold current (Figure 15.43). Warm currents carry water from the tropics towards the poles, e.g the North Atlantic Drift. They raise the temperature so that coastal places are warmer than would be expected for their latitude. Cold currents carry water from polar areas back towards the Equator. They lower temperatures so that coastal areas are colder than would be expected for their latitude (e.g. Californian Current).

The *North Atlantic Drift* is a warm current of water which originates in the Caribbean Sea and Gulf of Mexico. It passes up the east coast of the USA, where it is known as the *Gulf Stream*, before making its way across the Atlantic Ocean towards North-west Europe. The current affects the climate of coastal places, like the British Isles, by:

- Raising winter temperatures by several degrees. The seas off the coast of Britain and Norway are kept ice-free whereas those off the coast of Newfoundland, in the same latitude, freeze for several months each year.
- Warming the temperature of the prevailing south-westerly winds as they blow over it in winter, but lowering their temperatures in summer (page 191). These prevailing winds help give Britain its mild winters and cool summers.
- Enabling winds which blow over its warm surface to pick up large amounts of moisture which is later deposited, as relief or frontal rainfall, on coastal areas (page 192). West coasts receive large and reliable amounts of rainfall spread evenly throughout the year.

The *Californian Current* is a cold current flowing southwards along the west coast of North America. It affects the climate of coastal areas by:

- Lowering temperatures, especially in summer. Although San Francisco is much further south than London, it has the same summer temperature.
- Cooling down winds which blow across it from the sea.
- Limiting the amount of moisture which winds blowing over it can collect. Cold currents are a major reason why hot deserts are located near the west coasts of continents (page 202).
- Causing fog when warm air from the land drifts seawards and meets colder air above the current. Fog often pours through San Francisco's Golden Gate (Figure 15.45).

Figure 15.44 Relationship between prevailing winds and ocean currents

50°N
25°N
Equator 0°
25°S
50°S
Westerlies
North-east Trades
South-east Trades
Westerlies

Figure 15.45
Fog over the Golden Gate Bridge, San Francisco

1 *(Page 190)*

Four climate graphs have been drawn in Figure 15.1.

a i) What is the maximum temperature for Fort William? *(1)*
ii) What is the minimum temperature for Fort William? *(1)*
iii) What is the annual range of temperature for Fort William? *(1)*

b Which of the four places has the
i) coolest summer?
ii) warmest summer?
iii) mildest winter?
iv) coldest winter?
v) most sunshine in a year? *(5)*

c i) What is the annual average rainfall for Penzance? *(1)*
ii) Which is the wettest season in Penzance? *(1)*
iii) Which is the wettest month in Penzance? *(1)*

2 *(Pages 190 to 193)*

Five places are shown on the map below.

a Give the missing temperature for:
i) January.
ii) July. *(2)*

b With the help of a diagram explain why place B is cooler than place A in summer. *(3)*

c Give two reasons why place C is warmer during the winter than place D. *(4)*

d Why does place E have snow lying for over 50 days in an average year? *(2)*

e Why does place C receive more rainfall throughout the year than place D? *(3)*

f Draw fully labelled diagrams to show the formation of:
i) relief rainfall.
ii) frontal rainfall.
iii) convectional rainfall. *(9)*

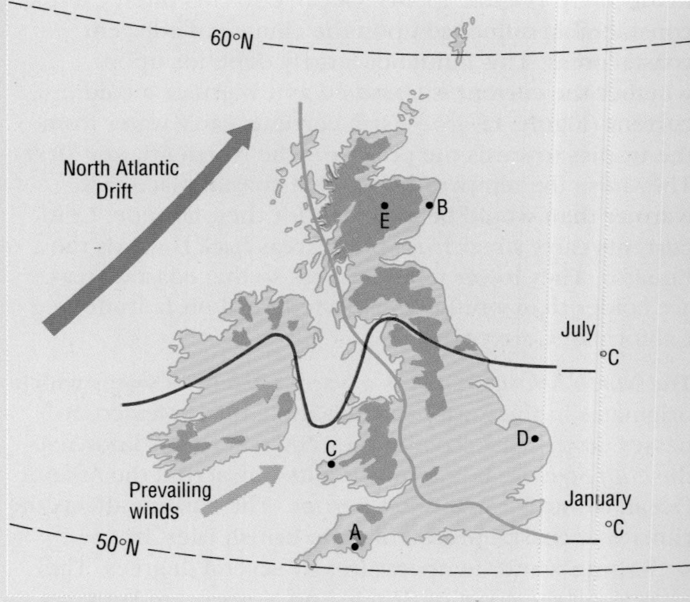

3 *(Pages 194 and 195)*

a i) Why do depressions form over the Atlantic Ocean? *(2)*
ii) What happens to warm and cold air at:
a) a warm front?
b) a cold front? *(2)*

b There is usually a recognisable weather pattern as a depression passes over the British Isles. Describe, on an enlarged copy of diagram A below, the likely weather conditions
i) as a warm front passes.
ii) in a warm sector.
iii) just after a cold front passes. *(18)*

c Using diagram B as a guide, list six differences between the expected weather conditions in SUMMER between a depression and an anticyclone. *(6)*

d What are three likely differences in the weather of an anticyclone in winter and an anticyclone in summer? *(3)*

	A			B	
Weather Conditions	**As a warm front passes**	**In a warm sector**	**Just after a cold front passes**	**Depression in summer**	**Anticyclone in summer**
Temperature					
Cloud cover					
Precipitation					
Wind speed					
Wind direction					
Pressure					

4 *(Page 195)*

On the weather map opposite:

a i) Name the weather symbols labelled A and B. *(2)*
ii) Is C an area of high pressure or low pressure? *(1)*

b What is the temperature, cloud cover, precipitation, wind speed, wind direction and pressure at:
i) Belfast?
ii) Manchester?
iii) Aberdeen? *(18)*

c What do you think will be the forecast for the London area for the next few hours? *(3)*

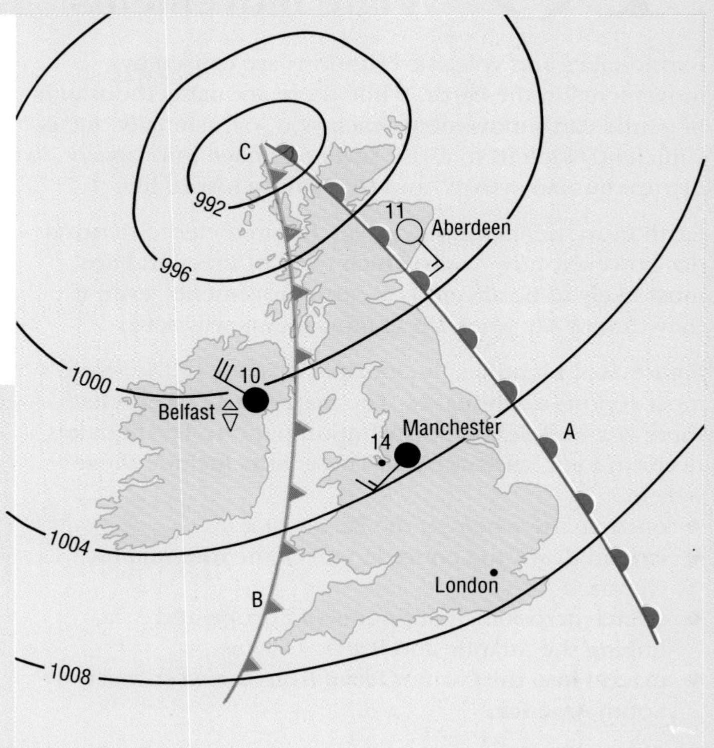

5 *(Pages 190 to 204)*

The locations of the six climates described in this chapter are shown on Figure 15.39 (page 204). Match each of the six climates with the following descriptions: *(6)*

- hot, dry summers; warm, wet winters
- long cold winters; short cool summers
- hot and dry throughout the year
- hot, wet and humid all year
- cool summers; mild winters; rain all year
- hot, wet summers; warm, dry winters

6 *(Pages 196 to 205)*

a Make a copy of the table below.
i) Fill in the left hand column by choosing THREE of the following types of climate:
Equatorial; Mediterranean; Tropical continental (savanna); Hot desert; and Cold climate.
ii) Complete the table by using information from the relevant graph for each climatic type. *(18)*

b For EACH of the three climates types which you selected in part **a**
i) Name three parts of the world where it is located. *(9)*
ii) Explain how it is affected by:
– latitude (angle of the sun).
– distance from the sea.
– prevailing winds. *(9)*

c i) Describe, with the help of annotated diagrams, the main characteristics of its natural vegetation. *(9)*
ii) Describe how the natural vegetation:
– has adapted to the climatic conditions.
– has been altered by human activity. *(9)*

Climatic type	Temperatures			Precipitation		
	Maximum	Minimum	Annual range	Annual total	Season with most rain	Type of rain
1						
2						
3						

7 *(Pages 204 to 207)*

a Why is pressure:
i) low at the Equator?
ii) high about 30° from the Equator?
iii) low about 60° from the Equator? *(3)*

b i) Draw a simple diagram to show the general circulation of the atmosphere (your diagram should show three circulation 'cells'). *(3)*
ii) What is the relationship between the circulation of the atmosphere and the pattern of world climatic types? *(6)*

c Why do many of the least economically developed countries, especially those in Africa, experience a 'high variability and uncertainty of rainfall'? *(4)*

d The diagram shows an ocean lying north of the Equator.
i) Are the currents flowing in a clockwise or an anticlockwise direction? *(1)*
ii) Is current A a warm or a cold current? *(1)*
iii) Is current B a warm or a cold current? *(1)*
iv) Ocean currents influence the climate of adjacent coasts. What will be the differences in temperature and precipitation between places X and Y on the coast of continent D? *(6)*

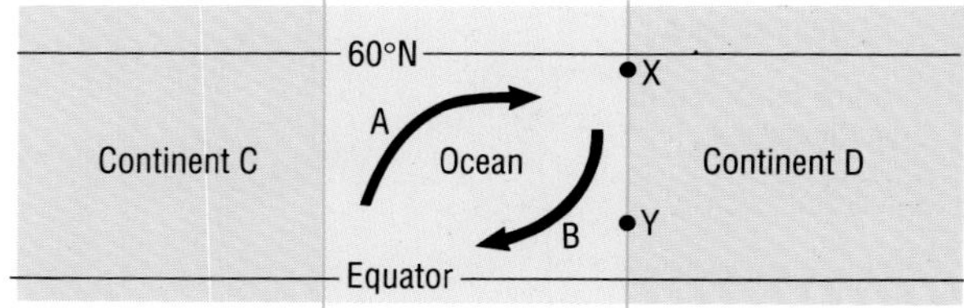

Plate movements

Earthquakes and volcanic eruptions are caused by movements in the earth. While there are many thousands of gentle earth movements each year, occasionally one is sufficiently violent to cause severe damage to property, to disrupt human activity, and to result in loss of life.

Earth movements cannot, as yet, be predicted. Scientists do, however, now know which parts of the world are most likely to be affected by earth movements, even if they cannot say when these movements will occur.

Figure 16.2 identifies the location of some of the world's most serious earthquakes. The map clearly shows that there is a well-defined distribution pattern. Earthquakes occur in long, narrow belts. These belts include those which:

- encircle the whole of the Pacific Ocean.
- extend down the entire length of the mid-Atlantic Ocean.
- stretch across the continents of Europe and Asia, linking the Atlantic and Pacific Oceans.
- extend into the Pacific Ocean from the west coast of South America.

The location of the world's major centres of volcanic activity, including some recent eruptions, is shown on Figure 16.2. This map shows that volcanoes also occur in long narrow belts. The two most obvious belts:

- encircle the whole of the Pacific Ocean.
- extend down the entire length of the mid-Atlantic Ocean.

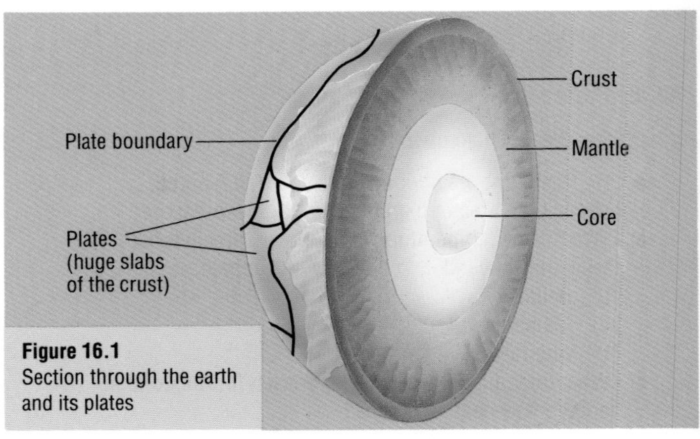

Figure 16.1 Section through the earth and its plates

The two maps show that earthquakes and volcanoes often occur at the same place on the earth's crust and in narrow *zones of activity*. If the earth were the size of an apple, its crust would be no thicker than the apple's skin. Underneath the crust is the *mantle* (Figure 16.1). Here temperatures are so high that rock exists in a semi-molten state. The crust is broken into some large and several smaller segments called *plates* (Figure 16.3) which float, like rafts, on the mantle. Heat from within the earth sets up convection currents which cause the plates on the surface to move, perhaps by only a few centimetres a year. Plates may either move away from, towards, or sideways past, neighbouring plates. Plates meet at *plate boundaries* and it is at these boundaries that most of the world's earthquakes, volcanic eruptions and high mountains ranges are located (compare Figure 16.3 with Figure 16.2). Very little activity takes place in the rigid centres of the plates.

Figure 16.2 World distribution of earthquakes and volcanoes

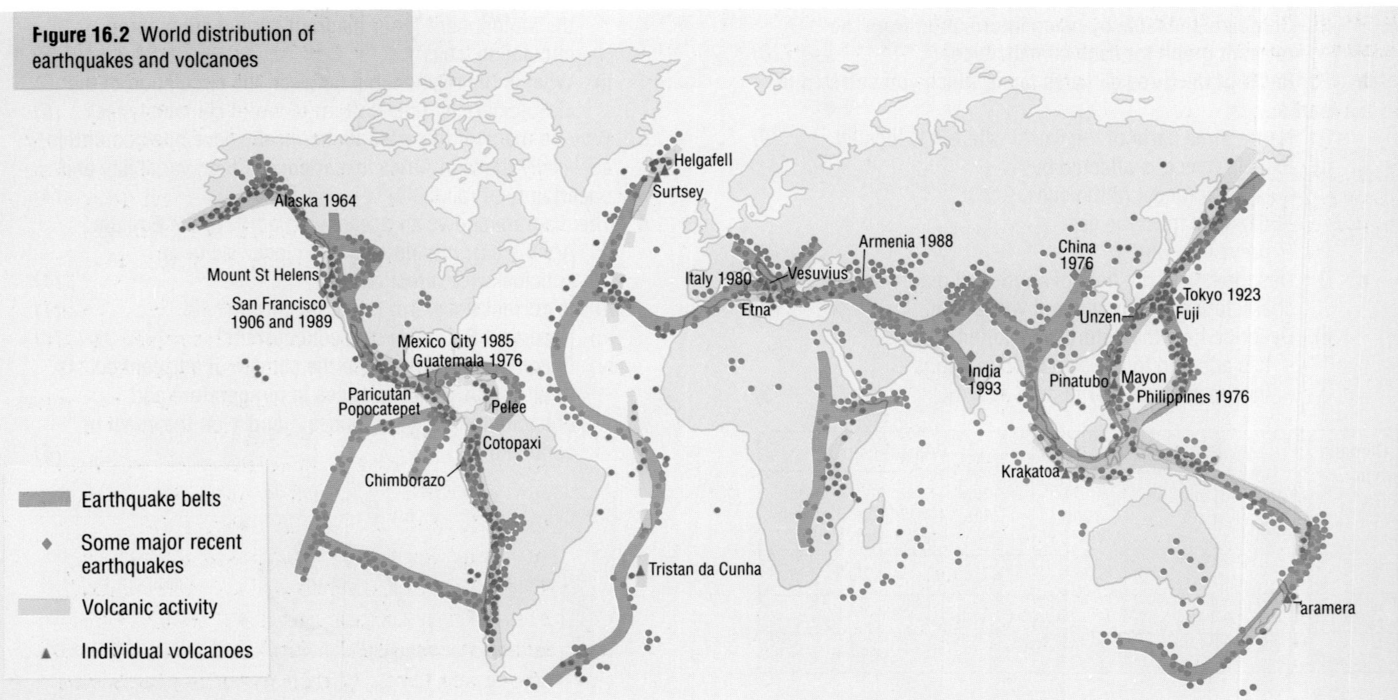

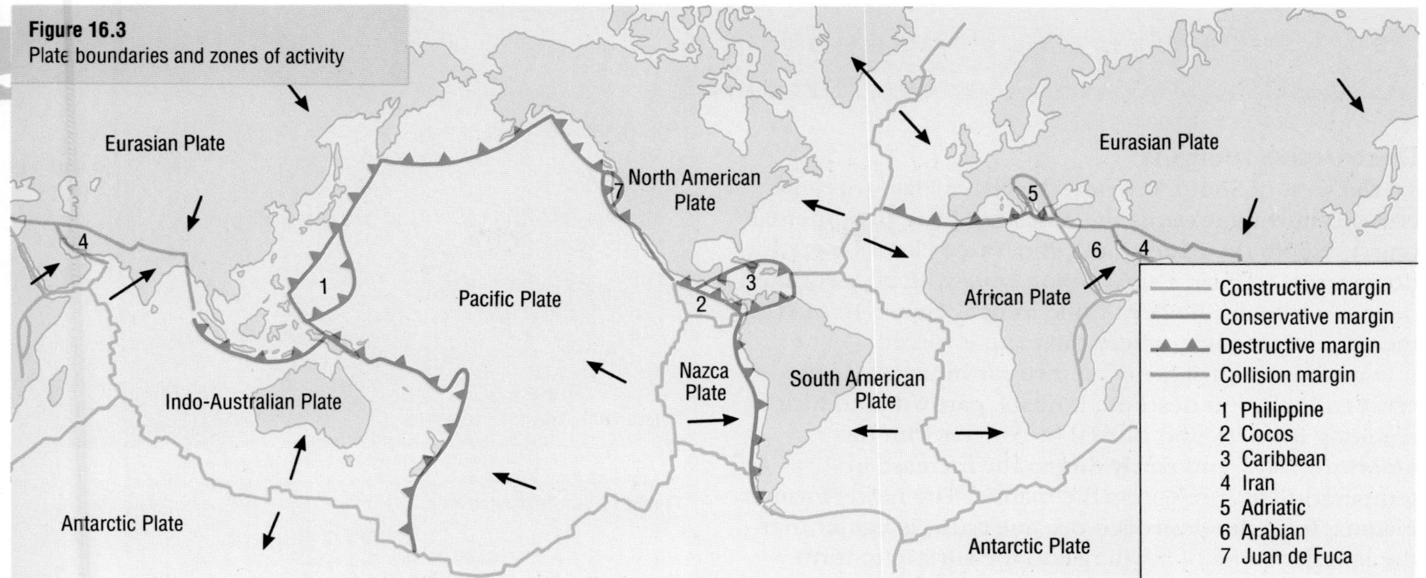

Figure 16.3
Plate boundaries and zones of activity

Type of plate boundary	Description of changes	Earthquake/volcanic activity	Examples
A Constructive margins	Two plates move away from each other. New oceanic crust appears, forming mid-ocean ridges with volcanoes	Gentle volcanic and earthquake activity	Mid-Atlantic Ridge, e.g. Iceland
B i) Destructive margins	Oceanic crust moves towards continental crust but being heavier sinks and is destroyed, forming deep-sea trenches and island arcs with volcanoes	Violent volcanic and earthquake activity	Nazca and South American Plates Cocos and North American Plates Juan de Fuca and North American Plates
ii) Collision zones	Two continental crusts collide and as neither can sink, are forced up into fold mountains	Earthquake activity (no volcanic activity)	Indo-Australian and Eurasian Plates, e.g. Himalayas
C Conservative margins	Two plates move sideways past each other – land is neither formed nor destroyed	Can be violent earthquake activity (no volcanic activity)	Pacific and North American Plates, e.g. San Andreas, California

Figure 16.4 Activities at the plate boundaries

Plates consist of two types of crust: *continental* and *oceanic*. Continental crust is older, lighter, is permanent and cannot sink. Oceanic crust is younger, heavier, can sink and is constantly being destroyed and replaced. It is these differences which account for the variation in landforms and the level of activity at plate boundaries (Figure 16.4).

Figure 16.5
The Mid-Atlantic Ridge, a constructive margin

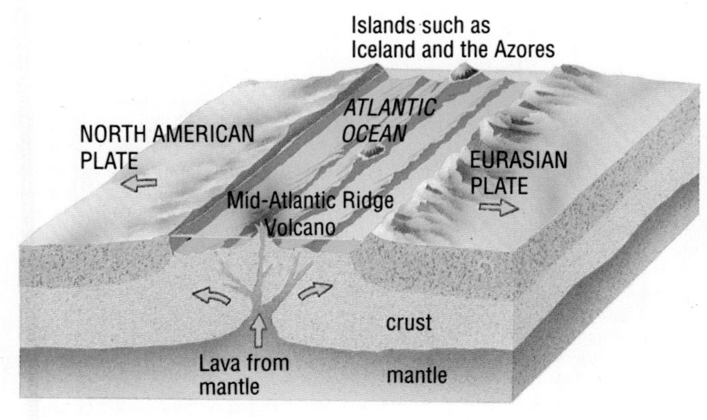

Constructive margins

At constructive margins, such as the Mid-Atlantic Ridge (Figure 16.5), two plates move away from each other. Molten rock, or magma, immediately rises to fill any possible 'gap', forming new oceanic crust. The Atlantic Ocean is widening by about 9 centimetres a year, which means that the Americas are moving away from Eurasia and Africa.

In November 1963 an Icelandic fishing crew reported an explosion under the sea south-west of the Westman Islands. This was followed by further explosions, accompanied by steam and ash, which gave birth to the island of Surtsey. The submarine eruptions initially built up an ash cone 130 metres high from the sea bed. In April 1964 the permanence of the island was guaranteed when lava began to flow from the central vent. When eruptions ended in 1967 the island measured 2.8 km^2 and rose 178 metres above sea level. Within months plants and insects had begun colonisation.

Destructive margins

To the west of South America, the Nazca Plate (oceanic crust) is moving towards the American Plate (continental crust). Where the plates meet, the Nazca Plate is forced downwards to form a *subduction zone* with an associated deep-sea trench (the Peru-Chile trench, Figure 16.6). The increase in pressure, where the plate is forced downwards, can trigger off severe earthquakes. As the crust continues to descend, it melts, partly due to heat resulting from friction caused by contact with the American Plate, and partly due to the increase in temperature as it re-enters the mantle. The newly-formed magma, from the destroyed oceanic crust, is lighter than the mantle. Some of it will rise to the surface to form volcanoes (Chimborazo and Cotopaxi) and long chains of fold mountains (Andes). Usually volcanic eruptions are at their most violent at destructive margins. Melting snow, caused by the eruption of Nevado del Ruiz in Colombia in 1985, created mudflows which killed 21,000 inhabitants of the town of Armero.

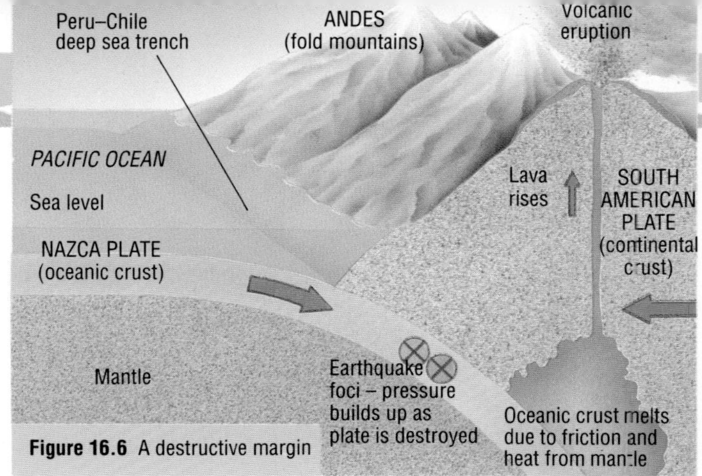

Figure 16.6 A destructive margin

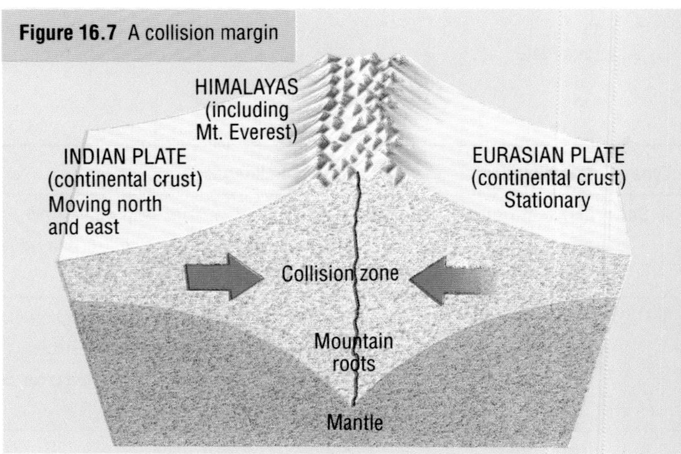

Figure 16.7 A collision margin

Collision margins

The Indian Plate is moving into the Eurasian Plate at a rate of 5 cm a year. As both plates consist of continental crust, neither can sink. The land between them has been buckled and pushed upwards to form the Himalayas (Figure 16.7). This movement, which is still taking place, accounts for massive earthquakes which periodically occur where the plates meet. Evidence suggests that Mount Everest is increasing in height. Less obvious, however, is the effect of the collision felt by the whole of India. In September 1993 an earthquake in central India caused the death of 22,000 people and left another 150,000 homeless (Figure 16.8).

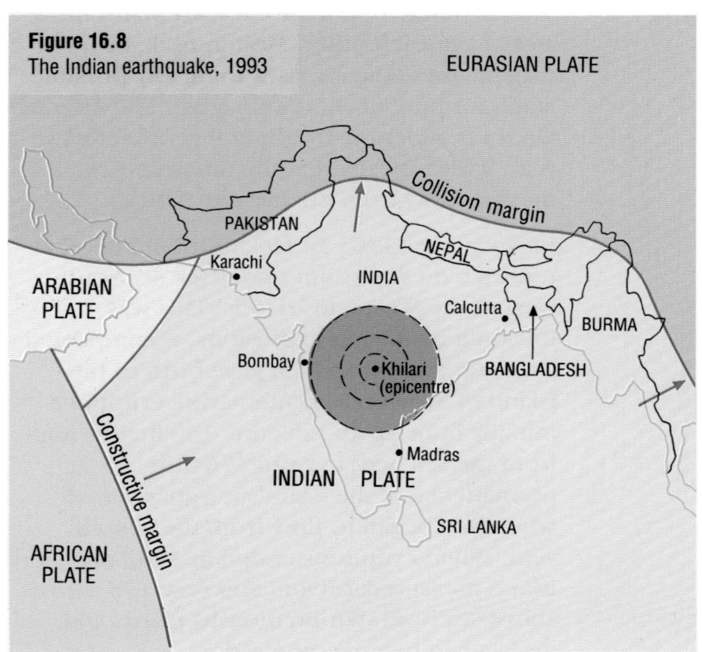

Figure 16.8 The Indian earthquake, 1993

Conservative margins

These margins are found where two plates are forced to slide past one another. Although crust is neither formed nor destroyed at this point, earthquakes can occur if the plates 'stick'. The San Andreas Fault, which passes through California, marks the junction of the Pacific and North American Plates (Figure 16.9). The American Plate moves more slowly than, and at a slight angle into, the Pacific Plate. Instead of the plates slipping past each other, they tend to stick, like a machine without oil. When sufficient pressure builds up, one plate is jerked forward, sending shockwaves to the surface. These shockwaves caused earthquakes in San Francisco in 1989 and in 1906, when the ground moved by 6 metres.

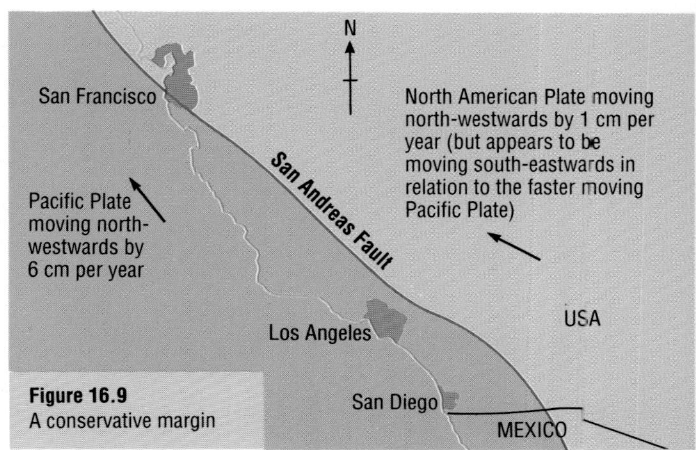

Figure 16.9 A conservative margin

Earthquakes

Earthquakes occur where two areas of the earth's crust try to move in different directions. If friction prevents movement between these two areas then pressure will build up. When pressure is eventually released by a sudden earth movement, the result is an earthquake. Earthquakes are measured on the *Richter* scale (Figure 16.10). Each level of magnitude on the scale is ten times greater than the level below it. This means that the Lisbon earthquake of 1755 was ten times stronger than the one which affected Mexico City in 1985 and nearly 100 times stronger than that which hit San Francisco in 1989.

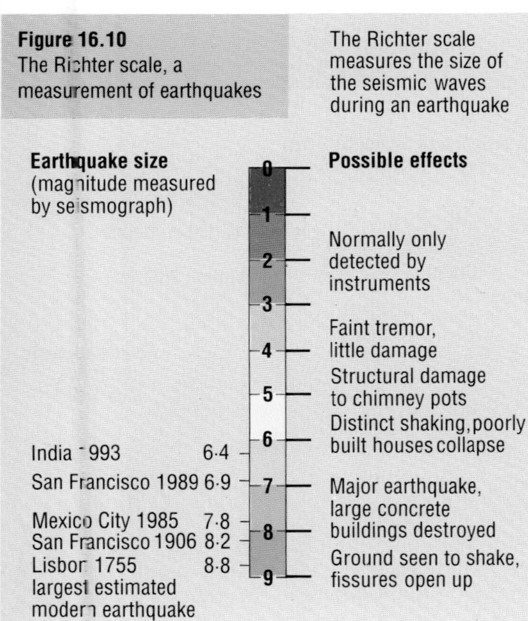

Figure 16.10
The Richter scale, a measurement of earthquakes

The Richter scale measures the size of the seismic waves during an earthquake

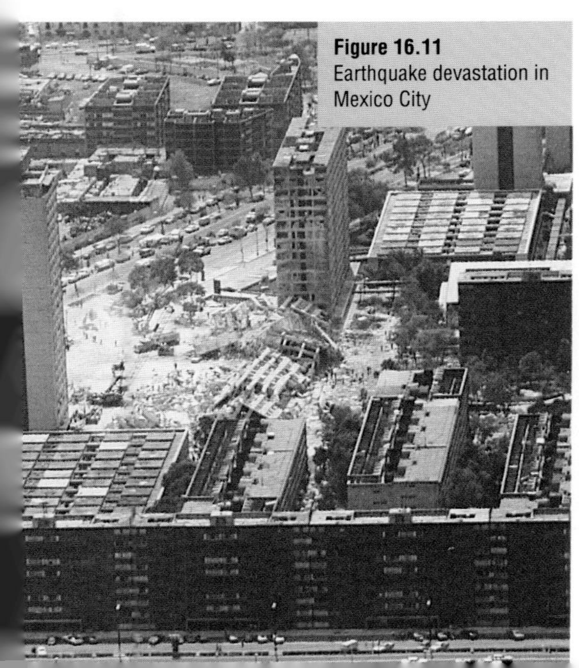

Figure 16.11
Earthquake devastation in Mexico City

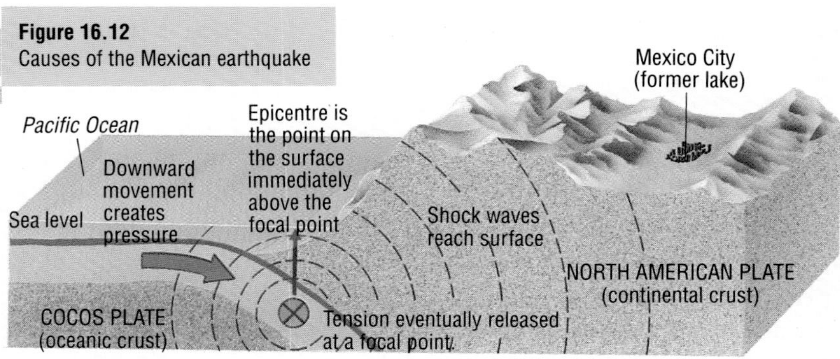

Figure 16.12
Causes of the Mexican earthquake

Mexico City, 1985

Two weeks before the Mexico City earthquake, two Mexican seismologists published a map showing that there was a 160 km gap which had been free of small earthquakes for several years along the junction of the Cocos and North American plates (Figure 16.12). It was probable that this lack of earthquake activity resulted in the build up of pressure that was suddenly released in September 1985. Although the epicentre was just off the west coast, shock waves reached Mexico City. Unfortunately, several parts of the city had been built upon silt and peat that had accumulated when the site was previously a shallow lake. The shock waves brought water to the surface, turning the silt into mud. As Mexico City 'wobbled like a jelly', over 1000 large buildings, all without rock foundations, collapsed and sank into the mud. Nearly 30 km^2 of the city was devastated (Figure 16.13).

Figure 16.13
The primary and secondary effects of the Mexican earthquake

Primary Effects

According to police figures, the quake had claimed 4596 lives by yesterday morning, with another 1500 people thought to be still trapped.

Four hundred buildings have been destroyed, 700 are severely damaged and 57 are on the verge of collapse. About 31,000 people are homeless.

At least three hospitals were among buildings either seriously damaged or destroyed with doctors and patients trapped under wreckage. Several churches had caved in only minutes before they would be filling for morning mass.

Secondary Effects

The confusion which dominated the first 24 hours of the earthquake, whose epicentre 250 miles south-west of Mexico City registered 7.8 on the Richter scale, continued yesterday. Fires caused by gas leaks added smoke to the normally polluted city air.

The three minutes of terror caused by the earthquake were followed by explosions as petrol stations blew up and fires were started by ruptured power and gas lines.

With rail, road and telephone links cut or badly disrupted, contact with nearby villages was impossible.

Thirty fishing vessels, mostly Colombian, were also reported missing, while reports from Spain listed 19 trawlers and four freighters as unaccounted for and feared sunk by waves which "boiled up" to heights reaching 20 metres.

Mexico City was struck by fresh tremors last night. Little extra damage was reported but the tremors hampered the rescue work by 50,000 troops, police and firemen already struggling with dwindling supplies of water and medicine against fire, fear of disease and the cries of the trapped and injured. The threat of diseases from contaminated water was increasing.

Meanwhile it was suggested that 1 million jobs were lost due to destroyed factories and shops.

Volcanic eruptions

Mount St Helens

Figure 16.14 shows the causes of the Mount St Helens eruption. The Juan de Fuca Plate (oceanic crust) moves eastwards towards the North American Plate (continental crust), and is forced downwards. This movement creates friction which produces earthquakes and, due to an increase in temperature, destroys the oceanic crust. Volcanic eruptions take place where, and when, the magma rises to the earth's surface. Through the centuries, a series of volcanic eruptions had formed the Cascades mountain range. Mount St Helens (2950 metres high) is one peak within this range. As, by 1980, it had been inactive for over 120 years most people living near to it did not accept that one day it might erupt again.

Figure 16.14
Causes of Mount St Helens eruption

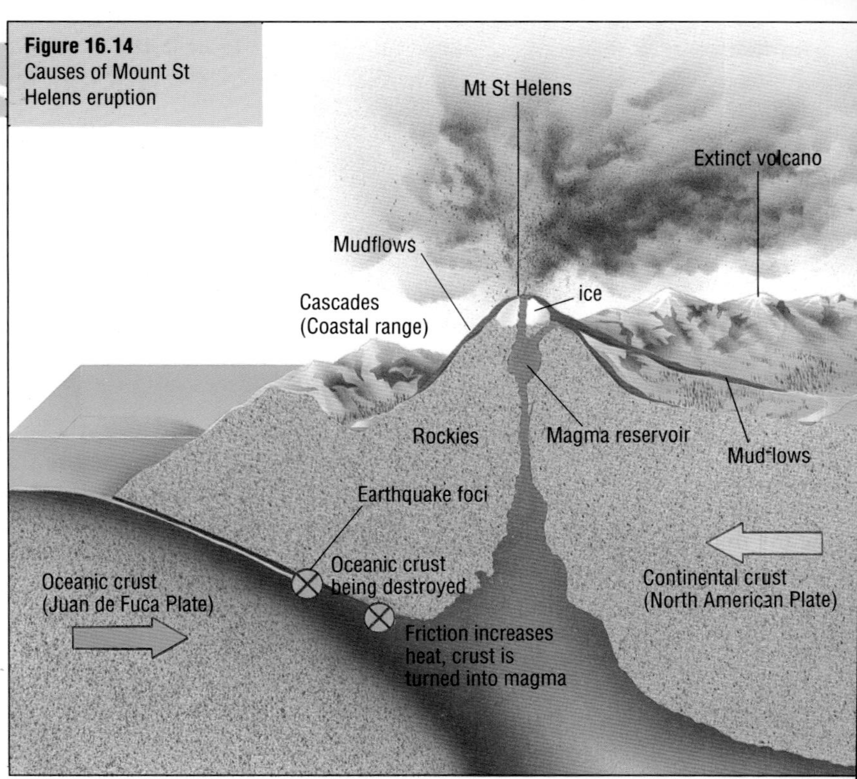

Timetable of events

Spring 1980

On 20 March there was a minor earthquake which measured 4.1 on the Richter scale. There were many more tremors over the next few days until, on 27 March, there was a small eruption of steam and ash. Minor eruptions occurred daily, attracting an increasing number of tourists. By early May the north side of the mountain began bulging by 1.5 m a day, indicating a build-up of magma and an increase in pressure. This reached a peak on the morning of 18 May.

18 May

0830 hours Ash and steam erupted

0832 hours An earthquake (magnitude 5 on the Richter scale) caused the bulge to move forwards and downwards (Figure 16.15a). The released material formed a landslide of rock, glacier ice and soil. This raced downhill to fill in Spirit Lake and then, reinforced by the water displaced from this lake, moved rapidly down the northern fork of the Toutle Valley (Figure 16.16). The mudflow reached Baker Camp, but floodwater continued down the valley and sediment blocked the port of Portland on the Columbia River.

0833 hours The exposed magma exploded sideways sending out blast waves of volcanic gas, steam and dust (called a *nuée ardente*) which moved northwards for 25 km. Within this range every form of life – vegetation and animal – was destroyed (Figure 16.17).

Rest of morning A series of eruptions ejected gas, ash and volcanic 'bombs' (rocks). The thicker ash rose 20 km and drifted eastwards before settling. Inhabitants at Yakima, 120 km away, could only go out if they wore face masks.

Three days later The volcanic 'plume' (cloud) of fine ash reached the east coast of the USA.

Several days later The ash had completely encircled the world.

Figure 16.15 The eruption of Mount St Helens

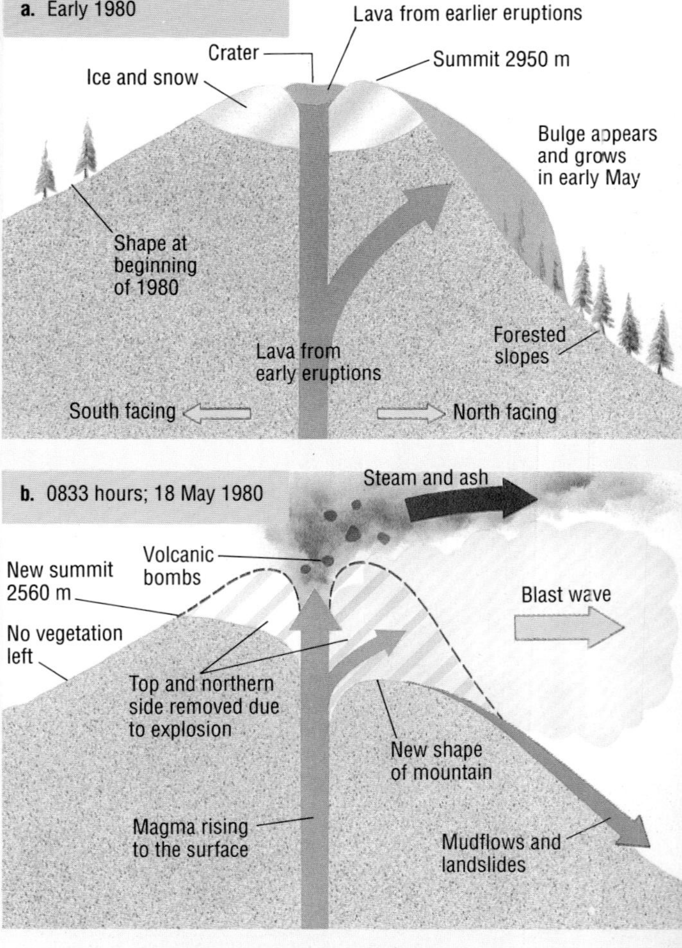

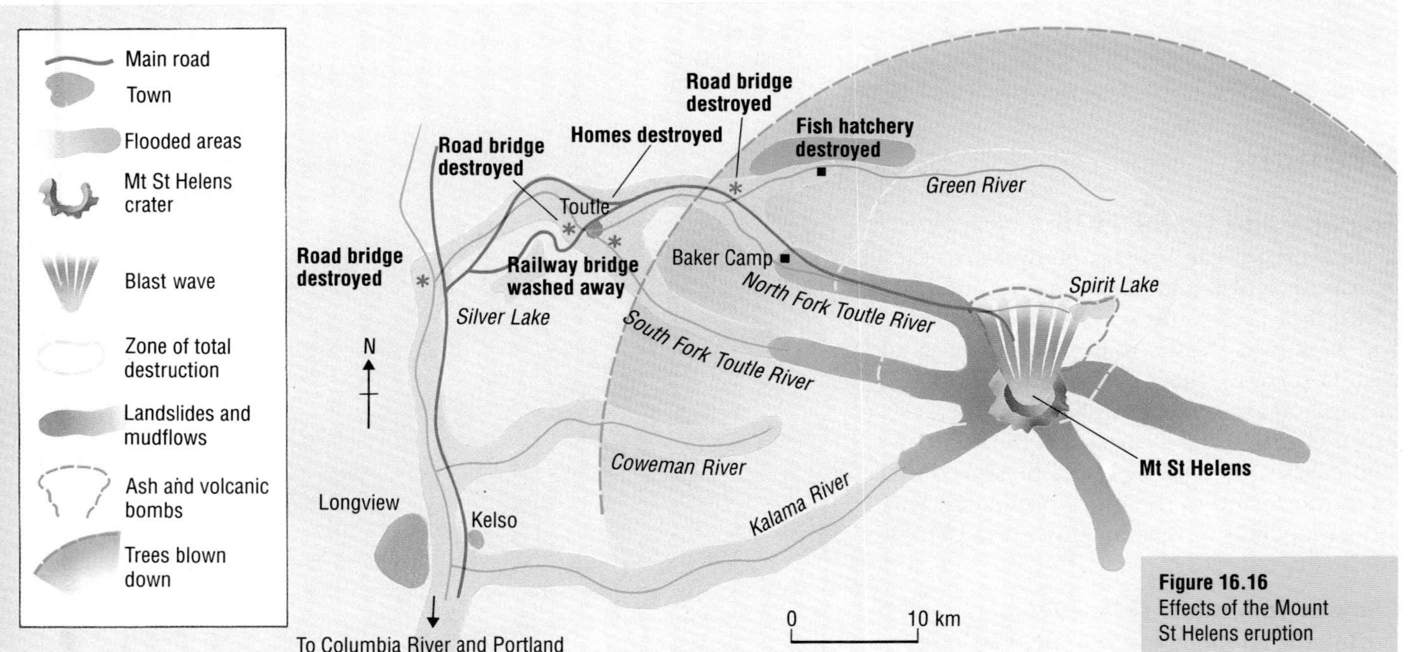

Figure 16.16
Effects of the Mount St Helens eruption

Figure 16.17
Destruction resulting from Mount St Helens eruption

Figure 16.18
View of Mount St Helens crater following eruption

Consequences of the eruption (Figure 16.16)

Mount St Helens itself had been reduced by 390 m to 2560 m. A crater (more like an amphitheatre in appearance) 3 km long and 0.5 km deep had been created on the north facing slope (Figure 16.18).

Human life Sixty-one deaths were reported, most of them caused by the release of poisonous gases which accompanied the blast waves.

Settlements Several logging camps were destroyed – luckily, it being a Sunday, no-one was working or living there.

Rivers and lakes Ash which fell into rivers and lakes raised the water temperature, while sediment and mud also choked channels. The combined effect was the death of all fish, including those in a hatchery, and the loss of 250 km of former top-class salmon and trout rivers. Spirit Lake was filled in.

Communications Floodwaters washed away several road and railway bridges. Falling ash hindered the smooth running of car engines in three states.

Forestry Every tree in the 250 km² forest and lying within the 25 km blast zone north of the volcano was totally flattened and destroyed (Figure 16.17). Trees, carried down by rivers in flood, caused a log jam 60 km away. Some 10 million trees had to be replanted.

Services Electricity supplies were interrupted and telephone wires cut.

Wildlife As with the trees, nothing survived within the blast zone.

Farming Estimates suggested that 12 per cent of the total crop was ruined by settling dust. Fruit and alfalfa were hardest hit. Crops and livestock on valley floors were lost due to flooding.

Drought

England and Wales 1976

In an average year, due to the uneven distribution of rainfall in Britain (Figure 15.6), there is a water surplus in the north and west, and a water deficit in the south and east. Reservoirs, therefore, had to be built in the upland areas of Central Wales, the Pennines, the Lake District and the Scottish Highlands so that water could be stored and then transferred to the more populated and industrial areas of Britain. However, 1976 was not an average year.

Climatic conditions 1975–1976

During the summer of 1975, depressions which usually bring cloud and rain from the Atlantic were diverted to the north of Britain. The result was a hot, dry summer causing reservoirs and underground supplies of water to run low. The winter of 1975–76 remained mild and dry. Apart from a wet May in northern England, the dry weather continued throughout the country until the last few days of August 1976. During June, July and August, all of England and Wales received over 30 per cent more than their expected amounts of sunshine, with some areas in eastern England getting almost 50 per cent more. Water, already in the soil and reservoirs, was lost due to the high rates of evaporation. Rainfall totals were also well below average. Figure 16.19 shows that only the extreme north-west of England received anywhere near its usual amount of rainfall.

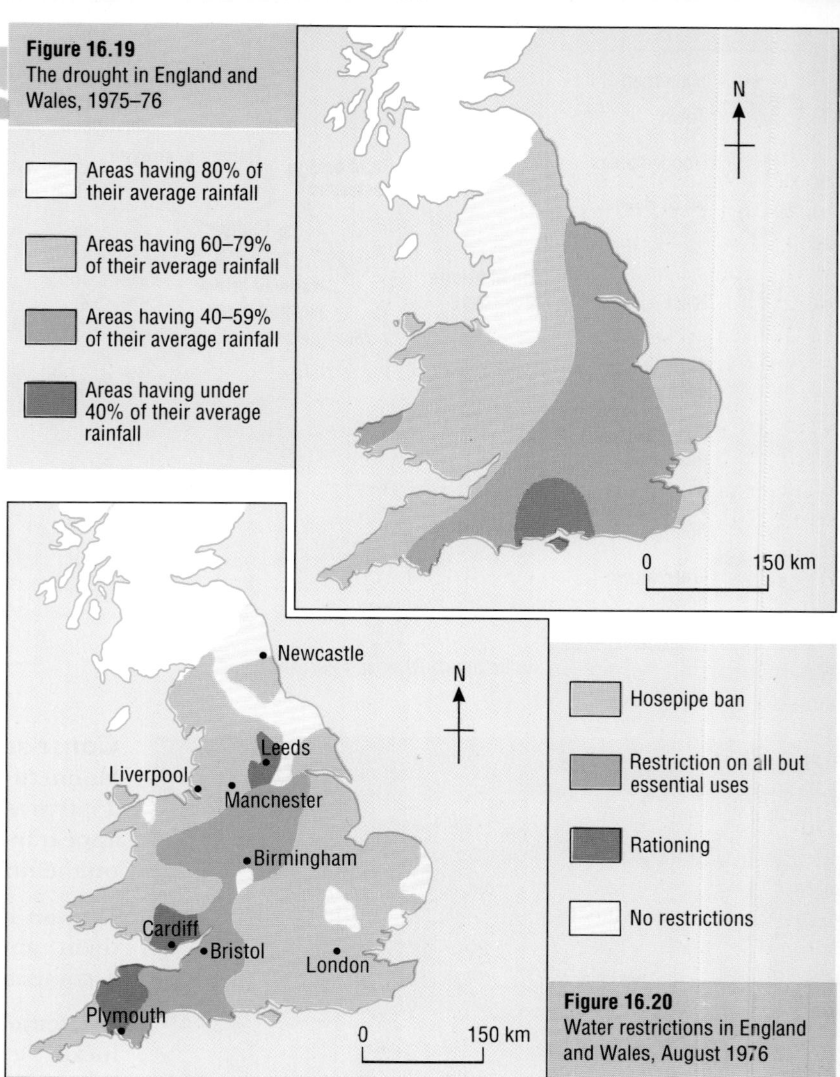

Figure 16.19
The drought in England and Wales, 1975–76

Figure 16.20
Water restrictions in England and Wales, August 1976

Figure 16.21
Haweswater Reservoir (Lake District) during the 1976 drought

Consequences of the drought

Figure 16.20 shows some of the problems caused by the drought:

- A hosepipe ban for gardens and cars was imposed in some areas by June, and by August several parts of the country were affected by rationing. Parts of Devon could only obtain water through standpipes for two weeks in late August.
- People were encouraged to take showers rather than baths, and even to share their bathwater.
- Clay soils in southern England dried out and shrank. This caused buildings to be damaged as their foundations moved.
- Farmers were badly hit as grass turned brown and stopped growing, and crops wilted under the hot sun. Yields of all crops fell, there was insufficient grass for cattle, and winter fodder was in short supply due to a poor hay harvest.
- Recreation and sport were affected. Cricket pitches and bowling greens could not be watered, while the drop in the level of lakes and reservoirs curtailed water-based activities.
- In southern England areas of heathland became tinder dry. Fires broke out and large areas were destroyed. Visitors in northern England and Wales were asked to avoid coniferous forests in the hope of reducing the fire risk.
- Two reservoirs, Haweswater in Cumbria (Figure 16.21) and Derwent in Derbyshire, fell to their lowest levels since they had been built. In both cases 'lost' villages, which had been drowned as the reservoirs filled, were exposed again.

Some parts of Britain are occasionally inconvenienced by a lack of rain. In comparison, drought is a major environmental hazard across an estimated 30 per cent of the earth's land surface (Figure 16.22). Since the late 1960s, the worst affected area has been the Sahel.

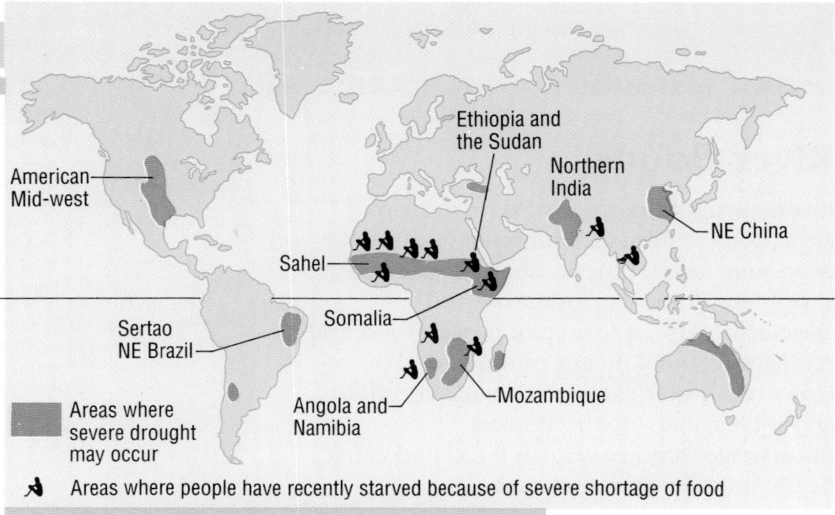

Figure 16.22
World distribution of drought-stricken areas

The Sahel

The Sahel is a narrow belt of land which extends across Africa, and which borders the southern edge of the Sahara Desert. Normally its climate can be described as semi-arid, a transition between the tropical continental region (page 200) and the desert. Rainfall is confined to only one or two months. The total amount of rain and the length of the wet season are both very unreliable (page 206). For some years the total rainfall may all fall in several downpours where the water is immediately lost through surface run-off. During other years the rains may fail altogether. The present drought, and associated famine, began in the Sahel in 1968. In some places it has continued since then almost without interruption. Pictures of starving and dying people have become all too common in our television news reports (Figure 16.23). Some of the worst drought affected places have been:

- 1968 to 1973 – mainly the western Sahel countries.
- 1983 – Ethiopia (Figure 16.24). Thousands of people who lived in the northern district of Tigre were forced to leave their homes to try to find food. Each day up to 3000 Tigreans set off on a walk of up to six weeks over mountains, through deserts with temperatures over 45°C, and without food and water, to reach refugee camps in the Sudan. Many died on the way (an estimated 200,000) through hunger, exhaustion and attack by enemy planes. A fifth of those who stayed behind in Tigre did so because they were too weak to move.
- 1984 to 1991 – There were three major droughts and famines in the Sudan (interrupted by serious flooding in the capital of Khartoum in 1989).
- 1990s – Somalia. This led to UN intervention.

Drought can now be detected from space. Satellite images can show the 'greenness' of an area and therefore the level of its vegetation cover. From this data, maps can be drawn and computer models produced to show 'average' vegetation conditions. Later satellite images will show changes in this vegetation cover. If there are signs of a decrease, presumably caused by a lack of rain, then national governments and international relief agencies can be alerted to possible future food shortages. This, hopefully, will give the afflicted nation time to find alternative supplies of food.

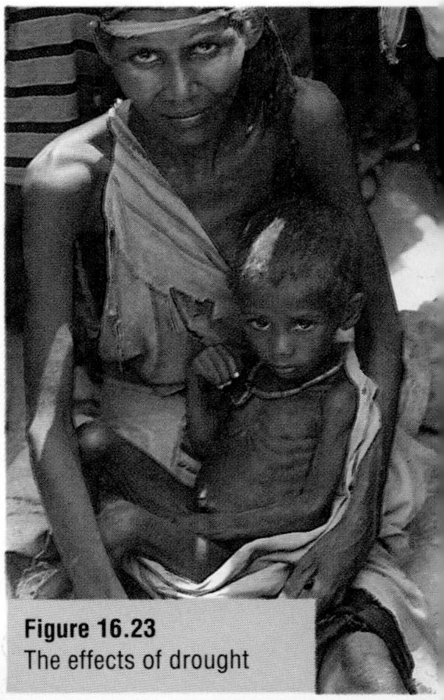

Figure 16.23
The effects of drought

Figure 16.24
Refugees leaving Tigre during the 1980s

River floods

Rivers throughout the world provide an attraction for human settlement and economic development. They provide a water supply for domestic, industrial and agricultural use, a source of power, food and recreation, and a means of transport. However, under extreme climatic conditions, and increasingly due to human mismanagement, rivers can flood and cause death and widespread damage.

Lynmouth 1952

One of the worst floods in living memory in Britain devastated the North Devon village of Lynmouth in 1952 (Figure 16.26).

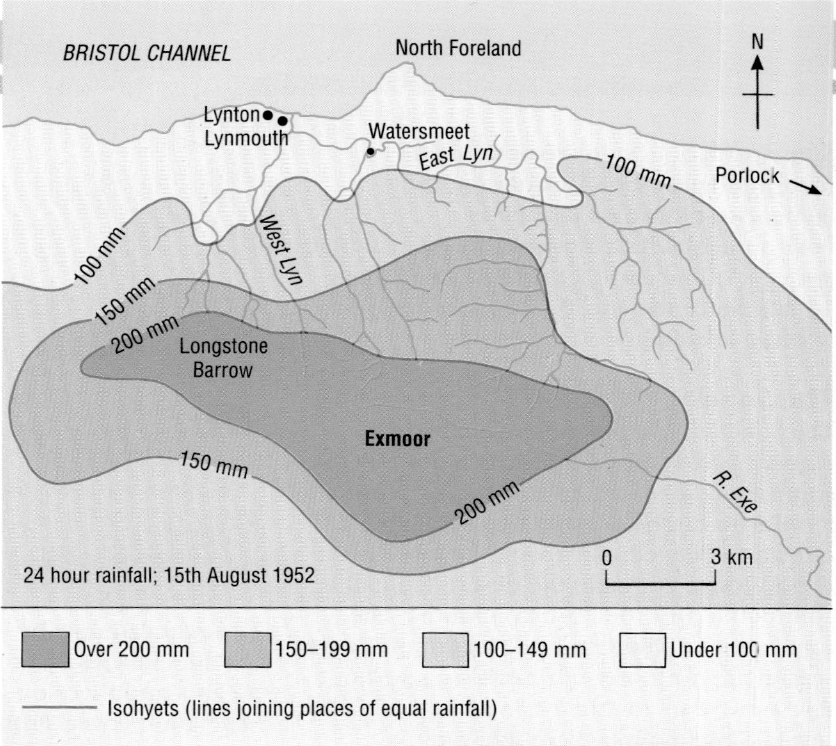

BRISTOL CHANNEL
North Foreland
N
Lynton
Lynmouth
Watersmeet
East Lyn
West Lyn
100 mm
Porlock
100 mm
150 mm
200 mm
Longstone Barrow
Exmoor
150 mm
200 mm
R. Exe
0 3 km
24 hour rainfall; 15th August 1952

Over 200 mm | 150–199 mm | 100–149 mm | Under 100 mm

Isohyets (lines joining places of equal rainfall)

Figure 16.25
Drainage basin of East and West Lyn

Figure 16.26
Devastation in Lynmouth, 1952

Exmoor — impermeable rock causing surface run-off

August very wet. Rained 12 of first 14 days. Ground totally saturated. Any extra rain meant surface run-off.

Heavy thunderstorms and frontal rain: over 200 mm in 14 hours (some parts over 300 mm). One of the three heaviest falls of rain ever recorded in Britain.

No recording or early flood warning system

Peak discharge of River Lyn so great that only twice in the last century had it ever been exceeded by River Thames (with its drainage basin 100 times larger)

Steep river gradient. Some 50-tonne boulders moved by the river

1 Small catchment basin and
2 Narrow, steep-sided valleys; water soon collects in rivers

N

Bridges trapped boulders and trees causing temporary dams which later 'broke' causing a wave 12 m high to travel downstream at 30 km/hr

West Lyn River

Lynmouth Hill

East Lyn River

Carried more water than West Lyn River but did not have to change direction in Lynmouth

Church

LYNMOUTH

River had been diverted and its channel made narrower due to building of tourist accommodation and amenities. It flowed through a narrow culvert

Lyndale Hotel

Road

Flood occurred at night while people asleep

West Lyn River changed direction to an older course: triangle of destruction

Road

Cliffs

Bristol Channel

Delta of River Lyn enlarged after 1952 flood

Lynmouth:
34 dead, 1000 homeless,
90 houses and hotels destroyed,
130 cars and 19 boats lost

Figure 16.27
Causes and effects of the River Lyn flood, 15 August 1952

Course of West Lyn River before flood

H Lyndale Hotel

B1 Bridge over West Lyn River

B2 Bridge over East Lyn River

Figure 16.28
River Lyn changing course while in flood

Figure 16.29
The River Lyn floods, 1952

"Cause of the 1952 flood

The first fortnight of August 1952 was exceptionally wet throughout southwest England. This meant that if any more rain fell on the already saturated soils of Exmoor it would very quickly reach the various tributaries of the East and West Lyn and, within a few hours, would be rushing through Lynmouth since this village lay at the junction of the two rivers. Tragically for the people of Lynmouth an unprecedented deluge of rain fell on the 15th August – one of the three heaviest falls of rain ever recorded in 24 hours in the British Isles. Thunderstorms associated with a small frontal depression produced torrential rain as the Exmoor plateau squeezed every drop of rainfall from the overlying moist atmosphere: 9 inches [229 mm] was measured near Longstone Barrow about 5 miles [8 km] south of Lynmouth, and some localities may have suffered as much as 12 inches [305 mm]. Over 3,000 million gallons of water fell into the drainage area of the two Lyn rivers. The river channels could not cope with such an overwhelming amount of water and devastating floods were inevitable."

[Keene and Elsom]

Figure 16.30 Lynmouth in 1993

A West Lyn allowed to follow its natural route (the one taken during the flood)
B Flood plain left open to take excess water
C Larger bridges with much larger spans
D Land where hotel was is now left open. (Car park)
E East Lyn channel has been straightened to allow flood water to flow off more quickly

A flood of this size may occur only once in every 100 or even 200 years. There were several physical reasons why the situation of Lynmouth was a flood risk. Figure 16.28 shows a small river basin with a high drainage density (page 168) in an area which can expect heavy rainfall. The rocks in the basin are impermeable, and the valley sides and the gradient of the rivers are both steep (Figure 16.27). The flood risk had, however, been increased by human activity (Figure 16.27). Even so, no-one was prepared for the events of 15 August 1952 (Figure 16.29). The real cause of the damage was the huge volume of water which enabled the West Lyn to move gigantic boulders and to transport vast amounts of material. The river also changed its course so that it flowed through the centre of the village (Figure 16.28).

The flood has had a lasting impact upon the village, both physically and emotionally. Lynmouth has a different appearance today, as it was rebuilt to try to ensure the safety of its inhabitants rather than to try to recapture all of its former character. The flood management plan has, to date, managed to cope with any excess water in the Lyn drainage basin despite exceptionally heavy rainfall on three occasions since it was implemented (Figure 16.30).

Coastal floods

Bangladesh

May 1985

"Three days after the tropical cyclone hit the coastal islands of Bangladesh, countless bodies are floating in the Bay of Bengal. Hundreds of survivors on bamboo rafts and floating roof tops, stalked by sharks and crocodiles, are awaiting rescue. The Red Cross suggested that the tidal wave, 9 m in height and extending 150 km inland, may have claimed the lives of 40,000 people. An official source in Hatia claimed that 6000 people, many in their sleep, were washed out to sea and the only survivors were those who climbed to the top of palm trees and clung on despite the 180 km per hour winds. No links have yet been made with the more remote islands. Already there is the threat of typhoid and cholera, as fresh water has been contaminated. Famine could result as the rice crop has been lost, and it will take next year's monsoon rains to wash the salt out of the soil. Thousands of animals and most of the coastal fishing fleet seem likely to have been lost. The people of Bangladesh, already amongst the world's poorest, will be even more destitute."

Tropical cyclones (typhoons), similar to the one described above, occur mainly in autumn. One storm in 1991 killed 150,000 people.

Coastal areas can also be affected by flooding caused by the rivers Ganges, Jumana (called the Brahmaputra in India) and Meghna (Figure 16.34). In a geographical sense these rivers created the country by carrying soil from the Himalayas and forming a vast delta. The country owes its continued existence to the water which the rivers bring down and which is needed by the two main crops of rice and jute. The rivers, when in flood, also threaten the country's existence. In both 1987 and 1988, flood water in the rivers rose by over 8 metres in ten days (Figure 16.31). Over the two years, 3000 people died, farm animals were drowned, and homes and crops destroyed. Flooding in Bangladesh appears to be increasing, both in frequency and severity.

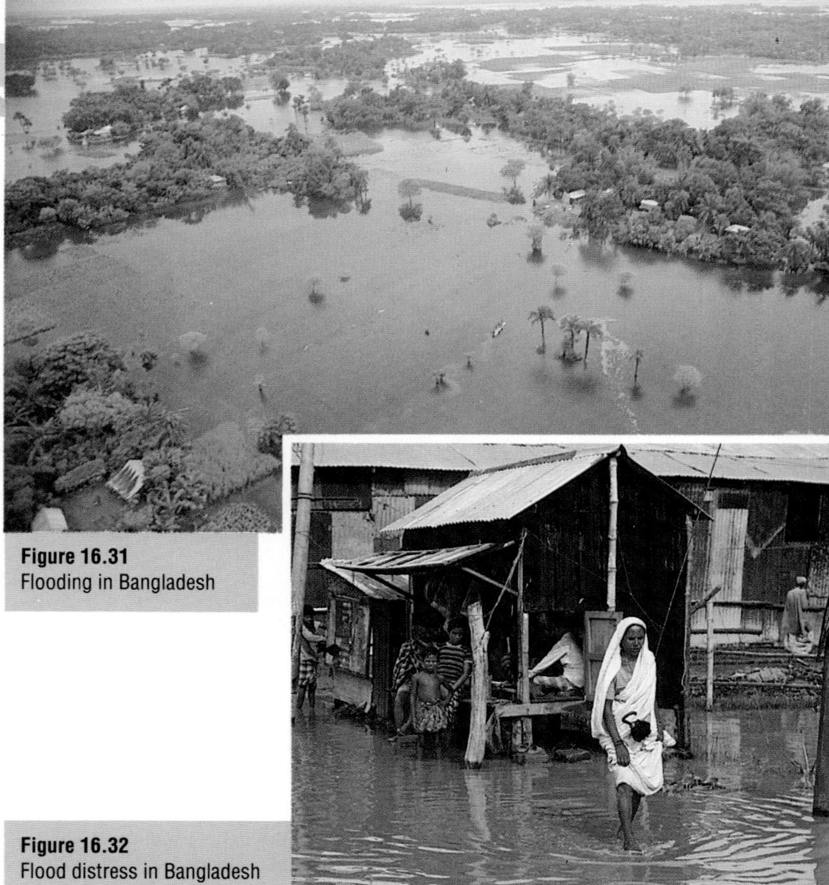

Figure 16.31
Flooding in Bangladesh

Figure 16.32
Flood distress in Bangladesh

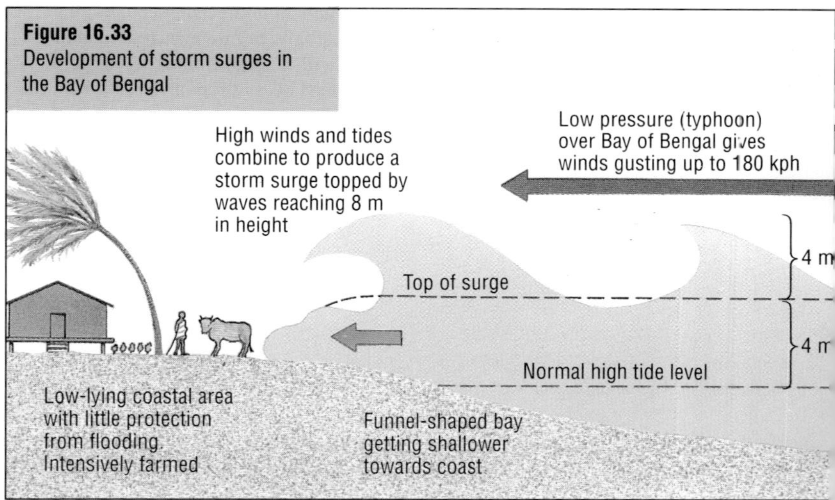
High winds and tides combine to produce a storm surge topped by waves reaching 8 m in height
Low pressure (typhoon) over Bay of Bengal gives winds gusting up to 180 kph
4 m
Top of surge
4 m
Normal high tide level
Low-lying coastal area with little protection from flooding. Intensively farmed
Funnel-shaped bay getting shallower towards coast

Figure 16.33
Development of storm surges in the Bay of Bengal

Why are coastal areas prone to flooding?

Bangladesh is trapped between two sets of floods: one caused by tidal surges and a rising sea level, and the other by rivers (Figure 16.34).

- Silt, deposited at the mouth of the Ganges and the other rivers, has formed a large delta (page 175). As the silt accumulated upwards and outwards, it created many flat islands which divide the several rivers into numerous distributaries. As the marshy islands are ideal for rice growing, they have attracted large numbers of farmers. Further deposition of silt blocks the main channels and increases the flood risk by raising the beds of the rivers. Flooding is most likely to occur in late summer following the heavy, seasonal monsoon rains and snow melt in the Himalayas. Deforestation in the Himalayas may be a contributory factor.

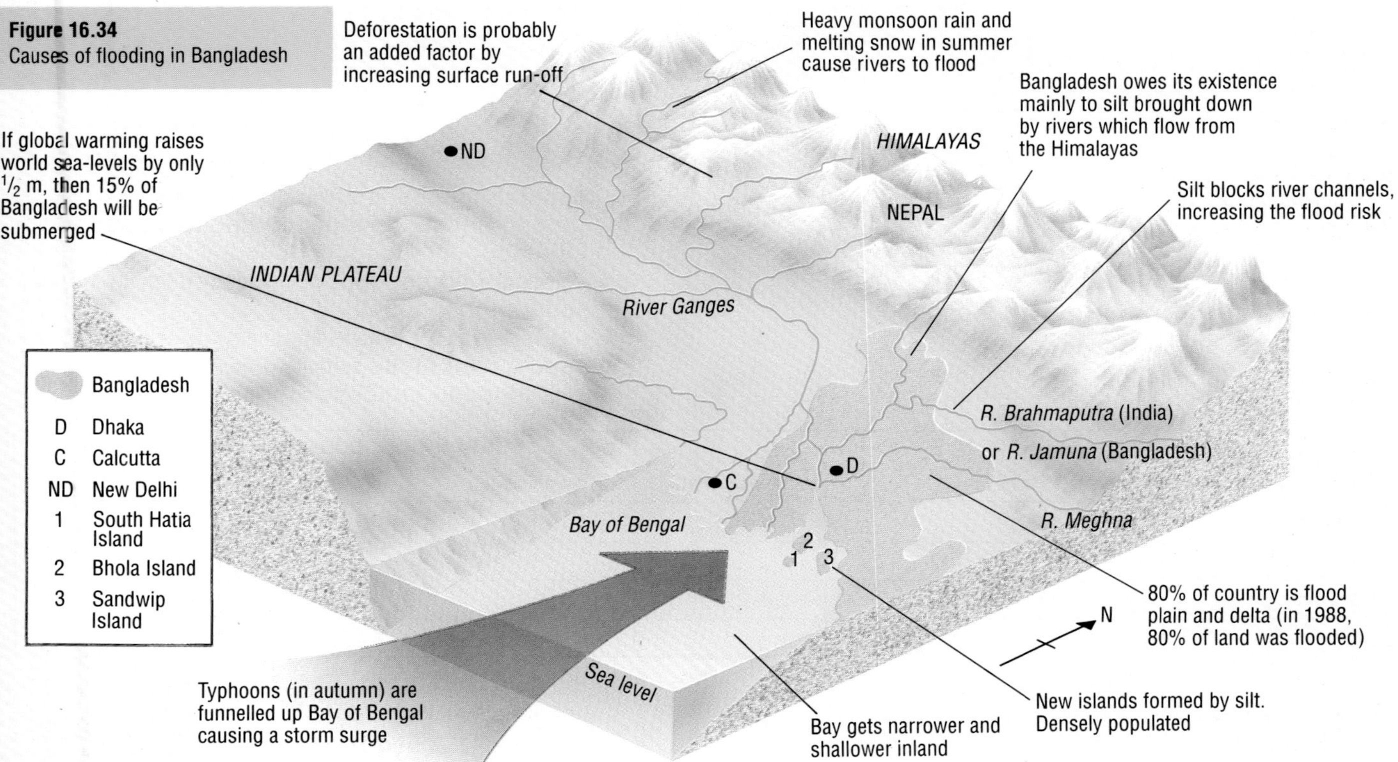
Deforestation is probably an added factor by increasing surface run-off
Heavy monsoon rain and melting snow in summer cause rivers to flood
Bangladesh owes its existence mainly to silt brought down by rivers which flow from the Himalayas
If global warming raises world sea-levels by only 1/2 m, then 15% of Bangladesh will be submerged
ND
HIMALAYAS
NEPAL
Silt blocks river channels, increasing the flood risk
INDIAN PLATEAU
River Ganges
Bangladesh
D Dhaka
C Calcutta
ND New Delhi
1 South Hatia Island
2 Bhola Island
3 Sandwip Island
R. Brahmaputra (India)
or R. Jamuna (Bangladesh)
D
C
Bay of Bengal
R. Meghna
1 2 3
80% of country is flood plain and delta (in 1988, 80% of land was flooded)
N
Sea level
Typhoons (in autumn) are funnelled up Bay of Bengal causing a storm surge
Bay gets narrower and shallower inland
New islands formed by silt. Densely populated

Figure 16.34
Causes of flooding in Bangladesh

- As tropical cyclones are funnelled up the Bay of Bengal, the force of the wind increases and water is pushed northwards. Towards Bangladesh, the Bay of Bengal becomes narrower and the sea shallower (due to deposition of silt by the rivers), so that the water builds up to form a *storm surge* (Figure 16.33). The surge may be 4 metres in height and topped by waves reaching another 4 metres. The wall of water sweeps over the flat, defenceless islands of the delta carrying away the flimsy buildings and any life-form in its path. Local inhabitants, many without telephones or televisions, may not get any advance warning or, even if they do, they cannot find land high enough upon which to escape the rising water.
- Although Bangladesh's contribution to global warming is minimal (page 226), the effects of this process upon the country are expected to be considerable. As global temperatures increase and ice caps melt, the predicted rise in the world's sea-level will result in many parts of Bangladesh, including the whole delta region, being totally submerged. For every few centimetres that sea-level rises, the more frequent and serious will flooding be along the coast of Bangladesh.

What can be done to reduce the flood risk?

In the USA levees (flood banks) have been built to try to stop the Mississippi river from flooding. In the Netherlands, large dykes have been constructed to protect the land from being flooded by the sea. Both schemes were expensive to implement and are expensive to maintain. Similar schemes have recently been proposed for Bangladesh (Figure 16.35), but, unlike the USA and the Netherlands, Bangladesh is one of the world's poorest of countries. Three different proposals have been made:

1 That a massive scheme, financed by the World Bank, be implemented, to construct flood banks to protect the land from coastal and river flooding. The scheme does not make any provision for the maintenance of the flood banks, while the 1993 Mississippi floods suggest that attempts to try to control flooding often only increase its effects.

2 That the early warning system be improved and more shelters above the expected flood level be provided.

3 That flooding should be allowed since it is essential for agriculture and coastal fishing, but to have some control, through appropriate technology (page 123), over the flooding process.

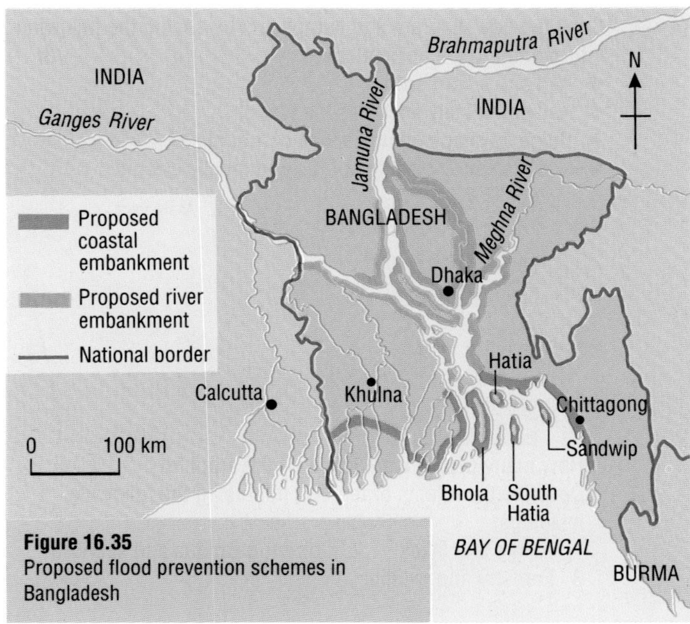
Brahmaputra River
INDIA
Ganges River
INDIA
N
Jamuna River
Meghna River
BANGLADESH
Proposed coastal embankment
Proposed river embankment
National border
Dhaka
Hatia
Calcutta
Khulna
Chittagong
Sandwip
0 100 km
Bhola
South Hatia
BAY OF BENGAL
BURMA

Figure 16.35
Proposed flood prevention schemes in Bangladesh

QUESTIONS

1 *(Pages 220 to 212)*

a What are plates? What causes them to move? *(2)*

b Give three differences between continental and oceanic crust. *(3)*

c Copy and complete the following table by:

i) naming the two types of plate involved (continental or oceanic).

ii) giving the direction of movement (away from, towards or sideways past).

iii) giving an actual example or location.

iv) putting one tick in the earthquake column.

v) putting one tick in the volcano column. *(5 x 4)*

Plate margin	Two types of plates involved	Direction of plate movement	Example/location	Earthquake			Volcano		
				Violent	Less Violent	Rare	Violent	Less Violent	Rare
Constructive									
Destructive									
Collision									
Conservative									

2 *(Page 213)*

a i) What is an earthquake?

ii) How are earthquakes measured?

iii) Why is an earthquake of 7.0 on the Richter scale 100 times more severe than one which measures 5.0? *(3)*

b i) Name two plates that meet off the west coast of Mexico.

ii) Which town was closest to the epicentre?

iii) Why was this town not badly damaged? *(3)*

c i) Describe the primary effects of the earthquake. *(3)*

ii) Describe the secondary effects of the earthquake. *(3)*

iii) What could be done to minimise the effects of any future earthquake? *(2)*

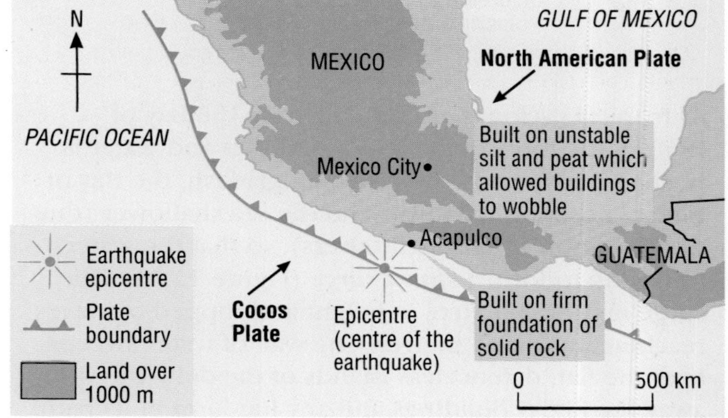

3 *(Pages 214 and 215)*

a Why did Mount St Helens erupt in 1980? *(2)*

b Copy the flow diagram and complete it by adding the following information to the correct boxes: *(8)*

- ◆ Ash and steam erupts.
- ◆ Ash completely encircles the world.
- ◆ Bulge develops on north side of mountain.
- ◆ Gas, ash and volcanic bombs continually ejected.
- ◆ Earthquake causes bulge to move outwards.
- ◆ Ash plume reaches east coast of USA.
- ◆ Blast wave from main explosion kills everything within 25 km to north.
- ◆ Landslides, mudflows and floodwaters affect surrounding area.

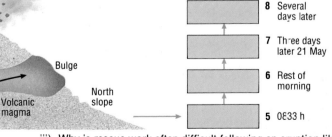

1 Spring 1980
2 18 May 0830 h
3 0832 h
4 0832 h
5 0833 h
6 Rest of morning
7 Three days later 21 May
8 Several days later

Main vent
Bulge
Mt St Helens
Volcanic magma
North slope

c i) How many people were killed by the eruption? *(1)*

ii) Describe the effects of the eruption using the following headings:
1. Rivers and lakes 2. Communications and services
3. Forestry and wildlife *(6)*

iii) Why is rescue work often difficult following an eruption like that of Mount St Helens? *(3)*

4 *(Page 216)*

a i) Which parts of England and Wales usually get the most rainfall? *(1)*
ii) Which parts received most of their usual amount of rain in the summers of 1975 and 1976? *(1)*
iii) Which parts of Britain suffered most from the drought? *(1)*
iv) Name three cities which experienced water rationing. *(3)*

b What problems did the drought of 1976 create for each of the following groups of people? *(5)*

farmers • sports enthusiasts • industrialists
forestry workers • householders

c Name two groups of people who might have benefited from the drought. *(2)*

5 *(Pages 218 and 219)*

The River Exe, like the Lyn, has its source on Exmoor. Heavy rainfall on Exmoor takes 24 hours to reach Exeter which, over the centuries, has experienced frequent flooding. During 1960, the wettest year this century in the West Country, 1000 homes in Exeter were flooded on 27 October and 1200 houses and business premises on 4 December. Residents demanded action. Once costs had been balanced against risks, the Exeter Flood Defence Scheme was built. (The more the money spent on prevention schemes, the less likely should be the risk of future flooding.) The scheme was completed in 1977. Since then, although the flood relief channels have been needed on average 3 to 4 times a year, no property has been flooded.

a Describe the main points of the scheme. *(5)*
b How successful has the scheme been to date? *(2)*
c Do you consider that the scheme was quite cheap, very costly, or somewhere in between to implement? *(1)*

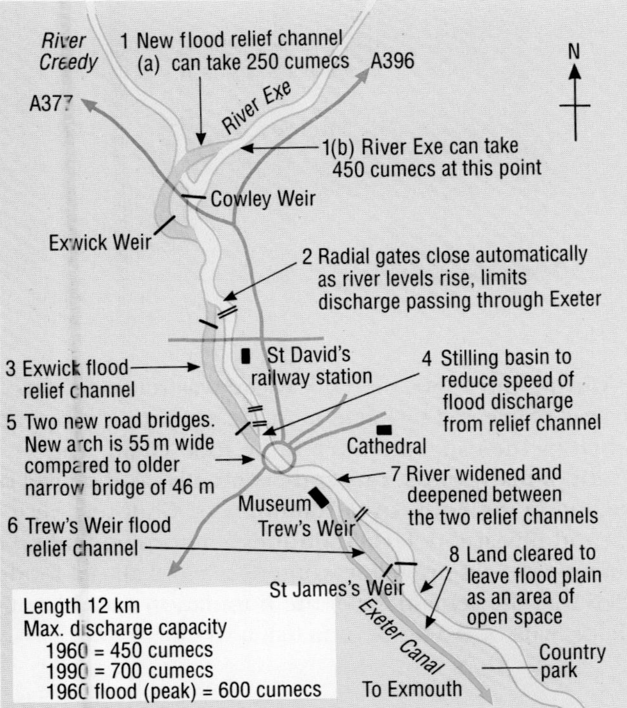

6 *(Pages 218 and 219)*

One of the worst floods in living memory in Britain hit Lynmouth in August 1952.

a What natural (physical) features of the River Lyn drainage basin made Lynmouth vulnerable to a possible flood? *(6)*
b How had the development of Lynmouth increased the risk of damage from flooding? *(3)*
c How did extreme weather conditions cause the worst flood in the area for over 200 years? *(3)*
d What was the scale of the damage to:
i) human life?
ii) property?
iii) the economy of the town? *(3)*

A flood the size of that which hit Lynmouth may only occur once in every 100 or even 200 years. After the flood you were put in charge of a scheme to try to prevent a repetition of flooding in Lynmouth. The following suggestions were put to you. How appropriate do you think each one is? Give reasons for your answers (think of safety, suitability, costs, jobs, and the environment). *(10)*

1. Widen the river so that it can hold more water.
2. Straighten the river to reduce friction and to carry away excess water more quickly.
3. Build large flood banks (levees) alongside the river.
4. Build wider arches to any bridges.
5. Plant trees on Exmoor and in the drainage basin to reduce the speed of surface run-off.
6. Install a flood warning system.
7. Divert the course of the river away from Lynmouth.
8. Move the buildings in Lynmouth to a new site away from the river.
9. Build a dam on the river to hold back any floodwater.
10. Do nothing and just pray that it will not happen again in your lifetime.

7 *(Pages 220 and 221)*

The coastal areas of Bangladesh suffer frequently from two natural hazards – tropical cyclones and flooding.

a What is a tropical cyclone? *(1)*
b i) Give three reasons why the coast of Bangladesh is vulnerable to flooding. *(3)*
ii) Why do so many people live in this flood-prone area? *(2)*
iii) Why is it difficult to warn people about the imminent threat of a flood? Why do relatively few people heed the warning? *(2)*
c i) Why are the waves which hit the coast so high? *(2)*
ii) What are the primary (immediate) problems which result from flooding? *(2)*
iii) What are the secondary (longer term) problems caused by flooding? *(2)*
d i) What might be done to try to reduce the risk of flooding? *(2)*
ii) Why is it difficult to implement flood prevention schemes in countries like Bangladesh? *(2)*

Air and water pollution in Japan

Before 1980

In its attempts to industrialise, Japan initially paid little attention to the effects air and water pollution would have upon its environment. Water resources and the atmosphere, in particular, became severely polluted. This led to serious human health problems and adversely affected the habitats of plants and wildlife. What were the main causes of water and air pollution?

Farming Fertiliser and pesticides were washed through the soil by the heavy Japanese rainfall, and made their way into paddy-fields, rivers, lakes and, eventually, the sea. Phosphates and nitrates encouraged the growth of algae and other water plants which used up oxygen and left insufficient for fish to survive (page 84).

Domestic sewage and rubbish Many rural areas were still too isolated to have mains sewerage, while urban areas were growing too rapidly for the authorities to keep pace with the demand for extra drains. Untreated sewage in rural areas escaped into water intended for either drinking purposes or for the paddy-fields. Untreated sewage from urban areas, most of which are on the coast, was often allowed to escape into the sea. The worst affected areas were the Inland Sea and Tokyo Bay (Figure 17.1) where the tides were insufficient to carry the sewage out to sea. Figure 17.2 shows how sewage increases the amount of ammonia and nitrates in the water, and reduces oxygen and plant life. The disposal of domestic rubbish was a major problem. Tokyo built 16 incinerators to burn rubbish but this only added to air pollution and caused smog. Rubbish was also deliberately dumped into Tokyo Bay to be used in later land reclamation schemes.

Industry Industry also dumped its waste into water or released it into the air (Figure 17.3). Water in inland lakes such as Lake Biwa (Figure 17.1) became dull, lifeless and unsuitable for domestic consumption and plant and animal life. The largest industries – steel, cars, engineering and chemicals – were all located on the coast where they could discharge their effluent directly into the sea. One of the consequences was the rapid decline in the number of fish caught in what had previously been one of the world's major fishing grounds. During the 1950s mercury waste was released into Minamata Bay. It was converted by bacteria in the sea into a substance which was absorbed by the fish, and entered the food chain. The result was the death of many birds, cats and eventually, as the level of mercury accumulated in the body, over 100 humans. Children were born with mental and physical defects (blindness, deformed limbs). In 1973 the government advised pregnant women to avoid all sea foods, and recommended that the remainder of the population should not eat more than six prawns or 0.5 kg of tuna fish a week.

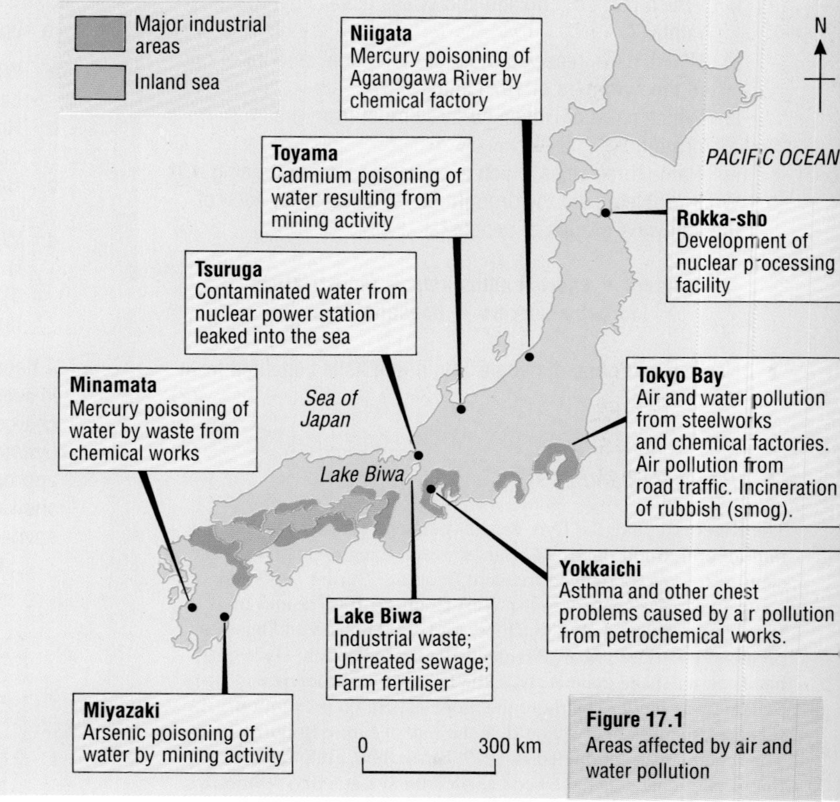

Figure 17.1 Areas affected by air and water pollution

Figure 17.2 Water pollution in Japan

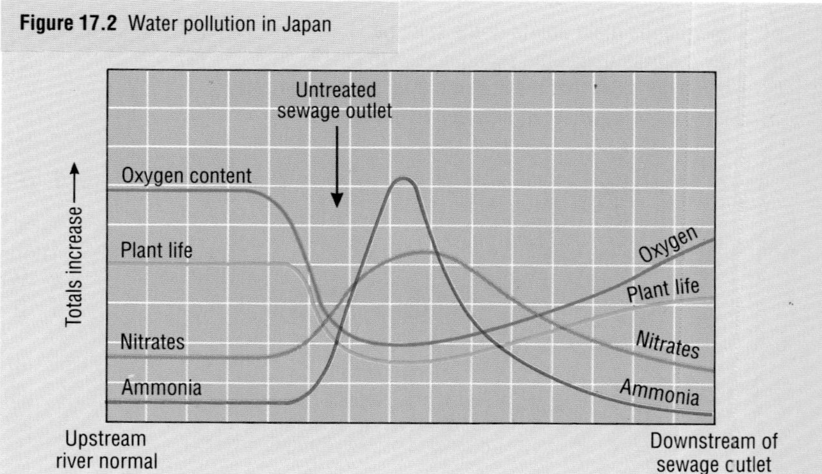

Figure 17.3
Industrial pollution in Japan

Power stations Thermal power stations ejected hot water into rivers and seas, raised the temperature beyond that usually tolerated by plants and fish, and reduced the oxygen content. Japan increased its number of nuclear power stations (page 100) and although, as yet, there have been no major radio-active leakages, the threat remains.

Transport As road traffic increased, so too did the emissions of exhaust fumes and the volume of noise.

Since 1980

In the early 1970s, the Japanese government produced standards for the quality of their environment. These standards were designed to control the levels of water, air and noise pollution. Fortunately for Japan, it had both the technology and capital needed to tackle its environmental problems. At the same time, further legislation designated a larger number of wilderness conservation areas.

Figure 17.4 Lake Biwa

Figure 17.5 Oyster beds off Hiroshima

Figure 17.6 Reduction in gaseous emissions

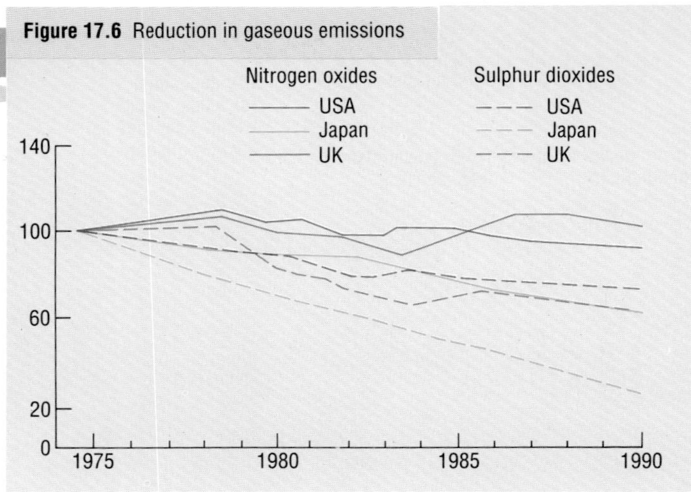

Since 1980 many formerly polluted areas have been cleaned up. Lake Biwa is now a major tourist area which allows swimming and other water activities (Figure 17.4). Fish have returned to the Inland Sea where the Japanese have also set up numerous fish farms and oyster beds (Figure 17.5). Air quality in Japan has improved considerably. Despite the continued increase in the number of cars, factories and power stations, emissions of nitrogen oxides and sulphur dioxides have been reduced far more than in other industrialised countries (Figure 17.6). Apart from cars being fitted with catalytic converters and using unleaded petrol, Mazda are now working on a hydrogen rotary engine which, if successful, would produce only water vapour as a waste. Steps have been taken to reduce sulphur emissions from thermal power stations, as well as turning increasingly to nuclear power which, arguably, contributes less to global warming and acid rain (pages 226 to 229). To reduce the amount of domestic waste and to reduce imports, Japan has adopted a policy of recycling waste products in a big way. It recycles 50 per cent of its used paper, 55 per cent of its glass and 70 per cent of its cans (the corresponding figures for the UK are 25 per cent, 15 per cent and 5 per cent). Industry is also moving to cleaner and more pleasant surroundings such as Tsukuba Science City (page 117). One of Japan's two religions, Shintu, is based upon a concern for the environment, and increasingly Japanese are taking time to visit their numerous National Parks (Figure 17.7), especially during spring (cherry blossom time) and autumn (when leaves change colour).

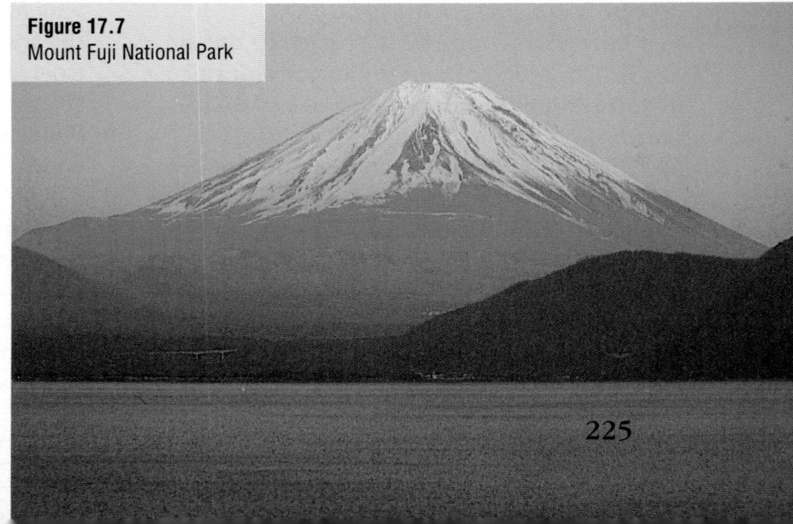

Figure 17.7
Mount Fuji National Park

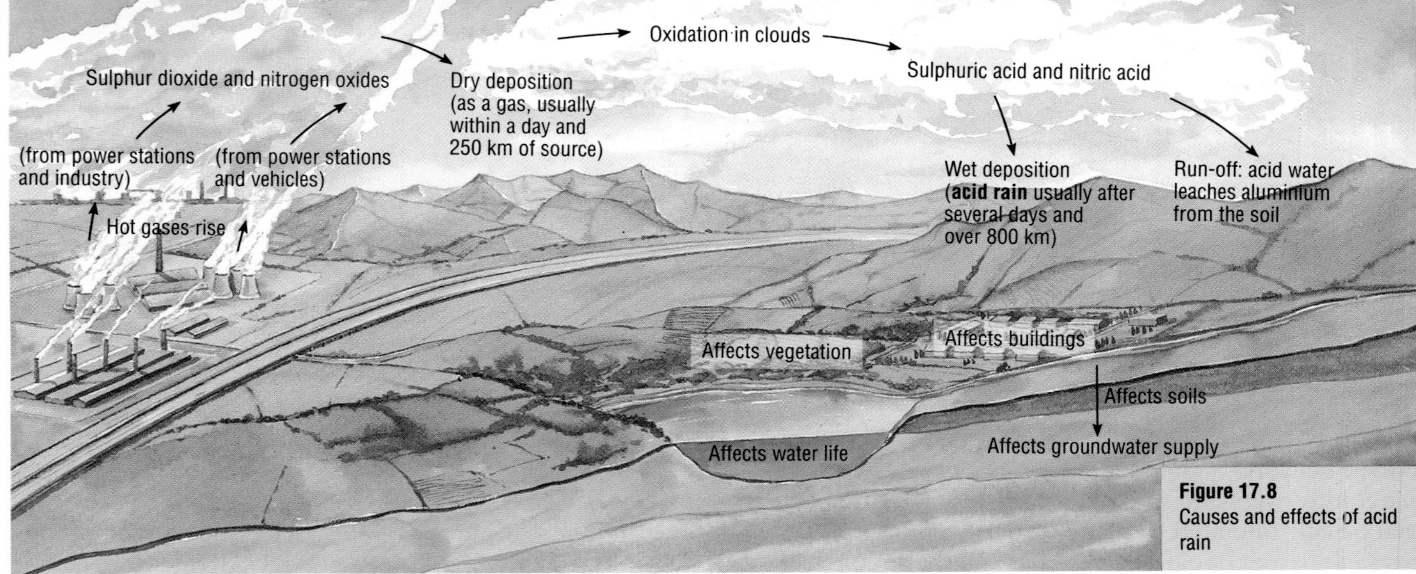

Figure 17.8
Causes and effects of acid rain

Acid rain

Acid rain was first noticed in Scandinavia in the 1950s when large numbers of freshwater fish died. Research showed that the water in which these fish had lived contained more than average amounts of acid. Later it was discovered that this extra acid had been carried by rain, hence the term *acid rain*. The acid is formed in the air from sulphur dioxide and nitrogen oxide which are emitted by thermal power stations, industry and motor vehicles (Figure 17.8). These gases are either carried by prevailing winds across seas and national frontiers to be deposited directly on to the earth's surface (dry deposition), or are converted into acids (sulphuric and nitric acid) which then fall to the ground in the rain (wet deposition). Clean rainwater has a pH value of between 5.5 and 6 (pH 7 is neutral). Today the pH readings are between 4 and 4.5 through much of north-west Europe, with the lowest ever recorded being 2.4 (Figure 17.9). A falling pH is the sign of increasing acidity. (Remember: when pH falls by one unit it means that the level of acid has increased ten times.)

Europe's pollution budget

Most European countries add acids to the air, with Britain being one of the major culprits. However, only about one-third of Britain's contribution actually lands back on British soil. Some falls into the North Sea but most is carried by the prevailing south-westerly winds towards Scandinavia. Figure 17.11 shows how acidity increased between 1960 and 1990. It also shows how Scandinavia, despite being one of the least of the offenders, is one of the main sufferers from acid rain. It is because acid rain crosses national frontiers that it is an international problem which can only be solved through global management and co-operation.

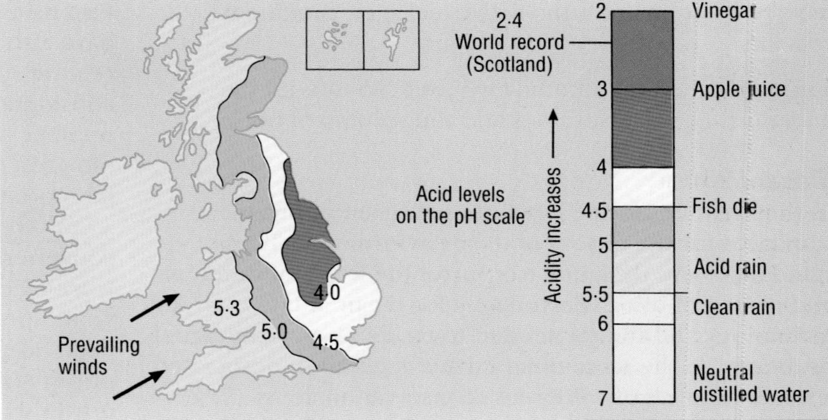

Figure 17.9
Acidity of rainfall in the UK, 1990

The effects of acid rain

- The acidity of lakes has increased. Large concentrations kill fish and plant life.
- An increase in the acidity of soils reduces the number of crops that can be grown.
- Forests are being destroyed as important nutrients (calcium and potassium) are washed away (leached). These are replaced by manganese and aluminium which are harmful to root growth. In time, the trees become less resistant to drought, frost and disease, and shed their needles (Figure 17.10).
- Water supplies are more acidic and this could become a future health hazard; e.g. the release of extra aluminium has been linked to Alzheimer's disease.
- Buildings are being eroded by chemical action caused by acid rain (Figure 17.12). The Acropolis in Athens and Taj Mahal in India have both deteriorated rapidly in recent years.

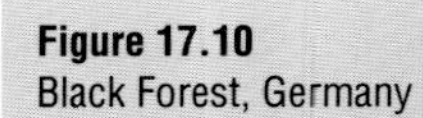

Figure 17.10
Black Forest, Germany

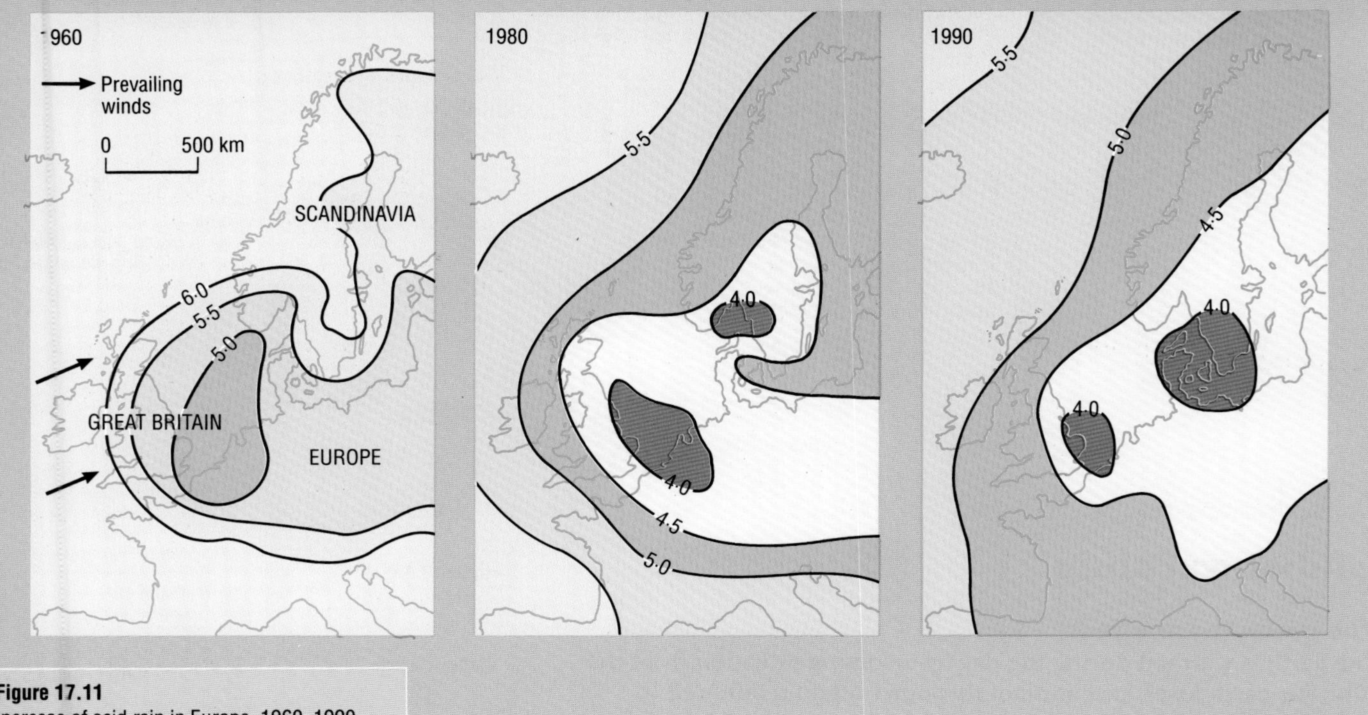

Figure 17.11
Increase of acid rain in Europe, 1960–1990

Prevention or cure?

Trees have been sprayed in Germany to try to wash off the acid, and lime has been added to soils, lakes and rivers in Scandinavia to try to reduce acidity. These procedures are, however, expensive and are not a sustainable solution as the processes have to be continually repeated. Prevention, as always, is preferable to the cure, and can be achieved by reducing the emissions of sulphur dioxide and nitrogen oxides. In Britain, over 60 per cent of these gases are produced by thermal (fossil-fuel burning) power stations. Several options as to how existing power stations can reduce emission are given in Figure 17.13. Although the British government has increased the money available to combat these emissions, many people consider that far more needs to be done. The government is committed to reducing sulphur dioxide emissions to 60 per cent of their 1980 levels by the year 2000. This could be achieved by either using improved technology to reduce the release of sulphur dioxide from existing power stations, turning coal-fired stations into gas-fired stations, or becoming more reliant upon nuclear power. Each method meets with considerable opposition, namely, from consumers (increase in electricity prices), coalminers (more pit closures) and conservationists (anti-nuclear). In reality, Britain could meet its commitments and still burn domestic coal, provided that power stations are fitted with equipment to remove sulphur dioxide. At present, the generators prefer to switch to gas, which is cheaper.

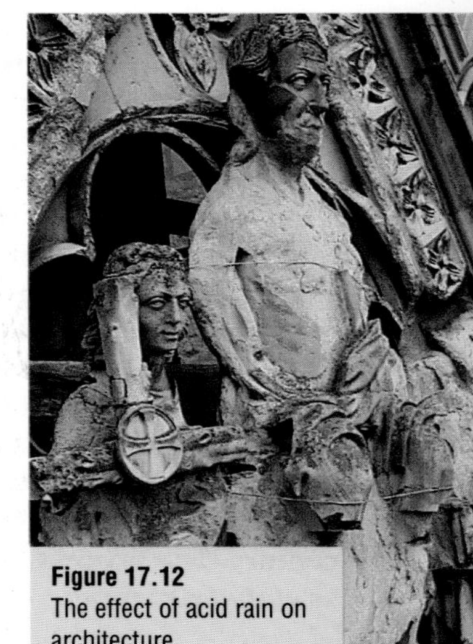

Figure 17.12
The effect of acid rain on architecture

Figure 17.13 How emissions can be reduced

Options for reducing sulphur dioxide (SO_2) emissions	**Problems**
1 Burn non-fossil fuels (nuclear/renewable)	Would mean closure of even more of the few remaining British coalmines.
2 Burn coal which contains less sulphur	This type of coal would have to be imported, forcing British pits to close.
3 Remove sulphur from coal before it is used. Desulphurisation can be done either by a) washing finely ground coal; b) treating coal with chemicals.	Extra processes means extra time and costs.
4 Install new boilers in power stations which allow SO_2 to remain in ash. "Fluidised bed technology" burns coal and limestone together so that the sulphur "sticks" to the limestone	Extra processes add to the expense. Problem of disposing of waste (ash). Expensive.
5 Remove SO_2 from waste gases after use. *Flue gas desulphurisation*: gas is sprayed with water turning it into sulphuric acid, which is then neutralised after being treated with lime.	Extra process. Extremely expensive.

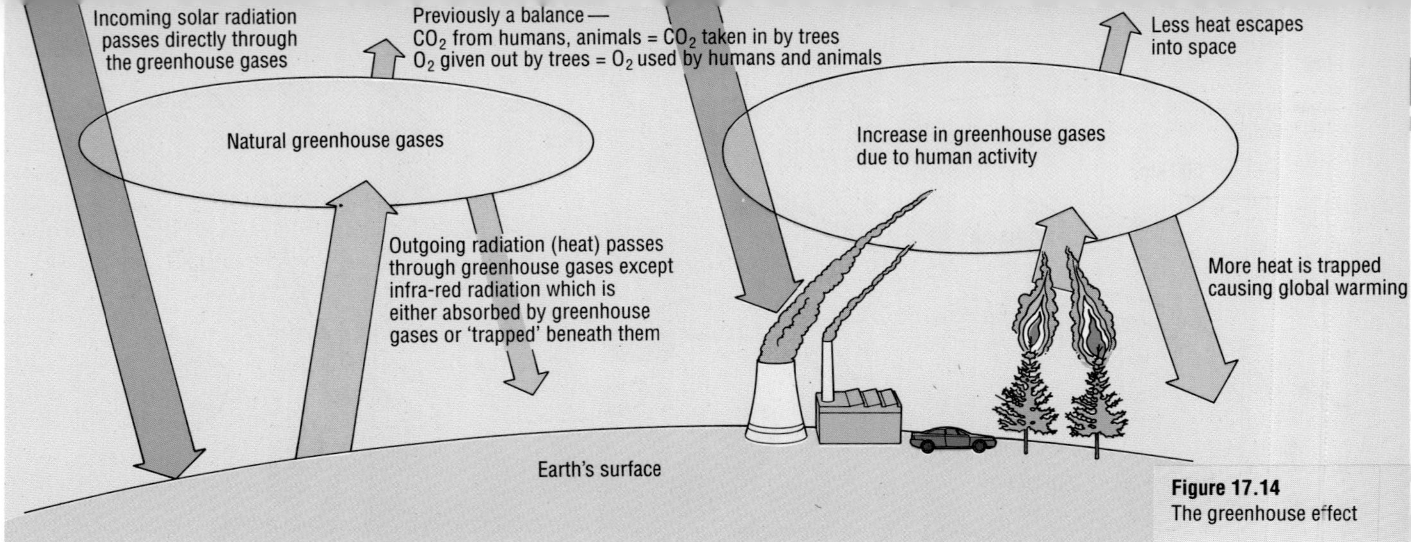
Incoming solar radiation passes directly through the greenhouse gases
Previously a balance —
CO_2 from humans, animals = CO_2 taken in by trees
O_2 given out by trees = O_2 used by humans and animals
Less heat escapes into space
Natural greenhouse gases
Increase in greenhouse gases due to human activity
Outgoing radiation (heat) passes through greenhouse gases except infra-red radiation which is either absorbed by greenhouse gases or 'trapped' beneath them
More heat is trapped causing global warming
Earth's surface

Figure 17.14
The greenhouse effect

Global warming

The greenhouse effect

The earth is warmed during the day by incoming radiation from the sun. The earth loses heat at night through outgoing infra-red radiation. Over a lengthy period of time, because there is a balance between incoming and outgoing radiation, the earth's temperatures remain constant.

On cloudy nights, temperatures do not drop as low as on clear nights. This is because the clouds act as a blanket and trap some of the heat. Greenhouse gases in the atmosphere also act as a blanket, as they prevent the escape of infra-red radiation. Without these greenhouse gases, which include carbon dioxide, the earth's average temperature would be 33°C colder than it is today (during the ice-age temperatures were only 4°C colder than at present). Recent human activity has led to a significant increase in the amount, and type, of greenhouse gases in the atmosphere. This is preventing heat from escaping into space, and is believed to be responsible for a rise in world temperatures (Figure 17.14). World temperatures have risen by 0.5°C this century (Figure 17.16). Seven of this century's warmest ten years were in the 1980s. Estimates suggest that a further rise of between 1.5°C and 4.5°C could take place by the end of the next century. The process by which world temperatures are rising is known as *global warming*.

Figure 17.16 The rise in global temperatures since 1860

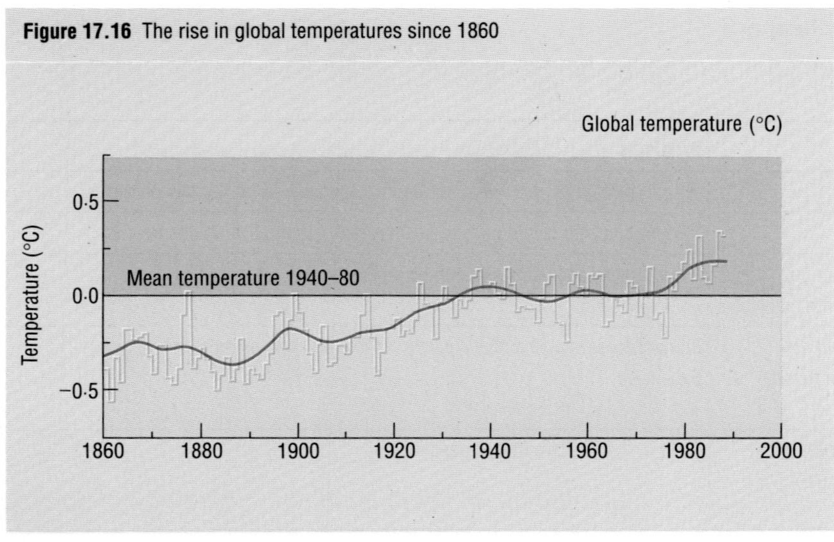
Global temperature (°C)
Temperature (°C)
0·5
0·0
−0·5
Mean temperature 1940–80
1860
1880
1900
1920
1940
1960
1980
2000

Figure 17.15
Greenhouse gases

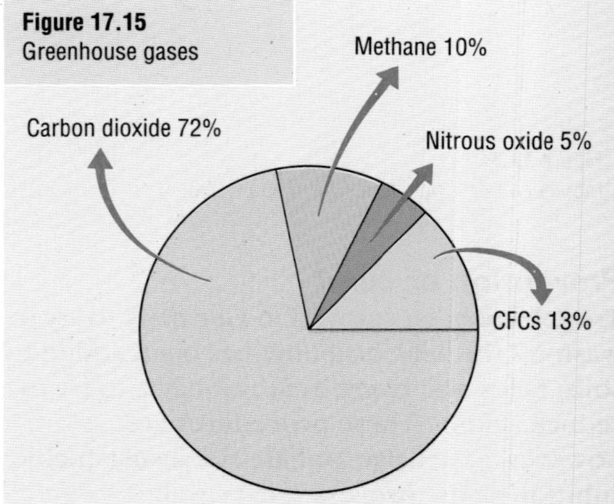
Methane 10%
Carbon dioxide 72%
Nitrous oxide 5%
CFCs 13%

Causes of global warming

The major contributors to global warming are carbon dioxide and other pollutants released into the atmosphere (Figure 17.15).

- Carbon dioxide is the most important single factor in global warming. It is produced by road transport and by burning fossil fuels in power stations, in factories and in the home (Figure 17.18). Since the economically more developed countries consume three-quarters of the world's energy, they are largely responsible for global warming. A secondary source of carbon dioxide is deforestation and the burning of the tropical rainforests (page 230).
- CFCs (chlorofluorocarbons) from aerosols, air conditioners, foam packaging and refrigerators are the most damaging of the greenhouse gases.
- Methane is released from decaying organic matter such as peat bogs, swamps, waste dumps, animal dung and farms (e.g. ricefields in South-east Asia).
- Nitrous oxide is emitted from car exhausts, power stations and agricultural fertiliser.

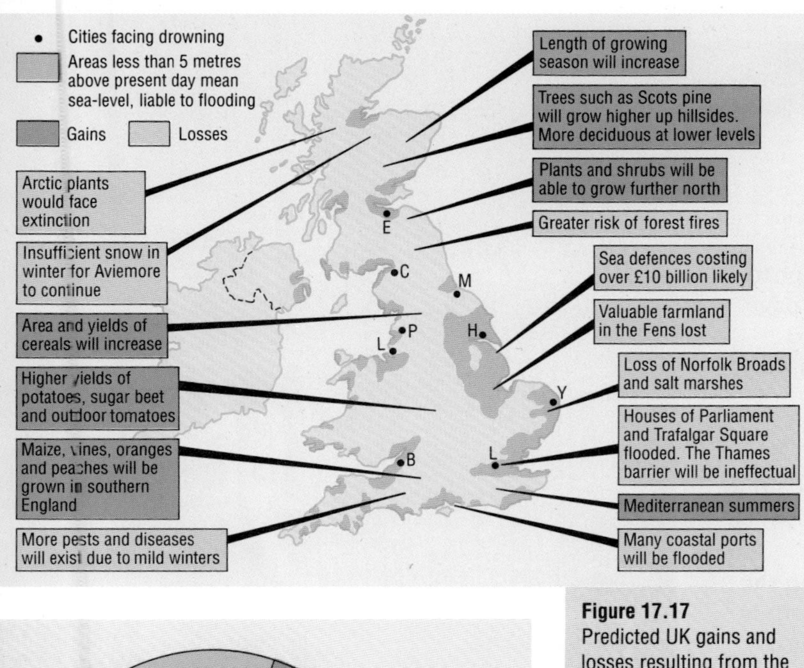

Cities facing drowning
Areas less than 5 metres above present day mean sea-level, liable to flooding
Gains
Losses
Arctic plants would face extinction
Insufficient snow in winter for Aviemore to continue
Area and yields of cereals will increase
Higher yields of potatoes, sugar beet and outdoor tomatoes
Maize, vines, oranges and peaches will be grown in southern England
More pests and diseases will exist due to mild winters
Length of growing season will increase
Trees such as Scots pine will grow higher up hillsides. More deciduous at lower levels
Plants and shrubs will be able to grow further north
Greater risk of forest fires
Sea defences costing over £10 billion likely
Valuable farmland in the Fens lost
Loss of Norfolk Broads and salt marshes
Houses of Parliament and Trafalgar Square flooded. The Thames barrier will be ineffectual
Mediterranean summers
Many coastal ports will be flooded
E
C
M
P
L
H
Y
B
L

Figure 17.17
Predicted UK gains and losses resulting from the greenhouse effect

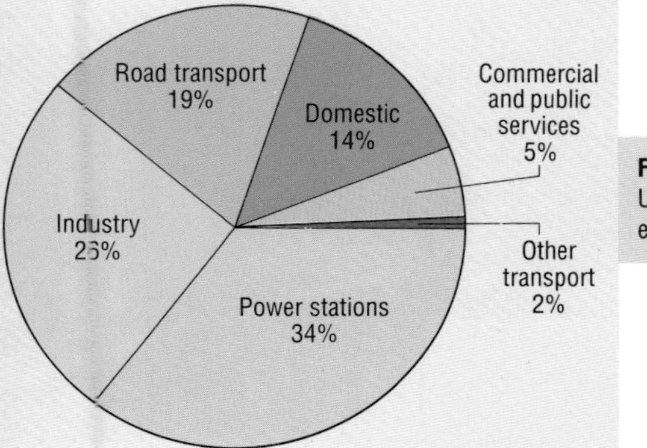

Road transport 19%
Domestic 14%
Commercial and public services 5%
Industry 25%
Other transport 2%
Power stations 34%

Figure 17.18
UK carbon dioxide emissions, 1990

Effects of global warming

The major consequences of global warming are the predicted world changes in climate and sea-levels. Scientists are suggesting that as air temperatures increase:

- Sea temperatures will also rise. As the sea gets warmer it will expand causing its level to rise by between 0.25 and 1.5 metres.
- Ice caps and glaciers, especially in polar areas, will melt. The release of water at present held in storage as ice and snow in the hydrological cycle (page 168) could raise the world's sea-level by another 5 metres. Even a rise of one metre could flood 25 per cent of Bangladesh (page 220), 30 per cent of Egypt's arable land and totally submerge several low-lying islands in the Indian and Pacific Oceans (e.g. Maldives).
- The distribution of precipitation will alter with some places becoming wetter and stormier, others becoming drier and with a less reliable rainfall.

Figure 17.17 shows some predicted effects of global warming on the British Isles, and Figure 17.19 on the wider world.

Figure 17.19
Predicted effects of global warming on the world

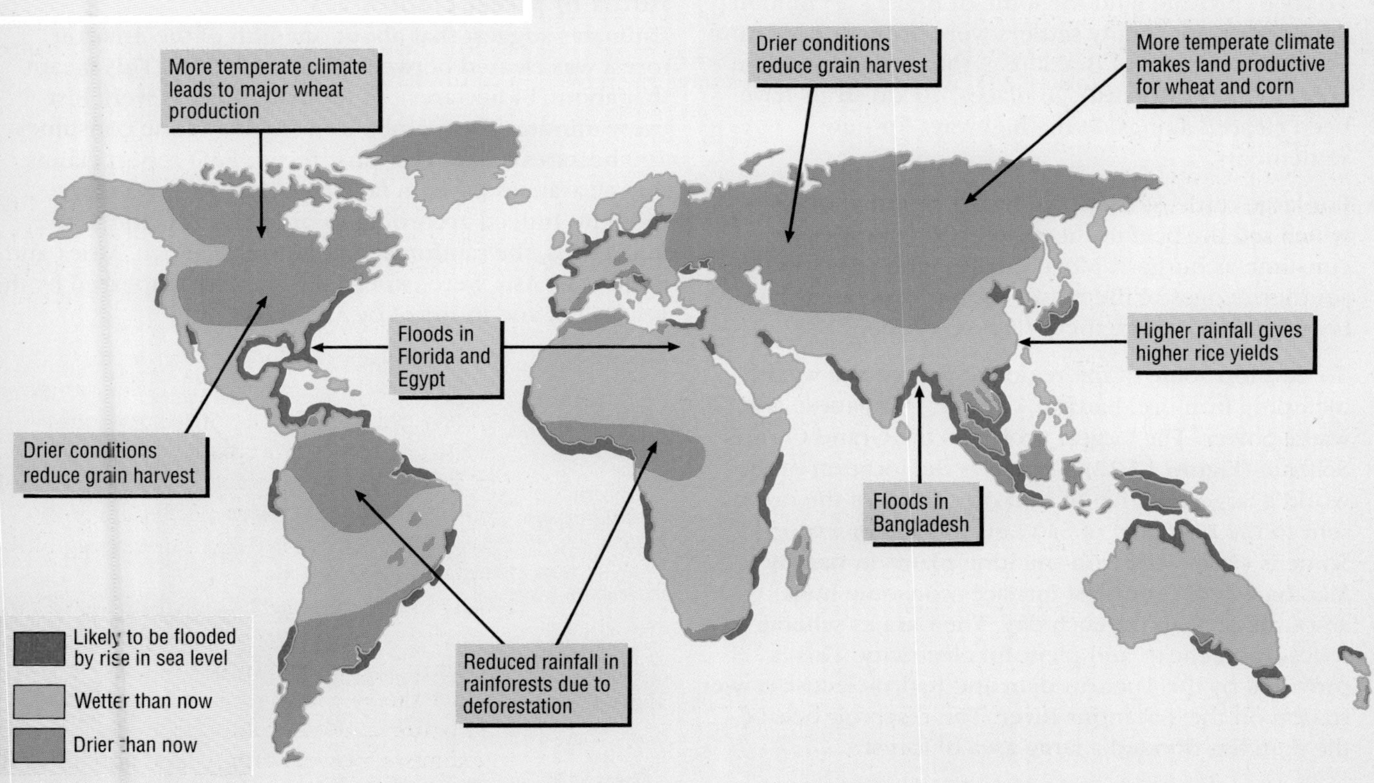

More temperate climate leads to major wheat production
Drier conditions reduce grain harvest
More temperate climate makes land productive for wheat and corn
Floods in Florida and Egypt
Higher rainfall gives higher rice yields
Drier conditions reduce grain harvest
Floods in Bangladesh
Reduced rainfall in rainforests due to deforestation
Likely to be flooded by rise in sea level
Wetter than now
Drier than now

Deforestation in the Amazon basin

The trees in the tropical rainforest have had to adapt to a climate which is hot and wet throughout the year (page 197). One-third of the world's trees still grow in the Brazilian rainforest, but their numbers are being rapidly reduced due to deforestation.

Why are the rainforests being cleared?

- To provide space for farming: Rainforests are found in economically less developed countries, most of which have a rapid population growth. Land has to be cleared for extra settlement and farming. Even in the Amazon forest, where the local population growth is less, land is constantly cleared for use by shifting cultivators (page 82).
- To help satisfy the needs of the developed world for an increasing amount of timber, especially for hardwoods such as mahogany: The felled timber provides an essential income for less wealthy countries. Most clearances have taken place along the more accessible rivers and beside the new highways.
- To build an increasing number of highways in an attempt to develop the interior of Brazil and to tap its natural resources: The Trans-Amazonian Highway extends inland for 6000 km (Figure 17.20).
- To try to provide land for some of Brazil's 25 million landless people: Many settlers were brought here from even poorer parts of Brazil (e.g. the drought stricken areas in the north-east). In places, 10 km strips have been cleared alongside the highways for new settlements.
- For large cattle ranches run by the multinationals which sell the beef to the developed countries to consume as burgers: Most ranches tend to be on the southern edges of the rainforest but large areas have been burnt to create them (Figure 17.21).
- To develop some of the region's vast natural wealth including iron ore, bauxite, copper, manganese and water power: The largest project is the Grand Carajas Scheme (Figure 17.22). Carajas is the location of the world's largest source of iron ore. Much of the ore is sent to the new port of São Luis by rail, for export. Some is sent to the iron-smelting plants in nearby Maraba where four blast furnaces consume huge amounts of charcoal each day. The Carajas scheme relies upon cheap and plentiful electricity. This is provided by the Tucurui dam and hydro-electric power station on the Tocantins River. The reservoir behind the dam has flooded a large area of forest.

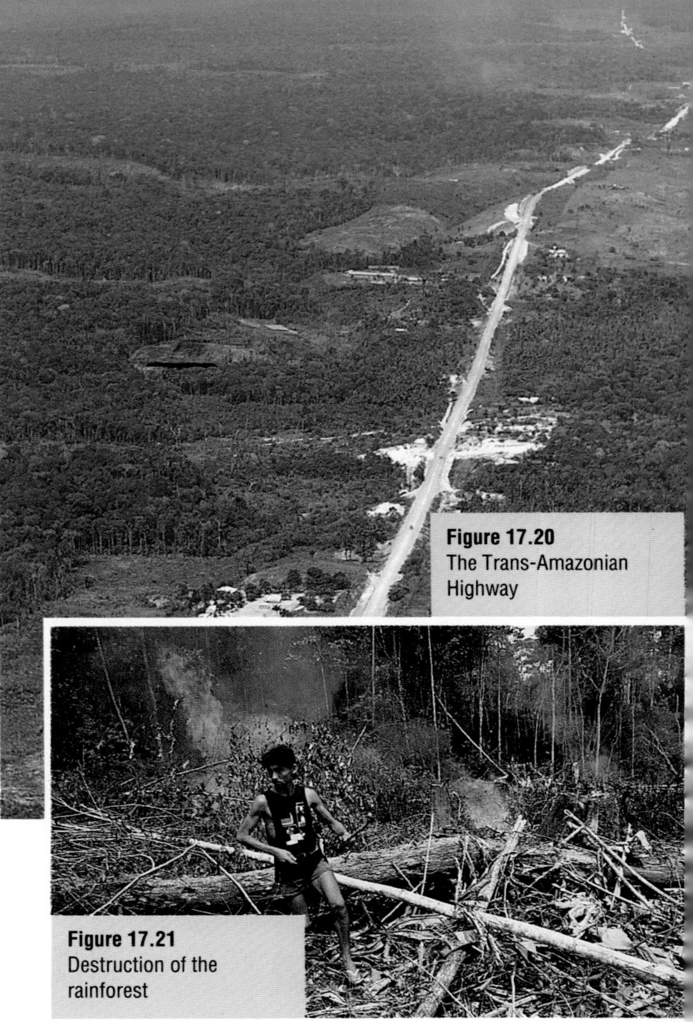

Figure 17.20 The Trans-Amazonian Highway

Figure 17.21 Destruction of the rainforest

Rates of forest clearances

Estimates suggest that about one-fifth of the Amazon forest was cleared between 1960 and 1990. This meant that about 14 hectares (14 football pitches) were lost every minute. The Maraba iron smelter alone consumes 160 hectares a day! The most recent FAO report claims that clearances have, in fact, been less than was first thought. Indeed according to predictions made in the mid-1980s, the rainforests in Central America, Africa and South-east Asia were expected to have disappeared by the year 2000, and in Brazil by AD 2020.

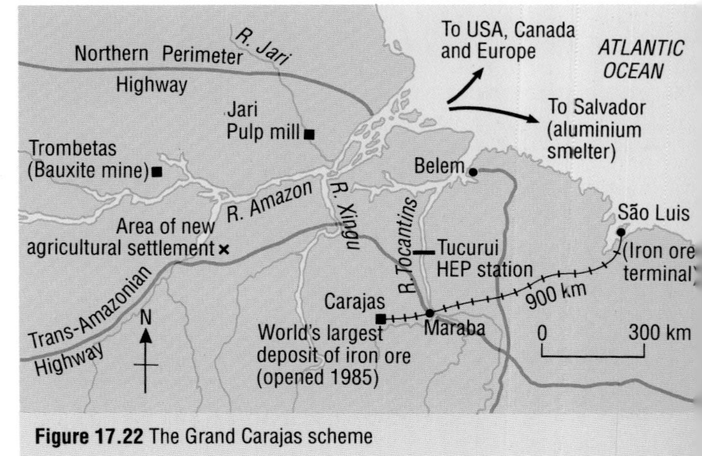

Figure 17.22 The Grand Carajas scheme

Effects of the clearances

- There has been a countless loss of birds, insects, reptiles and mammals which found their food and shelter in the forest, together with numerous species of tree. A typical patch of rainforest, 10 km², may contain as many as 1500 species of flowering plant, 750 species of tree, 400 species of bird, 150 varieties of butterfly, 100 different reptiles and 60 types of amphibian. Many types have still to be identified and studied. How many of these may be of value? Over half of our modern medicines have their origin in the rainforest. Recently one plant, a periwinkle, has been used successfully to treat child leukaemia, reducing deaths from 80 per cent of total cases to 20 per cent. Some species of tree, such as mahogany, are becoming endangered.
- Large-scale destruction of the traditional Indian ways of life has occurred and the possibility of their extinction threatens. When Europeans arrived in the Amazon there were an estimated 6 million Amerindians. Now there are only about 200,000 – a decrease of 96 per cent. Many have been killed by Europeans, others have died from western illnesses, such as measles, against which they had no immunity. Those remaining have been forced to live in reservations, or to become 'tourist attractions'. The Kayapo are one of several tribes (Figure 17.25) who have suffered massacres from illegal settlers.
- In the hot, wet climate fallen leaves soon decompose, and the nutrients released are taken up again by the vegetation. If trees are removed, the nutrient cycle is broken, and existing nutrients are rapidly washed (leached) out of the soil leaving it infertile (Figure 17.23).
- The tree canopy protects the soil from the heavy rain, while tree roots help to bind the soil together and to retain moisture. Without the protective tree cover, there will be less interception and infiltration, and more surface run-off and soil erosion. Soil erosion leads to an increase in the extent and frequency of flooding.
- Some of the cattle ranches and new settlements along the highways have already been abandoned as the soil becomes increasingly leached and infertile. Many settlers have left their farms due to a drop in yields, and have moved to swell the number of urban favela dwellers (page 32).
- Recent investigations suggest that over one-third of the world's oxygen supply comes from trees in the rainforest, and that one-quarter of the world's fresh water is stored in the Amazon Basin (Figure 17.24). Both resources would be lost if Amazonia was totally deforested.

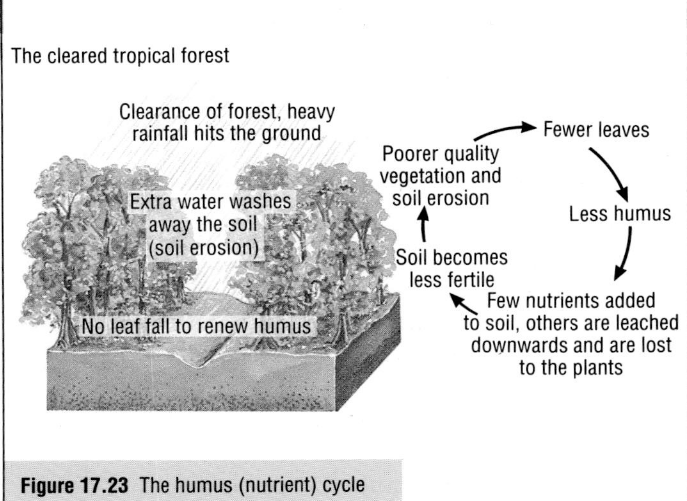

Figure 17.23 The humus (nutrient) cycle

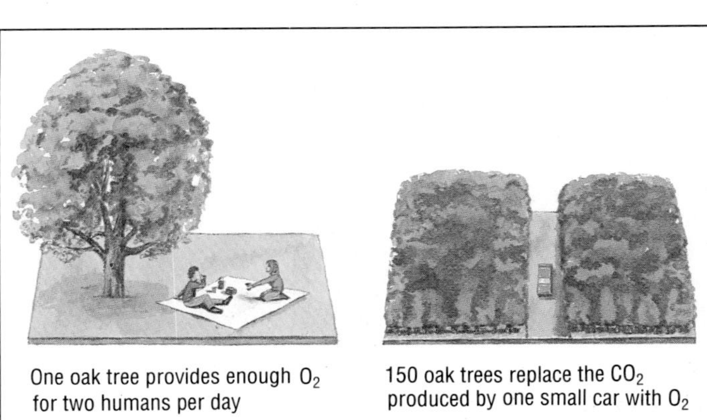

One oak tree provides enough O_2 for two humans per day
150 oak trees replace the CO_2 produced by one small car with O_2

Figure 17.24 The oxygen-carbon dioxide balance

- Deforestation is believed to be contributing to changes in the world's climate. Without trees there will be a decrease in evapotranspiration and, therefore, of water vapour in the air. This in turn will reduce rainfall totals and, according to many experts, will increase the possibility of the Amazon basin being turned into a desert. The release of carbon by the burning of trees contributes to the greenhouse effect and to global warming (page 228).

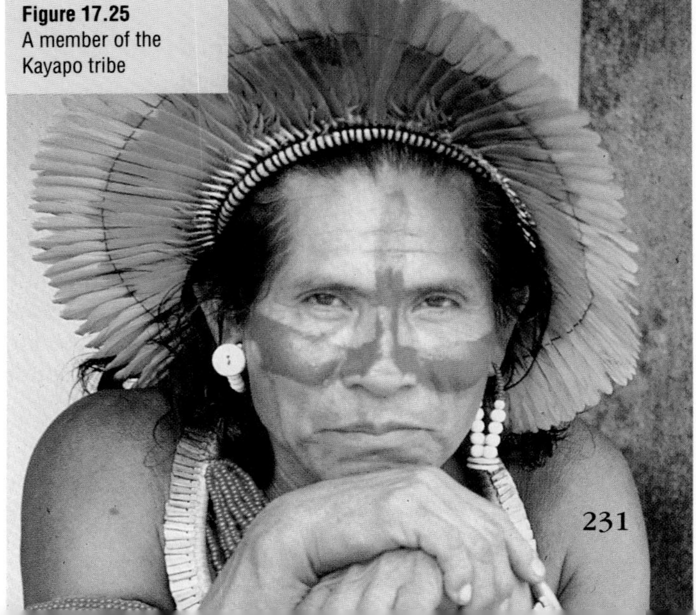

Figure 17.25 A member of the Kayapo tribe

Soil erosion

Thirty per cent of the earth's surface is land, and only 11 per cent of this is classed as prime agricultural land. It can take one to four centuries to produce 1 cm of soil, and between 30 and 120 to produce a sufficient depth for farming. Yet, as Figure 17.26 shows, human development is ruining this essential ingredient. It is estimated that by AD 2000 one-third of the area that was ploughed in 1980 will have been reduced to dust. By the year 2020 another 30 per cent could be lost. Erosion is most rapid in areas where the land is mismanaged and where climatic conditions are extreme, especially in places where the rainfall is seasonal and unreliable. Where the vegetation cover is removed there will be no replacement of humus, no interception by plants, no roots to bind the soil together, and the surface will be left exposed to wind and rain. If the climate is dry and the winds are strong they will pick up the finer material (Figure 17.28). If rainfall occurs as heavy thunderstorms and in areas of steep slopes, the soil will be washed downwards. In both cases, the land will be reduced to bare rock or left with deep, unusable gulleys (Figure 17.27).

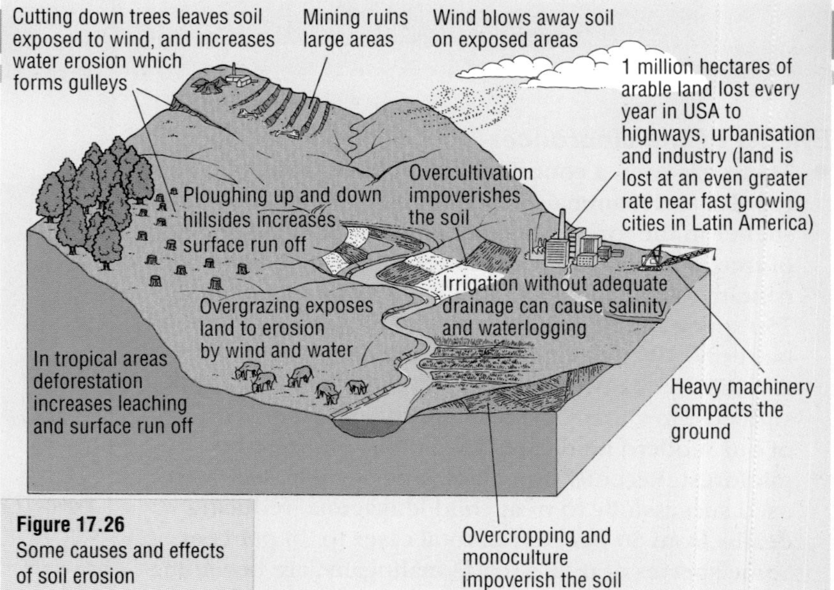

Figure 17.26
Some causes and effects of soil erosion

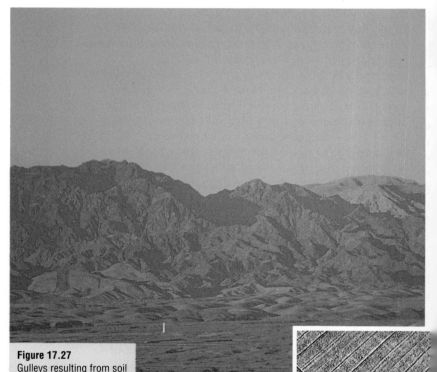

Figure 17.27
Gulleys resulting from soil erosion

The dust-bowl, USA

The American Mid-West suffers from fluctuations in its annual amounts of precipitation (Figure 17.30). John Steinbeck's book, *The Grapes of Wrath*, gives a dramatic picture of the effect of a drought in the 1930s on the land and its people. The book begins with a description of how the soil was blown away to form a dust-bowl. He describes how, by May, clouds had disappeared to allow the sun to beat down daily upon the corn (maize). By June, the vegetation had turned pale through lack of moisture, and teams of horses drawing carts caused clouds of dust. With the passing of each day this dust seemed to rise higher into the sky and to take longer to settle. The rain clouds of mid-May came and went without giving rain, and were replaced by a wind which grew daily in strength. The topsoil was picked up and carried away. The sun became an increasingly dim red ring in a darkening sky. People put handkerchiefs around their noses and mouths and goggles over their eyes before going out, and unsuccessfully tried to stop the dust coming in through the doors and windows of their homes. Suddenly, one night, the wind dropped. The people waited for the morning (Figure 17.29).

Some of the dust was carried by the wind as far as Washington DC, 2000 km to the east, while in the worst-affected states such as Oklahoma, many farms were left abandoned. Those farmers who remained were to suffer extreme poverty for many years.

During a similar drought in 1989, dust from the American Mid-West again settled on cities on the east coast of the USA.

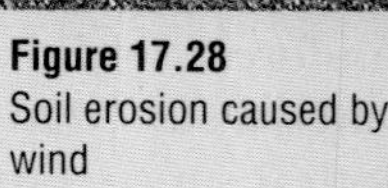

Figure 17.28
Soil erosion caused by wind

Figure 17.29
The dust-bowl

"They knew it would take a long time for the dust to settle out of the air. In the morning the dust hung like fog, and the sun was as red as ripe new blood. All day the dust sifted down from the sky, and the next day it sifted down. An even blanket covered the earth. It settled on the corn, piled up on the tops of the fence posts, piled up on the wires; it settled on roofs, blanketed the weeds and trees".

John Steinbeck, *The Grapes of Wrath*

How can soil erosion be reduced?

Soil is a renewable resource, but only if it is carefully managed. Without careful management soil, which may have taken centuries to form, can be lost within days and sometimes even minutes. As the world's population continues to grow at a rapid rate, greater pressure will be put on the land to produce food for the extra people. Often population growth is greatest in those places where the soil is at greatest risk. Some suggested methods by which soil erosion may be reduced and its productivity sustained are given in Figure 17.31.

Figure 17.30
Annual precipitation in the American Mid-West since 1900

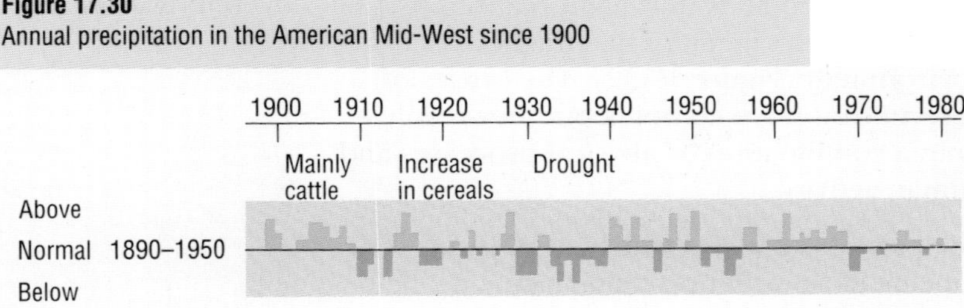
1900
1910
1920
1930
1940
1950
1960
1970
1980
Mainly cattle
Increase in cereals
Drought
Above
Normal 1890–1950
Below

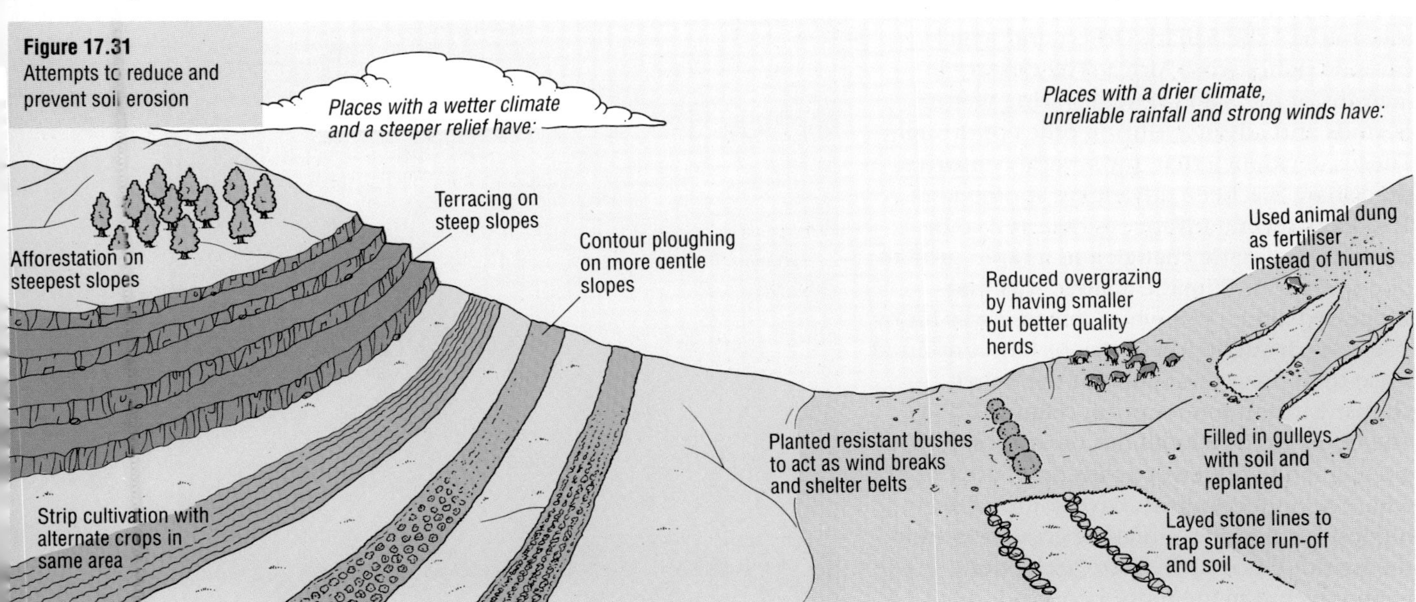
Places with a wetter climate and a steeper relief have:
Places with a drier climate, unreliable rainfall and strong winds have:
Afforestation on steepest slopes
Terracing on steep slopes
Contour ploughing on more gentle slopes
Strip cultivation with alternate crops in same area
Reduced overgrazing by having smaller but better quality herds
Used animal dung as fertiliser instead of humus
Planted resistant bushes to act as wind breaks and shelter belts
Filled in gulleys with soil and replanted
Layed stone lines to trap surface run-off and soil

Figure 17.31
Attempts to reduce and prevent soil erosion

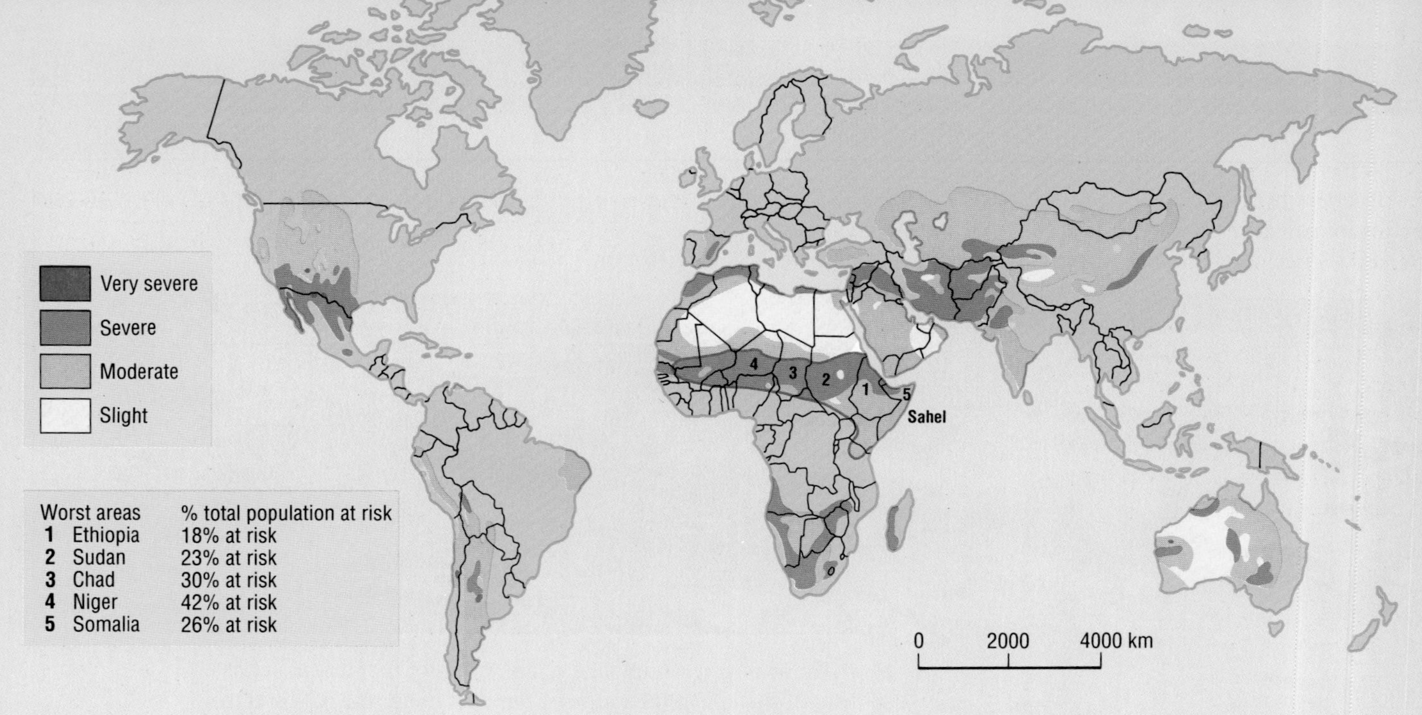

Figure 17.32 Areas at risk from desertification

Desertification

There are several definitions of the term *desertification*. Taken literally it means turning the land into desert. It is a process of land degradation, mainly in semi-arid lands where the rainfall is unreliable, caused by human mismanagement of a fragile environment (Figure 17.32). The causes of desertification are complex but they result from a combination of physical processes and human activity.

The part of the world which, at present, appears to be suffering most from desertification is the Sahel. The Sahel is a narrow fringe of semi-arid land which lies to the south of the Sahara Desert and which extends right across Africa. The desert margins of the Sahel retreat during wetter periods and advance during times of drought. There is evidence that, for several centuries, the Sahara has been advancing southwards. The most recent advance is believed to be caused by climatic change and a rapid growth in population. Climatic change was first suggested after 1968 when the area was hit by a serious drought. The drought has continued since then, in several parts of the Sahel, almost without interruption (Figure 17.34). The decrease in rainfall has meant less grazing land and fewer crops in an area where several countries have some of the highest birth and population growth rates in the world. Put simply, there are fewer resources but many more people.

Causes of desertification in the Sahel

It is suggested that desertification is the result of climatic change (decrease in rainfall and, possibly, global warming) and population growth (which has led to overgrazing, overcultivation and deforestation).

Figure 17.33 Desertification in Niger

Climatic change

Even at the best of times, water supply is always a problem in these semi-arid lands. Since the late 1960s there has been a decrease in the amount of rainfall and in its reliability (Figure 17.34). The resultant drought has caused rivers and water holes to dry up, and the water table to fall. Vegetation has died leaving the soil exposed to erosion by wind and water. Some scientists suggest that global warming may be a contributory factor. As temperatures rise, the warmer air can now hold more water vapour, and so evaporation is more likely to occur than condensation.

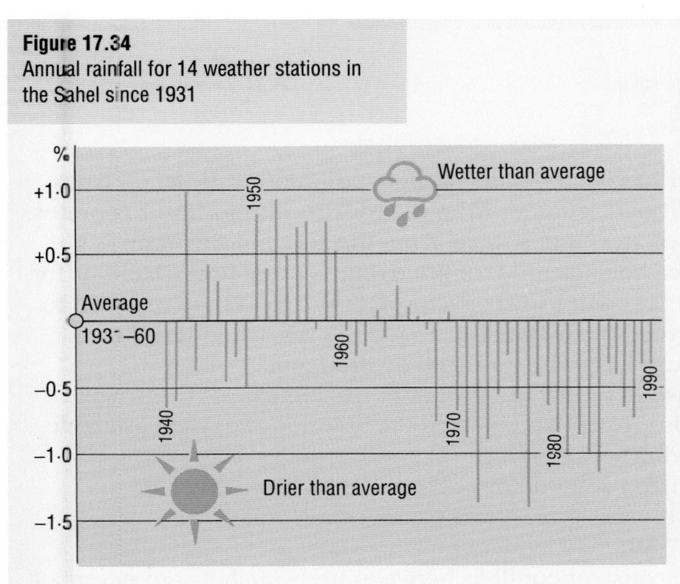

Figure 17.34
Annual rainfall for 14 weather stations in the Sahel since 1931

Figure 17.35
Comparative population change in the UK and Sahel areas

Map number		Population (millions) 1950	1990	Est 2000	Growth per decade 1950–1990	Estimated growth for decade 1990–2000
1	Ethiopia	19.6	49.2	66.4	26%	35%
2	Sudan	9.2	25.2	33.6	29%	33%
3	Chad	2.7	5.7	7.3	21%	29%
4	Niger	2.4	7.7	10.8	34%	39%
5	Somalia	2.4	7.5	9.7	33%	30%
	(UK)	50.6	57.2	58.4	3%	2%

Figure 17.36
The results of overgrazing

Population growth

Ethiopia's population had grown from 20 million in 1950 to 50 million in 1990. The latest estimate for the year 2000 is 66 million (Figure 17.35). The recent population increase of 2.5 per cent per year has outstripped the 1.7 per cent annual increase in food production. As population has grown, so too has pressure on the land. This has forced some farmers to cultivate marginal areas which are more vulnerable to erosion. Elsewhere other farmers grow the same crop year after year on the same piece of land which had previously been allowed 'rest', or *fallow*, periods. This method of farming, known as *overcultivation*, rapidly exhausts the soil. Overgrazing also encourages soil erosion. The many nomadic tribes of the Sahel measure their wealth in terms of the number of animals they own. The drought has concentrated the nomads near to the few remaining water holes, and their large herds have been too great for the amount of grass available. This has caused a loss of the natural vegetation cover to leave the soil, once again, exposed to erosion. As population increases, there is a greater need for wood for cooking. Villagers must walk further each year in their search for fuelwood (page 91). The collection of fuelwood increases deforestation while the soil, no longer protected from the occasional, but heavy, downpour, is exposed to the sun, dries, cracks and becomes loose. It is then blown away by the wind in the dry season, or washed away by the rain during the short, wet season.

The problems have been made worse in several Sahel countries by civil war. Some countries spend over half of their limited total annual expenditure on arms; money which could be better spent developing agriculture and services. Wars also increase the number of refugees who need feeding but who do not produce any food themselves.

Is the Sahara advancing?

Recent evidence, based upon the use of satellite images, has indicated that, contrary to common belief, the Sahara has not made any significant advance in the last few decades. While this suggests that the threat of desertification may be less than was previously feared, it does not mean that the risk has disappeared. Indeed, if true, it should have increased our awareness that the semi-arid lands are a very fragile environment which needs careful management.

Disappearing wetlands

Wetlands are transition zones between land and sea where the soil is frequently waterlogged and the water table is at or near the surface:

> "This in-between country, neither sea nor lake, nor dry land, is a curious zone, sometimes inhospitable, often highly productive, always a haven for a special kind of flora and fauna. But the wetlands are fragile places, subject to mounting pressures which threaten their existence."
>
> (*Geographical Magazine*)

Figure 17.37
A non-tourist scene of the Norfolk Broads

Figure 17.38
A tourist scene of the Norfolk Broads

The Broads (Norfolk)

This is an area of 200 km of navigable waterways, near to the mouth of the River Yare. It is the largest area of wetland left in Britain. The surrounding land is either unreclaimed marsh or drained marsh used as pastureland (Figure 17.37). The area is a now a National Park in everything but name.

Environmental problems

- The water table has been lowered recently as modern pumps are more efficient at extracting water than the traditional windmills. The land has 'sunk' below river levels and has to be protected by floodbanks, many of which need urgent, expensive repairs.
- The water has become increasingly polluted by diesel oil from the motorboats, effluent from the tourists and fertiliser (nitrates and phosphates) and sewage from the surrounding farms.
- Reeds have been cleared, or are dying, leaving fewer habitats for birds, animals and insects. As more of the banks are exposed to waves formed by the passing boats, soil is washed into the channel and has to be removed by dredging.
- An increase in nitrates in the water has increased the growth of algae. This growth has reduced the amount of oxygen available to fish and other plant life.
- The estimated 250,000 motorboats, carrying nearly half a million tourists a year, cause congestion and noise (Figure 17.38).
- There are constant conflicts between users such as preservers of wildlife and councils which dredge channels for motorboats, and between anglers and motorboat users.

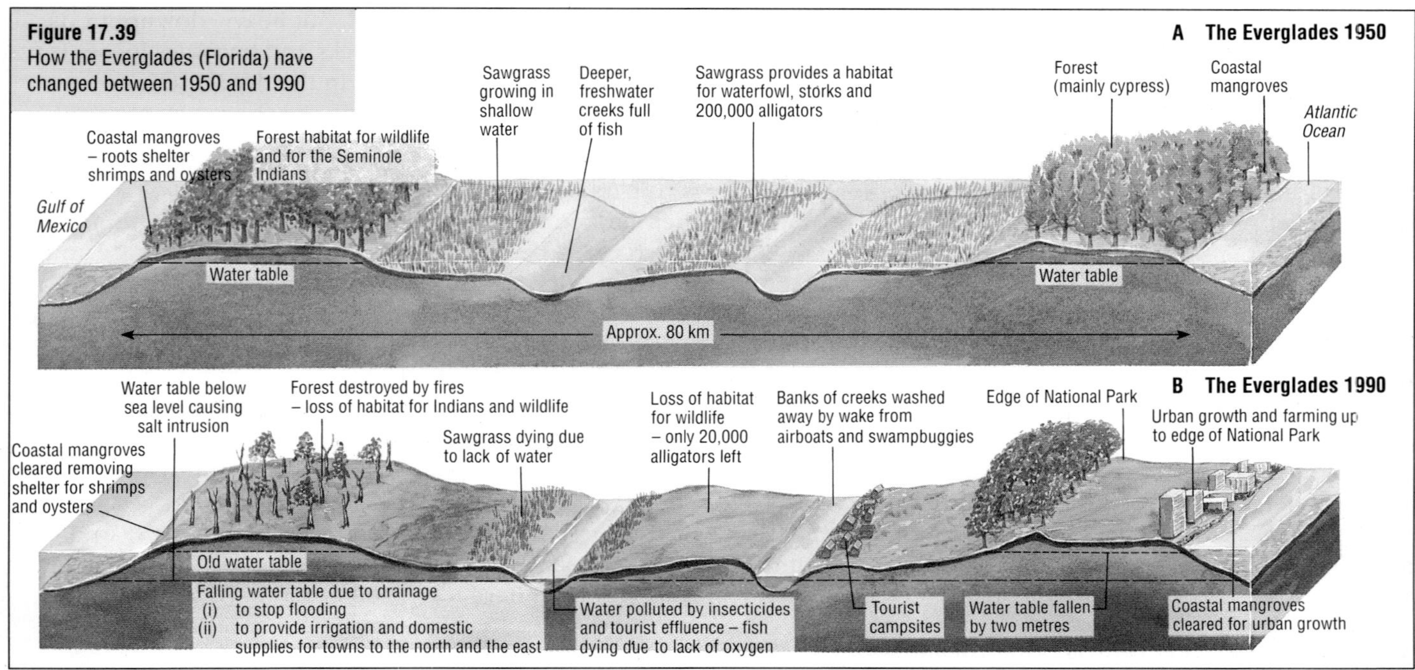
A The Everglades 1950
Coastal mangroves – roots shelter shrimps and oysters
Forest habitat for wildlife and for the Seminole Indians
Sawgrass growing in shallow water
Deeper, freshwater creeks full of fish
Sawgrass provides a habitat for waterfowl, storks and 200,000 alligators
Forest (mainly cypress)
Coastal mangroves
Atlantic Ocean
Gulf of Mexico
Water table
Water table
Approx. 80 km
B The Everglades 1990
Water table below sea level causing salt intrusion
Forest destroyed by fires – loss of habitat for Indians and wildlife
Coastal mangroves cleared removing shelter for shrimps and oysters
Sawgrass dying due to lack of water
Loss of habitat for wildlife – only 20,000 alligators left
Banks of creeks washed away by wake from airboats and swampbuggies
Edge of National Park
Urban growth and farming up to edge of National Park
Old water table
Falling water table due to drainage
(i) to stop flooding
(ii) to provide irrigation and domestic supplies for towns to the north and the east
Water polluted by insecticides and tourist effluence – fish dying due to lack of oxygen
Tourist campsites
Water table fallen by two metres
Coastal mangroves cleared for urban growth

Figure 17.39
How the Everglades (Florida) have changed between 1950 and 1990

1 *(Pages 224 and 225)*

a How did the rapid economic development of Japan put each of the following at risk from pollution?
i) rivers and lakes
ii) inland sea areas and bays
iii) the atmosphere *(9)*

b The graph shows that since the early 1970s, Japan has managed to improve the quality of its environment.
i) How has it managed to improve the quality of its
1. water resources?
2. atmosphere? *(6)*
ii) What do you consider to be the likely cause of the increase in the level of pollution in rural rivers? *(1)*

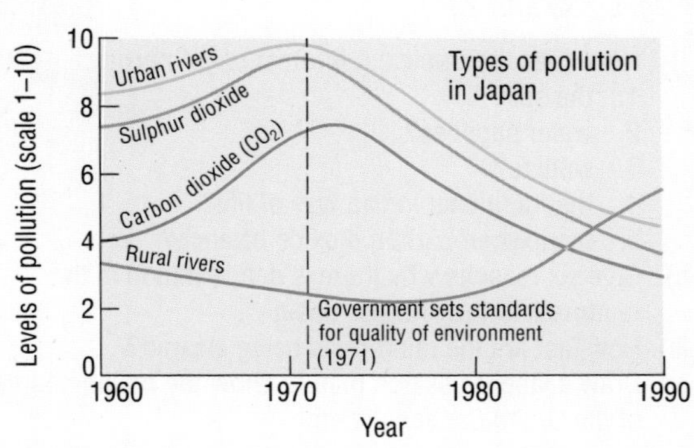

2 *(Pages 226 and 227)*

a i) What are the two main causes of acid rain?
ii) Which two chemicals cause rain to be acidic? *(4)*

b i) Give three ways in which acid rain affects the natural environment.
ii) How can acid rain affect buildings and people's health? *(5)*

c i) How is the level of acidity in rain measured?
ii) How have the levels and distribution of acid rain in Europe changed between 1960 and 1990?
iii) Which parts of Europe suffered most from acid rain in 1990?
iv) Why were these areas the worst affected? *(7)*

d The map shows the origin of the sulphur content of acid rain that poisons lakes in Norway and Sweden.
i) Which two countries were probably the source of most of the sulphur?
ii) Suggest reasons for the production of sulphur in the source countries. *(4)*

e i) Why is international co-operation needed if the effects of acid rain are to be controlled?
ii) How could the problems of acid rain be reduced? *(4)*

f It has been estimated that reducing acid rain by eliminating harmful chemicals released by power stations could increase the cost of electricity in Germany and Britain by 20 per cent.
i) What effects would this have upon industry and domestic users?
ii) Would you support such a move? Give reasons for your answer (include the benefits and drawbacks of your choice). *(6)*

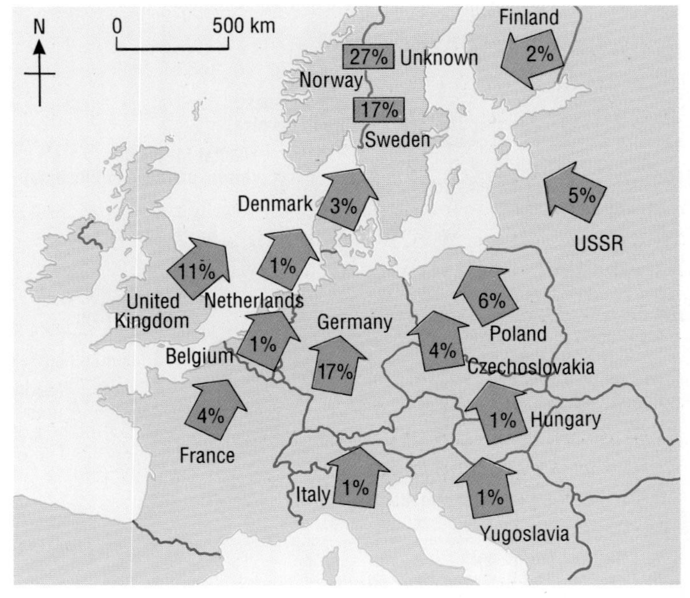

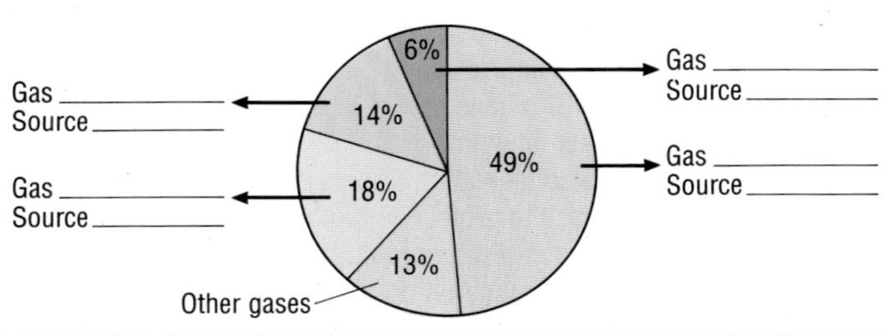

3 *(Pages 228 and 229)*

a Copy and complete the pie graph by:
i) inserting the names of the four missing greenhouse gases.
ii) naming one source for each of the four missing gases. *(8)*

b i) By how many degrees has the global temperature risen this century?
ii) By how many degrees is it predicted to rise by the end of the next century?
iii) Why are global temperatures rising? *(4)*

c i) List four advantages to Britain which are likely to result from global warming.
ii) List four problems likely to face Britain as a result of global warming.
iii) How is global warming likely to affect people living in each of Bangladesh, the Amazon basin, the central parts of the USA, and northern Canada? *(12)*

4 *(Pages 230 and 231)*

a i) How does the tropical rainforest help to protect
1. the soil?
2. water supplies?
3. wildlife?
4. the traditional Indian way of life?
5. the oxygen-carbon dioxide balance? *(10)*

ii) Give six reasons why there is deforestation in the rainforest in the Amazon Basin. *(6)*

iii) How fast are the rainforests being cleared? *(1)*

iv) Draw a labelled sketch map to show the main features of the Grand Carajas Scheme *(4)*

b i) Describe how the removal of trees can affect
1. the soil.
2. water supplies.
3. wildlife.
4. the traditional Indian way of life.
5. plant life.
6. local climate.
7. global climate.
8. oxygen supplies. *(16)*

ii) Draw annotated diagrams to show the humus (nutrient) cycle before and after deforestation. *(4)*

Evapotranspiration from trees adds moisture to the air
Forested area
Heavy convectional storms most afternoons
Forested slopes, nature in balance
Shifting cultivators live in harmony with nature, only limited deforestation in Amazonia for fuel
Habitat for wildlife (birds, animals and insects)
Fragile soils shielded from heavy rain by trees
Movement of rain-water through soil regulates river flow, prevents flooding and stores water for drier periods
Clean river useable for drinking
Muddy water undrinkable
Tree roots control flow of water and stabilise the soil preventing landslides
Little economic gain
Considerable environmental gain
Deforested area
Fewer trees mean less evapotranspiration
Ranching
Mainly for poor quality meat for hamburgers and frankfurters
Heavy rainfall (both in amount and intensity) washes away the unprotected surface soil
Plantation crops
Highways
Mining
Timber
Loss of wildlife and many species of trees
Lack of trees creates a fuel shortage
Rapid surface runoff causes gulley erosion and flooding
No roots to hold soil together results in landslides
Heavy rainfall causes leaching ruining the soil
Silt blocks rivers and fills reservoirs
Reasonable short term economic gain
Considerable environmental loss

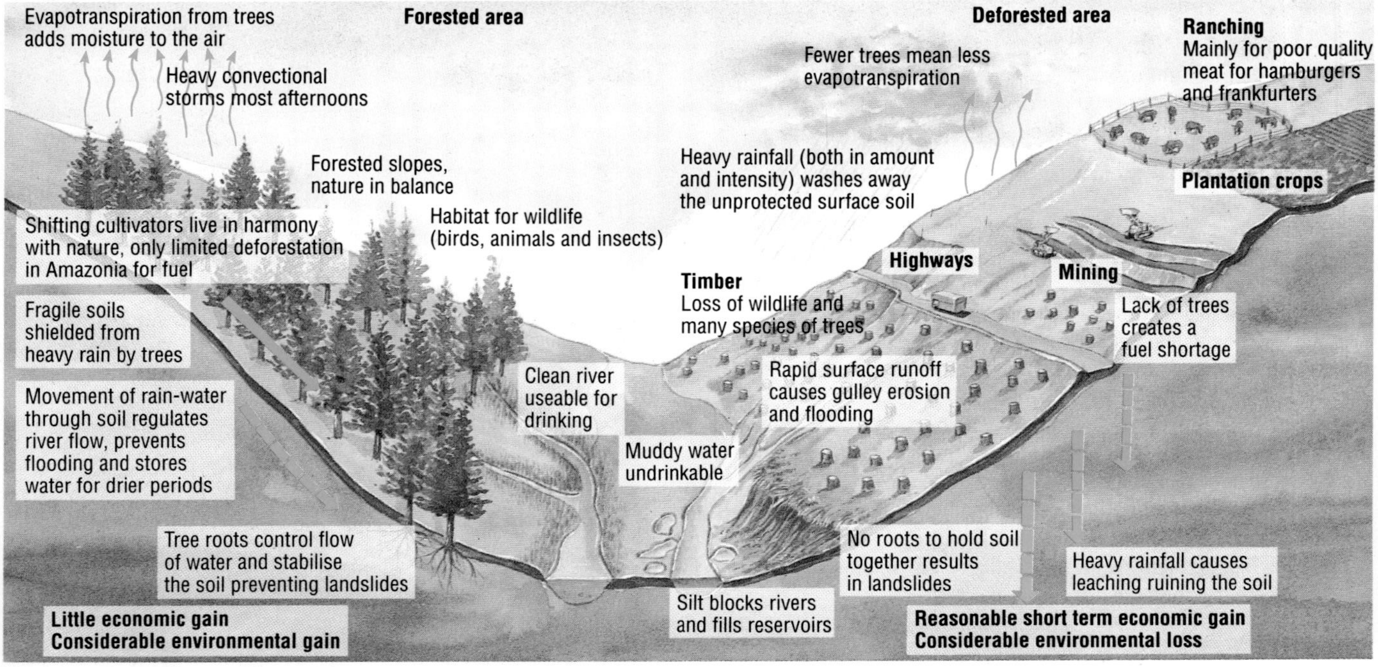

c Brazilians often express different views to those of people who live in the more economically developed countries:

A Brazilian tour guide: "Europeans have exploited us for years and now they expect us not to develop or to use our own resources."

An Indian guide: "It is western propaganda. What is the point in clearing the forest when the Amazon and its tributaries rise by 15 metres a year and flood 60% of the forest for several months?"

A Geography lecturer at São Paulo University: "It is an over-reaction by the western world. At present we are making various studies of the forest to see how we can organise its development on a sustainable basis. Development cannot be stopped, but it should be made to harmonise with the environment."

A Brazilian doctor: "Conservation groups have to exaggerate if they are to raise funds."

These views contrast with conservation groups:

Friends of the Earth: "Every minute, an area of rainforest the size of 30 football pitches is being destroyed which means an area the size of England and Wales is lost every year. At the present rate of destruction, in 40 years' time there will be virtually no more rainforests. That means the Earth's climate will change. We will lose a precious source of medicine. We will be deprived of an important source of food and industrial products. And we will lose over half the world's animal and plant species."

(October 1993)

i) Why do some Brazilians feel the western world has over-reacted to deforestation? *(4)*

ii) Why do Brazilians resent the western world telling them to protect the rainforest? *(2)*

iii) Why do conservation groups like Friends of the Earth want Brazil to protect its rainforest? *(4)*

iv) Can you suggest a compromise that will benefit Brazil AND protect the rainforest? *(4)*

5 *(Pages 232 and 233)*

a i) In which country is the dust-bowl?
ii) What were the differences in rainfall between the years 1900–1910 and 1930–1940? *(3)*

b Conditions were ideal for cereal farming between 1900 and 1910 and many new settlers arrived to farm in the area. Soil erosion became a problem in the 1930s and many of the farms were abandoned.
i) What was the main type of farming in 1900?
ii) Why did the rainfall between 1900 and 1910 encourage farmers to grow cereals?
iii) Why was soil erosion in the 1930s the result of rainfall and cereal farming?
iv) Why did the area become known as the dust-bowl? *(5)*

c i) Describe five other causes of soil erosion which occur elsewhere in the world. *(5)*
ii) Describe how each of the eight methods named in the diagram may reduce soil erosion. *(8)*

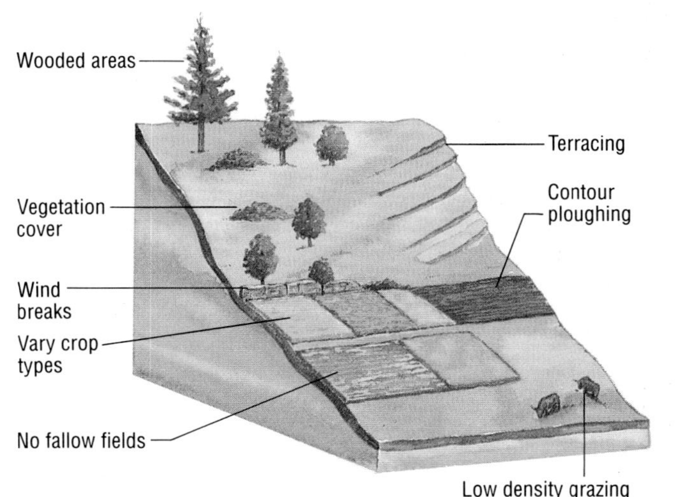

6 *(Pages 234 and 235)*

a i) What is desertification?
ii) Where is the Sahel?
iii) Name four countries in the Sahel which are at great risk from desertification. *(6)*

b Copy the flow diagram below to show the processes which are believed to cause desertification. Complete it by putting the following phrases into the correct boxes: *(9)*

vegetation dies • deforestation
less rainfall and increased drought
soil exposed to wind and rain • overgrazing
increased risk of soil erosion • vegetation cover removed
overcultivation • vegetation cannot re-establish itself

c Explain how overgrazing, overcultivation and deforestation can all lead to desertification. *(9)*

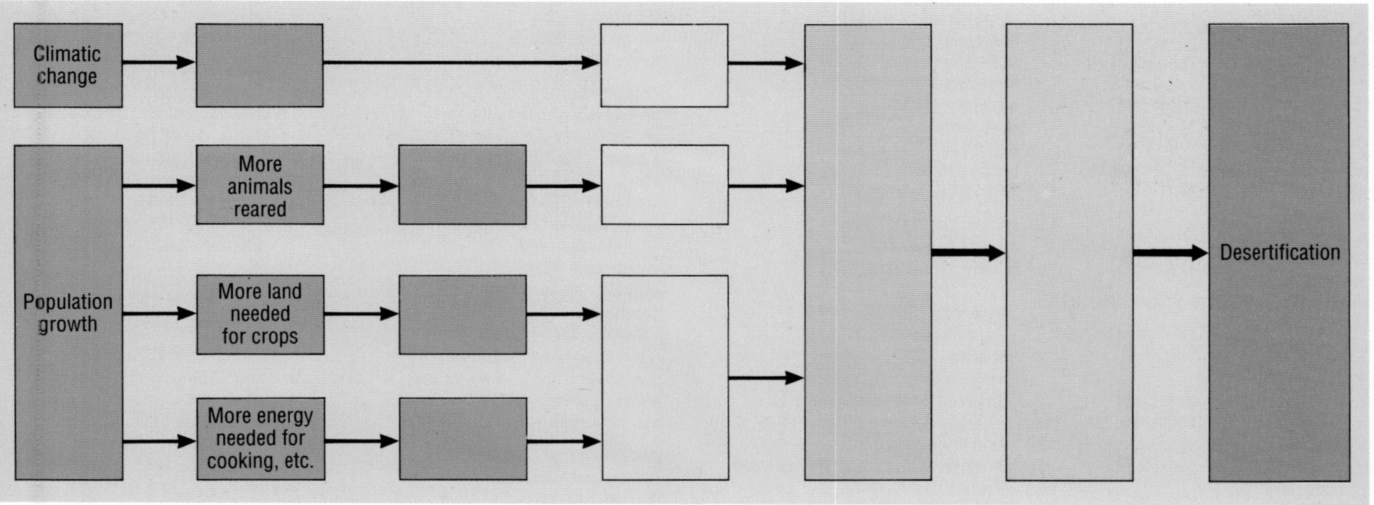

7 *(Page 236)*

a i) What is meant by the term wetland?
ii) Why are wetlands under threat?
iii) Why is it important to conserve wetlands? *(5)*

b Why do the Norfolk Broads attract tourists? *(2)*

c i) Why might the following groups object to large numbers of tourists visiting the Broads?
1. Farmers 2. Villagers 3. Bird-watchers
ii) Why might the following groups welcome tourists to the Broads?
1. Teenagers 2. Shopkeepers 3. Marina owners *(6)*

d i) Where are the Everglades?
ii) Give six changes which have taken place in the Everglades between 1950 and 1990.
iii) Give one reason for each of the six changes. *(13)*

INDEX

accessibility 26, 60, 115.
acid rain 226-27, 237.
aid 160-61, 167.
Alaska 103, 107.
altitude 191.
Amazon basin 7, 82, 88, 196-97, 230-31, 138.
Amsterdam 61, 68.
anticyclones 195, 208
apartheid 51.
arches 177.
arêtes 181.
Athens 146-47.
atmospheric circulation 204-05, 209.
atmospheric pressure 194-95, 204-05, 209.

Bangladesh 11, 109, 162, 220-21, 223.
Belfast 52.
birth rates 8-9, 17, 162, 167.
Brasilia 7, 130-31
Brazil 6-7, 11, 13, 15, 34-36,67, 82-83, 88, 92, 95, 109, 125, 154,162,196-97, 230-31, 238.
Burgess model 26.
business parks 117, 130-31

California 49, 53, 61, 212.
caves 177, 184-85
census data 28-29, 40, 45, 51, 164.
central business district (CBD) 26, 34.
chemical weathering 184.
Chernobyl 102.
cliffs 177.
climate 190, 196, 198, 200, 202-05.
coal 90, 96-98.
coasts 176-79, 220-21, 223.
cold climates 203, 205.
Common Agricultural Policy (CAP) 73.
commuting 37, 60-61, 68.
coniferous forest 203.
core-periphery model 164-65.
corries 181, 189.
Costa del Sol 142-43, 152.

death rates 8-9, 162.
deforestation 199, 230-31, 238.
deltas 175.
demographic transition model 8-9, 11, 15.
Denmark 76-77, 87.
deposition 173-75, 178-79, 183, 185, 220, 232.
depressions 194, 208.
desert climate and vegetation 202-03, 205.
desertification 234-35, 239.
diet 85, 162.
discharge 170-71.
drainage basins 168-71, 186.
drainage density 168, 186.
drought 199, 201-22, 216-17, 223, 134, 239.
drumlins 183.
Dust bowl (USA) 232, 239.

earthquakes 210-13, 222.
EC 72-73, 87, 105, 140-41, 157, 164.
employment structures 108-09, 126, 162.
electricity 98.
energy 90-107.
  biomass and biogas 95.
  coal 90, 96-98, 100.
  distribution and reserves 96-97.
  environment 102-03.
  fuelwood 92.
  geothermal 94, 100.
  Ghana 101, 106.
  hydro-electricity 92, 96, 98, 100-01.
  Japan 100, 106.
  non-renewable 90-91.
  nuclear 91, 96-98, 100, 102.
  oil and natural gas 91, 96-98, 100, 103.
  renewable 92-93.
  solar 94,100.
  tidal 95.
  wave 95.
  wind 93,104.
enterprise zones 118.
equatorial climate 196, 205.
erosion 172-74, 176-77, 180-82, 232.
erratics 183.
ethnic groups 44-45, 50-51.
Eurotunnel 65, 68.
evapotranspiration 169.
Everglades (Florida) 236.
Exe (river) 168, 223.

farming 70-89.
  Brazil 82-83, 88.
  Denmark 76-77, 87.
  EC 72-73, 87.
  environment 84, 89, 224.
  Japan 80-81, 88.
  Mezzogiorno (Italy) 78-79.
  Netherlands 74-75.
  systems 70-71, 86.
  types 71, 86.
favelas 35.
Felixstowe 62, 69.
flood hydrograph 170-71, 186-87.
flood plains 175.
floods 218-23.
  coastal 220-21, 223.
  rivers 218-19, 223.
food supplies 85.
footloose industries 115, 127.
fragile environments 197, 231, 236, 238-39.
freeze-thaw 180.
fronts 193-94, 208.

Germany 48.
Ghana 101, 106, 109.
glacial trough 182.
glaciation 180-83.
global warming 221, 228-29, 231, 237.
government policies 118-119.
Greece 146-47.
greenhouse effect 228-29, 231, 237.

hanging valleys 182.
headlands and bays 176-77.
hedgerows 84.
high-tech industries 115-17, 128.
hierarchies 22-23, 54, 57.
honeypots 139.
Hong Kong 63.
Hoyt model 26.
hydro-electricity 92, 96, 98, 101.
hydrological cycle 168.

Iceland 94, 211.
India 109, 162, 212.
industry 108-129.
  cars 121.
  developing countries 122-25.
  edge-of-city 115, 127.
  footloose 64.
  formal and informal 124-25, 129.
  government intervention 118-19.
  industrial location 110-11, 114-15, 127.
  inner cities 114.
  intermediate technology (IT) 123, 129.
  iron and steel 112-13.
  multinationals 122.
infant mortality 51, 162-63, 167.
inner cities 28, 46, 114, 132-34.
Intermediate technology (IT) 123, 129.
Italy 47, 78-79, 108, 119, 128, 144-45, 152, 162.
Itaipu 92.

Jamaica 153.
Japan 11, 30-31, 55, 64, 67, 80-81, 88, 100, 106, 109, 117,120-1,129,154, 157-59, 162, 165, 224-25, 237.

Kenya 67, 109, 123, 129, 148-49, 153, 154, 162.

Land and sea (climate) 191.
land use 26-29, 34, 39.
land values 26, 31, 39, 115.
latitude 191.
leaching 82, 231.
levées 175.
life expectancy 10, 162-63, 167.
limestone 184-85.
literacy 162-63, 167.
location quotient 111, 127.
London 45-46,132-33, 135.
longshore drift 178.
Lynmouth (Devon) 218-19, 223.

M4 corridor 116.
meanders 174.
Mediterranean climate 142, 198, 205.
Mediterranean vegetation 198-99.
MetroCentre 56.
Mexico City 24, 213, 222.
Mezzogiorno 78-79,119, 128.
migration 42-53.
  guestworkers 48-49, 53.
  international 42, 52.
  rural depopulation 32-33, 40.
  urban depopulation 46.
million cities 24, 38.
models 26-27, 34, 39, 41, 164-67.
moraines 181, 183.
Mt St Helens 214-15, 222.
multinationals 122.

national parks 138-39, 151.
natural increase (population) 8.
Netherlands 61, 68, 74-75.
networks 66-67.
New Commonwealth immigrants 44-45, 52.
new towns 130-31.
Norfolk Broads 236, 239.
non-renewable resources 90-91.
nuclear energy 91, 96-98, 102.

ocean currents 191, 207, 209.
oil and natural gas 90, 96-99.
OS maps 21, 23.
overgrazing 235.
oxbow lakes 174.

Peak District 151.
permeable and impermeable rock 184, 219.
physical quality of life index (PQLI) 163.
planning 118-19, 130-35.
plates 210-14, 222.
  collision 211-12.
  conservative 211-12.
  constructive 211.
  destructive 211-12.
pollution 84, 89, 103, 107, 224-26, 237.
population 4-17.
  density 4-6, 17.
  distribution 4-6, 165.
  pyramids 10-11, 16, 48, 53.
prevailing winds 191, 205.
pyramidal peaks 181.

rainfall reliability 206, 229.
rainfall types 206, 229.
refugees 43, 217.
renewable resources 92-95.
residential environments 28-29, 34-36, 39, 41.
ribbon lakes 182.
Rio de Janeiro 6, 125.
rivers 168-75, 186-87, 218-19.
Rostow model 166-67.

Sahel 217, 223, 234-35, 239.
San Francisco 61, 212.
São Paulo 7, 24, 34-36.
satellite images 195.
savanna grasslands 201.
science parks 117, 128.
sea-level changes 179, 229.
self-help housing schemes 36, 41.
Sellafield (Cumbria) 102.
settlement 18-23.
  functions 19, 23, 26.
  hierarchy 22-23.
  patterns 20.
site and situation 18, 23.
Shetland Islands 99.
shopping 54-57.
soil erosion 231-33, 235, 238.
South Africa 50-51.
Spain 142-43, 152.
spits 179.
stacks 177.
stalagtites and stalagmites 184-85.
storm surges 220.
swallow holes 184.
synoptic charts 195, 209.

technological developments 61-62, 99.
temperatures 190-91.
threshold population 22, 54.
Tokyo 30-31, 55, 165.
topographical maps 7.
topological maps 65.
tourism 136-153.
  coasts 142-43, 152.
  cultural 146-47.
  developing countries 148-50, 153.
  EC 140-41.
  growth 136-37.
  mountains 144-45.
  national parks 138-39.
trade 154-59.
transport 58-69.
  air 58, 63.
  commuting 60-61.
  developing countries 35, 67, 70.
  networks 66-67.
  ports 58, 62.
  rail 58-59, 64-65.
  road 68-69.
transportation 172, 178, 183.
tropical continental climate 200, 205.
tropical rainforest 197, 230-31, 238

urbanisation 24-41, 162.
  developed countries 24-27, 30-31.
  developing countries 24-25, 32-35.
  problems 30-31, 34-35, 40.
urban planning 118, 130-34.
urban redevelopment 28, 132-33, 135.
urban renewal 134-35.
USA 49, 53, 61, 103, 107, 109, 157, 162, 212, 232, 239.

vegetation 197-99, 201-03, 209, 230-31.
volcanoes 210-12, 214, 222.
V-shaped valleys 173.

Wales 112-13, 189.
waterfalls 173.
watershed 168.
wave-cut platform 177.
waves 176, 188.
weather 190-95, 208.
weather maps 195, 209.
weathering 180, 184.
West Indies 150, 153.
wetlands 236, 239.
wildlife habitats 148-49, 231.
wind power 93, 104.
world development 160-67.